MW00652359

What physicians, psychologists, scientists, meditation teachers, educators, and leaders are saying about *Full Catastrophe Living*

"Jon Kabat-Zinn's classic work on the practice of mindfulness to alleviate stress and human suffering stands the test of time, a most useful resource and practical guide. I recommend this new edition enthusiastically to doctors, patients, and anyone interested in learning to use the power of focused awareness to meet life's challenges, whether great or small."

—ANDREW WEIL, M.D., author of *Spontaneous Happiness* and *8 Weeks to Optimum Health*

"How wonderful to have a new and updated version of this classic book that invited so many of us down a path that transformed our minds and awakened us to the beauty of each moment, day-by-day, through our lives. This second edition, building on the first, is sure to become a treasured sourcebook and traveling companion for new generations who seek the wisdom to live full and fulfilling lives."

—DIANA CHAPMAN WALSH, PH.D., president emerita of Wellesley College

"When first published, *Full Catastrophe Living* provided the language, attitude, and pragmatics—indeed an entire weltanschauung—to enable those of us drawn to these ideas to refine their application and increase their clinical impact. The second edition of *Full Catastrophe Living* builds on this foundation by seamlessly extending and expanding Jon Kabat-Zinn's visionary work, a singular beacon of clarity for integrating a 2,500-year-old science of mind with twenty-first century management of stress, pain, and related disorders."

—Zindel V. Segal, Ph.D., distinguished professor of psychology in mood disorders, University of Toronto, and co-developer of Mindfulness Based Cognitive Therapy

"*Full Catastrophe Living* is a timeless classic, a door opener to the world of mindfulness. The revised edition gives the cutting edge view on stress science, within historical context, followed by wise instruction on the simple grace of mindful living."

—Elissa Eppel, Ph.D., professor, Department of Psychiatry, University of California, San Francisco, and stress scientist

"In this revision and expansion of his landmark *Full Catastrophe Living,* Jon Kabat-Zinn charts for us a wise path of living with nuance, care, and irrepressible wonder. Drawing upon decades of experience working with thousands of individuals, he connects personal stories with up-to-the-minute research findings to teach us how to harness intelligent awareness in ways that will profoundly lessen our loads and help us find joy even in the hardest things in life. This book can change your life. Take the invitation!"

—Clifford Saron, Ph.D., UC Davis Center for Mind and Brain, and principal investigator, The Shamantha Project

"Jon Kabat-Zinn's impact on transforming the lives of millions of people worldwide to experience inner peace and joy via mindfulness meditation is truly epic. *Full Catastrophe Living* shows you how."

—Dean Ornish, M.D., founder and president, Preventive Medicine Research Institute, clinical professor of medicine, University of California, San Francisco, and author of *The Spectrum*

"Every mindfulness teacher I know considers this book indispensable, and frequently consults it even after they have been teaching for several years. Yet it is also easily accessible to the lay reader who is brand-new to mindfulness. For people without access to an actual MBSR program, this book provides an invaluable tool to begin transforming their lives."

—Sara Lazar, Ph.D., Massachusetts General Hospital and Harvard Medical School

"This book represents a revolution in the way we now think of stress, change, and our capacity for presence and love. Filled with new research, new insights, and new stories, *Full Catastrophe Living* is again defining the forward edge of thinking about happiness and how we can experience it—for our own deep benefit and for the benefit of our friends, families and communities."

—Sharon Salzberg, author of *Lovingkindness* and *Real Happiness*

"In this brilliant and comprehensive book, Jon Kabat-Zinn shares the depth of his meditation experience and the breadth of its application in the world. Through the concise and extremely pragmatic meditation exercises, the wealth of the science explaining their benefits, and the many compelling personal stories, *Full Catastrophe Living* offers the way to a balanced and mindful life."

—Joseph Goldstein, author of *Mindfulness: A Practical Guide to Awakening* and *One Dharma: The Emerging Western Buddhism*

"With beautiful and compassionate clarity, Jon Kabat-Zinn shows us how to cultivate mindful awareness, to learn from the obstacles that arise in nourishing it, and to recognize its fruits. Updated in the light of the latest evidence, we see clearly the extraordinary transformation in evidence-based integrative medicine that his work has brought about throughout the world. The first edition was the turning point in the field of medicine for the end of the twentieth century, and this edition will inspire a new generation in the twenty-first. An extraordinary achievement."

—Mark Williams, Ph.D., professor of clinical psychology, University of Oxford

"With cutting-edge neuroscience research presented along the journey, this book is a trusted companion to the heart of MBSR. A foundational book in the modern canon of mindfulness."

—Amishi Jha, Ph.D., director of contemplative neuroscience, University of Miami Mindfulness Research and Practice Initiative

"Neuroscience is teaching us that positive experiences can change the architecture of our brains and, through that, improve the health of our bodies. *Full Catastrophe Living* is a highly readable and practical guide for harnessing the power of mindfulness to enhance brain and body health."

—Bruce McEwen, Ph.D., Alfred E. Mirsky Professor, head, Harold and Margaret Milliken Hatch Laboratory of Neuroendocrinology, The Rockefeller University

"The second edition of *Full Catastrophe Living* is a masterpiece of mindfulness, science, and practice. In precise, yet poetic, language Jon Kabat-Zinn presents us with a guide to Participatory Medicine: actively and fully engaging in taking charge of our health and well-being by building on our already existing inner resources for learning, growing, and healing. Truly a new paradigm for living and healing."

—Bessel van der Kolk, M.D., medical director of Trauma Center at JRI, co-director of National Complex Trauma Treatment Network, and professor of psychiatry, Boston University School of Medicine

"We are at a critical moment in the health and healing of our country—for our veterans, for the public, for healthcare professionals, and the system itself. I believe the fundamental element of this healing is mindfulness, and once again Jon Kabat-Zinn teaches us—as only he can—the way forward. He shows us the way to open our hearts in every moment of every day, and gives our lives and our well-being back to us—as individuals, and as a society."

—Tracy W. Gaudet, M.D., director,
VHA Office of Patient Centered Care and
Cultural Transformation

"Twenty-five years after the first edition of *Full Catastrophe Living,* the hundreds of thousands of people all over the world who have utilized Kabat-Zinn's Mindfulness-Based Stress Reduction program to improve their lives will want to read this thoughtful update and recommend it to their friends."

—James E. Dalen, M.D., MPH, dean and professor
emeritus of medicine and public health,
University of Arizona, and
executive director of
the Weil Foundation

"*Full Catastrophe Living* enriches one's understanding of mindfulness and provides scientific evidence for its benefits in improving one's life and in dealing with the difficult challenges one often encounters throughout life. Jon Kabat-Zinn has carefully and lovingly laid out his vision with numerous compelling stories and instructional guides. In doing so, he has created a potentially life changing gift for the readers of this book. This edition provides a comprehensive and compelling case for making mindfulness meditation a part of one's life. It is an excellent guide to enable one to have a far fuller and healthier life."

—Ralph Snyderman, M.D., James B. Duke
Professor of Medicine and chancellor
emeritus, Duke University

"In developing MBSR, Jon Kabat-Zinn created a vehicle to make the practice and benefits of mindfulness available and accessible to many people who otherwise may not have come to mindfulness. In this revised edition of his seminal work, Jon adds to the earlier edition with beautiful, wise, and moving perspectives on mindfulness and health from his many years of personal practice and teaching in mindfulness. A remarkable and valuable book!"

—Jeffrey Brantley, M.D., DFAPA, founder and director of the Mindfulness-Based Stress Reduction Program at Duke Integrative Medicine

"Using a scientifically tested combination of mindfulness meditation, yoga, and other complementary practices, Kabat-Zinn's approach has helped revolutionize the field of integrative medicine while greatly benefitting literally hundreds of thousands and even millions of individuals through his program of Mindfulness-Based Stress Reduction. It is thus a time for joy and gratitude that a new, revised, and updated revision of this wonderful book has become available to the public."

—David E. Meyer, Ph.D., distinguished professor of mathematical psychology and cognitive science, University of Michigan

"With *Full Catastrophe Living,* Jon Kabat-Zinn shows how our own pain and challenges are not something we must just 'bear with' or endure, but the very ingredients for waking up. For all those who wish to learn the art of strength with gentleness, of fierceness with compassion, and of truly living amidst the ups and downs of life. In a world where our attention is continually directed to outer devices and technologies, Jon gives us an exquisite map of the inner dimension that is the heart of learning and growth."

—Soren Gordhamer, founder, Wisdom 2.0

"A wonderful treasure! Full of immense practical wisdom, kind heart, and revolutionary science, this book has changed medicine, science, and psychology."

—Jack Kornfield, Ph.D., author of *A Path with Heart*

"This book is a great gift. I turned to it after injury, for the work I do, and for my life. In it I have found tools that I try to practice each day. I am grateful to Jon for the clarity and love with which it is written, and encourage anyone who reads it to find in it what speaks to them so it can help light their path."

—ARTURO BEJAR, director of engineering, Facebook

"A landmark book that has changed the life of millions!"

—ARTHUR ZAJONC, PH.D., president of the Mind and Life Institute

"*Full Catastrophe Living* is a classic, launching and sustaining an extraordinary worldwide surge of interest in the healing powers of mindfulness. With generosity and compassion, Jon Kabat-Zinn offers superbly skillful guidance on the practices of mindfulness, wise and heartful advice on responding mindfully to a wide range of stresses, and a deep knowledge of supporting scientific research. Please read this revolutionary book."

—JOHN TEASDALE, PH.D., co-author of *The Mindful Way Through Depression, Mindfulness-Based Cognitive Therapy for Depression,* and *The Mindful Way Workbook*

"*Full Catastrophe Living* has been the doorway to wisdom and healing for so many people. Re-reading this classic now in its updated form, I am struck by how trailblazing and prescient it was when it first appeared. Jon is a pioneer in this field, and this book remains a must-read for anyone interested in understanding the mind-body connection and using mindfulness to heal themselves."

—ELIZABETH A. STANLEY, PH.D., associate professor of security studies, Georgetown University, founder of the Mind Fitness Training Institute

"*Full Catastrophe Living* is for everyone! A comprehensive practical guide to living fully in the present moment, this masterful book, originally published in 1990, has now been thoroughly updated with descriptions of modern research, references to our pressing global predicaments, and documentation of the spread and influence of mindfulness-based approaches in a wide range of healthcare, educational, and workplace settings. Jon Kabat-Zinn has done more than any other person on the planet to spread the power of mindfulness in the lives of ordinary people and major societal institutions and this book compellingly tells the story of that monumental achievement."

—Richard J. Davidson, Ph.D., founder and chair, Center for Investigating Healthy Minds, University of Wisconsin–Madison

"This is the ultimate owner's manual for our lives. Kabat-Zinn's brilliant description of mindfulness practice gives us the tools to meet both ordinary stress and extraordinary difficulties in a way that heals us profoundly. It is essential reading—putting our happiness in our own hands, leading us to feel more vividly, gratefully alive in every moment. What a gift!"

—Amy Gross, former editor in chief of *O, The Oprah Magazine,* MBSR teacher

"I first read *Full Catastrophe Living* in my early twenties and it changed my life. I learned about mindfulness, I learned how to develop profound calmness and clarity of mind, and most importantly, I learned the difference between pain and suffering. It set me on the path to becoming one of the key pioneers in bringing mindfulness to the corporate world. In person, Jon Kabat-Zinn is a wise, compassionate, and skillful teacher. He is my hero."

—Chade-Meng Tan, Jolly Good Fellow of Google and author of *Search Inside Yourself*

"One of the greatest classics of mind/body medicine. More than any other, *Full Catastrophe Living* is the book that enabled Americans to discover the inner life."

—Rachel Naomi Remen, M.D., author of *Kitchen Table Wisdom*

"To say that this wise, deep book is helpful to those who face the challenges of human crisis would be a vast understatement. It is essential, unique, and, above all, fundamentally healing."

—Donald M. Berwick, M.D., president emeritus and senior fellow, Institute for Healthcare Improvement

"Looking back in time a hundred or five hundred years from now we may come to realize more fully the incalculable ripples that the being and work of Jon Kabat-Zinn catalyzed in the world."

—Saki F. Santorelli, Ed.D., M.A., professor of medicine, executive director, Center for Mindfulness in Medicine, Health Care, and Society, and author of *Heal Thy Self*

"This book challenges each American to slow down and pay attention to the power of their own mind and the impact it has on our physical and emotional health. By actively participating in your own health and wellness you will, by extension, increase the health and wellness of our country. As Jon Kabat-Zinn teaches us how to heal our body and boost our immune system, we can actively contribute to the healing of our body politic and strengthen our nation's ability to attack the many challenges of our time. Join us in this quiet revolution! It has the potential to transform our country from the inside out, one courageous American at a time."

—Congressman Tim Ryan, 13th district, Ohio, author of *A Mindful Nation*

BY JON KABAT-ZINN

Full Catastrophe Living

Wherever You Go, There You Are

Everyday Blessings (co-author with Myla Kabat-Zinn)

Coming to Our Senses

The Mindful Way Through Depression (co-author with Mark Williams, John Teasdale, and Zindel Segal)

Arriving at Your Own Door

Letting Everything Become Your Teacher

Mindfulness for Beginners

The Mind's Own Physician (co-editor with Richard Davidson)

Mindfulness (co-editor with Mark Williams)

FULL CATASTROPHE LIVING

FULL CATASTROPHE LIVING

How to cope with stress, pain and illness
using mindfulness meditation

Revised and Updated Edition

JON KABAT-ZINN, Ph.D.

piatkus

PIATKUS

First published in the US in 1990 by Bantam Books,
An imprint of The Random House Publishing Group
This revised edition first published in the US in 2013 Bantam Books,
An imprint of The Random House Publishing Group
First published in Great Britain in 1996 by Piatkus Books Ltd
This revised edition first published in Great Britain in 2013 by Piatkus

9 10 8

Copyright © 1990, 2013 by Jon Kabat-Zinn

The moral right of the authors has been asserted.

All rights reserved.
No part of this publication may be reproduced, stored in a retrieval system, or transmitted in any form or by any means, without the prior permission in writing of the publisher, nor be otherwise circulated in any form of binding or cover other than that in which it is published and without a similar condition including this condition being imposed on the subsequent purchaser.

Grateful acknowledgment is made to the following for permission to reprint previously published material: Bantam Books, an imprint of The Random House Publishing Group, a division of Random House LLC: Excerpt from Is It Worth Dying For? By Robert S. Eliot, M.D. and Dennis L. Breo, copyright © 1984 by Robert S. Eliot, M.D. and Dennis L. Breo. Reprinted by permission of Bantam Books, an imprint of The Random House Publishing Group, a division of Random House LLC. Houghton Miffl in Harcourt Publishing Company and Faber and Faber Limited: Excerpts from "Burnt Norton" from Four Quartets by T. S. Eliot, copyright © 1936 by Houghton Miffl in Harcourt Publishing Company and copyright renewed © 1964 by T. S. Eliot. Rights outside of the United States and digital rights are controlled by Faber and Faber Limited. Reprinted by permission of Houghton Miffl in Harcourt Publishing Company and Faber and Faber Limited.

A CIP catalogue record for this book is available from the British Library.

ISBN 978-0-7499-5841-1

Printed and bound by CPI Group (UK) Ltd, Croydon, CR0 4YY

Papers used by Piatkus are from well-managed forests
and other responsible sources.

FSC www.fsc.org
MIX
Paper from
responsible sources
FSC® C104740

Piatkus
An imprint of
Little, Brown Book Group
Carmelite House
50 Victoria Embankment
London EC4Y 0DZ

An Hachette UK Company
www.hachette.co.uk

www.littlebrown.co.uk

Important Note
This book is not intended as a substitute for medical advice or treatment.
Any person with a condition requiring medical attention should consult a qualified medical practitioner or suitable therapist.

for
my family

for
all the people in the Stress Reduction Clinic
at UMass who came to face the full catastrophe and grow

for
past, present, and future participants
in MBSR programs and other
mindfulness-based programs
everywhere

and for
mindfulness teachers and researchers
throughout the world—a deep bow to you for your dedication, integrity,
and love of this work

This book describes the Mindfulness-Based Stress Reduction program of the Stress Reduction Clinic at the University of Massachusetts Medical Center. The content does not necessarily reflect the position or policy of the University of Massachusetts, and no official institutional endorsement of the content should be inferred.

The recommendations made in this book are generic and are not meant to replace formal medical or psychiatric treatment. Individuals with medical problems should consult their physicians about the appropriateness of following the MBSR program, and in particular some of the yoga postures, and discuss appropriate modifications relevant to their unique circumstances and conditions.

Contents

II The Paradigm: A New Way of Thinking About Health and Illness

III Stress

IV The Applications: Taking on the Full Catastrophe

V The Way of Awareness

Preface

This very readable and practical book will be helpful in many ways. I believe many people will profit from it. Reading it, you will see that meditation is something that deals with our daily life. The book can be described as a door opening both on the dharma (from the side of the world) and on the world (from the side of the dharma). When the dharma is really taking care of the problems of life, it is true dharma. And this is what I appreciate most about the book. I thank the author for having written it.

THICH NHAT HANH
PLUM VILLAGE, FRANCE
1989

As countless people have discovered over the past twenty-five years, mindfulness is the most reliable source of peace and joy. Anyone can do it. And it's become increasingly clear that not only our health and well-being as individuals, but our continuation as a civilization and a planet depend on it. This book's invitation for each one of us to wake up and savor every moment we are given to live has never been more needed than it is today.

THICH NHAT HANH
PLUM VILLAGE, FRANCE
2013

Introduction to the Second Edition

Welcome to this new edition of *Full Catastrophe Living*. My intention in revising the book for the first time in twenty-five years has been to update it and, perhaps more importantly, to refine and deepen the meditation instructions and the description of mindfulness-based approaches to life and to suffering, given the many years that have elapsed since the first writing. The updating felt necessary because the scientific investigation of mindfulness and its effects on health and well-being has grown tremendously over this period. Still, the more I entered into the actual process of revising the text, the more it felt to me that the basic message and content of the book needed to remain essentially the same, simply amplified and deepened where appropriate. In spite of its seductiveness, I didn't want the tail of the exploding scientific evidence for the efficacy of mindfulness and how it might exert its effects to wag the dog of the interior adventure and potential value that mindfulness-based stress reduction (MBSR) offers. In the end, the book remains what it was intended to be from the start—a practical guide to commonsensical ways in which to cultivate mindfulness and its deeply optimistic and transformative view of human nature.

Personally, from my very first exposure to the practice of mindfulness, I was astonished and heartened by its nurturing effects in my own life. That sense has not diminished over the past forty-five-plus years. It has only deepened and grown more reliable, like an old and trustworthy friendship, sustaining in even the hardest of times, and at the same time, hugely humbling.

At the time I was working on the original version of this book, my editor suggested that it would not be wise to put the word *catastrophe* in the title. He was concerned that it might repel many potential readers right from the start. So I tried hard, very hard, to come up with a different title. I thought of and discarded dozens. *Paying Attention: The Healing Power of Mindfulness* was high on the list. It certainly conveyed for me what the book was about. But the title *Full Catastrophe Living* just kept coming back over and over again. It simply wouldn't go away.

In the end, it wound up being okay. To this day, people come up to me and tell me that this book saved their life, or the life of a relative or friend. It happened again recently, at a Mindfulness in Education conference I was attending in Cambridge, Massachusetts, and then again at a mindfulness conference in Chester, England, the following week. I am always deeply moved, often beyond words, as I try to take in the full import of what people are communicating back to me about its effects on their lives. Sometimes the stories are hard to hear—very hard—the suffering that led them to this book inconceivable. And yet, that was its original purpose, to touch something very special that lies within us, our capacity for embracing the actuality of things, often when it seems utterly impossible, in ways that are healing and transforming, even in the face of the full catastrophe of the human condition. Bill Moyers, who filmed our program as part of his public television series *Healing and the Mind,* told me that when he was covering the Oakland fire of 1991, a year after the book came out, he saw a man clutching a copy under his arm after his house burned down. And somehow New Yorkers seem to get the title right away.

Such responses affirm what I sensed from the very beginning of the work in the Stress Reduction Clinic, watching the effect that the practice of mindfulness had on our patients—many of whom were falling through the cracks of the health care system and not getting entirely better, if at all, from the various treatments they were receiving for their chronic medical conditions.* It was clear that there is something about the cultivation of mindfulness that is healing, that is transformative, and that can serve to give our lives back to us, not in some romantic pie-in-the-sky way, but because simply by virtue of being human, to quote William James, the father of American psychology, ". . . we all have reservoirs of life to draw upon of which we do not dream."

Like subterranean water, or vast oil deposits, or minerals buried deep within the rock of the planet, we are talking here of interior resources deep within ourselves, innate to us as human beings, resources that can be tapped and utilized, brought to the fore—such as our lifelong capacities for learning, for growing, for healing, and for transforming ourselves. And how might such transformation come about? It comes directly out of our ability to take a larger perspective, to realize that we are bigger than who we think we are. It comes directly out of recognizing and inhabiting the full dimensionality of our being, of being who and what we *actually* are. It turns out that these innate internal resources—that we can discover for ourselves and draw upon—all rest on our capacity for embodied awareness and on our ability to *cultivate* our relationship to that awareness. We go about this discovery and cultivation through paying attention in a particular way: on purpose, in the present moment, and non-judgmentally.

I was familiar with this domain of being from my own experiences with meditation long before there was a science of mindfulness. And if a science of mindfulness had never emerged, meditation would still be just as

* The clinic was set up to serve as a kind of safety net in the hospital to catch people who were falling through those cracks and challenge them to do something for themselves as a complement to whatever their doctors and their health care team were doing for them. Now those cracks are more like chasms. For a powerful indictment of the current state of our health care (really disease care) system and the case for making it much more patient-centered and based on mind-body and integrative approaches, see the 2013 CNN documentary *Escape Fire*.

important to me. Such meditative practices stand on their own. They have their own compelling logic, their own empirical validity, their own wisdom which can be known only from the inside, through their actual purposeful and intentional cultivation over time in one's own life. This book and the MBSR program it describes are offered as a framework and guide for navigating often unfamiliar and sometimes difficult territory with a degree of clarity and equanimity. You will find other potentially useful books listed in the Appendix. They are offered so that your journey within this domain, should you choose to make it a lifelong one, will have rich, varied, and continual support and nurturance, and so that you can benefit from multiple perspectives on the territory, its opportunities, and its challenges. For it is truly the journey and adventure of a lifetime lived fully—or maybe I should say, *wakefully*.

Since no map completely describes a territory, ultimately it has to be *experienced* in order for us to know it, navigate within it, and benefit from its unique gifts. It has to be *inhabited* or, at the very least, visited from time to time, so that we can experience it directly, firsthand, for ourselves.

In the case of mindfulness, that direct experiencing is nothing less than the great adventure of your life unfolding moment by moment, starting now, where you already are, wherever that is, however difficult or challenging your situation. As we often say to our patients in the Stress Reduction Clinic in our very first encounter with them:

> . . . from our point of view, as long as you are breathing, there is more right with you than wrong with you, no matter what is wrong. Over the next eight weeks, we are going to pour energy in the form of attention into what is right with you—much of which we never notice or take for granted, or don't fully develop in ourselves—and let the rest of the medical center and your health care team take care of what is "wrong," and just see what happens.

In this spirit, mindfulness, and in particular the MBSR program described in this book, is an invitation to become more familiar with the field of your own body, mind, heart, and life by paying attention in new, more systematic and more loving ways—and thereby discover important dimensions of your own life that you may not have noticed or that, for some reason, you have ignored until now.

Paying attention in new ways is a very healthy and potentially healing thing to do, although, as you will come to see, it isn't really about *doing* at all, or about getting somewhere else. It is much more about *being*—about allowing yourself to be as you already are, and discovering the fullness and the vast potential within such an approach. Interestingly, the eight-week MBSR program is really just a beginning, or a new beginning. The real adventure is and has always been your whole life. In a sense, MBSR is only a way-station, and hopefully also a launching platform into a new way of being in relationship with things as they are. The practice of mindfulness has the potential to become a lifelong companion and ally. And whether you know it or not when you start, by engaging in these mindfulness practices you are also joining a worldwide community of others whose hearts have been drawn to this way of being, this way of interfacing with life and with the world.

Above all, this book is about the cultivation of mindfulness *through practice*. It is an engagement we will have to undertake with huge resolve and, at the same time, with the lightest of touches. Everything in this book we will touch on is meant to support you in that engagement.

It turns out that this book and the work of the Stress Reduction Clinic that it describes—the work of MBSR—were instrumental, along with the efforts of many others, in launching a new field within medicine, health care, and psychology, and, in parallel, a growing science of mindfulness and its effects on health and well-being at every level of our biology, psychology, and social connectedness. Mindfulness is also increasingly influencing many other fields, such as education, law, business, technology, leadership, sports, economics, and even politics, policy, and government. This is an exciting and promising development because of its potential healing benefits for our world.

In 2005, there were more than a hundred papers on mindfulness and its clinical applications in the scientific and medical literature. Now, in 2013, there are more than 1,500, plus an ever-increasing number of books on the subject. There is even a new scientific journal called *Mindfulness.* Other scientific journals have followed suit, publishing special issues or special sections on mindfulness. In fact, so high is professional interest in mindfulness, its clinical applications for health and well-being, and the mechanisms by which it might be exerting its effects, that the research in this area is expanding exponentially. What is more, the scientific findings and their implications for our well-being and for our understanding of the mind-body connection as well as stress, pain, and illness are becoming more intriguing by the day.

Still, this second edition has less to do with understanding the psychological mechanisms and neural pathways through which the cultivation of mindfulness might be affecting us—interesting as they may be—than it has to do with our ability to seize hold of our lives and life circumstances, with huge tenderness and kindness toward ourselves, and find ways to honor the full dimensionality of our possibilities for living sane, satisfying, and meaningful lives. None of us, hopefully, will be cultivating mindfulness for the sake of generating colorful brain scans, even though the practice of mindfulness may very well result in beneficial changes not just to the activity in certain regions of our brain, but in the very structure of the brain and its connectivity, along with other potential biological benefits that we will touch on. Such possible benefits take care of themselves. They arise naturally through the practice of mindfulness. Our motivation for cultivating mindfulness, should you choose to pursue it in your own life, will need to be much more basic: perhaps to live a more integrated and satisfying life, to be healthier and perhaps happier and wiser. Other motivations might include the desire to face and cope more effectively and compassionately with our own suffering and that of others, with the stress, pain, and illness in our lives—what I am calling here the *full catastrophe* of the human condition*—and to be the fully integrated and emotionally

* You will find this expression and its origin explained in the Introduction.

intelligent beings that we already are but sometimes lose touch with and drift away from.

Over the course of my own meditation practice and of doing the work I do in the world, I have come to see the cultivation of mindfulness as a radical act—a radical act of sanity, of self-compassion, and, ultimately, of love. As you will see, it involves a willingness to drop in on yourself, to live more in the present moment, to stop at times and simply *be* rather than getting caught up in endless doing while forgetting who is doing all the doing, and why. It has to do with not "mis-taking" our thoughts for the truth of things, and not being so susceptible to getting caught in emotional storms, storms that so often only compound pain and suffering, our own and that of others. This approach to life is indeed a radical act of love on every level. And part of the beauty of it, as we shall see, is that you don't have to *do* anything other than to pay attention and stay awake and aware. These domains of being are already who and what you are.

Even though the meditation practice is really about being rather than doing, it can seem as if it is a major undertaking, and it is. After all, we have to make the time to practice and that does take some doing and requires intentionality and discipline, as we shall see. We sometimes put it this way to prospective participants before we admit them to the MBSR program:

> You don't have to like the daily meditation practice schedule; you just have to do it [on the disciplined schedule you are agreeing to by signing up and then doing the best you can]. Then, at the end of the eight weeks, you can tell us whether it was a waste of time or not. But in the interim, even if your mind is telling you constantly that it is stupid or a waste of time, practice anyway, and as wholeheartedly as possible, as if your life depended on it. Because it does—in more ways than you think.

A recent headline in *Science,* one of the most prestigious and high-impact scientific journals in the world, read: "A Wandering Mind Is an Unhappy Mind." Here is the first paragraph of that paper:

> Unlike other animals, human beings spend a lot of time thinking about what is not going on around them, and contemplating events that happened in the past, might happen in the future, or will never happen at all. Indeed, "stimulus-independent thought" or "mind wandering" appears to be the brain's default mode of operation. Although this ability is a remarkable evolutionary achievement that allows people to learn, reason, and plan, it may have an emotional cost. Many philosophical and religious traditions teach that happiness is to be found by living in the moment, and practitioners are trained to resist mind wandering and "to be here now." These traditions suggest that a wandering mind is an unhappy mind. Are they right?*

The Harvard researchers concluded, as the headline itself suggests, that indeed, those ancient traditions, which emphasize the power of the present moment and how to cultivate it, were onto something.

The findings of this study have interesting and potentially profound implications for all of us. It was the first large-scale study of happiness in daily life ever conducted. To pull it off, the researchers developed an iPhone app to randomly sample responses from several thousand people to questions about their happiness, what they were doing at that particular moment, and mind wandering ("Are you thinking about something other than what you are currently doing?"). It turned out that people's minds wandered nearly half the time, according to Matthew Killingsworth, one

* Killingsworth MA, Gilbert DT. A wandering mind is an unhappy mind. *Science.* 2010;330:932.

of the study's authors, and that the mind wandering, especially when it involved negative or neutral thoughts, appears to contribute to people being less happy. His overall conclusion: "No matter what people are doing, they are much less happy when their minds are wandering than when their minds are focused," and "we should pay at least as much attention to where our minds are as to what our bodies are doing—yet for most of us, the focus of our thoughts isn't part of our daily planning . . . we ought to [also] ask, 'What am I going to do with my mind today?' "*

As you will see, becoming aware of what is on our minds from moment to moment, and of how our experience is transformed when we do, is precisely what mindfulness practice, MBSR, and this book are all about. And just for the record, mindfulness is not about forcing your mind not to wander. That would just give you a big headache. It is more about being aware of when the mind is wandering and, as best you can, and as gently as you can, redirecting your attention and reconnecting with what is most salient and important for you in that moment, in the here and now of your life unfolding.

Mindfulness is a skill that can be developed through practice, just like any other skill. You could also think of it as a muscle. The muscle of mindfulness grows both stronger and more supple and flexible as you use it. And like a muscle, it grows best when working with a certain amount of resistance to challenge it and thereby help it become stronger. Our bodies, our minds, and the stress of our daily lives certainly provide us with plenty of resistance to work with in that regard. Indeed, you might say they provide just the right conditions for developing our innate capacities for knowing our own mind and shaping its ability to stay present to what is most germane and important in our lives, and, by doing so, discover new dimensions of well-being and even happiness without having to change anything.

The very fact that studies such as this one, which make use of emergent consumer technologies to sample the experience of very large numbers of people in real time, are now being conducted with scientific rigor and

* *Harvard Business Review.* Jan-Feb 2012:88.

published in top-tier journals is itself an indicator of a new era in the science of the mind. Recognizing that what is on our mind may have a greater influence on our sense of well-being than what we are doing in particular moments has profound implications for understanding our own humanness, and for shaping, in very practical and yet very personal, even intimate ways, our understanding of what is involved in being healthy and genuinely happy. The intimacy, of course, is with ourselves. This is the essence of mindfulness and its cultivation through MBSR.

Many streams within science—from genomics and proteomics to epigenetics and neuroscience—are revealing in new and indisputable ways that the world and *our own ways of being in relationship to it* exert significant and meaningful effects at every level of our being, including on our genes and chromosomes, on our cells and tissues, on specialized regions of our brain and the neural networks that link those regions, as well as on our thoughts and emotions and our social networks. All these dynamical elements of our lives, and many more as well, are interconnected. Together they constitute who we are and define our degrees of freedom to develop to our full human capacity—always unknown and always infinitely close.

What it means for each of us to be human, coupled with the Harvard researchers' question, "What am I going to do with my mind today?" lie at the heart of mindfulness as a way of being. Only, for our purposes here, I would rephrase that question slightly, putting it in the present tense: "How is it in my mind *right now*?" We can also extend the question to ask: "How is it in my heart right now?" And "How is it in my body right now?" We don't even have to ask using thought alone, for we are capable of *feeling* how it is in the mind, in the heart, in the body—right in this moment. This feeling, this apprehending, is another way of knowing for us, beyond merely thought-based knowing. We have a word for it in English: *awareness.* Making use of this innate capacity for knowing, we can investigate, inquire, and apprehend what is so for us in profoundly liberating ways.

To cultivate mindfulness, requires that we pay attention and inhabit the present moment, and make good use of what we see and feel and know and learn in the process. As you will see, I define mindfulness operationally as *the awareness that arises by paying attention on purpose, in the present moment, and non-judgmentally.* Awareness is not the same as thinking. It is a complementary form of intelligence, a way of knowing that is at least as wonderful and as powerful, if not more so, than thinking. What is more, we can hold our thoughts in awareness, and that gives us an entirely new perspective on them and on their content. And just as our thinking can be refined and developed, so our access to awareness can be refined and developed, although as a rule, we get precious little schooling in how to go about it, or even that it is possible. It can be developed through exercising our capacity for attention and discernment.

Moreover, when we speak of *mindfulness,* it is important to keep in mind that we equally mean *heartfulness.* In fact, in Asian languages, the word for "mind" and the word for "heart" are usually the same. So if you are not hearing or feeling the word *heartfulness* when you encounter or use the word *mindfulness,* you are in all likelihood missing its essence. Mindfulness is not merely a concept or a good idea. It is a way of being. And its synonym, *awareness,* is a kind of knowing that is simply bigger than thought and gives us many more options for how we might choose to be in relationship to whatever arises in our minds and hearts, our bodies and our lives. It is a more-than-conceptual knowing. It is more akin to wisdom, and to the freedom a wisdom perspective provides.

As you will see further on, when it comes to the cultivation of mindfulness, paying attention to our thoughts and emotions in the present moment is only one part of a larger picture. But it is an extremely important part. Recent work from the University of California, San Francisco, by Elissa Epel, Elizabeth Blackburn (Blackburn shared in the 2009 Nobel Prize for the discovery of the antiaging enzyme telomerase), and their colleagues is showing that our thoughts and emotions, especially highly stressful thoughts that involve worrying about the future or ruminating obsessively about the past, seem to influence the rate at which we age, right down to the level of our cells and our telomeres—the specialized DNA repeat sequences at the tips of all of our chromosomes that are essential for cell division and that shorten over time as we age. They and their colleagues showed that telomere shortening is much more rapid under conditions of chronic stress. But they also showed that *how we perceive that stress* makes all the difference in how quickly our telomeres degrade and shorten. And it can make many years' worth of difference. Importantly, this means we don't have to make the sources of our stress go away. In fact, some sources of stress in our lives will not go away. Still, research is showing that we can change our attitude, and thereby our relationship to our circumstances, in ways that can make a difference in our health and well-being, and possibly to our longevity.

The evidence to date suggests that longer telomeres are associated with the difference between a rating of how present you are ("In the past week, have you had moments when you felt totally focused on or engaged in doing what you are doing at the moment?") and a rating of how much mind wandering you experienced in the past week ("Not wanting to be where you are at the moment or doing what you are doing"). This calculated difference in the ratings on these two questions, which the researchers are provisionally calling "state of awareness," is very closely related to mindfulness.

Other studies that looked at levels of the enzyme telomerase rather than at telomere length suggest that our thoughts—especially when we perceive situations as threatening to our well-being, whether they are or not—can have an influence all the way down to the level of this one specific molecule, measured in immune cells circulating in the blood, which apparently plays a major role in how healthy we are and even in how long we might live. The implications of this research may prompt us to wake up a bit more and to pay more attention to the stress in our lives and to how we might shape our relationship to it over the long haul with greater intentionality and wisdom.

This book is about you and your life. It is about your mind and your body and how you might actually learn to be in wiser relationship to both. It is an invitation to experiment with the practice of mindfulness and its applications in everyday life. I wrote it primarily for our patients and for people like them everywhere—in other words, it was written for *regular people.* And by regular people, I basically mean you and me, anybody and everybody. For when you boil away the narrative of our travails and accomplishments and get down to the essence of being alive and having to deal with the enormity of what life throws at us, we are all just regular people, dealing with that enormity as best we can. And I am not just referring to the hard stuff and the unwanted in our lives—I mean *everything* that arises: the good, the bad, and the ugly.

And the good is enormous—to my mind, enormous enough to deal with the bad and the ugly, the difficult and the impossible—and it is not just found outwardly, but inwardly as well. The practice of mindfulness involves finding, recognizing, and making use of that in us which is already okay, already beautiful, already whole by virtue of our being human—and drawing upon it to live our lives as if it really mattered *how* we stand in relationship to what arises, whatever it is.

Over the years, I have increasingly come to realize that mindfulness is essentially about relationality—in other words, *how we are in relationship to everything,* including our own minds and bodies, our thoughts and emotions, our past and what transpired to bring us, still breathing, into this moment—and how we can learn to live our way into every aspect of life with integrity, with kindness toward ourselves and others, and with wisdom. This is not easy. In fact, it is just about the hardest work in the world. It is difficult and messy at times, just as life is difficult and messy. But stop for a moment and reflect on the alternative. What are the implications of *not* fully embracing and inhabiting the life that is yours to live in the only moment you ever get to experience it? How much loss and grief and suffering might there be in that?

Coming back to the happiness iPhone app study for a moment, the Harvard researchers had a number of things to say that are germane to us as we embark on our own adventures in mindfulness and MBSR:

> "We know that people are happiest when they're appropriately challenged—when they're trying to achieve goals that are difficult but not out of reach. Challenge and threat are not the same thing. People blossom when challenged and wither when threatened."

MBSR is exceedingly challenging. In many ways, being in the present moment with a spacious orientation toward what is happening may really be the hardest work in the world for us humans. At the same time, it is also infinitely doable, as so many people around the world have demonstrated through their participation in MBSR programs and in then continuing to keep up the practice and cultivation of mindfulness as an integral part of their daily lives for years afterward. As you will see, the cultivation of greater mindfulness also gives us new ways of working with what we find threatening, and of learning how to respond intelligently to such perceived threats rather than react automatically and trigger potentially unhealthy consequences.

> "If I wanted to predict your happiness, and I could know only one thing about you, I wouldn't want to know your gender, religion, health, or income. I'd want to know about your social network—about your friends and family, and the strength of your bonds with them."

The strength of those bonds is also known to be highly associated with overall health and well-being. They get deeper and stronger with mindfulness, because mindfulness, as we've seen, is all about relationality and relationship—with yourself and with others.

> "We imagine that one or two big things will have a profound effect [on our happiness]. But it looks like happiness is the sum of hundreds of small things. . . . The small stuff matters."

Not only does the small stuff matter. The small stuff isn't so small. It turns out to be huge. Tiny shifts in viewpoint, in attitude, and in your efforts to be present can have enormous effects on your body, on your mind, and in the world. Even the tiniest manifestation of mindfulness in any moment might give rise to an intuition or insight that could be hugely transforming. If nurtured consistently, those nascent efforts to be more mindful often grow into a new and more robust, more stable way of being.

What are some of the little things we can do to increase happiness and well-being? According to Dan Gilbert, one of the authors of the happiness study:

> "The main things are to commit to some simple behaviors—meditating, exercising, getting enough sleep—and to practice altruism. . . . And nurture your social connections."

If what I said earlier about meditation being a radical act of love is true, then meditation itself is also a basic altruistic gesture of kindness and acceptance—starting with but not limited to yourself!

The world has changed hugely, unthinkably, since this book first appeared, perhaps more than it has ever changed before in a twenty-five-year interval. Just think of laptops, smart phones, the Internet, Google, Facebook, Twitter, ubiquitous wireless access to information and people, the impact of this ever-expanding digital revolution on just about everything we do, the speeding up of the pace of life, and our 24/7 lifestyles, to say nothing of the huge social, economic, and political changes that have occurred globally during this period. The ever-accelerating speed at which things are changing nowadays is not likely to abate. Its effects will be increasingly felt and will be increasingly unavoidable. You could say that the revolution in science and technology (and its effects on the way we live our lives) has hardly gotten started. Certainly the stress of adjusting to it on top of everything else will only mount in the coming decades.

This book and the MBSR program it describes are meant to serve as an effective counterbalance to all the ways we get pulled out of ourselves and wind up losing sight of what is most important. We are apt to get so caught up in the urgency of everything we have to do, and so caught up in our heads and in what we *think* is important, that it is easy to fall into a state of chronic tension, anxiety, and perpetual distraction that continually drives our lives and easily becomes our default mode of operating, our autopilot. Our stress is further compounded when we are faced with a serious medical condition, chronic pain, or a chronic disease, whether our own or that of a loved one. Mindfulness is now more relevant than ever as an effective and dependable counterbalance to strengthen our health and well-being, and perhaps our very sanity.

For while we are now blessed with 24/7 connectivity, which allows us to be in touch with anybody anywhere at any time, we may be finding, ironically enough, that it is more difficult than ever to actually be in touch with ourselves and with the inner landscape of our own lives. What is more, we may feel that we have less time in which to be in touch with ourselves, although each of us still gets the same twenty-four hours a day. It's just that we fill up those hours with so much *doing* that we scarcely have time for *being* anymore, or even for catching our breath, literally and metaphorically—to say nothing of time for knowing what we are doing as we are doing it, and why.

The first chapter of this book is called "You Have Only Moments to Live." This is an undeniable statement of fact. It will continue to be true, for all of us, no matter how digital the world becomes. Yet so much of the time, we are out of touch with the richness of the present moment and with the fact that inhabiting this moment with greater awareness shapes the moment that follows. Thus, if we can *sustain* our awareness, it shapes the future—and the quality of our lives and relationships, often in ways we simply cannot anticipate.

The only way we have of influencing the future is to own the present, however we find it. If we inhabit this moment with full awareness, the next moment will be very different because of our very presence in this one. Then we just might find imaginative ways to fully live the life that is actually ours to live.

Can we experience joy and satisfaction as well as suffering? What about being more at home in our own skin within the maelstrom? What about tasting ease of well-being, even genuine happiness? This is what is at stake here. This is the gift of the present moment, held in awareness, nonjudgmentally, with a little kindness.

Before we launch into this exploration together, you might be interested to know that a number of recent studies of MBSR have shown highly intriguing and promising results. While, as we've said, mindfulness has its own internal logic and poetry, and offers many compelling reasons for you to bring it into your life and cultivate it systematically, the scientific findings outlined below, together with those presented elsewhere in the book might provide extra incentive, if any is needed, for following the MBSR curriculum with the commitment and resolve that our patients tend to bring to it.

- Researchers at Massachusetts General Hospital and Harvard University have shown, using fMRI brain scanning technology, that eight weeks of MBSR training leads to thickening of a number of different regions of the brain associated with learning and memory, emotion regulation, the sense of self, and perspective taking. They also found that the amygdala, a region deep in the brain that is responsible for appraising and reacting to perceived threats, was thinner after MBSR, and that the degree of thinning was related to the degree of improvement on a perceived stress scale.[*†] These preliminary findings show that

* Hölzel BK, Carmody J, Vangel M, Congleton C, Yerramsetti SM, Gard T, Lazar SW. Mindfulness practice leads to increases in regional brain gray matter density. *Psychiatry Research: Neuroimaging.* 2010. doi:10.1016/j.psychresns.2010.08.006.

† Hölzel BK, Carmody J, Evans KC, Hoge EA, Dusek JA, Morgan L, Pitman R, Lazar

at least certain regions of the brain respond to mindfulness meditation training by reorganizing their structure, an example of the phenomenon known as *neuroplasticity.* They also show that functions vital to our well-being and quality of life, such as perspective taking, attention regulation, learning and memory, emotion regulation, and threat appraisal, can be positively influenced by training in MBSR.

- Researchers at the University of Toronto, also using fMRI, found that people who had completed an MBSR program showed increases in neuronal activity in a brain network associated with embodied present-moment experience, and decreases in another brain network associated with the self as experienced across time (described as the "narrative network," because it usually involves the story of who we think we are). The latter network is the one most implicated in mind wandering, the trait that, as we just saw, plays such a big role in whether we are actually happy in the present moment or not. This study also showed that MBSR could unlink these two forms of self-referencing, which usually function in tandem.* These findings imply that by learning to inhabit the present moment in an embodied way, people can learn how not to get so caught up in the drama of their narrative self, or, for that matter, lost in thought or mind wandering—and when they do get lost in these ways, that they can recognize what is happening and return their attention to what is most salient and important in the present moment. They also suggest that non-judgmental awareness of our wandering mind may actually be a gateway to greater happiness and well-being right in the present moment, without anything at all having to change. These findings have important

---

SW. Stress reduction correlates with structural changes in the amygdala. *Social Cognitive and Affective Neurosciences Advances.* 2010;5(1):11–17.

* Farb NAS, Segal ZV, Mayberg H, Bean J, McKeon D, Fatima Z, Anderson AK. Attending to the present: mindfulness meditation reveals distinct neural modes of self-reference. *Social Cognitive and Affective Neuroscience.* 2007;2:313–322.

implications not only for people suffering from mood disorders, including anxiety and depression, but for all of us. They also offer a significant step toward clarifying what psychologists mean when they speak of "the self." Differentiating between these two brain networks—one with an ongoing "story of me" and one without—and showing how they work together and how mindfulness can influence their relationship to each other may shed at least a bit of light on the mystery of who and what we consider ourselves to be, and how we manage to live and function as an integrated whole being, grounded at least some of the time in self-knowing.

- Researchers at the University of Wisconsin have shown that training a group of healthy volunteers in MBSR reduced the effect of psychological stress (caused by having to give a talk in front of a panel of unknown and emotionally impassive people) on a laboratory-induced inflammatory process that produced blistering of the skin. This study was the first to employ a carefully constructed comparison control condition (the Health Enhancement Program, or HEP) that matched MBSR in all respects except for the mindfulness practices themselves. The groups were indistinguishable on all self-reported measures of change in psychological stress and physical symptoms following MBSR or HEP. However, blister size was uniformly smaller in the MBSR group following training than in the HEP group. What is more, those individuals who spent more time practicing mindfulness showed a greater buffering of the effect of psychological stress on inflammation (blister size) than those who practiced less.* The authors relate these preliminary findings of so-called neurogenic inflammation to those we reported for patients with the skin disease, psoriasis, also a neurogenic inflammatory condition. That study, described in

* Rosenkranz MA, Davidson RJ, MacCoon DG, Sheridan JF, Kalin NH, Lutz A. A comparison of mindfulness-based stress reduction and an active control in modulation of neurogenic inflammation. *Brain, Behavior, and Immunity.* 2013;27:174–184.

Chapter 13, showed that people who were meditating while receiving ultraviolet light therapy for their psoriasis healed at four times the rate of those receiving the light treatment by itself without meditating.*

- In a study we collaborated on with this same group at the University of Wisconsin, looking at the effects of MBSR delivered in a corporate setting during working hours with healthy but stressed employees rather than with medical patients, we found that the electrical activity in certain areas of the brain known to be involved in the expression of emotions (within the prefrontal cerebral cortex) shifted in the MBSR participants in a direction (right-sided to left-sided) that suggested that the meditators were handling emotions such as anxiety and frustration more effectively—in ways that we can think of as being more emotionally intelligent—than the control subjects, who were waiting to take the MBSR program after the study was completed but being tested in the lab on the same schedule and in the same ways as the MBSR group. The right-to-left brain shift in the MBSR group was still apparent four months after the program ended. This study also found that when the people in the study in both groups were given a flu vaccine at the end of the eight weeks of training, the MBSR group mounted a significantly stronger antibody response in their immune system in the following weeks than did the waiting list control subjects. The MBSR group also showed a consistent relationship between the degree of right-to-left brain shift and the amount of antibody produced in response to the vaccine. No such relationship was found in the control group.† This was the first study to show that people could actually change, through

* Kabat-Zinn J, Wheeler E, Light T, Skillings A, Scharf M, Cropley TC, Hosmer D, Bernhard J. Influence of a mindfulness-based stress reduction intervention on rates of skin clearing in patients with moderate to severe psoriasis undergoing phototherapy (UVB) and photochemotherapy (PUVA). *Psychosomatic Medicine.* 1998;60: 625–632.

† Davidson RJ, Kabat-Zinn J, Schumacher J, Rosenkranz MA, Muller D, Santorelli SF,

MBSR training, in eight short weeks, a signature ratio of brain activity between the two sides of the prefrontal cortex, characteristic of emotional style, a ratio that had been thought of as a relatively fixed and invariant "set point" in adults. It was also the first MBSR study to show immune changes.

- A study conducted at UCLA and Carnegie Mellon University showed that participating in an MBSR program actually reduced loneliness, a major risk factor for health problems, especially in the elderly. The study, conducted in adults ranging in age from fifty-five to eighty-five, showed that in addition to reducing their loneliness, the program resulted in reduced expression of genes related to inflammation, measured in immune cells sampled from blood draws. It also resulted in lowering an indicator of inflammation known as C-reactive protein. These findings are potentially important because inflammation is increasingly thought to be a core element of cancer, cardiovascular disease, and Alzheimer's disease,* and because many different programs designed specifically to target social isolation and decrease loneliness have failed.

In summary, mindfulness is not merely a good idea or a nice philosophy. If it is to have any value for us at all, it needs to be embodied in our everyday lives, to whatever degree we can manage without forcing or straining—in other words, with a light and gentle touch, thereby nurturing self-acceptance, kindness, and self-compassion. Mindfulness meditation is increasingly becoming an integral part of both the American

---

Urbanowski R, Harrington A, Bonus K, Sheridan JF. Alterations in brain and immune function produced by mindfulness meditation, *Psychosomatic Medicine.* 2003;65:564–570.

* Creswell JD, Irwin MR, Burklund LJ, Lieberman MD, Arevalo JMG, Ma J, Breen EC, Cole SW. Mindfulness-Based Stress Reduction training reduces loneliness and pro-inflammatory gene expression in older adults: A small randomized controlled trial. *Brain, Behavior, and Immunity.* 2012;26:1095–1101.

and the world landscape. It is with this recognition, and in this context and spirit, that I welcome you to this revised edition of *Full Catastrophe Living.*

May your mindfulness practice grow and flower and nourish your life from moment to moment and from day to day.

Jon Kabat-Zinn
May 28, 2013

INTRODUCTION

Stress, Pain, and Illness: Facing the Full Catastrophe

This book is an invitation to the reader to embark upon a journey of self-development, self-discovery, learning, and healing. It is based on thirty-four years of clinical experience with more than twenty thousand people who have begun this lifelong journey via their participation in an eight-week course known as Mindfulness-Based Stress Reduction (MBSR) offered through the Stress Reduction Clinic at the University of Massachusetts Medical Center in Worcester, Massachusetts. Now, as of this writing, there are over 720 mindfulness-based programs modeled on MBSR in hospitals, medical centers, and clinics across the United States and around the world. Many more thousands of people have participated in these programs worldwide.

Since the founding of the clinic in 1979, MBSR has contributed steadily to a new and growing movement within medicine, psychiatry, and psychology that might best be called *participatory medicine.* Mindfulness-based programs have become an opportunity for people to engage more fully in their own movement toward greater levels of health and well-being as a complement to whatever medical treatments they may be receiving, starting of course from where they are at the moment they decide to take up this challenge: namely, to do something for themselves that no one else on the planet can do for them.

In 1979, MBSR was a new kind of clinical program in a new branch of medicine known as behavioral medicine or, more broadly now, *mind-body and integrative medicine.* From the perspective of mind-body medicine, mental and emotional factors, the ways in which we think and behave, can have a significant effect, for better or for worse, on our physical health and our capacity to recover from illness and injury and lead lives of high quality and satisfaction, even in the face of chronic disease, chronic pain conditions, and endemically stressful lifestyles.

This perspective, radical in 1979, is now axiomatic throughout medicine. So we can simply say at this juncture that MBSR is just one more aspect of the practice of good medicine. In this day and age, that means, as we just saw, that its use and value are supported by increasingly strong scientific evidence of its efficacy. That was much less the case when this book was first published. This edition summarizes some of the salient scientific evidence in support of mindfulness-based programs and their effectiveness for stress reduction, symptom regulation, and emotional balance in a wide variety of ways, in addition to its effects on the brain and immune system. It also touches on some of the ways in which mindfulness training has become integral both to good medical practice and to effective medical education.

The people who embark on this journey of self-development, self-discovery, learning, and healing that is MBSR do so in an effort to regain control of their health and to attain at least some peace of mind. They come referred by their doctors—or, increasingly now, self-referred—for a wide range of life problems and medical problems ranging from headaches, high blood pressure, and back pain to heart disease, cancer, AIDS, and anxiety. They are young and old and in-between. What they learn in MBSR is *the how of taking care of themselves,* not as a replacement for their medical treatment but as a vitally important complement to it.

Over the years, numerous people have made inquiries about how they can learn what our patients learn in this eight-week course, which amounts to an intensive self-directed training program in the art of conscious living. This book is above all a response to those inquiries. It is meant to be a practical guide for anyone, well or ill, stressed or in pain, who seeks to transcend his or her limitations and move toward greater levels of health and well-being.

MBSR is based on rigorous and systematic training in mindfulness, a form of meditation originally developed in the Buddhist traditions of Asia. Simply put, mindfulness is moment-to-moment non-judgmental awareness. It is cultivated by purposefully paying attention to things we ordinarily never give a moment's thought to. It is a systematic approach to developing new kinds of agency, control, and wisdom in our lives, based on our inner capacity for paying attention and on the awareness, insight, and compassion that naturally arise from paying attention in specific ways.

The Stress Reduction Clinic is not a rescue service in which people are passive recipients of support and therapeutic advice. Rather, the MBSR program is a vehicle for active learning, in which people can build on the strengths that they already have and, as we noted, come to do something for themselves to improve their own health and well-being, both physical and psychological.

As we just saw, in this learning process we assume from the start that as long as you are breathing, there is more right with you than wrong with you, no matter how ill or how despairing you may be feeling in a given moment. But if you hope to mobilize your inner capacities for growth and for healing and to take charge in your life on a new level, a certain kind of effort and energy on your part will be required. The way we put it is that it can be stressful to take the stress reduction program.

I sometimes explain this by saying that there are times when you have to light one fire to put out another. There are no drugs that will make you immune to stress or to pain, or that will by themselves magically solve your life's problems or promote healing. It will take conscious effort on your part to move in a direction of healing, inner peace, and well-being. This means learning to work with the very stress and pain that are causing you to suffer.

The stress in our lives is now so great and so insidious that more and more people are making the deliberate decision to understand it better and to find imaginative and creative ways to change how they are in relationship to it. This is especially relevant to those aspects of stress that cannot be entirely controlled but can be lived with differently if we learn to bring them into at least momentary balance and integrate them into a larger strategy for living in a healthier way. People who choose to work with stress in this way realize the futility of waiting for someone else to make things better for them. Such a personal commitment is all the more important if you are suffering from a chronic illness or disability that imposes additional stress in your life on top of the usual pressures of living.

The problem of stress does not admit to simpleminded solutions or quick fixes. At root, stress is a natural part of living from which there is no more escape than from the human condition itself. Yet some people try to avoid stress by walling themselves off from life experience; others attempt to anesthetize themselves one way or another to escape it. Of course, it is only sensible to avoid undergoing unnecessary pain and hardship. Certainly we all need to distance ourselves from our troubles now and again. But if escape and avoidance become our habitual ways of dealing with our problems, the problems just multiply. They don't magically go away. What does go away or gets covered over when we tune out our problems, run away from them, or simply go numb is our power to continue to learn and grow, to change and to heal. When it comes right down to it, facing our problems is usually the only way to get past them.

There is an art to facing difficulties in ways that lead to effective solutions and to inner peace and harmony. When we are able to mobilize our inner resources to face our problems artfully, we find we are usually able to orient ourselves in such a way that we can use the pressure of the problem itself to propel us through it, just as a sailor can position a sail to make the best use of the pressure of the wind to propel the boat. You can't sail straight into the wind, and if you only know how to sail with the wind at your back, you will only go where the wind blows you. But if you know how to use the wind's energy and are patient, you can sometimes get where you want to go. You can still be in control.

If you hope to make use of the force of your own problems to propel you in this way, you will have to be tuned in, just as the sailor is tuned in to the feel of the boat, the water, the wind, and his or her course. You will have to learn how to handle yourself under all kinds of stressful conditions, not just when the weather is sunny and the wind blowing exactly the way you want it to.

We all accept that no one controls the weather. Good sailors learn to read it carefully and respect its power. They will avoid storms if possible, but when caught in one, they know when to take down the sails, batten down the hatches, drop anchor, and ride things out, controlling what is controllable and letting go of the rest. Training, practice, and a lot of firsthand experience in all sorts of weather are required to develop such skills so that they work for you when you need them. Developing skill and flexibility in facing and effectively navigating the various "weather conditions" in your life is what we mean by the art of conscious living.

The issue of control is central to coping with problems and with stress. There are many forces at work in the world that are totally beyond our control and others that we sometimes think are beyond our control but really aren't. To a great extent, our ability to influence our circumstances depends on how we see things. Our beliefs about ourselves and about our own capabilities as well as how we see the world and the forces at play in it all affect what we will find possible. How we see things affects how much energy we have for doing things and our choices about where to channel what energy we do have.

For instance, at those times when you are feeling completely overwhelmed by the pressures in your life and you see your own efforts as ineffectual, it is very easy to fall into patterns of what is called *depressive rumination,* in which your unexamined thought processes wind up generating increasingly persistent feelings of inadequacy, depression, and helplessness. Nothing will seem controllable or even worth trying to control. On the other hand, at those times when you are seeing the world as threatening but only potentially overwhelming, then feelings of insecurity and anxiety rather than depression may predominate, causing you to worry incessantly about all the things you think threaten or might threaten your sense of control and well-being. These could be real or imagined; it hardly matters in terms of the stress you will feel and the effect it will have on your life.

Feeling threatened can easily lead to feelings of anger and hostility and from there to outright aggressive behavior, driven by deep instincts to protect your position and maintain your sense of things being under control. When things do feel "under control," we might feel content for a moment. But when they go out of control again, or even *seem* to be getting out of control, our deepest insecurities can erupt. At such times we might even act in ways that are self-destructive and hurtful to others. And we will feel anything but content and at peace within ourselves.

If you have a chronic illness or a disability that prevents you from doing what you used to be able to do, whole areas of control may go up in smoke. And if your condition causes you physical pain that has not responded well to medical treatment, the distress you might be feeling can be compounded by emotional turmoil caused by knowing that your condition seems to be beyond even your doctor's control.

What is more, our worries about control are hardly limited to our major life problems. Some of our biggest stresses actually come from our reactions to the smallest, most insignificant events when they threaten our sense of control in one way or another: the car breaking down just when you have someplace important to go, your children not listening to you for the tenth time in as many minutes, long lines at the supermarket checkout.

It is not that easy to find a single word or phrase that really captures the broad range of experiences in life that cause us distress and pain and that promote in us an underlying sense of fear, insecurity, and loss of control. If we were to make a list, it would certainly include our own vulnerability, our wounds, whatever they may be, and our mortality. It might also include our collective capacity for cruelty and violence, as well as the colossal levels of ignorance, greed, delusion, and deception that seem to drive us and the world much of the time. What could we possibly call the sum total of our vulnerabilities and inadequacies, our limitations and weaknesses and foibles, the illnesses and injuries and disabilities we may have to live with, the personal defeats and failures we have felt or fear in the future, the injustices and exploitations we suffer or fear, the losses of people we love and of our own bodies sooner or later? It would have to be a metaphor that would not be maudlin, something that would also convey the understanding that it is not a disaster to be alive just because we feel fear and we suffer; it would have to convey the understanding that there is joy as well as suffering, hope as well as despair, calm as well as agitation, love as well as hatred, health as well as illness.

In groping to describe that aspect of the human condition that the patients in the stress clinic and, in fact, most of us at one time or another need to come to terms with and in some way transcend, I keep coming back to one line from the movie of Nikos Kazantzakis's novel *Zorba the Greek*. Zorba's young companion (Alan Bates) turns to him at a certain point and inquires, "Zorba, have you ever been married?" to which Zorba (played by the great Anthony Quinn) replies, growling (paraphrasing somewhat), "Am I not a man? Of course I've been married. Wife, house, kids . . . the *full catastrophe*!"

It was not meant to be a lament, nor does it mean that being married or having children is a catastrophe. Zorba's response embodies a supreme appreciation for the richness of life and the inevitability of all its dilemmas, sorrows, traumas, tragedies, and ironies. His way is to "dance" in the gale of the full catastrophe, to celebrate life, to laugh with it and at himself, even in the face of personal failure and defeat. In doing so, he is never weighed down for long, never ultimately defeated either by the world or by his own considerable folly.

Anybody who knows the book can imagine that living with Zorba must in itself have been quite "the full catastrophe" for his wife and children. As is so often the case, the public hero that others admire can leave quite a trail of private hurt in his wake. Yet ever since I first heard it, I have felt that the phrase "the full catastrophe" captures something positive about the human spirit's ability to come to grips with what is most difficult in life and to find within it room to grow in strength and wisdom. For me, facing the full catastrophe means finding and coming to terms with what is deepest and best and ultimately, what is most human within ourselves. There is not one person on the planet who does not have his or her own version of the full catastrophe.

Catastrophe here does not mean disaster. Rather, it means the poignant enormity of our life experience. It includes crisis and disaster, the unthinkable and the unacceptable, but it also includes all the little things that go wrong and that add up. The phrase reminds us that life is always in flux, that everything we think is permanent is actually only temporary and constantly changing. This includes our ideas, our opinions, our relationships, our jobs, our possessions, our creations, our bodies, everything.

In this book, we will be learning and practicing the art of embracing the full catastrophe. We will be doing this so that rather than destroying us or robbing us of our power and our hope, the storms of life will strengthen us as they teach us about living, growing, and healing in a world of flux, change, and sometimes great pain. This art will involve learning to see ourselves and the world in new ways, learning to work in new ways with our bodies and our thoughts and feelings and perceptions, and learning to laugh at things a little more, including ourselves, as we practice finding and maintaining our balance as best we can.

In our era, the full catastrophe is very much in evidence on all fronts. A brief reading of any morning newspaper will drive home the impression of an unending stream of human suffering and misery in the world, much of it inflicted by one human being or group of human beings on another. If you listen with an attentive ear to what you hear on radio or television news programs, you will find yourself assaulted daily by a steady barrage of terrible and heartbreaking images of human violence and misery, reported in the always matter-of-fact tones of polished broadcast journalism, as if the suffering and death of people in Syria, Afghanistan, Iraq, Darfur, Central Africa, Zimbabwe, South Africa, Libya, Egypt, Cambodia, El Salvador, Northern Ireland, Chile, Nicaragua, Bolivia, Ethiopia, the Philippines, in Gaza or Jerusalem or Paris or Beijing or Boston, or Tucson, Aurora, or Newtown, and whatever community is next on that list—and the list, sadly, appears endless—were just part of the prevailing climatic conditions that follow on the local weather report in the same matter-of-fact tones, without so much as a nod to the incomprehensible juxtaposition of the two. Even if we don't read or listen to or watch the news, we are never far from the full catastrophe of living. The pressures we feel at work and at home, the problems we run into and the frustrations we feel, the balancing and juggling that are required to keep our heads above water in this increasingly fast-paced world, are all part of it. We might extend Zorba's list to include not only wife or husband, house and children, but also work, paying the bills, parents, lovers, in-laws, death, loss, poverty, illness, injury, injustice, anger, guilt, fear, dishonesty, confusion, and on and on. The list of stressful situations in our lives and of our reactions to them is very long. It is also constantly changing as new and unexpected events demanding some form of response continue to surface.

No one who works in a hospital can be unmoved by the infinite variations of the full catastrophe that are encountered every day. Each person who comes to the Stress Reduction Clinic has his or her own unique version, just as do all the people who work in the hospital. Although people are referred for training in MBSR with specific medical problems, including heart disease, cancer, lung disease, hypertension, headaches, chronic pain, seizures, sleep disorders, anxiety and panic attacks, stress-related digestive problems, skin problems, voice problems, and many more, the diagnostic labels they come with mask more about them as people than they reveal. The full catastrophe lies within the complex web of their past and present experiences and relationships, their hopes and their fears, and their views of what is happening to them. Each person, without exception, has a unique story that gives meaning and coherence to that person's perception of his or her life, illness, and pain, and what he or she believes is possible.

Often these stories are heartbreaking. Not infrequently, our patients come feeling that not only their bodies but their very lives are out of control. They feel overwhelmed by fears and worries, often caused or compounded by painful family relationships and histories, and also by tremendous feelings of loss. We hear accounts of physical and emotional suffering, of frustration with the medical system; poignant stories of people overwhelmed by feelings of anger or guilt, sometimes deeply lacking in self-confidence and self-esteem from having been beaten down by circumstances, often since childhood. And many times we see people who were or are literally beaten down through physical and psychological abuse.

Many of the people who come to the Stress Reduction Clinic have not seen much improvement in their physical condition despite years of medical treatment. Many do not even know where to turn for help anymore and come to the clinic as a last resort, often skeptical about it but willing to do anything to get some relief.

Yet by the time they have been in the program for a few weeks, the majority of these people are taking major steps toward transforming their relationship to their bodies and minds and to their problems. From week to week, there is a noticeable difference in their faces and their bodies. By the end of eight weeks, when the program comes to an end, their smiles and more relaxed bodies are evident to even the most casual observer. Although they were originally referred to the clinic to learn how to relax and to cope better with their stress, it is apparent that they have learned a lot more than that. Our outcome studies over many years, as well as participants' anecdotal reports, show that they often leave with fewer and less severe physical symptoms and with greater self-confidence, optimism, and assertiveness. They are more patient with and more accepting of themselves and their limitations and disabilities. They are more confident about their ability to handle physical and emotional pain, as well as the other forces in their lives. They are also less anxious, less depressed, and less angry. They feel more in control, even in very stressful situations that previously would have sent them spinning out of control. In a word, they are handling "the full catastrophe" of their lives, the entire range of life experience, including impending death in some cases, much more skillfully.

One man who came into the program had had a heart attack that had forced him to retire from his work. For forty years he had owned a large business and lived right next door to it. For forty years, as he described it, he worked every day, never taking a vacation. He loved his work. He was sent to stress reduction by his cardiologist following cardiac catheterization (a procedure for diagnosing coronary artery disease), angioplasty (a procedure for expanding the coronary artery at the point of narrowing), and participation in a cardiac rehabilitation program. As I walked by him in the waiting room, I saw a look of utter despair and bewilderment on his face. He seemed on the verge of tears. He was waiting for my colleague

Saki Santorelli to see him, but his sadness was so apparent that I sat down and talked with him then and there. He said, half to me and half to the air, that he no longer wanted to live, that he didn't know what he was doing in the Stress Reduction Clinic, that his life was over—there was no more meaning in it, he had no joy in anything, not even his wife and children, and no desire to do anything anymore.

After eight weeks, this same man had an unmistakable sparkle in his eyes. When I met with him following the MBSR program, he told me that work had consumed his entire life without him realizing what he had been missing, and that it had damn near killed him in the process. He went on to say that he realized that he had never told his children he loved them when they were growing up but was going to get started now, while he still had the chance. He was hopeful and enthusiastic about his life and was able for the first time to think about selling his business. He also gave me a big hug when he left, probably the first he had ever given another man.

This man still had the same degree of heart disease that he had had when he started, but at that time he saw himself as a sick man. He was a depressed cardiac patient. In eight weeks he had become healthier and happier. He was enthusiastic about living, even though he still had heart disease and plenty of problems in his life. In his own mind he had gone from seeing himself as a heart patient to seeing himself as a whole person again.

What happened in between to bring about such a transformation? We can't say with certainty. Many different factors were involved. But he did take the MBSR program during that time, and he took it seriously. It crossed my mind that he would probably drop out after the first week because, on top of everything else, he had to travel fifty miles to come to the hospital, and when a person is depressed, that is hard to do. But he stayed and did the work we challenged him to do, even though at the beginning he had no idea of how it could possibly help him.

Another man, in his early seventies, came to the clinic with severe pain in his feet. He came to the first class in a wheelchair. His wife came with him to each class and sat outside the room for the two and a half hours it lasted. That first day, he told the class that the pain was so bad he just wanted to cut off his feet. He didn't see what meditating could possibly do for him, but things were so bad that he was willing to give anything a try. Everybody felt incredibly sorry for him.

Something about that first class must have touched him, because this man showed a remarkable determination to work with his pain in the weeks that followed. He came to the second class on crutches rather than in the wheelchair. After that he used only a cane. The transition from wheelchair to crutches to cane spoke volumes to us all as we watched him from week to week. He said at the end that the pain hadn't changed much but that his attitude toward his pain had changed a lot. He said it just seemed more bearable after he started meditating and that by the end of the program, his feet were less of a problem. When the eight weeks were over, his wife confirmed that he was much happier and more active.

A young physician's story comes to mind as another example of embracing the full catastrophe. She was sent to the program for high blood pressure and extreme anxiety. She was going through a difficult period in her life, which she described as full of anger, depression, and self-destructive tendencies. She had come from another part of the country to finish her residency training. She was feeling isolated and burned out. Her doctor had urged her to give MBSR a try, saying, "What can it hurt?" But she was scornful and dubious of a program that didn't actually "do something to you." And the fact that it involved meditation just made it worse. She didn't show up for the first class on the day she was scheduled, but Kathy Brady, one of the clinic secretaries, who had been through the program herself as a patient years before, had called her to find out why, and was so nice to her and sounded so concerned on the phone, she told me later, that she sheepishly showed up for another class the next evening.

As part of her job, this young doctor had to fly in the medical center helicopter on a regular basis to the scene of accidents and bring back severely injured patients. She hated the helicopter. It terrified her, and she always got nauseous flying in it. But by the end of eight weeks in the Stress Reduction Clinic, she was able to fly in the helicopter without getting nauseous. She still hated it with a passion, but she was able to tolerate it and get her job done. Her blood pressure came down to the point where she took herself off her medication to see if it would stay down (doctors can get away with this), and it did. By this time she was in the last few months of her residency training and was exhausted a good deal of the time. On top of that, she continued to be emotionally hypersensitive and reactive. But now she was much more aware of her fluctuating states of body and mind. She decided to repeat the entire course because she felt she was just getting into it when it ended. She did, and continued to keep up her meditation practice for many years afterward.

This doctor's experience in the Stress Reduction Clinic also led her to a newfound respect for patients in general and for her own patients in particular. During the program, she was among medical patients every week in class, not in her usual role as "the doctor" but as just another person with her own problems. She did the same things they were doing in the course week by week. She listened to them talking about their experiences with the meditation practices, and she watched them change over the weeks. She said she was astonished to see how much some people had suffered and what they were able to do for themselves with a little encouragement and training. She also came to respect the value of meditation as her view that people could only be helped by *doing something to them* yielded to what she was seeing. In fact, she came to see that she was no different from the other people in the class and that what she could do, they could do, and what they could do, she could also do.

Transformations similar to the ones these three people experienced occur frequently in the Stress Reduction Clinic. They are usually major turning points in the lives of our patients because they expand the range of what they thought was possible for them.

Usually people leave the program thanking us for their improvement. But actually the progress they make is entirely due to their own efforts. What they are really thanking us for is the opportunity to get in touch with their own inner strength and resources, and also for believing in them and not giving up on them, and for giving them the tools for making such transformations possible.

We take pleasure in pointing out to them that to get through the program, they had to not give up on themselves. They had to be willing to face the full catastrophe of their own lives, in both pleasant and unpleasant circumstances, when things were going the way they wanted and when they were not, when they felt things were under control and when they didn't, and to use these very experiences and their own thoughts and feelings as the raw materials for healing themselves. When they began, it was with thoughts that the program could or might or probably wouldn't do something for them. But what they found was that they could do something very important for themselves that no one else on the planet could possibly do for them.

In the above examples, each person took up the challenge we extended to them to live life as if each moment was important, as if each moment counted and could be worked with, even if it was a moment of pain, sadness, despair, or fear. This "work" involves above all the regular, disciplined cultivation of moment-to-moment awareness, or *mindfulness*—the complete "owning" and "inhabiting" of each moment of your experience, good, bad, or ugly. This is the essence of full catastrophe living.

All of us have the capacity to be mindful. All it involves is cultivating our ability to pay attention in the present moment as we suspend our judging, or at least, as we become aware of how much judging is usually going on within us. Cultivating mindfulness plays a central role in the changes that the people who come to the Stress Reduction Clinic experience. One way to think of this process of transformation is to think of mindfulness as a lens, taking the scattered and reactive energies of your mind and focusing them into a coherent source of energy for living, for problem solving, and for healing.

We routinely and unknowingly waste enormous amounts of energy in reacting automatically and unconsciously to the outside world and to our own inner experiences. Cultivating mindfulness means learning to tap into and focus our own wasted energies. In doing so, we learn to calm down enough to enter and dwell in extended moments of deep well-being and relaxation, of feeling whole and wholly integrated as a person. This tasting and inhabiting of one's own wholeness nourishes and restores both the body and the mind. At the same time, it makes it easier for us to see with greater clarity the way we actually live, and therefore how to make changes to enhance our health and the quality of our life. In addition, it helps us to channel our energy more effectively in stressful situations, or when we are feeling threatened or helpless. This energy comes from inside us, and is therefore always available to us to be put to use wisely, especially if we cultivate it through training and personal practice.

Cultivating mindfulness can lead to the discovery of deep realms of well-being, calmness, clarity, and insight within yourself. It is as if you were to come upon a new territory, previously unknown to you or only vaguely suspected, which contains a veritable wellspring of positive energy for self-understanding and healing. Moreover, it is easy to familiarize yourself with this territory and learn to inhabit it more frequently. The path to it in any moment lies no further than your own body and mind and your own breathing. This domain of pure being, of wakefulness, is always accessible to you. It is always here, independent of your problems. Whether you are facing heart disease or cancer or pain or just a very stressful life, its energies can be of great value to you.

The systematic cultivation of mindfulness has been called the heart of Buddhist meditation. It has flourished over the past 2,600 years in both monastic and secular settings in many Asian countries. In the 1960s and 1970s, the practice of this kind of meditation became much more widespread in the world. This was due in part to the Chinese invasion of Tibet and the decades of war in Southeast Asia, both of which made exiles of many Buddhist monks and teachers; in part to young Westerners who went to Asia to learn and practice meditation in monasteries and then became teachers in the West; and in part to Zen masters and other meditation teachers who came to the West to visit and teach, drawn by the remarkable level of interest in Western countries in meditative practices. This trend has only gotten stronger in the past thirty years.

Although, until recently, mindfulness meditation was most commonly taught and practiced within the context of Buddhism, its essence is and always has been universal. In this era, it is increasingly finding its way into the mainstream of society globally, now at a virtually exponential rate. Given the state of the world, that is a very good thing. You might say the world is starving for it, both literally and metaphorically. We will explore this subject further in Chapter 32, when we examine what we are calling *world stress*.

Mindfulness is basically just a particular way of paying attention and the awareness that arises through paying attention in that way. It is a way of looking deeply into oneself in the spirit of self-inquiry and self-understanding. For this reason it can be learned and practiced, as is done in mindfulness-based programs throughout the world, without appealing to Asian culture or Buddhist authority to enrich it or authenticate it. Mindfulness stands on its own as a powerful vehicle for self-understanding and healing. In fact, one of the major strengths of MBSR and of all other specialized mindfulness-based programs such as mindfulness-based cognitive therapy (MBCT) is that they are not dependent on any belief system or ideology. Their potential benefits are therefore accessible for anyone to test for himself or herself. Yet it is no accident that mindfulness comes out of Buddhism, which has as its overriding concerns the relief of suffering and the dispelling of illusions. We will touch on the ramifications of this conjunction in the Afterword.

This book is designed to give the reader full access to the MBSR training program our patients engage in at the Stress Reduction Clinic. Above all, it is a manual for helping you to develop your own personal meditation practice and for learning how to use mindfulness to promote improved health and healing in your own life. Part I, "The Practice of Mindfulness," describes what takes place in the MBSR program and the experiences of people who have participated in it. It guides you through the major meditation practices we use in the clinic and gives explicit and easily followed directions for how to make practical and daily use of them, as well as how to integrate mindfulness into your everyday life activities. It also provides a detailed eight-week practice schedule so that, if you choose, you can follow the exact MBSR curriculum that our patients undergo, while you are reading other sections of the book to amplify and deepen your experience with the practice of mindfulness itself. This is the way we recommend you proceed.

Part II, "The Paradigm," provides a simple but revealing look at some of the latest research findings in medicine, psychology, and neuroscience as background for understanding how the practice of mindfulness is related to physical and mental health. This section develops an overall "philosophy of health" based on the notions of "wholeness" and "interconnectedness" and on what science and medicine are learning about the relationship of the mind to health and the process of healing.

The section called simply "Stress," Part III, discusses what stress is and how our awareness and understanding of it can help us to recognize it and deal with it more appropriately in this era that is so defined by the challenges of just getting through the day in our ever-more complex and fast-moving society. It includes a model for understanding the value of bringing moment-to-moment awareness to stressful situations in order to navigate and cope with them more effectively, minimizing the toll in wear and tear they exact from us and optimizing as best we can our well-being and health.

Part IV, "The Applications," provides detailed information and guidance for utilizing mindfulness in a wide range of specific areas that cause people significant distress, including medical symptoms, physical and emotional pain, anxiety and panic, time pressures, relationships, work, food, and events in the greater world.

The last section, "The Way of Awareness," Part V, will give you practical suggestions for maintaining momentum in the meditation practice once you understand the basics and have begun practicing, as well as for bringing mindfulness effectively into all aspects of your everyday life. It also contains information about how to find groups of people to practice with, as well as hospitals and community-based institutions that have programs nurturing meditative awareness. The Appendix contains several awareness calendars described in the text, an extensive reading list to support your continued practice and understanding of mindfulness, as well as a short listing of useful resources and websites for the same purpose.

If you wish to transform your relationship to stress, pain, and chronic illness by engaging fully in the MBSR program—whether over a period of eight weeks or on another schedule of your own devising—I encourage you to go through the book in concert with the Series 1 guided mindfulness meditation practice CDs (www.mindfulnesscds.com) that the patients in my classes use when practicing the formal meditations described here. Almost everybody finds it easier, when embarking for the first time on a daily meditation practice, to listen to an instructor-guided audio program and let it "carry them along" in the early stages, until they get the hang of it from the inside, rather than attempting to follow instructions from a book, however clear and detailed they may be. The CDs are an essential element of the MBSR curriculum and learning curve. They significantly increase your chances of giving the formal meditation practices a fair try—which basically means sticking with them on a daily basis over eight weeks—and your chances of connecting with the essence of mindfulness itself. Of course, once you understand what is involved, you can always practice on your own without my guidance whenever you feel like it, as many of our patients do. I hear from many people who continue to use these CDs regularly long after they have completed the eight-week MBSR curriculum, and I am invariably profoundly moved by their ongoing commitment to practice and by their stories of how the various practices have touched and transformed their lives.

But whether you use the CDs (also available as downloads and iPhone apps) or not, anybody who is interested in experiencing the kind of major shifts seen in the majority of participants in the Stress Reduction Clinic at UMass or in MBSR, wherever it is well taught, should understand that the medical patients and others who participate in the program make a strong commitment *to themselves* to engage in the formal mindfulness practices as described in this book on virtually a daily basis. Just making the time to engage in the MBSR curriculum in this way involves a major lifestyle change from the very outset. Our patients are required to practice with the CDs for forty-five minutes a day, six days a week, over the eight weeks. From follow-up studies, we know that most of them continue to practice on their own long after the eight weeks are over. For many, mindfulness rapidly becomes a way of being—and a way of life.

As you embark on your own journey of self-development and discovery of your inner resources for healing and for working with the full catastrophe, all you need to remember is to suspend judgment for the time being—including any strong attachment you might have to a desired outcome, however worthy and desirable and important it may be—and simply commit yourself to practice in a disciplined way, observing for yourself what is happening as you go along. What you will be learning will be coming primarily from inside you, from your own experience as your life unfolds from moment to moment, rather than from some external authority, teacher, or belief system. Our philosophy is that you are the world expert on your life, your body, and your mind, or at least you are in the best position to become that expert if you observe carefully. Part of the adventure of meditation is to use yourself as a laboratory to find out who you are and what you are capable of. As the legendary New York Yankees catcher Yogi Berra once put it in his unique and charmingly quirky way, "You can observe a lot by just watching."

I

The Practice of Mindfulness: Paying Attention

1

You Have Only Moments to Live

Oh, I've had my moments, and if I had to do it over again, I'd have more of them. In fact, I'd try to have nothing else. Just moments, one after another, instead of living so many years ahead of each day.

—NADINE STAIR, EIGHTY-FIVE YEARS OLD,
LOUISVILLE, KENTUCKY

As I look around at the thirty or so people in this new class in the Stress Reduction Clinic, I marvel at what we are coming to engage in together. I assume they all must be wondering to some extent what the hell they are doing here in this room full of total strangers this morning. I see Edward's bright and kind face and ponder what he must be carrying around daily. He is a thirty-four-year-old insurance executive with AIDS. I see Peter, a forty-seven-year-old businessman who had a heart attack eighteen months ago and is here to learn how to take it easy so that he doesn't have another one. Next to Peter is Beverly, bright, cheerful, and talkative; sitting next to her is her husband. At forty-two Beverly's life changed radically when she had a cerebral aneurysm that burst, leaving her uncertain about how much she is her real self. Then there is Marge, forty-four years old, referred from the pain clinic. She had been an oncology nurse until she injured her back and both knees several years ago trying to prevent a patient from falling. Now she is in so much pain that she can't work and walks only with great effort, using a cane. She has already had surgery on one knee and now, on top of everything else, faces surgery for a mass in her abdomen. The doctors won't know for sure what it is until they operate. Her injury knocked her for a loop from which she has yet to recover. She feels wound up like a spring and has been exploding at the littlest things.

Next to Marge is Arthur, fifty-six, a policeman who suffers from severe migraine headaches and frequent panic attacks, and sitting next to him is Margaret, seventy-five, a retired schoolteacher who is having trouble sleeping. A French Canadian truck driver named Phil is on the other side of her. Phil was also referred here by the pain clinic. He injured himself lifting a pallet and is out on disability from chronic low-back pain. He will not be able to drive a truck anymore and needs to learn how to handle this pain better and figure out what other type of work he will be able to do to support his family, which includes four small children.

Next to Phil is Roger, a thirty-year-old carpenter who injured his back at work and is also in pain. According to his wife, he has been abusing pain medications for several years. She is enrolled in another class. She makes no bones about Roger being the major source of her stress. She is so fed up with him that she is certain they are going to get divorced. I wonder, as I look over at him, where his life will carry him and whether he will be able to do what is necessary to get his life on an even keel.

Hector sits facing me across the room. He wrestled professionally for years in Puerto Rico and has come here today because he has a hard time controlling his temper and is feeling the consequences of it in the form of violent outbursts and chest pains. His large frame is an imposing presence in the room.

Their doctors have sent them all here for stress reduction, and we have invited them to come together one morning a week at the medical center for the next eight weeks in this class. *For what, really?* I find myself asking as I look around the room. They don't know it as well as I do yet, but the level of collective suffering in the room this morning is immense. It is truly a gathering of people suffering not only physically but emotionally as well from the full catastrophe of their lives.

In a moment of wonder before the class gets under way, I marvel at our chutzpah in inviting all these people to embark on this journey. I find myself thinking, *What can we possibly do for the people gathered here this morning and for the 120 others who are beginning the MBSR program in different classes this week—*

young people and older people; single, married, or divorced; people who are working, others who are retired or on disability; people on Medicaid and people who are well off? How much can we influence the course of even one person's life? What can we possibly do for all these people in eight short weeks?

The interesting thing about this work is that we don't really *do* anything for them. If we tried, I think, we would fail miserably. Instead we invite them to do something radically new for themselves, namely to experiment with living intentionally from moment to moment. When I was talking to a reporter, she said, "Oh, you mean to live for the moment." I said, "No, it isn't that. That has a hedonistic ring to it. I mean to live *in* the moment."

The work that goes on in the Stress Reduction Clinic is deceptively simple, so much so that it is difficult to grasp what it is really about unless you become involved in it personally. We start with where people are in their lives right now, no matter where that is. We are willing to work with them if they are ready and willing to engage in a certain kind of work with and *on* themselves. And we never give up on anyone, even if they get discouraged, have setbacks, or are "failing" in their own eyes. We see each moment as a new beginning, a new opportunity to start over, to tune in, to reconnect.

In some ways our job is hardly more than giving people permission to live their moments fully and completely and providing them with some tools for going about it systematically. We introduce them to ways that they can use to listen to their own bodies and minds and to begin trusting their own experience more. What we really offer people is a sense that there is a way of being, a way of looking at problems, a way of coming to terms with the full catastrophe that can make life more joyful and rich than it otherwise might be, and a sense also of being somehow more in control. We call this way of being *the way of awareness* or *the way of mindfulness.* The people gathered here this morning are about to encounter this new way of being and seeing as they embark on this journey in the Stress Reduction Clinic, this journey of mindfulness-based stress reduction. We will have occasion to meet them again and others as well along the way as we now embark upon our own exploration of mindfulness and healing.

If you were to look in on one of our classes at the hospital, the chances are you would find us with our eyes closed, sitting quietly or lying motionless on the floor. This can go on for anywhere from ten minutes to forty-five minutes at a stretch.

To the outside observer it might look strange, if not a little crazy. It looks like nothing is going on. And in a way nothing is. But it is a very rich and complex nothing. These people you would be looking in on are not just passing time daydreaming or sleeping. You cannot see what they are doing, but they are working hard. They are practicing *non-doing.* They are actively tuning in to each moment in an effort to remain awake and aware from one moment to the next. They are practicing mindfulness.

Another way to say it is that they are "practicing being." For once, they are purposefully stopping all the doing in their lives and relaxing into the present without trying to fill it up with anything. They are purposefully allowing body and mind to come to rest in the moment, no matter what is on their mind or how their body feels. They are tuning in to the basic experiences of living. They are simply allowing themselves to be in the moment with things exactly as they are, without trying to change anything.

In order to be admitted to the stress clinic in the first place, each person had to agree to make a major personal commitment to spend some time every day practicing this "just being." The basic idea is to create an island of being in the sea of constant doing in which our lives are usually immersed, a time in which we allow all the doing to stop.

Learning how to suspend all your doing and shift over to *a being mode,* how to make time for yourself, how to slow down and nurture calmness and self-acceptance in yourself, learning to observe what your mind is up to from moment to moment, how to watch your thoughts and how to let go of them without getting caught up and driven by them, how to make room for new ways of seeing old problems and for perceiving the interconnectedness of things—these are some of the lessons of mindfulness. This kind of learning involves turning toward and settling into moments of being, and simply cultivating awareness.

The more systematically and regularly you practice, the more the power of mindfulness will grow and the more it will work for you. This book is meant to serve as a guide in this process, just as the weekly classes are a guide to the people who come to the Stress Reduction Clinic at the urging of their doctors.

As you know, a map is not the territory it portrays. In the same way, you should not mistake reading this book for the actual journey. That journey you have to live yourself, by cultivating mindfulness in your own life.

If you think about it for a moment, how could it be otherwise? Who could possibly do this kind of work for you? Your doctor? Your relatives or your friends? No matter how much other people want to help you and can help you in your efforts to move toward greater levels of health and well-being, the basic effort still has to come from you. After all, no one is living your life for you, and no one's care for you could or should replace the care you can give to yourself.

In this regard, cultivating mindfulness is not unlike the process of eating. It would be absurd to propose that someone else eat for you. And when you go to a restaurant, you don't eat the menu, mistaking it for the meal, nor are you nourished by listening to the waiter describe the food. You have to actually eat the food for it to nourish you. In the same way, you have to actually *practice* mindfulness, by which I mean cultivate it systematically in your own life, in order to reap its benefits and come to understand why it is so valuable.

Even if you send away for the CDs or download the guided meditations to support your efforts in practicing, you will still have to use them. CDs sit on shelves and gather dust very nicely. Audio files go unlistened to for ages. Nor is there any magic in them. Just listening to them from time to time will not help you much, although it can be relaxing. To benefit deeply from this work, you will have to *do* the CDs, as we say to our patients, not just listen to them. If there is magic anywhere, it is in you, not in any CD or in a particular practice.

Until recently, the very word *meditation* tended to evoke raised eyebrows and thoughts about mysticism and hocus-pocus in many people. In part, that was because people did not understand that meditation is really about paying attention. This is now more widely known. And since paying attention is something that everybody does, at least occasionally, meditation is not as foreign or irrelevant to our life experience as we might once have thought.

However, when we start paying attention a little more closely to the way our own mind actually works, as we do when we meditate, we are likely to find that much of the time our mind is more in the past or the future than it is in the present. This is the endemic mind wandering we all experience, which was investigated in the Harvard happiness iPhone app study. As a consequence, in any moment we may be only partially aware of what is actually occurring in the present. We can miss many of our moments because we are not fully here for them. This is true not just while we are meditating. Unawareness can dominate the mind in any moment; consequently, it can affect everything we do. We may find that much of the time we are really on automatic pilot, functioning mechanically without being fully aware of what we are doing or experiencing. It's as if we are not really at home a lot of the time or, put another way, only half awake.

You might verify for yourself whether this description applies to your mind the next time you are driving a car. It is a very common experience to drive someplace and have little or no awareness of what you saw along the way. You may have been on automatic pilot for much of the drive, not really fully there but there enough, one would hope, to drive safely and uneventfully.

Even if you deliberately try to concentrate on a particular task, whether it's driving or something else, you might find it difficult to be in the present for very long. Ordinarily our attention is easily distracted. The mind tends to wander. It drifts into thought and reverie.

Our thoughts are so overpowering, particularly in times of crisis or emotional upheaval, that they easily cloud our awareness of the present. Even in relatively relaxed moments they can carry our senses along with them whenever they take off, as when driving, we find ourselves looking intently at something we have passed long after we should have brought our attention back to the road in front of us. For that moment, we were not actually driving. We were on autopilot. The thinking mind was "captured" by a sense impression—a sight, a sound, something that attracted its attention—and was pulled away. It was back with the cow, or the tow truck, or whatever it was that caught our attention. As a consequence, at that moment, and for however long our attention was captured, we were literally "lost" in our thoughts and unaware of other sense impressions.

Is it not true that the same thing happens most of the time, whatever you are doing? Try observing how easily your awareness is carried away from the present moment by your thoughts, no matter where you find yourself, no matter what the circumstances. Notice how much of the time during the day you find yourself thinking about the past or about the future. You may be shocked at the result.

You can experience this pull of the thinking mind for yourself right now if you perform the following experiment. Close your eyes, sit so that your back is straight but not stiff, and become aware of your breathing. Don't try to control your breathing. Just let it happen and be aware of it, feeling how it feels, witnessing it as it flows in and out. Try being with your breath in this way for three minutes.

If, at some point, you think that it is foolish or boring to just sit here and watch your breath go in and out, note to yourself that this is just a thought, a judgment that your mind is creating. Then simply let go of it and bring your attention back to your breathing. If the feeling is very strong, try the following additional experiment, which we sometimes suggest to our patients who feel similarly bored with watching their breathing: take the thumb and first finger of either hand, clamp them tightly over your nose, keep your mouth closed, and notice how long it takes before your breathing becomes very interesting to you!

When you have completed three minutes of watching your breath go in and out, reflect on how you felt during this time and how much or how little your mind wandered away from your breathing. What do you think would have happened if you had continued for five or ten minutes, or for half an hour, or an hour?

For most of us, our minds tend to wander a lot and to jump quite rapidly from one thing to another. This makes it difficult to keep our attention focused on our breathing for any length of time unless we train ourselves to stabilize and calm our own mind. This little three-minute experiment can give you a taste of what meditation is. It is the process of observing body and mind intentionally, of letting your experiences unfold from moment to moment and accepting them *as they are.* It does not involve rejecting your thoughts, trying to clamp down on them or suppress them, or trying to regulate anything at all other than the focus and direction of your attention.

Yet it would be incorrect to think of meditation as a passive process. It takes a good deal of energy and effort to regulate your attention and to remain genuinely calm and non-reactive. But, paradoxically, mindfulness does not involve trying to get anywhere or feel anything special. Rather, it involves allowing yourself to be where you already are, to become more familiar with your actual experience moment by moment. So if you didn't feel particularly relaxed in these three minutes or if the thought of doing it for half an hour is inconceivable to you, you don't need to worry. The relaxation, the sense of being more at home in your own skin, comes by itself with continued practice. The point of this three-minute exercise was simply to try to pay attention to your breathing and to note what actually happened when you did. It was not to become more relaxed. The relaxation, the equanimity, the well-being emerge all by themselves when we attend wholeheartedly in this way.

If you start paying attention to where your mind is from moment to moment throughout the day, as the researchers in the iPhone app study suggested might be critically important for our quality of life, chances are you will find that considerable amounts of your time and energy are expended in clinging to memories, being absorbed in reverie, and regretting things that have already happened and are over. And you will probably find that as much or more energy is expended in anticipating, planning, worrying, and fantasizing about the future and what you want to happen or don't want to happen.

Because of this inner busyness, which is going on almost all the time, we are liable either to miss a lot of the texture of our life experience or to discount its value and meaning. For example, let's say you are not too preoccupied to look at a sunset, and are struck by the play of light and color among the clouds and in the sky. For that moment, you are just there with it, taking it in, really seeing it. Then thinking comes in and perhaps you find yourself saying something to a companion, either about the sunset and how beautiful it is or about something else that it reminded you of. In speaking, you disturb the direct experiencing of the moment. You have been drawn away from the sun and sky and the light. You have been captured by your own thought and by your impulse to voice it. Your comment breaks the silence. Or even if you don't say anything, the thought or memory that came up had already carried you away to some degree from the actual sunset in that moment. So now you are really enjoying the sunset in your head rather than the sunset that is actually happening. You may be *thinking* you are enjoying the sunset itself, but actually you are only experiencing it through the veil of your embellishments with past sunsets and other memories and ideas that this one triggered in you. All this may happen completely below the level of your conscious awareness. What is more, this entire episode might last only a moment or so. It will fade rapidly as one thing leads to the next.

Much of the time you may get away with being only partially conscious like this. At least it seems that way. But what you are missing is more important than you realize. If you are only partially conscious over a period of years, if you habitually run through your moments without being fully in them, you may miss some of the most precious experiences of your life, such as connecting with the people you love, or with sunsets or the crisp morning air.

Why? Because you were "too busy" and your mind too encumbered with what you *thought* was important in that moment to take the time to stop, to listen, to notice things. Perhaps you were going too fast to slow down, too fast to know the importance of making eye contact, of touching, of being in your body. When we are functioning in this mode, we may eat without really tasting, see without really seeing, hear without really hearing, touch without really feeling, and talk without really knowing what we are saying. And, of course, in the case of driving, if your mind or somebody else's happens to check out at the wrong moment, the immediate consequences can be dramatic and very unfortunate.

So the value of cultivating mindfulness is not just a matter of getting more out of sunsets. When unawareness dominates the mind, all our decisions and actions are affected by it. Unawareness can keep us from being in touch with our own body, its signals and messages. This in turn can create many physical problems for us, problems we don't even know we are generating ourselves. And living in a chronic state of unawareness can cause us to miss much of what is most beautiful and meaningful in our lives—and, as a consequence, be significantly less happy than we might be otherwise. What is more, as in the driving example, or in the case of alcohol and drug abuse or habits such as workaholism, our tendency toward unawareness may also be lethal, either rapidly or slowly.

When you begin paying attention to what your mind is doing, you will probably find that there is a great deal of mental and emotional activity going on beneath the surface. These incessant thoughts and feelings can drain a lot of your energy. They can be obstacles to experiencing even brief moments of stillness and contentment.

When the mind is dominated by dissatisfaction and unawareness, which is much more often than most of us are willing to admit, it is difficult to feel calm or relaxed. Instead, we are likely to feel fragmented and driven. We will think this *and* that, we want this *and* that. Often the *this* and the *that* are in conflict. This mind state can severely affect our ability to do anything or even to see situations clearly. In such moments we may not know *what* we are thinking, feeling, or doing. What is worse, we probably won't know that we don't know. We may think we know what we are thinking and feeling and doing and what is happening. But it is an incomplete knowing at best. In reality we are being driven by our likes and dislikes, totally unaware of the tyranny of our own thoughts and the self-destructive behaviors they often result in.

Socrates was famous in Athens for saying, "Know thyself." It is said that one of his students said to him: "Socrates, you go around saying

'Know thyself,' but do you know yourself?" Socrates was said to have replied, "No, but I understand something about this not knowing."

As you embark upon your practice of mindfulness meditation, you will come to know something for yourself about your own not knowing. It is not that mindfulness is the "answer" to all life's problems. Rather, it is that all life's problems can be seen more clearly through the lens of a clear mind. Just being aware of the mind that thinks it knows all the time is a major step toward learning how to see through your opinions and perceive things as they actually are.

One very important domain of our lives and experience that we tend to miss, ignore, abuse, or lose control of as a result of being in the automatic pilot mode is our own body. We may be barely in touch with our body, unaware of how it is feeling most of the time. As a consequence, we can be insensitive to how our body is being affected by the environment, by our actions, and even by our thoughts and emotions. If we are unaware of these connections, we might easily feel that our body is out of control and we will have no idea why. As you will see in Chapter 21, physical symptoms are messages the body is giving us that allow us to know how it is doing and what its needs are. When we are more in touch with our body as a result of paying attention to it systematically, we will be far more attuned to what it is telling us and better equipped to respond appropriately. Learning to listen to your body is vital to improving your health and the quality of your life.

Even something as simple as relaxation can be frustratingly elusive if you are unaware of your body. The stress of daily living often produces tension that tends to localize in particular muscle groups, such as the shoulders, the jaw, and the forehead. In order to release this tension, you first have to know it is there. You have to feel it. Then you have to know how to shut off the automatic pilot and how to take over the controls of your own body and mind. As we will see further on, this involves zeroing in on your body with a focused mind, experiencing the sensations coming from within the muscles themselves, and sending them messages to let the tension dissolve and release. This is something that can be done at the time the tension is accumulating if you are mindful enough to sense it. There is no need to wait until it has built to the point that your body feels like a two-by-four. If you let it go that long, the tension will have become so ingrained that you will have probably forgotten what it feels like to be relaxed, and you may have little hope of ever feeling relaxed again.

One Vietnam war veteran who came to the clinic years ago with back pain put the dilemma in a nutshell. While testing his range of motion and flexibility, I noticed that he was very stiff and his legs were as hard as rocks, even when I asked him to relax them. They had been that way ever since he was wounded when he stepped on a booby trap in Vietnam. When his doctor told him that he needed to relax, he had responded, "Doc, telling me to relax is about as useful as telling me to be a surgeon."

The point is, it didn't do this man any good to be told to relax. He knew he needed to relax more. But he had to learn how to relax. He had to experience the process of letting go within his own body and mind. Once he started meditating, he was able to *learn* to relax, and his leg muscles eventually regained a healthy tone.

When something goes wrong with our body or our mind, we have the natural expectation that medicine can make it right, and often it can. But as we will see further on, our active collaboration is essential in almost all forms of medical treatment. It is particularly vital in the case of chronic diseases or conditions for which medicine has no cures. In such cases the quality of your life may greatly depend on your ability to know your own body and mind well enough to work at optimizing your own health within the bounds, always unknown, of what may be possible. Whatever your age, taking responsibility for learning more about your body by listening to it carefully and by cultivating your inner resources for healing and for maintaining health is the best way to hold up your end of this collaboration with your doctors and with medicine. This is where the meditation practice comes in. It gives power and substance to such efforts. It catalyzes the work of healing.

The first introduction to the meditation practice in MBSR always comes as a surprise to our patients. More often than not, people come with the idea that meditation means doing something unusual, something mystical and out of the ordinary, or, at the very least, something relaxing. To relieve them of these expectations right off the bat, we give everybody three raisins and we eat them one at a time, paying attention to what we are actually doing and experiencing from moment to moment. You might wish to try it yourself after you see how we go about it.

First we bring our attention to seeing one of the raisins, observing it carefully as if we had never seen one before. We feel its texture between our fingers and notice its colors and surfaces. We are also aware of any thoughts we might be having about raisins or food in general. We note any thoughts and feelings of liking or disliking raisins if they come up while we are looking at it. We then smell it for a while, and finally, with awareness, we bring it to our lips, being aware of the arm moving the hand to position it correctly, and of salivating as the mind and body anticipate eating. The process continues as we take it into our mouth and chew it slowly, experiencing the actual taste of one raisin. And when we feel ready to swallow, we watch the impulse to swallow as it comes up, so that even that is experienced consciously. We even imagine, or "sense," that now our bodies are one raisin heavier. Then we do it again with another raisin, this time without any verbal guidance, in other words, in silence. And then with the third.

The response to this exercise is invariably positive, even among the people who don't like raisins. People report that it is satisfying to eat this way for a change, that they actually experienced what a raisin tasted like for the first time that they could remember, and that even one raisin could be satisfying. Often someone makes the connection that if we ate like that all the time, we would eat less and have more pleasant and satisfying experiences of food. Some people usually comment that they caught themselves automatically moving to eat the other raisins before finishing the one that was in their mouth, and recognized in that moment that this is the way they normally eat.

Since many of us use food for emotional comfort, especially when we feel anxious or depressed or even just bored, this little exercise in slowing things down and paying careful attention to what we are doing illustrates how powerful, uncontrolled, and unhelpful many of our impulses are when it comes to food, and how simple and satisfying it can be and how much more in control we can feel when we bring awareness to what we are actually doing while we are doing it.

The fact is, when you start to pay attention in this way, your relationship to things changes. You see more, and you see more deeply and clearly. You may start seeing an intrinsic order and connectedness between things that were not apparent before, such as the connection between impulses that come up in your mind and finding yourself overeating and disregarding the messages your body is giving you. By paying attention, you literally become more awake. It is an emerging from the usual ways in which we all tend to see things and do things mechanically, without full awareness. When you eat mindfully, you are in touch with your food because your mind is not distracted, or at least it is *less* distracted. It is not thinking about other things. It is attending to eating. When you look at the raisin, you really see it. When you chew it, you really taste it.

Knowing what you are doing while you are doing it is the essence of mindfulness practice. This knowing is a non-conceptual knowing, or a bigger than conceptual knowing. It is awareness itself. It is a capacity you already have. That's why we call the raisin-eating exercise "eating meditation." It helps make the point that there is nothing particularly unusual or mystical about meditating or being mindful. All it involves is paying attention to your experience from moment to moment. This leads directly to new ways of seeing and being in your life because the present moment, whenever it is recognized and honored, reveals a very special, indeed magical power: *it is the only time that any of us ever has.* The present is the only time that we have to know anything. It is the only time we have to perceive, to learn, to act, to change, to heal, to love. That is why we value moment-to-moment awareness so highly. While we may have to teach ourselves how to inhabit this capacity of our own mind for this kind of knowing through practicing, the effort itself is its own end. It makes our experiences more vivid and our lives more real.

As you will see in the next chapter, to embark on the practice of mindfulness meditation it is helpful to deliberately introduce a note of simplicity into your life. This can be done by setting aside a time during the day for moments of relative peace and quiet, moments you can use to focus on the basic experiences of living such as your breathing, the sensations you feel in your body, and the flowing movement of thoughts in your mind. It doesn't take long for this formal meditation practice to spill over into your daily life in the form of intentionally paying greater attention from one moment to the next, no matter what you are doing. You might find yourself spontaneously paying attention more of the time in your life, not just when you are "meditating."

We practice mindfulness by remembering as best we can—and that means with considerable kindness toward ourselves as well as with some resolve and discipline—to be present in all our waking moments. We can practice taking out the garbage mindfully, eating mindfully, driving mindfully. We can practice navigating through all the ups and downs we encounter, the storms of the mind and the storms of our bodies, the storms of the outer life and of the inner life. We learn to be aware of our fears and our pain, yet at the same time stabilized and empowered by a connection to something deeper within ourselves, a discerning wisdom that helps to penetrate and transcend the fear and the pain, and to discover some peace and hope within our situation *as it is.*

We are using the word *practice* here in a special way. It does not mean a rehearsal or a perfecting of some skill so that we can put it to use at some other time. In the meditative context, practice means "being in the present on purpose." The means and the end of meditation are really the same. We are not trying to get somewhere else, only working at being where we already are and being here fully. Our meditation practice may very well deepen over the years, but actually we are not practicing for this to happen. Our journey toward greater health and well-being is really a natural progression. Awareness, insight, and indeed health as well, ripen on their own if we are willing to pay attention in the moment and remember that we have only moments to live.

2

The Foundations of Mindfulness Practice: Attitudes and Commitment

To cultivate the healing power of mindfulness requires much more than mechanically following a recipe or a set of instructions. No real process of learning is like that. It is only when the mind is open and receptive that learning and seeing and change can occur. In practicing mindfulness you will have to bring your whole being to the process. You can't just assume a meditative posture and hope that something will magically just happen, nor can you play a CD and think that the CD is going to "do something" for you.

The attitude with which you undertake the practice of paying attention and being in the present is crucial. It is the soil in which you will be cultivating your ability to calm your mind and to relax your body, to concentrate and to see more clearly. If the attitudinal soil is depleted, that is, if your energy and commitment to practice are low, it will be hard to develop calmness and relaxation with any consistency. If the soil is really polluted, that is, if you are trying to force yourself to feel relaxed and demand of yourself that "something happen," nothing will grow at all and you will quickly conclude that "meditation doesn't work."

To cultivate meditative awareness requires an entirely new way of looking at the process of learning. Since thinking that we know what we need and where we want to get are so ingrained in our minds, we can easily get caught up in trying to control things to make them turn out "our way," the way we want them to. But this attitude is antithetical to the work of awareness and healing. Awareness requires only that we pay attention and see things as they are. It doesn't require that we change anything. And healing requires receptivity and acceptance, a tuning to connectedness and wholeness. None of this can be forced, just as you cannot force yourself to go to sleep. You have to create the right conditions for falling asleep and then you have to let go. The same is true for relaxation. It cannot be achieved through force of will. That kind of effort will only produce tension and frustration.

If you come to the meditation practice thinking to yourself, "This won't work but I'll do it anyway," the chances are it will not be very helpful. The first time you feel any pain or discomfort, you will be able to say to yourself, "See, I knew my pain wouldn't go away," or "I knew I wouldn't be able to focus or concentrate," and that will confirm your suspicion that it wasn't going to work and you will drop it.

If you come as a "true believer," certain that this is the right path for you, that mindfulness is "the answer," the chances are you will soon become disappointed too. As soon as you find that you are the same person you always were and that this work requires effort and consistency and not just a romantic belief in the value of meditation, relaxation, or mindfulness, you may find yourself with considerably less enthusiasm than before.

In the Stress Reduction Clinic, we find that those people who come with a skeptical but open-minded attitude do the best. Their attitude is "I don't know whether this will work or not, I have my doubts, but I am going to give it my best shot and see what happens."

So the attitude that we bring to the practice of mindfulness will to a large extent determine its long-term value to us. This is why consciously cultivating certain attitudes can be very helpful in getting the most out of the process of meditation. Your intentions set the stage for what is possible. They remind you from moment to moment of why you are practicing in the first place. Keeping particular attitudes in mind is actually part of the training itself, a way of directing and channeling your energies so that they can be most effectively brought to bear in the work of growing and healing.

Seven attitudinal factors constitute the major pillars of mindfulness practice as we teach it in MBSR. They are non-judging, patience, a beginner's mind, trust, non-striving, acceptance, and letting go. These attitudes are to be cultivated consciously when you practice. They are not independent of each other. Each one relies on and influences the degree to which you are able to cultivate the others. Working on any one will rapidly lead you to the others. Since together they constitute the foundation upon which you will be able to build a strong meditation practice of your own, we are introducing them before you encounter the meditation practices themselves so that you can become familiar with these attitudes from the very beginning. Once you are engaged in the practice itself, this chapter will merit rereading to remind you of ways you might continue to fertilize this attitudinal soil so that your mindfulness practice will flourish.

THE ATTITUDINAL FOUNDATION OF MINDFULNESS PRACTICE

1. Non-judging

Mindfulness is cultivated by paying close attention to your moment-to-moment experience while, as best you can, not getting caught up in your ideas and opinions, likes and dislikes. This orientation allows us to see things more as they may actually be rather than through our own distorted lenses and agendas. To adopt such a stance toward your own experience requires that you become aware of the constant stream of judging and reacting to the inner and outer experiences that we are all normally caught up in, and learn to step back from it. When we begin practicing paying attention to the activity of our own mind, it is common to discover and to be surprised, even astonished, by the fact that we are constantly generating judgments about our experience. Almost everything we see is labeled and categorized by the mind. We react to everything we experience in terms of what we think its value is to us. Some things, people, and events are judged as "good" because they make us feel good for some reason. Others are equally quickly condemned as "bad" because they make us feel bad. The rest is categorized as "neutral" because we don't think it has much relevance. Neutral things, people, and events are almost completely tuned out of our consciousness. We usually find them the most boring to give attention to.

This habit of categorizing and judging our experience locks us into automatic reactions that we are not even aware of and that often have no objective basis at all. These judgments tend to dominate our minds, making it difficult for us ever to find any peace within ourselves, or to develop any discernment as to what may actually be going on, inwardly or outwardly. It's as if the mind were a yo-yo, going up and down on the string of our own judging thoughts all day long. If you doubt this description of your mind, just observe how much you are preoccupied with liking and disliking during, say, any given ten-minute period as you go about your business.

If we are to find a more effective way of handling the stress in our lives, the first thing we will need to do is to be aware of these automatic judgments so that we can see through our own usually unexperienced prejudices and fears and liberate ourselves from their tyranny.

When practicing mindfulness, it is important to recognize this judging quality of mind when it appears and assume a broader perspective by intentionally suspending judgment and assuming a stance of impartiality, reminding yourself to, as best you can, simply observe what is unfolding, including your reactions to it. When you find the mind judging, you don't have to stop it from doing that, and it would be unwise to try. All that is required is to be aware of it happening. No need to judge the judging and make matters even more complicated for yourself.

As an example, let's say you are practicing watching your breathing, as we did in the last chapter and as we will do a lot more in the next. At a certain point you may find your mind saying something like, "This is boring," or "This isn't working," or "I can't do this." These are judgments. When they come up in your mind, it is very important to recognize them as judgmental thinking and remind yourself that the practice involves suspending judgment and just watching *whatever* comes up, including your own judging thoughts, without pursuing them or acting on them in any way. Then go back to riding the waves of your breathing with full awareness once again.

2. *Patience*

Patience is a form of wisdom. It demonstrates that we understand and accept the fact that sometimes things must unfold in their own time. A child may try to help a butterfly to emerge by breaking open its chrysalis. Usually the butterfly doesn't benefit from this. Any adult knows that the butterfly can only emerge in its own time, that the process cannot be hurried.

In the same way, we cultivate patience toward our own minds and bodies when practicing mindfulness. We intentionally remind ourselves that there is no need to be impatient with ourselves because we find the mind judging all the time, or because we are tense or agitated or frightened, or because we have been practicing for some time and nothing positive seems to have happened. We give ourselves room to have these experiences. Why? Because we are having them anyway! When they come up, they are our reality; they are part of our life unfolding in this moment. So we treat ourselves as well as we would treat the butterfly. Why rush through some moments to get to other, "better" ones? After all, each one is your life in that moment.

When you practice being with yourself in this way, you are bound to find that your mind has "a mind of its own." We have already seen in Chapter 1 that one of its favorite activities is to wander into the past and the future and lose itself in thinking. Some of its thoughts are pleasant. Others are painful and anxiety-producing. In either case thinking itself exerts a strong pull on our awareness, eclipsing it. Much of the time our thoughts overwhelm our perception of the present moment. They may cause us to lose our connection to the present entirely.

Patience can be a particularly helpful quality to invoke when the mind is agitated. It can help us to accept this wandering tendency of the mind while reminding us that we don't have to get caught up in its travels. Practicing patience reminds us that we don't have to fill up our moments with activity and with more thinking in order for them to be rich. In fact, it helps us to remember that quite the opposite is true. To be patient is simply to be completely open to each moment, accepting it in its fullness, knowing that, like the butterfly, things can only unfold in their own time.

3. Beginner's Mind

The richness of present-moment experience is the richness of life itself. Too often we let our thinking and our beliefs about what we "know" prevent us from seeing things as they really are. We tend to take the ordinary for granted and fail to grasp the extraordinariness of the ordinary. To see the richness of the present moment, we need to cultivate what has been called "beginner's mind," a mind that is willing to see everything as if for the first time.

This attitude will be particularly important when we engage in the formal meditation practices described in the following chapters. Whatever the particular practices we might be using, whether it is the body scan, the sitting meditation, or the yoga, we can resolve to bring our beginner's mind with us each time we practice, so that we can be free of our expectations based on our past experiences. An open, "beginner's" mind allows us to be receptive to new possibilities and prevents us from getting stuck in the rut of our own expertise, which often thinks it knows more than it does. No moment is the same as any other. Each is unique and contains unique possibilities. Beginner's mind reminds us of this simple truth.

You might try to cultivate your own beginner's mind in your daily life as an experiment. The next time you see somebody who is familiar to you, ask yourself if you are seeing this person with fresh eyes, as he or she really is, or if you are only seeing the reflection of your own thoughts about this person, and your feelings as well. Try it with your children, your spouse, friends, and co-workers, and even with your dog or cat if you have one. Try it with problems when they arise. Try it when you are outdoors in nature. Are you able to see the sky, the stars, the trees, the water, and the rocks as they are right now, with a clear and uncluttered mind? Or are you actually seeing them only through the veil of your own thoughts, opinions, and emotions?

4. Trust

Developing a basic trust in yourself and your feelings is an integral part of meditation training. It is far better to trust in your intuition and your own authority, even if you make some "mistakes" along the way, than always to look outside yourself for guidance. If at any time something doesn't feel right to you, why not honor your feelings? Why should you discount them or write them off as invalid because some authority or some group of people thinks or says differently? This attitude of trusting yourself and your own basic wisdom and goodness is very important in all aspects of the meditation practice. It will be particularly useful in the yoga. When practicing yoga, you will have to honor your feelings when your body tells you to stop or to back off in a particular stretch. If you don't listen, you might injure yourself.

Some people who become involved in meditation get so caught up in the reputation and authority of their teachers that they don't honor their own feelings and intuition. They believe that their teacher must be a much wiser and more advanced person, so they think they should venerate the teacher as a model of perfect wisdom and do exactly what he or she says without question. This attitude is completely contrary to the spirit of meditation, which emphasizes being your own person and understanding what it means to be yourself. Anybody who is imitating somebody else, no matter who it is, is heading in the wrong direction.

It is impossible to become like somebody else. Your only hope is to become more fully yourself. That is the reason for practicing meditation in the first place. Teachers, books, CDs, and apps can only be guides and offer signposts and suggestions. It is important to be open and receptive to what you can learn from other sources, but ultimately you still have to live your own life, every moment of it. In practicing mindfulness, you are practicing taking responsibility for being yourself and learning to listen to and trust your own being. The more you cultivate this trust in yourself, the easier you will find it will be to trust other people more and to see their basic goodness as well.

5. Non-striving

Almost everything we do we do for a purpose, to get something or somewhere. But in meditation this attitude can be a real obstacle. That is because meditation is different from all other human activities. Although it takes a lot of work and energy of a certain kind, ultimately meditation is a non-doing. It has no goal other than for you to be yourself. The irony is that you already are. This sounds paradoxical and a little crazy. Yet this paradox and craziness may be pointing you toward a new way of seeing yourself, one in which you are trying less and being more. This comes from intentionally cultivating the attitude of non-striving.

For example, if you sit down to meditate and you think, "I am going to get relaxed, or get enlightened, or control my pain, or become a better person," then you have introduced an idea into your mind of where you should be, and along with it comes the notion that you are not okay right now. "If only I were calmer, or more intelligent, or a harder worker, or more this or more that, if only my heart were healthier or my knee were better, then I would be okay. But right now, I am not okay."

This attitude undermines the cultivation of mindfulness, which involves simply paying attention to whatever is happening. If you are tense, then just pay attention to the tension. If you are in pain, then be with the pain as best you can. If you are criticizing yourself, then observe the activity of the judging mind. Just watch. Remember, we are simply allowing anything and everything that we experience from moment to moment to be here, because it already is. The invitation is to simply embrace it and hold it in awareness. You do not have to *do* anything with it.

People are either referred to the Stress Reduction Clinic by their doctors or come on their own because something is the matter. The first time they come, we ask them to identify three goals that they want to work toward in the program. But then, often to their surprise, we encourage them not to try to make any progress toward their goals over the eight weeks. In particular, if one of their goals is to lower their blood pressure or to reduce their pain or anxiety, they are instructed not to try to lower their blood pressure nor to try to make their pain or anxiety go away, but simply to stay in the present and carefully follow the meditation instructions.

As you will see shortly, in the meditative domain, the best way to achieve your goals is to back off from striving for results and instead to start focusing carefully on seeing and accepting things as they are, moment by moment. With patience and regular practice, movement toward your goals will take place by itself. This movement becomes an unfolding that you are inviting to happen within you.

6. Acceptance

Acceptance means seeing things as they actually are in the present. If you have a headache, accept that you have a headache. If you are overweight, why not accept it as a description of your body at this time? Sooner or later we have to come to terms with things as they are and accept them, whether it is a diagnosis of cancer or learning of someone's death. Often acceptance is reached only after we have gone through very emotion-filled periods of denial and then anger. These stages are a natural progression in the process of coming to terms with what is. They are all part of the healing process. In fact, my working definition of healing is *coming to terms with things as they are.*

However, putting aside for the moment the major calamities that usually take a great deal of time to heal from, in the course of our daily lives we often waste a lot of energy denying and resisting what is already fact. When we do that, we are basically trying to force situations to be the way we would like them to be, which only makes for more tension. This actually prevents positive change from occurring. We may be so busy denying and forcing and struggling that we have little energy left for healing and growing, and what little we have may be dissipated by our lack of awareness and intentionality.

If you are overweight and feel bad about your body, it's no good to wait until you are the weight you think you should be before you start liking your body and yourself. At a certain point, if you don't want to remain stuck in a frustrating vicious cycle, you might realize that it is all right to love yourself at the weight that you are now because this is the only time you can love yourself. Remember, now is the only time you have for anything. You have to accept yourself as you are before you can really change. Your choosing to do so becomes an act of self-compassion and intelligence.

When you start thinking this way, losing weight becomes less important. It also becomes a lot easier. By intentionally cultivating acceptance, you are creating the preconditions for healing.

Acceptance does not mean that you have to like everything or that you have to take a passive attitude toward everything and abandon your principles and values. It does not mean that you are satisfied with things as they are or that you are resigned to tolerating things as they "have to be." It does not mean that you should stop trying to break free of your self-destructive habits or to give up on your desire to change and grow, or that you should tolerate injustice, for instance, or avoid getting involved in changing the world around you because it is the way it is and therefore hopeless. It has nothing to do with passive resignation. Acceptance as we are speaking of it simply means that, sooner or later, you have come around to a willingness to see things as they are. This attitude sets the stage for acting appropriately in your life, no matter what is happening. You are much more likely to know what to do and have the inner conviction to act when you have a clear picture of what is actually happening versus when your vision is clouded by your mind's self-serving judgments and desires or its fears and prejudices.

In the meditation practice, we cultivate acceptance by taking each moment as it comes and being with it fully, as it is. We try not to impose our ideas about what we "should" be feeling or thinking or seeing in our experience. Instead, we just remind ourselves to be receptive and open to whatever we are feeling, thinking, or seeing, and to accept it because it is here right now. If we keep our attention focused on the present, we can be sure of one thing, namely, that whatever we are attending to in this moment will change, giving us the opportunity to practice accepting whatever it is that will emerge in the next moment. Clearly there is wisdom in cultivating acceptance.

7. *Letting Go*

They say that in India there is a particularly clever way of catching monkeys. As the story goes, hunters will cut a hole in a coconut that is just big enough for a monkey to put its hand through. Then they will drill two smaller holes in the other end, pass a wire through, and secure the coconut to the base of a tree. Then they slip a banana inside the coconut through the hole and hide. The monkey comes down, puts his hand in, and takes hold of the banana. The hole is cleverly crafted so that the open hand can go in but the fist cannot get out. All the monkey has to do to be free is to let go of the banana. But it seems most monkeys don't let go.

Often our minds get us caught in very much the same way in spite of all our intelligence. For this reason, cultivating the attitude of letting go, or non-attachment, is fundamental to the practice of mindfulness. When we start paying attention to our inner experience, we rapidly discover that there are certain thoughts, feelings, and situations that the mind seems to want to hold on to. If they are pleasant, we try to prolong these thoughts or feelings or situations, stretch them out, and conjure them up again and again.

Similarly, there are many thoughts and feelings and experiences that we try to get rid of or prevent ourselves from having because they are unpleasant, painful, or frightening in one way or another and we want to protect ourselves from them.

In the meditation practice we intentionally put aside the tendency to elevate some aspects of our experience and reject others. Instead we just let our experience be what it is, and practice observing it from moment to moment. Letting go is a way of letting things be, of accepting things as they are. When we observe our mind grasping and pushing away, we remind ourselves to let go of those impulses on purpose, just to see what will happen if we do. When we find ourselves judging our experience, we let go of those judging thoughts. We recognize them and we just don't pursue them any further. We let them be, and in doing so we let them go. Similarly, when thoughts of the past or of the future come up, we let go of them. We just watch—resting in awareness itself.

If we find it particularly difficult to let go of something because it has such a strong hold over our mind, we can direct our attention to what "holding on" feels like. Holding on, or "clinging," is the opposite of letting go. We can become an expert on our own attachments, whatever they may be and whatever their consequences in our lives, as well as how it feels in those moments when we finally do let go and what the consequences of that are. Being willing to look at the ways we hold on ultimately shows us a lot about the experience of its opposite. So whether we are "successful" at letting go or not, mindfulness continues to teach us if we are willing to look.

Letting go is not such a foreign experience. We do it every night when we go to sleep. We lie down on a padded surface, with the lights out, in a quiet place, and we let go of our mind and body. If you can't let go, you can't go to sleep.

Most of us have experienced times when the mind just would not shut down when we got into bed. This is one of the first signs of elevated stress. At these times we may be unable to free ourselves from certain thoughts because our involvement in them is just too powerful. If we try to force ourselves to sleep, it just makes things worse. So if you can go to sleep, you are already an expert in letting go. Now you just need to practice applying this skill in waking situations as well.

In addition to these seven foundational attitudinal elements of mindfulness practice, there are other qualities of mind and heart that also contribute to broadening as well as deepening the embodiment of mindfulness in our lives. These include cultivating attitudes of *non-harming, generosity, gratitude, forbearance, forgiveness, kindness, compassion, empathic joy,* and *equanimity.* In many ways, these are not separate from the seven we just explored, and arise naturally out of them and from paying attention to how we conduct ourselves in the face of challenging circumstances. The underlying power of these attitudes is easily discovered by experimenting with them, especially in easy, relatively stress-free moments. We can do this simply by keeping them in mind as best we can, and noticing how difficult it can be to be in touch with our gratitude, our impulses to be generous, our inclination to be kind, especially to ourselves . . . in other words, to be mindful of our *lack* of trust, or patience, or non-striving, or of generosity, kindness, empathic joy, or equanimity for that matter, in key moments. Mindfulness of being mistrustful, or impatient, or of clinging rather than letting go, of harming rather than non-harming, or of self-centeredness rather than generosity, is still mindfulness, and it is out of our intentional cultivation of the non-judging awareness that mindfulness is that a shift can slowly emerge, tilting us bit by bit toward these more spacious, even virtuous qualities that already reside within us by virtue of our being human. We can then notice how much they "affect the quality of the day," in Thoreau's famous words.*

COMMITMENT, SELF-DISCIPLINE, AND INTENTIONALITY

Purposefully cultivating the attitudes of non-judging, patience, trust, beginner's mind, non-striving, acceptance, and letting go will greatly support and deepen your engagement with the meditation practices you will be encountering in the following chapters.

In addition to these attitudes, you will also need to bring a particular kind of energy or *motivation* to your practice. Mindfulness doesn't just

* "To affect the quality of the day, that is the highest of arts." Thoreau HD. *Walden.* New York: Modern Library; 1937:81.

come about by itself because you have decided that it is a good idea to be more aware of things. A strong commitment to working on yourself and enough self-discipline to persevere in the process are essential to developing a strong meditation practice and a high degree of mindfulness.

In the MBSR classroom, the basic ground rule is that everybody practices. Nobody goes along for the ride. We don't let in any observers or spouses unless they are willing to practice the meditation just as the patients are doing, that is, forty-five minutes a day, six days a week. Doctors, medical students, therapists, nurses, and other health professionals who go through the program as part of an internship training program* all have to agree to practice the meditation on the same schedule as the patients. Without this personal experience, it would not be possible for them really to understand what the patients are going through and how much effort it takes to work with the energies of one's own mind and body.

The spirit of engaged commitment we ask of our patients during their eight weeks in the MBSR program is similar to that required in athletic training. The athlete who is training for a particular event doesn't practice only when he or she feels like it—for instance, only when the weather is nice, or there are other people to keep him or her company, or there is enough time to fit in a workout. The athlete trains regularly, every day, rain or shine, whether she feels good or not, whether the goal seems worth it or not on any particular day.

We encourage our patients to develop the same attitude. As already mentioned, we tell them from the very start, "You don't have to like it; you just have to do it. When the eight weeks are over, then you can tell us whether it was of any use or not. For now, just keep practicing."

Their own suffering and the possibility of being able to do something themselves to improve their health are usually motivation enough for the patients signing up for MBSR to invest this degree of personal commitment, at least for the eight weeks we require it of them. For most, it is a new experience to be in intensive mind-body training, to say nothing of working systematically within the domain of being. The discipline requires

* Now called the Practicum.

that people rearrange their lives to a certain extent around the training program. It takes a major and immediate lifestyle change just to make the time to engage in the formal meditation practices for forty-five minutes each day, never mind bringing mindfulness more and more into everyday life.

This time does not appear magically in anyone's life. You have to rearrange your schedule and your priorities and plan how you will free it up for practice. This is one of the ways in which enrolling in the stress reduction program can increase the stress in a person's life in the short run.

Those of us who teach in the clinic see meditation practice as an integral part of our own lives and of our own growth as people. So we are not asking our patients to do something that we don't do on a regular basis ourselves. We know what we are asking of them because we do it too. We know the effort that it takes to make space in one's life for meditation practice, and we know the value of living in this way. No one is ever considered for a staff position in the clinic unless he or she has had years of meditation training and has a strong daily meditation practice. The people referred to the clinic sense that what they are being asked to do is not something "remedial" but rather "advanced training" in mobilizing their deep inner resources for coping and for healing. You might think of it as advanced training in the art of living. Our own commitment to the practice as MBSR instructors conveys wordlessly our conviction that the journey we are inviting our patients to undertake is a true life adventure, one that we can engage in and pursue together over the eight weeks of the MBSR program. This feeling of involvement in a common pursuit makes it a lot easier for everyone to keep up the discipline of the daily practice. Ultimately, however, we are asking even more of our patients and of ourselves than just a time for formal meditation practice on a daily basis. For it is only by making the practice a "way of being" that its power can be put to practical use. The real mindfulness practice is how we live our lives from moment to moment, whatever we are doing, whatever our circumstances. Even the eight weeks of MBSR is just the beginning. We see the MBSR program as a launching platform for the rest of one's life. The ongoing cultivation and embodiment of mindfulness is that important.

To tap this power in your own life, we recommend that you set aside a particular block of time—every day, or at least six days a week, for at least eight consecutive weeks—to practice. Just making this amount of time every day for yourself is already a profound and very positive lifestyle change. Our lives are so complex and our minds so busy and agitated most of the time that it is necessary, especially at the beginning, to protect and support your meditation practice by making a special time for it and, if possible, by making a special place in your home where you will feel particularly comfortable and truly "at home" while practicing.

This time needs to be protected from interruptions and from other commitments so that you can just be yourself, without having to do or respond to anything. Although it is not always possible to set things up in this way, it is hugely helpful if you can manage to do it. One measure of your commitment is whether you can bring yourself to shut off your various electronic devices for the time you will be practicing.* It is a great letting go in and of itself to be home only for yourself at those times. Great peace can follow from this alone.

Once you make the commitment to yourself to practice in this way, the self-discipline comes in carrying it out. Committing yourself to goals that are in your own self-interest is easy. But keeping to the path you have chosen when you run into obstacles and may not see "results" right away is the real measure of your commitment. This is where conscious intentionality comes in, the intention to practice whether you feel like it or not on a particular day, whether it is convenient or not, with the determination of an athlete.

Regular formal meditation practice is not as hard as you might think

* In the process, you can bring mindfulness to just how difficult this may be, and how much of the time your mind wants to check your email or your text messages or post a tweet. You might become aware of how addicted we can be to our devices, and to that 24/7 connectivity that has us always available and immediately responsive to everybody else, clutching our phones as if they were our oxygen line to life itself, and in the process, perhaps losing touch more and more with ourselves and with our moments—so that, ironically, some of the most important connections of all, namely, with our own deepest analog self, with our body, and with our present-moment experience, can be seriously eclipsed.

once you make up your mind to do it and pick an appropriate time. Most people are inwardly disciplined already to a certain extent. Getting dinner on the table every night requires discipline. Getting up in the morning and going to work requires discipline. And taking time for yourself certainly does too. You are not going to be paid for it, and chances are you will not be enrolled in an MBSR program in which you know that everybody else is doing it and so feel some social pressure to keep up your end of things. You will have to do it for better reasons than those. Perhaps the ability to function more effectively under pressure, or to be healthier and feel better, or to be more relaxed, self-confident, and happy will suffice. Ultimately you have to decide for yourself why you are making such a commitment.

Some people have resistance to the whole idea of taking time for themselves. In the United States at least, the Puritan ethic has left a legacy of guilt when we do something for ourselves. Some people discover that they have a little voice inside that tells them that it is selfish or that they are undeserving of this kind of time and energy. Usually they recognize it as a message they were given very early on in their lives: "Live for others, not for yourself." "Help others; don't dwell on yourself."

If you do feel undeserving of taking time for yourself, why not look at that as part of your mindfulness practice? Where do such feelings come from? What are the thoughts behind them? Can you observe them with acceptance? Are they accurate?

Certainly the degree to which you can really be of help to others, if that is what you believe is most important, depends directly on how balanced you are yourself. Taking time to "tune" your own instrument and restore your energy reserves can hardly be considered selfish. *Intelligent* would be a more apt description.

Happily, once people start practicing mindfulness, most quickly get over the idea that it is "selfish" or "narcissistic" to take time for themselves. They come to see the difference that making some time to just be has on the quality of their lives and their self-esteem, as well as on their relationships.

We suggest that everyone find their own best time to practice. Mine is early in the morning. I like to get up an hour or so before I would otherwise and meditate and do yoga. I like the quiet of this time. It feels very good to be up and have nothing to do, by agreement with myself, except to dwell in the present, being with things as they are, my mind open and aware—and staying away from the Internet and all electronic devices, no matter how strong their pull. I know the phone won't ring at that hour. I know the rest of my family is asleep, so my meditation practice is not taking time away from them. When our children were young, for years the littlest one in the family always seemed to sense when there was awake energy in the house, no matter what time it was, and so there were periods when I had to push my meditation time back as far as 4:00 a.m. to be sure to get some uninterrupted time. As they got older, at times they would meditate or do yoga with me. I never pushed it. It was just something Daddy did, so it was natural for them to know about it and to do it with me from time to time.

Practicing meditation and yoga in the early morning invariably has a positive influence on the rest of the day for me. When I start off the day dwelling in stillness, resting in awareness, inhabiting and thereby nourishing the domain of being, and cultivating some degree of calmness and concentration, I seem to be more mindful and relaxed the rest of the day as well, and better able to recognize stress and handle it more effectively. When I tune in to my body and work it gently to stretch my joints and feel my muscles, my body feels more alive and vibrant than on the days I don't do it. I also know with much greater sensitivity what condition my body is in that day and what I might want to watch out for, such as my lower back or my neck if they are particularly stiff or painful that morning.

Some of our patients like to practice early in the morning, but a lot don't or can't. We leave it to each individual to experiment with times to practice and to choose the best one for his or her schedule. Practicing late at night is not recommended in the beginning, however, because it is very hard to keep up the alert attention required when you are tired.

In the first weeks of the stress reduction program, many people have trouble staying awake when they do the body scan (see Chapter 5), even when they do it in the daytime, because they get so relaxed. If I feel groggy when I wake up in the morning, I might splash cold water on my face until

I know I am really awake. I don't want to meditate in a daze. I want to be alert. This may seem somewhat extreme, but really it is just affirming the value of being awake before engaging in a period of formal practice. It helps to remember that mindfulness is about being fully awake. It is not cultivated by relaxing to the point where unawareness and sleep take over. So we advocate doing anything necessary to wake up, even taking a cold shower if that is what it takes.

Your meditation practice will only be as powerful as your motivation to dispel the fog of your own lack of awareness. When you are in this fog, it is hard to remember the importance of practicing mindfulness, and it is hard to locate your attitudinal bearings. Confusion, fatigue, depression, and anxiety are powerful mental states that can undermine your best intentions to practice regularly. You can easily get caught up and then stuck in them and not even know it.

That is when your commitment to practice is of greatest value. It keeps you engaged in the process. The momentum of regular practice helps to maintain a certain mental stability and resilience even as you feel under tremendous pressure to get things done, or find yourself going through states of turmoil, confusion, lack of clarity, and procrastination. These are actually some of the most fruitful times to practice—not to get rid of your confusion or your feelings but just to be conscious and accepting of them.

Most people who come to the Stress Reduction Clinic, no matter what their medical problem is, tell us that they are really coming to attain peace of mind. This is an understandable goal, given their mental and physical pain. But to achieve peace of mind, people have to kindle a vision of what they really want for themselves and keep that vision alive in the face of inner and outer hardships, obstacles, and setbacks.

I used to think that meditation practice was so powerful in itself and so healing that as long as you devoted yourself to it on a regular basis, you would eventually see growth and change. But time has taught me that some kind of personal vision is also necessary. Perhaps it could be a vision of what or who you might be if you were to see more clearly into the ways in which your own mind might be limiting your possibilities for growth, even around what your body might be capable of if you were to accept and learn to work within its limitations of the moment. Such a personal vision or aspiration can be essential in carrying you through the inevitable periods of low motivation and give continuity to your practice.

For some, that vision might be one of vibrancy and health. For others, it might be one of relaxation, or kindness, or peacefulness, or harmony, or wisdom. Your vision should be what you believe is most fundamental to your ability to be your best self, to be at peace with yourself, to be fully integrated as a person, to be whole.

The price of wholeness is nothing less than a total commitment to recognizing your intrinsic wholeness and an unswerving belief in your capacity to embody it in any moment. In our view, you are already perfect just as you are, in the sense of already being perfectly who you are, including all the imperfections. The present moment is the perfect moment for opening to this dimension of your being, for embodying the full dimensionality of who you already are—in awareness. Carl Jung put it this way: "The attainment of wholeness requires one to stake one's whole being. Nothing less will do; there can be no easier conditions, no substitutes, no compromises."

With this perspective on the spirit and the attitudes that are most helpful to cultivate in your meditation practice, we are now ready to explore the practice itself.

3

The Power of Breathing: Your Unsuspected Ally in the Healing Process

Poets and scientists alike are aware that our organism pulsates with the rhythms of its ancestry. Rhythm and pulsation are intrinsic to all life, from the beating of bacterial cilia to the alternating cycles of photosynthesis and respiration in plants, to the circadian rhythms of our own body and its biochemistry. These rhythms of the living world are embedded within the larger rhythms of the planet itself, the ebb and flow of the tides, the carbon, nitrogen, and oxygen cycles of the biosphere, the cycles of night and day, the seasons. Our very bodies are joined with the planet in a continual rhythmic exchange as matter and energy flow back and forth between our bodies and what we call "the environment." Someone once calculated that, on average, every seven years all the atoms in our body have come and gone, replaced by others from outside us. This in itself is interesting to think about. What am I if little of the substance of my body is the same in any decade of my life?

One way this exchange of matter and energy happens is through breathing. With each breath, we exchange carbon dioxide molecules from inside our bodies for oxygen molecules from the surrounding air. Waste disposal with each outbreath, renewal with each inbreath. If this process is interrupted for more than a few minutes, the brain becomes starved for oxygen and undergoes irreversible damage. And, of course, without the breath, we die.

The breath has a very important partner in its work, namely the heart. Think of it: this amazing muscle never stops pumping during our entire lifetime. It begins beating in us long before we are born and it just keeps on beating, day in and day out, year in and year out without a pause, without a rest for our entire life. And it can even be kept alive by artificial means for some time after we are dead.

As with the breath, the heartbeat is a fundamental life rhythm. The heart pumps the oxygen-rich blood from the lungs via the arteries and their smaller capillaries to all the cells of the body, supplying them with the oxygen they need to function. As the red blood cells give up their oxygen, they load up with the carbon dioxide that is the major waste product of all living tissue. The carbon dioxide is then transported back to the heart through the veins and from there pumped to the lungs, where it is discharged into the atmosphere on the outbreath. This is followed by another inbreath, which again oxygenates the hemoglobin carrier molecules that will be pumped throughout the body with the next contraction of the heart. This is literally the pulse of life in us, the rhythm of the primordial sea internalized, the ebb and flow of matter and energy in our bodies.

From the moment we are born to the moment we die, we breathe. The rhythm of our breathing varies considerably as a function of our activities and our feelings. It quickens with physical exertion or emotional upset, and it slows down during sleep or periods of relaxation. As an experiment, you might try to be aware of your breathing when you are excited, angry, surprised, and relaxed and notice how it changes. Sometimes our breathing is very regular. At other times it is irregular, even labored.

We have some measure of conscious control over our breathing. If we choose to, we can hold our breath for a short while or voluntarily control the rate and depth at which we breathe.

But slow or rapid, controlled or left to itself, the breath keeps going, day and night, year in, year out, through all the experiences and stages of life we traverse. Usually we take it completely for granted. We don't pay any attention to our breathing unless something happens to prevent us from breathing normally. That is, unless we start to meditate.

The breath plays an extremely important role in meditation and in healing. Breathing is an incredibly powerful ally and teacher in the work of meditation, although people who have no training in meditation think nothing of it and find it uninteresting.

The fundamental pulsations of the body are particularly fruitful to focus on during meditation because they are so intimately connected with the experience of being alive. While we could theoretically focus on our heart beating instead of on our breathing, the breath is much easier to be aware of. The fact that it is a rhythmic process and that it is constantly changing will make it even more valuable to us. In focusing on the breath when we meditate, we are learning right from the start to get comfortable with change. We see that we will have to be flexible. We will have to train ourselves to attend to a process that not only cycles and flows but also responds to our emotional state by changing its rhythm, sometimes quite dramatically.

Our breathing has the added virtue of being a very convenient process to support ongoing awareness in our daily lives. As long as we are alive, it is always with us. We can't leave home without it. It is always here to be attended to, no matter what we are doing or feeling or experiencing, no matter where we are. Tuning in to it brings us right into the here and now. It immediately anchors our awareness in the body, in a fundamental, rhythmic, flowing life process.

Some people have trouble breathing when they get anxious. They start to breathe faster and faster and more and more shallowly and wind up hyperventilating, that is, not getting enough oxygen and blowing off too much carbon dioxide. This brings on feelings of light-headedness, often accompanied by a feeling of pressure in the chest. When, all of a sudden, you feel like you are not getting in enough air, an overwhelming wave of fear or panic can arise. When you panic, of course, it just makes it that much harder to get control of your breathing.

People who experience episodes of hyperventilation can think they are having a heart attack and are going to die. Actually, the worst that can happen is that they will black out, which is dangerous enough. But passing out is the body's way of breaking the vicious cycle that begins when you feel unable to breathe, which leads to panic, which leads to a stronger feeling of being unable to breathe. When you pass out, your breathing returns to normal on its own. If you are unable to get your breathing under control, your body and brain will do it for you, if necessary by short-circuiting your consciousness for a while.

When patients who suffer from hyperventilation are sent to the stress reduction clinic, they are asked, along with everyone else, to focus on their breathing as the first step in getting into the formal meditation practice. For many, just the thought of focusing on their breathing produces feelings of anxiety; they may have a lot of trouble *watching* their breath without trying to regulate it. But with perseverance, most regain confidence in their breathing as they get more familiar with it in the meditation practice.

A thirty-seven-year-old firefighter named Gregg came to the clinic referred by a psychiatrist after a year-long history of hyperventilation episodes and unsuccessful drug treatments for anxiety. His problem started when he was overcome by smoke in a burning building. From that day on, every time he tried to put on his gas mask to go into a burning building, his breathing would become rapid and shallow and he would be unable to put on the mask. Several times he was rushed from fires to the emergency room of the local hospital because he thought he was having a heart attack. But it was always diagnosed as hyperventilation. At the time he was referred to the Stress Reduction Clinic, he had been unable to go into buildings to fight fires for over a year.

In the first class, Gregg, along with everybody else, was introduced to the basic approach of watching his breathing. As soon as he started focusing on the feeling of it moving in and out, he felt anxiety building. He was reluctant to run out of the room, so he held on and made it through the class somehow. He also managed to force himself to practice every day that week, mostly out of desperation, in spite of his discomfort and his fear. That first week practicing the body scan, which as you will soon see involves a lot of focusing on breathing, was torture for him. Every time he would tune in to his breathing, he would feel terrible, as if his breath were an enemy. He saw it as an undependable and potentially uncontrollable force that had already made it impossible for him to work, thus changing his relationship to his fellow firefighters and his view of himself as a man.

Yet after just two weeks of doggedly working with his breathing while doing the body scan, he discovered that he could put on his mask and go into burning buildings again.

Gregg later described to the class how this dramatic change came about. As he spent time watching it, he became more confident in his breathing. Even though he was unaware of it at first, he was relaxing a little during the body scan, and as he got more relaxed, his feelings about his breathing started to change. By spending time just watching his breath flowing in and out as he moved his focus of attention through his body, he began to know what his breathing actually felt like. At the same time, he found that he was getting less caught up in his thoughts and fears about his breathing. From his own direct experience, he came to see that his breathing was not his enemy and that he could even use it to relax.

It was not a big jump for him to practice being aware of his breathing at other times of the day and to use it in the same way to become calmer wherever he was. One day it occurred to him to try it at a fire. He had been going out with the trucks on occasion but had only been able to do support activities. As he put on the mask, he purposefully focused on his breathing, watching it, letting it be as it was, accepting the feeling of the mask as he put it on his face, just as he worked with accepting his breathing and whatever feelings he was experiencing when he practiced the body scan at home. What he discovered was that it was okay.

From that day on, Gregg was able to put on his mask and go into burning buildings without panicking or hyperventilating. He had several moments in the first three years after he took the program when he experienced fear of being trapped when he was in closed, smoky places. But when this happened, he was able to become aware of his fear, slow down his breathing, and maintain his balance of mind. He never had another hyperventilation episode.

The easiest and most effective way to begin cultivating mindfulness as a formal meditative practice is to simply focus your attention on your breathing and see what happens as you attempt to keep it there, just as we did in Chapter 1 but for longer than three minutes. There are a number of different places in the body where we can focus our attention on the sensations associated with breathing. Obviously one is the nostrils. If you are watching your breathing from here, you will be focusing on the feeling of the breath as it flows past the nostrils. Another place to focus on is the chest as it expands and contracts, and another is the belly, which, if it is relaxed, moves in and out with each breath.

No matter which location you choose, the idea is to be aware of the sensations that accompany your breathing at that particular place and to hold them in the forefront of your awareness from moment to moment. Doing this, we *feel* the air as it flows in and out past the nostrils; we *feel* the movement of the muscles associated with breathing; we *feel* the belly as it moves in and out.

Paying attention to your breathing means just paying attention. Nothing more. It doesn't mean that you should "push" or force your breathing, or try to make it deeper, or change its pattern or rhythm. The chances are your breath has been moving in and out of your body very well for years without your having thought about it at all. There is no need to try to *control* it now just because you have decided to pay attention to it. In fact, trying to control it is counterproductive. The effort we make in being mindful of the breathing is simply to be aware of the *feeling* of each inbreath and each outbreath. If you like, you can also be aware of the feeling of the breath as the direction of flow reverses.

Another common mistake that people make when they first hear the meditation instructions about breathing is to assume that we are telling them to *think about* their breathing. But this is absolutely incorrect. Focusing on the breath does not mean you should think about your breathing! On the contrary, it means *becoming aware* of the breath by *feeling* the sensations associated with it, and by *attending* to the changing qualities of those breath sensations.

In MBSR, we generally focus on the sensations of breathing at the belly rather than at the nostrils or in the chest. This is partly because doing so tends to be particularly relaxing and calming in the early stages of practice. All professionals who make special use of their breathing as part of their work, such as opera singers, wind instrument players, dancers, actors, and martial artists, know the value of breathing from the belly and of "grounding" or anchoring their awareness in this region. They know from first-hand experience that they will have more breath and be better able to modulate it effectively if the breath comes from the belly.

Focusing on the breath at your belly can be calming. Just as the surface of the ocean tends to be choppy when the wind is blowing, so too the "atmospheric conditions" in our own mind can influence the waves of the breath. Our breathing tends to be reactive and agitated when either the outside environment or the inner environment is not calm and peaceful. In the case of the ocean, if you go down ten or twenty feet, there is only a gentle undulation; there is calm even when the surface is agitated. Similarly, when we focus on our breathing down in the belly, we are tuning in to a region of the body that is far from the head and thus far below the agitations of our thinking mind. It is intrinsically calmer. So tuning in to the breath at the belly is a valuable way of reestablishing inner calmness and balance in the face of emotional upset or when you have a lot on your mind.

In meditation, the breath can serve as a reliable and ever-present anchor for our attention. Tuning to the sensations of breathing anywhere we can feel them in the body allows us to drop below the surface agitations of the mind into relaxation, calmness, and stability, without having to change anything at all. The agitation and choppiness may still be at the surface of the mind, just as the waves and turbulence are at the surface of the water during stormy conditions. But in resting in awareness of the breath sensations, even for a moment or two, we are out of the wind and protected from the buffeting action of the waves and their tension-producing effects. This is an extremely effective way to reconnect with the potential for calmness within you. It enhances the overall stability of your mind, even in very difficult moments, when you most need some stability and clarity of mind.

When you touch base in any moment with that part of your mind that is already calm and stable, your perspective immediately changes. You can see things more clearly and act from inner balance rather than being tossed about by the agitations of your mind. This is one reason why focusing on the breath at your belly is so useful. Your belly is literally the center of gravity of your body, far below the head and the turmoil of your thinking mind. For this reason we "befriend" the belly right from the beginning as an ally in establishing calmness and awareness. But what we are really befriending is awareness itself. We are becoming intimate with this deep capacity that is an innate and priceless dimension of our human life. We are learning to *inhabit* awareness, and to embody awareness moment by moment and breath by breath.

Any moment during the day when you bring your attention to your breathing in this way becomes a moment of meditative awareness. It is an effective way of tuning in to the present and orienting yourself to your body and to what you are feeling, not only while you are meditating but also while you are going about living your life.

When you practice mindfulness of breathing, you may find that closing your eyes is helpful in deepening your concentration. However, it is not necessary always to meditate with your eyes closed. If you decide to keep them open, let your gaze be unfocused on the surface in front of you or on the floor, and keep it steady, but without staring. Bring the same kind of sensitivity to feeling your breathing that we brought to eating the raisins, as described in Chapter 1. In other words, be mindful of what you are actually feeling from moment to moment. Keep your attention on the breath for the full duration of the inbreath and the full duration of the outbreath as best you can. When you notice that your mind has wandered and is no longer attending to your breathing at all, just notice what *is* on your mind in that moment, and then gently and firmly bring it back to the breath at the belly.

DIAPHRAGMATIC BREATHING

Many of our patients have found it beneficial to breathe in a particular way that involves relaxing the belly. This is known as diaphragmatic breathing. It may or may not be the way you are already breathing. If it isn't, as you become more aware of your breathing pattern by focusing on your belly, you may find yourself breathing more this way naturally because it is slower and deeper than chest breathing, which tends to be rapid and shallow. If you watch infants breathe, you will see that diaphragmatic breathing is the way we all start out when we are babies.

Diaphragmatic breathing is better described as abdominal or belly breathing, because all respiratory patterns involve the diaphragm. To visualize this particular way of breathing, it helps to know a little about how your body gets air in and out of your lungs in the first place.

The diaphragm is a large, umbrella-shaped sheet of muscle that is attached all around the lower edges of the rib cage. It separates the contents of the chest (the heart, the lungs, and the great blood vessels) from the contents of the abdomen (the stomach, the liver, the intestines, etc.). When it contracts, it tightens and draws downward (see Figure 1) because it is anchored all along the rim of the rib cage. This downward movement increases the volume of the chest cavity, in which the lungs are located on either side of the heart. The increased volume in the chest produces a decrease in the air pressure in the lungs. Because of the decreased pressure inside the lungs, air from outside the body, which is at a higher pressure, flows into the lungs to equalize the pressure. This is the inbreath.

After the diaphragm contracts, it goes through a relaxation. As the diaphragm muscle relaxes, it gets looser and returns to its original position higher up in the chest, thereby decreasing the volume of the chest cavity. This increases the pressure in the chest, which forces the air in the lungs out through the nose (and mouth if it is open). This is the outbreath. So in all breathing, the air is drawn into the lungs as the diaphragm contracts and lowers and it is expelled as the diaphragm relaxes and comes back up.

Now, suppose the muscles that form the wall of your belly (the abdomen) are tight rather than relaxed when the diaphragm is contracting. As

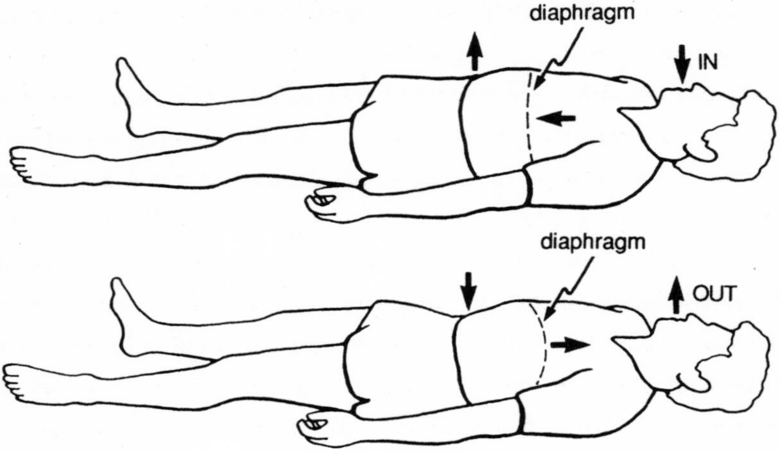

FIGURE 1

the diaphragm pushes down on the stomach and the liver and the other organs that are in your abdomen, it will meet resistance and will not be able to descend very far. Your breathing will tend to be shallow and rather high up in the chest.

In abdominal or diaphragmatic breathing, the idea is to intentionally relax your belly as much as you can. Then, as the breath comes in, the belly expands slightly (on its own) in an outward direction as the diaphragm pushes down on the contents of the abdomen from above. The diaphragm can go down farther when this happens, so the inbreath is a little longer and the lungs fill with a little more air. Then a little more air is expelled on the outbreath. Overall, the full cycle of your breathing will be slower and deeper.

If you are not accustomed to relaxing your belly, you may find your first attempts to breathe in this way to be frustrating and confusing. But if you persevere without forcing it, it soon comes naturally. Babies aren't trying to relax their bellies when they breathe; they are already relaxed. But once our bodies have developed a certain amount of chronic tension, as can happen as we get older, it can take a while to get the hang of softening the belly. However, it is definitely a skill worth cultivating, and it comes about just by paying some friendly attention to your breathing now and again.

At the beginning, you may find it helpful to lie down on your back or stretch out in a recliner, close your eyes, and put one hand on your belly. Bring your attention to your hand and feel it move as the breath flows in and out. If your hand is rising during the inhalation and falling during the exhalation, then you have it. It should not be a violent or forced movement and it need not be very big. It will feel like a balloon, expanding gently on the inbreath, deflating gently on the outbreath. If you feel it now, good. If you don't, that's fine too. It will come with time all by itself as you continue to practice tuning in to your breathing. And for the record, keep in mind that there is no balloon in your belly. That's just a way of visualizing the movement. If anything resembles balloons, it's your lungs, and they are in your chest!

When we surveyed several hundred patients who had been out of the stress reduction program for a number of years and asked them what the single most important thing they got out of the program was, the majority said, "The breathing." I find this response amusing, since every one of them was breathing long before they came for stress reduction training. Why would breathing, which they were doing before anyway, be so important and so valuable all of a sudden?

The answer is that once you start meditating, breathing is no longer just breathing. When we start paying attention to our breathing on a regular basis, our relationship to it changes dramatically. As we have already seen, tuning in to it helps us to gather our often unfocused energies and center ourselves. The breath reminds us to tune in to our body and to encounter the rest of our experience with mindfulness, in this very moment.

When we are mindful of our breathing, it automatically helps us to establish greater calmness in both the body and the mind. Then we are better able to be aware of our thoughts and feelings with a greater degree of calm and with a more discerning eye. We are able to see things more clearly and within a larger perspective, all because we are a little more awake, a little more aware. And with this awareness comes a feeling of having more room to move, of having more options, of being free to choose effective and appropriate responses in stressful situations rather than losing our equilibrium and sense of self as a result of feeling overwhelmed, thrown off balance by our own knee-jerk reactions.

This all comes from the simple practice of paying attention to your breathing when you dedicate yourself to practicing it regularly. In addition, you will discover that it is possible to direct your breath with great precision to various parts of your body in such a way that it will penetrate and soothe regions that are injured or in pain, at the same time that it calms and stabilizes the mind.

We also can use the breath to refine our innate capacity to rest for stretches of time in calmness and focused attention. Giving the mind *one thing* to keep track of—namely, the breath—to replace the whole range of things that it usually finds to preoccupy itself enhances our powers of concentration. Staying with the breath during meditation, no matter what, ultimately leads to deep experiences of calmness and awareness. It is as if the breath contains, folded into itself, a power that we can come to simply by giving ourselves over to it and following it as if it were a path.

This power is uncovered when we systematically bring awareness to the breath and sustain it for extended periods. With it comes a growing sense of the breath as a dependable ally. I suspect this is why our patients so often say that the breathing is the most important thing they get out of the course. Right in the simple old breath (I won't say "right beneath our noses") lies a completely overlooked source of power to transform our lives. All we need to do to make use of it is to deepen our attentional skills and our patience.

It is the very simplicity of the practice of mindfulness of breathing that gives it its power to disentangle us from the compulsive and habitual hold of the mind's many preoccupations. Yogis have known this for centuries. Breathing is the universal foundation for meditation practice.

Eventually, through ongoing practice, we may discover that it is not the breath that is actually the most important element in this equation—it is awareness itself that is most important and where the real transformative potential lies. The breath is simply an extremely useful object of attention in cultivating our ability to dwell in awareness and act out of embodied awareness. But it does have all the unique virtues we have been talking about, and many others as well, that make it a very special object of attention, one worthy of far greater intimacy and familiarity than we usually accord it. Plus, as our patients figure out for themselves, breathing as a primary object of attention can catalyze the discovery of the overriding importance of awareness itself. Breathing is no longer "just" breathing. Held in awareness, it is transformed, as is everything else. *It is all in how we are in relationship to experience.*

There are two major ways of practicing mindfulness of breathing. One involves the formal discipline of making a specific time in which you stop all activity, assume a special posture, and dwell for some time in moment-to-moment awareness of the inbreath and the outbreath, as described above. By practicing in this way regularly, you naturally deepen your ability to keep your attention on the breath for a sustained period of time. This will improve your ability to concentrate in general, as the mind becomes more focused and calmer, less reactive both to its own thoughts and to outside pressures. As you continue practicing, the calmness that comes with just being with your breathing over a period of time develops a stability of its own and becomes much more robust and dependable. Then, whatever practice you choose to engage in, and whatever object of attention you might choose to feature center-stage in the field of awareness, making time to meditate becomes nothing other than making time to come home to the deeper dimensions of your being, a time of inner peace and renewal.

The second way of practicing using the breath is to be mindful of it from time to time during the day, or even all day long, wherever you are and whatever you are doing. In this way the thread of meditative awareness, including the physical relaxation, the emotional calm, and the insight that come with it, is woven into every aspect of your daily life. We call this *informal meditation* practice. It is at least as valuable as the formal practice, but is easily neglected and loses much of its ability to stabilize the mind if it is not combined with regular formal meditation practice. The formal and informal practices using the breath complement and enrich each other. It is best to let them work together. Of course, the second way takes no time at all, just remembering. Then the real meditation practice becomes simply life itself, unfolding in awareness.

Mindfulness of breathing is central to all aspects of meditation practice. We will be using it when we practice the sitting meditation, the body scan, the yoga, and the walking meditation, which are all formal meditation practices. We will also be using it throughout the day as we practice developing a continuity of awareness in our lives. If you keep at it, the day will soon come when you will look upon your breathing as an old, familiar friend and a powerful ally in the healing process—and in living your life as if it really mattered, moment by moment by moment, and breath by breath by breath.

EXERCISE 1

1. Assume a comfortable posture lying on your back or sitting. If you are sitting, as best you can sit in a posture that embodies dignity, keeping the spine straight and letting your shoulders drop.
2. Allow your eyes to close, if it feels comfortable to you.
3. Allow your attention to gently alight on your belly, as if you were coming upon a shy animal sunning itself on a tree stump in a clearing in the forest. Feel your belly rise or expand gently on the inbreath, and fall or recede on the outbreath.
4. As best you can, maintain the focus on the various sensations associated with breathing, "being with" each inbreath for its full duration and "being with" each outbreath for its full duration, as if you were riding the waves of your own breathing.
5. Every time you notice that your mind has wandered off the breath, notice what it was that carried you away, and then gently bring your attention back to your belly and to the sensations

associated with the breath coming in and with the breath going out.

6. If your mind wanders away from the breath a thousand times, then your "job" is simply to notice what is on your mind at the moment that you come to realize that it is no longer on your breathing, and then to bring your attention back to the breath each and every time, no matter what it becomes preoccupied with. As best you can, continually rest in the awareness of the feeling of the breath moving in and out of the body, or come back to it over and over again.
7. Practice this exercise for fifteen minutes at a convenient time every day, whether you feel like it or not, for one week and see how it feels to incorporate a disciplined meditation practice into your life. Be aware of how it feels to spend some time each day just being with your breath without having to do anything.

EXERCISE 2

1. Tune in to your breathing at different times during the day, feeling the belly go through one or two risings and fallings.
2. Become aware of your thoughts and emotions in these moments, just observing them with kindness, without judging them or yourself.
3. At the same time, be aware of any changes in the way you are seeing things and feeling about yourself.
4. Ask yourself and look deeply into whether your awareness of an emotion or thought that arises is actually *caught* in the feeling of the emotion or in the content of the thought.

4

Sitting Meditation: Nourishing the Domain of Being

In the first class in MBSR, each person gets a chance to say why he or she has come to the program and what he or she hopes to get from participating. Linda described feeling as if a large truck were always right on her heels, driving just faster than she can walk. It was an image people could relate to; the vividness of it sent a wave of acknowledging nods and smiles through the room.

"What do you think the truck actually is?" I asked. She responded that it was her impulses, her cravings (she was very overweight), her desires—in a word, her mind. Her mind was the truck. It was always right behind her, pushing her, driving her, allowing her no rest, no peace.

We have already mentioned how our behavior and our emotional states can be driven by the play of the mind's likes and dislikes, by our addictions and aversions. When you look, is it not accurate to say that your mind is constantly seeking satisfaction, making plans to ensure that things will go your way, trying to get what you want or think you need and at the same time trying to ward off the things you fear, the things you don't want to happen? As a consequence of this common play of our minds, don't we all tend to fill up our days with things that just *have* to be done and then run around desperately trying to do them all, while in the process not really enjoying much of the doing because we are too pressed for time, too rushed, too busy, too anxious? We can feel overwhelmed by our schedules, our responsibilities, and our roles at times, even when everything we are doing is important, even when we have chosen to do them all. We live immersed in a world of constant doing. Rarely are we in touch with who is doing the doing—or, put otherwise, with the world of being.

To get back in touch with being is not that difficult. We only need to remind ourselves to be mindful. Moments of mindfulness are moments of peace and stillness, even in the midst of activity. When your whole life is driven by doing, formal meditation practice can provide a refuge of sanity and stability that can be used to restore some balance and perspective. It can be a way of stopping the headlong momentum of all the doing, giving yourself some time to dwell in deep relaxation and well-being and to remember who you are. The formal practice can give you the strength and the self-knowledge to return to what you need or want to do and let the doing come out of your grounding in the domain of being. Then at least a certain degree of patience, inner stillness, clarity, and balance of mind will infuse what you are doing, and the busyness and pressure will be less onerous. In fact, they might just disappear entirely as you step out of clock time altogether and take up residence even for brief moments in the timeless quality of now.

Meditation is really a non-doing. It is the only human endeavor I know of that does not involve trying to get somewhere else but, rather, emphasizes being where you already are. Much of the time we are so carried away by all the doing, the striving, the planning, the reacting, the busyness—that when we stop just to feel where we are, it can seem a little peculiar at first. For one thing, we tend to have little awareness of the incessant and relentless activity of our own mind and how much we are driven by it. That is not too surprising, given that we hardly ever stop and observe the mind directly to see what it is up to. We seldom look dispassionately at the reactions and habits of our own mind, at its fears and its desires.

It takes a while to get comfortable with the richness of allowing yourself to just *be* with your own mind. It's a little like meeting an old friend for the first time in years. There may be some awkwardness in the beginning, not knowing who this person is anymore, not knowing quite how to be with him or her. It may take some time to reestablish the bond, to refamiliarize yourselves with each other.

Ironically, although we all have minds, we seem to need to "re-mind" ourselves of who we are from time to time. If we don't, the momentum of all the doing can take over and have us living its agenda rather than our own, almost as if we were robots, and frenetic robots at that. The momentum of unbridled doing can carry us for decades, even to the grave, without our quite knowing that we are living out our lives and that we have only moments to live.

Given all the momentum behind our doing, getting ourselves to remember the preciousness of the present moment seems to require somewhat unusual and even drastic steps. This is why we make a special time each day for formal meditation practice. It is a way of stopping, a way of "re-minding" ourselves, of nourishing the domain of being for a change.

To make time in your life for being, for non-doing, may at first feel stilted and artificial. Until you actually get into it, it can sound like just one more thing to do. "Now I have to find time to meditate on top of all the obligations and stresses I already have in my life." And on one level, there is no getting around the fact that this is true.

But once you see the critical need to nourish your being, once you see the need to calm your heart and your mind and find an inner balance with which to face the storms of life, your commitment to make that time a priority and the requisite discipline to make it a reality develop naturally. Making time to meditate becomes easier. After all, if you discover for yourself that it really does nourish what is deepest and best in you, you will certainly find a way. You may even find yourself *wanting* to meditate, and looking forward to your times for formal practice.

We call the heart of the formal meditation practice "sitting meditation" or simply "sitting." As with breathing, sitting is not foreign to anyone. We all sit—nothing special about that. But mindful sitting is different from ordinary sitting in the same way that mindful breathing is different from ordinary breathing. The difference, of course, is your awareness.

To practice sitting, we make a special time and place for non-doing, as suggested in Chapter 2. We consciously adopt an alert and relaxed body posture so that we can feel relatively comfortable without moving. Then we simply reside with calm acceptance in the present without trying to fill it with anything. You have already tried this in the various exercises in which you have been watching your breathing.

It helps a lot to adopt an erect and dignified posture, with your head, neck, and back aligned vertically. This allows the breath to flow most easily. It is also the physical counterpart of the inner attitudes of self-reliance, self-acceptance, and alert attention that we are cultivating.

We usually practice the sitting meditation either on a chair or on the floor. If you choose a chair, the ideal is to use one that has a straight back and that allows your feet to be flat on the floor. We often recommend that, if possible, you sit away from the back of the chair so that your spine is self-supporting (see Figure 2A). But if you have to, leaning against the back of the chair is also fine. If you choose to sit on the floor, do so on a firm, thick cushion that raises your buttocks off the floor three to six inches (a pillow folded over once or twice does nicely, or you can purchase a meditation cushion, or zafu, specifically for this purpose).

There are a number of cross-legged sitting postures and kneeling postures that we can choose from if we wish to sit on the floor. The one I use most is the so-called Burmese posture (see Figure 2B), which involves drawing one heel in close to the body and draping the other leg in front of it. Depending on how flexible your hips, knees, and ankles are, your knees may or may not be touching the floor; it is somewhat more comfortable when they are. Others use a kneeling posture, placing the cushion between the feet (see Figure 2C) or using a bench designed for the purpose.

Sitting on the floor can give you a reassuring feeling of being "rooted" or "grounded" and completely self-supporting in the meditation posture. But it is not at all necessary to meditate sitting on the floor or in a cross-legged posture. Some of our patients prefer the floor, but most sit on straight-backed chairs. Ultimately it is not what you are sitting on that matters but the sincerity of your effort.

Whether you choose the floor or a chair, posture is very important in meditation practice. It can be an outward support in cultivating an inner attitude of dignity, patience, presence, and self-acceptance. The main points to keep in mind about your posture are to keep the back, neck, and head aligned vertically to whatever degree possible, to relax the shoulders, and to do something comfortable with your hands. Usually we place them on the knees, as in Figure 2, or we rest them in the lap with the fingers of the left hand above the fingers of the right and the tips of the thumbs just touching each other.

When we have assumed the posture we have selected, we bring our attention to our breathing. We *feel* it come in, we *feel* it go out. We dwell in the present, moment by moment, breath by breath. It sounds simple—and it is. Full awareness on the inbreath, full awareness on the outbreath—letting the breath just happen, observing it, and feeling all the sensations, gross and subtle, associated with it, as best we can.

It is simple but it is not easy. You can probably sit in front of a TV or in a car on a trip for hours at a time without giving it a thought. But when you try sitting in your house with nothing to watch but your breath, your body, and your mind, with nothing to entertain you and no place to go, the first thing you will probably notice is that at least part of you doesn't want to stay at this for very long.

After perhaps a minute or two or three or four, either the body or the mind will have had enough and will demand something else, either to shift to some other posture or to do something else entirely. This is inevitable. It happens to everybody, not just to novices.

It is at this point that the work of self-observation gets particularly interesting and fruitful. Normally every time the mind moves, the body follows. If the mind is restless, the body is restless. If the mind wants a drink, the body goes to the kitchen sink or the refrigerator. If the mind says, "This is boring," then before you know it, the body is up and looking around for the next thing to do to keep the mind happy, usually by entertaining it or distracting it and thus diverting you from your original inten-

FIGURE 2

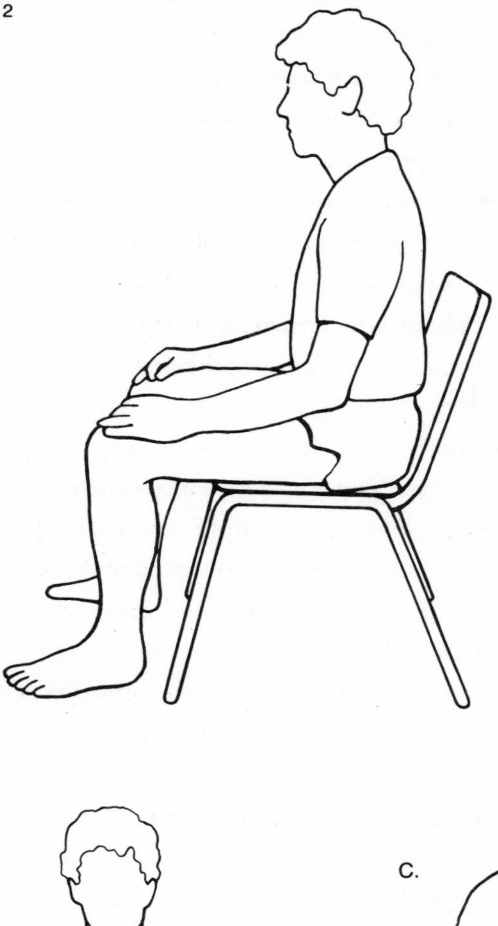

A.

B.

C.

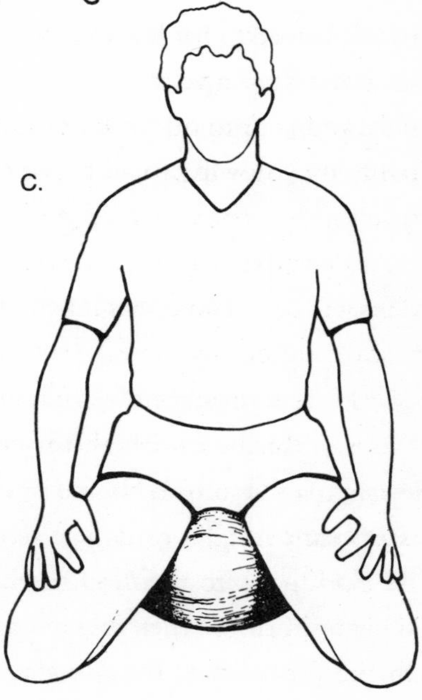

tion to stay with the meditation practice. It also works the other way around. If the body feels the slightest discomfort, it will shift to be more comfortable or it will call on the mind to find something else for it to do, and again, you will be standing up, literally before you know it. Alternatively, you may find yourself perpetually lost in thought or daydreaming.

If you are genuinely committed to being more peaceful and relaxed, you might wonder why it is that your mind is so quick to be bored with being with itself and why your body is so restless and uncomfortable. You might wonder what is behind your impulses to fill each moment with something, what is behind your need to jump up and get going or be entertained whenever you have an "empty" moment. What drives the body and mind to reject being still?

In practicing meditation we don't try to answer such questions. Rather we just observe the impulse to get up or the thoughts and emotions that come into the mind. And instead of jumping up and doing whatever the mind decides is next on the agenda, we gently but firmly bring our attention back to the belly, back to the breathing, and just continue to watch and feel and ride on the waves of the breath, moment by moment by moment. We may ponder why the mind is like this for a moment or two, but basically we are practicing accepting each moment as it is without reacting to how it is. And so, we keep sitting, attending to the breath sensations and being the knowing that awareness already is.

THE BASIC MEDITATION INSTRUCTIONS

The basic instructions for practicing the sitting meditation are very simple. We observe the breath as it flows in and out. We give full attention to the *feeling* of the breath as it comes in and full attention to the *feeling* of the breath as it goes out, just as we did in Chapters 1 and 3. And whenever we find that our attention has been carried elsewhere, wherever that may be, we simply note it, then let go and gently escort our attention back to the breath, back to the rising and falling of our own belly.

If you have been trying it, perhaps you will have already noticed that your mind tends to move around a lot. You may have contracted with yourself to keep your attention focused on the breath no matter what. But before long, you will undoubtedly find that the mind is off someplace else. It has forgotten the breath; it has been drawn away.

Each time you become aware of this while you are sitting, the instruction is to first note briefly what is on your mind or what carried you away from attending to the breath, and then to gently bring your attention back to your belly and back to your breathing, no matter what carried it away. If it moves off the breath a hundred times, then you just calmly and gently bring it back a hundred times.

By doing so, you are training your mind to be less reactive and more stable. You are making each moment count. You are taking each moment as it comes, not valuing any one above any other. In this way you are cultivating your natural ability to concentrate your mind. By repeatedly bringing your attention back to the breath each time it wanders off, concentration builds and deepens, much as muscles develop by repetitively lifting weights. Working regularly with (rather than struggling against) the resistance of your own mind builds inner strength. At the same time you are also developing patience and practicing being non-judgmental. You are not giving yourself a hard time because your mind wandered away from the breath. You simply and matter-of-factly return it to the breath, gently but firmly.

WHAT TO DO ABOUT YOUR BODY'S DISCOMFORT

As you will quickly see when you sit down to meditate, almost anything can carry your attention away from your breathing. One big source of distracting impulses is your body. As a rule, if you sit still for a while in any position, your body will become uncomfortable. Normally we are continually shifting our posture in response to this discomfort, without much, if any, awareness of it. But when practicing formal sitting meditation, it is actually useful to resist the first impulse to shift position in response to bodily discomfort. Instead, we direct our attention to these very sensations of discomfort and mentally welcome them.

Why? Because at the moment they come into awareness, these sensations of discomfort become part of our present-moment experience and thus worthy objects of observation and inquiry in and of themselves. They give us the opportunity to look directly at our automatic reactions and at the whole process of what happens as the mind loses its balance and becomes agitated as it is carried off and gets lost in the thought stream in one way or another, far away from any awareness of the breath.

In this way, the pain in your knee or the aching in your back or the tension in your shoulders, rather than being treated as distractions preventing you from staying with your breath, can be included in the field of your awareness and simply accepted without reacting to them as undesirable and trying to make them go away. This approach gives you an alternative way of seeing discomfort. Uncomfortable as they may be, these bodily sensations are now potential teachers and allies in learning about yourself. They can help you to develop your powers of concentration, calmness, and awareness rather than just being frustrating impediments to the goal of trying to keep your attention fixed on your breathing.

The cultivation of this kind of flexibility, which allows you to welcome *whatever* comes up and be with it rather than insisting on paying attention to only one thing, say the breath, is one of the most characteristic and valuable features of mindfulness meditation. This is the case because, as we noted earlier, it is not the breath that is most important here, but the awareness itself. And the awareness can be of *any* aspect of your experience, not just your breathing—because it is always the same awareness, whatever the chosen object or objects of attention.

What this means in practice is that we make some effort to sit *with* sensations of discomfort when they come up during our attempts to meditate, not necessarily to the point of pain but at least past where we might ordinarily react to them. We breathe *with* them. We breathe *into* them. We put out the welcome mat for them and actually try to maintain a continuity of awareness from moment to moment in their presence. Then, if we have to, we shift our body to reduce the discomfort, but even that we do mindfully, with moment-to-moment awareness as we are moving the body.

It's not that the meditative process considers messages about discomfort and pain that the body produces to be unimportant. On the contrary, as you will see in Chapters 22 and 23, we consider pain and discomfort to be important enough to merit a far deeper exploration. The best way to explore sensations of pain and discomfort is to welcome them when they arise rather than resisting them or trying to make them go away because we don't like them. By sitting with some discomfort and accepting it as part of our experience in the present moment, even if we don't like it, which we don't, we discover that it is actually possible to turn toward and relax into physical discomfort, to embrace it in awareness as it is. This is one example of how discomfort or even pain can become your teacher and help you to heal.

Relaxing and softening into discomfort sometimes actually reduces pain intensity. The more you practice, the more skill you can develop in reducing pain or at least becoming more transparent to it, so that it is less eroding of your quality of life. But whether you experience pain reduction or not during the sitting meditation, intentionally working with your reactions to discomfort and to whatever arises that is unpleasant and unwanted will help you to develop some degree of calmness, equanimity, and flexibility of mind, qualities that will prove useful in facing many different challenges and stressful situations as well as pain (see Parts II and III).

HOW TO WORK WITH THOUGHTS IN MEDITATION

Aside from physical discomfort and pain, there are numerous other occurrences during meditation that can carry your attention away from the breath. The primary one is thinking. Just because you decide to still your body and observe your breath from moment to moment doesn't mean that your thinking mind is going to cooperate. It doesn't necessarily quiet down just because you have decided to meditate! Quite the contrary.

What does happen as we intentionally pay attention to our breathing is that we realize pretty quickly that we are immersed in a seemingly never-ending stream of thoughts, coming willy-nilly one after another in rapid succession. Many people are greatly relieved when they come back after practicing meditation on their own during their first week of MBSR and discover that they were not the only ones who found that their thoughts cascaded through their mind like a torrent or a waterfall, completely beyond their control. They are reassured to learn that everybody in the class has a mind that behaves in this way. It is just the way the mind is.

This discovery amounts to a revelation for many of the people in the Stress Reduction Clinic. It becomes the occasion of or sets the stage for a profound learning experience that many claim is the most valuable thing they get out of their mindfulness training: the realization that they are not their thoughts. This discovery means that they can consciously choose to relate (or not) to their thoughts in a variety of ways that were not available to them when they were unaware of this simple fact.

In the early stages of our meditation practice, the activity of thought is constantly pulling our attention away from the primary task we have set ourselves in the developing of some degree of calmness and concentration, namely, to be with the breath. In order to build continuity and momentum in the meditation practice, you will need to keep reminding yourself to come back to the breath over and over again, no matter what the mind is up to from one moment to the next.

The things you find yourself thinking about during meditation may or may not be important to you, but important or not, they do seem to lead a life of their own, as we have seen. If you are in a period of high stress, the mind will tend to obsess about your predicament—what you should do or should have done, what you shouldn't do or shouldn't have done. At such times your thoughts may be highly charged with anxiety and worry.

At less stressful times, the thoughts that go through your mind may be less anxious in nature, but they can be just as powerful in taking your attention away from the breath. You may find yourself thinking about a movie you saw, or fall captive to a song in your head that stubbornly refuses to leave. Or you may be thinking about dinner, work, your parents, your children, other people, your vacation, your health, death, the bills you have to pay, or just about anything else. Thoughts of one kind or another will cascade through the mind as you sit, most of them below the level of your awareness, until finally you realize that you are not watching your breathing anymore and you don't even know how long it's been since you were aware of it, nor how you got to what you are thinking now.

It's at this point that you might say to yourself, "Okay, let's just go back to the breath right now and let go of these thoughts I'm having, no matter what they are. But first, let me recognize that they are actually thoughts, events in the field of my awareness." It is helpful to remind yourself that letting go of your thoughts doesn't mean pushing them away. It means simply letting them be here as they are, as we once again place the breath sensations center stage in the field of awareness. It also helps at such moments to check your posture and to sit up straight again if your body has slumped over, which it tends to do when dullness and self-distraction set in.

During meditation, we intentionally treat all our thoughts as if they are of equal value. As best we can, and with the lightest of touches, we bring awareness to them when they arise, and then we intentionally return our attention to the breath as the primary focus of our attention, *regardless of the content of the thought and its emotional charge.* In other words, we intentionally practice letting go of each thought that attracts our attention, whether it seems important and insightful or unimportant and trivial. We just observe them as thoughts, as discrete and exceedingly transient events that appear in the field of our awareness. We are aware of them because they are here, but we intentionally decline to get caught up in the content of the thoughts during meditation, no matter how meaningful or enticing the content may be for us in any given moment. Instead, we remind ourselves to see them simply as thoughts, as seemingly independently occurring events in the field of our awareness. We note their content and their "emotional charge"—in other words, whether they are weak or strong in their power to dominate the mind at that moment. Then, no matter how charged they may be for us in that moment, and regardless of whether they are primarily pleasant or primarily unpleasant, we intentionally let go of them and refocus on our breathing once again and on the experience of being "in our body" as we sit here. We repeat this hundreds of thousands of times, millions of times, as necessary. And it will be necessary.

It's important to reiterate that letting go of our thoughts does not mean suppressing them. Many people hear it this way and make the mistake of thinking that meditation requires them to shut off their thinking or their feelings. They somehow hear the instructions as meaning that if they are thinking, that is "bad," and that a "good meditation" is one in which there is little or no thinking. *Thinking is not bad, nor is it even undesirable during meditation. What matters is whether you are aware of your thoughts and feelings during meditation and how you are in relationship to them.* Trying to suppress them will only result in greater tension and frustration and more problems, not in calmness, insight, clarity, and peace.

Mindfulness does not involve pushing thoughts away or walling yourself off from them to quiet your mind. We are not trying to stop our thoughts as they cascade through the mind. We are simply making room for them, observing them as thoughts, and letting them be, using the breath as our anchor or "home base" for observing, for reminding us to stay focused and calm. It might help to keep in mind that the awareness of our thoughts and emotions is *the same awareness* as the awareness of our breathing.

In bringing this orientation to the cultivation of mindfulness, you will find that every period of formal meditation practice is different. Sometimes you may feel relatively calm and relaxed, undisturbed by thoughts or strong emotions. At other times, the thoughts and emotions may be so strong and recurrent that all you can do is watch them as best you can and be with your breath as much as you can in between. *Meditation is not so concerned with how much thinking is going on as it is with how much room you are making for it to take place within the field of your awareness from one moment to the next.*

It is remarkable how liberating it feels to be able to see that your thoughts are just thoughts and that they are not "you" or "reality." For instance, if you have the thought that you have to get a certain number of things done today and you don't recognize it as a thought but act as if it's "the truth," then you have created a reality *in that moment* in which you really believe that those things must all be done today.

Peter, who, as we saw in Chapter 1, had come to MBSR training because he had had a heart attack and wanted to prevent another one, came to a dramatic realization of this one night when he found himself washing his car at ten o'clock at night with the floodlights on in the driveway. It struck him that he didn't *have* to be doing this. It was just the inevitable result of a whole day spent trying to fit everything in that he *thought* needed doing. As he saw what he was doing to himself, he also saw that he had been unable to question the truth of his original conviction that everything had to get done today, because he was already so completely caught up in believing it.

If you find yourself behaving in similar ways, it is likely that you will also feel driven, tense, and anxious without even knowing why, just as Peter did. So if the thought of how much you have to get done today comes up while you are meditating, you will have to be very attentive to it *as a thought* or you may be up and doing things before you know it, without any awareness that you decided to stop sitting simply because a thought came through your mind.

On the other hand, when such a thought comes up, if you are able to step back from it and see it clearly, then you will be able to prioritize things and make sensible decisions about what really does need doing. You will know when to call it quits during the day, and when to take breaks while you are working so you can restore yourself and work most effectively. So the simple act of recognizing your thoughts as *thoughts* can free you from the distorted reality they often create, and allow for more clear-sightedness and a greater sense of manageability and even productivity in your life.

This liberation from the tyranny of the thinking mind comes directly out of the meditation practice itself. When we spend some time each day in non-doing, resting in awareness, observing the flow of the breath and the activity of our mind and body without getting caught up in that activity, we are cultivating calmness and mindfulness hand in hand. As the mind develops stability and is less caught up in the content of thinking, we strengthen the mind's ability to concentrate and to be calm. Each time we recognize a thought as a thought when it arises and we register its content and discern the strength of its hold on us, as well as the accuracy of its content, we are strengthening the mindfulness muscle. Each time we then let go of it and come back to our breathing and to a sense of our body, we are strengthening the mindfulness muscle. In the process, we are coming to know ourselves better and becoming more accepting of ourselves, not as we would like to be but as we actually are. This is an expression of our innate wisdom and compassion.

OTHER OBJECTS OF ATTENTION IN THE SITTING MEDITATION PRACTICE

We usually introduce the sitting meditation practice in the second class of the MBSR curriculum. People practice it for homework for ten minutes once a day in the second week, in addition to the forty-five-minute body scan you will encounter in the next chapter. Over the weeks, we increase the sitting time until we can sit for up to forty-five minutes at a stretch. As we do, we also expand the range of experiences we invite into the field of awareness and attend to in the sitting.

For the first few weeks, we just watch the breath come in and go out. You could practice in this way for a very long time and never come to the end of its richness. It just gets deeper and deeper. The mind gradually becomes calmer and more supple, and mindfulness—moment-to-moment non-judgmental awareness—stronger and stronger.

In the domain of meditation instructions, the simplest practices, such as mindfulness of breathing, are as profoundly healing and liberating as more elaborate methods, which sometimes people mistakenly think are more "advanced." In no sense is being with your breath any less advanced than paying attention to other aspects of inner and outer experience. All have a place and value in cultivating mindfulness and wisdom. Fundamentally, it is the quality and sincerity of your effort in practicing and the depth of your seeing that are important, rather than what "technique" you are using or what you are paying attention to. If you are really paying attention, any object can become a door into direct moment-to-moment awareness. Remember, it is the same awareness, no matter what the objects of attention may be to which we are according primacy in any particular practice. Nevertheless, mindfulness of breathing can be a very powerful and effective foundation for all the other meditation practices you will be encountering in MBSR. For this reason, we will be returning to it over and over again.

As the MBSR curriculum unfolds over the eight weeks of the program, we gradually expand the field of attention in the sitting meditation in a stepwise fashion to include, in addition to breathing, body sensations in particular regions, a sense of the body as a whole, sounds, and finally the thought process itself and our emotions. Sometimes we focus on just one of these as the primary object of attention. At other times we may cover all of them sequentially in one practice period and finish by sitting with awareness of whatever comes up, not looking for anything in particular to focus on, whether it be sounds or thoughts or even the breath. This way of practicing is called *choiceless awareness* or, alternatively, *open presence.* You can think of it as simply being present with and receptive to whatever unfolds in each moment as you rest in awareness. Simple as it may sound, practicing in this way requires developing at least a degree of stability of mind, including a relatively strong calmness and attentiveness. These are qualities of mind that are best cultivated, as we have seen, by choosing one object, most commonly the breath, and working with it over a period of months and even years. For this reason, some people might benefit most by staying with the breath and a sense of the body as a whole in the early stages of their meditation practice, especially if they are taking more than eight weeks to work their way through the MBSR curriculum. You can practice the awareness of breathing on your own without using a CD or its audio program equivalent for guidance. Alternatively, you can find other guided meditations (for instance, Series 2 and 3) that might help you at this or other stages of your practice. However, for now, we suggest that you practice as described in the exercises at the end of this chapter. Then in Chapter 10, and also in Chapters 34 and 35, you will find the outlines of a comprehensive program for developing the meditation practice, formally and informally, over an eight-week period, following the schedule we use in the MBSR classes themselves. In this way, all the meditation practices develop and are deepened in tandem as we are introduced to them in sequence. Many people wind up doing the entire eight-week program on their own using the guided meditation CDs along with this book as a manual. I know this because I hear from them and meet them quite often in my travels.

When we introduce the sitting meditation in the second class, there is usually a lot of shifting around, fidgeting, and opening and closing of the eyes as people get accustomed to the idea of not doing anything and learn to settle into just being. For those people who come with pain diagnoses or with anxiety or ADHD (attention deficit hyperactivity disorder), or who are exclusively action-oriented, sitting still may at first seem like an impossibility. They often think, not surprisingly, that they will be in too much pain, or too nervous, or too bored to be able to do it. But after a few weeks of practicing on their own in between the classes, the collective stillness in the room is deafening—even though by that time we may be sitting for twenty or thirty minutes at a stretch. There is very little shifting and fidgeting, even among the people with pain and anxiety problems and the "go-getters" who usually never rest for a minute. These are clear signs that they are indeed practicing at home and that they are developing some degree of intimacy with stillness, both of the body and of the mind.

Before long, most people discover that it can be quite exhilarating to meditate. Sometimes it doesn't even seem like work. It's just an effortless opening and releasing into the stillness of being, accepting each moment as it unfolds, resting in awareness.

These are true moments of wholeness, accessible to all of us. Where do they come from? Nowhere. They are here all the time. Each time you sit in an alert and dignified posture and turn your attention to your breathing, for however long, you are returning to your own wholeness, affirming your intrinsic balance of mind and body, independent of the passing state of either your mind or your body in any moment. Sitting becomes an easing into stillness and peace beneath the surface agitations of your mind. It's as easy as seeing and letting be, seeing and letting go, seeing and letting be.

EXERCISE 1

Sitting with the Breath

1. Continue to practice awareness of your breathing in a comfortable and dignified sitting posture for at least ten minutes at least once a day.
2. Each time you notice that your mind is no longer on your breath, just notice what is on your mind. Then, whatever it is, let it be as it is and once again feature the breath sensations in your belly center stage in the field of awareness.
3. Over time, try extending the time you sit until you can sit for thirty minutes or longer. But remember, when you are really in the present moment, there is no time, so clock time is not as important as your willingness to pay attention and ride the waves of your breathing as best you can, moment by moment and breath by breath.

EXERCISE 2

Sitting with the Breath and the Body as a Whole

1. When your practice feels strong in the sense that you can sustain some continuity of attention on the breath, try expanding the field of your awareness "around" your breathing and "around" your belly to include a sense of your body as a whole sitting and breathing.
2. Maintain this awareness of the body sitting and breathing. When the mind wanders, noticing what is on your mind, and

then gently bringing it back to an awareness of sitting and breathing.

EXERCISE 3

Sitting with Sound

1. If you feel like it, try featuring hearing itself center stage in the field of awareness during periods of formal sitting meditation. This does not mean listening for sounds, but rather simply hearing what is here to be heard, moment by moment, without judging or thinking about what you are hearing—just hearing sounds as sounds. Imagine the mind as a "sound mirror," simply reflecting whatever arises in the domain of hearing. You can also experiment with hearing the silences within and between the sounds as well.
2. You can practice this way with music too, hearing each note as it comes and also hearing as best you can the spaces *between* the notes. Try breathing the sounds into your body on an inbreath and letting them flow out again on the outbreath. Imagine that your body is transparent to sounds, that sounds can move in and out of your body through the pores of your skin. Imagine that sounds can be "heard" and felt by your very bones. How does this feel?

EXERCISE 4

Sitting with Thoughts and Feelings

1. When your attention is relatively stable on the breath, try shifting your focus to feature the process of thinking itself. Let the breath sensations move into the background and allow the

thinking process itself to come to the foreground, placing it center stage in the field of awareness—observing thoughts arise and pass away like clouds in the sky or like writing on water—allowing the mind to function as a "thought mirror" simply reflecting and registering whatever comes, as it comes, and whatever goes, as it goes.

2. See if you can perceive these thoughts as discrete events in the field of awareness, arising, lingering perhaps, and then passing away.
3. As best you can, note their content and their emotional charge while, if possible, not being drawn into thinking about them, or thinking the next thought, but just maintaining the "frame" through which you are observing the process of thought.
4. Note that an individual thought does not last long. It is impermanent. If it comes, it will go. It is helpful to be aware of this observation and let its import register with you in awareness.
5. Note how some thoughts keep coming back.
6. It can be especially instructive to take note of those thoughts that are centered on or driven by personal pronouns, especially *I, me,* or *mine* thoughts, observing carefully how self-centered the content of those thoughts may be. How are you in relationship to those thoughts when you simply note them as thoughts in the field of awareness and don't take them quite so personally? How do you feel about them when you observe them in this non-judgmental way? Is there something to be learned from this?
7. Note those moments when the mind creates a "self" to be preoccupied with how well or how badly your life is going.
8. Note thoughts about the past and thoughts about the future.
9. Note thoughts that are about greed, wanting, grasping, or clinging.
10. Note thoughts that are about anger, disliking, hatred, aversion, or rejection.
11. Note feelings and moods as they come and go.

12. Note what feelings and moods are associated with different thought contents.
13. If you get lost in all this, just go back to your breathing until the attention stabilizes itself, and then, if you care to, reestablishing thinking as the primary object of attention. Remember, this is not an invitation to generate thoughts, simply an invitation to attend to their arising, their lingering if they linger, and their passing away in the field of awareness.

This exercise requires a degree of stability in your attention. It might be best to practice this for relatively short periods of time in the early stages of practice. But even two or three minutes of mindfulness of the process of thinking can be extremely valuable.

EXERCISE 5

Sitting with Choiceless Awareness

1. Just sit. Don't hold on to anything. Don't look for anything. Practice being completely open and receptive to whatever comes into the field of awareness, letting it all come and go, watching, witnessing, attending in stillness. Allow yourself to be the non-conceptual knowing (and the not-knowing) that awareness already is.

5

Being in Your Body: The Body-Scan Meditation

It is amazing to me that we can be simultaneously completely preoccupied with the appearance of our own body and at the same time completely out of touch with it as well. This goes for our relationship to other people's bodies too. As a society, we seem to be overwhelmingly preoccupied with appearances in general and appearance of bodies in particular. Bodies are used in advertisements to sell everything from cars to smart phones to beer. Why? Because the advertisers are capitalizing on people's strong identification with particular body images at particular stages of life. Images of attractive men and seductive women generate in viewers thoughts about looking a certain way themselves to feel special, or better, or younger, or happy.

Much of our preoccupation with how we look comes from a deep-seated insecurity about our bodies. Many of us grew up feeling awkward and unattractive and disliking our body for one reason or another. Usually it was because there was a particular ideal "look" that someone else had and we didn't, perhaps when we were adolescents, when such preoccupations are at a feverish peak. So if we didn't look a certain way, we were obsessed with what we could do to look that way or to compensate for not looking that way, or we were overwhelmed with the impossibility of "being right." For many people, at one point in their lives the *appearance* of their body was elevated to supreme social importance, leading to feeling somehow inadequate, and troubled by how they thought they looked. At the other extreme were those who did look "the right way." As a result, they were frequently infatuated with themselves or overwhelmed in one way or another by all the attention they got.

Sooner or later people get over such preoccupations, but the root insecurity can remain about one's body. Many adults feel deep down that their body is either too fat or too short or too tall or too old or too "ugly," as if there were some perfect way that it should be. Sad to say, we may never feel completely comfortable with the way our body is, never completely at home in it. This may give rise to problems with touching and with being touched and therefore with intimacy. And as we get older, this malaise may be compounded by the awareness that our body is aging, that it is inexorably losing its youthful appearance and qualities.

Any deep feelings of this kind that you might have about your body can't change until the way you actually experience your body changes. These feelings stem from a restricted way of looking at your body in the first place. Our *thoughts about* our body can limit drastically the range of feelings we allow ourselves to experience.

When we put energy into actually *experiencing* our body and we refuse to get caught up in the overlay of judgmental *thinking about* it, our whole view of it and of ourself can change dramatically. To begin with, what it does is remarkable! It can walk and talk and sit up and reach for things; it can judge distance and digest food and know things through touch. Usually we take these abilities completely for granted and don't appreciate what our bodies can actually do until we are injured or sick. Then we realize how nice it was when we could do the things we can't do anymore.

So before we convince ourselves that our bodies are too this or too that, shouldn't we get more in touch with how wonderful it is to have a body in the first place, no matter what it looks or feels like?

The way to do this is to tune in to your body and be mindful of it without judging it. You have already begun this process by becoming mindful of your breathing in the sitting meditation. When you place your attention in your belly and you feel the belly moving, or you place it at the nostrils and you feel the air passing in and out, you are tuning in to the sensations your body generates associated with life itself. We usually tune out these sensations because they are so familiar. When you tune in to them, you are reclaiming your life in that very moment, and your body as well, making yourself more real and more alive. You are living your life in real time as it unfolds, moment by moment in awareness. You are present for it and with it and in it. Your experience is *embodied.*

THE BODY SCAN MEDITATION

One very powerful meditation practice that we use in MBSR to reestablish contact with the body is known as the body scan. Because of the thorough and minute focus on the body in the body scan, it is an effective method for developing both concentration and flexibility of attention simultaneously. It is most commonly practiced by lying on your back and moving your mind systematically through the different regions of your body.

We start with the toes of the left foot and slowly move our attention to the different regions of the foot and the left leg, inhabiting each region for a stretch of time in full awareness, which means tuning in to any and all sensations we might encounter—(including numbness or absence of sensation), whatever our experience of that region of the body is as we tune in to it and take up residency in it in awareness. The focusing on a particular region is often coupled with an intentional directing of the breath in to and out from that region. Once we arrive at the left hip and the pelvis, we move our attention to the toes of the right foot and then slowly move up the right leg to the right hip and back to the pelvis. From here, we move up through the torso, the low back and abdomen, the upper back and chest, the shoulder blades, the armpits, and the shoulders.

At this point, we direct our attention to any and all sensations in the fingers of both hands, and the thumbs (we usually do both hands and arms at the same time), then the palms and backs of the hands, then in turn, the wrists, the forearms, the elbows, the upper arms, then returning to the shoulders. Then we move into the neck and throat, and finally all the regions of the face, the back of the head, and the top of the head.

We wind up breathing through an imaginary "hole" in the very top of the head, as if we were a whale with a blowhole. We let our breathing move through the entire body from one end to the other, as if the air were flowing in through the top of the head and out through the soles of the feet, and then in through the soles of the feet and out through the top of the head. Sometimes we hold the entire envelope of the skin in awareness and imagine or feel it breathing as well.

By the time we have completed the body scan, it can feel as if the entire body has dropped away or has become transparent, as if its substance were in some way erased. It can feel as if there is nothing but breath flowing freely across all the boundaries of the body. We are not trying to "achieve" such an experience, because, in the spirit of non-doing, we are not trying to achieve anything at all, nor attain any "special state" of being. We are simply attending to our experience of the body moment by moment as we bring awareness to it in the ways just described. In awareness, every moment and every experience we have is special, even the more trying and difficult ones, so there is no need to try to "attain" anything at all. This becomes clearer the more we practice.

As we complete the body scan, we let ourselves dwell in silence and stillness, in an awareness that may have by this point expanded beyond the body altogether. After a time, when we feel ready, we return to our body, to a sense of it as a whole. Perhaps we get in touch with its solidity once again. Then we slowly and gently experiment with intentionally moving our hands and feet, feeling whatever sensations arise as we do. We might also massage the face and rock a little from side to side before opening our eyes, finally coming to a sitting position for a time and then to standing, as we transition to whatever is next in our day.

The idea in scanning your body is to actually *feel* and *inhabit* each region you focus on and linger in it in the timeless present as best you can. You breathe in *to* and out *from* each region a few times and then let go of it in your mind's eye as your attention moves on to the next region. As you let go of the sensations you find in each region and of any of the thoughts and images you may have found associated with that part of the body, the muscles in that region literally let go too, lengthening and releasing much of the tension they may have accumulated. It helps if you can feel or imagine that the tension in your body and the feelings of fatigue associated with it are *flowing out* on each outbreath and that, on each inbreath, you are breathing in vitality and energy and openness.

In MBSR, we practice the body scan intensively for at least the first four weeks of the program. It is the first formal mindfulness practice that our patients in the clinic engage in for a sustained period of time. Along with awareness of breathing, it provides the foundation for all the other meditation practices that they will work with later, including the sitting meditation. It is in the body scan that our patients first learn to keep their attention focused over an extended period of time. It is the first practice they engage in systematically that nurtures and develops greater stability of mind (concentration), calmness, and mindfulness. For many people, it is the body scan that catalyzes their first experience of well-being and timelessness in the meditation practice. It is an excellent place for anyone to begin formal mindfulness meditation practice, following the schedule outlined in Chapter 10. It is particularly valuable for people suffering from chronic pain conditions or other problems with the body that make it necessary to lie down a good deal of the time.

In the first two weeks of the program, our patients practice the body scan at least once a day, six days a week, using the Body Scan Meditation CD in the Series 1 guided mindfulness meditations. That means forty-five minutes a day scanning slowly through the body. In the next two weeks they do it every other day, alternating with the Mindful Yoga 1 CD (lying-down yoga) if they are able to do it. If not, they just continue with the body scan every day. They are using the same guided meditation CD day after day, and it's the same body day after day too. The challenge, of course, is to bring your beginner's mind to it, to let each time be as if you were encountering your body for the first time. That means taking it moment by moment by moment, and letting go of all your expectations and preconceptions, including the memory of how it was for you yesterday. Every time you practice, the meditation is different even if the guidance is always the same. Every time you practice, you are different too.

We start out using the body scan in the early weeks of the MBSR program for a number of reasons. First, it is done lying down. That makes it more comfortable and therefore more doable than sitting up straight for forty-five minutes. Many people find it easier, especially at the beginning, to let go and relax deeply when they are lying down. On occasion, when guiding the body scan, I might even suggest, following Shakespeare, that we let our "too too solid flesh . . . melt, thaw, and resolve itself into a dew."

In addition, the inner work of healing is greatly enhanced if you can develop your ability to place your attention systematically anywhere in your body that you want it to go and purposefully direct energy of various kinds, in the form of attention, kindness, friendliness, and acceptance, into that region or regions. This requires a degree of sensitivity to your body and an intimacy with the range of sensations you may be experiencing in different locations. In conjunction with your breathing, the body scan is a perfect vehicle for developing and refining this kind of sensitivity, intimacy, and befriending. For quite a number of the participants in our MBSR classes, the body scan provides the first positive experience of their body that they have had for many, many years.

At the same time, practicing the body scan is tantamount to cultivating moment-to-moment non-judgmental awareness. If we are practicing without external guidance, each time the mind wanders and we notice it, we simply bring it back to the part of the body that we were working with when our attention drifted off, just as we bring the mind back to the breath when it wanders in the sitting meditation. If you are practicing with the body-scan CD, you bring your mind back to wherever in the body the voice is pointing to when you realize your attention has wandered off.

When you practice the body scan regularly for a while, you come to notice that your body isn't quite the same every time you do it. You become aware that your body is changing constantly, that even the sensations in, say, your toes may be different each time you practice, or even from one moment to the next. You may also hear the instructions differently each time. Many people don't hear certain words on the CD until weeks have passed, even with daily practice. Such realizations, when they occur, can tell people a lot about how they feel about their bodies.

Mary religiously practiced the body scan every day for the first four weeks in an early cycle of the MBSR program at the hospital many years ago. After four weeks, she commented in class that she could do it fine until she got to her neck and head. She reported that she felt "blocked" in this region each time she did it and was unable to get past her neck and up to the top of her head. I suggested that she might want to experiment with imagining that her attention and her breathing could flow out of her shoulders and around the blocked region. That week she came in to see me to discuss what had happened.

She had tried the body scan again, intending to flow around the "blockage" in the neck. However, when she was scanning through the pelvic region, she heard the word *genitals* for the first time. Hearing the word triggered a flashback of an experience that Mary immediately realized she had repressed since the age of nine. It reawakened in her a memory of having been frequently molested sexually by her father between the ages of five and nine. When she was nine years old, her father had a heart attack in her presence in the living room and died. As she recounted it to me, she (the little girl) didn't know what to do. It is easy to imagine the conflicted feelings of a child torn between relief at the helplessness of her tormentor and concern for her father. She did nothing.

The flashback concluded with her mother coming downstairs to find her husband dead and Mary huddled up in a corner. Her mother blamed her for her father's death because she had not called for help and proceeded to beat her about the head and neck in a fury with a broom.

The entire experience, including the four-year history of childhood sexual abuse, had been repressed for more than fifty years and had not emerged during more than five years of psychotherapy. But the connection between the feeling of blockage in the neck during the body scan and the beating she received decades earlier is obvious. One cannot but marvel at her strength as a young girl to repress what she was unable to cope with in any other way. She grew up and raised five children in a reasonably happy marriage. But her body suffered over the years from a number of worsening chronic problems, including hypertension, coronary disease, ulcers, arthritis, lupus, and recurrent urinary tract infections. When she came to the Stress Reduction Clinic at the age of fifty-four, her medical record was four feet thick, and in it her physicians made reference to her medical problems by using a two-digit numbering system. She was referred to the Stress Reduction Clinic to learn to control her blood pressure, which was not well regulated with drugs, in part because she proved highly allergic to most medications. She had had bypass surgery on one blocked coronary artery the previous year. Several of her other coronary arteries were also blocked but were considered inoperable. She attended the MBSR program with her husband, a local electrical contractor who also had hypertension. One of her biggest complaints at the time was that she was unable to sleep well and was awake for long stretches in the middle of the night.

By the time she finished the program, Mary reported that she was sleeping through the night routinely (see Figure 3), her blood pressure had come down from 165/105 to 110/70 (see Figure 4), and she was reporting significantly less pain in her back and shoulders (see Figures 5A and B). At the same time, the number of *physical* symptoms she complained of in the previous two months had decreased dramatically, while the number of *emotional* symptoms that were causing her distress had increased. This was due to the flux of emotions unleashed by her flashback experience. To cope with it, she increased her psychotherapy sessions from one to two per week. At the same time she continued to practice the body scan. She returned for a two-month follow-up after the program ended. At that time the number of emotional symptoms she reported over that period had decreased dramatically as well, a result of articulating and working through some of her feelings. Her neck, shoulder, and back pain had all decreased even further as well (Figure 5C).

Mary had always been extremely shy in groups. She had been practically incapable of even saying her name when it was her turn to talk during the

FIGURE 3

MARY'S SLEEP GRAPHS, BEFORE AND AFTER THE PROGRAM

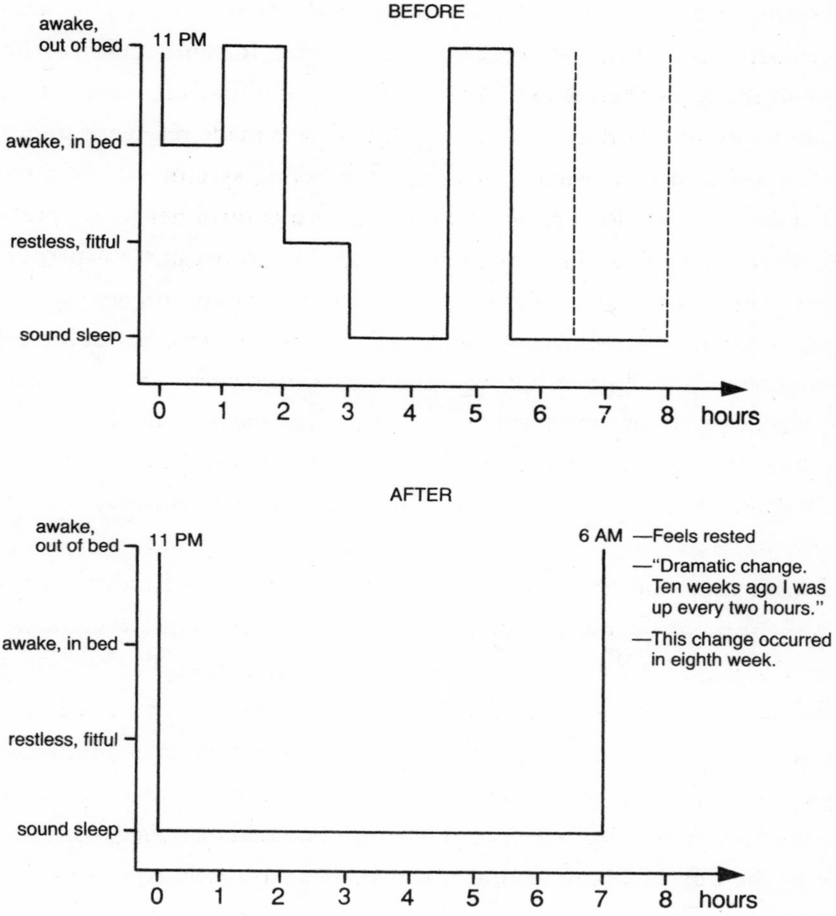

first class. In the years that followed, she kept up a regular meditation practice, using primarily the body scan. She returned many times to speak in the first class to other patients who were just beginning the MBSR program, telling them about how it had helped her and recommending that they practice regularly. She fielded questions gracefully and marveled at her newfound ability to speak in front of groups. She was nervous, but she wanted to share some of her experience with others. Her discovery also

FIGURE 4

MARY'S BLOOD PRESSURE MEASUREMENTS OVER THE YEAR IN WHICH SHE TOOK THE STRESS REDUCTION PROGRAM

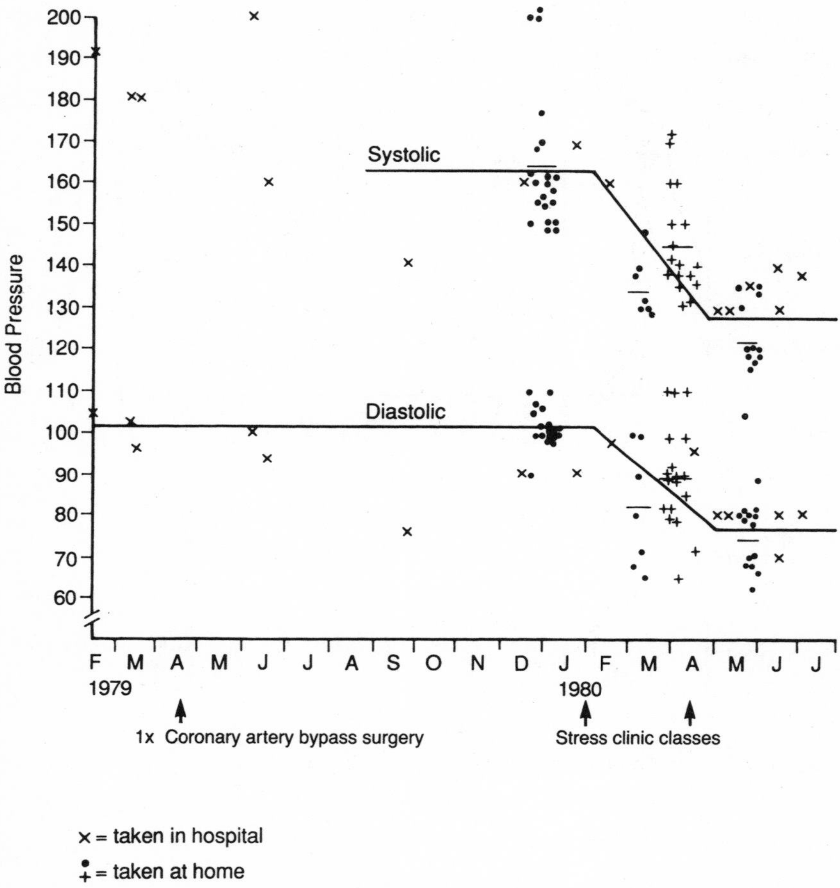

led to her joining an incest survivors' group, in which she was able to share her feelings with people who had had similar experiences.

In the years that followed, Mary was often hospitalized, either for her heart disease or for the lupus. It seemed that she was always going into the hospital for tests, only to wind up having to stay for weeks without anybody being able to tell her when she could go home. On at least one occasion her body swelled up to the point where her face seemed to be twice its normal size. She was almost unrecognizable.

FIGURE 5

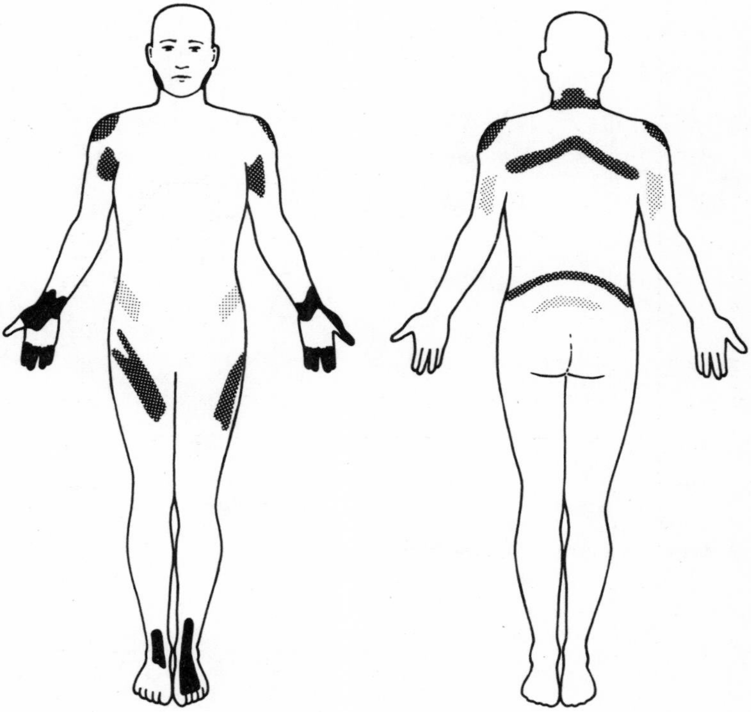

A. Mary's pain drawing before the program started.

solid = intense pain
crosshatch = intermediate pain
dots = dull or aching pain

Through it all, Mary managed to maintain a remarkable acceptance and equanimity. She felt she almost *had* to make continual use of her meditation training in order to cope with her spiraling health problems. She amazed the physicians taking care of her with her ability to control her blood pressure with her meditation practice and to handle the very stressful procedures she had to undergo. Sometimes they would say to her be-

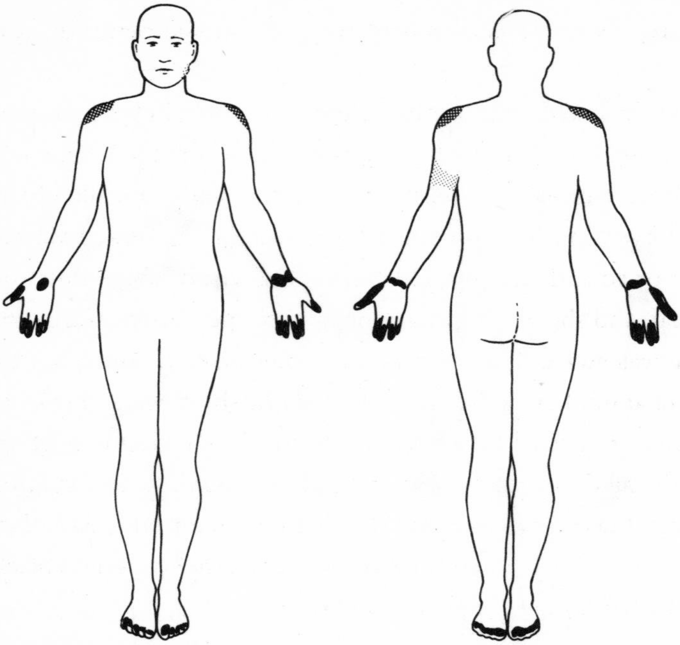

B. Mary's pain drawing ten weeks later.

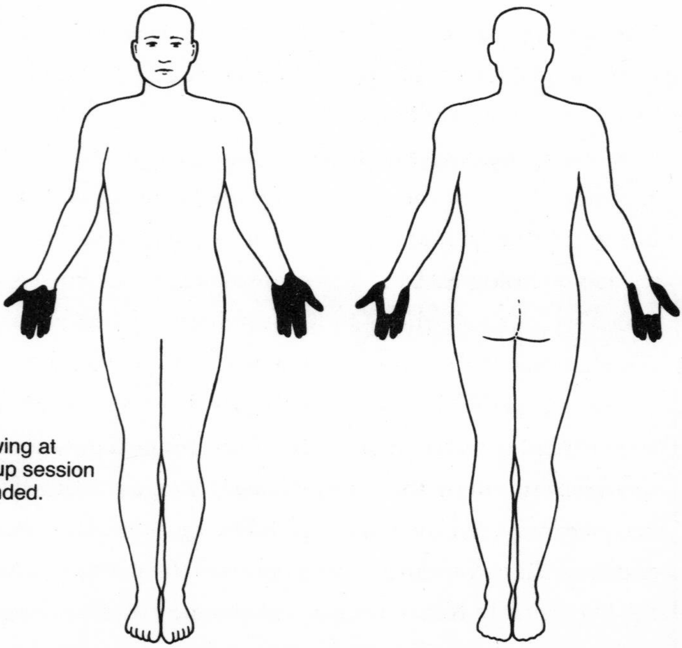

C. Mary's pain drawing at a two-month follow-up session after the program ended.

fore a procedure, "Now, Mary, this may hurt, so you had better do your meditation."

I learned that she had died early one Saturday morning in June, on a day that we were having one of our all-day sessions (described in Chapter 8). I went to her hospital room as soon as I heard the news, and silently offered my good-byes and my love and admiration for her. When we had spoken a week or so earlier, she said that had known for some time that the end was near, and she was approaching it with a peacefulness that surprised her. She was aware that her suffering would soon be over, but she expressed regret at not having had more than a few short years to revel in, as she put it, her "newfound liberated, aware self" outside the hospital. We dedicated the all-day session that day to Mary's memory. In the Stress Reduction Clinic, the old-timers who knew her miss her to this day. Many of her doctors came to her funeral and cried openly. She wound up teaching us all about what is really important in life.

Over the years, we have seen quite a few people in the clinic with severe medical problems who had similar stories of repeated sexual and psychological abuse as children. This certainly suggests a possible connection between repressing this kind of trauma in childhood, when repression and denial may be the only coping mechanisms available to the child victim, and future somatic disease. The retaining and walling off of such traumatic psychological experiences must induce enormous stress in the body, which, years down the road, undermines physical health. As we shall see, there are many mechanisms by which this can happen.

Mary attended the MBSR program in 1980, in the very year that the term *PTSD* (post-traumatic stress disorder) was coined and included in the third edition of the *Diagnostic and Statistical Manual of Mental Disorders,* a key handbook for mental health professionals that is periodically updated and revised. It took many years, though, for PTSD to be understood, and for high-quality research to be conducted on the biological, neurological, and psychological effects of childhood and adult trauma. None of what is known now was widely known in the early and mid-1980s. The condition often went unrecognized, as in Mary's case, and treatments were rudimentary and undeveloped compared to what is available now. Today, mindfulness practices are increasingly being applied as part of the treatment of PTSD in both adults and children.

Mary's experience with the body scan is not meant to imply that everybody who practices the body scan will have flashbacks of repressed material. Such experiences are rare.* People find the body scan beneficial because it reconnects their conscious mind to the feeling states of their body. By practicing regularly, people usually feel more in touch with sensations in parts of their body they had never felt or thought much about before. They also feel much more relaxed and more at home in their bodies. In a word, the body scan can help us all befriend our bodies, nurture them with appropriate, we might even say *wise* attention, and live more fully embodied lives.

INITIAL CHALLENGES PRACTICING THE BODY SCAN

Some people have a hard time feeling their toes or other parts of their body when they begin practicing the body scan. Others, especially people with chronic pain problems, may at first feel so overwhelmed by the pain that they have trouble concentrating on any other region of their body. And some people find that they keep falling asleep in the body scan, no matter what they do. They have a hard time maintaining awareness as they get more and more relaxed, and just doze off.

These experiences, if they do come up for you, can all provide important messages about your body and your mind. None of them is a serious

* But they do occur. If they arise, they are best worked with in concert with a trauma-oriented psychotherapist. Nevertheless, MBSR instructors should have sufficient background and training to recognize the signs and symptoms of latent traumatic experiences if they surface as a consequence of mindfulness practice, and to respond quickly and appropriately to support the person experiencing these potentially retraumatizing memories, which also have potential for initiating healing if they are met with kindness in a safe therapeutic environment.

obstacle if you are prepared to work with and accept whatever arises as a valid object of affectionate attention in its own right. Whatever it is, it can teach us important things about ourselves as we give ourselves over to entering more deeply into the practice of mindfulness. Remember that whatever arises in a very real way becomes the curriculum of the moment, if we can simply hold it in awareness, with kindness. We will now look into how to do this in more detail.

HOW TO USE THE BODY SCAN WHEN YOU DON'T FEEL ANYTHING OR WHEN YOU ARE IN PAIN

In practicing the body scan, you are invited and encouraged to tune in to the various regions of the body one by one and feel whatever sensations are apparent in each region. If, for instance, you tune in to your toes and you don't feel anything, then "not feeling anything" is your experience of your toes at that particular moment. That is neither bad nor good; it's simply your experience in that moment. So we note it, and accept it, and move on. It is not necessary to wiggle your toes to try to stir up sensations in that region so you can feel them, although that is okay too, at the beginning.

The body scan is especially powerful in cases where there is a particular region of your body that is problematic or painful. Take chronic low-back pain as one example. Let's say that when you lie down on your back to do the body scan, you feel considerable pain in your lower back that is not relieved by minor shifts in your position. You start off with awareness of your breathing nevertheless, and then try to move your attention to the left foot, breathing in and out to the toes. But the pain in your back keeps drawing your attention to that region and prevents you from concentrating on the toes or on any other regions. You just keep coming back to your lower back and to the pain.

One way to proceed when this happens is to keep bringing your attention back to your toes and redirecting the breath to that region each time the back captures your attention. You continue to move up systematically through your left leg, then your right leg, then the pelvis, all the while paying meticulous attention to the sensations in the various regions and to whatever thoughts and feelings you become aware of, regardless of their content. Of course, much of the content of your thinking may concern your lower back and how it is feeling. So, as you move through the pelvis and approach the problem region, as best you can, you attempt to remain open and receptive, noting with precision the sensations you are experiencing as you move into this region, just as you did for all preceding regions.

Now, again, as best you can, you breathe into the back and out from the back, at the same time being aware of any thoughts and emotions as they arise. You dwell here breathing for a period of time until, when you are ready, you let go of the lower back on purpose and move the focus of your attention to the upper back and the chest. In this way you are practicing *moving through* the region of maximum intensity, experiencing it fully *in its turn* when you come to focus on it, to whatever degree you find you can manage that. As always, the invitation is to be gentle with yourself, and not push beyond your limits of the moment, or your intuition. Still, you are allowing yourself to be curious about and open to all of the sensations that may be present in that region, in all their intensity, watching them, breathing with them, and then letting them go as you move on.

Another way to work with pain when it comes up during the body scan is to let your attention go to the region of greatest intensity. This strategy is best when you find it difficult to concentrate on different parts of your body because the pain in one region is so great. Instead of scanning, you just breathe in *to* and out *from* the pain itself. Try to imagine or feel the inbreath penetrating into the tissue until it is completely absorbed, and imagine the outbreath as a channel allowing the region to discharge to the outside whatever pain, toxic elements, and "dis-ease" it is willing to or capable of surrendering. As you do this, you continue to pay attention from moment to moment and breath by breath, noticing that even in the most problematic regions of your body the sensations you are attending to from moment to moment change in quality. You may notice that the intensity of the sensations can change as well. If it subsides a little, you can try going back to your toes and scanning the whole body, as described above. In Chapters 22 and 23 you will find further suggestions for how to use mindfulness to work with pain.

THE BODY SCAN AS A PURIFICATION PROCESS

One of the people who influenced my developing the MBSR version of the body scan had been an aerospace engineer before he became a meditation teacher. He liked to describe the body scan the way he taught it as a metaphorical "zone purification" of the body. Zone purification is an industrial technique for purifying certain metals by moving a circular furnace the length of a metal ingot. The heat liquefies the metal in the zone that is in the ring of the furnace, and the impurities become concentrated in the liquid phase. As the zone of melted metal moves along the length of the bar, the impurities stay in the liquid metal. The resolidified metal coming out the back end of the furnace is of much greater purity than it was before the process began. When the whole bar has been treated in this way, the end region of the bar that was the last to melt and resolidify (and which now contains all the impurities) is cut off and thrown away, leaving a purified bar.

Similarly, the body scan can be thought of in one way as an active purification of the body. The moving zone of your attention harvests tension and pain as it passes through various regions and carries them to the top of your head, where, with the aid of your breathing, you allow them to discharge out of your body, leaving it lighter and more transparent. Each time you scan your body in this way, you can think of it or visualize it as a purification or detoxification process, a process that is promoting healing by restoring a feeling of wholeness and integration to your body.

Although this metaphor can make it sound as if the body scan is being used to achieve a specific end—namely, to purify your body—the spirit in which we practice it is still entirely one of non-striving. As you will see in Chapter 13, we let any purification that might occur take care of itself. We just persevere in the practice on a daily basis for its own sake, or, you could say, for the sake of being fully who we already are but too often lose track of.

Through repeated practice of the body scan over time, we come to grasp the reality of our body as whole in the present moment. This feeling of wholeness can be experienced no matter what is wrong with your body. One part of your body, or many parts of your body, may be affected by disease, or in pain, or even missing. Yet it is still possible to cradle them in awareness and recognize and nurture the innate and intrinsic wholeness of the body and of your being.

Each time you scan your body, you are letting what will flow out flow out. You are not trying to force either "letting go" or purification to happen, which of course is impossible anyway. Letting go is really an act of acceptance of your situation. It is not a surrender to your fears about it. It is a seeing of yourself as larger than your problems and your pain, larger than your cancer, larger than your heart disease, larger than your body, and identifying with the totality of your being rather than with your body or your heart or your back or your fears. The experience of wholeness transcending your problems comes naturally out of regular practice of the body scan. It is nurtured every time you breathe out from a particular region and let it go.

ACCEPTANCE AND NON-STRIVING IN THE BODY SCAN PRACTICE

When practicing the body scan, the key point is to maintain awareness in every moment as best you can, experiencing your breath and your body, region by region, as you scan from your feet to the top of your head. We do this with the lightest of touches, not trying to force anything, and as best we can, not turning away from anything either, although you are always the ultimate decision maker on this score. The quality of your attention and your willingness just to feel what is here to be felt and be with it no matter what is much more important than imagining the tension leaving your body or the inbreath revitalizing your body. If you just work at getting rid of tension, you may or may not succeed, but you are not practicing mindfulness. But if you are practicing being present in each moment and at the same time you are allowing your breathing and your attention to purify the body within this context of awareness and with a willingness to experience and accept whatever happens, then you are truly practicing mindfulness and tapping its power to heal.

The distinction is important. In the introduction to the body scan practice CD, it says that the best way to get results from the meditation is not to try to get anything from it but just to do it for its own sake. When our patients use the body scan CD, they hear this message every day. Every one of them has a serious problem for which he or she is seeking some kind of help. Yet they are being given the message that the best way to get something out of the meditation practice is just to practice every day and to let go of their expectations, their goals, even their reasons for coming.

In framing the work of meditation in this way, we are putting them in a paradoxical situation. They have come to the clinic hopeful of having something positive happen, yet they are instructed to practice without trying to get anywhere. Instead, we encourage them to try to be fully where they already are, with acceptance. In addition, we suggest they suspend judgment as best they can for the eight weeks that they are in the program and decide only at the end whether it was a worthwhile undertaking or not.

Why do we take this approach? Creating this paradoxical situation invites people to explore non-striving and self-acceptance as ways of being. It gives them permission to start from scratch, to tap a new way of seeing and feeling without holding up standards of success and failure based on a habitual and limited way of seeing their problems and their expectations about what they *should* be feeling. We practice the meditation in this way because the effort to try to "get somewhere" is so often the wrong kind of effort for catalyzing change or growth or healing, coming as it usually does from a rejection of present-moment reality without having a full awareness and understanding of that reality.

A desire for things to be other than the way they actually are is simply wishful thinking. It is not a very effective way of bringing about real change. At the first signs of what you think is "failure," when you see that you are not "getting anywhere" or have not gotten where you thought you should be, you are likely to get discouraged or feel overwhelmed, lose hope, blame external forces, and give up. Therefore no real change ever happens.

The meditative view is that it is only through the acceptance of the actuality of the present, no matter how painful or frightening or undesirable it may be, that change and growth and healing can come about. As we shall see in Part II, "The Paradigm," new possibilities can be thought of as already contained within present-moment reality. They need only be nurtured in order to unfold and be dis-covered.

If this is true, then you don't need to try to get anywhere when you practice the body scan or any of the other mindfulness practices. You only need to really be where you already are and realize it (i.e., make it real). In fact, in this way of looking at things, *there is truly no place else to go,* so efforts to get anywhere else are ill conceived. They are bound to lead to frustration and failure. On the other hand, you cannot fail to be where you already are. So you cannot "fail" in your meditation practice if you are willing to be with things as they are.

In its truest expression, meditation goes beyond notions of success and failure, and this is why it is such a powerful vehicle for growth and change and healing. This does not mean that you cannot progress in your meditation practice, nor does it mean that it is impossible to make mistakes that will reduce its value to you. A particular kind of effort is necessary in the practice of meditation, but it is not an effort of striving to achieve some special state, whether it be relaxation, freedom from pain, healing, or insight. These come naturally with practice because they are already inherent in the present moment and in every moment. Therefore, any moment is as good as any other for experiencing their presence within yourself.

If you see things in this light, it makes perfect sense to take each moment as it comes and accept it as it is, seeing it clearly in its fullness, and letting it go.

If you are unsure of whether you are practicing "correctly" or not, here is a good litmus test. When you notice thoughts about getting somewhere, about wanting something, or about having gotten somewhere, about "success" or "failure," are you able to honor each one as you observe it as an aspect of present-moment reality? Can you see it clearly as an impulse, a thought, a desire, a judgment, and let it be here and let it go without being drawn into it, without investing it with a power it doesn't have, without losing yourself in the process? This is the way to cultivate mindfulness.

So we scan the body over and over, day by day, ultimately not to purify it, not to get rid of anything, not even to relax or attain peace of mind. These may be the motives that bring us to practice in the first place and that keep us at it day after day in the early stages. And, in fact, we may *feel* more relaxed and better from doing it. But in order to practice correctly *in each moment,* sooner or later we will have to let go of even these motives. Then practicing the body scan is just a way of being with your body as it is, a way of being with yourself as you are in this moment, a way of being whole right now.

EXERCISE

1. Lie down on your back in a comfortable place, such as on a foam mat or pad on the floor or on your bed. Keep in mind from the very beginning that in this lying-down practice, the intention is to "fall awake" rather than to fall asleep. Make sure that you will be warm enough. You might want to cover yourself with a blanket or do it in a sleeping bag if the room is cold.
2. Allow your eyes to gently close. But if and when you find any drowsiness creeping in, feel free to open your eyes and continue with them open.
3. Gently let your attention settle on your abdomen, feeling the rising and falling of your belly with each inbreath and each out-

breath; in other words, "riding the waves" of your own breathing with full awareness for the full duration of each inbreath, and the full duration of each outbreath.

4. Take a few moments to feel your body as a whole, from head to toe; the "envelope" of your skin; the sensations associated with touch in the places you are in contact with the floor or the bed.
5. Bring your attention to the toes of the left foot. As you direct your attention to them, see if you can direct or channel your breathing to them as well, so that it feels as if you are breathing in *to* your toes and out *from* your toes. It may take a while for you to get the hang of this so that it doesn't feel effortful or contrived. It may help to imagine your breath traveling down the body from your nose into the lungs and continuing through the torso and down the left leg all the way to the toes, and then back again and out through your nose. Actually, the breath does take this and every other route in the body, through the bloodstream.
6. Allow yourself to *feel* any and all sensations from your toes, perhaps distinguishing between them and watching the flux of sensations in this region. If you don't feel anything at the moment, that is fine too. Just allow yourself to feel "not feeling anything."
7. When you are ready to leave the toes and move on, take a deeper, more intentional breath in all the way down to the toes and, on the outbreath, allow them to "dissolve" in your mind's eye. Stay with your breathing for a few breaths at least, and then move on in turn to the sole of the foot, the heel, the top of the foot, and then the ankle, continuing to breathe in *to* and out *from* each region as you observe the sensations that you are experiencing, and then letting go of that region and moving on.
8. As with the awareness-of-breathing exercises (Chapter 3) and the sitting meditation practices (Chapter 4), bring your mind back to the breath and to the region you are focusing on each time you notice that your attention has wandered off, after first

taking note of what carried you away in the first place or what is on your mind when you realize it has wandered away from the focus on the body.

9. In this way, as described in the text of this chapter, continue moving slowly up your left leg and through the rest of your body as you maintain the focus on the breath and on the sensations within the individual regions as you come to them, breathe with them, and let go of them. If you are experiencing pain or discomfort of any kind, consult the sections in this chapter that suggest how to work with discomfort, as well as Chapters 22 and 23.
10. Practice the body scan at least once a day. Again, it helps to use the CD for guidance in the beginning stages of your practice so that the pace is slow enough, and to help you remember the instructions and their tonal quality accurately.
11. Remember that the body scan is the first formal mindfulness practice that our patients engage in intensively and that they do it forty-five minutes a day, six days a week, for at least two weeks straight in the beginning of their training in MBSR. So when you are ready, that would be a good strategy for undertaking the next steps in your own developing meditation practice, especially if you want to follow the full curriculum of MBSR and give it and yourself a fair chance.
12. If you have trouble staying awake, try doing the body scan with your eyes open, as noted in step 2 above.
13. The most important point is to get down on the floor and practice. How much or for how long is not as important as that you make the time for it at all, every day if possible.

6

Cultivating Strength, Balance, and Flexibility: Yoga Is Meditation

As you have probably gathered by now, bringing mindfulness to any activity transforms it into a kind of meditation. Mindfulness dramatically amplifies the probability that any activity in which you are engaged will result in an expansion of your perspective and your understanding of who you are. Much of the practice is simply a remembering, a reminding yourself to be fully awake, not lost in waking sleep or enshrouded in the veils of your thinking mind. Intentional practice is crucial to this process because the automatic pilot mode takes over so quickly when we forget to remember.

I like the words *remember* and *remind* because they imply connections that already exist but need to be acknowledged anew. To remember, then, can be thought of as *reconnecting* with membership, with the set to which what one *already knows* belongs. That which we have forgotten is still here, somewhere within us. It is *access* to it that is temporarily veiled. What has been forgotten needs to renew its membership in consciousness. For instance, when we "re-member" to pay attention, to be in the present, to be in our body, we are already awake right in that moment of remembering. The membership completes itself as we remember our wholeness.

The same can be said for reminding ourselves. It reconnects us with what some people call "big mind," with a mind of wholeness, a mind that sees the entire forest as well as individual trees. Since we are always whole anyway, it's not that we have to do anything. We just have to "re-mind" ourself of it.

I believe that a major reason people in the Stress Reduction Clinic take so quickly to the meditation practice and find it healing is that the cultivation of mindfulness reminds them of what they already knew but somehow didn't know they knew or weren't able to make use of, namely that they are already whole.

We remember wholeness so readily because we don't have far to look for it. It is always within us, usually as a vague feeling or memory left over from when we were children. But it is a deeply familiar memory, one you recognize immediately as soon as you feel it again, like coming home after being away a long time. When you are immersed in doing without being centered, it feels like being away from home. And when you reconnect with being, even for a few moments, you know it immediately. You feel like you are at home no matter where you are and what problems you face.

Part of the feeling in such moments is that you are at home in your body too. So it is a little peculiar that the English language doesn't allow us to "rebody" ourselves. It seems on the face of it to be just as necessary and useful a concept as to remind ourselves. In one way or another all the work we do in MBSR involves rebodying.

Bodies are subject to inevitable breakdown. But they do seem to break down sooner and to heal less rapidly and less completely if they are not cared for and listened to in some basic ways. For this reason, taking proper care of your body is of great importance both in the prevention of disease and in the work of healing from illness, disease, or injury.

Step number one in caring for your body, whether you are sick or injured or healthy, is to practice being "in" it, to actually *inhabit* it with full awareness. Tuning in to your breathing and to the sensations that you can feel in your body is one very practical way to work at being in your body. It helps you to stay in close touch with it and then to act on what you learn as you listen to its messages. The body scan is a very powerful form of "rebodying," since you are regularly checking in with, listening to, befriending, and embracing every region of your body systematically. You can't help developing greater familiarity with and confidence in your body when you do this, and for the most part, your body can't but soften in response, without your *trying* to relax or soften anything at all.

There are many different ways to practice being in your body. All enhance growth and change and healing, especially if they are done with meditative awareness. One of the most powerful in terms of its ability to transform the body, and most wonderful in terms of how good it feels to do it, is *hatha yoga.*

Mindful hatha yoga is the third major formal meditation practice that we make use of in MBSR, along with the body scan and sitting meditation. It consists of gentle stretching, strengthening, and balancing exercises, done very slowly, with moment-to-moment awareness of breathing and of the sensations that arise as you put your body into various configurations known as "postures." Many of the participants in the Stress Reduction Clinic swear by the yoga practice and prefer it to the sitting and the body scan, at least in the beginning. They are drawn to the relaxation and increased musculoskeletal strength and flexibility that come from regular yoga practice. What is more, after enduring the stillness of the sitting and the body scan for several weeks, it allows them at last to move!

It also allows them, as they often do, to realize that the posture we adopt in practicing the body scan is itself a yoga posture, known as the corpse pose. In fact, it is said to be the most difficult of the entire array of traditional yoga postures, numbering in the thousands, some of which may be impossible for us to imagine ourselves ever doing. Why is it considered to be the most difficult posture of all? Because it is at one and the same time so simple but yet so challenging to be fully awake—to die to the past and to the future (this is why it is called "corpse pose") and thus to be fully alive in the present moment.

Aside from being a powerful way in which to explore the body and help it to grow more supple and relaxed, stronger and more flexible and balanced, mindful yoga is also an extremely effective way in which you can learn about yourself and come to experience yourself as whole, regardless of your physical condition or level of fitness. Although it looks like exercise and conveys the benefits of exercise, yoga is far more than exercise. Done mindfully, it is meditation just as much as the sitting practice or the body scan are meditation.

In MBSR, we practice the yoga with exactly the same attitude that we bring to the sitting meditation or the body scan. We do it without striving and without forcing. We practice accepting our body as we find it, in the present, from one moment to the next. While stretching or lifting or balancing, we learn to work with and dwell at our limits while maintaining moment-to-moment awareness. We are patient with ourselves. As we carefully move up to our limits in a stretch, for instance, we practice breathing at that limit, residing in the creative space between not challenging the body at all and pushing it too far.

This is a far cry from most exercise and aerobics classes and even many yoga classes, which only focus on what the body is *doing*. These approaches tend to emphasize progress. They like to push, push, push. Not much attention is paid to the art of non-doing and non-striving in exercise classes, nor to the present moment, nor to the mind, for that matter. In exercise that is totally body-oriented, there tends to be little explicit care given to the domain of being, which is just as important when working with the body as when doing anything else. Of course, anybody can come upon the domain of being on their own, because it is always here. But it is a lot harder to find if the prevailing atmosphere and attitude are diametrically opposed to such experiences. Still, nowadays things are changing, and many yoga teachers do incorporate mindfulness instructions skillfully into their teaching. In fact, many yoga teachers practice mindfulness and attend meditation retreats at mindfulness centers.

Most of us need to be given permission to switch from the doing mode to the being mode, in large measure because we have been conditioned since we were little to value doing over being. We were never taught how to work with the being mode or even how to find it. So most of us need at least a few pointers on how to let go into it and inhabit it more reliably.

It's not all that easy to get in touch with the being mode on your own when you are exercising, especially in a class that is strongly oriented toward doing and achievement. On top of that, it is also difficult because we carry our mind's usual preoccupations, reactivity, and lack of awareness around with us when we are exercising.

To locate and inhabit the domain of being, we need to learn and practice mobilizing our powers of attention and awareness while we are exercising. Professional and even amateur athletes are now realizing that unless they pay attention to the mind as well as the body, they are disregarding an entire realm of personal power and engagement that can make a critical difference in performance.

Even physical therapy, which is specifically oriented toward teaching and prescribing stretching and strengthening exercises for people who are recovering from surgery or who have chronic pain, is usually taught without paying much attention to breathing, and without enlisting the person's innate ability to relax into the stretching and strengthening exercises. Often physical therapists undertake to teach people to do healing things for their bodies while neglecting two of the most powerful allies people have for healing: the breath and the mind. Time and again our patients with pain problems report that their physical therapy sessions go much better when they use mindfulness of breathing as they perform their exercises. It's as if a whole new dimension of what they are being asked to do is revealed to them. And their physical therapists often comment on the dramatic changes they seem to have undergone.

When the domain of being is actively cultivated during slow and gentle stretching and strengthening exercises such as yoga or in physical therapy, what people traditionally think of as "exercise" is transformed into meditation. This allows it to be done and even enjoyed by people who could not tolerate the same level of physical activity in a more accelerated and progress-oriented context.

In MBSR, the ground rule is that every individual has to consciously take responsibility for reading his or her own body's signals while doing the yoga. This means listening carefully to what your body is telling you and honoring its messages, always *erring on the side of being conservative.* No one can listen to your body for you. If you want to grow and heal, you have to take some responsibility for listening to it yourself. Each person's body is different, so each person has to come to know his or her own limits. And the only way to find out about those limits is to explore them carefully and mindfully yourself, over an extended period of time.

What you learn from doing this is that, no matter what the state of your body, when you bring awareness to it and work at your limits, those limits tend to recede over time. You discover that the boundaries of how far your body can stretch or how long you can hold a particular posture are not fixed or static. So your thoughts about what you can and can't do shouldn't be too fixed or static either, because your own body can teach you differently, if you listen carefully to it.

This observation is nothing new. Athletes use this principle all the time to improve their performances. They are always exploring their limits. But they are doing it to get somewhere, whereas we are using it to be where we already are and discover where that is. We will find, paradoxically, that we get somewhere too, but without the relentless striving.

The reason it is so important for people with health problems to work at their limits in a similar way to the way athletes do is that when there is something "wrong" with one part of your body, there is a tendency to back off and not use *any* of it. This is a sensible short-term protection mechanism when you are sick or injured. The body needs periods of rest for recuperation and recovery.

But often what was a commonsensical short-term solution can unwittingly evolve into a long-term sedentary lifestyle. Over time, especially if we have an injury or a problem with our body, a restricted body image can creep into our view of ourself. If we are unaware of this inner process, we can come to identify ourself in that diminished way and believe it. Rather than finding out what our limits and limitations are by directly experiencing them, we declare them to be a certain way, on the basis of what we think or what we were told by a doctor or by family members concerned for our well-being. Unwittingly we may be driving a wedge between ourself and our own well-being.

Such thinking can lead to a rigid and fixed view of ourself as "out of shape," "over the hill," having something "wrong" with us, perhaps even "disabled"—reasons enough to dwell in inactivity and neglect our body in its entirety. Maybe we have an exaggerated belief that we have to stay in bed just to get through the day or that we can't go out of the house and do things. Views like these lead readily to what is sometimes referred to as "illness behavior." We begin to build our psychological life around our preoccupations with our illness, injury, or disability, while the rest of our life is on hold and unfortunately atrophying along with the body. In fact, even if there is nothing "wrong" with your body, if you do not challenge it much, you may be carrying around a highly restricted image of what it (and you) are capable of doing. This reduced self-image/body image is only compounded by the burden of excessive weight, a condition that is becoming increasingly common, given the obesity epidemic the developed world finds itself in the midst of at this time.

Physical therapists have two wonderful maxims that are extremely relevant for people seeking to take better care of their bodies. One is "If it's physical, it's therapy." The other is "If you don't use it, you lose it." The first implies that it's not so much what you do that is important, it's that you are doing *something* with your body. The second maxim reminds us that the body is never in a fixed state. It is constantly changing, responding to the demands placed upon it. If it is never asked to bend or squat or twist or stretch or run, then its ability to do these things doesn't just stay the same—it actually decreases over time. Sometimes this is called being "out of shape," but that implies a fixed state. In fact, the longer you are "out of shape," the worse shape your body is in. It declines.

This decline is technically known as *disuse atrophy.* When the body is given complete bed rest—say, when you are recuperating from surgery in the hospital—it rapidly loses a good deal of muscle mass, especially in the legs. You can actually see the thighs get smaller day by day. When not maintained by constant use, muscle tissue atrophies. It breaks down and is reabsorbed by the body. When you get out of bed and start moving around and exercising your legs, it slowly builds up again.

It's not just the leg muscles that atrophy with disuse. All skeletal muscles do. They also tend to get shorter, lose their tone, and become more prone to injury in people who lead a sedentary lifestyle. Moreover, protracted periods of disuse or underuse probably also affect joints, bones, the blood vessels feeding the regions in question, and even the nerves supplying them. It is likely that with disuse, all these tissues undergo changes in structure and function that are in the direction of degeneration and atrophy.

In an earlier era of medical practice, extended bed rest was the treatment of choice following a heart attack. Now people are out of bed, walking, and exercising within days of a heart attack because medicine has come to recognize that inactivity only compounds the heart patient's problems. Even a heart that has atherosclerosis responds to the challenge of regular, graduated exercise and benefits from it by becoming functionally stronger (even more so if the person goes on a very low-fat diet, as we shall see in Chapter 31).

Of course, the level of exercise has to be adjusted to the physical state of your body so that you are not pushing beyond your limits at any time but are working in a target range for heart rate that produces what is called a "training effect" on the heart. Then you gradually increase your exercise as your heart becomes stronger. Nowadays, it's not unheard of for people who have had a heart attack to build themselves up to the point where they can complete a marathon, that is, run 26.2 miles!

Yoga is a wonderful form of exercise for a number of reasons. To begin with, it is very gentle. It can be beneficial at any level of physical conditioning and, if practiced regularly, counteracts the process of disuse atrophy. It can be practiced in bed, in a chair, or in a wheelchair. It can be done standing up, lying down, or sitting. In fact, the whole point of hatha yoga is that it can be done in any position. Any posture can become a starting place for practice. All that is required is that you are breathing and that some voluntary movement is possible.

Yoga is also good exercise because it is a type of full-body conditioning. It improves strength, balance, and flexibility in the entire body. It's like swimming, in that every part of your body is involved and benefits. It can even have cardiovascular benefits when done vigorously. But in MBSR, the way we do it is not as cardiovascular exercise. We do it primarily for stretching and strengthening your muscles and joints, to wake up the body to its full range of motion and potential for movement and balance. People in need of greater cardiovascular exercise or who want to include it in their daily routine walk, swim, bike, run, or row in addition to doing the yoga. Those activities can also be done mindfully, to very great advantage.

Perhaps the most remarkable thing about yoga is how much energy you feel *after* you do it. You can be feeling exhausted, do some yoga, and feel completely rejuvenated in a short period of time. Those people who have been practicing the body scan every day for two weeks in a row and found it difficult to feel relaxed or present in their bodies are thrilled to discover in the third week of the program that they can easily drop into deep feelings of relaxation and embodied presence with the yoga; it's almost impossible not to (unless you are dealing with a chronic pain condition, in which case you have to be particularly careful of how you approach the yoga and what you do, as we will see in a moment). They also find, as a rule, that they stay awake during the yoga and get to taste feelings of stillness and peace that they did not experience in the body scan because they fell asleep or were unable to concentrate. And once they have had an experience of this kind, many come to feel more positively toward the body scan as well. They understand it better and have an easier time staying awake and in touch with their moment-to-moment experience while doing it.

I do yoga almost every day and have for over forty-five years. I get out of bed and splash some cold water on my face to make sure I'm awake. Then I work with my body mindfully by doing some yoga. Some days it feels like my body is literally putting itself together as I practice. Other days it doesn't feel that way. But it always feels like I know how my body is today because I have spent some time with it in the morning, being with it, nourishing it, strengthening it, stretching it, listening to it. This feeling is very reassuring when you have physical problems and limitations and are never quite sure what your body is going to be like on any given day.

Some days I'll do fifteen minutes, just some basic back, leg, shoulder, and neck work, especially if I have to get to work early or have to travel. Mostly I will practice for at least half an hour or an hour, using a routine and sequence of postures and movements that I find particularly beneficial and that I developed over the years from listening to my body and sensing what it most needs in any given moment. When I am teaching yoga, my classes are usually two hours long, because I want people to take their time and to luxuriate in the experience of anchoring themselves in their bodies as they practice exploring their limits in various postures. But even five or ten minutes a day can be very useful as a regular routine. If, however, you intend to immerse yourself in the MBSR curriculum, or are thinking about doing so, I recommend that you practice for forty-five minutes a day, starting in Week 3, alternating mindful yoga one day with the body scan on the next, just as our patients do, and as is described in Chapter 10.

Yoga is a Sanskrit word that literally means "yoke." The practice of yoga is the practice of yoking together or unifying body and mind, which really means penetrating into the experience of them not being separate in the first place. You can also think of it as experiencing the unity or connectedness between the individual and the universe as a whole.* The word has other specialized meanings, which do not concern us here, but the basic thrust is always the same: realizing connectedness, non-separation, integration—in other words, realizing wholeness through disciplined prac-

* See the Einstein quote in Chapter 12.

tice. The image of the yoke goes nicely with what we were saying about re-minding and re-bodying.

The trouble with yoga is that talking about it doesn't help you to do it, and instructions from a book, even under the best of circumstances, can't really convey the feeling of what it is like to practice. One of the most enjoyable and relaxing aspects of doing yoga mindfully is the sense of your body flowing from one posture to the next and through periods of stillness while lying on your back or on your belly. This cannot be achieved when you are going back and forth between the illustrations and descriptions in a book and your body on the floor. It always exasperated me the few times that I tried to learn yoga from a book, no matter how good the book was. That is why we strongly recommend that if you are following the MBSR curriculum, or are even just drawn to practicing mindful yoga, you use the Mindful Yoga 1 and Mindful Yoga 2 practice CDs to get started. Then all you have to do is play one of them and let it guide you through the various sequences of postures. This leaves you free to just practice, to put all your energy into cultivating moment-to-moment awareness of your body, your breath, and your mind. The illustrations and the instructions in this chapter can then be used to clarify any uncertainties you may have and to supplement your own understanding, which will grow mostly out of your personal experiences engaging in the practice itself. Once you know what is involved, you can continue on your own, without my guidance, and make up different sequences of postures for yourself.

In MBSR, we tend to do the yoga very, very slowly, as a moment by moment mindful exploration of the body. And because we are doing it with people with a wide range of medical conditions, we only make use of a small number of postures, for the purpose of introducing this venerable gateway into greater awareness of the body and of the mind-body connection. Some of our patients are so taken with it that they later take up the practice within one of the various schools of yoga, which all have somewhat different approaches, some of which can be quite aerobic, strenuous, even acrobatic. But for our purposes, we see the yoga we do as its own form of meditation, which, of course, all yoga is when understood properly. And by the same token, there is no separation between yoga and life. Life itself is the real yoga practice, and every way in which you carry your body is a yoga posture, if it is held in awareness.

We have already seen that posture is very important in the sitting meditation and that positioning your body in certain ways can have immediate effects on your mental and emotional state. Being aware of the carriage of the body and of your body language, including facial expressions, and what they reveal about your attitudes and feelings, can help you to change your attitudes and feelings just by adjusting your physical posture. Even something as simple as curling up the mouth into a half smile in a particular posture can invoke feelings of happiness and relaxation that weren't present before the facial muscles were mobilized to mimic the smile.

This is important to remember when you are practicing the mindful yoga. Every time you intentionally assume a different posture, you are literally changing your physical orientation, the carriage of the body, and therefore your inner perspective as well. So you can think of all the positions in which you find yourself while doing yoga as opportunities to practice mindfulness of your thoughts, feelings, and mood states as well as of your breathing and the sensations associated with stretching and lifting different parts of your body. After all, it is always the same awareness, whether you are moving or still, using one practice or another. In some sense, the various formal practices of MBSR, including the yoga postures, are all different doors into the same room. Feel free, therefore, to skip certain postures if they aren't appropriate for you. You can always come back to them later. Remember, this is potentially a lifetime engagement—if for no other reason than because your relationship with your body certainly is.

For example, rolling up into a fetal position upside down on the back of your head, neck, and shoulders (posture 21 in Figure 6) may not be a posture that you can easily move into and maintain. In fact, you may find it impossible. Please consider it optional, as noted, and instead, repeat postures 9 and 10. Moreover, an inverted posture of this kind is not advisable if you have any kind of neck problem or hypertension. But if these are not concerns for you and you find you can do it easily and without strain, being in this position can provide a significant and welcome change in perspective and can result in a positive mood change, even as it stretches out the lower back and gives you a different angle on the interior experiencing of your body, moment by moment. The same is true for each and every one of the postures if you are willing to give yourself over to them with full awareness, even for a few minutes. If undertaken with appropriate caution and respect, they are perspective-changing and perspective-enhancing, in addition to whatever their physical effects on the body may be. They invite and catalyze greater embodiment.

Even such simple things as what you do with your hands when you are sitting—how you position them, whether the palms are open to the ceiling or are facing down on your knees, whether the palms are touching in your lap or not, whether the thumbs are touching or not—can all have an effect on how you feel in a particular posture. Experimenting with such shifts in positioning within a posture can be a very fruitful area for developing an awareness of energy flow in your body.

When you practice the yoga, you should be on the lookout for the many ways, some quite subtle, in which your perspective on your body, your thoughts, and your whole sense of self can change as you are drawn to adopt different postures and stay in them for a time, paying full attention from moment to moment. Practicing in this way enriches the inner work enormously and takes it far beyond the physical benefits that come naturally with the stretching, strengthening, and balancing. In my experience, this kind of gentle mindful yoga is a lifetime practice. It is a veritable laboratory in which to get to know your body in ever deeper ways. When it is approached with ease and respect for your body as the final arbiter of what you should be doing on any particular day (with input from your doctor, if that is appropriate, and from a yoga teacher if you have one), it can yield rich ongoing revelations as we grow older.

HOW TO GET STARTED

1. Lie on your back in the corpse pose on a mat or pad that cushions you from the floor. If you can't lie on your back, lie in whatever way you can.

2. Become aware of the flow of your breathing and feel the abdomen rising and falling with each inbreath and outbreath.
3. Take a few moments to feel your body as a whole, from head to toe, the envelope of your skin, and the sensations associated with touch in the places your body is in contact with the floor.
4. As with the sitting meditation and the body scan, keep your attention focused in the present moment as best you can, and bring it back to the breath when it wanders off, noting first what drew it away or what is on your mind now, before letting go of it.
5. Position your body as best you can in the various postures illustrated on the following pages and try to stay in each one for a time while you focus on your breathing at the abdomen. Figures 6 and 7 give you the sequences of postures we do in MBSR. On the CDs (Mindful Yoga 1 and Mindful Yoga 2), some of the postures are repeated at different points in the sequence. These repeats are not included in the drawings. When a posture is pictured as being on either the right side or the left side, do both, as indicated.
6. While in each posture, be aware of the sensations that you are experiencing in various parts of your body, and if you like, direct your breath in to and out from the region of greatest intensity in a particular stretch or posture. The idea is to relax into each posture as best you can and breathe with what you are feeling.
7. Feel free to skip any of the postures that you know will exacerbate a problem you may have. *It is important and prudent to check with your doctor, physical therapist, or yoga teacher about particular postures if you have a neck problem or a back problem. This is an area in which you have to use your judgment and take responsibility for your own body.* Many of the people in the program who have back and neck problems report that they can do at least some of these postures, but they do them *very carefully,* not pushing or forcing or pulling. Although these exercises are relatively gentle and

can be healing if practiced systematically over time, they are also deceptively powerful and can lead to muscle pulls and more serious setbacks if they are not done slowly, mindfully, and gradually.

8. Do not get into competing with yourself, and if you do, notice it and let go of it. The spirit of mindful yoga is the spirit of self-acceptance in the present moment. The idea is to explore your limits gently, lovingly, with respect for your body. It is not to try to break through your body's limits because you want to look better or fit better into your bathing suit next summer. Such outcomes may well happen naturally if you keep up the practice, but they are hardly in the spirit of non-striving and befriending your body as it is. What is more, if you tend to push beyond your limits of the moment instead of relaxing and softening into them, you may wind up injuring yourself. This would just set you back and discourage you about keeping up the practice, in which case you might find yourself blaming the yoga instead of seeing that it was the striving attitude that led to your overdoing it. Certain people tend to get into a vicious cycle of overdoing it when they are feeling good and full of enthusiasm, and then not being able to do anything for a time and becoming discouraged. So it is worth paying careful attention if you have this tendency, always erring on the side of being conservative.

9. Although it is not shown in the sequences of postures illustrated in Figures 6 and 7 simply in the interest of space, *you should rest between postures.* Depending on what you are doing, you can do this either lying on your back in the corpse pose or in another comfortable posture. At these times, be aware of the flow of your breathing from moment to moment, feeling your belly as it gently expands on the inbreath and then falls back toward the spine on the outbreath. If you are lying on the floor, feel your muscles let go as you settle more and more deeply into your mat with each outbreath. Ride the waves of your

breathing with full awareness as you melt into the floor. You can practice in a similar way as you rest in the standing postures in Figure 7, feeling the contact that your feet make with the floor and letting your shoulders drop each time you breathe out. In both cases, as your muscles let go and relax, allow yourself to notice and let go of any thoughts you might be having as you continue to ride the waves of your breathing.

10. There are two general rules that you may find helpful if you keep them in mind as you do the yoga. The first is that you breathe *out* as you do any movements that contract the belly and the front of your body, and you breathe *in* as you engage in any movements that expand the front of your body and contract the back. For example, if you are lifting one leg while lying on your back (see Figure 6, posture 14), you would breathe out as you lift it. But if you are lying on your belly and lifting the leg (Figure 6, posture 19), you would breathe in. This applies just for the movement itself. Once the leg is up, you just continue observing the natural flow of your breath.

    The other rule is to dwell in each posture long enough to release into it. The idea is to gentle yourself into each posture and "take up residency" within it with full awareness—even if for just a few breaths at first—and skip the ones that your body is telling you are not for you at the present time. If you find yourself struggling and fighting within a particular posture, see if you can simply rest in an awareness of your breathing. In the beginning, you may find that you are unconsciously bracing yourself in many areas while you are in a particular posture. After a while, your body will realize this in some way, and you will find yourself relaxing and either sinking or expanding further into it. Let each inbreath expand the posture slightly in all directions. On each outbreath settling a little more deeply into it, allowing gravity to be your friend and help you to explore your limits of the moment. Try not to use any muscles that don't need to be involved in what you are doing. For instance, you might practice relaxing your face when you notice that it is tense.

11. Work at or within your body's limits at all times, with the intention to both observe and explore the boundary between what your body can do and where it says, "Stop for now." Never stretch beyond this limit to the point of pain. Some discomfort is inevitable when you are working intimately, gently, and carefully up close to but this side of your limits. But you will need to learn how to enter this healthy stretching zone slowly and mindfully, so that you are nourishing your body, not damaging it, as you lovingly and mindfully explore and inhabit your body and get to know from the inside what it is capable of.
12. Once again, as with the body scan, the most important point is to get down on the floor and practice. How much or for how long is not as important as that you make the time for it at all, every day if possible.

FIGURE 6

SEQUENCE OF YOGA POSTURES (SERIES 1, CD 2)

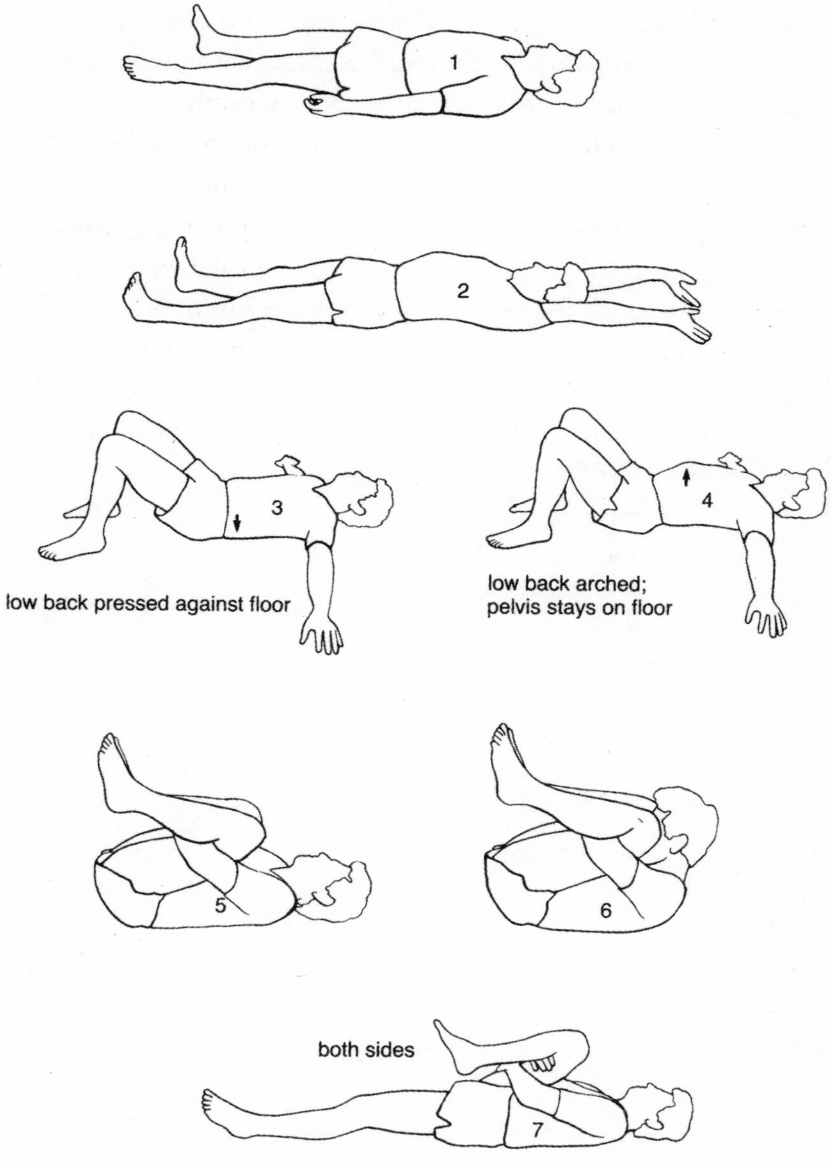

both sides

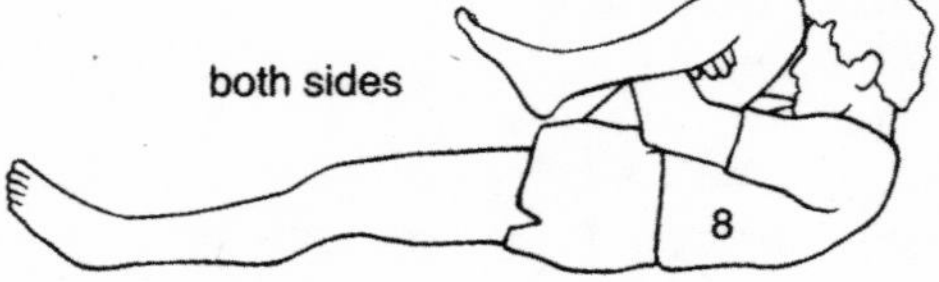

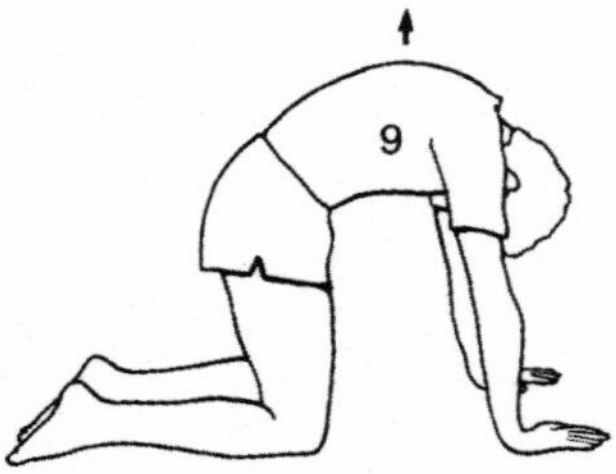

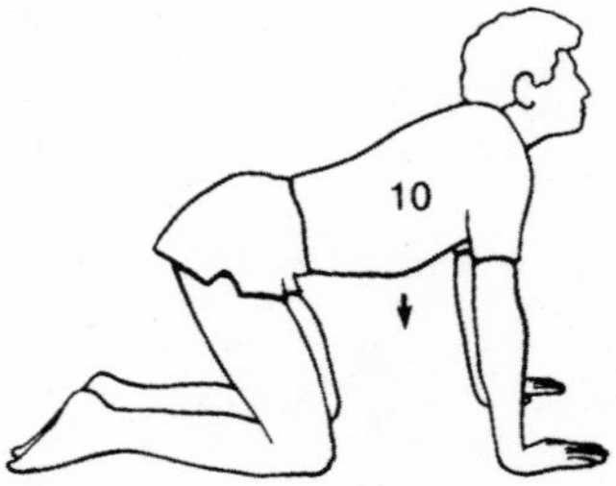

both sides

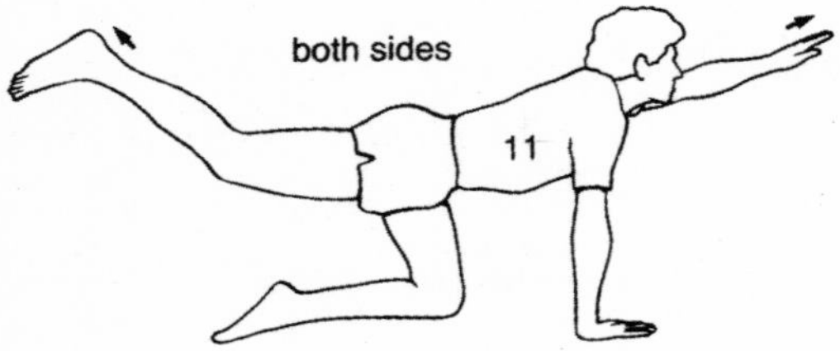

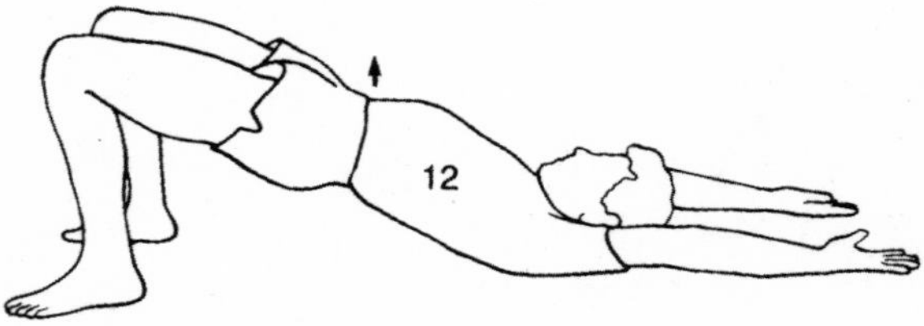

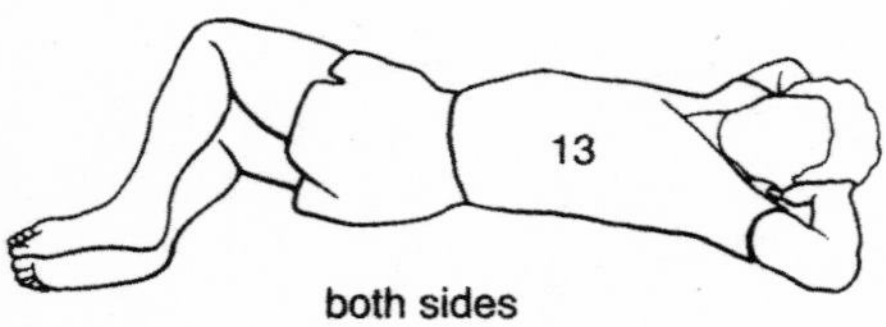

both sides

both sides

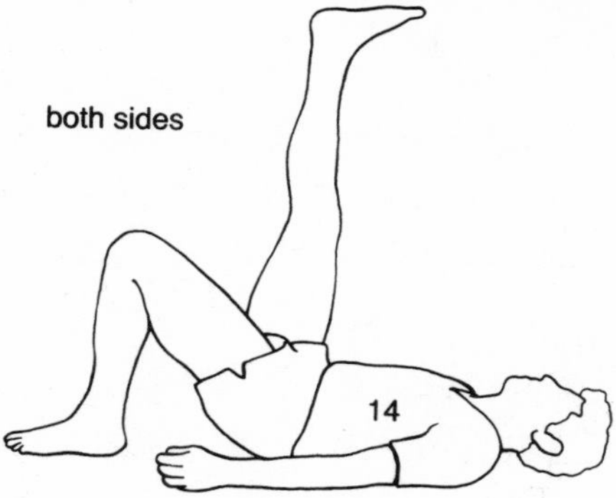

both sides

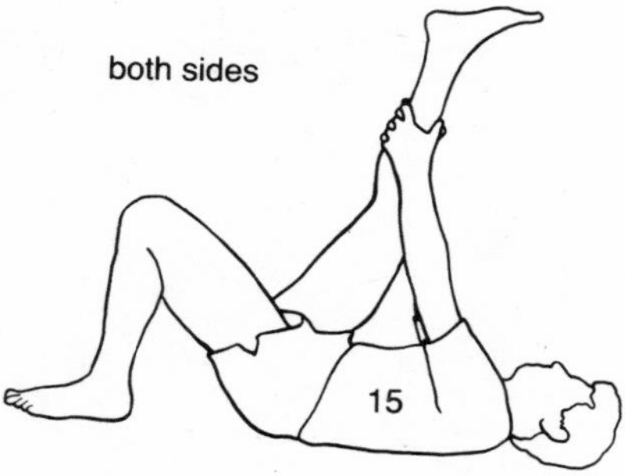

both sides

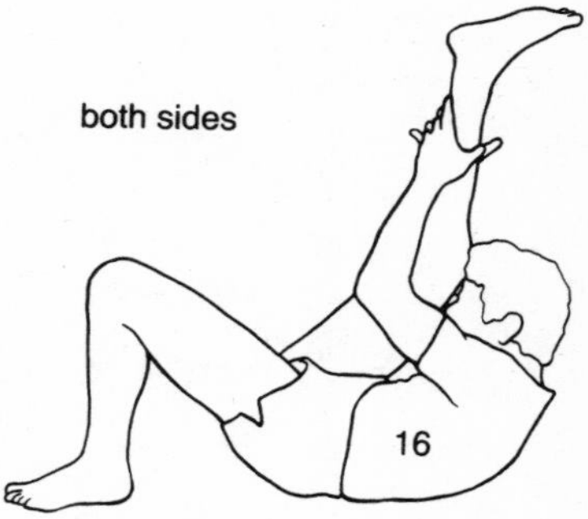

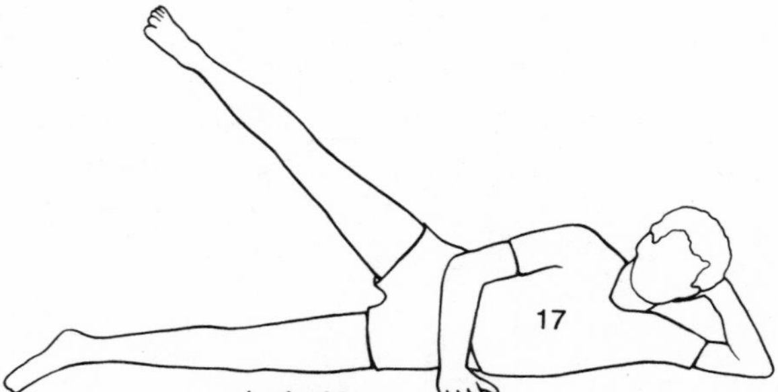

both sides

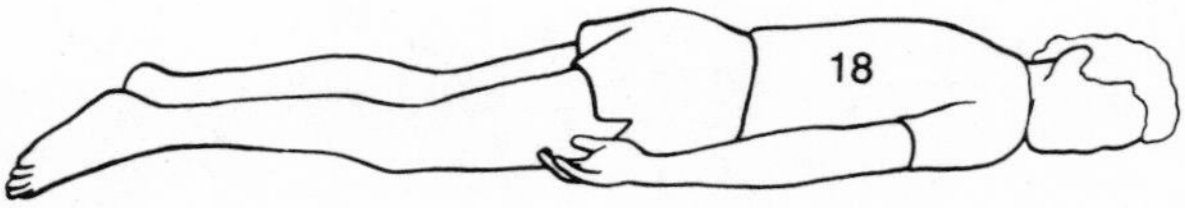

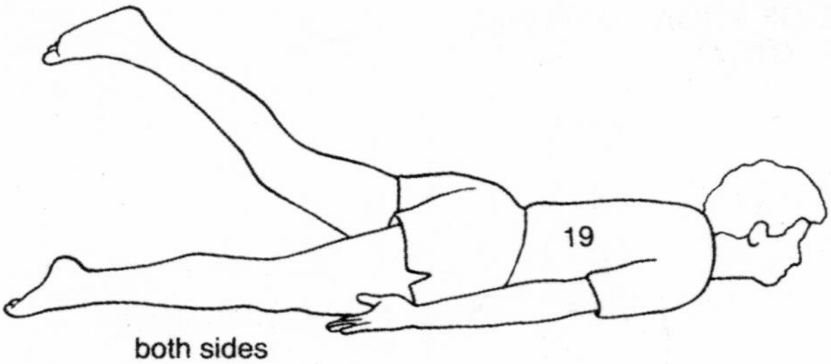

both sides

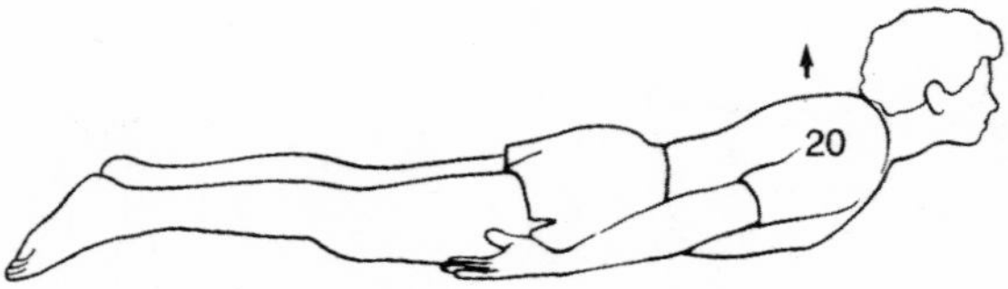

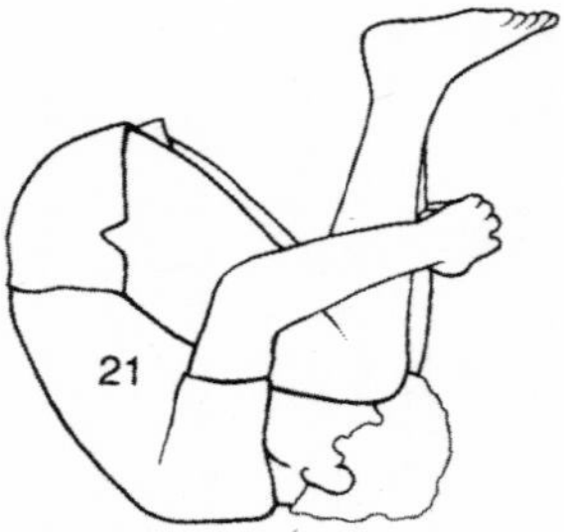

optional

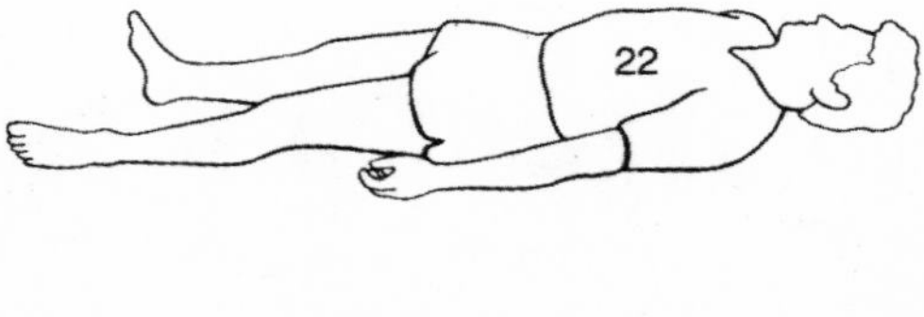

FIGURE 7

SEQUENCE OF YOGA POSTURES (SERIES 1, CD 4)

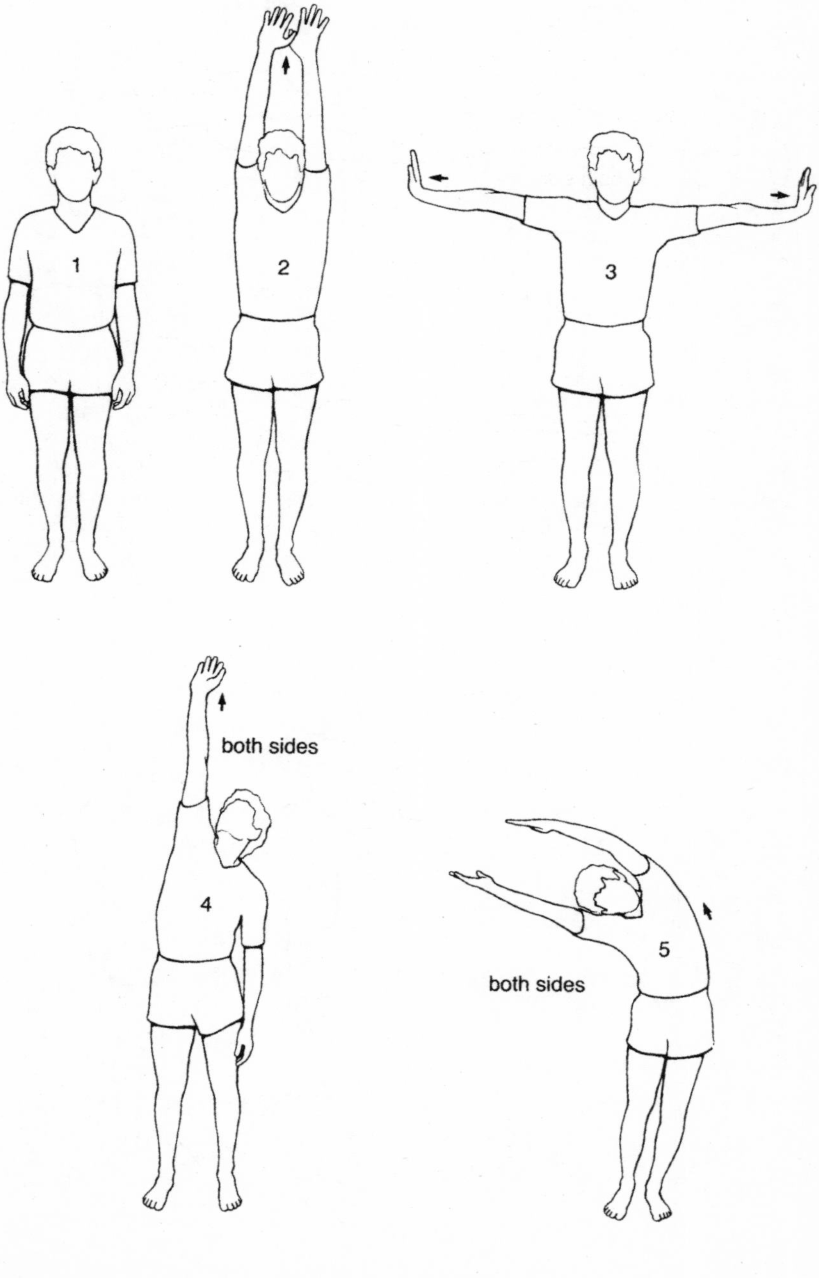

shoulder rolls: do in forward, then backward directions

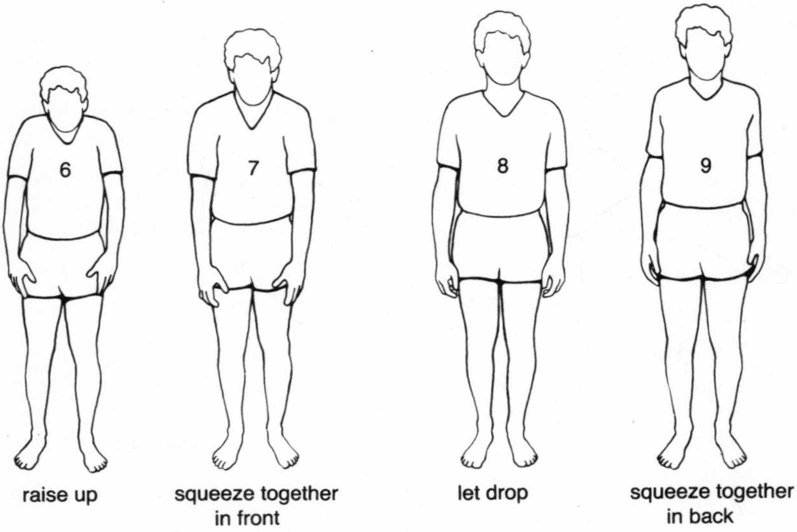

neck rolls: do in one direction, then the other

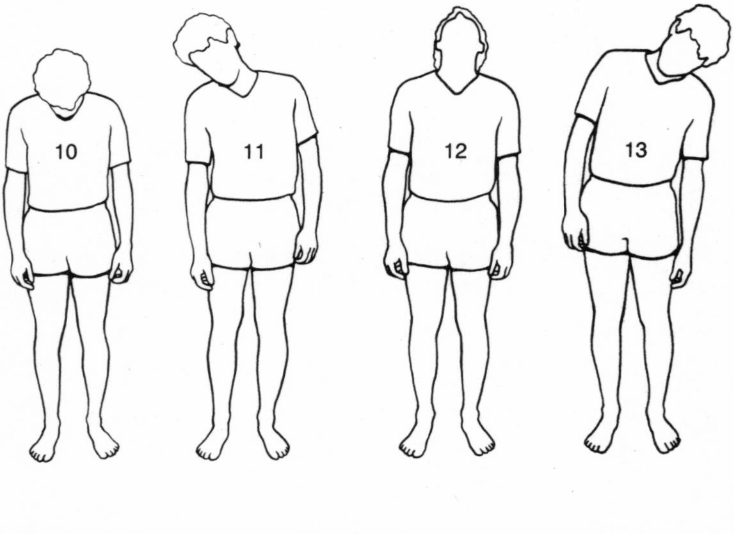

both sides

both sides

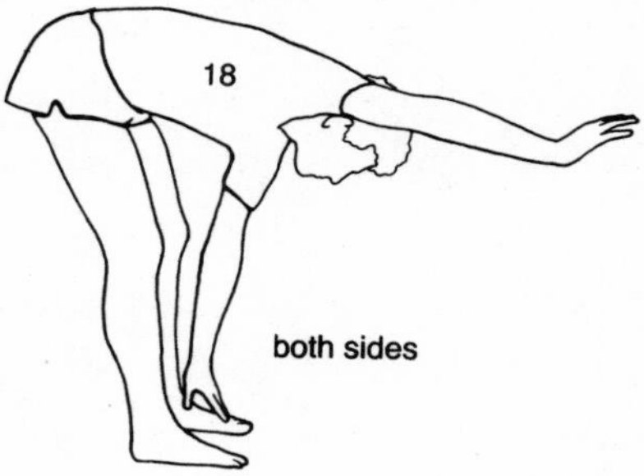

both sides

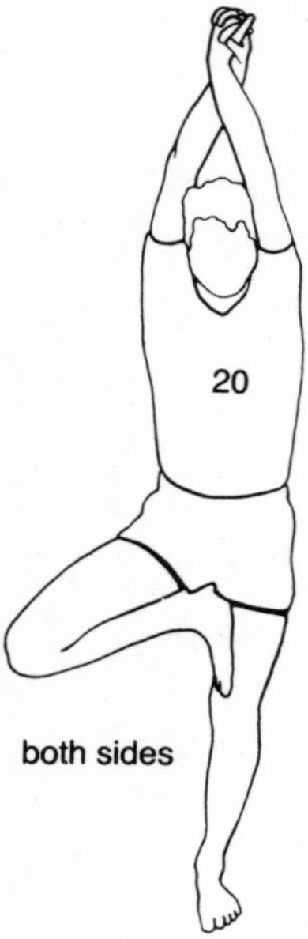

both sides

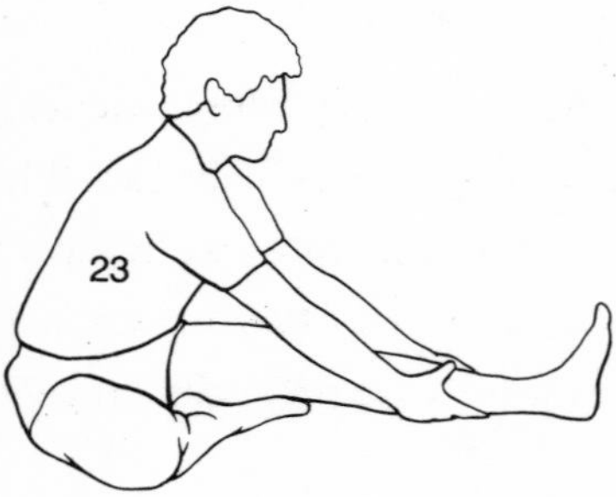

repeat 22 to 24 on other side

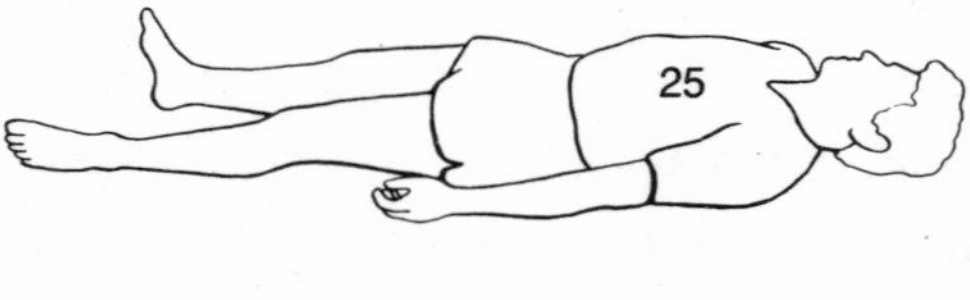

7

Walking Meditation

One simple way of bringing awareness into your daily life is to practice mindful walking, or more formally, walking meditation. As you might guess, this means bringing your attention to the actual experience of walking as you are engaged in it. It means simply walking *and* knowing that you are walking. It does *not* mean looking at your feet!

One of the things that you find out when you have been practicing mindfulness for a while is that nothing is quite as simple as it appears. This is as true for walking as it is for anything else. For one thing, we carry our mind with us when we walk, so we are usually absorbed in our own thoughts to one extent or another. We are hardly ever just walking, even when we are "just going for a walk."

Usually we walk for a reason. The most common one is that we want to go from one place to another and walking is how we can best do it. Of course the mind tends to think about where it wants to go and what it is going to do once it gets there, and it presses the body into service to deliver it to its destination, so to speak. So we could say that often the body is really the chauffeur of the mind, willingly (or reluctantly) transporting it and doing its bidding. If the mind is in a hurry, then the body rushes. If the mind is attracted to something it finds interesting, then the head turns and your body may change direction or stop. Thoughts of all kinds are, as usual, cascading through the mind while you are walking, just as they are when you are sitting still and breathing. As a rule, all this happens without the least awareness on our part.

Walking meditation involves intentionally attending to the experience of walking itself. It involves focusing on the sensations in your feet or in your legs, or, alternatively, feeling your whole body moving. You can also integrate awareness of your breathing with the experience of walking.

We begin by standing still and becoming aware of the body as a whole standing and, of course, breathing. At a certain point we become aware of the impulse to begin walking, and we note that initiating impulse. We also note that in preparation for lifting one foot, the other foot stabilizes itself as the weight of the body begins to shift onto it. We continue to experience in awareness the sensations in the body as the other foot lifts, moves ahead, and then comes down and makes contact with the floor or the ground in its turn. Then we become aware of the weight slowly shifting onto that foot as the other foot lifts and swings out in front of us to take a step. And so we walk, step by step, with full awareness of the gait cycle: the lifting, the moving, the placing, and the shifting of our weight. Not that we need to say those words to ourselves; instead, we can simply be in touch with the feet and the legs and the entire body walking. In MBSR, we tend to walk extremely slowly, so that we can really experience the various aspects of the gait cycle, which is, when all is said and done, a continually controlled falling forward and catching oneself.

As with all the other mindfulness practices we have been exploring, when the mind wanders away from the feet or the legs or the feeling of the whole body walking, we simply notice what is on our mind in that moment and then gently bring it back to where we are in the walking when we become aware of it. Alternatively, we can simply stop altogether, gather ourself, feel the body standing and breathing, and then begin walking again, aware once again of the impulse to begin.

To deepen our concentration when practicing walking meditation, we do not look around at the sights, but keep our gaze focused in front of us. We also don't look down at our feet; they know how to walk quite well on their own. It is an internal observation that is being cultivated, just the felt sensations associated with walking, nothing more. That doesn't mean that mindful walking has to be somber or serious. We can approach it, as with all the meditation practices, with a light touch and a sense of ease. After all, it is nothing special, just walking and knowing that you are walking—and thus, also very special.

Because we tend to live so unconsciously, we take things such as the ability to walk very much for granted. When you start paying more attention to it, you will appreciate that it is an amazing balancing act, given the small surface area of our two feet. It took us about a year as a baby to be ready to learn this dynamic balancing act of locomotion, which, as we have noted, is essentially an exquisitely coordinated and elegant falling forward and catching oneself.

Although we all know how to walk, if we are conscious of being observed by other people or even when we observe ourselves sometimes, we can feel self-conscious and awkward, even to the point of losing our balance. It's as if, when we look at it closely, we don't really know what we are doing when we are walking. You could say we don't even know how to walk! Aspiring actors have to learn to walk all over again when it comes time to "just walk" across a stage. Even walking is not so simple.

On any given day in the hospital there are many people who are unable to walk because of injury or illness, and some who will never walk again. For all these people, just being able to take one step unassisted—much less walk down the hall or out to a car—is a miracle. Yet we hardly ever appreciate the great marvel of walking.

Most importantly, when we engage in the practice of walking meditation, it is helpful to keep in mind that we are not trying to get anywhere! We are simply inviting ourselves to experiment with being where we already are in this moment, with *this* step, and not get out ahead of ourselves. The trick is to be completely present where we are, step by step.

To reinforce the message that we are not trying to get anywhere in the formal walking practice, we walk in circles around the room or back and forth in lanes. This helps put the mind to rest because it literally has no place to go and nothing interesting happening to keep it entertained. Either you are going in circles or you are going back and forth; under these circumstances, the mind just may grasp that there is no point in hurrying to get somewhere else and it may be willing to just be wherever you actually find yourself in each moment, with each step, and feel the sensations in your feet, the air on your skin, the whole body walking in concert with the breath moving.

This doesn't mean that your mind will go along with your intention to just be with each step for very long, not without a concerted effort to keep it focused. You might soon find it condemning the whole exercise, calling it stupid, useless, idiotic. Or your mind might start to play games with the pace or with balancing, or have you looking around or thinking of other things. But if your commitment to the practice of mindfulness in the walking is strong, you will quickly become aware of these impulses and simply note them and return your attention to your feet and legs, and to the whole body walking. It's a good idea to start with awareness of the feet and legs and practice that for a while. Then, when your concentration is stronger, you can expand the field of awareness to include a sense of the entirety of your body walking and breathing. You can also include, if you care to, the air on your face and skin, the sights in front of you, and the sounds around you. Remember, it is the same awareness, whatever the specific objects you are focusing on, and that awareness can hold the entire experience of walking in each and every moment.

You can practice mindful walking at any pace. We sometimes do it very slowly, so that one step might take a minute. This allows you to really be with each movement from moment to moment. But we also practice it at a more natural pace. During the day-long session in the sixth week of the program, described in the next chapter, there are times when we do the walking meditation at a very fast pace. The point here is to practice being aware even when moving quickly. If you try it, you will find that you won't be able to be with each step so easily, but you can shift your awareness instead to a sense of your body as a whole moving through space. So, even rushing, you can be mindful, if you can remember.

To begin walking as a formal meditation practice, it is helpful to form the intention to do it for a specific period of time, say ten minutes, in a place where you can walk slowly back and forth in a lane. To keep mindfulness strong, it's a good idea to focus your attention on *one* aspect of your walking rather than changing it all the time. So if you have decided to pay attention to your feet, for instance, then you might experiment with staying with your feet for that entire walking period, rather than changing to the breath or the legs or the full gait. Since it looks weird to other people to walk back and forth without any apparent purpose, especially if you are doing it slowly, you should do it someplace where you will not be observed, such as your bedroom or living room. Choose a pace that maximizes your ability to pay attention. This might differ from one time to another, but in general it should be slower than you normally walk.

One young woman was so nervous when she started the stress reduction program that she couldn't tolerate any stillness at all. She was unable to keep still and would twitch and pace and pound the walls, or fiddle incessantly with the telephone cord on the desk as we talked. Practicing the body scan and the sitting, even for short periods of time, was out of the question for her. Even the yoga was too static. But in spite of her extreme anxiety, this woman intuitively knew that connecting with mindfulness was a route toward sanity for her, if only she could find a way to do it. It turned out that the walking meditation became her lifeline; she used it to anchor her mind as she engaged in working mindfully with her demons at a time when things were totally out of control. Gradually her condition improved over a period of months and years, and she was able to get into the other practices as well. But it was the walking meditation that came through for her when nothing else was possible. Mindful walking can be just as profound a meditation practice as sitting or doing the body scan or the yoga.

When our children were babies, I did a lot of "enforced" walking meditation. It took place in the house late at night, holding one of them on my shoulder. Back and forth, back and forth. Since I had to be walking the floor with them anyway, using it as an occasion to meditate helped me to be present 100 percent with what was happening.

Of course, a lot of the time my mind resisted being up in the middle of the night. It didn't like being sleep-deprived and wanted badly to go back to bed. Every parent knows what this is like, especially when a child is sick.

The reality of the situation was that I had to be up. So it made sense in my mind to decide to be up completely—in other words, to practice being fully present holding the baby and walking slowly back and forth, and to work at letting go of whether I wanted to be doing this or not. Sometimes this walking went on for what seemed like hours. The mindfulness practice made it a lot easier to do what had to be done anyway, and it also brought me into much closer contact with my children at those times, since I would include in the field of my awareness the sense of the little body snuggled over my shoulder or in my arms and of our bodies breathing together. When a parent is fully present, it is very reassuring and comforting for the child, who feels the calmness and presence and love coming in through his or her own body.

There are probably circumstances of one kind or another in your life in which you have to be walking, whether you like it or not. These can be wonderful occasions to bring awareness to your walking and thereby transform it from a dull, mostly unconscious chore into something rich and nurturing.

Once you have practiced walking mindfully as a formal exercise and you have some experience of what is involved, you will find that you can easily practice a more informal mindfulness of walking in many different circumstances. For instance, when you park your car and go into stores to shop or run errands, that is a good occasion to try walking to where you are going with a continuity of awareness. So often we feel impelled to rush from one routine errand to the next until we get them all done. This can be exhausting, even depressing, because of the monotony of going to the same old places we find ourselves in all the time. The mind craves something new. But if we bring awareness to our walking during these routine tasks, it will short-circuit the automatic pilot mode, making our routine experiences more vivid and actually more interesting, and leaving us calmer and less exhausted at the end. In this spirit, it is a good idea to stay off your cell phone entirely and just be present with what you are doing. If that is impossible, then at the very least, keeping incoming and outgoing calls to a bare minimum.

I usually practice mindful walking in everyday life by tuning in to a sense of the whole body walking and breathing. You can walk at a normal pace, or you can decide to walk just a little bit slower than usual to be more attentive. No one will notice anything unusual if you do this, but it might make a great deal of difference in your state of mind.

Many of our patients walk for exercise on a regular basis. They find that they enjoy it much more when they intentionally practice being aware of their breathing and of their feet and legs with every step. Some do this early every morning as a regular routine. John, a forty-four-year-old stockbroker and father of two who had been referred to the Stress Reduction Clinic with idiopathic cardiomyopathy (a poorly understood and very dangerous disease that weakens and enlarges the heart and causes the myocardium, the heart muscle itself, to dilate and perform poorly) was, by his own description, a wreck when he came to the MBSR program. His diagnosis two years earlier, after experiencing severe problems with his heart, sent him into a deep depression and self-destructive behaviors. His attitude then had been "I'm going to die anyway, so why bother trying to take care of myself?" He loved all the things that were bad for him: alcohol, for instance, and fatty and salty foods. His wild mood swings would trigger a vicious cycle of anxiety followed by shortness of breath. Then he would eat things he knew he shouldn't. These behaviors would often bring on severe pulmonary edema (a dangerous condition in which the lungs fill up with fluid), requiring hospitalization.

At a three-month follow-up session we held for his class, he reported that when he had started in the program, he had been incapable of walking for more than five minutes. By the time it ended, he was getting up at 5:15 a.m. and walking mindfully for forty-five minutes every day before going to work. Now, three months later, he was still doing it. His pulse rate was down below 70 beats per minute, and his cardiologist had told him his heart had decreased in size, a very good sign.

John called me six months later to let me know that his practice was going well and was still "working for him." He said he knew it was because he had had a lot of stress in his life recently and had handled it, he thought, very well. His mother had died several weeks before, and he felt he had been able to accept her death, stay conscious during that entire time, and help his family with it. He had also just come out of a very intense period of studying for a professional exam, during which he was getting only three hours of sleep a night. He said the meditation practice helped him to get through this time without resorting to any drugs for anxiety. He is continuing to practice the body scan with the CD about three nights a week. On those days, as soon as he gets home from work, he goes upstairs and does it immediately. Before the stress reduction program, he said, he spent two years just feeling sorry for himself. He would just sit home and say, "Oh God, I'm dying." Now he is out walking every morning—even in the cold New England winter—and he is feeling healthier every day. His cardiologist told me recently that mindfulness is the perfect thing for John. According to him, John has to be mindful in his life. When he really pays attention to every aspect of his life, he does very well. When he doesn't, he can unwittingly trigger a severe medical emergency.

At that same three-month follow-up session, several other people commented that the meditation had improved their ability to walk and increased their enjoyment of it. Rose said that she has been doing the walking meditation regularly since the classes ended and that she usually does it focusing on sensations of touch, such as the warmth of the sun on her skin or the feeling of the wind. Karen, a woman in her mid-forties, reported that she is walking three to four miles every night as part of her meditation practice. For twenty-two years she had gone without doing any regular exercise, and she is thrilled to be "using her body" again.

In summary, anytime you find yourself walking is a good time to practice mindfulness. But sometimes it's good to find an isolated spot and do it formally as well, and a bit more slowly—back and forth, step by step, moment by moment, walking gently on the earth, in step with your life, being exactly where you are.

8

A Day of Mindfulness

It is a beautiful New England morning in early June. The sky is blue and cloudless. At 8:15 a.m. people start arriving at the hospital, carrying sleeping bags, pillows, blankets, and lunch, looking much more like a group of campers than medical patients. The Faculty Conference Room is set up with blue straight-backed plastic and metal chairs in a large square around the sides of the room. By 8:45 a.m. there are 120 people in this large, friendly, sunny space, stowing their coats, shoes, purses, and lunches under the seats and sitting on the chairs or on the colorful meditation cushions scattered throughout the room. About fifteen people who have already been through the stress reduction program—we call them "graduates"—are returning to do the day again, or because they missed it the first time. Sam, seventy-four years old, comes in with his son, Ken, forty. Both had taken the program in previous years and decided to come back for a "booster." They thought it would be fun to do it together.

Sam looks terrific. A retired truck driver, he is grinning from ear to ear as he comes over to hug me and to say how happy he is to be back. He is short and lean, and he appears relaxed and jovial. He looks so different from the drawn, tense, angry man who first entered my class two years earlier with his face knotted and his jaw characteristically clenched. I marvel at the transformation as I recall momentarily his problems with anger and the story of how hard he was on his wife and children—by his own admission he had been "impossible to live with" since his retirement, "a real son of a bitch" around the house but a total "nice guy" to everybody else.

I comment on how good he looks, and he says, "Jon, I'm a different person." His son, Ken, nods his agreement, saying that Sam is no longer hostile, cantankerous, and hard to reach. He is getting along well with his family now, happy and relaxed at home, even easygoing. We banter a little before the session gets down to business at nine o'clock sharp.

As the teaching staff of the clinic gets ready to start the day rolling, we look around the room. Aside from the graduates such as Sam and Ken, the rest of the people are currently in their sixth week of the MBSR program. They have two more weeks to go to finish it after today. We have combined all the separate clinic classes this Saturday for the all-day session. It is an integral and required part of the course and always takes place between the sixth and seventh classes.

There are a number of physicians in the room, all of whom are enrolled in the program. One is a senior cardiologist who decided to take the program himself after sending a number of his patients. He is wearing a cut-off football jersey and sweatpants and has his shoes off, as we all do. This is quite a change from his usual hospital attire, with the necktie, the white coat, and the stethoscope hanging out of the pocket. Today the doctors in the room are just regular people, even though they work here. Today they are here for themselves.

Norma Rosiello is here today as well. She first took the program as a pain patient, in the same class as Mary, who we met in Chapter 5. Now she works as our secretary and receptionist in the clinic office. In many ways, Norma is the heart of the clinic. She is the first person the patients usually talk with about the program after they have been referred by their doctor, so she has spoken with most of the people in the room at one time or another, often providing them with comfort, reassurance, and hope. She does her work with such grace, poise, and independence that we hardly notice how much work she actually does and how critical her work is in ensuring that things run smoothly.

When she first came as a patient with diagnoses of facial pain and headaches, she was winding up in the emergency room like clockwork, at least once a month, with pain that she could not bear and had no way of relieving. She was working as a hairdresser a few times a week but was constantly missing work because of her pain condition, which she had had for fifteen years and for which she had sought help from many specialists. In the Stress Reduction Clinic, over a relatively short period of time, she was able to get her pain under control using meditation instead of hospital visits and medications. Then she started working with us as a volunteer, coming in from time to time to help out. I finally persuaded her to take on the job as our secretary and receptionist even though she was a hairdresser, couldn't type, and knew nothing about working in an office. I thought she would be the perfect person for the job because she had been through the clinic herself and would be able to talk with the patients in a way that someone doing the work as "a job" wouldn't be able to do. I figured she could learn to type and to do the other things the job required, and she did. Moreover, from the time she began working in the clinic, she missed only a small number of days in the first few years due to headaches and facial pain, and none after that. As I look over at her now, I marvel at her and am very happy to see her here. She has come on her own time to practice with us today.

As I look around the room, I see a mix of ages. Some people have shining white hair, while others look about twenty-five years old. Most are between thirty and fifty. Some come on crutches or with canes. Amy, a graduate of the program who has cerebral palsy and who has come to each one of our all-day sessions in her wheelchair since she took the program several years ago, is not here, and I feel her absence. She moved to Boston recently, where she is in graduate school. She called yesterday to say she wouldn't be coming because she couldn't find someone who could come with her for the whole day. She has her own van with a special wheelchair lift, but she needs another person to drive her. As I look around the circle of faces, I find myself recalling her determination to participate fully in the activities of the day each time she came, even though it meant letting one of us feed her lunch, wipe her mouth, and take her to the bathroom. Her courage, perseverance, and lack of self-consciousness about her condition had become part of the meaning of the all-day session for me, and I am sorry she isn't able to come this time because she always taught us a lot through her being. Although it is sometimes difficult to understand her when she talks, her willingness and courage to speak out, to ask questions, and to share her experiences at the end of the day in such a large group had been inspiring to all of us.

At nine o'clock my colleague and friend Saki Santorelli welcomes the group and invites us to sit, that is, to begin meditating. The sounds in the room from everybody talking quiet some when he speaks, but they disappear completely as he suggests that we sit up in our chairs or on the floor and come to our breathing. You can actually hear a wave of silence rise in the room as 120 people bring their attention to their breathing. It is a crescendo of stillness. I am always moved by it.

So begin six hours of silent mindfulness practice on this beautiful Saturday. All of us have other things we might be doing today, yet we have all chosen to be here together, befriending our own minds and bodies as we practice paying attention from moment to moment for an entire day, gently exploring and perhaps deepening our ability to be still and simply rest in awareness with whatever might unfold inwardly and outwardly, in other words, relaxing into just being ourselves, just being present.

We have drastically simplified our lives for today just by coming, as Saki explains after our first sitting. By being here, we have made the choice not to run around doing the usual things we do on the weekend, such as errands, cleaning the house, going away, or working. To simplify things even further so that we can benefit the most from this very special day, Saki now reviews certain ground rules for the day, among which are no talking and no eye contact. He explains that these rules will allow us to go more deeply into the meditation practice and to conserve our energy for the work of mindfulness. In six very concentrated hours of "non-doing," just sitting and walking and lying down and eating and stretching, a lot of different feelings can come up. We like to stress that whatever arises during the day becomes de facto the "curriculum" of the day, because it is already here, it is what has arisen, and therefore it is what we get to work with. Many of the feelings that arise can be quite intense, especially when all of our usual outlets such as talking, doing things, moving around, reading, or listening to the radio are intentionally suspended and unavailable to as outlets or distractors. While many people find the all-day session enjoyable from the very start, for others the moments of relaxation and peace, if any, may be interspersed with other experiences that may be a lot less enjoyable. Physical pain can well up for extended stretches; so can emotional pain or discomfort in the form of anxiety, boredom, or feelings of guilt about being here rather than someplace else, especially if someone had to give up a lot to come today. It's all part of the curriculum.

Rather than commenting on such feelings to a neighbor and perhaps disturbing someone else's experience as well as compounding our own emotional reactions, Saki counsels us for today just to watch whatever comes up and simply to accept our feelings and our experiences in each moment. The silence and ban on eye contact will support this process of looking into and accepting ourselves, he says. They will help us to become more intimate and familiar with the actual comings and goings of our own minds and bodies, even those that are sad or painful. We can't talk with our neighbor about them; we can't complain or comment about how things are going or what we are feeling. What we can do is practice just being with things as they are. We can practice being calm. We can practice putting out the welcome mat for whatever arises. We can practice in the exact same way that we have been practicing the meditation over the past six weeks in the MBSR classes, only now over a more extended period of time and under more intense, perhaps even stressful circumstances.

Saki reminds us we are intentionally making time for this very process to occur. This is to be a day of mindfulness, a day to be with ourselves in a way we usually don't have time for because of all our obligations and entanglements and busyness—and also because, when you come right down to it, a lot of the time we don't feel like paying too much attention to our being, especially if we are hurting, and because in general we would prefer not being still and quiet. So, when we do have some "free" time, ordinarily we tend to want to fill it up right away with something to keep us occupied. We entertain or distract ourselves to "pass" the time; sometimes we even talk about "killing time."

Today will be different, he concludes. Today we will have no props to help us pass the time or distract us. We will pull on everything we have learned in the program so far, from our five weeks of mindfulness practice. The invitation is to be with whatever we are feeling in any moment and to accept it as we practice staying with our breathing, with walking, with stretching, with whatever the instructors are guiding us through. He points out that today is not a day for trying to feel a certain way but for just letting things unfold. So he counsels us to let go of all our expectations, including that we should have a relaxing and pleasant day, and to practice being fully awake and aware of whatever happens, moment by moment.

Elana Rosenbaum and Kacey Carmichael, the other instructors in the stress clinic today, guide the flow of the day along with Saki and myself. After Saki's talk, we all get down on the floor on our mats to do an hour of yoga. We do it slowly, gently, mindfully, listening to our bodies. As I begin to guide this part of the day, I emphasize the importance of remembering to listen to our own bodies carefully and honoring them by not doing anything that we know to be inappropriate for a particular condition we might have. Some of the patients, particularly those with low-back or neck problems, don't do the yoga at all but just sit on the side of the room and watch or meditate. Others do a little but only what they know they can handle. The heart patients are monitoring their pulse, as they learned to do in cardiac rehabilitation, and hold the postures only as long as their pulse rate is in the appropriate range. Then they rest and do repetitions as the rest of us hold the postures a little longer, seeing if we can drop "behind" the intensity of the sensations, noticing how they change as we maintain each pose, resting in awareness.

Everybody is doing as much or as little as he or she feels comfortable with. We are working at our limits, moment by moment with full awareness, then backing off from them just as mindfully, not forcing, not striving, as we go through a slow sequence of yoga postures. We are breathing in to those limits and out from those limits, and becoming intimate with any and all sensations in various parts of our body as we move: lifting, stretching, bending, twisting, rolling, with long stretches of resting in between, all held as best we can within a seamless continuity of awareness. At the same time, we are noting our thoughts and feelings as they arise and practicing seeing them and letting them be, seeing them and letting them go, bringing the mind back to the breath every time it distracts itself and wanders off.

After the yoga, we sit for thirty minutes. Then we walk mindfully in a circle around the room for ten minutes or so. Then we sit again for twenty minutes. Everything we do this day we do with awareness and in silence. Even lunch is in silence, so that we can eat our food knowing that we are eating, chewing, tasting, swallowing, pausing. It is not so easy to do this. It requires a lot of energy to stay focused and concentrated in the present.

During lunch, I notice one man who is reading a newspaper in spite of the spirit of the day and our explicit ground rule of no reading. Our hope is that everyone will see the value, at least as an experiment, of going along with the ground rules for the day and taking responsibility for keeping them. But perhaps it's too much intensity for him to handle eating mindfully right now. So I smile to myself, observing my self-righteous impulse to insist he do it "our way" today, and let it go. After all, he is here, isn't he? Perhaps that is enough. Who knows what his morning was like?

One year we had a group of district court judges, for whom we ran a special stress reduction program. They were in a class by themselves so that they could speak freely about their unique stresses and problems. Since the job description for judges is that they "sit" on the bench, it seemed fitting that they were getting some formal training in how to sit and also in how to cultivate being intentionally non-judgmental.* Some were strongly drawn to the concept of mindfulness when we first discussed the possibility of a program for them. To do their job well requires enormous concentration and patience, and both compassion and dispassion. They have to listen to a steady stream of sometimes painful and

* See "Sitting on the Bench," in *Coming to Our Senses.* New York: Hyperion; 2005:451–455.

repugnant but mostly boring and predictable testimony while maintaining equanimity and, above all, paying careful attention to what is actually unfolding moment by moment in the courtroom. Having a systematic way of handling one's intrusive thoughts and feelings and perhaps strong emotional reactions at times might be particularly useful professionally for a judge, to say nothing of its value in reducing his or her own stress levels.

When they came for the all-day session, the judges were anonymous within the large group of patients. I noticed that they sat next to each other and that they ate lunch together out on the lawn. They commented later, in their next class together, that they had felt a special closeness to each other during lunch as they sat together without talking or looking at each other, a very unusual experience for them.

The energy in the room today feels very crisp. Most people are clearly awake and focused during the sitting and the walking. You can feel the efforts being made to be present and to stay focused. The stillness up to now has been exquisite.

After a period of silent walking following lunch, in which people are free to walk where they please for a half hour on their own, we begin the afternoon with a lovingkindness and forgiveness meditation. This simple meditation (see Chapter 13) often has people sobbing with sadness or joy. Following it, we move once again seamlessly into sitting quietly, and then more slow walking.

We used to do "crazy walking" in the middle of the afternoon to keep the energy up. Almost everybody enjoyed the change of pace, although some people had to sit this one out and just watch. The crazy walking involved walking very quickly, changing direction every seven steps, then every four, then three, with our jaws and fists clenched, not making eye contact, all done with moment-to-moment awareness. Then we did it making intentional eye contact, at the same pace, minding the differences this time. Then we walked backward very slowly with our eyes closed, changing direction when we bumped into someone, after we allowed ourselves to feel the bump, the contact with another body. The crazy-walking period ended with everybody backing up slowly into what they thought was the center of the room with their eyes closed, until we were all in one big mass. Then we leaned our heads on whatever was available for support. There was a lot of laughing at this point. It eased some of the intensity that built as the level of concentration deepened during the afternoon.

Over the years, we have come to abandon this period of fast crazy walking in favor of cycles of simply sitting and walking in silence. It was almost as if the practice itself and the priceless opportunity of these few short hours together in one day had their own compelling logic, calling for less rather than more, no matter how appealing the more was. This is a general principle of MBSR: to leave as much space as possible rather than filling it up, even with compelling and potentially relevant exercises to convey one thing or another. As instructors, we have learned to trust that everything that needs to emerge or be understood by the participants comes on its own with time, out of the basic simplicity of mindfulness practice. So we keep the curriculum of MBSR as simple as possible and leave as much space as possible within it, realizing that in this case less really is more, and that the real curriculum is life itself, and whatever emerges in our experience, moment by moment, when we give ourselves over to it with awareness and with basic kindness toward ourselves.

The longest sitting of the afternoon starts off with what we call the "mountain meditation." We use the image of a mountain to help people remember what the sitting is all about as the day goes on and a certain fatigue sets in. The image is uplifting, suggesting as it does that we sit like mountains, feeling rooted, massive, and unmoving in our posture. Our arms are the sloping sides of the mountain, our head the lofty peak, the whole body majestic and magnificent, as mountains tend to be. We are sitting in stillness, just being what we are, just as a mountain "sits" unmoved by the changing of day into night and the changes of the weather and of the seasons. The mountain is always itself, always present, grounded, rooted in the earth, always still, always beautiful. It is beautiful just being what it is, seen or unseen, snow-covered or green, rained on or wrapped in clouds.

This image of the mountain sitting sometimes helps us to remember and feel our own strength and intentionality within the sitting meditation practice as the sunlight begins to wane in the room in the late afternoon and our day together moves toward its natural conclusion. It reminds us that we might look upon some of the changes we are experiencing in our own minds and bodies as internal weather patterns. The mountain reminds us that we can remain stable and balanced in our sitting and in our lives in the face of the storms that sometimes arise within our minds and bodies.*

People like the mountain meditation because it gives them an image that they can use to anchor themselves in the sitting practice and deepen their calmness and equanimity. But the image has its limits too, since we are the kind of mountain that can walk and talk and dance and sing and think and act as well as just be still.

And so the day unfolds, moment by moment and breath by breath. Many people showed up this morning anxious about whether they would be able to make it through six hours of silence, whether they would be able to endure just sitting and walking and breathing in silence for much of a day. But here it is three o'clock already, and everybody is still here and seemingly very much with it.

Now we dissolve the silence and the injunction against making eye contact. We do so in a particular way. First we gaze around the room in silence, making eye contact with others and feeling what arises in doing so. Often it is big, wide-open smiles. Then, still in silence, we find a partner and get in fairly close so that we can whisper together, for it is in whispering that we will dissolve the silence of the day. We speak about what, if anything, we saw, felt, learned, and struggled with; how we worked with what arose, especially if it was difficult; what surprised us; and how we feel now. First

* For more on the mountain meditation, see *Wherever You Go, There You Are,* and Series 2 Guided Mindfulness Meditation Practice CDs, CD #3.

one person speaks and the other just listens. Then they switch. One hundred and twenty people scattered in dyads throughout the room engage in intimate conversations, all in a whisper, about our direct and very personal experiences of the day. The feeling in the room during the whispering is both calm and electric, like the buzzing of an industrious beehive. After these whispered conversations, we come together again as a group for a larger sharing, this time, in our normal speaking voice. People are invited to speak about their experience of the day in whatever ways they care to, including in relationship to what brought them to the Stress Reduction Clinic and to MBSR in the first place. As hands go up and people begin speaking, the calmness and peacefulness in the room are palpable. There is a feeling of exquisite intimacy, even with so many people. It almost feels as if we are sharing one big mind together around the circle and mirroring different aspects of it back and forth to each other. People are really listening, really hearing and feeling what is being voiced.

One woman says that during the lovingkindness and forgiveness meditation she was able to direct some love and kindness toward herself and that she found she was able to forgive her husband just a little for years of violence and physical abuse. She says it feels good to let go of it in this way, even just a little bit, for it feels as if something is being healed inside her by forgiving him. She says she sees now that she doesn't have to carry her anger around with her like an enormous weight forever, and that she can move on with her life as she lets this be behind her.

At this, another woman wonders for herself whether it is always appropriate to forgive. She says she doesn't think it is healthy for her to practice forgiveness right now; she was a "professional victim" most of her adult life and was always forgiving people and making herself the object of other people's needs at the expense of her own. She says that what she thinks she needs is to feel her anger. She says she has gotten in touch with it today for the first time and sees that she was unwilling to face it in the past. She has come to realize today that she needs to pay attention to and honor the dominant feeling that she has at this time, which is a lot of anger, and that "forgiveness can wait."

Several graduates say that they came to "recharge their batteries," as a way of getting back into a daily meditation routine, which some have moved away from. Janet says that our day of practicing together reminded her of how much better she feels when she meditates regularly. Mark says that his regular sitting practice helps him to trust his body and listen to it too, rather than exclusively to his doctors. He says his doctors told him that there were many things he would no longer be able to do because of his worsening spinal condition, known as ankylosing spondylosis, in which the vertebrae fuse together to form a rodlike structure, but he finds he is now able to do many of those things again.

During our hour-long conversation among these 120 people, all present, all listening intently, there are frequent stretches of silence in the group, as if we have collectively transcended the need for talk. It feels as if the silence is communicating something deeper than what we are able to express with words. It binds us together. We feel peaceful in it, comfortable, at home. We don't have to fill it with anything.

And so the day comes to an end. We sit for a final fifteen minutes in silence and then say our good-byes. Sam still has a big grin on his face. It is obvious that he has had a good day. We hug once more and promise to keep in touch. Some people stay to help us roll up the mats and put them away.

Later in the week, in our regular classes, we discussed the all-day session some more. Bernice said she had been so nervous about coming that she'd gotten practically no sleep the night before. Around five in the morning she'd done the body scan on her own, without the CD for the first time, in a last-ditch attempt to relax enough to feel able to come. To her surprise it worked. But she said that when she got up she still had been in a somewhat deranged state from lack of sleep and almost decided that it would be too hard for her to sit for a whole day with so many people without talking. For some reason that she could not really explain, at some point she decided that she might be able to do it. She got into her car and played the body scan CD the whole way to the medical center, using the sound of my voice to reassure her. She said this sheepishly and laughed along with the rest of the class, because everybody knew that they were not supposed to use the guided meditation CDs while driving.

During the morning, Bernice went on, there had been three separate times that she almost bolted from the room in a state of sheer panic. But she didn't. Each time she told herself that she could always leave if she had to, that there was nothing holding her prisoner in the room. Reframing the situation this way was enough to help her stay with her anxious feelings and breathe with them when they welled up. In the afternoon, she experienced no feelings of panic at all. Instead she felt peaceful. She discovered for the first time in her life, she said, that she could actually stay with her feelings and watch them without running from them.

Not only did she discover that they eventually subside by themselves, she also discovered a new feeling of confidence in her ability to handle such episodes. She saw that she could have long stretches of relaxation and peace in the afternoon, even though she had had almost no sleep the night before and therefore had every "reason" to expect things to be "bad." She was thrilled to make this discovery and feels that it is going to have relevance to other situations in which, in the past, she has been controlled by her fears.

Bernice was particularly pleased with this discovery because she suffers from Crohn's disease, a chronic ulcerative disorder of the intestines that gives rise to intense abdominal pain whenever she is tense and stressed. She had had none of her usual symptoms during the all-day session, as she managed to ride out and regulate her feelings of panic that morning.

Ralph then told a story about jumping out of his parents' car as a child when it was stuck in traffic in a long tunnel and running toward the end of the tunnel, driven by an uncontrollable fear. This recollection struck a chord in Bernice, who confessed that she won't go to Logan Airport in Boston because she has to go through either the Callahan or the Ted Williams Tunnel. But later, before the class ended, she said that going through a tunnel would probably be similar to making it through the all-day session. Since she did that, she decided, she can probably go through one of those tunnels. It seems she is thinking about doing it now, almost as a homework assignment for herself, a rite of passage to test her growth in the program.

Fran said that her experience of the all-day session was one of having a "funny" feeling that she didn't want to call relaxation or peace; it was more like feeling "solid" and "free." She said that even lying down on the grass outside after lunch felt special. She hadn't lain on grass and just looked up at the sky since she was a little girl. Now she is forty-seven. Her first thought after she realized how good she was feeling was "What a waste," meaning all those years she had felt out of touch with herself. I suggested that those years were what led up to this present experience of freedom and solidity and that she might bring her awareness to the impulse to label them as "bad" or "a waste" just as she would if we were meditating. Perhaps then she could see those years with greater acceptance, as what she was able to do then, seeing things as she did at that time.

The cardiologist said he realized that his whole life was spent trying to get somewhere else, using the present to achieve results that would bring him what he wanted sometime later. During the all-day session, he had seen that nothing bad would happen to him if he started living in the present and appreciating it for its own sake.

A young psychiatrist spoke of how discouraged she had felt on Saturday doing the meditation. She had had a hard time keeping her attention focused on her breath or on her body. She described it as feeling just like "slogging through mud." She said she kept having to "start over, again and again, from the bottom."

This image became the subject of some discussion, since there is a big difference between "starting over" and "starting from the bottom." Starting over implies just being in the moment, the possibility of a fresh beginning with each inbreath. Seeing things this way, coming back to the breath in each moment that the mind wanders, would be relatively effortless, or at least neutral. Each breath really is a new beginning of the rest of our lives. But the words she used carried a strong negative judgment. "Starting from the bottom" implies that she felt she had lost ground, has been submerged, has to rise up. Taken with the weight and resistance of the mud image, it was easy to see why she might have felt discouraged about bringing her mind back to her breathing when it wandered.

When she saw this, she laughed good-naturedly. The meditation practice is a perfect mirror. It allows us to look at the problems our thinking creates for us, those little or not-so-little traps that our own minds set for us and in which we get caught and sometimes stuck. What we ourselves have made laborious and difficult becomes easier the moment we see the reflection of our mind in the mirror of mindfulness. In a moment of insight, her confusion and difficulty dissolved, leaving the mirror empty, at least for a moment, and her laughing.

9

Really Doing What You're Doing: Mindfulness in Daily Life

Jackie returned home from the all-day intensive late in the afternoon on Saturday. Although she was tired from the effort she had put in, she felt it had been a good day. She had made it through and had enjoyed being silent and alone with all those people. In fact, she was pleasantly surprised by how good she felt about herself after seven and a half hours of mostly just sitting and walking, seven and a half hours of simply being present with her own experience, of doing nothing really.

Arriving home, she discovered a note from her husband saying he had gone off overnight to take care of things at their summer home in a neighboring state. He had mentioned that he might do this, but she had not taken it seriously because he knew very well that she would not want to be alone that night. Had she known in advance that he was going to be away, she could have arranged not to be alone, as she had always done in the past. Jackie had spent very little time alone in her life, and she was well aware that the prospect frightened her. When her daughters were younger and still living at home, she had always encouraged them to get out of the house and do things, to get together with friends, anything rather than being alone in the house, to which they had always responded, "But Mom, we *like* being alone." Jackie could never understand how they could like being alone. The prospect simply terrified her.

When she got home and found the note from her husband, her first impulse was to reach for the telephone and invite a friend over for dinner and to spend the night. In the middle of dialing, she stopped herself and thought, "Why am I in such a rush to fill up this time? Why not really take seriously what those people in the Stress Reduction Clinic are saying about living your moments fully?" She hung up and decided just to let the momentum of her day of mindfulness that had begun that morning at the hospital continue. She decided she would allow herself to be in her house all alone for the first time in her adult life and just feel what it was like.

As she described it to me a few days later, it turned out to be a special time. Rather than experiencing loneliness and anxiety, she was filled with a feeling of joy that lasted all evening. With some effort, she moved her mattress and box spring to another room, where she knew she would feel more secure keeping her windows open on a Saturday night alone. She stayed up late, enjoying herself in her own house. She got up early the next morning, before sunrise, still feeling exuberant, and watched the sun come up.

Jackie had made a very important discovery. In her mid-fifties, she had discovered that all her time is really her own. Her experience that night and the next morning helped her to see that she is really living her own life all the time, that all her moments are hers, available to be felt and lived if she chooses to. When we talked, she expressed concern that she wouldn't be able to duplicate the feeling of peace that she had had that night and the next day. I reminded her that this very concern was itself just another worried thought about the future, and she agreed, mindful that it had been her willingness to be in the present that night that had brought about her experience of inner peace in the first place, and that having such a positive experience under such conditions was in itself a breakthrough for her.

The discovery that she could be happy by herself came about because she had chosen to use the momentum she had built up in her meditation practice during the day-long session. We reviewed how she had kept the "being mode" alive when she got home and encountered the unexpected.

She had caught herself thinking first of filling up that time to escape from being with herself and had chosen instead, quite intentionally, to dwell in the present, to accept it as it was at that moment. This being the case, we discussed the possibility that perhaps she didn't need to worry about either duplicating her experience or losing it. The happiness she experienced came from inside herself in the first place. It was released by her courage and her intention to bring awareness to her situation and to be mindful in the face of her insecurities. As we talked, she began to see that she can tap into this dimension of her being at any time, that it is a part of her, and that all it really takes is a willingness to be mindful and to adjust her priorities so that time by herself is valued and protected.

The peacefulness Jackie experienced that night is something that can be felt in any moment, under any circumstances, if the commitment to practice mindfulness is strong. It is a great gift we can give to ourself. It means we can reclaim our entire life rather than just living for our vacations or the other "special" times when everything will be "perfectly arranged" to bring on those hoped-for feelings of well-being, inner peace, and serenity. Of course, it hardly ever works out that way anyway, even on vacation.

The challenge is to make calmness, inner balance, and clear seeing a part of everyday life. In the same way that it is possible to be mindful *whenever* we are walking, not just when we are practicing walking meditation, we can attempt to bring moment-to-moment attention to the tasks, experiences, and encounters of ordinary living, such as cooking dinner, setting the table, eating, washing the dishes, doing the laundry, cleaning the house, taking out the garbage, working in the garden, mowing the lawn, brushing our teeth, shaving, taking a shower or a bath, drying off with the towel, playing with the children or helping them to get ready for school, communicating through email and texting, talking on the phone, cleaning out the garage, taking the car in to be fixed or fixing it ourselves, riding a bike, taking the subway, getting on a bus, stroking the cat, walking the dog, hugging, kissing, touching, making love, taking care of people who depend on us, going to work, working, or just sitting on the front steps or in a park.

If you can name something or even feel it, you can be mindful of it. As we have already seen a number of times, in bringing mindfulness to an activity or an experience, whatever it may be, you flesh it out. It becomes more vivid, brighter, more real for you. In part things become more vivid because the stream of your thinking subsides a little and is less likely to interpose itself between you and what is actually happening. This greater clarity and fullness can be experienced in the activities of daily living in the very same way that we have felt it practicing the body scan, the sitting, and the yoga. Your formal mindfulness practice heightens your ability to encounter the whole of your life with moment-to-moment awareness. When you are practicing regularly, mindfulness will tend naturally to spill over into all the various contours of your daily life. You might find your mind altogether calmer and less reactive.

As encountering each moment with awareness becomes more familiar to you, you will find that it is not only possible but actually enjoyable to be in the moment, even with ordinary tasks such as washing the dishes. You come to see that you don't have to rush to finish the dishes so that you can get on to something better or more important because, at the moment that you are doing the dishes, that is your life. As we have seen, if you miss these moments because your mind is somewhere else, in an important way you are shortchanging your life. So try taking each pot and each cup and each plate as it comes, being aware of the movements of your body in holding and scrubbing and rinsing, the movements of the breath, and the movements of your mind. This also applies to when you are setting the table or putting the dishes away after they are washed and dried.

You can follow a similar approach with anything and everything you find yourself doing, whether it be alone or with other people. As long as you are doing something, doesn't it make sense to be fully present as you do it, with the whole of your being? If you choose to do things mindfully, then your doing will be coming out of non-doing. It will feel more meaningful and requires less effort.

If you are able to be present in the routine daily activities of your life, if you are willing to remember that those moments can be moments of calm and alert attention as well as times of doing things that have to be done, you may find that not only do you enjoy the process more but you are also more likely to have insights into yourself and your life while you are engaged in these routine activities.

For instance, in doing the dishes mindfully, you may come to see with great vividness the reality of impermanence. Here you are, doing the dishes again. How many times have you done the dishes? How many more times will you do them in your life? What is this activity we call doing the dishes? *Who* is it who is actually doing the dishes?

By inquiring in this way without looking for answers, especially conceptual answers, but instead looking deeply into and holding in awareness this totally ordinary routine of "doing the dishes," you may find that the whole world is represented in it. You can learn a lot about yourself and about the world by doing the dishes with your whole being, with alert interest and an inquiring mind. The dishes can teach you something important in this way. They become a mirror of your own mind.

We are not talking about simply seeing that life is a stream of dirty dishes, after which you go back to doing the dishes mechanically. The point is to really do the dishes when you are doing them, to be awake and alive as you do them, mindful of the tendency to slip back into autopilot and do them unconsciously, perhaps also aware of your resistance to get to them, to procrastinate, or to resent other people who you may want to help you with them but who don't. Mindfulness can also lead to decisions to make changes in your life based on your insights. Perhaps you might even get others to do their fair share of the dishes! Or if you don't wash the dishes yourself, because you use a dishwasher, you can let the loading of the dishes in the dishwasher become part of your mindfulness practice. One thing you might notice is how attached you may be to loading it the right way ("my way," of course), and that nobody knows how to load the dishwasher properly except yourself. Sometimes watching the mind in this way is both humbling and hysterically funny, no matter what you are engaged in.

Take cleaning the house as another example of an activity of daily living. If you have to clean your house, why not clean it mindfully? So many people tell me that their houses are spotless, that they cannot live with mess, with disorder, that they are always cleaning and picking up and straightening and dusting. But how much of the time are they doing it with awareness? How much of the time are they aware of their bodies as they are cleaning? And are they inquiring at all about how clean is clean, about their attachment to the house looking a certain way, about what they get out of doing it or whether they resent doing it? Are they inquiring about when they should stop, or about what else they might be doing with their energy instead of keeping the house like a showpiece? Or about why they are driven to clean compulsively? Or about who will be cleaning their house after they are dead twenty years, or whether it will matter to them?

By making cleaning the house into part of your meditation practice, this routine chore can become an entirely new experience. You may also wind up doing it differently, or less, and not because you have stopped caring about order and cleanliness. These do not need to be sacrificed. But you may change *how* you clean the house because you have seen more deeply into your relationship to order and cleanliness and into yourself and your own needs, priorities, and attachments. Inquiry here means simply non-judgmental awareness, a seeing through the unawareness that usually veils our activities, especially those we do routinely.

Perhaps these suggestions for how to do the dishes mindfully or to clean your house mindfully will give you some ideas for ways to do whatever you find yourself doing with greater awareness and for ways to nurture a clearer seeing into your own mind and life situation. The important point to keep in mind is that each moment that you are alive is a moment that you can live fully, a moment not to be missed. Why *not* live life as if it really mattered?

George does the grocery shopping for himself and his wife every week. He does it mindfully. He has to. With his condition, almost anything he does can send him into a severe episode of shortness of breath. Moment-to-moment awareness helps him to keep his body and his breathing under control. George has chronic obstructive pulmonary disease (COPD). He cannot work, so he at least tries to help out with things around the house while his wife is at work. He is sixty-six years old and has had the disease for the past six years. He was a smoker, on top of which he had worked his whole adult life in a poorly ventilated machine shop, continually breathing chemicals and abrasive dust. Recently he has had to go on oxygen twenty-four hours a day. He has a portable oxygen canister on wheels that he pulls along. A tube brings the oxygen to his nostrils. He is able to get around this way.

George learned to practice mindfulness when he took the pulmonary rehabilitation program in our hospital. Part of the program involves using mindfulness of breathing to control shortness of breath and the panic that occurs when you find you can't get the next breath into your lungs. For the past four years he has been practicing faithfully four or five mornings a week for fifteen minutes. While he is meditating, his breathing is unlabored and he doesn't feel he needs the oxygen, although he still uses it.

For George, practicing the meditation has made a big difference in the quality of his life. For one thing, he has learned to reduce the frequency of the episodes of shortness of breath by bringing awareness to his breathing. "My breathing is not so hard, let's put it that way. It sort of lets down a little bit and I don't have to go after it, it just stabilizes itself." Although he knows that his condition will not get better and that there are many things he cannot do, George has come to accept this and has learned that he can move along at the slow pace he is capable of and still be happy. He is acutely aware of his limits and tries to be mindful of his body and his breathing throughout the day.

When he came in to the hospital today, he parked his car, walked slowly into the building, and then stopped in the men's room to rest and breathe for a few minutes. Then he went to the elevator and rested for another few minutes. He consciously paces himself and takes his time everywhere he goes. He has to. Otherwise he would be in the emergency room all the time.

It took him a while to adjust psychologically to needing the oxygen twenty-four hours a day. At first he had stopped going to stores because he felt self-conscious and embarrassed by his oxygen tank, but finally he said to himself, "This is crazy! I am only hurting myself." So now he is back doing the grocery shopping again. He gets everything put in small bags with handles. He can lift these smaller bags and put them into the trunk of his car if he does everything slowly, with awareness.

When he gets home, he has to walk about fifty feet from the car to the side entrance of the house. He can pull his oxygen bottle and carry a few bags if they are not too heavy. The heavy ones he leaves in the car for his wife to bring in later. He says, "The folks in the store know me now and they give me those shopping bags with no problem. So I kind of licked that problem. That is the routine; there's a way to cut corners, ya know. I say to myself, 'If I can do it, I'm going to do it. If I can't, I'm going to leave it,' and that's the general idea."

By doing the shopping for the family, George is contributing to the work that needs to be done to keep the household going as well as saving his wife from having to do it on top of working. This helps him to continue to feel engaged in his own life. Within the limits of his disease, he is actively meeting life's challenges rather than sitting at home and bemoaning his fate. He takes each moment as it comes and figures out how he can work with it and stay relaxed and aware. By living this way, by exploring his limits and by pacing himself, staying with his breathing right through the day, George is functioning extremely well in his life despite a level of physiological lung impairment that might completely disable somebody else. For in this disease in particular, the degree of disability at a given level of lung damage depends more on psychological factors than on anything else once the person is receiving proper medical treatment.

Just as George found a way to make use of mindfulness in his day-to-day life and adapt it to his situation and physical condition, so might each one of us begin to take some responsibility for cultivating mindfulness in our own daily lives, whatever our circumstances. As we will see in the chapter on time and time stress (Chapter 26), bringing full awareness to each moment is a particularly effective way to make the best use of the time that we have. Living in this way, life naturally becomes more balanced and the mind steadier and calmer.

When it comes right down to it, the challenge of mindfulness is to realize that, *"This is it."* Right now is my life. This realization immediately gives rise to a number of vital questions: "What is my relationship to my own life going to be? Does my life just automatically 'happen' to me? Am I a total prisoner of my circumstances or my obligations, my body or my illness or my past, or even of my to-do lists? Do I become hostile, defensive, or depressed if certain buttons get pushed, happy if other buttons are pushed, and anxious or frightened if something else happens? What are my choices? Do I have any options?"

We will be looking into these questions more deeply when we take up the subject of our reactions to stress and how our emotions affect our health. For now, the important point is to grasp the value of bringing the practice of mindfulness into the conduct of our everyday lives. Is there any waking moment of your life that would not be richer and more alive for you if you were more fully awake for it while it was happening?

10

Getting Started in the Practice

If you are interested in further developing your own mindfulness meditation practice and have been experimenting with the various suggestions we have been making up to this point in our journey together, perhaps you are wondering what the best way to proceed from here on out might be. Should you start with the sitting meditation practice or the body scan? What about the yoga? Where do the recommendations about the breathing fit in, and the instructions about sitting? How often should you practice, and at what times, and for how long? What about the walking meditation and practicing mindfulness in everyday life?

We have already given some indications about how we combine the various aspects of the formal practices in MBSR. This chapter provides specific recommendations for getting started in your own daily mindfulness practice based on exactly what we do with the participants in the Stress Reduction Clinic—in other words, based on the formal curriculum of MBSR. In this way, as you continue to move through the rest of the book, you can also be practicing as you would if you were enrolled in the clinic. Alternatively, you may wish to read through to the end before you decide whether to engage in the practice itself in a regular way. You will find further details about developing and maintaining a regular mindfulness practice in Chapters 34 and 35.

It is not a bad idea for you to start practicing at this point if what has come before speaks to you. This is certainly what you would have to do were you to enroll in an MBSR program anywhere. All the talk about the practice, the instructions for how to practice, the discussion of the applications of mindfulness in the case of specific illnesses and problems, what its relationship is to the larger areas of medicine and health and illness, to the mind and the body, to the brain and to stress—all these are secondary to the regular cultivation of the meditation practice in your own life. It is your engagement in the daily formal practice of mindfulness that is most fundamental, and out of which everything else in the way of learning, growing, healing, and transformation arises.

In MBSR, we begin practicing in the very first class. The material you will be encountering in the following sections of this book will be richer and make more sense to you if you are already at work cultivating mindfulness in your own life. So if you feel inclined at this point to get started on a structured program, this chapter will give you guidelines for how to proceed over the next eight weeks. You may only get as far as the first two or three weeks before you complete the book. That is fine. There is no need to take eight weeks to read the book, although that is also a credible way to proceed as you follow the curriculum. The most important thing is just to get started, if you are ready to make this kind of commitment to yourself. Hopefully, once you begin, you will be motivated by your experience to keep up the momentum and intentionality you are developing and proceed through the entire eight weeks. That is certainly what we would recommend. Remember, we tell our patients, "You don't have to like it; you just have to do it." By the time you have been practicing for eight weeks, you will have enough momentum and direct personal experience with the practice to keep going with it for years, perhaps even for the rest of your life, if you choose to. Tens of thousands of people have used the book in this way since it was first published. And hundreds of thousands have completed MBSR and related mindfulness-based programs around the world.

The place to start, of course, is with your breathing. If you haven't done the three-minute experiment on paying attention to your breathing (see Chapter 1) and watching what your mind does, then you might want to do that now, just to make sure you know what we mean about keeping the mind on the breath and bringing it back when it wanders. We recommend that at the very least you do this every day for five or ten minutes, either sitting or lying down, at a time that is convenient for you. Review Chapter 3, on breathing, and start getting comfortable with feeling your belly rise and fall as you breathe. Then follow the instructions in exercises 1 and 2 at the end of that chapter.

The most important thing to remember is to practice every day. Even if you can make only five minutes to practice during your day, five minutes of mindfulness can be very restorative and healing. But keep in mind that we require the people in the Stress Reduction Clinic to commit to between forty-five minutes and an hour of practice a day, six days a week, for at least eight weeks, and we strongly recommend that you commit yourself to a similar schedule, and that you make use of the Series 1 CDs in the same way our patients do. As we have mentioned, making time to practice with the CDs is a significant lifestyle change right from the very beginning. Nobody has an extra hour a day lying around, especially to devote to non-doing, which looks an awful lot like nothing to our thinking mind, but turns out to positively influence just about everything in our lives. You have to actually *make* the time to practice every day, because otherwise you will not *find* it. And remember, from our point of view, given the pain and suffering that may have brought you to this juncture, it is essential to *practice* mindfulness—and to make time for formal practice every day—as if your life depended on it. Because, as we have said, it does.

The Series 1 guided mindfulness meditation practice CDs can be a powerful aid in getting started and in deepening your practice over the eight weeks of the MBSR program, and can serve you well beyond those eight weeks. Guided mindfulness practice CDs, usually voiced by their particular instructors, are used by all the participants in MBSR programs. Many people continue to practice with them for years after completing the program. Following along with the voice and the instructions allows you to simply attend to what you are being asked to attend to, without having to remember what you are supposed to be doing—especially since it is not about *doing* but about *being,* which is much harder for us to remember to trust when we are caught up in the activity of our own minds and, at times, the stress and travails of the body. In this section, you will find specific indications for which CD to use at which times.

If you choose not to use the practice CDs but would prefer to gentle yourself into the practice of mindfulness and aspects of the MBSR curriculum on your own and at your own pace, there are ample instructions in this section of the book for you to develop a formal mindfulness practice without the guidance of the CDs. And whether or not you are using the CDs, we recommend that you study all the chapters in this section from time to time to review the descriptions and suggestions they contain.

MBSR CURRICULUM - PROGRAM SCHEDULE

Weeks 1 and 2

For the first two weeks of your formal practice of MBSR, we recommend that you do the body scan as described in Chapter 5 (Series 1, CD #1). Do it every day, whether you feel like it or not. It takes approximately forty-five minutes by the clock, although the invitation is always to reside as best you can in the timeless quality of the present moment. As we have seen, you will have to experiment to determine the best time of day for you to practice, but keep in mind that the overarching invitation with the body scan is to "fall awake," not to fall asleep! Let each time you come to the body scan be as if for the first time, letting go as best you can of any expectations at all. The most important thing is to just do it. If you have a lot of trouble with sleepiness, practice with your eyes open. In addition to the body scan, practice mindfulness of breathing while sitting for ten minutes at some other time during the day.

To cultivate mindfulness in your daily life—what we have been calling "informal practice"—you might try bringing moment-to-moment awareness to routine activities such as waking up in the morning, waking up your children, brushing your teeth, taking a shower, drying your body, getting dressed, eating, driving, taking out the garbage, shopping, cooking, doing the dishes, even checking your email—the list is endless. The point is simply to drop in and *experience what you are doing in a fully embodied way as you are actually doing it;* in other words, being fully present, as best you can, moment by moment, for the unfolding of your life. This would also include awareness of the thoughts and emotions that arise in the mind from moment to moment and how they express themselves in your body.

If this seems a bit overwhelming, just pick out one routine activity each week, such as taking a shower, and see if you can remember to just be fully in the shower when you are in the shower—to feel the water on your skin, the movements of your body, the whole of the experience. You may be astonished at how hard this is, at how you may already be at work while you are still in the shower, maybe even having a meeting in the shower, in spite of the fact that you are the only person there. And, if you care to, you might try to eat at least one meal mindfully in each of these two weeks as well.

Weeks 3 and 4

After practicing in this way for two weeks, start alternating the body scan one day with the first sequence of mindful hatha yoga postures (Series 1, CD #2) the next, and keep this up during weeks 3 and 4. Follow the recommendations for the yoga as described in Chapter 6. Remember only to do what you feel your body is capable of, and always to err on the side of being conservative, listening carefully to your body's messages as you practice. Remember also to check with your doctor or physical therapist before undertaking the yoga if you have a chronic pain condition or some kind of musculoskeletal problem or lung or heart disease.

Continue to practice mindfulness of breathing in the sitting posture for fifteen to twenty minutes a day in week 3 and up to thirty minutes a day in week 4.

For informal practice in week 3, try to be aware of *one pleasant event* a day in your life *as it is happening*. Keep a calendar for the week, jotting down what the experience was, whether you were actually aware of it at the time it was happening (that's the assignment but it doesn't always work out that way), how your body felt at the time, what thoughts and feelings were present, and what it means to you at the time you write it down. A sample calendar is provided in the Appendix. In week 4, do the same thing for one unpleasant or stressful event a day, again bringing awareness to it as it is happening.

Weeks 5 and 6

In weeks 5 and 6, we recommend that you stop doing the body scan for a while and replace it with the forty-five-minute guided sitting meditation practice (Series 1, CD # 3), alternating with the yoga. By this point you are probably ready to sit for forty-five minutes, although you might not think so on any given day. The guidance on the CD will carry you through paying attention to an expanding field of objects of attention: the breath, other body sensations, a sense of the body as a whole sitting and breathing, sounds, thoughts and emotions, and then a choiceless awareness of whatever is most vivid in your experience in the present moment—what is sometimes called "open presence."

If you choose to practice without the guidance, you can practice as described in the exercises at the end of Chapter 4. You can sit the whole time just focusing on your breathing (Exercise 1) or you can gradually expand the field of your awareness to include other objects such as bodily sensations and a sense of the body as a whole sitting and breathing (Exercise 2), sounds (Exercise 3), thoughts and emotions (Exercise 4), or no particular object—choiceless awareness (Exercise 5). Remember to let your breathing serve as the anchor for your attention in all of these practices.

If you chose to modify the timeline of the MBSR curriculum, you might experiment with staying with the breath as the primary object of attention in the sitting meditation (especially if you are not using the CD for guidance) for weeks, or even months. In the early stages of the sitting practice, it is possible to be uncertain as to where to focus your attention when, and to worry inordinately about whether you are doing it "right."

For the record, if your energy is continually going into patiently attending to the unfolding of experience from moment to moment, whether your attention is focused on the breath sensations in the body or on other objects, and if you are attempting to observe what is on your mind when you realize it is far from the breath, and are then bringing it back each time it wanders, gently, with a light touch, without giving yourself a hard time, then you are doing it right. If you are looking for a special feeling to occur, whether it be relaxation, calmness, concentration, or insight, that is a sign you are trying to get somewhere other than where you already are. When your notice this, it is helpful to remind yourself in such moments just to be with the breath sensations in the present. Paradoxically, as we have seen, not trying to get somewhere is the most effective way to get somewhere in the sense of greater well-being, relaxation, calmness, concentration, and insight. These will flourish by themselves in time if you keep up the daily discipline and practice according to these guidelines.

In weeks 5 and 6 the people in the Stress Reduction Clinic alternate a forty-five-minute sitting one day with the yoga practice the next. If you aren't doing the yoga, then you might like to alternate the sitting with the body scan during these weeks, or just sit every day. This is also a good time to start practicing some walking meditation, as described in Chapter 7.

By this time you will probably want to be making the decisions for yourself about when and what to practice and for how long. After four or five weeks, many people feel ready to start crafting and personalizing their own meditation practice, using our guidelines merely as suggestions. By the end of the eight weeks, the aim of MBSR is for you to have made the practice *your own* by adapting it to suit your schedule, your body's needs and capabilities, and your temperament, in terms of which combination of formal and informal practices you find most effective, and even how long you practice.

Week 7

To encourage self-directed practice and increasing self-reliance, week 7 of MBSR is dedicated to practicing without the CDs for guidance if at all possible. People devote a total of forty-five minutes a day to a combination of sitting, yoga, and body scanning, but they have to decide on the mix themselves. They are encouraged to experiment, perhaps by using two or even three of the different practices together on the same day, say thirty minutes of yoga followed by fifteen minutes of sitting, or twenty minutes of sitting followed by yoga either right after it or at another time of day entirely.

Some people find they do not feel ready for practicing in this way at this point. They prefer to continue using the CDs. They find the guidance comforting and reassuring and are better able to focus and to rest in awareness in a relaxed and spacious way when it is not up to them to decide what to do next, particularly in the body scan and the yoga. From our point of view this is not a problem. Our hope is that with time you will internalize the practice and be comfortable practicing on your own, without CDs or books for guidance. However, the development of this kind of confidence and faith in your capacity to guide yourself in the meditation does take time, and it varies from one individual to another. Many of our patients can meditate quite well on their own but still prefer to use the CDs, even years after they complete the program.

Week 8

In week 8 of MBSR, we come back to the CDs. Leaving them in week 7, to whatever degree we can manage to practice on our own, and then coming back to them in this way can be quite revealing. You are likely to hear things on the CDs that you never heard before and to perceive the deep structure of the meditation practice in new ways. In this week, you are encouraged to practice with the CDs even if you prefer doing it without them. But now *you* are in charge of deciding what practice or practices you wish to engage in. You may just be practicing the sitting meditation or the yoga or the body scan, depending on your situation, or you may be combining two or all three in various ways, and including formal walking meditation practice as well.

At this point in the development of your mindfulness practice, it is important for you to recognize that, you now have at least some familiarity, if not intimacy, with all four of the formal mindfulness practices of MBSR. You are likely to find this familiarity beneficial in very practical ways, for you now have a knowledge base to call upon in particular circumstances. For instance, you may find yourself drawn from time to time to practice the yoga or the body scan even if your daily practice is mainly sitting. What is more, the body scan can be particularly useful when you are sick in bed, in acute pain, or unable to sleep. Likewise, a little mindful yoga can be particularly helpful at certain times, such as when you are very tired and need to revitalize yourself, when there is stiffness in particular regions of your body, or when you happen to find yourself in a particularly beautiful spot in nature where the conditions are just right, nobody is around, and the freshness of the air is calling you to drop into a yoga pose and hold it in this very instant.

The eighth week brings us to the end of our formal recommendations for practicing mindfulness, and thus, we hope, to the first week of your practicing on your own. We tell our patients that the eighth week of MBSR lasts the rest of their lives. We see it as a beginning much more than an ending. The practice doesn't end just because we have stopped guiding you in such a formal way. The eight weeks of MBSR function simply as a launching platform into the practice and into the rest of your life. The adventure simply continues.

So by this point, I hope that you will be firmly in the driver's seat yourself and, if you have been practicing in a regular, disciplined way as you have been reading along, you will now have enough familiarity and experience to keep up the momentum you have developed and guide your own mindfulness practice. At the end of the book, you will find more suggestions for how to keep up the momentum and deepen it over the years. This includes not only a review of the formal practices but more suggestions for bringing mindfulness into daily life and using it to help you to cope with the situations you might be facing. But in all likelihood, by the time you get to that part of the book, you will probably have invented better ones for yourself.

In the next section we will be looking at a new way of thinking about health and illness and how it relates directly to your own efforts to develop a personal mindfulness meditation practice. From there we will go on to explore ways of looking at stress and change from a meditative perspective, as well as specific applications of mindfulness for different medical problems and for handling stress in its many different guises. As we proceed, we recommend that you keep to the practice schedule outlined above, so that as you read more about the process and its ramifications, it is actually unfolding simultaneously in your own life and in your own heart.

II

The Paradigm: A New Way of Thinking About Health and Illness

11

Introduction to the Paradigm

In order for the meditation practice to take root in your life and flourish, you will have to know why you are practicing. How else will you be able to sustain non-doing in a world where only doing seems to count? What will get you up early in the morning to sit, taking up residency in the present moment in awareness, perhaps simply by befriending your breathing for a time, when everybody else is snug in bed? What will motivate you to practice when the wheels of the doing world are turning, your obligations and responsibilities are beckoning, and a part of you decides or remembers to take some time for "just being"? What will motivate you to bring moment-to-moment awareness into your daily life? What will prevent your practice from losing energy and becoming stale or from petering out altogether after an initial burst of enthusiasm?

To sustain your commitment and keep your meditation practice fresh over a period of months, years, and decades, it is important to develop your own personal vision that can guide you in your efforts and remind you at critical times of the value of charting such an unusual course in your life. There may be times when your vision will be the only support you have in keeping up your practice.

In part, that vision will be molded by your unique life circumstances, by your personal beliefs and values. Another part will develop from your experience of the meditation practice itself, from letting everything become your teacher: your body, your attitudes, your mind, your pain, your joy, other people, your mistakes, your failures, your successes, nature—in short, all your moments. If you are cultivating mindfulness in your life, there is not one thing that you do or experience that cannot teach you about yourself by mirroring back to you the reflections of your own mind and body.

Still another element of your vision will have to come from your embeddedness in the world and from your beliefs about where and how you fit into it. If your health is a major part of your motivation for coming to meditation practice, then your knowledge of and respect for your body and how it works, your perspective on what medicine can and cannot do for you, and your understanding of the role of the mind in health and healing may contribute important elements to your vision. The strength of your personal vision will depend in great measure on what you know in these areas and on how much you are willing to learn. As with the meditation practice itself, this kind of learning requires a lifelong commitment to continual inquiry and a willingness to modify your perspective as you acquire new knowledge and arrive at new levels of understanding and insight.

In MBSR, we try to inspire people to learn more about their own bodies and about the role of the mind in health and illness as a fundamental element of their ongoing adventure in learning, growing, and healing. We do this by touching on the ways in which new scientific research and thinking are transforming the practice of medicine itself, and by exploring the direct relevance of these new developments to our lives as individuals and to the meditation practice. This is now made infinitely easier by Internet searches you can do yourself periodically, if you care to keep up with the latest findings.

The Stress Reduction Clinic and MBSR do not exist in a vacuum. The clinic took shape originally in 1979, under the aegis of the Department of Ambulatory Care at the University of Massachusetts Medical

Center's hospital. It was soon given an academic home within the Department of Medicine, and then, a few years later, within its newly formed Division of Preventive and Behavioral Medicine. At that time, behavioral medicine represented a new current within medicine itself, one that contributed to a rapid expansion of our ideas and knowledge about health and illness. New research findings and new ways of thinking about health and illness from this perspective, and later, through the lens of what later became known as *integrative medicine,* gave rise over time to a more comprehensive perspective within medicine itself, one that recognizes the fundamental unity of mind and body, and how essential it is for people to be active participants, whenever possible, in their own health care—by learning more about health in general and how to maintain and optimize it through their own efforts—in close collaboration with their doctors and the rest of the health care team. As we have already seen, this perspective has come to be called *participatory medicine.* It is based on the view that all of us, by virtue of being alive, have deep interior resources for learning, growing, healing, and transformation that can be tapped, nurtured, and mobilized in the service of living a fuller and more optimal life on every level: from the most basic molecular and cellular levels (our genes, chromosomes, and cells) to higher levels of organization of the body (our tissues, organs, and organ systems, including the brain and the nervous system), to the psychological level (the domain of our thoughts and emotions), to the level of the interpersonal (the domain of the social and cultural, including our relationships with others, with society as a whole, and, of course, with the environment—the natural world of which we are an intimate part).

This new lens of a more participatory medicine recognizes and emphasizes the importance of people learning to communicate more effectively with their doctors in order to ensure that they understand as much as they want to about what their doctor is telling them about their condition and possible treatment options. It also emphasizes the importance for patients to be seen, met, and understood by their doctors, and to know that their needs will be acknowledged, taken seriously, and whenever possible, honored.* It is in this spirit and from this perspective that we introduce the participants in the Stress Reduction Clinic to some of the more prominent and compelling research developments in the fields of neuroscience, psychology, and medicine that may be relevant to their engagement in MBSR, as well as to the new perspective developing within medicine itself, so that they will have a better understanding of what we are asking of them and why it is so important.

Perhaps the most fundamental development in medicine over the past decades is the recognition that we can no longer think about health as being solely a characteristic of the body or the mind, because body and mind are not two separate domains—they are intimately interconnected and completely integrated. The new perspective acknowledges the central importance of thinking in terms of *wholeness* and *interconnectedness* and the need to pay attention to the interactions of mind, body, and behavior in any comprehensive effort to understand and treat illness. This view emphasizes that science will never be able fully to describe a complex dynamical process such as health, or even a relatively simple chronic disease, without looking at the functioning of the whole organism, rather than restricting itself solely to an analysis of parts and components, no matter how important that domain may be as well.

Medicine is presently expanding its own working model of what health and illness are and how lifestyle, patterns of thinking and feeling, relationships, and environmental factors all interact to influence health. The new model explicitly rejects the view that mind and body are fundamentally and inexorably separate. In its place, medicine is presently seeking to ar-

* When patients come to the hospital, each visit generates an "encounter form" in order to ensure payment. From the perspective of participatory medicine, it is important for both medical and ethical reasons that a true encounter takes place, one in which the patient feels that she or he has been seen, met, and heard as a person, and that his or her concerns will be taken seriously and honored by the physician and by the entire health care team, to whatever degree possible. This principle and perspective is becoming more and more the new standard of practice in medicine, as medicine and health care are coming to recognize the unique individuality of human beings and how person-specific biological, psychological, social, and cultural factors can influence the choice of treatment options and the degree of buy-in, participation, and adherence on the part of the patient.

ticulate an alternative, more encompassing vision for understanding what we actually mean by "mind" and "body," and by "health" and "disease."

This transformation in medicine is sometimes referred to as a *paradigm shift,* a movement from one entire worldview to another. There is little doubt that not only medicine but all of science is going through such a shift as the implications of the revolutionary changes in our understanding of nature and of ourselves that have come about in the twentieth and twenty-first centuries become clearer. For the most part, our day-to-day thinking about physical reality—our tacit assumptions about the world, the body, matter, and energy—is based on an outmoded view of reality, one that has changed little in the past three hundred years. Science is now searching for more comprehensive models that are truer to our understanding of the interconnectedness of space and time, matter and energy, mind and body, even consciousness and the universe, and what role the human brain, by far the most complex, interconnected, specialized, and ever-changing organization of matter in the known-by-us universe, plays in all of it.

In this section, you will encounter some of these new ways of looking at the world based on the principles of wholeness and interconnectedness, as well as their implications for medicine, health care, and your own life. We will follow two major threads, both of which are intimately related to the practice of mindfulness, and to each other. The first has to do with the whole process of paying attention. In the next chapter we will take a closer look at how we see things (or don't see things) and how we think about them and represent them to ourselves. This has direct bearing on how we conceptualize our problems and on our ability to face, understand, cope with, and possibly befriend and transcend some of the most rending and toxic effects of stress and illness. We will explore what we mean by wholeness and interconnectedness and why they are so important for health and healing. We return to this theme in the last chapter in this section.

The second thread we will follow has to do with the new perspective that is developing based on research in behavioral and integrative medicine, health psychology, and neuroscience. It addresses the question of how the mind and body interact to influence health and illness, what the implications of this new understanding are for health care, and what we mean when we speak of "health" and "healing" in the first place.

Taken together, these two threads may help you to expand your perspective on the meditation practice and the value of cultivating greater mindfulness in your own life. They underscore the importance of paying attention both to personal experience *and* to current developments in medical research if you hope to enhance and optimize your own health.

However, if the information and the perspective presented in this section are only assimilated by your thinking mind, they will be of little practical value. This section and the following one on stress are meant to encourage a growing interest in, respect for, and appreciation of the exquisite beauty and complexity of your own body and its remarkable ability to self-regulate and heal at every level. The aim is not to give you detailed information about specialized disciplines such as physiology or psychology, psychoneuroimmunology or neuroscience. Rather, it is to expand your perspective on who you are and on your relationship to the world, and perhaps even to inspire you to reflect more deeply on and develop greater confidence in your own body and mind, and to know yourself as a wholly integrated thinking, feeling, and socially interacting being. It is hoped that the views and information presented here will help you to develop your own view of why you might undertake to practice meditation regularly, a personal vision within which you can put the healing power of mindfulness to practical use in your own life.

12

Glimpses of Wholeness, Delusions of Separateness

Have you ever looked at a dog and really seen it in its total "dogness"? A dog is quite miraculous when you really see it. What is it? Where did it come from? Where is it going? What is it doing here? Why is it shaped the way it is? What is its "view" of things, of the neighborhood? What are its feelings?

Children tend to think about things this way. Their vision is fresh. They see things as if for the first time every time. Sometimes our seeing gets tired. We just see a dog: "If you've seen one dog, you've seen them all." So we barely see it at all. We tend to see more through our thoughts and opinions than through our eyes. Our thoughts act as a kind of veil, preventing us from seeing things with fresh eyes. What comes into view is identified by the thinking, categorizing mind and quickly framed: a dog. This frame of mind actually prevents us from seeing the dog in its fullness. It processes and categorizes the "dog" signal and all its various associations very quickly in our brain and then moves on to do the same with the next perception or thought.

When our son was two years old, he wanted to know if there was a person inside our dog. It warmed my heart to see through his eyes in that moment. I knew why he was asking. Sage was a real family member. He had his rightful place. His presence was felt. He was a complete being. He participated along with everyone else in the psychic space of the home, as much a "personality" as any of the people in the family. What could I say to him?

Never mind dogs. What about a bird, or a cat, or a tree, or a flower, or a rhinoceros? They are all quite miraculous really. When you really look at one, when you truly apprehend it, you can hardly believe it exists; here it is, this perfect thing, alive, just being what it is, complete in itself. Any imaginative child could have dreamed up a rhinoceros, or an elephant, or a giraffe. But they didn't get here as the product of a child's imagination. The universe is spinning these dreams. They come out of the universe, as do we.

It doesn't hurt to keep this in mind on a daily basis. It would help us to be more mindful. All life is fascinating and beautiful when the veil of our routinized thinking lifts, even for a moment.

There are many different ways of looking at any thing or event or process. In one way, a dog is just a dog, and there is nothing special about it; at the same time, it is extraordinary, even miraculous. It all depends on how you are looking at it. We might say that it is both ordinary and extraordinary. The dog doesn't change when you change the way you look—and therefore what you see. It is always just what it is. That is why dogs and flowers and mountains and the sea are such great teachers. They reflect your own mind. It is your mind that changes.

When your mind changes, new possibilities tend to arise. In fact, everything changes when you can see things on different levels simultaneously, when you can see fullness and connectedness as well as individuality and separateness. Your thinking expands in scope. This can be a profoundly liberating experience. It can take you beyond your limited preoccupations with yourself. It can put things in a larger perspective. It will certainly change the way you relate to the dog.

When you observe things through the lens of mindfulness, whether it be during formal meditation practice or in daily living, you invariably begin to appreciate things in a new way because your very perceptions change.

Ordinary experiences may suddenly be seen as extraordinary. This does not mean that they stop being ordinary. Each is still just what it is. It's just that now you are appreciating them more in their fullness, and that, it turns out, changes everything.

Let's take eating as an example once again. Eating is an ordinary activity. We do it all the time, usually without much awareness and without thinking much about it. We have seen this already in the eating meditation exercise with the raisins. But the fact that your body can digest food and derive energy from it is extraordinary. The process by which this is accomplished is exquisitely organized and regulated at every level, from the ability of your tongue and cheeks to keep the food between your teeth so that it can be chewed, to the stepwise biochemical processes by which it is broken down and absorbed and used to fuel your body and rebuild its cells, to the effective elimination of the waste products of this process so that toxins do not accumulate and the body remains in metabolic and biochemical balance.

In fact, everything your body normally does is quite wonderful and extraordinary, though you may hardly ever think of it this way. Walking is another good example. If you have ever been unable to walk, you will know how precious and miraculous walking is. It is an extraordinary capability. So are seeing and talking, thinking and breathing, being able to turn over in bed, and anything else your body does that you choose to focus on.

A little reflecting on your body will easily lead you to conclude that it does wondrous things, all of which you probably take completely for granted. When was the last time you gave some thought to the remarkable job your liver is doing, for instance? It is the largest internal organ in your body, performing more than thirty thousand enzymatic reactions per second to ensure metabolic harmony. Dr. Lewis Thomas, a great immunologist and former chancellor of Memorial Sloan-Kettering Cancer Center, wrote in his classic book *The Lives of a Cell* that he would rather be given the controls of a 747, knowing nothing about how to fly, than be responsible for the functioning of his liver.

And what about your heart, or your brain and the rest of your nervous system? Do you ever think about them when they are doing their job well?

If you do, do you see them as ordinary or extraordinary? What about your eyes' ability to see, your ears' ability to hear, the ability of your arms and legs to move just where you want them to, the ability of your feet to keep your whole body balanced when standing and to carry your weight and transport you without losing your balance and stumbling while walking? These capacities of the body are quite extraordinary. Our well-being depends intimately and entirely on the integrated functioning of all our senses—of which we have well more than five—along with our muscles and nerves, our cells, our organs, and organ systems at all times. Yet we tend not to see and think in this way, and so we forget or are ignorant of the fact that our body is truly wondrous. It is a universe in itself, consisting of more than 10 trillion cells that all ultimately derive from one single cell, organized into tissues and organs and systems and structures, and with a built-in ability to regulate itself as a whole to maintain internal balance and order down to the nano level of interacting molecular structures. In a word, our bodies are undeniably self-organizing and self-healing at every level you care to look at. This is one reason why we see the participants in MBSR classes as "miraculous beings"—it turns out we all are.

The body accomplishes and maintains this inner balance through finely tuned feedback loops that interconnect and integrate all aspects of the organism. For instance, when you exert yourself, as in running or climbing stairs, your heart will automatically pump more blood to provide more oxygen to your muscles so that they can perform the task. When the exertion is over, the output of the heart returns to a resting level and the muscles that got you up the stairs, including, of course, your heart, recuperate. The exertion may also have generated a lot of heat if it lasted awhile. This might have caused you to sweat. This is your body's way of cooling off. If you did sweat a lot, you will feel thirsty and drink something, your body's way of ensuring that the lost fluid will be replaced. All these are highly integrated, interconnected regulatory processes operating through elaborate feedback loops.

Such interconnections are built into living systems. When the skin is cut, biochemical signals are sent out and cellular blood-clotting processes set in motion that stop the bleeding and heal the wound. When the body is infected by microorganisms such as bacteria and viruses, the immune system goes into action to identify, isolate, and neutralize them. If any of our own cells lose the feedback loops that control cell growth and become cancerous, a healthy immune system will mobilize specific types of lymphocytes, called natural killer cells, that can recognize structural changes on the surface of the cancerous cells and destroy them before they can cause damage.

On every level of organization, from the molecular biology of the interior of our cells right down to the level of our genome and to the functioning of entire organs and organ systems, our biology is regulated by information flow, which connects each part of the system to the other parts that are important for its functioning. The incredible network of interconnections by which the nervous system monitors, regulates, and integrates all of our organ functions, the countless hormones and neurotransmitters released by specialized glands, by the brain itself, and by the entire nervous system, which in concert transmit chemical messages to targets throughout the body via the bloodstream and nerve fibers, as well as the panoply of different specialized cells in the immune system—all play varied but crucial roles in organizing and regulating this flow of information in the body so that you can function as an integrated, coherent, whole being.

If interconnectedness is crucial for physical integration and health, it is equally important psychologically and socially. Our senses allow us to connect with external reality as well as with our internal states. They give us essential information about the environment and about other people that allows us to organize a coherent impression of the world, to function in "psychological space," to learn, to remember things, to reason, to respond or react with emotion—everything that we mean when we use the word *mind.* Without these coherent impressions, we would be unable to function in even the most basic ways in the world. So the organization of the body allows for a psychological order that arises out of the physical order and also contains it. How amazing! At each level of our being there is a wholeness that is itself embedded in a larger wholeness. And that wholeness is always embodied. It cannot be separated from the body and from an exquisite and intimate belonging to the larger expression of life unfolding. This can be seen in the discovery of what are called "mirror neurons," networks of cells in the brain that fire in us when we see someone else engaged in a particular intentional action. These mirror neurons may underlie our biological capacity for empathy, for "feeling with" another individual.

This web of interconnectedness extends well beyond our individual psychological self. While we are whole ourselves as individual beings, we are also part of a larger whole, interconnected through our family and our friends and acquaintances to the larger society and, ultimately, to the whole of humanity and life on the planet. Beyond the ways in which we can perceive through our senses and through our emotions that we are connected with the world, there are also the countless ways in which our being is intimately woven into the larger patterns and cycles of nature that we only know about through science and through thinking (although even here, indigenous peoples always knew and respected these aspects of interconnectedness in their own ways as natural laws). To mention just a few, we depend on the ozone layer in the atmosphere to protect us from lethal ultraviolet radiation; we depend on the rain forests and oceans to recycle the oxygen we breathe; we depend on a relatively stable carbon dioxide concentration in the atmosphere to buffer global temperature changes. In fact, one scientific view, known as the Gaia hypothesis, is that the earth as a whole behaves as one single self-regulating living organism, given the name Gaia after the Greek goddess of the earth. This hypothesis affirms a view based on strong scientific evidence and reasoning that was, in essence, also held by all traditional cultures and peoples, a world in which all life, including human life, is interconnected and interdependent—and that interconnectedness and interdependence extends to the very earth itself.

The ability to perceive interconnectedness and wholeness in addition to separateness and fragmentation can be cultivated through mindfulness practice. Partly it comes from recognizing how quick our mind is to jump to a particular way of seeing things out of habit or out of unawareness, how easily our views of events and of ourselves are shaped by prejudices, beliefs, likes, and dislikes that we acquired at earlier times. If we hope to see things more clearly, as they actually are, and thereby perceive their intrinsic wholeness and interconnectedness, we have to be mindful of the ruts our thinking gets us into and the tacit assumptions we make all the time about things and people. We have to learn to see and approach things somewhat differently.

To illustrate the automatic nature of our patterns of seeing and thinking, as well as the power inherent in keeping wholeness in mind, we give the following exercise to the people in the Stress Reduction Clinic as a homework "problem" in the very first class. It usually generates a good deal of stress during the week, because some people invariably think that they are going to be judged by their answers—a holdover, no doubt, from our days in school. By design we don't say anything until the next class about how this puzzle might relate to what they are doing in the program. We leave that for them to come to on their own. We call it the problem of the nine dots. You may know it from your own childhood. It is a vivid and easily grasped example of how the way we perceive a problem tends to limit our ability to see solutions to it.

The problem is as follows: Below is an arrangement of nine dots. Your assignment is to connect up all the dots by making four straight lines without lifting your pencil and without retracing along any line. Before you turn the page, spend five or ten minutes trying to solve this puzzle yourself if you don't already know the answer.

What invariably happens with most people is that they start out in one

FIGURE 8

A.

corner and draw three lines around the square. Then the light dawns! One of the dots will be left out this way.

At this point the mind can experience a modicum of distress. The more solutions you try that don't work, the more frustrated you can become.

B.

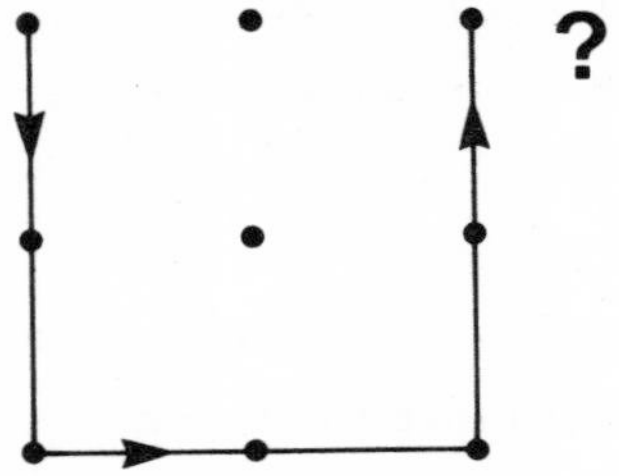

When we go over it in class the following week, we ask all those people who do not know the answer to watch carefully what their reaction is when all of a sudden they "see" the solution when a volunteer draws it on the blackboard.

When you see or discover for yourself the solution to this problem, especially after you have been struggling with it for a while, there is usually an "aha!" experience at the moment of discovery. This is associated with the realization that the solution lies in extending the lines you draw *beyond* the imaginary square that the dots make. The problem as stated does not prevent you from going outside the dots, but the "normal" tendency is to see the nine-dot square pattern as the field of the problem, rather than seeing the dots in the context of the paper and recognizing that the field of the problem is the whole surface that contains the dots.

If you isolate the nine dots by themselves as the domain of the problem because of the automatic way in which you perceive things and think about them, you will never find a satisfactory solution to this problem. As a consequence, you may wind up blaming yourself for being stupid, or getting angry at the problem and proclaiming it impossible or foolish, and certainly irrelevant to your health concerns. All the while, you are putting your energy in the wrong place. You are not seeing the full domain of the problem. You are missing the larger context and therefore, possibly, the potential relevance of the problem to your own situation.

The problem of the nine dots suggests that we may need to take a

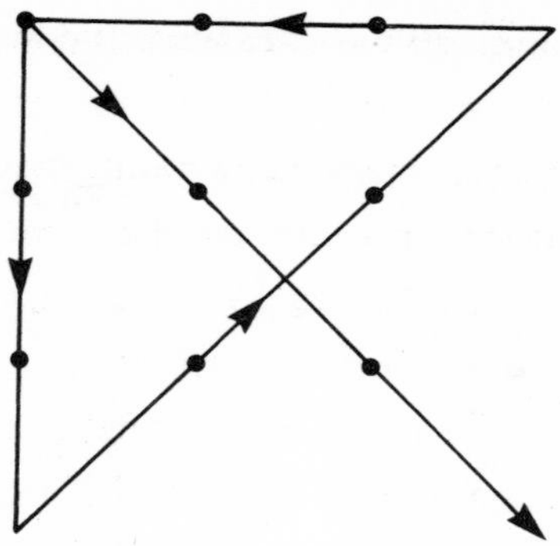

C.

broader view of certain problems if we hope to solve them. This approach involves asking ourselves what the extent of the problem actually is and discerning the relationship between the various isolated parts of the problem and the problem as a whole. This is called adopting a *systems perspective.* If we do not identify the system correctly in its entirety, we will never be able to come to a satisfactory solution of the problem because a key domain will always be missing: the domain of the whole.

The problem of the nine dots teaches us that we may have to expand beyond our habitual, highly conditioned ways of seeing, thinking, and acting in order to solve, resolve, or even dissolve certain kinds of problems. If we don't, our attempts to identify and solve our problems will usually be thwarted by our own prejudices and preconceptions. Our lack of awareness of the system as a whole will often prevent us from seeing new options and new ways of approaching problems. We will have a tendency to get stuck in our problems and our crises and to make faulty decisions and choices by misapprehending the actuality of things and circumstances. Rather than penetrating *through* problems to the point where solutions are reached, when we get stuck there is a tendency to make more problems, and to make them worse, and also to give up trying to solve them. Such experiences can lead to feelings of frustration, inadequacy, and insecurity. When self-confidence becomes eroded, it just makes it harder to solve any other problems that come along. Our doubts about our own abilities become self-fulfilling prophecies. They can come to dominate our lives. In this way, we effectively impose limits on ourselves via our own thought processes. Then, too often, we forget that we have created these boundaries all on our own. Consequently, we get stuck and feel we can't get beyond them.

You can get a closer look at this process on a day-to-day level by being mindful of your own inner dialogue and beliefs and how they affect what you wind up doing in certain situations. Unless we are practicing mindfulness, we rarely observe our inner dialogue with any clarity and ponder its validity, especially when it concerns our thoughts and beliefs about ourselves. For instance, if you have the habit of saying to yourself "I could never do that" when you encounter some kind of problem or dilemma, such as learning to use a tool, or fixing a mechanical device, or speaking up for yourself in front of a group of people, one thing is pretty certain—you won't be able to do it. At that moment, your thought fulfills or makes real its own content. Saying "I can't . . ." or "I could never . . ." is a self-fulfilling prophecy.

If you are in the habit of thinking about yourself in this way, by the time you have a chance to act or to do something to solve a challenging problem you may be facing, you may have already put yourself in a box of your own creation and limited your possibilities. The fact is, in many situations you really do not know what you are capable of doing at any particular moment. You might surprise yourself if you took on a problem, just for fun, and tried something new, even if you didn't know what you were doing and even if you inwardly doubted your ability to do it. I have fixed many a clock and car door that way, sometimes learning about clocks and doors in the process but sometimes managing to fix it just by fiddling with it without having the foggiest idea about how it got fixed.

The point is that we don't always know what our true limits are. However, if your beliefs, attitudes, thoughts, and feelings are always producing reasons for not taking on new challenges, for not taking risks, for not exploring what might be possible for you at the limits of your understanding and your beliefs, for not looking at what the entire scope of a problem might be and at your relationship to it, then you may be severely and unnecessarily limiting your own learning, your own growth, and your ability to make positive changes in your life. Whether it is losing weight, giving up cigarettes once and for all, not yelling at your kids all the time, going back to school, starting your own business, or finding out what there is to live for when you have experienced a deep personal loss or are in the middle of a momentous change in your life that threatens your well-being and everything you hold dear, what you can do will very strongly depend on how you see things, on your beliefs about your own limits and resources, and on your views concerning life itself. As we will see in Chapter 15, our beliefs and attitudes, our thoughts and emotions, can actually have a major influence on our health. In the Stress Reduction Clinic, most people rise to the challenge and take on the risks of turning toward and facing the full catastrophe of their situations with greater mindfulness and heartfulness. In the process, they often surprise themselves and their families with their newfound courage and clarity; they discover their limits receding; and they find themselves capable of doing things they never thought they could do, buoyed up by a new sense of wholeness and connectedness within themselves.

Wholeness and connectedness are what are most fundamental in our nature as living beings. No matter how many scars we carry from what we have gone through and suffered in the past, our intrinsic wholeness is still here: what else contains the scars? None of us has to be a helpless victim of what was done to us or what was not done for us in the past, nor do we have to be helpless in the face of what we may be suffering now. We are also what was present before the scarring—our original wholeness, what was born whole. And we can reconnect with that intrinsic wholeness at any time, because its very nature is that it is always present. It is who we truly are. So when we make contact with the domain of being in the meditation practice, we are already, in a profound sense, beyond the scarring, beyond the isolation and fragmentation and suffering we may be experiencing. This means that as long as we are breathing, it is always possible to make meaningful inroads into the harmful effects of past trauma to at least some degree, and that degree is always unknown when we begin. It means that it is always possible for us to recognize, work with, and possibly transcend fragmentation, fear, vulnerability, insecurity, even despair, if we can manage to come to see differently, to see with eyes of wholeness.

Perhaps more than anything else, the work of MBSR involves helping people to see and feel and believe in their wholeness, helping them to tend, befriend, and mend the wounds of disconnectedness and the pain of feeling isolated, fragmented, and separate, and helping them to discover an underlying fabric of wholeness and connectedness *within themselves.* Obviously this is the work of a lifetime. For our patients, the Stress Reduction Clinic is often the first conscious, intentional step as an adult in this lifelong process.

Clearly the body is an ideal place to begin. In the first place, as we have seen, it is convenient. It is also a door to the larger world, in that what we see in the workings of our body teaches us many lessons that apply in other domains of our lives. What's more, our bodies usually require some healing. We all carry around at least some physical and psychological tension and armor. At the very least, it is likely that most of us have encountered some degree of personal harm or injury, some stress to the system that was traumatic, either physically, emotionally, or both. Some psychologists speak of this as "little-*t* trauma," to distinguish it from the catastrophe of "big-*T* trauma," such as that experienced by Mary, as described in Chapter 5. Whatever we have experienced and have survived, whether it took the form of big-T trauma or little-t trauma, our body, our mind, and our heart, which only *seem* separate, constitute a profound resource for healing. If we listen carefully to the body, it can teach us a great deal about what is most difficult for us to recognize and come to terms with from the past, and how we might approach our hurt with kindness and wisdom. It has a great deal to teach us about stress and pain, illness and health, and about suffering and the possibility of freeing ourselves from suffering. Mindfulness is a key ingredient in approaching and nurturing what is deepest and best and forever unharmed within ourselves.

Given the centrality of the body in the healing process, and how much pain and hurt it may be carrying (the root meaning in Latin of the verb "to suffer"), it is not surprising that we devote a good deal of attention to the breath, which you could think of as a bridge between the body and our emotional life. It also explains why MBSR starts out with two weeks of practicing the body scan every day, why we tune in so systematically to sensations in different regions of our body, why we cultivate a sense of our body as a whole, why we pay attention to such basics as eating, walking, moving, and stretching. All these facets of our body's experience are doors through which, from the beginning, we can catch glimpses of our own wholeness. In time and through daily practice, we can walk through those doors more and more frequently and inhabit that wholeness in full awareness. This process of befriending awareness itself and learning how to inhabit it is always much more important than the particular objects of attention we choose to focus on, important as they are. Through ongoing practice, we can come to live in a more integrated way from day to day and from moment to moment, in touch with our own wholeness and connectedness and aware of our *interconnectedness* with others, with the larger world in which we find ourselves, and with life itself. Feeling whole, even for brief moments, nourishes us on a deep level. It is a source of healing and wisdom when we are faced with stress and pain in all the various forms that stress and pain can take.

You probably won't be too surprised to learn that the very word *health* itself means "whole." *Whole* implies integration, an interconnectedness of all parts of a system or organism, a completeness. The nature of wholeness is that it is always present. Someone who has had an arm amputated or has lost some other part of the body, or who faces death from an incurable disease, is still fundamentally whole. Yet he or she will have to *come to terms* with the physical loss or the meaning of the prognosis to experience that wholeness. This will certainly entail profound changes in one's view of oneself and of the world and of time, even of life itself. It is this process of coming to terms with things as they are that embodies the process of healing.

While every living organism is whole in itself, it is also embedded in a larger wholeness. We are whole in our bodies, but as we have already seen, our bodies are constantly exchanging matter and energy with the environment. So although our bodies are complete, they are also constantly changing. Our bodies are literally immersed in a larger whole, namely, the environment, the planet, the universe. Looked at in this way, health is a dynamical process. It is not a fixed state that you "get" and then hold on to.

The notion of wholeness is found not only in the meaning of the words *health* and *healing* (and, of course, in the word *holy*); we also find it embedded in the deep meaning of the words *meditation* and *medicine,* words that are obviously related to each other in some way. According to renowned polymath David Bohm, a theoretical physicist whose work involved exploring wholeness as a fundamental property of nature, the words *medicine* and *meditation* come from the Latin *mederi,* which means "to cure." *Mederi* itself derives from an earlier Indo-European root meaning "to measure."

Now what might the concept of measure have to do with either meditation or medicine? Nothing, if we are thinking of measure in the usual way, as the process of comparing the dimensions of an object to an external standard. But the concept of "measure" has another ancient, more Platonic meaning. This is the notion that all things have, in Bohm's words, their own "right inward measure" that makes them what they are, that gives them their properties. Medicine, seen in this light, is basically the means by which right inward measure is restored when it is disturbed by disease, illness, or injury. Meditation, by the same token, is the process of perceiving directly the right inward measure of one's own being through careful, non-judgmental self-observation. Right inward measure, in this context, is another way of saying wholeness. So it may not be as farfetched as it may first appear to have a clinic based on training in meditation in a medical center.

The choice of meditation training, and in particular mindfulness meditation training, as the central and unifying element of MBSR and the program of the Stress Reduction Clinic was not arbitrary. Mindfulness meditation training as it is taught in MBSR has unique characteristics that distinguish it from the many relaxation techniques and stress reduction approaches in common use. The most important is that it is a door into direct experiences of wholeness, experiences not so easily tapped and deepened by methods that perpetually focus on doing and on getting somewhere rather than on non-doing and being. According to Dr. Roger Walsh, professor of psychiatry and behavioral sciences at the School of Medicine of the University of California at Irvine, meditation is best described as a *consciousness discipline.* Dr. Walsh, a longtime mindfulness practitioner himself and student of the interface between Eastern and Western psychologies, emphasizes that the consciousness disciplines are based on a profoundly different paradigm from that of mainstream Western psychology. From the perspective of the consciousness disciplines, our ordinary state of waking consciousness is severely suboptimal. Rather than contradicting the Western paradigm, this perspective simply extends it beyond psychology's dominant concern, at least until very recently, with pathology and with therapies aimed at restoring people to "normal" functioning in the usual waking state of consciousness. At the heart of this "orthogonal," paradigm-breaking perspective lies the conviction that it is essential for a person to engage in a personal, intensive, and systematic training of the mind through the discipline of meditation practice to free himself or herself from the incessant and highly conditioned distortions characteristic of our everyday emotional and thought processes, distortions that, as we have seen, can continually undermine the experiencing of our intrinsic wholeness.

Many great minds have been preoccupied with the notion of wholeness and how to realize it in one's own life. Carl Jung, the great Swiss psychiatrist, held the meditative traditions of Asia in very high regard in this connection. He wrote, "This question [of coming to wholeness] has occupied the most adventurous minds of the East for more than two thousand years, and in this respect, methods and philosophical doctrines have been developed that simply put all Western attempts along these lines into the shade." Jung well understood the relationship between meditation practice and the realization of wholeness.

Albert Einstein also clearly articulated the importance of seeing with eyes of wholeness. In the last class of the eight-week MBSR program, we give our patients a booklet that closes with the following quotation from a letter of Einstein's that appeared in the *New York Times* on March 29, 1972. I cut it out of the newspaper on that day and still have it tucked away, now yellowed with age and brittle to the touch. This statement is particularly meaningful to me, in part because it captures so well the essence of the meditation practice, and also because it comes from the scientist who, more than any other, revolutionized our understanding of physical reality and demonstrated the unity of space and time and of matter and energy.

When Einstein was living in Princeton, working at the Institute for Advanced Study, he used to receive letters from people from all over the world asking for his advice about their personal problems. He had a unique reputation for wisdom among laypeople throughout the world because of his scientific achievements, which few understood but most people knew were revolutionary. But he also had a profound reputation for compassion because of his kindly face and his outspoken involvement in humanitarian causes. He was thought of by many people as "the smartest man in the world," although he himself could never understand the big fuss people made over him. The following passage comes from a letter he wrote in response to a rabbi who had written explaining that he had sought in vain to comfort his nineteen-year-old daughter over the death of her sister, a "sinless, beautiful, sixteen-year-old child." The letter to Einstein was clearly a cry for help, coming out of one of the most painful of human experiences, the death of a child. Einstein replied:

> A human being is a part of the whole, called by us "Universe," a part limited in time and space. He experiences himself, his thoughts and feelings as something separated from the rest—a kind of optical delusion of his consciousness. This delusion is a kind of prison for us, restricting us to our personal desires and to affection for a few persons nearest to us. Our task must be to free ourselves from this prison by widening our circle of compassion to embrace all living creatures and the whole nature in its beauty. Nobody is able to achieve this completely, but

> the striving for such achievement is in itself a part of the liberation and a foundation for inner security.

In his reply, Einstein is suggesting that we can easily become imprisoned in and blinded by our own thoughts and feelings because they are so endemically self-centered, concerned solely with the particulars of our own lives and our own desires. He is not belittling the suffering we experience at such a loss. Not at all. But he *is* saying that our overwhelming preoccupation with our own separate lives imprisons us by ignoring and obscuring another, more fundamental level of reality. In his view, we all come into and go out of this world as quickly passing gatherings of highly structured energy. Einstein is reminding us to see wholeness as more fundamental than separateness. He is reminding us that our experience of ourselves as separate and enduring is a delusion, and ultimately, imprisoning.

Of course we *are* separate in the sense that our lives are localized in time (a lifetime) and space (a body). We *do* have particular thoughts and feelings and unique, wonderful, love-filled relationships, and we suffer greatly and understandably when those bonds and connections are ruptured, especially when death comes to the young. But at the same time, is it not equally true that we are all here and gone in an instant, little eddies or whirlpools in a flowing current, waves briefly rising on an ocean of wholeness? As eddies and waves, our lives do have a certain uniqueness, but they are also the stuff of a larger wholeness expressing itself in ways that ultimately surpass our comprehension.

Einstein is reminding us that when we neglect the perspective of wholeness and connectedness, we see only one side of being alive. This view inflates the sense of *my* life, *my* problems, *my* loss, *my* pain as what is supremely important and prevents us from seeing another, very real dimension of our own being that is not so separate or unique. When we identify ourselves with a permanent, solid "self," it is a delusion of consciousness, a form of self-imprisonment, according to Einstein. Elsewhere he wrote that "the true value of a human being is determined primarily by the measure and sense in which he has attained liberation from the self."

Einstein's remedy for this dilemma of the delusion and tyranny of what we might call the small self, which he exemplified in large measure in his own life, is for us to break out of this "optical delusion" of consciousness by intentionally cultivating compassion for all life, and an appreciation of ourselves and of "all living creatures" as part of the infinitely interconnected natural world in all its beauty. In suggesting this as a way to freedom and inner security, Einstein was not merely speaking romantically or philosophically. He understood that it takes a certain kind of *work* to achieve liberation from the prison of our own thought habits and delusions. He also knew that such work is intrinsically healing.

Coming back to the problem of the nine dots, we have seen that how we perceive a problem, and by extension how we perceive the world and also ourselves, can have a profound influence over what we are capable of doing and how much we are capable of loving. Seeing with eyes of wholeness means recognizing that nothing occurs in isolation, that problems need to be seen within the context of whole systems. Seeing in this way, we can perceive the intrinsic web of interconnectedness underlying our experience and merge with it. Seeing in this way is healing. It helps us to acknowledge the ways in which we are extraordinary and miraculous, without losing sight of the ways in which we are simultaneously nothing special, just part of a larger whole unfolding, waves on the sea, rising up and falling back in brief moments we call life spans.

13

On Healing

When we use the word *healing* to describe the experiences of people engaging in mindfulness training through MBSR, what we mean above all is that they are undergoing a profound transformation of view, what I sometimes refer to as a "rotation in consciousness." This transformation is brought about by the encounter with one's own wholeness, catalyzed by the meditation practice itself. When we glimpse our own completeness in the stillness of any moment, when we directly experience ourself during the body scan or the sitting meditation, or while practicing the yoga as whole in this very moment and also as part of a larger whole, a new and profound encountering and coming to terms with our problems and our suffering begins to take place. We begin to see both ourselves and our problems differently, namely from the perspective of wholeness. This transformation of view creates an entirely different context within which we can see and work with our problems, however serious they may be. It is a perceptual shift away from fragmentation and isolation and toward wholeness and interconnectedness. With this change of perspective comes a shift from feeling out of control and beyond help (helpless and pessimistic) to a sense of the possible, a sense that this situation might just be workable if you yourself are willing to do a certain amount of work. We can discover a sense of acceptance and inner peace, and even control, if by control we mean manageability or workability within a larger framework and embrace. Healing always involves an attitudinal and emotional transformation. Sometimes, but not always, it is also accompanied by a major reduction in physical symptoms and by improvement in a person's physical condition.

This transformation of view comes about in many different ways as people immerse themselves in the MBSR curriculum and in mindfulness meditation practice. In the Stress Reduction Clinic, sometimes people have sudden and dramatic experiences during meditation that lead them to new ways of seeing. More frequently, people speak of moments of simply feeling deeply relaxed or confident. Many times they don't even recognize such experiences at the time they are happening as being particularly important, although they often can't remember ever having had such an experience before. These incremental transformations can be quite subtle. Yet they can be as profound or even more so as the more dramatic ones. Dramatic or subtle, such shifts in perspective are signs of seeing with eyes of wholeness. Out of this shift in perspective comes an ability to act with greater balance and inner security in the world, especially when encountering stress or pain.

In the first week of the program Phil, a forty-seven-year-old French Canadian truck driver who had injured his back three years previously in a lifting accident, and who had been referred to the Stress Reduction Clinic by his doctors in the Pain Clinic, had a breakthrough while practicing the body scan. He started out listening to the CD while lying on his back. He was in a lot of pain, and he said to himself, "Oh my God, I don't know if I can do this." But because he had made the commitment to "do it right" in spite of his pain, he stayed with the voice on the CD. After about twenty minutes, he started feeling his breathing "all over his body," and he found himself completely focused on that extraordinary feeling of his body breathing. He said to himself, "Wow, this is great!" Then he realized something else: he wasn't feeling any pain at all. Phil found that he was able to tap into a similar experience with the body scan practice each day that week. He came to the second class ecstatic.

The next week turned out to be just the opposite. Nothing he did made any difference. He practiced the body scan with the CD every day, but his pain was just as bad as it had ever been. Nothing he did could bring back the feelings he had had the first week. I suggested that perhaps he was trying too hard to bring back his experiences of the first week. Perhaps he was fighting with his pain now, trying to get rid of it so that he could regain those good feelings. He went home determined to look into what I had suggested. He made up his mind that he would simply try to let whatever was going to happen during the body scan happen, and not try to achieve a particular outcome. After that, things went more smoothly. When he ceased fighting with his pain, he was able to concentrate and be a lot calmer during the body scan. He discovered that the pain would diminish as his concentration deepened. On average, he said, it would be about 40 to 50 percent less severe, sometimes even more, by the end of the forty-five minutes.

Joyce came to the Stress Reduction Clinic referred by her oncologist, shortly after having been treated for a cancerous tumor on her leg. At the time she was fifty years old. Her husband had died from esophageal cancer two years earlier, a "horrendous and painful death," and on the day he died, her mother also died unexpectedly. Her own medical problems had started while she was taking care of her husband. With increasing frequency, she felt pain in her right thigh that would travel down her leg. She consulted several doctors, who said that it was nothing serious, either varicose veins or just part of getting older. One day, two years after the death of her husband and her mother, as she was picking out a Christmas tree with her son, her thighbone broke. When she was operated on, a tumor called a plasmacytoma was discovered that had eaten away the bone to the point where it had just crumbled. They removed the tumor and rebuilt the bone with a bone graft. During the surgery, Joyce bled so much that the surgeon told her children that he did not expect her to survive. But she did. She then underwent six weeks of radiation therapy and, soon after, was referred to the Stress Reduction Clinic.

When Joyce took the CD home from her first class, she said to herself that she was going to do everything that she was told to do in the course and that she was really going to get into it. The first time she did the body scan, she had what she described as "a very powerful experience of some otherness." This feeling came up toward the end of the CD, during an extended stretch of silence. She remembered saying to herself at the time, "Oh, so this is what God is." In describing it, she said "it felt like a nothingness and an everything at the same time. It wasn't any kind of person or anything that I had ever thought of as God."

Joyce still remembered this feeling ten years later and said that it was what kept her going through some very difficult times, which included multiple surgeries to repair her bone graft, a hip replacement, and severe family stresses. She was convinced that her meditation practice was responsible for keeping her plasmacytoma in remission and preventing it from progressing to multiple myeloma, which it does in almost all cases within five years. Her oncologist said that he had never seen another case in which a plasmacytoma did not cross over to become multiple myeloma in that period of time. He was not convinced that Joyce's meditating was responsible for her remission, but he admitted that he didn't have any idea why the disease had not progressed. Whatever the reason, he was happy about it and hoped things would continue that way. He supported Joyce in doing everything of a positive nature that she believes in to keep mind and body in harmony.

Both Phil and Joyce had strong experiences with the body scan right off the bat. Others sometimes go for weeks before experiencing even a little relaxation or stillness or change in perspective. Yet we find that if we explore their experience together in dialogue, something positive is usually stirring beneath the surface for most people as a result of practicing the body scan regularly in the first two weeks, even if it is not so dramatic. Interestingly enough, sometimes these stirrings don't manifest fully until the person switches over and starts doing the yoga. The change to a more active use of the body can trigger a change in perspective that has been slowly building below the person's level of awareness during weeks of working with the body scan.

Ultimately the trajectory of healing will be different in its details for each individual. Healing is always a unique and deeply personal experience. Each of us, whether well or ill, has to face our own particular life circumstances and cope with them. The meditation practice, taken on in the spirit of self-exploration and self-inquiry, can transform our capacity to face, embrace, and work with and within the full catastrophe. But to make this transformation a reality in your life requires that you take responsibility for adapting the basic practice so that it becomes yours; so that you "own" it; so that it fits with your life and your needs! The particular choices you make will depend on your unique life circumstances and on your temperament.

Here is where your imagination and creativity come in. As we have seen, meditation practice is, more than anything, a way of being. It is not a set of techniques for healing. Healing comes out of the practice itself when it is engaged in *as a way of being*. Meditation is much less likely to be healing if you are using it as a way of getting somewhere, even to wholeness. From this perspective, you already are whole, so what is the point of trying to become what you already are? What is required above all is that we *let go into* the domain of being and reside in that wholeness with awareness, outside time. This is what is fundamentally healing.

In the stress clinic we are constantly astonished by the many ways in which our patients adapt the practice in their own lives, as well as by the effects that the practice of mindfulness comes to have on them. These effects are completely unpredictable. This is one powerful reason to give yourself over completely to the meditation practice and, as best you can, let go of any attachment you may have to specific outcomes, even though those outcomes are what draw people to MBSR in the first place.

Most people come to the clinic hoping to attain peace of mind. They want to learn to relax, and to be able to deal more effectively with their stress and pain. But they often leave transformed beyond anything they had hoped to accomplish in the first place. For example, Hector, a wrestler from Puerto Rico, who took the program because he was having frequent outbursts of anger, accompanied by chest pain, left eight short weeks later having found ways to regulate and control both his chest pain and his anger, and having discovered a deep strain of gentleness he never knew he had. Bill, a butcher, came to the clinic at the urging of his psychiatrist when he was left to raise six children on his own after his wife committed suicide. Bill became a vegetarian and told me one day, "Jon, the practice has deepened in me to the point that I can't even lie anymore." After completing the program, he started his own meditation practice group. Edith learned mindfulness meditation in the pulmonary rehabilitation program in order to control her shortness of breath; she kept up the practice on her own, and proudly recounted at a reunion of her pulmonary rehab class several years later how she had used it during cataract surgery to successfully control pain when told by her doctors at the last minute that they couldn't use anesthesia because of her lung disease, and then proceeded to stick needles into her eye. Henry came to MBSR with anxiety, heart disease, and high blood pressure. In the fourth week of the program, he had an episode of vomiting blood due to ulcers. Taken to the Intensive Care Unit thinking he might very well die, Henry calmed himself down using awareness of his breathing as he lay in bed with tubes coming out of his arms and nose. Nat was a middle-aged businessman who came in an extreme state of distress due to a combination of severe high blood pressure, even on medication (he had been fired from his job two weeks earlier) and from having tested positive for the HIV virus after his wife contracted AIDS (presumably from a blood transfusion she received during an appendectomy) and died; he was in such bad shape that a nurse in the primary care clinic personally marched him down to the Stress Reduction Clinic office to make sure he enrolled. Eight weeks later, Nat had his blood pressure back to normal, had gotten his bad temper under control, was relating much better to his only child, and was looking at his life more optimistically in spite of the enormity of his situation and his loss. Edward was a young man with AIDS. Six months after he completed the MBSR program, he told me that he had not missed a day of meditation practice in those six months, and said that he was no longer a "nervous wreck" at work. When he had to undergo another bone marrow test, he thought to use his breathing to let go of his fear of the pain and found that he didn't feel any. None of these individual outcomes of mindfulness practice was predictable. But they all grew directly out of the meditation practice.

Of course, part of making the practice your own, as we will see further on, will include paying attention to the particular behaviors and habits in your life that may directly or indirectly influence your health for better or for worse. These include diet and exercise; habits such as smoking and abusing alcohol and drugs; negative and destructive attitudes, especially hostility and cynicism; and the unique constellation of stresses and difficulties you face and how you handle them. Cultivating greater awareness in these particular areas or ingrained habit can enhance and amplify the process of personal transformation that grows naturally out of dwelling regularly in the domain of being.

Healing, as we are using the word here, does not mean "curing," although the two words are often used interchangeably in common speech. However, it is important for us to be able to differentiate between the two, as they have profoundly different implications.* As we shall see in the next chapter, there are few outright cures for chronic diseases or for stress-

* In some languages, such as French, they cannot be distinguished. There is only one word that means both: *guérir.*

related disorders. While it may not be possible for us to cure ourselves or to find someone who can, it is possible for us to *heal* ourselves—to learn to live with and work with the conditions that present themselves in the present moment. Healing implies the possibility that we can relate differently to illness, disability, even death, as we learn to see with eyes of wholeness. As we have seen, this comes from practicing such basic skills as entering and dwelling in the open spaciousness of awareness, itself associated with deep physiological and psychological relaxation, as well as with the possibility of seeing our fears and limitations and vulnerability within that larger embrace. In even brief moments of stillness, you may come to realize that you are already whole, already complete in your being, even if your body has cancer or heart disease or AIDS or pain, even if you don't know how long you will live or what will happen to you.

Experiences of wholeness are as accessible to people with chronic illness or stress-related problems as they are to anyone else. Moments of experiencing wholeness, moments when you connect with the domain of your own being, often include a palpable sense of being larger than your illness or your problems and in a much better position to come to terms with them. Thus, to think that you are a "failure" if you "still" have pain, or heart disease, or cancer, or AIDS after you have been meditating for a while is to completely misunderstand the practice of mindfulness and MBSR. *We are not meditating to make anything go away,* any more than we are meditating to attain some special state or feeling. Whether we are basically healthy at the moment or have a terminal illness, none of us knows how long we have to live. Life only unfolds in moments. The healing power of mindfulness lies in living each of those moments as fully as we can, accepting it as it is as we open to what comes next—in the next moment of now.

Paradoxically, this shift in orientation and in awareness has the power to transform everything. Remember, acceptance does not mean passive resignation. Not at all. It means taking a reading of a situation, feeling it and embracing it in awareness as completely as one can manage, however challenging or horrible it may be, and recognizing that things are as they are, independent of our liking or disliking the situation and wanting it to be different. Then we can either intentionally or intuitively *choose* to be in what might be a wiser relationship to the present moment. This could include, when necessary or possible, taking some action or other. But it might also include simply being still, keeping in mind that everything is always changing and that our mind, our attitude, and our ability to rest in the open spaciousness of awareness all contribute to the understanding of our circumstances and to the coming to terms with them that underlies the process of healing. That non-doing is itself a powerful form of action.

One woman with breast cancer had the insight while she was meditating one day that she was not her cancer. She saw vividly in one moment that she was a whole person and that the cancer was a process that was going on within her body. Prior to that, her life had been consumed with identifying with the disease and with being a "cancer patient." Realizing that she was not her cancer made her feel freer. She was able to think more clearly about her life, and decided that she could use having cancer as an opportunity to grow and to live more fully, for however long she had to live. In making the commitment to live each moment of her life as fully as possible and to use her cancer to help her, rather than showering blame or pity on herself for having it, she was setting the stage for healing, for dissolving the mental boundaries that confined her, for coming to terms with what she was facing. She understood that although she had hope that this approach might influence the cancer itself, there was no guarantee or even suggestion that the tumor would shrink or that she would live any longer. Her commitment to live with greater awareness was not chosen for those reasons. It was chosen because she wished to live life as fully as possible no matter what. At the same time, she wanted to remain open to the possibility that the course of the disease might be positively influenced by a more profound integration of her mind and body through the practice of mindfulness.

There is mounting evidence that the mind might indeed be able to influence the course of at least some diseases. A whole new field known as psychoneuroimmunology, or PNI, has emerged, in which studies are showing that our body's many exquisite defense mechanisms against infection and disease, known collectively as the immune system, do not operate in a vacuum to keep us healthy. As the term *psychoneuroimmunology* itself implies, the immune system is now known to be regulated at least in part by the brain and nervous system, which themselves integrate all the body's organ systems. And, of course, the brain and nervous system make the life of the mind possible. So there appear to be important interconnections between the brain and the immune system, and these connections allow for information to flow in both directions. In other words, while the brain can influence and modulate the functioning of the immune system, the condition of the immune system can also influence the brain in particular ways. The discovery of these connections means that science now has a plausible working model for elucidating the biological pathways and mechanisms by which our thoughts, emotions, and life experiences can influence our susceptibility or resistance to disease.

There is now a large body of studies showing that stressful life experiences can influence the activity of the immune system, which is known to play a critical role in the body's defense mechanisms against cancer and infection. Drs. Janice Kiecolt-Glaser and Ron Glaser of Ohio State University College of Medicine showed that the natural killer (NK) cell activity of medical students clearly went down and then back up as a function of how much stress they were under. During exam periods, NK activity and other immune functions were diminished compared to levels when the students did not have exams. These researchers and others have also shown that loneliness, separation, divorce, and caring for a spouse with dementia are all associated with reduced immune functioning, and that various relaxation techniques and coping approaches can help protect or even enhance the immune system. Immune functions measured in studies of this kind, such as natural killer cell activity, are thought to play an important role in the body's defense mechanisms against cancer and viral infection.

Other studies have shown a connection between MBSR training and enhanced immune function. In a collaborative study with Richard Davidson and his colleagues at the University of Wisconsin, mentioned in the Introduction, we conducted the first randomized trial of MBSR. In addition to gathering measures of psychological well-being reported on questionnaires filled out by the participants, our study looked at aspects of the participants' biology, namely electrical activity in certain regions of the prefrontal cortex measured using EEG, as well as immune response to an influenza vaccine (measured by antibody levels in the blood). We studied a healthy group of employees in a high-stress corporate work setting and found that those employees who underwent the eight weeks of MBSR training showed a significantly higher antibody response to the flu virus challenge than those in the control group, who were waiting to take the program at a later date but being tested on the same schedule as the MBSR group. We also found that the immune response was correlated with the amount of change we saw in a person's brain activity. In the MBSR group, the more the brain activity shifted from the right hemisphere to the left (an indicator of less emotional reactivity and greater emotional resilience), the stronger the antibody response to the flu vaccine in that person. There was no such relationship in the control group.

A remarkable series of experiments conducted by Robert Ader and Nicholas Cohen at the University of Rochester Medical School starting in the mid-1970s launched the field of psychoneuroimmunology and generated an explosion of interest and wide-ranging research in this area. Ader and Cohen used a clever experimental design to reveal an undeniable and dramatic relationship between the brain and the immune system. They showed that immunosuppression (a lowering of the immune response) in rats could actually be psychologically *conditioned.* They paired treatment of the animals with an immunosuppressant drug with exposure to a sweet-tasting chemical (saccharin) in their drinking water. Later, the animals received only saccharin alone in their drinking water—but they still showed immunosuppression, even though they were no longer receiving the immunosuppressing drug! It appeared that their bodies had somehow *learned* to suppress immune functioning in response to tasting the saccharin when it was given with the immunosuppressing drug. Control animals did not show this conditioned response. This suggested that in the conditioned animals, immune functioning was affected by a kind of psychological learning, which could only have come through the nervous system.

Many experiments have now been conducted that suggest that experiences of uncontrollable stress in animals can produce deficits in immune function and decrease natural resistance to cancers and tumor growth. Recent studies with people are also showing intriguing connections between stress, feelings of helplessness, immune system deficits, and diseases such as cancer. Ultimately, a major question for future research is the extent to which the mind might influence the *healing* of specific diseases, not simply indirectly by changing lifestyle, important as such changes are, but also by directly influencing the functioning of the immune system and the brain itself. However, we need to exercise caution in interpreting the meaning of specific immune system changes in such studies because there is as yet no firm evidence that the many changes observed in various studies are directly related to changes in any specific disease process or illness. And while both animal and human studies have shown that chronic stress, in many different forms, suppresses immune function and leads to heightened sensitivity to a range of infectious agents, other studies have demonstrated that stress actually enhances the immune response rather than suppressing it. So further work is necessary to understand exactly what is going on.

In 1998 we published the results of a study that looked directly at the question of whether the mind can be shown to have a direct effect on a well-recognized healing endpoint.* In collaboration with Dr. Jeffrey Bernhard and his colleagues in the Division of Dermatology at the University of Massachusetts Medical Center, we decided to look at people with the skin disease psoriasis while they were undergoing ultraviolet light therapy.

* Kabat-Zinn J, Wheeler E, Light T, et al. Influence of a mindfulness meditation-based stress reduction intervention on rates of skin clearing in patients with moderate to severe psoriasis undergoing phototherapy (UVB) and photochemotherapy (PUVA). *Psychosomatic Medicine.* 1998;60:625–632.

People who have psoriasis suffer from an increased rate of growth of their skin cells that produces scaly patches. The cause of the disease remains unknown, and there is no cure for it at present. We do know that the extent of the disease fluctuates and is related to emotional stress as well as to other factors. The scaly patches can disappear completely and then return. Psoriasis is characterized by an uncontrolled cell proliferation in the epidermal layer of skin. It is not cancerous, but it does involve similar growth factors as skin cancer. For this reason, understanding more about how psoriasis works might have broader medical implications. It was certainly a good model for studying the question we wanted to ask: can the mind influence a healing process that we can actually see and photograph?

The standard therapy for psoriasis is ultraviolet light treatment, known as *phototherapy.* Ultraviolet light in a particular frequency band (UVB) is used because it slows down the growth of the cells in the scaly patches of skin, which, when severe, can cover large areas of the body. Sometimes a drug called psoralin is used systemically in concert with the ultraviolet light if a more powerful treatment is necessary. Then a different frequency of light (UVA) is used. The UVA exposure activates the psoralin that gets into the skin, and this activated molecule accelerates the skin clearing by preventing the skin cells from dividing. This treatment is known as *photochemotherapy.* In our study, we followed patients going through either phototherapy or photochemotherapy. In both cases, treatment requires the patient to stand almost naked in a cylindrical light box, about the size of an old-fashioned telephone booth, for increasing periods of time, up to about ten minutes, during which their skin is exposed to the ultraviolet light. The walls of the light box have head-to-toe ultraviolet lightbulbs. Treatments usually take place three times a week over about four months. They start out very brief and get progressively longer, so as not to burn the skin. It can take quite a few treatments for the skin to clear completely.

In our study, thirty-seven people about to undergo ultraviolet light treatments in the phototherapy clinic were randomly assigned to two groups. One group practiced mindfulness meditation while they were in the light box, with guidance from an audio program that focused sequentially, as the light exposures got longer, on mindfulness of breathing, body sensations (from standing and from the intense heat from the lights, and from the air currents from blowers), and on sounds, thoughts, and emotions. As the treatment sessions got longer, the meditators also were encouraged to visualize that the ultraviolet light was slowing down the growth of their skin cells by "jamming the machinery" those cells depend on to divide. They also had the option of practicing mindfulness without the guidance after twenty treatment sessions, and hearing meditative harp music instead. People in the comparison control group received the standard light treatment protocol without engaging in any mindfulness practices or listening to music.

While this study design had its flaws, it did replicate as well as extend the results of an earlier pilot study. We found that over the treatment period, the meditators' skin cleared approximately four times faster than the skin of those patients getting just the light treatment in the control group. This was true whether the treatment was phototherapy or photochemotherapy. This is all the more remarkable because the longest people were in the light box at any given time was about twelve minutes, so they were only meditating for relatively short periods of time. What is more, unlike the participants in MBSR, the participants in the psoriasis study did not get guided meditation CDs to take home and practice with, and were asked not to meditate at other times. The fact that we saw such dramatic improvements may be an indication of the power of mindfulness to positively influence various mind-body factors, even with relatively brief practice times. It suggests that even a little mindfulness practice may be highly beneficial. We shall see a similar use of short periods of meditation practice when we look at studies of laboratory-induced pain in Chapter 23.

The findings of the psoriasis study, while still preliminary until they are replicated by other researchers, do suggest a number of intriguing implications. The most obvious is that the mind can positively influence a healing process, at least under some circumstances. We can't say with certainty that it was the mindfulness practice itself that was responsible, because we also included the visualization of the skin clearing in response to the light exposure, as well as music, and the control group was not tailored to match all the conditions of the meditation group except for the mindfulness. For instance, they did not listen to any audio program at all, including music. Still, the results suggest that some dimension of the mind played a significant role in accelerating the healing of the skin. Since we now know that the brain can influence inflammatory processes in the body and various epigenetic and immune factors that may play a role in psoriasis, it is likely that the effects of the mind can work all the way down to the level of gene expression and cellular and humeral immune activity. These are fruitful areas for future studies to elucidate.

Our study was also a built-in cost-effectiveness study, in the sense that the meditation group reached clearing faster than the people in the control group. They thus required fewer treatments and therefore cost the system less. The study was also a classic example of participatory medicine, in that the patients were actively participating in their own possible trajectory toward greater levels of health and well-being, just as MBSR is itself an example of participatory medicine on a larger scale. It is also an example of integrative medicine, in that the meditative practice was integrated right into the medical treatment protocol itself. Moreover, since ultraviolet light is itself a risk factor for skin cancer (basal cell carcinoma), reducing the number of treatments necessary to reach skin clearing reduced the intrinsic risk associated with the phototherapy treatment itself.

Every so often, the mind-body connection and healing receive widespread coverage in the popular press. This is becoming ever more the case with mind-body approaches in general and mindfulness in particular, now that there are so many studies coming out in the fields of neuroscience, health psychology, and psychoneuroimmunology. Having heard about the results of these studies, many people with cancer or AIDS now want to learn meditation to control their stress, both to improve their quality of life and with the expectation that they will be able to stimulate their immune system to combat their disease more effectively. But while it is entirely possible that practicing meditation and specific visualizations might significantly influence immune function and stimulate healing, that conjecture is still far from proven at this time, as we have noted.

From our point of view, an individual who comes for training in MBSR with the strong expectation that his or her immune system can be strengthened by meditating might actually be creating impediments to his or her own healing, both psychologically and physically. Too strong an investment in making your immune system respond the way you want it to might be more of a problem than a help, because the quality and the spirit of the meditation practice can be easily undermined by *any* goal orientation, however understandable and worthy that goal might be—as we have been emphasizing repeatedly. If the essence of meditation is non-doing, then trying to work it around to getting what you want, even subtly, can distort and undermine the very qualities of letting go and acceptance that allow you to experience wholeness directly, in our view the foundation for healing. This would be true even if it is ultimately shown that meditation can lead to positive changes in immune function that result in an increased ability of the body to heal disease processes.

This is not to say that you cannot use meditation for specific ends. There are countless ways of incorporating specific visualizations and goals into meditation practice, as in the use of the mountain meditation (described in Chapter 8), in the psoriasis experiment we just reviewed, and in the lovingkindness meditation we will visit shortly. In all the meditative traditions of the world, visualizations and imagery are used to invoke particular qualities of mind and heart. There are meditations on love, God, lovingkindness, peace, forgiveness, selflessness, impermanence, and suffering. There are meditations on energy, body states, particular emotions, equanimity, compassion, generosity, joy, wisdom, death, and of course healing. Imagery and specific channeling of one's energy and attention are integral to these practices.

However, it is important to emphasize that they are all *practices*. They are always undertaken with a systematic discipline and commitment, and always within the larger context of meditation *as a way of being*. When we take them up as isolated techniques that we utilize only when we feel bad or when we want something, we invariably ignore or discard this greater context; in fact, we may not even realize that it exists. In any event, the wisdom and power inherent in the non-doing perspective can be easily lost or overlooked and, with it, the deeper power of the particular visualization. There is little wisdom in this approach, and potentially a great deal of frustration, disappointment, and wasted energy.

In order to be maximally effective for healing, the use of visualization and imagery is best embedded in a larger context, one that understands and honors non-doing and non-striving. Otherwise, visualization exercises can too easily degenerate from meditation into wishful thinking, and the intrinsic healing power and wisdom of the simple mindfulness practice itself can remain untapped or be trivialized in the quest for something more elaborate and goal-oriented. Even in the simple case of lowering blood pressure, which meditation has been shown to do in numerous clinical studies, it is not wise to meditate primarily for that purpose. It tends to make the meditation mechanical and too oriented toward success or failure. We believe that it is far more effective just to practice the meditation regularly and let your blood pressure take care of itself.

When you are practicing meditation as a way of being and not as a means to a particular end, then the use of specific visualizations to work on particular areas of concern within that larger context can sometimes be very helpful. Not enough research has yet been done to be able to determine the relative importance of specific visualizations in the healing process compared with the simple practice of moment-to-moment awareness. The psoriasis experiment may lead to further studies of this kind.

From our experiences with MBSR, we find that symptom reduction and a transformation of perspective are more likely to occur if you actively cultivate non-doing in the meditation practice rather than preoccupy yourself with what your blood pressure, particular symptoms, or your immune system is doing.

We tell our patients in the stress clinic, whether they have high blood pressure or cancer or AIDS, that it is fine to come with the hope of controlling their blood pressure or improving their immune function, just as it is fine to come wanting to learn to relax and be calmer. But once they decide to commit to the program, they need to let go of their goals for the moment and just practice mindfulness for its own sake. Then, if their blood pressure comes down, if their natural killer cells or helper T-cells increase in number and activity, or if their pain lessens, so much the better. We want our patients to experiment with what their bodies and minds are capable of, without feeling they have to influence or improve a specific physiologic function by a specific time. To bring calmness to the mind and body requires that at a certain point we be willing to let go of wanting anything at all to happen and accept things as they are and ourselves as we are with an open and receptive heart. This inner peace and acceptance lie at the heart of both health and wisdom.

Ideally, hospitals should be environments in which there is an appreciation for and nourishing of a person's own inner capacity for healing as a complement to the medical management of his or her problems. Many doctors and nurses honor this perspective and try to nurture it as best they can, given the less-than-ideal conditions under which they often work and to which their patients come seeking help. Finding creative ways to mobilize the patient's own interior resources for moving toward greater levels of health and well-being is, as we have seen, an important element of a more participatory medicine.

To provide a resource for the individual patient to participate more directly in his or her own healing while in the hospital, and to give busy and overworked physicians and nurses a resource that they could offer to their patients, in the early years of the Stress Reduction Clinic I developed a televised outreach program to teach hospitalized patients how to meditate. The hope was that inpatients lying in bed would be able to engage in a similar kind of meditative work on themselves as do the people who come to the Stress Reduction Clinic as outpatients for MBSR training.

Ordinarily, television functions to distract us or absorb us. It easily carries us away from ourselves and away from the moment (we discuss this subject in more detail in Chapter 32). With this TV program, which is called *The World of Relaxation,* I was attempting to use the medium in a new way—you might think of it as person-to-person interactive television.

Many patients have their televisions on most of the time while they are in the hospital, though often the person isn't even watching. The constant barrage of noise and images is hardly conducive to overall well-being and healing, even if it does function to help the time pass more quickly. Silence would probably be better, especially if people knew what to do with it—knew *how* to be in silence, *how* to concentrate their energies for being in the moment and for dwelling in calmness and stillness.

If you are hospitalized in a room with another person, you might have to put up with whatever is on your roommate's TV, even if your own is off. For people in pain, or who are dying, or who are in a crisis of some kind, it can be dehumanizing, degrading, and demoralizing to have to tolerate soap operas and game shows as the ambient audio backdrop to their real-life problems. It is hardly a dignified atmosphere in which to die or to suffer, and hardly the best conditions under which to try to recuperate and heal.

The World of Relaxation was a way for me to reach out to the patient lying in bed from the television up on the wall and propose something like this: "Look, as long as you are lying here in the hospital with time on your hands, perhaps you might be interested in using some of this time to exercise certain muscles you many not even know you have—for instance, the muscle of attention, the muscle of mindfulness, and the muscle of working with the present moment, whatever your circumstances. It might be interesting to purposefully explore learning how to systematically enter into and dwell in a condition of deep relaxation and well-being. At the very least, engaging in this program might give you a greater sense of being able to control and reduce some of the stress, pain, and anxiety that you might be experiencing. What is more, it might also enhance the healing process itself."

The World of Relaxation is an unusual use of television. Visually it is simply my face on the screen for an hour—not exactly high drama or entertainment. Even worse, after a brief introduction, I ask the viewer to close his or her eyes, and then I close my eyes too. So for most of the hour the image is just my face on the screen with my eyes closed. I am meditating and guiding the listener in an extended healing-oriented meditation that includes mindfulness of breathing, a modified body scan, and directing the breath to the regions the patient feels require the most attention. The verbal guidance is entwined with soothing harp music composed and played by Georgia Kelly, a musician and composer committed to using music and sound for healing.

You might ask, "Why a television program at all if the patient has his or her eyes closed for most of it?" The answer is that even the image of another person in the room and reaching out to the patient in an inviting way may contribute to a feeling of trust and acceptance. If the person gets disoriented or bored at a particular point during the program, he or she always has the option of opening the eyes and seeing a real person up on the screen meditating—and thus perhaps be reassured that it is possible to return once again to the breath, to the present moment, and to the sounds of the harp, and drop back into some degree of calm and well-being.

I encourage the viewer to tune in and out of what is being said as he or she feels like it and to just give oneself over to bathing in the sounds themselves, the notes, and the spaces between them. The harp is an instrument that has been associated with healing since biblical times. The notes of the harp in this particular piece of music sound as if they are coming out of nowhere and going back into nowhere. There is a deep silence inside, in between, and underneath the plucking of the strings, giving the music a timeless quality, very different from music, however wonderful, that has a dominant melody or theme that might tend to carry the listener off somewhere else. Kelly's sound track provides an effective background for the cultivation of mindfulness as a formal practice, especially for someone attempting it for the very first time, mirroring as it does the way in which our thoughts and feelings and perceptions also appear to arise out of nowhere and dissolve back into nowhere, moment by moment.

The World of Relaxation plays on the in-house cable channel in our hospital seven times each twenty-four hours. It has been there for decades. Doctors can "prescribe" it for their patients to help them with pain, anxiety, or sleep problems, or to enhance relaxation and well-being and reduce the stress of hospitalization. To do this, they give their patients a little bookmark with the times when the program is on and a few suggestions for how to use it, and suggest they "do" it twice a day during their hospital stay. In our view, regular meditation practice using this program is a far better diet for patients in the hospital than the usual fare they are served up on TV. Over the years, we have heard numerous reports from patients that bear this out. The program has now been purchased by hundreds of hospitals in the United States and Canada, and it is also available on the Web (www.betterlisten.com).

Long ago, I was contacted by a woman who used *The World of Relaxation* when she was a patient at New York University Medical Center. We had an extended conversation, at the end of which I asked her if she would be willing to write down the circumstances under which she used it. This is how she described her experience:

> *Dear Dr. Kabat-Zinn:*
>
> *"There is more right with you than wrong with you"—those words of yours have stayed with me through two frightening cancer surgeries. So many other comforting thoughts that you offer on your video have helped me keep my sanity.*
>
> *At night, when alone after my visitors were gone, I couldn't wait to turn on the NYU Medical Center in-house channel because, somehow, I became dependent on the comfort you would offer. I can still see your face before me, almost as though my experience was a personal one. You offer a meaningful philosophy that puts everything into perspective for a frightened human being. Thank you so much for that. I tried so hard to remember how to practice the relaxation technique, but I still need the help that the program provides.*
>
> *So many other patients during my hospital stay were taking comfort from your voice. When I took my required walks along the hospital corridor, I could hear the program coming out of different rooms. Whenever I had the chance to talk to a patient who was suffering, I told them to turn it on and was thanked. (My first hospital stay was for twenty-three days. I had lots of time to meet others.)*

I am still hurting from my most recent surgery, and I am still scared, but I have so many good, in fact wonderful, moments because of your help. I am really very grateful.

LOVINGKINDNESS MEDITATION

Healing energy in the form of mindfulness and heartfulness can be directed toward others and toward our relationships as well as toward our own body. The process of uncovering in ourselves deep feelings of empathy, compassion, and love toward others has its own purifying effects on the mind and heart. When such feelings are invited to come into the heart to whatever degree they will, without any forcing, they can be experienced for oneself and then effectively directed toward others. Doing so can offer enormous benefit, and you, in all likelihood, will be the first beneficiary.

We usually offer a guided lovingkindness meditation in the all-day session in week six of MBSR to give people a taste of the power of evoking feelings of kindness, generosity, goodwill, love, and forgiveness, and directing them first and foremost toward oneself. The response is invariably moving. A great many tears are shed, both in joy and in sorrow. This type of meditation strikes a deep chord in many people. It can help us to cultivate strong positive emotions within ourselves, and to let go of ill will and resentment. Some of the participants' feelings about this form of meditation have already been voiced in Chapter 8. To practice lovingkindness meditation, we begin with awareness of our breathing. Then we consciously invite feelings of love and kindness toward ourselves to arise, perhaps by remembering a moment when we felt completely seen and accepted by another human being and inviting those feelings of kindness and love received to re-emerge out of the memory and be held in awareness and felt in the body; and then perhaps by saying inwardly to ourselves simple phrases that you can either make up for yourself or take from others, phrases such as "May I be free from inner and outer harm; may I be happy; may I be healthy; may I live with ease." Imagine what saying these things to yourself might do if you really, really, really inclined your heart in the direction the words are pointing—not to get anywhere or to pretend to feel anything, or even to think that you should feeling anything, but just as an experiment, to see what already resides within you when you give yourself over to the process wholeheartedly, or even just a little.

After a time, we can then go on, if we care to, to invoke someone else, perhaps a particular person we are close to and care deeply about. We can visualize that person in our mind's eye or hold the feeling of the person in our heart as we wish that person well: "May he or she be happy, may he (she) be free from pain and suffering, may he (she) experience love and joy, may he or she live with ease." In the same vein, we may then include others we know and love: parents, children, friends.

Next we can identify a person with whom we may have a particularly difficult time for whatever reason, for whom feelings of aversion or antipathy arise. It should not be someone who has caused us harm in a major way, just someone we don't really care for and really don't like to feel kindness toward. Again, and only if you care to, we can intentionally cultivate feelings of kindness, generosity, and compassion toward that person, intentionally recognizing and letting go of our feelings of resentment and dislike for him or her and reminding ourself instead to see that person as another human being, someone just as deserving of love and kindness as yourself, someone who also has feelings and hopes and fears, someone who feels pain and anxiety just as you do, someone who also suffers.

The practice can then move on to invoke a person who indeed *has* caused us harm in some way. This is always optional. It does not mean that you are being asked to forgive the person for what he or she has done to hurt you or to cause harm to others. Not at all. You are simply recognizing that he or she is also a human being, however damaged; that he or she also has aspirations, just like you; that he or she also suffers; that he or she also has the desire to be safe and to be happy. Since it is only we ourselves who suffer by carrying around feelings of hurt and anger, or even hatred, a willingness to experiment—even the tiniest bit, if and only if you feel receptive to the idea—with directing a modicum of kindness toward this person who is so difficult for us, who has hurt us, is really a way to bring our suffering to the fore and release it into the larger field of our own wholeness. The other person may not benefit from this at all. But you may benefit from it enormously. At this point, there is also the option of purposefully forgiving this person. This impulse may or may not develop spontaneously over time with ongoing practice of the lovingkindness meditation. It is always entirely up to you to decide who to include in the practice and to what degree. And if we have harmed others, knowingly or unknowingly, we can also bring them to mind at some point and ask them to forgive us.

The lovingkindness practice can be done with people whether they are alive or have already died. There can be a strong release of long-carried negative emotions as we ask for forgiveness and explore forgiving them. It is a profound process of coming to terms in your own heart and mind with the way things are in this moment, a deep letting go of past feelings and hurt. The cultivation of lovingkindness in this way can be deeply liberating if we follow our own lead, if we are careful not to force anything, if we honor our own boundaries and limits of the moment, just as we do in the yoga.

The practice continues further as we expand the field of people we might be willing to include. We can direct lovingkindness toward other individuals, known and unknown, perhaps to people we may see regularly but don't really know, such as the people who take our clothes at the cleaners, or the toll booth collector, or waiters and waitresses. We can extend the scope still further, radiating feelings of lovingkindness to people anywhere and everywhere in the world who are suffering, who have been severely traumatized, who are oppressed, who are so deeply in need of human kindness and caring. The meditation can be carried even further if we care to, expanding the field of lovingkindness out from our own heart in all directions until it includes all living creatures on the planet, not just people, and the life-giving planet itself.

Finally, we return to our own body, we come back to our breathing for a time, and end by simply resting in the aftermath of the process itself, cradling and accepting whatever feelings may be present, and taking particular note of whatever feelings of warmth, generosity, and love we may find flowing out of our own hearts.

When I first encountered the practice of lovingkindness, I thought it was a little strange and contrived. It felt very different from the spirit of mindfulness practice because it seemed to be suggesting that the meditator generate certain emotions instead of being aware of and accepting of any all emotions that might arise and according them all lovingkindness. Since I saw the cultivation of mindfulness as itself a radical act of love and of lovingkindness, it seemed superfluous at best to supplement it with a more specialized practice that might be confusing to people training in mindfulness because, on the face of it, it seems to contradict the non-striving and non-doing orientation of mindfulness itself.

I changed my mind when I saw and felt the power that purposefully cultivating lovingkindness had. When practiced regularly, it can have a remarkable softening effect on the heart. It can help you to be kinder to yourself and to others. It can help you to see all beings as deserving of kindness and compassion, so that even if disputes do arise, your mind can see clearly and your heart does not close down and become lost in self-serving yet ultimately self-destructive negative feeling states.

Under the best of circumstances, it sometimes takes years and years of chipping away at our more confining habits of mind to grow out of them. For some of us, at least, wisdom practices need to be softened with compassion and kindness practices, beginning with ourselves. Otherwise, they may not actually nurture wisdom in any real way, because wisdom and compassion are not separate, they enfold each other. As we shall see, because of the interconnectedness of all things—and therefore, because there is no absolute separation between self and other—there can be no real wisdom without kindness and compassion, and no real kindness and compassion without wisdom.

In summary, healing is a transformation of view rather than a cure. It involves recognizing your intrinsic wholeness and, simultaneously, your interconnectedness with everything else. Above all, it involves learning to feel at home and at peace within yourself. As we have seen and will explore more in later sections of the book, this way of being, grounded in the practices of MBSR, can lead to dramatic improvements in symptoms, a renewed ability to move toward greater levels of health and well-being, and even to changes in the brain that may play a role in these vital transformations.

14

Doctors, Patients, and People: Moving Toward a Unified Perspective on Health and Illness

The past decade and a half have seen three extremely exciting major discoveries in basic science that are transforming the way we understand the body and the mind and how they influence each other and our health.

The first is the phenomenon of *neuroplasticity*. It has now been demonstrated that the brain is an organ of ongoing experience. It continues to grow and change and reshape itself across our entire life span in response to experience, right into old age. Systematic training of all sorts, as well as repetitive exposure to challenges, is known to drive this intrinsic capacity of the brain. The discovery of neuroplasticity upended the long-standing central dogma of neurobiology, which held that after about the age of two, we only lost neurons in the brain and central nervous system, and at an ever-increasing rate as we grew older. Now, however, it seems that at least certain regions of the brain can generate new functional neurons even into old age, as well as continually making new synaptic connections driven by experience and lifelong learning. A new field called *contemplative neuroscience* has arisen to investigate what might be learned about brain functioning, consciousness, and the mind-body connection by studying both long-term meditators and also those who are relatively new to regular meditation practices, such as those taking mindfulness-based programs like MBSR.

The second new area of emergence is the field of *epigenetics*. It turns out that the genome is equally "plastic" in ways that were unimaginable even a short time ago. Epigenetics explores in detail how our experience, our behaviors, our lifestyle choices, and even our attitudes can potentially influence which genes in our chromosomes are turned on (the technical term is *upregulated*), and which genes in our chromosomes are turned off (*downregulated*). The implications of this are profound. They suggest that we are not entirely the prisoners of our genetic inheritance in the way we classically thought we were—that we can work with our genetic inheritance in ways that can modulate its expression, and thus potentially influence our susceptibility to particular diseases. It also suggests that in the fetus and in children, the developing brain is extremely sensitive to stress and other environmental factors that can influence, for better or for worse, how well and how completely it develops. This means that all the capacities required for optimal development into a full human being can be compromised because of stress at key moments of development, from before birth to well into adolescence. Those key capacities have to do with our ability to learn (executive functioning, working memory capacity), to grow optimally (embodiment, including basic gross and fine motor coordination), to regulate our emotions and social relationships (the development of empathy and the decoding of emotions and underlying motivations in oneself and others—sometimes called *emotional intelligence*), and to heal (functions of perspective taking, empathy for oneself, processing of self-relevant stimuli).

The third recent revolution in science and medicine came with the discovery of telomeres and the enzyme telomerase that repairs the telomeres. Telomeres are structures at the ends of all of our chromosomes that are necessary for our cells to divide. The telomeres shorten a bit with each cell division, and over time, when they are completely gone, the cell can no longer replicate. This work was recognized by a Nobel Prize in 2009 to Elizabeth Blackburn of the University of California, San Francisco, and others. After discovering that stress shortens telomeres, she and her colleagues began to investigate the effects of mindfulness and other meditative practices on protecting against telomere shortening, with promising early results. It is now known that telomere length is directly related to aging on the cellular level, and therefore, to how long we may live. The rate at which our telomeres degrade and shorten is very much affected by how much stress we are under and how well we cope with it.

Because of these recent breakthrough discoveries and the overall momentum of discovery in the life sciences over the past seven decades, we find ourselves at a very promising juncture in the evolution of medicine, the medical sciences, and our health care institutions. With the completion of the Human Genome Project and the development of the fields of genomics and proteomics, more is known about the details of the structure and functioning of living organisms on every level, and especially in humans, than ever before. Biological research is being carried out at a feverish pace, and more is being learned every day. Since 1944, the year that DNA was shown to be the genetic material, molecular biology has completely revolutionized the practice of medicine, providing it with a comprehensive and ever-deepening scientific foundation that has proved to be enormously successful in many areas and continues to hold great promise for future breakthroughs.

We now know a great deal about the genetic and molecular basis of a number of diseases, including many kinds of cancer, and are realizing that because of our unique genomes, different people may experience the same disease differently, and therefore might require different, specifically targeted drug interventions. We also have an elaborate and continually growing array of drugs for controlling infectious diseases and for regulating many of the physiological responses of the body when they get out of control. We know that our cells harbor certain genes, known as proto-oncogenes, that control normal functions within cells but which, when altered by a mutational event, can lead to tumor growth and cancer. We know a great deal more about the prevention and treatment of heart disease than was known even ten years ago. If caught in time, a person having a heart attack, or who has just had one, can now have a specific enzyme (TPA or streptokinase) injected into the bloodstream that will dissolve the culprit blood clot in one of the coronary arteries and greatly reduce damage to the heart muscle. In fact, we know a great deal about disease prevention in general. And yet in this domain, our medical system and health care policy have fallen far short of the mark when it comes to implementing what is already known about disease prevention. Educating people about how to optimize health and well-being across the life span would lead to huge cost savings for society. Here is where participatory medicine, including MBSR and other mindfulness-based approaches to health and well-being, can play an ever-increasing role in improving the overall health of the society and, at the same time, reduce significantly the enormous cost burden on the society, incurred when preventable illness due to poverty, lack of education, or lack of political will is not prevented. One shocking symptom of this is that the United States ranks about thirty-seventh among nations in life expectancy, and about fiftieth in infant mortality.

Health care and medicine now routinely make use of ever more sophisticated computer-controlled diagnostic technologies, including sonography, CAT scans, PET scans, and MRI, allowing doctors to look inside the body in various ways and determine what might be going on. Comparable technological advances have been made in surgical procedures: lasers are routinely used to do fine repair on detached retinas and to preserve vision; artificial hip and knee joints have been developed that can restore the ability of people suffering with severe arthritis to walk, and increasingly, even to run; cardiac bypass surgery and organ transplants are now common occurrences.

However, while more is known about disease than ever before and while we have improved ways of diagnosing and treating many diseases, far more still remains unknown. Modern medicine is nowhere near putting itself out of business by eradicating or even controlling disease. In spite of the rapid progress in genetics, molecular and cell biology, and neuroscience, our understanding of the biology of living organisms, even the simplest ones, is still rudimentary. And when it comes down to medicine's ability to treat certain diseases and the people who have them, we discover very real limits and major areas of ignorance, even today.

We naturally put enormous faith in modern medicine because of its spectacular successes. But at the same time we are often surprisingly uninformed about what medicine does not know and what it cannot do. Often we don't discover the very real limits of medicine until it is our own body that is in pain or dealing with a particular disease, disorder, or diagnosis, or when someone we love is suffering and there is no ready-made effective solution or treatment. Then we can become severely disillusioned, frustrated, and even angry at the discrepancy between our expectations of what medicine can do and the reality.

It is hardly fair to fault an individual doctor for the limits of medical knowledge. When you come right down to it, there are few medical cures at present or on the horizon for the chronic diseases and other chronic conditions (such as many forms of pain), although they are a major cause of suffering, disability, and death in our society. It is far better to prevent them in the first place, if possible, than to have to be treated for them. But true prevention, especially that involving lifestyle change and the restructuring of social priorities, remains an ongoing challenge. There are many diseases whose origins are completely mysterious or that are intimately linked to social factors such as poverty and social exploitation, dangerous working conditions, stressful and poisonous environmental conditions, and culturally entrenched habits, the rampant overuse of antibiotics with cattle leading to antibiotic-resistant superbugs, all of which are outside the direct influence of medicine and science as they are presently organized.

Although a great deal is known about the molecular biology of certain cancers and there are effective treatments, even cures, for some forms of cancer, many cancers are presently only very poorly understood and effective treatments do not exist. Yet even in such cases, there are always some people who survive much longer than expected. In some instances tumors have been known to regress or disappear altogether, even without medical treatment, though we know almost nothing about why or how this happens. Yet it is known to happen. This in itself can be a source of some hope for people when they have exhausted the options available in traditional medicine. Here is where our understanding of epigenetic factors and how we might mobilize them through lifestyle changes, including meditation, could make a profound difference.

Most physicians acknowledge the role of the mind and social factors in healing and health, and many doctors have observed this firsthand in their patients. Sometimes it gets talked about in fairly basic terms as simply "the will to live." Yet no one understands it, and it tends to be invoked in a hand-waving, mystical sort of way, usually only after all the medical options have been exhausted. It is a way of saying, "There is nothing more we can do, but I know that it is still possible for 'miracles' to happen, miracles that traditional medicine just doesn't have explanations for or know how to conjure up for people."

If a person believes she or he is going to die and loses hope, this emotional capitulation can itself tilt the system against recovery. Personal motivations to live are known to sometimes influence survival. Emotional disposition and support from family and friends can make a big difference in how people do in the face of serious illness and also in the face of aging.

Yet until recently, doctors did not receive much, if any, training in how to help patients make use of their own inner resources for healing, or even how to recognize when they themselves might be unwittingly undermining the very resources that are the patient's best allies in the healing process.

Too often, the scientific and technological sophistication of the traditional medical approach to disease leads to an impersonal, sometimes even disembodied approach to the patient, as if medicine's knowledge is so powerful that the patient's understanding, cooperation, and collaboration in treatment are of minor value. When this attitude is displayed by a physician in his or her relationship to a patient, when the patient is made to feel, either through omission or commission, inadequate, ignorant, or in some way to blame, either for his condition or for his lack of response to the treatment, or when the person's feelings are simply ignored, these are instances of grossly inadequate medical care.

A cardinal aphorism of traditional medicine, first voiced by Francis W.

Peabody of the Harvard Medical School in 1926, has always been that "the secret of the care of the patient is in caring for the patient." This aphorism needs to be more actively kept in mind by health professionals. In an optimal encounter between patient and physician, each has a vital area of expertise, and both parties have essential roles to play in the healing process, which ideally begins in the initial encounter, before any diagnosis and treatment plan are arrived at. The dignity of the patient needs to be honored and preserved throughout his or her entire sequence of medical encounters, whether they lead to a wholly "successful" outcome or not.

It is not uncommon for doctors who become ill to discover for the first time in their lives the little and not-so-little insensitivities in the health care system that rob people of their dignity and sense of agency. At such times, as they make the transition from "doctor" to "patient," they may be more likely to see that the latter role puts you at immediate risk for shame, loss of control, and reduced dignity, even though you are the same person you were before the role change. If this is true for physicians, who understand the process much better than most people, it is not hard to understand how alienating the health care system can be for people who have no background or understanding to help them sort out what they are going through.

When we become ill and seek medical care, and thereby inevitably take on the role of "patient," we are usually in a particularly vulnerable psychological state because we are naturally concerned about the larger implications of our illness. We are also, for the most part, in a position of substantial ignorance and little authority compared with our doctors, even though it is our body that is the subject of all the attention. In this situation, we may be unusually sensitive to the messages, both verbal and nonverbal, that we get from our doctors. These messages can either augment the healing process in us or subvert it altogether, if our doctor is insensitive to his or her own behaviors and the effects they can have on the person who is their patient.

A story told by Bernard Lown, a renowned cardiologist at the Harvard

Medical School and Brigham and Women's Hospital,* about an incident he observed while he was in training, illustrates this powerfully:

> The experience still provokes in me a shudder of disbelief. Some thirty years ago I had a postdoctorate fellowship with Dr. S. A. Levine, professor of cardiology at the Harvard Medical School and at the Peter Bent Brigham Hospital. He was a keen observer of the human scene, had an awesome presence, was precise in formulation, and was blessed with a prodigious memory. He was, in effect, the consummate clinician at the bedside. Dr. Levine conducted a weekly outpatient cardiac clinic at the hospital. After we young trainees examined the patient, he would drop in briefly to assess our findings and suggest further diagnostic workup or changes in the therapeutic program. With patients, he was invariably reassuring and convincing, and they venerated his every word. In one of my first clinics, I had as a patient Mrs. S., a well-preserved middle-aged librarian who had a narrowing of one of the valves on the right side of her heart, the tricuspid valve. She had been in low-grade congestive heart failure with modest edema [swelling] of the ankles, but was able to maintain her job and attend efficiently to household chores. She was receiving digitalis and weekly injections of a mercurial diuretic. Dr. Levine, who had followed her in the clinic for more than a decade, greeted Mrs. S. warmly, and then turned to the large entourage of visiting physicians and said, "This women has TS," and abruptly left.
>
> No sooner was Dr. Levine out of the door than Mrs. S.'s demeanor abruptly changed. She appeared anxious and frightened and was now breathing rapidly, clearly hyperventilating. Her skin was drenched with perspiration, and her pulse had acceler-

* Much later in his career, Dr. Lown accepted the 1985 Nobel Peace Prize on behalf of International Physicians Against Nuclear War.

ated to more than 150 a minute. In reexamining her, I found it astonishing that the lungs, which a few minutes earlier had been quite clear, now had moist crackles at the bases. This was extraordinary, for with obstruction of the right heart valve, the lungs are spared the accumulation of excess fluid.

I questioned Mrs. S. as to the reasons for her sudden upset. Her response was that Dr. Levine had said that she had TS, which she knew meant "terminal situation." I was initially amused at this misinterpretation of the medical acronym for "tricuspid stenosis." My amusement, however, rapidly yielded to apprehension, as my words failed to reassure and as her congestion continued to worsen. Shortly thereafter she was in massive pulmonary edema. Heroic measures did not reverse the frothing congestion. I tried to reach Dr. Levine, but he was nowhere to be located. Later that same day she died from intractable heart failure. To this day the recollection of this tragic happening causes me to tremble at the awesome power of the physician's word.

In this story we get to see the microanatomy of a dramatic and very rapid mind-body interaction that resulted, almost unbelievably, directly in death. We witness through Dr. Lown's eyes the appearance of a particular thought in the mind of the patient, triggered by the unexplained use of a technical term by her doctor, for whom she had the highest regard. The thought that her situation was terminal, although completely untrue, *was believed by her to be true.* It set off an immediate psychophysiological reaction. Her belief in that thought was so firmly entrenched that she was completely closed off even to authoritative reassurances from another physician that it was, in fact, a misunderstanding. By that point, her mind was in a state of turbulence, clearly overwhelmed by anxiety and fear. Apparently her emotional state overwhelmed her body's regulatory mechanisms that normally maintain physiological balance. As a result, her body went into a severe stress reaction, from which no one, not herself and not her doctors, were able to extricate her. Not even the heroic life-support and rescue measures of one of the best hospitals in the world could save her once this chain of events was unleashed, even though it had been triggered by a seemingly innocent, if insensitively delivered remark.

Dr. Lown's story graphically illustrates the enormous power that strongly held beliefs, which are in actuality just thoughts, can have on our health. Ultimately, the effects of our thoughts and emotions on our health comes down to the activity of the brain and nervous system, and how profoundly and immediately they can influence our physiology. This means that how we are in relationship to our thoughts and emotions can make a huge difference in the quality of our lives and our health, both in the present moment and over time. One thing is immediately clear from Dr. Lown's clinical anecdote: had this woman been a little less reactive, a little more willing to look at this suddenly acquired belief as a thought that might require some clarification or that might be inaccurate, had she been able to let go of her thought at least enough to entertain the notion that what Dr. Lown was telling her might be true, or to listen to his reassurances that she was mistaken, she might not have died. Unfortunately, she apparently lacked that flexibility of mind in the moment that Dr. Levine tried his best to set things straight. Perhaps she believed too strongly in her doctor and not enough in herself. In any event, we can clearly see through Dr. Lown's account that an emotional reaction to a misunderstood comment by her doctor was the direct cause of her death.

Had Dr. Levine not left her bedside so abruptly, he might have observed the effect of his words on his patient, as Dr. Lown had no trouble doing; he would have noticed that she was distressed. Had he asked her about her sudden anxiety reaction, he might have been able to allay her fears on the spot and prevent this entire sequence of events.

Although death under such circumstances is happily a rare occurrence in medical practice, the pain, anxiety, and on occasion humiliation that patients experience at the hands of the health care system, sadly are not. Much of it could be easily avoided if physicians were better trained to value making observations of a psychological and social nature in addition to attending to the physical aspects of patient care. Increasingly, they are receiving this kind of training.

Many physicians are naturally both sensitive and proactive in this dimension of the doctor-patient relationship, just from their own psychological constitution, coupled with the Hippocratic injunction to "first do no harm." Of course, not doing harm would require moment-to-moment awareness of how one's interactions with a patient are being received by the patient. Otherwise, the physician would have no yardstick for apprehending the effects of his or her communications and manner of being on the patient. Mindfulness provides that yardstick. What most patients want from their doctors is to be seen and heard and met. This, of course, requires that the doctor be skilled at truly listening to the patient's concerns, and even going to some lengths to elicit those that the patient may be reluctant to voice.

Nowadays, mindfulness in the physician-patient relationship and in clinical communications is becoming more and more a part of good medical training, both for medical students and for medical residents. And some physicians, such as Ron Epstein of the School of Medicine at the University of Rochester, are articulating the value of mindfulness in medical practice and publishing their views and research in premier medical journals. In an article in the Journal of the American Medical Society entitled "Mindful Practice," Dr. Epstein emphasizes the value of physicians attending to their "own physical and mental processes during ordinary, everyday tasks," and goes on to say that "this critical self-reflection [in their own lives] enables physicians to listen attentively to [their] patients' distress, recognize their own errors, refine their technical skills, make evidence-based decisions, and clarify their values so that they can act with compassion, technical competence, presence and insight." Together with his colleagues, Mick Krasner, Tim Quill, and others, these physician-researchers at the University of Rochester have pioneered a program for primary care physicians on mindful communication that was shown to reduce physician burnout (defined as emotional exhaustion), depersonalization (treatment patients as objects), and low sense of accomplishment.

The program "was associated with short-term and sustained improvements in well-being and attitudes associated with patient-centered care."*

This kind of participatory, mindfulness-based professional training program for physicians represents a remarkable sea change in medical education and practice. Along with other programs to promote physician well-being and meaning in novel heart-opening formats, such as Rachel Naomi Remen's "The Healer's Art" curriculum for medical students and physicians at the University of California San Francisco Medical School, now offered at medical schools around the country and abroad, such approaches are having an increasingly positive impact on how medicine is actually practiced at the personal and interpersonal levels.

The roots of this movement originated in part from the seminal work of Dr. George Engel, for decades a leading figure at the University of Rochester Medical School, where he revolutionized the teaching of medical students and residents by advocating the importance of training doctors to approach patients' psychological and social concerns with the same scientific care and rigor that they bring to their consideration of lab reports and X-rays. He articulated an expanded model for the practice of medicine that took into account the importance of psychological and social factors in health and disease and adopted a systems perspective (see Chapter 12) on health and illness, treating the patient as a whole person. Dr. Engel's *biopsychosocial model* influenced a whole generation of young doctors, including Dr. Krasner and Dr. Epstein, who were encouraged and trained to go beyond the limits of the traditional medical model of the time in the way they practiced medicine.

Until Dr. Engel's model was put forth, the effect of psychological factors on physical illness was not addressed in a major way in the curriculum of modern medical education, although it had been recognized since the days of Hippocrates that the mind plays a major and sometimes primary

* Remarkably, primary care physicians report alarming levels of professional and personal distress, and in some studies, up to 60 percent of practicing physicians report symptoms of burnout. Krasner, MS, Epstein, RM, Beckman, H et al. Association of an Educational Program in Mindful Communication With Burnout, Empathy, and Attitudes Among Primary Care Physicians *JAMA*. 2009;302:1284–1293.

role in disease and health. The virtual exclusion of the domain of the mind from the major currents in medical education was due mainly to the fact that, since the time of Descartes in the seventeenth century, Western scientific thinking has divided the intrinsic wholeness of being into separate, essentially non-interacting domains of soma (body) and psyche (mind). While these are convenient categories for facilitating understanding on one level, the tendency has been to forget that mind and body are separate in thought only. This dualistic way of thinking and seeing so permeated Western culture that it closed off the entire realm of mind-body interactions in health as a legitimate domain of scientific inquiry. Even our conventional use of language reflects this dualism, and thus limits the ways we can think about non-separation of mind and body. We talk about "my body" and "having a body" but fail to ask, "Who is separate from the body and claims to have it as a belonging or a possession?" Only in the past several decades has this old perspective and the language itself begun to change, as the major weaknesses and contradictions of the dualistic paradigm became more apparent and intellectually indefensible. This acceptance is coming about in part due to the advent of contemplative neuroscience, which is demonstrating that training of the mind through meditative practices produces neural patterns in the brain in long-term practitioners that have never been seen before—an example of the non-material mind (psyche) changing the material brain (soma) and thus being very much one seamless whole.

A notable weakness of the standard biomedical model was its failure to explain why, given the same exposure to disease agents and environmental conditions, some people get sick and others do not. While genetic variability might account for some differences in resistance to illness, other factors seemed to play a role as well. Engel's biopsychosocial model proposed that psychological and social factors could either protect a person from illness or increase his or her susceptibility to it. Such factors include a person's beliefs and attitudes, how supported and loved a person feels by family and friends, the psychological and environmental stresses to which one is exposed, and personal health behaviors. The discovery that the immune system can be influenced by psychological factors bolstered the biopsychosocial model by providing one plausible biological pathway for explaining such mind-body interactions. Now, with the advent of specialized disciplines such as cognitive neuroscience, affective neuroscience, and contemplative neuroscience, other plausible biological pathways linking mind and body, and therefore health and illness, may be elucidated as well.

Another important element pointing toward the need to include a role for the mind in a more accurate model of health and illness has always been the *placebo effect,* a very well-known phenomenon for which the standard biomedical model had no explanation. Numerous studies over the years have shown time and time again that when people believe that they are taking a drug of a particular potency, they show significant clinical effects typical of the drug in question, even when they did not actually receive the drug but only a sugar pill, known as a placebo. Sometimes the magnitude of the placebo effect comes close to the magnitude of the drug itself. This phenomenon can only be explained by assuming that the very *suggestion* that you are taking a powerful drug in some way influences the brain and nervous system to create conditions in the body similar to those produced on a molecular level by the presence of the drug. It suggests that, by whatever mechanism, a person's beliefs can either change his or her biochemistry or functionally mimic a change in biochemistry. The power of suggestion also lies at the root of the phenomenon of hypnosis, which has long been known to be able to dramatically affect many different human activities, including pain perception and memory. Of course, the standard medical model has no place for hypnotic phenomena either.

Another influence in the movement toward an expanded perspective on health and illness came through the acceptance of acupuncture in the West. The most dramatic moment came when James Reston of the *New York Times* suffered a ruptured appendix while in China and underwent an operation in which acupuncture was used for pain relief following the surgery, which was done under chemical anesthesia. Since acupuncture is based on a five-thousand-year-old classical Chinese model of health and disease, and treatment consists of stimulating energy pathways, called *meridians,* that have no anatomical basis in Western medical thought, the mind-set in the West was expanded to at least entertain the notion that a different way of looking at the body might lead to effective diagnostic and treatment methods

Studies by Dr. Herbert Benson of the Harvard Medical School in the early 1970s on people practicing a form of meditation known as Transcendental Meditation, or TM, demonstrated that meditation can produce a pattern of significant physiological changes, which he termed the *relaxation response.* These include a lowering of blood pressure, reduced oxygen consumption, and an overall decrease in arousal. Dr. Benson proposed that the relaxation response was the physiological opposite of *hyperarousal,* the state we experience when we are stressed or threatened. He hypothesized that if the relaxation response was elicited regularly, it could have a positive influence on health and protect us from some of the more damaging effects of stress. Dr. Benson pointed out that all religious traditions have ways of eliciting this response and that there is a kind of wisdom associated with prayer and meditation that is relevant to the health of the body and deserving of further study. More recent studies have demonstrated that training in the relaxation response can have dramatic epigenetic effects, upregulating and downregulating hundreds of genes. Similar epigenetic findings have been reported by Dr. Dean Ornish (see Chapter 31) in men with prostate cancer who were following his lifestyle change program which includes meditation and a low-fat vegetarian diet. Many of the genes that were downregulated in that study are known to be involved in inflammatory processes and cancer.

Going back in time to the late 1960s and the 1970s, early research in what was then called biofeedback and self-regulation showed that human beings could learn to control many physiological functions that had previously been considered involuntary, such as heart rate, skin temperature, skin conductance, blood pressure, and brain waves, when they were given feedback from a machine that told them how they were doing. This research was pioneered by Drs. Elmer and Alyce Green at the Menninger Foundation, Drs. David Shapiro and Gary Schwartz at the Harvard Medical School, Dr. Chandra Patel in England, and many others. Many of these biofeedback studies used relaxation, meditation, or yoga to help people to learn to regulate these bodily responses.

In 1977, a book appeared that brought together many of these various strands for the first time and made them accessible to the general public. Entitled *Mind as Healer, Mind as Slayer,* by Dr. Kenneth Pelletier, the book presented a wide range of compelling evidence that the mind was a major participant in illness and could be a major factor in health as well. It inspired widespread interest in mind-body interactions and in taking responsibility for one's own health rather than waiting for it to break down under stress and then counting on medical care to make things better. This book has since become a classic in the field.

In their time, Norman Cousins's writings also contributed to the growing public interest in taking charge of one's own health. Cousins's books recounting his experiences with illness and his determination to take the primary responsibility for healing out of the hands of his doctors and into his own created much controversy and debate within the medical establishment of the day. In *Anatomy of an Illness as Perceived by the Patient,* Cousins detailed his successful efforts to overcome a degenerative collagen disease using, among other things, large doses of self-prescribed laughter therapy. Laughter appears to be a profoundly healthful state of momentary body-mind integration and harmony. In Cousins's view, cultivating strong positive emotional states through humor and not taking oneself so seriously, even in the face of life-threatening circumstances, are of major therapeutic value in the healing process. Certainly this is very much in the spirit of Zorba, who dances and sings in the face of the full catastrophe.

In *The Healing Heart,* Cousins described his experiences following a heart attack that occurred some years after his experience with the collagen disease. In both books he recounts how he approached these illnesses by analyzing current medical knowledge and its limits in terms of his particular problems and circumstances, and then how he went on to chart his own intelligent and idiosyncratic course toward recovery, in close collaboration with his sometimes bemused doctors.

Because of his fame as the editor of the now long-defunct *Saturday*

Review and his sophistication about medical matters, Cousins received very special treatment from his doctors. On the whole, they were extraordinarily tolerant of his ideas and of his desire to be a full participant in all aspects of the decision-making process involving his medical treatment, long before this was common practice.

Not just Norman Cousins but *anybody* who wants to participate in the process of recovery from an illness in this way deserves this kind of treatment partnership with his or her doctors and with the health care system. To make this happen requires that we ask for information and explanations from our doctors and insist on being actively involved in the decisions that concern us. Many physicians welcome and encourage this kind of interaction with their patients. Cousins inspired many people with illnesses, as well as many of those treating them, to view the patient's role as a participant as essential to the healing process. Nevertheless, a lot of us tend to be intimidated by the authority of physicians. This is especially so when we feel vulnerable about our health and have little or no knowledge of medicine. If this is the case, you may have to work extra hard at asserting yourself and at maintaining your balance of mind and self-confidence. Bringing mindfulness to your interactions with your doctors, both before you see them and during your encounters with them, can help you to formulate and ask the questions you most want answers to, and to advocate more effectively for yourself.

Another influence that pushed medicine toward a new paradigm, if only indirectly, stemmed from the revolution in the science of physics that started around the beginning of the twentieth century and is still continuing, with the recent discovery of the Higgs Boson, and in the form of ongoing debates on string theory, supersymmetry, and the ultimate nature of matter, energy, and space itself, including the question of whether there is a single universe or many universes, of which ours is only one. The most rigorous of the physical sciences has had to come to terms with new discoveries showing that, at the deepest and most fundamental level, the natural world is neither describable nor understandable in conventional terms. Our basic notions that things are *what* they are, that they are *where* they are, and that one set of conditions always causes the same thing to happen, had to be completely revised to understand the world of the very small and the very fast. For instance, it is now known that the subatomic particles (electrons, protons, and neutrons) that make up the atoms of which all substances, including our bodies, are composed have properties that appear sometimes wave-like and sometimes particle-like; furthermore, they cannot be said with complete certainty to have a particular energy at a particular time; and the connections between events on this level of physical reality are only describable by probability.

Physicists had to drastically expand their view of reality in order to describe what they found inside the atom. They coined the term *complementarity* to convey the idea that one thing (say, an electron) can have two totally different and seemingly contradictory sets of physical properties (i.e., appear as either a wave or a particle), depending on what method you use to look at it. They were obliged to invoke a principle of *uncertainty* as a fundamental law of nature to explain that one can know either the position of a subatomic particle or its momentum, but not both at the same time. And they had to develop the idea of a *quantum field,* which posits that matter cannot be separated from the space surrounding it, that is, that particles are simply "condensations" of a continuous field that exists everywhere. In this description of the world, it may not be meaningful to ask what "causes" the appearance or disappearance of matter out of the void, although this is known to occur. These new descriptions of reality, of the internal structure of the very atoms that make up our own bodies and the world, are so far from our ordinary mode of thinking and experiencing that they require a major shift in how we conceive of the world.

These revolutionary concepts, which physicists have been grappling with for more than a hundred years now, have gradually filtered down in the culture, prompting us to think more in terms of complementary ways of knowing in general. This means that it is now more acceptable to posit, for instance, that while science and medicine offer a particular description of health, this description may not be the only possible valid one. The notion of complementarity reminds us that all systems of knowledge may be incomplete and need to be seen as aspects of a larger whole that lies beyond all the models and theories that attempt to describe it. Far from invalidating knowledge in a particular realm, complementarity merely points to the fact that knowledge is limited and needs to be used within the domains where its descriptions are valid and relevant.

One doctor's ideas about the implications that this new way of thinking in physics might have for medicine are presented in *Space, Time and Medicine,* by Larry Dossey. Dr. Dossey takes the position that "our ordinary view of life, death, health, and disease rests solidly on seventeenth-century physics, and if this physics has evolved to favor a more accurate and complete description of nature, an inescapable question occurs: must not our definitions of life, death, health, and disease themselves be in need of changing?" Dr. Dossey suggests that "we face the extraordinary possibility of fashioning a [health care] system going forward that emphasizes life instead of death, and unity and oneness instead of fragmentation, darkness, and isolation."

All the same, given the vicious political jockeying around health care reform in the United States (which is really more about health care reimbursement reform than true health care reform), it seems as though those of us who care—which should be all of us, of course—will have to patiently work as best we can for authentic and paradigmatic change with a long-term perspective. Every element of participatory medicine contributes to that long-term endeavor. Other countries are making more headway in the political arena than are we. For instance, mindfulness in the form of mindfulness-based cognitive therapy is officially mandated under the United Kingdom's National Health Service to help prevent relapse in people with a history of three or more episodes of major depression. We shall speak more about MBCT in Chapter 24.

Also in the United Kingdom, members of Parliament are now advocating greater mindfulness in addressing a broad range of social ills. Indeed, some members of Parliament in the House of Commons and the House of Lords have been participating in classes modeled on MBSR and MBCT to learn the practice of mindfulness. The chief medical officer of Scotland, Sir Harry Burns, is an advocate of using mindfulness to address social ills and health care disparities in that country. In the United States, Tim Ryan, a member of Congress from Ohio, recently wrote a book called

A Mindful Nation. Congressman Ryan is a strong advocate for greater mindfulness in health care as well as in other important areas such as education, the military, and criminal justice. In his book, he makes a very strong case for why we need greater mindfulness in these and other areas of our society.

As we have seen, the need to conceptualize health and illness in a larger framework than the traditional one has led to the formulation of a new paradigm, still in its infancy, but slowly coming to have substantial repercussions in the practice of medicine and in the wider society's view of health and illness, and what it wants out of medicine and health care. One of those repercussions has been the development of an expanded orientation within medicine, medical research, and clinical practice, known variously as *mind-body medicine, behavioral medicine,* or *integrative medicine,* that is devoted to a deeper understanding of what we mean by health and to exploring how we can best promote health and prevent disease, as well as how we can treat and heal the diseases and disabilities we do experience.

Behavioral medicine explicitly recognizes that mind and body are intimately interconnected and that an appreciation of these interconnections and their scientific study is vital to a fuller understanding of health and disease. It is an interdisciplinary field, uniting the behavioral sciences with the biomedical sciences in the hope that the cross-fertilization will yield a more comprehensive picture of health and illness than either could provide alone. Behavioral medicine recognizes that our thought patterns and emotions can play a significant role in health and disease, via mechanisms we have already discussed. It recognizes that what people believe about their bodies and their illnesses may be important for healing and that how we live our lives, what we think, and what we do may all influence our health in important ways.

The field of behavioral medicine offers new hope for people who ordinarily tend to fall through the cracks of the health care system and come away unhelped, frustrated, and bitter. As we have seen, clinical programs such as MBSR present people with the opportunity to try to do something for themselves as a complement to more traditional medical approaches. Patients are now being encouraged by their doctors to pursue such mindfulness-based programs and to learn meditation and yoga as effective aids for working with and minimizing stress, illness, and pain and their effects on one's quality of life and ability to function effectively. In mindfulness-based programs, people learn to face their life problems and develop personalized strategies for working with them rather than giving themselves over solely to "experts" who are supposed to just "fix them" or make their problems magically disappear. Such programs are vehicles in which people can work to become healthier and more resilient, change their beliefs about what they are capable of doing, and learn to relax and cope more effectively with life stress. At the same time, they can work at changing their lifestyles in key ways that might directly affect their health and physical well-being. Perhaps the most important step they can take in such programs is to expand the way they see themselves and their relationship to their life and to the world. In addition to MBSR and MBCT, there are now mindfulness-based programs modeled on MBSR specifically for binge drinking in college students (MBRP), for binge eating (MB-EAT), for working with veterans suffering from PTSD (MBTT), for deployed troops and their families (MMFT), for elder care (MBEC), for art therapy with cancer patients (MBSR-AT), for childbirth and parenting (MBCP) and for regulating anxiety in children (MBCT-C), to name a few.

Behavioral medicine, integrative medicine, mind-body medicine—whatever name you care to give to this orientation—it expands the traditional model of medical care so that it addresses mind as well as body, behavior and beliefs, thoughts and emotions, as well as the more traditional signs, symptoms, and drug- and surgery-based treatment procedures. By involving people in this expanded definition of medicine and health care in a participatory way, these new and increasingly evidence-based disciplines are helping people to shift the balance of responsibility for their well-being away from an exclusive dependency on their doctors and closer to their own personal efforts, over which they have more direct control than they do over hospitals, medical procedures, and doctors.

Thus, participating intimately in your own health and well-being as a complement to what your doctors and health care team are doing for you can help to restore and optimize your health, always starting from where you find yourself when you begin to take responsibility in this way.

Participating in an MBSR program, whether you have been referred by your physician or have taken the initiative to enroll on your own, is one way in which you or anyone with stress, pain, and medical problems of all kinds can take personal responsibility for participating in and contributing to the process of your own healing. As we have seen, a small but important element of the experience of MBSR involves learning about some of the latest research findings in all the various fields we have discussed that illustrate the importance of paying attention to mind-body interactions in your life.

When this book was first published, there was almost no science of mindfulness or mindfulness-based clinical programs such as MBSR. Now there is an ever-increasing body of scientific evidence suggesting that MBSR and other mindfulness-based interventions can affect specific regions in the brain, positively influence at least certain immune functions, regulate emotion under stress, reduce pain, and improve a wide range of health indicators across many different medical diagnostic categories as well as in healthy individuals. Thus, as we continue to deepen our engagement with the meditation practices of the MBSR curriculum as outlined in Part 1, with perhaps more of a sense of the new paradigm that is inexorably taking root within medicine and health care, we can now delve into some of the latest scientific evidence for the connections between mind and health, and the effects of training our own minds in attentional practices. This might give us an even better understanding of why it could be beneficial to practice mindfulness as if your life depended on it, and also of why health professionals make the recommendations for lifestyle change that they sometimes do. The scientific evidence can demystify medical knowledge by showing us where health professionals' knowledge comes from and how statements of medical "fact" are arrived at. In MBSR, we encourage people to think for themselves about the implications and limits of such knowledge, as well as to ask questions about its relevance to their own situation and condition. The results of studies investigating the relationship of psychological factors to health and illness can stimulate us to examine our own often limiting beliefs about ourselves and our health, and what might be possible if we tap deeply into our own interior resources for learning, growing, healing, and transformation. As long as we are breathing, it is never too late to give ourselves over, at least a bit, to this process and see what happens. We can see it as an adventure, in fact, the adventure of a lifetime.

Examining the evidence in support of mindfulness and of the mind-body connection in health and disease at any and every age, we may come to see that science is merely confirming what has long been known, namely, that each one of us has an important role to play in our own well-being. This role can be more effectively played if we can become conscious of and modify certain aspects of the way we live that influence our health either adversely or beneficially. These include our attitudes, thoughts, and beliefs; our emotions; our relationship to society and to the natural world; as well as our behaviors: how we actually act and conduct our lives. All can influence our health in different ways; all are related to stress and our attempts to cope with it; and all are directly influenced by the practice of mindfulness. In the next chapter we will examine a range of evidence that supports a new, unified mind-body perspective on health and illness and highlight the importance of becoming mindful of our own patterns of thinking, feeling, and behaving.

15

Mind and *Body: Evidence That Beliefs, Attitudes, Thoughts, and Emotions Can Harm or Heal*

THE ROLE OF PERCEPTIONS AND THOUGHT PATTERNS IN HEALTH

In the last chapter, we saw a dramatic example of how a thought, triggered by a misunderstood remark, led to an overwhelming mind-body crisis that resulted in a woman's death. Her single thought, although mistaken, precipitated a chain of events that rapidly and fatally disregulated the normally robust homeostatic processes of the body, including the regulation of how the heart and the lungs function in concert, such that physiological processes that almost never occur occurred, and with great and irreversible rapidity. Although we are often unaware of our thoughts as thoughts, they have a profound effect on everything we do, and they can have a profound effect on our health as well, which can be for better or for worse. Another case in point is the phenomenon of *depressive rumination,* negative thought patterns that, once they get going, can precipitate a downward spiral into the depths of depression, from which it is exceedingly difficult to extricate oneself. We will visit this subject in greater detail when we discuss how mindfulness training, in the form of MBCT, can make a huge difference in whether or not we let an initial negative thought trigger such an overwhelming chain of events.

Our thought patterns dictate the ways we perceive and explain reality, including our relationship to ourself and to the world. We all have particular ways in which we think about and explain to ourselves why things happen to us. Our thought patterns underlie our motives for doing things and for making choices. They influence the degree of confidence we have in our ability to make things happen. They are at the core of our beliefs about the world, how it works, and what our place in it is. Our thoughts can also carry a lot of emotion with them. Some carry very positive emotions such as joy, happiness, and contentment. Others carry sadness, feelings of isolation and hopelessness, even despair. Often our thoughts build themselves into extensive narratives, stories we tell ourselves about the world, about others, about ourselves, and about the past and the future. Still, when you really examine them by bringing mindfulness to the entire process of thinking and to our emotional lives, a lot of our thoughts are inaccurate, at best only partially true. Many are simply not true at all, although we invariably think they are. This can create huge problems for us, generating certain patterns of believing and behaving in which we can get caught for many, many years. It is very easy to be blind to the ways in which our thoughts create our reality. Our thought patterns can have a profound influence on how we see ourselves and others, what we think is possible, how confident we feel in our own ability to learn and grow and take action in our lives, even how happy we are, or aren't. Thought patterns can be grouped into categories and studied systematically by scientists to determine how people with a particular pattern compare with those with a different pattern.

Optimism and Pessimism: Basic Filters on the World

Dr. Martin Seligman is one of the principal founders of a new field known as positive psychology. For many years, he and his colleagues at the University of Pennsylvania and elsewhere studied the health differences between people who were identified as being basically optimistic or basically pessimistic in their thinking about why things happen to them. These two groups of people have very different ways of explaining the causes of what Dr. Seligman calls the "bad" events that happen to them in their lives. ("Bad" events include natural disasters, such as floods or earthquakes; personal defeats or setbacks, such as loss of a job or rejection by someone you care about; or an illness, injury, or other stressful occurrence.)

Some people tend to be pessimistic in the ways they explain the causes of a bad event to themselves. This pattern involves blaming themselves for the bad things that happen to them, thinking that the effects of whatever happened will last a long time and will affect many different aspects of their lives. Dr. Seligman refers to this attributional style, as it is technically called, as the "It's my fault, it's going to last forever, it's going to affect everything I do" pattern. In the extreme, this pattern reflects a person who is severely depressed, hopeless, and inordinately self-preoccupied. Some people call this mode of thinking *catastrophizing*. An example of this style might be the reaction "I always knew I was stupid, and this proves it; I can never do anything right" when you experience a failure of some kind.

An optimist experiencing the same event would see it quite differently. People who are optimists tend not to blame themselves for bad events or, if they do, they see them more as momentary occurrences that will get resolved. They tend to see bad events as limited in time and in how pervasive the damage they cause will be. In other words, they focus on the specific consequences of what happened and do not make sweeping global statements and projections that blow the event out of proportion. An example of this style might be "Well, I really blew it that time, but I'll figure out something, make some adjustments, and next time it will fly."

Dr. Seligman and his colleagues have shown that people who have a highly pessimistic attributional style are at significantly higher risk for becoming depressed when they encounter a bad event than are people who have an optimistic way of thinking. Pessimists are also more likely than optimists to come down with physical symptoms and show hormonal and immune system changes characteristic of increased susceptibility to disease following a bad event. In a study of cancer patients, these researchers showed that the worse the attributional style, the earlier the patient died of the disease. In another study they showed that baseball players in the Hall of Fame who had a pessimistic attributional style when they were young and healthy were more likely to die young than those who had an optimistic attributional style.

Dr. Seligman's overall conclusion from these and other studies is that it is not the world per se that puts us at increased risk of illness so much as how we see and think about what is happening to us. A highly pessimistic pattern of explaining the causes of bad or stressful events when they occur seems to have particularly toxic consequences. Dr. Seligman's work suggests that this way of thinking puts people at risk for illness and may explain why some people are more susceptible to illness and premature death than others, when other factors such as age, sex, smoking habits, and diet have been taken into account. A pattern of optimistic thinking in response to stressful events, on the other hand, appears to have a protective effect against depression, illness, and premature death.

Self-Efficacy: Your Confidence in Your Ability to Grow Influences Your Ability to Grow

One thought pattern that appears to be extremely powerful in improving health status is what is called *self-efficacy*. Self-efficacy is a belief in your ability to exercise control over specific events in your life. It reflects confidence in your ability to actually do things, a belief in your ability to make things happen, even when you might have to face new, unpredictable, and stressful occurrences. Classic studies by Dr. Albert Bandura and his colleagues at Stanford University Medical School showed that a strong sense of self-efficacy is the best and most consistent predictor of positive health outcomes in many different medical situations, including who will recover most successfully from a heart attack, who will be able to cope well with the pain of arthritis, and who will be able to successfully make lifestyle changes (such as quitting smoking). A strong belief in your ability to succeed at whatever you decide to do can influence the kinds of activities in which you will engage in the first place, how much effort you will put into something new and different before giving up, and how stressful your efforts to achieve control in important areas of your life will be.

Self-efficacy increases when you have experiences of succeeding at something you feel is important. For example, if you are practicing the body scan and, as a result, feel more in touch with your body and more relaxed, then that taste of success will lead you to feel more confident in your ability to relax when you want to. At the same time, such an experience will make it more likely that you will keep practicing the body scan.

Your self-efficacy can also increase if you are inspired by the examples of what other people are able to do. For instance, in the MBSR classes, when one person reports a positive experience with the body scan, say in regulating pain, it usually has a dramatic positive effect on other people in the class who may not yet have had such an experience. They are likely to say to themselves, "If that person can have such a positive experience, even with all of his problems, then I probably can as well, even with all of my problems" So seeing one person with a problem succeed, in the sense of having a positive experience, can boost everybody else's confidence in their own ability and in the efficacy of the practices they are working with.

Dr. Bandura and his colleagues studied self-efficacy in a group of men who had had heart attacks and were undergoing cardiac rehabilitation. They were able to show that those men who had a strong conviction that their heart was very robust and could recover fully were much less likely to be derailed from their exercise programs than were those who were less confident, even though the severity of heart disease in the two groups was the same. Those with high self-efficacy were able to exercise on the treadmill without worrying or feeling defeated by the discomfort, shortness of breath, and fatigue that are a natural and normal part of any exercise program. They were able to accept their discomfort without worrying that it was a "bad sign" and could focus instead on the positive benefits of their exercise program, such as feeling stronger and being able to do more. On the other hand, the men who did not have this kind of positive conviction tended to stop exercising, mistaking normal discomfort, shortness of breath, and fatigue for signs of an ailing heart. Further studies showed that when people who have low self-efficacy undergo training to develop mastery experiences, their confidence in their ability to function successfully and to positively influence areas of their lives that once felt out of their control grows and flourishes.

Another interesting line of research on the effects of thoughts and feelings on health involved studying people who seem to thrive on stress or who have survived extremely stressful situations. Here the goal was to see whether certain people have particular personality characteristics that may account for their apparent "immunity" to stress and to stress-related illnesses. Dr. Suzanne Kobasa of the City University of New York and her colleagues, and Dr. Aaron Antonovsky, a medical sociologist in Israel, both conducted studies in this area.

Hardiness

Dr. Kobasa studied business executives, lawyers, bus drivers, telephone company employees, and other groups of people who lead high-stress lives. In every group, as you might expect, she found some people who were much healthier than others experiencing the same amount of stress. She wondered whether the healthier people had some personality characteristic in common that might be protecting them from the negative effects of high stress. She found that a particular psychological characteristic differentiated those who got sick often from those who stayed healthy. She called this characteristic *psychological hardiness* (sometimes also referred to as *stress hardiness*).

As with the other psychological factors we have looked at, hardiness also involves a particular way of seeing oneself and the world. According to Dr. Kobasa, stress-hardy individuals show high levels of three psychological characteristics: *control, commitment,* and *challenge.* People who are high in control have a strong belief that they can exert an influence on their surroundings and can make things happen. This element is similar to Dr.

Bandura's notion of self-efficacy. People who are high in commitment tend to feel fully engaged in what they are doing from day to day and are committed to giving these activities their best effort. People who are high in challenge see change as a natural part of life that affords at least some chance for further development. This perspective allows stress-hardy individuals to see new situations more as opportunities and less as threats than might other people who do not share this orientation toward life as an ongoing challenge.

Dr. Kobasa emphasized that there are many things a person can do to increase his or her level of stress hardiness. The best way to develop greater hardiness is to come to grips with your own life by being willing to ask yourself hard questions about where your life is going and how it might be enriched by specific choices and changes you could make in the areas of control, commitment, and challenge. She also proposed that hardiness could be improved in high-stress work settings by restructuring roles and relationships within organizations to promote a greater sense of control, commitment, and a sense of challenge among employees. More and more, these principles are finding their way into present-day work settings as the complexity of work and its various challenges increases.

Sense of Coherence

Dr. Aaron Antonovsky's research focused on people who have survived extreme, almost unthinkable stress, such as prisoners in Nazi extermination camps. In Dr. Antonovsky's view, being healthy involves an ability to continuously restore balance in response to its continual disruption. He wondered what allowed some people to resist very high levels of stress even as their resources for coping with the stress and tension were constantly being disrupted during their imprisonment in the concentration camps. Dr. Antonovsky found that people who survive extreme stress have an inherent sense of coherence about the world and themselves. This sense of coherence is characterized by three components, which he termed *comprehensibility, manageability,* and *meaningfulness.* People who have a high sense of coherence have a strong feeling of confidence that they can make sense of their internal and external experience (that it is basically comprehensible), that they have the resources available to meet and manage the demands they encounter (manageability), and that these demands are challenges in which they can find meaning and to which they can commit themselves (meaningfulness). These qualities are beautifully encapsulated in the famous statement of Victor Frankl, himself a survivor of Auschwitz (and a neurologist and psychologist): "Everything can be taken from a man but one thing: the last of the human freedoms—to choose one's attitude in any given set of circumstances, to choose one's own way."

MBSR, Stress Hardiness, and Sense of Coherence

For a number of years we measured both stress hardiness and sense of coherence in our patients going through the MBSR program. We found that both measures increased over the eight weeks of the program. The increase wasn't large—it averaged about 5 percent—but it was significant. This was notable because both stress hardiness and sense of coherence are considered personality variables; in other words, they are traits that are unlikely to change in any significant way in adulthood. That is why, for instance, sense of coherence was used as a variable to distinguish those who seemed to survive the death camps with far less psychological damage from the trauma than other survivors who were more seriously affected. However, in MBSR, in eight short weeks, we were seeing a small but undeniable increase in these variables, which were not really supposed to change if they were fixed traits. Moreover, when we conducted follow-up studies, we found that even three years later, the increases in stress hardiness and sense of coherence had been maintained or had even increased slightly, up to about 8 percent on average. This was a rather remarkable finding. It suggested that something our patients were experiencing during MBSR was having a much more profound effect on them than merely reducing their physical and psychological symptoms—something more akin to a rearrangement in the way they were seeing themselves and their relationship to the world.

We shared these findings with Dr. Antonovsky a year or two before he died. He expressed surprise that we had observed such changes after such a brief intervention, especially one based primarily on non-doing. He had thought that only major social or political events on a large, disruptive, and transformative scale could result in such changes across the board in people. However, we had felt all along, based on anecdotal reports from our patients over the years, that they really were experiencing a profound shift in how they saw themselves as individual beings, as individual beings in relationship with other beings, and in relationship with the larger world. In fact, this intuition was the major reason we began looking at stress hardiness and sense of coherence in our patients in the first place, and specifically at the question of whether these measures would change over time. Perhaps future studies will support these early findings by correlating changes in these two measures with changes in particular brain regions known to be associated with the sense of self and relationality. But for our patients it won't matter. What matters is that such transformations can and do occur, regularly, and that they endure and even continue to deepen, especially with ongoing practice.

THE ROLE OF EMOTIONS IN HEALTH: CANCER

The studies we have looked at so far have had a predominantly cognitive focus, that is, they have looked primarily at thought patterns and beliefs and their effects on health and illness. A parallel line of research has concerned itself with the role of emotions in health and illness. Obviously our thought patterns and our emotions shape and influence each other. It is often difficult to determine in a particular situation whether one is more fundamental than the other. We will now take a look at some research findings from studies focusing primarily on the relationship between emotional patterns and health.

For some time now, there has been an ongoing debate about whether certain personality types are more prone to certain diseases. For instance, some studies suggested that there might be a "cancer-prone" personality, others that there is a "coronary-heart-disease-prone" personality. The cancer-prone pattern is frequently described as someone who tends to conceal his or her feelings and is very other-oriented while actually feeling deeply alienated from others and feeling unloved, and unlovable. Feeling a lack of closeness with one's parents when young is strongly associated with this pattern.

Much of the evidence in support of this link comes from a forty-year study conducted by Dr. Caroline Bedell Thomas of Johns Hopkins Medical School. Dr. Thomas collected large amounts of information on the psychological status of incoming medical students at Johns Hopkins starting in the 1940s and then followed these individuals periodically over the years as they got older and, in some cases, got sick and died. In this way she was able to correlate particular psychological characteristics and early family life experiences that these doctors reported when they were young (around age twenty-one) and healthy with a range of different diseases that some of them experienced over the next forty years. The results demonstrated, among other things, that *there was a particular constellation of features in early life that was associated with an increased likelihood of having cancer later in life.* Prominent among these characteristics were a lack of close relationship to parents and an ambivalent attitude toward life and human relationships. The conclusion, of course, is that our emotional experiences early in life may play a strong role in shaping our health later in life.

As we examine research relating thought patterns and emotional factors to health, it is important for us to keep firmly in mind that it is always dangerous and almost always wrong to assume that because a connection has been found between certain personality traits or behaviors and a disease, this means that being a certain way or thinking a certain way *causes* you to get a particular disease. It is more accurate to say that it may or may not increase to some extent (that extent depending on the strength of the correlation and a lot of other factors) your risk of getting the disease. This is because research studies always result in statistical relationships, not in a one-to-one correspondence. Not all people who have a particular personality trait that has been shown to be associated with cancer always get cancer. In fact, not all people who smoke cigarettes die from lung cancer, emphysema, or heart disease, even though smoking has been proven beyond all doubt to be a strong risk factor for all of these diseases. The relationship is a statistical one, having to do with probabilities.

Therefore it is wrong to conclude from any of the evidence pointing to a possible relationship between emotions and cancer that certain personality traits directly cause the disease. Nevertheless, there is mounting evidence that certain psychological and behavioral patterns may *predispose* a person to at least some forms of cancer, while other personality attributes may protect a person from cancer or increase the chances of surviving it. In this regard the feelings you experience toward yourself and other people and how you express or don't express them seem to be particularly important.

For example, Dr. David Kissen and his collaborators at the University of Glasgow in Scotland conducted a series of studies on men with lung cancer starting in the late 1950s. In one study they analyzed the personal histories of several hundred patients taken at the time they entered the hospital with chest complaints, but before any diagnosis was made. The men who were later found to have lung cancer reported significantly more adversities in childhood, such as an unhappy home or the death of a parent, than had those who turned out to have other diagnoses. This finding is consistent with Dr. Thomas's findings from the Johns Hopkins medical student study, in which she found that cancer later in life was associated with a lack of closeness to parents and ambivalent feelings toward relationships reported forty years earlier. In the Kissen study, those men who were found to have lung cancer had also reported more adversities as adults, including disturbed interpersonal relationships. The researchers observed that, as a group, those with lung cancer showed particular difficulty in expressing their emotions. They did not express their feelings about bad events, especially those that involved bonds with other people (such as marital problems or the death of somebody close to them), although, to the researchers, these were obviously sources of current emotional upset in their lives. Instead, the patients tended to deny that they were feeling emotional pain, and during the interviews they talked of their difficulties in matter-of-fact, emotionally flat tones that seemed inappropriate to the interviewers under the circumstances. This was in marked contrast to the patients in the control group (who were later found to have diseases other than lung cancer), who described similar situations with appropriate expressions of emotion.

The inability to express emotions was strongly linked to mortality among the lung cancer patients in this study. *Those lung cancer patients who had the poorest ability to express emotions had more than four and a half times the yearly death rate of those with the highest ability for emotional expression.* This finding held true regardless of whether or how much they smoked cigarettes, although, as you might expect, the heavy smokers had ten times the incidence of cancer as those who had never smoked.

More evidence relating emotional factors to cancer came from researchers at King's College Hospital in London, who conducted a similar study on women with breast cancer. Drs. S. Greer and Tina Morris conducted in-depth psychological interviews with 160 women when they were admitted to the hospital for a lump in the breast, before it was known whether or not it was cancerous. At the time of the interview, all the women were under the equal stress of not knowing whether they had cancer or not. The interviews with the women and with their husbands and other relatives were used as a means of measuring the degree to which the women concealed or expressed their feelings.

The majority of women who were later found not to have breast cancer had what these researchers termed a "normal" pattern of emotional expression. However, the majority of women who were later found to have breast cancer had a lifelong pattern of either extreme suppression of their feelings (for the most part, anger) or of "exploding" with emotion. Both extremes were associated with a higher risk of cancer. However, it was much more common for these women to suppress their feelings than to be "exploders."

In a five-year follow-up of fifty women with breast cancer, all of whom had been treated surgically, the researchers found that the women who were judged to be facing their situation three months after surgery with what they called a "fighting spirit," that is, a highly optimistic attitude and a belief in their own ability to survive, were much more likely to be alive than those who at three months post-surgery either had adopted an attitude of stoic acceptance toward their disease or were completely overwhelmed by it and felt helpless, hopeless, and defeated. Women who denied altogether that they had cancer, refused to discuss the subject, and showed no emotional distress about their situation also were much more likely to survive to five years. The results of this study suggest that emotions may play some role in cancer survival, with strong positive emotions (a fighting spirit, total denial) appearing protective and blocked emotional expression (stoicism or helplessness) decreasing survival. However, as these researchers themselves pointed out, their study was of a relatively small number of people and thus their findings can only be considered suggestive.

For unequivocal links to be established between a psychological characteristic and an illness, very large (and often extremely expensive) clinical trials need to be conducted. The results of one such study looked into the relationship of depression to cancer in more than six thousand men and women in the United States. Although many smaller and less well-designed studies had reported an association between depression and cancer, no link was found in this larger study. The group of people with symptoms of depression and the group that did not both had cancer rates of around 10 percent. Yet in animals, many well-designed studies do show an unequivocal link between the behavioral pattern of helplessness (which is related to depression), reduced immunological functions including natural killer cell levels, and increased tumor growth. Further research needs to be done on how these findings, along with work that has shown a link between helplessness in human beings and reduction in immune function, may relate to the apparent lack of correlation between depression and cancer seen in this clinical trial. This is an area of continued controversy.

Cancer is a condition in which cells within the body lose the biochemical mechanisms that keep their growth in check. Consequently, they multiply wildly, in many cases forming large masses called tumors. Many scientists believe that the production of cancerous cells in the body is happening at a low level all the time and that the immune system, when healthy, recognizes the abnormal cells and destroys them before they can do any damage. According to this model, it is when the immune system is weakened, either through direct physical damage or through the psychological effects of stress, and can no longer effectively identify and destroy these low levels of cancerous cells that the cancer cells multiply out of control. Then, depending on the type of cancer, either they develop a blood supply of their own and eventually form a solid tumor or they overwhelm the system with large numbers of circulating cancer cells, as in leukemia.

Of course, it is possible for a person to be exposed to such massive levels of carcinogenic substances that even a healthy immune system would be overwhelmed. This happened to people living in areas where there had been toxic dumping, such as the infamous Love Canal in New York State. Similarly, exposure to high doses of radiation, as occurred following the bombings of Hiroshima and Nagasaki and following the nuclear accident at Chernobyl, can provoke the formation of cancerous cells and at the same time weaken the immune system's ability to recognize and neutralize them. In short, the development of any kind of cancer is a multi-stage, complex occurrence involving our genes and cellular processes, the environment, and our individual behavior.

Even if it turns out that there is a statistically important relationship between negative emotions and cancer, to suggest to a person with cancer that his or her disease was caused by psychological stress, unresolved conflict, or unexpressed emotions would be totally unjustifiable. It amounts to subtly or not so subtly blaming the person for his or her disease. People often do this unwittingly, perhaps in an attempt to rationalize a painful reality and to cope with it better themselves. Whenever we can come up with an explanation for something, it makes us feel a little better because we can reassure ourselves, however wrongly, that we "understand" why that person "got" cancer. But doing this amounts to a violation of the other person's psychic integrity, based merely on ignorance and surmise. It also robs people of the present by directing their attention to the past just when they most need to focus and face the reality of having a life-threatening disease. Unfortunately, this kind of thinking, which seeks to attribute a subtle psychological deficiency as the "cause" of the cancer, has become fashionable in certain circles. This attitude is far more likely to result in increased suffering than in greater healing. From everything we know about the relationship between our emotions and our health, acceptance and forgiveness are what we need to cultivate to enhance healing, not self-condemnation and self-blame.

If a person who has cancer believes that stress or emotional factors may have been a factor in his or her illness, that is his or her prerogative. It may be very helpful to explore this question, and it may not be, depending on the person's life and on how the subject is approached. Some people are empowered by the realization that their handling of emotions in the past may have contributed to their illness. For them, it means that by becoming more aware of these particular issues and areas now, and making changes, they might be able to enhance their moment-to-moment quality of life and thereby, to whatever degree possible, their healing and recovery. But this perspective should not be imposed by someone else, however well-meaning the impulse behind the gesture may be. Explorations in this domain need to be undertaken with great compassion and caring, either by the person or with the help of a physician or therapist. Inquiry into possible factors that might have contributed to one's illness can help only if they come out of non-judging, out of generosity and compassion, and acceptance of one-self and of one's past, not out of condemnation.

Whether psychological factors played a causal or exacerbating role in a particular disease in a particular person will never be known with certainty. Since mind and body are not really separate in the first place, one's state of physical health will always be affected to some extent by psychological factors. But by the time a person has been diagnosed with a particular illness, the issue of causal psychological factors can be at best of secondary importance. At that juncture, it becomes much more important to take responsibility for what needs doing in the present. Since there is evidence that positive emotional factors can enhance healing, a diagnosis of cancer can be a particularly important turning point in a person's life, a time for mobilizing an optimistic, coherent, self-efficacious, and engaged perspective, and a time for working at being less susceptible to the pull of pessimistic, helpless, and ambivalent mind states. Purposefully directing gentleness, acceptance, and love toward oneself is a very good place to begin.

How do we go about that? We go about it by dropping in on ourselves in this moment, and befriending it; by taking up residency in awareness itself, resting in it, using any or all of the methods described in Part I to re-mind ourselves and re-body ourselves. In some profound sense, the rest takes care of itself.

MINDFULNESS AND CANCER

There are now a number of mindfulness-based approaches developed specifically for people who have cancer and want to work with it in the ways we have been describing. One is the Mindfulness-Based Cancer Recovery Program, developed by Linda Carlson and Michael Speca of the Tom Baker Cancer Center at the University of Calgary. They have published a number of papers showing major improvements in patients with breast cancer and prostate cancer on a range of physiological and psychological measures as a result of their cancer-oriented MBSR program. These include a one-year follow-up study showing enhanced quality of life, decreased stress symptoms, altered cortisol and immune patterns consistent with less stress and less mood disturbance, and decreased blood pressure. Another mindfulness-based program for cancer patients is MBCT for Cancer, a program developed by Trish Bartley and based on work at the University of North Wales in Bangor. Both teams have recently written books to make their programs more widely accessible.

HIGH BLOOD PRESSURE AND ANGER

There is evidence that suppressing emotional expression may play a role in hypertension as well as cancer. In this area the focus has been primarily on anger. People who habitually express anger when provoked by others have lower average blood pressures than people who habitually suppress such feelings. In a study of 431 adult men living in Detroit, Margaret Chesney, Doyle Gentry, and their collaborators found that blood pressure was highest in men reporting high job or family stress *and* a tendency to suppress feelings of anger. It seems that in high-stress situations, an ability to vent one's angry feelings is protective against high blood pressure. Other studies suggest that high blood pressure may be associated with both extremes of emotional behavior, either always suppressing anger or always expressing it overtly.

CORONARY HEART DISEASE, HOSTILITY, AND CYNICISM

Perhaps the greatest scientific scrutiny of personality factors in relationship to chronic disease has focused on the question of whether or not there is a heart-disease-prone personality. For some time it was thought that there was conclusive evidence of a particular behavior pattern associated with increased risk of coronary heart disease, known as type A behavior. Further research, however, showed that it was not the entire type A pattern that was related to heart disease, but only one aspect of it.

People with so-called type A personality are described as driven by a sense of time urgency and competitiveness. They are characteristically impatient, hostile, and aggressive. Their gestures and speech tend to be hurried and abrupt. In this terminology, people who do not show the type A pattern are referred to as type B. According to Dr. Meyer Friedman, one of the originators of the type A concept, type B's are more easygoing than type A's. They are not driven by time urgency and are free from a generalized irritability, hostility, and aggressiveness. They are also more inclined toward periods of contemplation. Yet there is no evidence that type B's are any less productive or less successful than type A's.

The original evidence relating type A behavior to coronary heart disease came from a large research project known as the Western Collaborative Group Study. This study characterized 3,500 men as either type A or type B when they were healthy and had no signs of disease. Eight years later they looked again to see who had developed heart disease and who had not. It turned out that the type A's developed coronary heart disease at two to four times the rate (depending on age, the younger men having the greater risk) of the type B's.

Many other studies confirmed the connection between the type A behavior pattern and coronary heart disease and demonstrated that it was true for women as well as for men. But other studies, particularly those by Dr. Redford Williams of Duke University Medical School and his collaborators, looked at just the hostility component of the type A behavior pattern and have found it to be a stronger predictor of heart disease all by itself than the full type A pattern. In other words, you are at less risk of heart disease as a type A if you are low in hostility, even if you feel a strong sense of time urgency and are competitive. What is more, *high hostility scores predicted not just myocardial infarction and death from heart disease but also increased risk of death from cancer and all other causes as well.*

In one fascinating study, Dr. Williams and his collaborators did a follow-up study on male physicians whose level of hostility on a particular psychological test had been measured when they were medical students twenty-five years earlier. They found that those men with low hostility scores when they were in medical school had about one-fourth the risk of having heart disease twenty-five years later as those with high hostility scores. When they looked at death from all causes, the results were also dramatic. Since they had graduated from medical school, only 2 percent of the men who were in the low-hostility group had died, whereas 13 percent of those in the high-hostility group had died in the same time period. In other words, those who showed high hostility on a psychological test they took twenty-five years in the past were dying at a rate six and a half times the rate of those whose hostility was low at that time.

Williams describes hostility as "an absence of trust in the basic goodness of others," grounded in "the belief that others are generally mean, selfish and undependable." He emphasizes that this attitude is usually acquired early in life from caregivers such as our parents or others and that it probably reflects an arrested development of basic trust. He points out that this attitude has a strong element of cynicism in it as well as hostility, as exemplified by two typical items on the questionnaire they used to measure hostility: "Most people make friends because friends are likely to be useful to them" and "I have frequently worked under people who seem to have things arranged so that they get credit for good work but are able to pass off mistakes onto those under them." Anyone who strongly believes these two statements probably has a very cynical view of people in general. With such a view of the world and other people, hostile and cynical people can be expected to feel anger and aggression much more frequently than others, whether they express it outwardly or attempt to suppress it under some circumstances.

The study of these doctors provides strong evidence that a hostile and cynical outlook on the world may, in and of itself, put one at much greater risk for illness and premature death than a more trusting view of people does. It seems that an ingrained cynical and hostile attitude is highly toxic to well-being. These and other findings are detailed in Dr. Williams's book *The Trusting Heart,* in which he also points out that all the major religious traditions of the world emphasize the value of developing qualities that science is now showing are good for your health, such as kindness, compassion, and generosity. In fact, there is a growing interest among researchers in studying the effects of such prosocial emotions (sometimes referred to as positive emotions) or virtuous qualities in parallel with research on the cultivation of mindfulness itself.

PROSOCIAL EMOTIONS AND HEALTH

For example, Barbara Fredrickson and her colleagues at the University of North Carolina at Chapel Hill have shown that nine weeks of training in lovingkindness meditation practice increased a sense of purpose and reduced symptoms of illness. The work of Paul Gilbert in the United Kingdom, Kristin Neff in Texas, and Christopher Germer at Harvard is showing that training in self-compassion and compassion for others results in major changes in physical, psychological, and relational well-being.

Interestingly enough, a recent clinical trial conducted by researchers from Northeastern University, Massachusetts General Hospital, and Harvard,* demonstrated that training in mindfulness over eight weeks, compared to training in compassion over the same time period, resulted in similar overt acts of coming to the aid of a person who appeared to be in a great deal of pain, even though others in the room were intentionally (because of the design of the experiment) ignoring that person's suffering. The meditators in both groups responded by helping more than five times as often as the subjects in a wait-list control condition who had not undergone either of the meditation trainings. There was no difference in the degree of helping displayed by the mindfulness group or the compassion group. This finding supports the view that mindfulness itself is an expression of kindness and compassion and can be deepened through ongoing practice.

Many other lines of evidence suggest that there is a strong relationship between emotions—and what is called *emotional style*—and health. These are expertly and compellingly described in the book *The Emotional Life of Your Brain,* by Richard Davidson, with Sharon Begley. Davidson's work has elucidated six dimensions of emotional style, which they describe as follows: *Resilience:* how slowly or quickly you recover from adversity; *Outlook*: how long you are able to sustain positive emotion; *Social Intuition:* how adept you are at picking up social signals from the people around you; *Self-Awareness:* how well you perceive bodily feelings that reflect emotions; *Sensitivity to Context:* how good you are at regulating your emotional responses to take into account the context you find yourself in; and *Attention:* how sharp and clear your focus is. As you can immediately see, these dimensions are all either aspects of the cultivation of mindfulness or stem from it. Most importantly, Davidson and Begley present convincing evidence that one's emotional style can be both accepted and, at the same time, transformed through meditation training.

* Condon, P, Desbordes, G, Miller, W, and DeStephano, D. Meditation Increases Compassionate Responses to Suffering. *Psychological Science,* 2013.

OTHER PERSONALITY TRAITS AND HEALTH

Motivation is another psychological characteristic that has been implicated in health. Dr. David McClelland, a renowned psychologist at Harvard in the 1960s and 1970s, identified a particular motivational profile that seemed to convey a greater susceptibility to disease than others. People who strongly display this characteristic, termed the *stressed power motivation,* demonstrate an intense need for power in their relationships with people. This power motive typically outweighs any need they might have for affiliation with people. They tend to be aggressive, argumentative, and competitive, and they are likely to join organizations in order to increase their personal status and prestige. But they also get very frustrated and feel blocked and threatened whenever stressful events occur that may challenge their sense of power. People with this particular motivational pattern get sick when under such stress much more readily than others who do not share this drive.

McClelland also identified an opposite motivational pattern that seems to confer hardiness or resistance to illness. He called it *unstressed affiliation motivation.* People who display high levels of unstressed affiliation are drawn to being with people and want to be friendly and liked by others, not as a means to an end (as with the cynical type A's) but as an end in its own right. They are also free to express their need for affiliation, since it is not blocked or threatened by the advent of stressful events. In a study of college students, those scoring above the average in stressed power motivation had more reported illness than other students, while those who were above average in unstressed affiliation motivation reported the least illness.

Once again, as with stress hardiness and sense of coherence, we find that there is convincing evidence that certain ways of looking at oneself and at the world can predispose a person to illness, while other ways seem to promote greater resilience and health. In an early pilot study in collaboration with Dr. McClelland and his colleagues, Joel Weinberger and Carolyn McCloud, we found that most people taking the MBSR program showed an increase on a measure of *affiliative trust* over eight weeks, while a group of patients waiting to get into the program and who were tested over the same time period showed no change on the same measure. This finding is emblematic of our patients' reports that their experience with MBSR often has a long-lasting and profoundly positive influence on their view of themselves and of the world, including an ability to be more trusting of themselves and of others.

SOCIAL INFLUENCES ON HEALTH

We have reviewed some of the evidence suggesting that our thought patterns, our beliefs, and our emotions—in short, our very personality—may affect our health in major ways. There is also considerable evidence that social factors, which of course are related to psychological factors, also play a major role in health and illness. It has long been known, for instance, that, statistically speaking, people who are socially isolated tend to be less healthy both psychologically and physically and more likely to die prematurely than people who have extensive social relationships. Death rates from all causes are higher in unmarried people than in married people at all ages. There seems to be something about having ties to others that is basic to health. Of course, this is intuitively understandable. It is deeply human to have a strong need to belong, to feel a part of something larger than oneself, to be in relationship with others in meaningful and supportive ways. The research on affiliative trust, compassion, and kindness suggest that these kinds of social bonds are extremely important for people's health and well-being.

Evidence supporting the importance of social connections for health has been bolstered by a number of major studies involving very large populations in this country and abroad. All show a relationship between ties to others and health. People who have a very low degree of social interaction in their lives, as measured by marital status, contacts with extended family and friends, church membership, and other group involvements, are between two and four times as likely to die in the succeeding ten-year period as are people who have a very high level of social interaction, when all other factors such as age, prior illness, income, health habits such as smoking and alcohol consumption, physical activity, race, and the like are taken into account. Social isolation and loneliness are now considered demonstrated risk factors for depression and cancer.

There are a number of studies that suggest why this might be so. Dr. James Lynch, of the University of Maryland and author of the classic text *The Broken Heart: The Medical Consequences of Loneliness,* has shown that physical contact with or even the presence of another person has a calming effect on cardiac physiology and reactivity in a stressful intensive care unit. More recently, as we saw earlier, David Creswell and his colleagues at Carnegie Mellon and UCLA have demonstrated that participation in an MBSR program can reduce loneliness in an elderly population. They were able to show not only that loneliness was reduced simply by participation in the MBSR program but also that the MBSR group had lower production of pro-inflammatory cytokines, compounds that are associated with many disease processes within the body, than those in a wait-list control group. Since loneliness is a major risk factor in the elderly for cardiovascular disease, Alzheimer's, and death, these findings are potentially very important, especially given the fact that, according to Dr. Creswell, efforts to diminish loneliness through social networking programs and developing community centers to encourage new relationships have not been effective.

In a series of on-going studies, Philippe Goldin, James Gross, and their colleagues at Stanford University are studying people diagnosed with what is called social anxiety disorder (SAD) before and after undergoing MBSR training, using fMRI brain scans. They found that people who completed MBSR showed improvements in anxiety and depression and an increase in self-esteem. When asked to practice awareness of breathing in the scanner, the MBSR group also showed what the researchers describe as decreased negative emotion experience, as well as marked reduction of activity in the amygdala, and increased activity in brain regions involved in regulating where one's attention goes. They also studied self-referential processing in the narrative brain region described earlier in the Toronto study (page xlii), which is involved in mind wandering in general and, in people with social anxiety, with an exaggerated and highly critical self-focus that makes social interactions very challenging and unsatisfying for them. They showed that activity in this narrative region was reduced after MBSR, suggesting greater control over such negative self-perspectives.*

In another classic study, Dr. Lynch showed that people lived longer after a myocardial infarction if they had a pet than if they didn't. He also showed that just the presence of a friendly animal can decrease one's blood pressure. This is suggestive evidence that *relationality* is key to our health. *And it is relationality above all else, we might say, that is at the heart of mindfulness.*

Interestingly, and not surprisingly, human-animal contact seems to benefit not only the humans but the pets as well. According to Dr. Lynch, petting reduces cardiovascular reactivity in stressful situations among dogs, cats, horses, and rabbits. One remarkable study of human-animal interaction came about after researchers at the University of Ohio noticed that rabbits on a high-fat, high-cholesterol diet designed to give them heart disease had much less severe heart disease if they were in lower cages in the room rather than higher ones. This finding didn't make any sense at all. Why should the position of their cages make a difference in the degree of heart disease when the rabbits were all genetically identical, were on the same diet, and were being treated the same way? Then one researcher observed that they were *not* being treated in exactly the same way. It turned out that one of the members of the team was taking out the rabbits in the lower cages from time to time, stroking them, and talking to them.

This led the researchers to perform a carefully controlled experiment, petting some rabbits and not others while keeping them all on the same high-fat, high-cholesterol diet. The results demonstrated conclusively that affectionate stroking of rabbits made them much more resistant to heart

* Goldin PR and Gross JJ. Effects of Mindfulness-based stress reduction (MBSR) on emotion regulation in social anxiety disorder. *Emotion* 2010; 10: 83-91.

disease than their unpetted kin. The petted rabbits had 60 percent less severe disease than the unpetted ones. They repeated the whole experiment a second time to make sure it wasn't a fluke and got exactly the same result.

To summarize, all the studies we have discussed and many others support the notion that our physical health is intimately connected with our patterns of thinking and feeling about ourselves and also with the quality of our relationships with other people and the world. The evidence suggests that certain patterns of thinking and certain ways of relating to our feelings can predispose us to illness. *Thoughts and beliefs that foster hopeless and helpless feelings, a sense of loss of control, hostility and cynicism toward others, a lack of commitment to meet life's challenges, an inability to express one's feelings, and social isolation all appear to be particularly toxic.*

On the other hand, other patterns of thinking, feeling, and relating appear to be associated with robust health. People who have a basically optimistic perspective, or at least those who have the ability to let go of a bad event, who can see that it is impermanent and that their situation will change, tend to be healthier than their pessimistic counterparts. Optimists know intuitively that there are always choices that can be made in life, that there is always the possibility of exercising some control or agency. They also tend to have a positive sense of humor and are able to laugh at themselves.

Other health-related psychological traits include a strong sense of coherence, the conviction that life can be comprehensible, manageable, and meaningful; a spirit of engagement in life, taking on obstacles as challenges; and confidence in one's ability to make changes that one decides are important; cultivating health-enhancing emotional styles, such as greater emotional resilience.

Healthy social traits include valuing relationships, honoring them, and feeling a sense of goodness and basic trust in people.

Since all the evidence we have looked at is only valid statistically, that is, for large populations of people, we cannot say that a particular belief or attitude or emotional style causes disease, only that more people get sick or die prematurely if they have strong patterns of thinking or behaving in such ways. As we will see in the next chapter, it makes more sense to think of health and illness as opposite poles of a continually changing and dynamical continuum rather than to think that you are either "healthy" or "sick." There will always be a flux of different forces at work in our lives at any given time; some may be driving us toward illness, others shifting the balance toward greater health. Some of these forces are under our control, or might be if we put all of our internal and external resources to work for us, whereas others lie beyond what any individual can influence. The degree of stress the system can take before it breaks down completely is not precisely known, and is very likely different for different people, and even different at different times for the same person. But this dynamical interplay of multiple forces that influence our health is happening wherever we are on the health-illness continuum at any particular time, and it goes on changing throughout our lives. The whole point of this book, and of MBSR, is that there is a lot that you can do to gently, lovingly, and firmly—through non-striving and non-doing, coupled with doing when taking action with awareness is called for—influence how things unfold across the life span, tilting them in the direction of greater well-being, self-compassion, and wisdom to whatever degree possible, always unknown.

HOW WE CAN USE THIS KNOWLEDGE IN OUR PRACTICE

The relevance of the evidence presented here to us as individuals lies primarily in our ability to bring awareness to our own thoughts and feelings and their physical, psychological, and social consequences *as we observe them.* If we can observe in ourselves the toxicity of certain beliefs, thought patterns, emotional patterns, and behaviors as they arise in the moment, then we can work to lessen their hold on us. Knowing something of the evidence, we might be motivated to look a little more closely at those moments when we find ourselves thinking pessimistically, suppressing our feelings of anger, or thinking cynically about other people or about ourselves. We might bring mindfulness to the consequences of these thoughts, feelings, and attitudes as they arise in us.

For instance, you might observe how your body feels when you hold in your anger. What happens when you let it out? What are its effects on other people? Can you see the immediate consequences of your hostility and distrust of others when these feelings surface? Do they cause you to jump to unwarranted conclusions or to think the worst of people and to say things you later regret? Can you see how such attitudes cause pain to others in the moment that they are happening? Can you see how these attitudes create unnecessary trouble and pain for you at the time that these feelings surface?

On the other hand, you might also be mindful of positive thoughts and affiliative emotions as they occur. How does your body feel when you see obstacles as challenges? How does it feel when you are experiencing joy? When you are trusting others? When you are generous and showing genuine kindness and concern? When you are loving? What are the effects of these inner experiences of yours and their outward manifestations on others? Can you see the immediate consequences of your positive emotional states and of your optimistic perspective at those times? Do these have an effect on other people's anxiety and pain? Is there a sense of greater peace within yourself in such moments?

If we can be aware—especially *in our own personal experience,* as well as from the evidence from scientific studies—that certain attitudes and ways of seeing ourselves and others are health-enhancing:—that affiliative trust, compassion, kindness, and seeing the basic goodness in others and in ourselves has intrinsic healing power, as does seeing crises and even threats as challenges and opportunities, then we can work mindfully to consciously develop these qualities in ourselves from moment to moment and from day to day. They become new options for us to cultivate. They become new and profoundly satisfying ways of seeing and being in the world.

16

Connectedness and Interconnectedness

Imagine the following famous experiment, which was carried out years ago by Judith Rodin and Ellen Langer, two very prominent social psychologists. They studied elderly residents in a nursing home. With the cooperation of the nursing home staff, Drs. Rodin and Langer divided the participants in the study into two groups that were the same in terms of age, sex, severity of illness, and kinds of illnesses. Then one group of people was explicitly encouraged to make more decisions for themselves about life in the nursing home, such as where to receive visitors and when to see movies, while the other group was explicitly encouraged to let the staff help them with these kinds of decisions.

As part of the study, each person was also given a plant for his or her room. However, the two groups of patients were told quite different things about the plant they were being given. People in the first group, those who were being encouraged to make more decisions for themselves, were told something like "This plant is to brighten up your room. It is your plant now, and whether it lives or dies is your responsibility. You decide when to water it and where it will do best." The people in the other group, who were encouraged to let the staff make decisions for them, were told something like "This plant is to brighten up your room a little. But don't worry, you don't have to water it or take care of it. The housekeeper will do that for you."

What Drs. Rodin and Langer found was that by the end of a year and a half, a certain number of people in both groups had died, as would have been predicted for these nursing home residents. But, remarkably, the two groups differed dramatically in how many people had died. It turned out that the people who were encouraged to let the staff help them with their decisions about visitors and other details of their lives and who were told that the staff would take care of the plant they had been given died at the same rate as was usually seen in that nursing home. But the people who were encouraged to make decisions for themselves and who were told that the plant was their responsibility died at about half the usual rate.

Rodin and Langer interpreted these findings to mean that enabling these nursing home residents to take more control in their lives, even over seemingly little decisions such as when to water the plant, protected them from an earlier death in some way. Anybody who is familiar with nursing homes knows that few things in that environment are ever really under a resident's control. This interpretation is consistent with Dr. Kobasa's work on psychological hardiness, which, as we saw in the preceding chapter, identified a sense of control as one important factor in resistance to illness.

There is a complementary interpretation to the nursing home experiment that I find myself drawn to, one that places the emphasis slightly differently. One might equally say that those people who were told that it was their responsibility to take care of the plant were given an opportunity to feel needed in some small way, and perhaps even to bond with the plant. In fact, they may have come to feel that the plant depended on them for its well-being. This way of looking at the experiment emphasizes the *connectedness* between the person and the plant rather than the exercise of control. It is at least plausible that the encouragement to make decisions for themselves about when and how to care for their plant, as well as decisions about where to meet visitors and when to go to the movies, led to them feeling as if they were participating more, were connected more with the nursing home, and *belonged* there more than the group that was not encouraged in this way.

When you feel connected to something, that connection immediately gives you a purpose for living. Relationship itself gives meaning to life. We have already seen that relationships, even relationships with pets, are protective of health. We have also seen that affiliation, meaning, and a sense of coherence are attributes of well-being. We have even said that at its core, mindfulness is about *relationality*.

Meaning and relationship are strands of connectedness and interconnectedness. They weave your life as an individual into a larger tapestry, a larger whole, which, you might say, actually gives your life its individuality. In the case of the plant experiment in the nursing home, we might suppose that those people who were given the plant but were not told that they were to be responsible for it would be less likely to develop this kind of connectedness with the plant. It is more likely that they saw the plant as just another neutral item in the room, like the furniture, rather than as something that depended on them for its well-being.

To my mind, connectedness (and interconnectedness, which emphasizes the intrinsic reciprocity of all relationships) may be what is most fundamental about the relationship of what we call *mind* to physical and emotional health. The studies of social involvement and health certainly suggest that this is so. They show that just the *number* of relationships and connections one has through marriage, family, church, and other organizations is a strong predictor of mortality. This is a very crude measure of relationship, since it does not take into account the *quality* of those relationships, their meaningfulness to the individuals studied, and how reciprocal they are experienced to be.

It would not be hard to imagine that a happy hermit, living in isolation, might feel connected to everything in nature and all people on the planet and not be at all affected by a dearth of human neighbors. We might speculate that such a person probably would not suffer ill health or premature death from such voluntary isolation. On the other hand, people who are married might have very rocky and tenuous connections, which might make for very high stress and a susceptibility to illness and premature death. Still, the fact that studies show a strong relationship between the sheer number of social connections and the death rate in large populations implies that our connections play very powerful roles in our lives. It suggests that even negative or stressful connections with people may be better for our health than isolation, unless we know how to be happy alone, which few of us do.

Many studies with animals also support the idea that connectedness is important for health. As we have seen, stroking and petting appear to be health-enhancing for both people and animals. Animals raised in isolation when they are young never function as normal adults and tend to die sooner than animals raised among littermates. Four-day-old monkeys will cling to a surrogate "mother" made of terry cloth if separated from their real mother. They will spend more time in physical contact with the soft cloth "mother" than with a wire-mesh surrogate, even when the wire one provides milk and the soft one doesn't. Dr. Harry Harlow of the University of Wisconsin performed such experiments in the late 1950s and clearly demonstrated the importance of warm physical contact between mother and infant in monkeys. Harlow's baby monkeys chose soft touch with an inanimate object over physical nourishment.

The renowned anthropologist Ashley Montagu documented the profound importance of touch and its relationship to physical and psychological well-being in a remarkable book called *Touching: The Human Significance of the Skin.* Physical touch is one of humanity's most basic ways of connecting. For instance, shaking hands and hugging are symbolic rituals that communicate an openness to connecting. They are formalized acknowledgments of relationship. And, when engaged in with mindful and heartful presence, they become much more, transcending mere formality and tapping a deeper domain of connectedness. They serve as a channel for mutual recognition and acknowledgment, giving rise to the possibility of expressing authentic feelings and even differences in views and aspirations in ways that might be mutually beneficial.

While physical touch is a wonderful way in which to communicate our feelings, it is hardly the only one. We have many other channels for touching besides the skin. We make contact with each other and connect through all our senses—with our eyes, our ears, our noses, our tongues—our bodies, and our minds. These are our doors of connection to each other and to the world. They can hold extraordinary meaning when the contact is made with awareness rather than out of habit.

When touching is perfunctory or habitual, the meaning embodied in it rapidly changes from connectedness to disconnectedness and from there to feelings of frustration or annoyance. No one likes to be treated mechanically, and we certainly do not like to be touched mechanically. If we think for a moment about making love, one of the most intimate expressions of human connectedness through touching, we might recognize and admit to ourselves that lovemaking suffers when the touching is automatic and mechanical. It is almost always felt as lacking in affection and true intimacy, an absence of connection, a sign that the other person is not fully present. This distance can be felt in all aspects of the touching: in body language, timing, movement, and speech. Perhaps one person's mind is elsewhere in a particular moment. This can lead to a break in the energy flow between the two people. When this happens, it seriously erodes positive feelings. If it becomes a chronic pattern, it can easily lead to resentment, resignation, and alienation. But usually an inability to bring awareness and embodied presence to making love and to experiencing a deep connectedness with the other person is only symptomatic of a larger pattern of disconnectedness, one likely to manifest itself in various ways in the relationship, not just in bed.

We might say that the degree to which a person's mind and body are connected and in harmony reflects the degree of awareness that person brings to present-moment experience. If you are not in touch with yourself, it is very unlikely that your connections with others will be satisfactory in the long run. The more centered you are within yourself, the easier it will be for you to be centered in your relationships with others, to appreciate the various threads of connection that give meaning to your world, and to fine-tune them as things change and life unfolds. This is a very fruitful area of application of the meditation practice, as you will see in Part IV.

In the last chapter we saw that a lack of closeness to one's parents during childhood was associated with an increased risk of cancer in Dr. Caroline Bedell Thomas's study of doctors. We might speculate that this has something to do with the extreme importance of early experiences of connectedness to later health as an adult. Perhaps it is in childhood that all the positive attitudes, beliefs, and emotional competencies that we looked at in the last chapter, and in particular, basic human trust and the need for affiliation, take root. If we were denied such experiences in childhood, for whatever reasons, it is likely that special attention to the cultivation of those qualities will be particularly important if we are to experience ourselves as whole when we are adults.

The fact is that everybody's original experiences of life were literally and biologically experiences of connectedness and oneness. Each of us came into the world through the body of another being. We were once part of our mother, connected to her body, contained within it. We all bear the sign of that connectedness. Surgeons know not to excise the belly button if they have to make a midline incision; nobody wants to lose his or her belly button, "useless" though it is. It's a sign of where we came from, our membership card in the human race.

After babies are born, they immediately seek another channel for connecting to their mother's body. They find it through nursing if their mothers are aware of this channel and value it. Nursing is reconnecting, a merging again into oneness, this time in a different way. Now the baby is on the outside, her body separate yet drawing life from the mother's body through the breast while touching her, being warmed by her body, enveloped in her gaze and sounds. These are early moments of connectedness, moments that cement and deepen the bond between mother and child even as the baby gradually learns about being separate.

Without parents or others to care for them, human babies are completely helpless. Yet protected and cared for within the web of connectedness that the family represents, babies thrive and grow, complete and perfect in themselves yet utterly dependent on others for their basic needs. Each one of us was at one time this complete and also this helpless.

As we grew older, we found out more and more about our separateness and individuality, about having a body, about "me," "my," and "mine," about having feelings, about being able to manipulate objects. As children learn to separate and to feel themselves as separate selves with increasing age, they also need to continue to feel connected in order to feel secure and in order to be psychologically healthy. *They need to feel that they belong.* It is not a matter of being dependent or independent, but of being *interdependent.* They can no longer be one with their mothers in the old ways, but they do need to experience ongoing emotional connections with them and with their fathers and others in order ultimately to feel whole themselves.

The energy that feeds this ongoing connectedness, of course, is love. But love itself needs nurturing to flower fully, even between children and parents. It's not that it isn't "always there" so much as that it can easily be taken for granted and remain underdeveloped in its expression. It needs to be "always here" as well as always there. It means little if you love your children (or your parents for that matter) deep in your heart but the expression of it is constantly being subverted or inhibited by strong feelings of anger, resentment, or alienation. Love means little if the major way you have to express it is to pressure others to conform to your views of how they should be or what they should do. It is particularly unfortunate if you have no awareness of what you are doing at such times and no sense of how it is being perceived by others, especially your child.

The path to developing our capacity to express love more fully is to bring awareness to our actual feelings, to observe them mindfully, to work at being non-judgmental and more patient and accepting. If we ignore our feelings and the ways in which we behave, and just coast in the belief that the love is there and that it is strong and good, sooner or later our connections with our children may become strained, badly frayed, or even broken. This is especially so if we are unable to see and accept them for who they actually are. This is an area in which regular practice of lovingkindness meditation (see Chapter 13), even for brief moments, can provide strong nourishment for the outward expression of our unconditional loving feelings. It also raises the possibility of bringing greater mindfulness to the ongoing adventure of parenting. Indeed, there is now a whole new field in psychology studying mindful parenting.

The majority of pediatricians and child psychologists used to believe that babies were senseless when they were born, that either they couldn't feel pain in the way adults do or that it wouldn't affect them if they did, because they wouldn't remember it later, and that therefore it didn't matter how you treated children when they were babies. What the mothers felt was probably quite different, but even a mother's instinctive responses to her baby are strongly influenced by cultural norms and especially by the authoritative pronouncements of pediatricians.

More recent studies of newborn babies have dispelled the viewpoint that they are insensitive to pain and unaware of the outside world at birth. They show that babies are alert and aware even in the womb. From the time they are born and even before, their view of the world and their feelings are being shaped by the messages they receive from the surrounding environment. Some studies suggest that if a newborn baby and its mother are separated at birth for a prolonged period, usually due to medical circumstances totally beyond the control of the mother, and if consequently the normal infant-maternal bonding process is unable to occur within that time, the future emotional relationship between the child and the mother may be more emotionally disturbed and distanced. The mother may never feel the strong attachment toward that child that mothers usually do. There may be a lack of feelings of deep connectedness. No one can say with certainty how this might translate into specific emotional or health problems for this child twenty or thirty years later, but there appears to be some connection.

The work of John Bowlby, Mary Ainsworth, D. W. Winnicott, and others has led to the emergence of a new field in psychology called *attachment research,* which emphasizes the quality of the parent-child relationship and its effects on the child's development. Secure attachment leads to a robust sense of well-being in the child as he or she gets older. Insecure attachment or other disordered forms of attachment often lead to significant problems right across the developmental spectrum and into adulthood. Psychiatrist Daniel Siegel has argued that the tenets of secure attachment exactly mirror the elements of mindfulness as taught in MBSR.

Early childhood experiences of isolation, cruelty, violence, and abuse, the exact opposite of secure attachment, can lead to severe emotional disabilities in later life. They strongly shape a person's view of the world as meaningful or meaningless, benevolent or uncaring, manageable or unmanageable, and of himself or herself as worthy or unworthy of love and esteem. While some children are true survivors and find ways of growing and healing from such experiences no matter what, countless others may not recover from the early rupture of their connections with warmth, acceptance, and love. They carry around scars that have never healed and that are seldom even understood or defined. This is now understood to be a signature of post-traumatic stress disorder. More and more therapies are now available to treat it, with mindfulness-based approaches increasingly at the forefront of these efforts, both for early childhood trauma and for veterans returning from the wars in Iraq and Afghanistan. And let us keep in mind, as we have already noted, that while the most horrific experiences in early childhood come from abuse of all kinds, accidents and loss, murderous assaults in schools, and all-out war often, what we have referred to as "big-*T* trauma," there is also increasing recognition that all of us, to one degree or another, may be suffering from "little-*t* trauma," disorganizing events from our past that may be harder to pinpoint but which, unrecognized and unmet, can also lead to significant suffering and a sense of being impaired or stuck in dysfunctional patterns of behavior. Children of alcoholics and drug addicts, as well as young victims of physical or sexual abuse, often suffer grievously in this way in addition to the big-T trauma they experience, but others who may have been less overtly abused can also carry deep emotional scars and wounds from simply feeling unseen or unmet by their parents or others while they were growing up.

A lack of closeness with your parents when you were a child can leave a deep wound, whether you are conscious of it or not. It is a healable wound, but it needs to be recognized as a wound, as a broken connection, if deep psychological healing is to occur. It may well express itself in feelings of alienation, even from your body. This too is healable. The woundedness of our connection to our own body at times cries out for healing. Yet too often these cries go unheeded or unrecognized, even unheard.

What would it take to initiate the healing of such wounds? First, an acknowledgment that they are here. Second, a systematic way of listening to and reestablishing a sense of connectedness with your own body, and with your positive feelings toward it and toward yourself.

We see such wounds and the scarring they produce every day in the Stress Reduction Clinic. Many people come to the clinic with much more pain than only that caused by their physical problems and by the stress in their lives. Many find it difficult to feel much, if any, love and compassion for themselves. Many feel unworthy of love and unable to express warmth toward members of their own family, even when they want to. Many feel disconnected from their bodies and have a hard time feeling anything, or knowing what they are feeling. Their lives may feel devoid of any sense of personal or interpersonal coherence or connectedness. Many got messages from their parents or from school, or from church, or sometimes from all three when they were children, that they were bad, stupid, ugly, unworthy, or selfish. Those messages were internalized, becoming part of their self-image and of their view of the world, and were carried into adulthood deep in their own psyches.

Of course, for the most part adults, whether they be parents, teachers, or clergy, don't *mean* to give children such messages. It is just that if we don't pay attention to this domain in our relationships, we may hardly ever be aware of the real import of what we are doing or saying. We have elaborate psychological defenses that allow us to believe unquestioningly that we know what is best for children, that we know exactly what we are doing and why. Most of us would be shocked if a neutral third party were to suddenly stop the action at certain times and point things out from the perspective of the child, or to highlight the likely consequences to the child of what we were saying or doing.

To take a simple example, when a parent calls a child a "bad boy" or a "bad girl," in all likelihood what is really meant is that the parent does not like what the child is doing. But that is not what is actually being communicated. What is being communicated is that the child is "bad." When a child hears this, the tendency is to take it literally: that he or she is unworthy of love. This message is all too easily internalized by the child. It is all too easy to think that there really is something wrong with you. Sometimes parents even say outright, "I don't know what is the matter with you!"

It is likely that the sum total of subtle psychological violence perpetrated on children by parents, teachers, and other adults who are not conscious of their actions and the effects of these actions on the self-esteem of children far exceeds the epidemic proportions of outright physical and psychological abuse of children in our society, and influences generation after generation of people in terms of how they feel about themselves and what they conceive of as possible in their lives. We carry around the scars of such treatment in the form of a lot of missed connections and sometimes imprisoning schemas we can continually recreate for ourselves related to core issues such as abandonment, unworthiness, failure, or victimization. We try to compensate in many ways in order to feel good deep in our hearts. But until the wounds are healed rather than covered over and denied, our efforts are not likely to result in wholeness or health. They are more likely to result in disease. We have already seen quite a few examples of this.

A MODEL OF CONNECTEDNESS AND HEALTH

In the late seventies, a general self-regulatory model was proposed by Gary Schwartz, then at Yale University, that attributed the ultimate origin of disease to disconnectedness and the maintenance of health to connectedness. This model was based on a systems perspective, which, as we saw in Chapter 12, considers complex systems of any kind as "wholes" rather than reducing the whole to its component parts and only considering the parts in isolation. This model has been developed and deepened over the years by Dr. Schwartz's student, Dr. Shauna Shapiro, of Santa Clara University, herself a mindfulness researcher, and is one example of how the new paradigm in science is finding ongoing expression within medicine.

We saw in Chapter 12 that living systems maintain inner balance, harmony, and order through their capacity to self-regulate via feedback loops between particular functions and systems. We saw that heart rate varies with the degree of muscle exertion, and when we eat varies as a function of hunger. Self-regulation is the process whereby a system maintains stability of functioning and, at the same time, adaptability to new circumstances. It includes regulating the flow of energy in and out of the system and the use of that energy to maintain the living system's organization and integrity in a complex and ever-changing dynamical state as it interacts with the environment—what is technically called *allostasis*. In order to achieve and maintain a condition of self-regulation, the individual parts of the system need to continually relay information about their status to the other parts of the system with which they interact. That information can be used to regulate, in other words, to selectively control or modulate the functioning of the network of individual parts to maintain an overall balance of energy and information flow within the system as a whole.

Dr. Schwartz used the term *disregulation** to describe what happens when a normally integrated self-regulating system, such as a human being, becomes imbalanced with regard to its feedback loops. Disregulation follows as a consequence of a disruption or *disconnection* of essential feedback loops. A disregulated system loses its dynamic stability, in other words, its inner balance. It tends to become less rhythmic and more *disordered* and is then less able to use whatever feedback loops are still intact to restore itself. This disorder can be seen in the behavior of the system as a whole and by observing its component parts in interaction. The disordered be-

* Commonly spelled *dysregulation* as well.

havior of a living system such as a person is usually described medically as a *disease.* The specific disease will depend on which particular subsystems are most disregulated.

The model emphasized that one major cause of disconnection in people is *disattention,* that is, not attending to the relevant feedback messages of our body and our mind that are necessary for their harmonious functioning. In his model, disattention leads to disconnection, disconnection to disregulation, disregulation to disorder, and disorder to disease.

Conversely, and very importantly from the point of view of healing, the process can work in the other direction as well. Attention leads to connection, connection to regulation, regulation to order, and order to ease (as opposed to dis-ease), or, more colloquially, to health. So, without going into all the physiological details of our feedback loops, we can simply say in general terms that the quality of the connections within us and between us and with the wider world determines our capacity for self-regulation and healing. And the quality of those connections is maintained and can be restored by paying attention to relevant feedback.

So it becomes important to ask, what does relevant feedback mean? What does it look like? Where should we be putting our attention in order to move from disease toward "ease," from disorder toward order, from disregulation toward self-regulation, from disconnectedness toward connectedness? Some concrete examples may help you to grasp the simplicity and power of this model in practical terms and relate it to the meditation practice. When your whole organism, your body and your mind together, is in a relatively healthy state, it takes care of itself without too much attention. For one thing, almost all of our self-regulatory functions are under the control of the brain and the nervous system and are ordinarily occurring without our conscious awareness. And we would hardly want to control them consciously for any length of time, even if it were possible. It would leave us no time for anything else.

The beauty of the body is that ordinarily our biology takes care of itself. Our brain is continually making adjustments in all of our organ systems in response to the feedback it gets from the outside world and from the organs themselves. But some vital functions do reach our consciousness and can be attended to with awareness. Our basic drives are one example. We eat when we are hungry. The message in the "hungry" feeling is feedback from the organism. We eat, and then we stop eating when we are full. The message in the "full" feeling is feedback from the body that it has had enough. This is an example of self-regulation.

If you eat for other reasons than because your body is producing a "hungry" message—perhaps because you are feeling anxious or depressed, emotionally empty or unfulfilled, and you seek to fill yourself in any way you can—a lack of attention to what you are doing and the consequences of it may throw your system seriously and dangerously out of whack, especially if it becomes a chronic behavior pattern. You might wind up eating compulsively, overriding the feedback messages from the body telling you that it has had enough. The simple process of eating when hungry and stopping when full can become highly disregulated in this way and lead to disease, in this case a range of eating disorders from binge eating to anorexia, as well as to the obesity epidemic in postindustrial societies.

Pain and feeling sick are also messages that should cause us to pay attention, because they help reconnect us to some basic needs of the organism. For example, if our response to stomach pain from repeatedly eating certain foods, from stress, or from too much alcohol or smoking, is simply to take antacids and continue to live in the same old way, we are not heeding this highly relevant message from our own body. Instead, we are unknowingly disconnecting from the body and thus overriding its efforts to restore balance and order. On the other hand, when we attend to such a message, we are likely to modify our behavior in some way or other in order to seek relief and restore regulation and order to the system. We will return to the whole question of paying appropriate attention to our body's messages in Chapter 21.

When we seek help from doctors, they become part of our feedback system. They pay attention to our complaints and to what they can detect in our bodies using their diagnostic tools. Then they prescribe whatever treatments they believe appropriate to reconnect the feedback loops within the organism so that it can self-regulate once again. And what we tell them about the effects of their treatment gives *them* feedback that might cause them to modify their approach, since we are usually closer to what is happening within our body than they are.

We function relatively well without awareness because so many of our connections and feedback loops within the body take care of themselves when we are relatively healthy. But when the system goes out of balance, *the restoring of health requires some attention to reestablish connectedness.* We must be aware of the feedback to know whether the responses we are making are moving us in a direction of greater health and well-being. And even when we are relatively healthy, the more we intentionally tune in to and establish sensitive connections with our body, our mind, and the world, the more likely we will be able to move the system as a whole to even greater levels of balance and stability. *Since the processes of healing and "diseasing" can be thought of as happening all the time within us, their relative balance at any point in our lives may hinge on the quality of attention we bring to the experience of our body and mind and the degree to which we can establish a comfortable level of connectedness and acceptance.* While this may happen automatically to some degree on its own, the intentional cultivation of attention and sustaining it over time in a disciplined way, as Shauna Shapiro emphasizes in her modification of Schwartz's original model, is usually necessary to drive the system in the direction of connection, regulation, order, and health. And this is, of course, where mindfulness comes into the picture, since mindfulness *is* the intentional cultivation of attention, coupled with the foundational attitudes presented in Chapter 2. Dr. Shapiro and her colleagues have developed this model, which they now call the IAA (intention, attention, attitude) model, over the years and have used it to great advantage to explore the ways in which mindfulness may be exerting the positive effects on health that are increasingly being seen in research studies at both the biological and psychological levels.

Most of us are not particularly sensitive to either our body or our thought processes. This becomes all too clear when we begin to practice mindfulness. We can be surprised at how difficult it is just to listen to the body or attend to our thoughts simply as events in the field of awareness. When we work systematically to bring our undivided attention into the body, as we do when we practice the body scan or the sitting meditation, or the yoga, we are increasing our connectedness with it. We inhabit it more fully; we befriend it. Therefore, we are more intimate with it. We know our body better as a result. We trust it more, we read its signals more accurately, and we know how good it can feel to be completely at one with our body, at home in our own skin, even for brief moments. We also learn to regulate its level of tension during the day, intentionally, in ways that are not possible without awareness.

The same is true for our thoughts and emotions and for our relationship to the environment. When we are mindful of the process of thought itself, we can more readily catch our own lapses of mind, the inaccuracies in our thinking, and the self-subverting behaviors that often follow from them. As we have seen, the great delusion of separateness that we indulge in, coupled with our deeply conditioned habits of mind, the scars we carry, and our general level of unawareness, can result in particularly toxic and disregulating consequences for both our body and our mind. The overall result is that we may feel deeply inadequate when it comes to facing, living within, and working with the full catastrophe of our lives.

On the other hand, the more conscious we are of the interconnectedness of our thoughts and emotions, our choices and our actions in the world, the more we can see with eyes of wholeness, the more effective we will be when faced with obstacles, challenges, and stress.

If we wish to mobilize our most powerful inner resources to help us to move toward greater levels of health and well-being, we will have to learn how to tap into them in the face of the sometimes blistering levels of stress that we live immersed in. Toward this end, in the following section we will examine what we mean by stress in the first place. We will look at the common ways we react to it and how stress can disregulate our bodies, our brains, our minds, and our very lives. We will also explore how we might make use of that very same stress to learn, to grow, to make new choices, and thus, to heal and to come to peace within ourselves.

III

Stress

17

Stress

The popular name for the full catastrophe nowadays is stress. Any concept that covers such a broad scope of life circumstances as does this particular term is bound to be somewhat complex. Yet at its heart the notion of stress is also very simple. It unifies a vast array of human responses into a single concept with which people strongly identify. As soon as I say to someone that my job is in stress reduction, the response is invariably, "Oh, I could really use that." People know exactly what stress means, at least to them.

But stress occurs on a multiplicity of levels and originates from many different sources. We all have our own version of it, one that may be continually changing in its details while its overall pattern remains the same. In order to understand what stress is in its broadest formulation and to know how to work with it effectively under many different circumstances, it makes sense to think about it from a systems perspective. In this chapter we will look at the origin of the concept of stress, at various ways of defining it, and at a unifying principle that will help us to handle it more effectively in our own lives.

Stress can be thought of as acting on different levels, including the physiological level, the psychological level, and the social level. As you might expect, all these levels interact with each other. These multiple interactions influence the actual state of your body and mind under specific circumstances. They also influence the range of options you have for facing and coping with stressful events. For simplicity, we will consider these various levels separately while keeping in mind that they are interconnected and are different aspects of one phenomenon.

Dr. Hans Selye first popularized the term *stress* in the 1950s based on his extensive physiological studies of what happens when animals are injured or placed under unusual or extreme conditions. In its popular usage the word has become an umbrella term connoting all the various pressures we experience in life. Unfortunately, this way of using the word does not indicate whether stress is the *cause* of the pressures we feel or the *effect* of those pressures, or in more scientific terms, whether stress is the stimulus or the response. We often say things like "I feel stressed," which implies that stress is what we are experiencing in response to whatever is making us feel that way. On the other hand, we may say something along the lines of "I've got a lot of stress in my life," which implies that stress is an outside stimulus that causes us to feel a certain way.

Selye opted to define stress as a response, and he coined another word, *stressor,* to describe the stimulus or event that produced the stress response. He defined stress as "the non-specific response of the organism to any pressure or demand." In his terminology, stress is the total response of your organism (mind *and* body) to whatever stressors you experience. But the picture is further complicated by the fact that a stressor can be an internal occurrence or event as well as an external one. For instance, a thought or a feeling can cause stress and therefore can be a stressor. Or, under other circumstances, that same thought or feeling might be a response to some outside stimulus and therefore be the stress itself.

The interplay of external and internal factors in identifying the ultimate cause of disease was very much in Selye's mind when he developed his theory of stress and the notion that diseases could originate from failed attempts to adapt to stressful conditions. Thirty years before the emergence of the field of psychoneuroimmunology, Selye was well aware that stress could compromise immunity and therefore resistance to infectious organisms:

> Significantly, an overwhelming stress (caused by prolonged starvation, worry, fatigue, or cold) can break down the body's protective mechanisms. This is true both of adaptation which depends on chemical immunity and of that due to inflammatory barricades. It is for this reason that so many maladies tend to become rampant during wars and famines. If a microbe is in or around us all the time and yet causes no disease until we are exposed to stress, what is the "cause" of our illness, the microbe or the stress? I think both are—and equally so. In most instances, disease is due neither to the germ as such, nor to our adaptive reactions as such, but to the inadequacy of our reactions against the germ.

The genius of Selye's insight was in emphasizing the non-specificity of the stress response. He claimed that the most interesting and fundamental aspect of stress was that the organism undergoes a generalized physiological response in its efforts to adapt to the demands and pressures it experiences, whatever they might be. Selye called this response the *general adaptation syndrome* and saw it as a pathway by which organisms are able to maintain fitness, even life itself, in the face of threat, trauma, and change. He emphasized that stress is a natural part of life and cannot be avoided. Yet at the same time, stress ultimately requires adaptation if the organism is to survive.

Selye saw that, under certain circumstances, stress might lead to what he called *diseases of adaptation.* In other words, our actual attempts to respond to change and to pressure, no matter what their particular source, might *in themselves* lead to breakdown and disease if they are inadequate or disregulated. From this it follows that the more we can bring attention to the effectiveness of our efforts to cope with the stressors we experience, the more we will be able to guard against disregulation and perhaps avoid making ourselves sick or sicker.

Of course now, sixty years later, a great deal more is known about the key roles that the brain, the nervous system, emotions, and cognitions play in all of this, and the various biological mechanisms that are at work in how we experience stress and deal with it for better (adaptively) or for worse (maladaptively). It turns out that we have a great deal of choice in the matter. Agency and awareness make a huge difference.

As we saw when we discussed Dr. Seligman's studies on optimism and health, *it is not the potential stressor itself but how you perceive it and then how you handle it that will determine whether or not it will lead to stress.* We all know this from personal experience. Sometimes the slightest little thing can trigger an emotional overreaction in us, completely out of proportion to the offending event itself. This is more likely to happen at times when we are under pressure and we feel anxious and vulnerable. At other times we might be able to handle not just little annoyances but major emergencies with almost no sense of effort. At such moments you may not even realize that you are under stress. It may only be later, after the event is over, that you feel the effects of what you went through, perhaps in the form of feeling emotionally drained or physically exhausted.

To some extent, our ability to cope with stressors depends on how virulent they are. At one end of the spectrum are stressors that, if not avoided, will destroy life regardless of the way we perceive them. Among these are exposure to high levels of toxic chemicals or radiation, or being hit by bullets that destroy vital organs. Absorption of high enough levels of energy of any kind into the body will kill or severely damage any living thing.

At the other end of the spectrum, there are many forces impinging on us that almost nobody finds particularly stressful. For instance, we are all continuously subjected to the gravitational pull of the earth, just as we are all continually exposed to the changing seasons and to the weather. Since gravity is always affecting us, we tend not to notice it. We are hardly aware of how we adapt to it by shifting the body from one leg to the other in the standing posture or by propping ourself up against a wall. But if you work for eight hours at a time standing in one place on a concrete floor, you will be very aware of gravity as a stressor.

Of course, unless you are an ironworker, a steeple painter, a trapeze artist, a ski jumper, or very advanced in years, gravity is usually the least of your stress problems. But it illustrates the point that some stressors are unavoidable, and that we are continually adapting to the demands they place on our body. As Selye pointed out, such stressors are a natural part of living. The example of gravity reminds us that, in and of itself, stress is neither good nor bad; it's just the way things are.

In the vast middle range of stressors, where exposure is neither immediately lethal, like bullets or high levels of radiation or poison, nor basically benign, like gravity, the general rule for those causing psychological stress is that *how you see things and how you handle them makes all the difference in terms of how much stress you will experience.* You have the power to affect the balance point between your internal resources for coping with stress and the stressors that are an unavoidable part of living. By exercising this capacity consciously and intelligently, to a large extent you can modulate and minimize the degree of stress you experience. Moreover, rather than having to invent a new way of dealing with every individual stressor that comes up in your life, you can develop a way of dealing with change *in general,* with problems *in general,* with pressures *in general.* The first step, of course, is recognizing when you are under stress in the first place.

Much of the early research on the physiological effects of stress was carried out on animals and did not distinguish between a psychological component of the stress reaction and a physiological component. For example, Selye's critics pointed out that the physiological damage seen in an animal forced to swim in freezing water might be due more to the animal's terror than to purely physiological reactions to either cold or water as the stressor. So Selye might have been measuring the effects of a psychological response to a harmful experience rather than a purely physiological response, as he thought. With this in mind, researchers set about to investigate the role of psychological factors in the stress response in animals as well as in people. These efforts led to the demonstration that psychological factors are an important part of an animal's response to physical stressors. In particular, it has now been shown conclusively that the extent to which an animal is given options to respond effectively to a particular stressor strongly influences how much physiological disregulation and breakdown will occur as a result of exposure to that stressor. Sense of control, a psychological factor, is a key factor in protecting an animal from stress-induced disease.

From everything we know about stress in human beings, the same relationship holds for us. (Recall that control was a major factor in the study of nursing home residents—the plant experiment described in Chapter 16, and in Dr. Kobasa's work on psychological hardiness, described in Chapter 15.) And since people usually have many more psychological options than do animals in laboratory experiments, it stands to reason that by becoming conscious of our options in stressful situations and by being mindful of the relevance and effectiveness of our responses in those situations, we may be able to exert considerable influence over our experience of the stress and thereby over whether or not it will lead to distress and even, over time, to disease.

Stress studies with animals demonstrated the extreme toxicity of learned helplessness, a term describing a condition in which we discover that nothing we do matters. But if helplessness can be learned, it can also be unlearned, at least by people. Even if there is no actual course of *external* action we can take that will have a meaningful effect under certain extremely stressful circumstances, human beings still have profound *internal* psychological resources that can give us a sense of being engaged and in control to some degree and thereby protect us from helplessness and despair. Certainly this is suggested by Dr. Antonovsky's studies of the survivors of concentration camps.

The late Richard Lazarus and his colleague Susan Folkman, who was later to play a prominent role in articulating the view that mindfulness lies at the very heart of integrative medicine, were stress researchers at the University of California at Berkeley when they proposed that a fruitful way to look at stress from a psychological point of view is to consider it as a transaction between a person and his or her environment. Lazarus defined psychological stress as "a particular relationship between the person and the environment that is appraised by the person as taxing or exceeding his or her resources and endangering his or her well-being." This was a particularly insightful approach because it emphasized relationality and thus the critical role of appraisal and conscious choice. And since relationality is fundamental to mindfulness, it eventually provided theoretical support for the use of mindfulness in facing whatever is unfolding in the present moment, appraising it, and choosing how one might be in wise relationship to it. It also explained why, as we have already discussed, an event can be more stressful for one person, who for one reason or another has fewer resources for dealing with it, than for another person, who has greater coping resources. It implied that the *meaning* we bring to the transaction, the way we see it and hold it in awareness, our perspective as a whole, can determine whether a situation is labeled as stressful or not. If you appraise or interpret an event as threatening your well-being, then it will be taxing to you. But if you see it differently, through a different set of lenses, then the same event might not be stressful at all for you, or a good deal less stressful, or even seen as potentially positive, as something you might actually handle well and grow from.

This is very good news because, given a particular situation, there are usually many ways of seeing it and many potential ways of handling it. As we shall see in greater detail as we go along, there are also many ways of living that contribute to building up your "bank account" of inner resources in advance, so that you are better prepared to handle intensely stressful experiences when they inevitably arise. A period of time devoted to formal meditation each day, coupled with the intentional cultivation of mindfulness throughout the day, is certainly one of those ways to make deposits into your account. I cannot tell you how many people have told me, after having had to cope with horrendously difficult and painful losses and challenges, "I don't know what I would have done without my mindfulness practice." And that rings true, in my experience. Once you have been practicing for a period of time, it is almost inconceivable that you ever could have managed without it in your life—it is that powerful, and also that subtle, because at the same time it doesn't seem like any kind of "big deal." Mindfulness is both nothing special and incredibly special, totally ordinary and completely extraordinary, all at the same time.

From a transactional perspective, the way we see, appraise, and evaluate our problems will determine how we respond to them and how much distress we will experience. It implies that we may have much more influence over things that potentially cause us stress than we might ordinarily think. While there will always be many potential stressors in our environment over which we cannot have immediate control, *by changing the way we see ourselves in relationship to them, we can actually expand our experience of the relationship, and therefore modify and modulate the extent to which it taxes or exceeds our resources or endangers our well-being.*

The transactional view of psychological stress reminds us that we can be more resistant to stress, more resilient, if we build up our resources and enhance our physical and psychological well-being in general (for example, via regular exercise, meditation, adequate sleep, and the deep connectedness of interpersonal intimacy, to name four of the most important ones) during times when we are not particularly taxed or overwhelmed. This is our biological and psychological "bank account" from which we can withdraw needed resources on some occasions, and to which we can make deposits at other times. This is really what the phrase "healthy lifestyle" implies. Our resources are the combination of inner and outer supports and strengths that help us to cope with an ever-changing field of experiences. Loving and supportive family relationships, friendships, and membership in groups that you care about are examples of external resources that could help buffer your experiences of stress. Inner resources might include your degree of confidence in your ability to handle adversity and challenges of all kinds (*self-efficacy*), your view of yourself as a person, your views on change and on what might be possible, your religious beliefs, your level of self-efficacy in terms of specific rather than general challenges, as well as your levels of stress hardiness, sense of coherence, and affiliative trust. All these can be strengthened, as we have seen, by practicing mindfulness.

As we have seen, stress-hardy individuals are more resilient. They have greater coping resources than other people under similar circumstances because they view life as a challenge, have a strong commitment to experiencing the fullness of life as it unfolds moment by moment, and assume an active role in interfacing with the actuality of what they are facing, with clarity and agency, which is what it means to exert meaningful control. The same is true of people with a high sense of coherence. Strong internal convictions about the comprehensibility, manageability, and meaningfulness of life experiences are powerful internal resources. People who cultivate such strengths are less likely to feel taxed or threatened by events than someone with fewer interior resources of this kind to call upon. This is also true for all the other health-enhancing cognitive and emotional patterns that we looked at in Chapter 15.

If, on the other hand, our reactions to things are usually clouded by fear, hopelessness, or anger, by underlying greed and distrust, by fear of loss or betrayal—ways of seeing the world and emotional patterns of reactivity that we develop early in life and then all too often carry with us relatively unexamined as fixed schemas, which rule our lives when they are triggered—then our actions will more than likely create additional problems and dig us deeper into a hole, to the point where it may be hard for us to see our way out of what seems more and more overwhelming. We bog down and get stuck. This can lead to feelings of vulnerability, being overwhelmed, and helplessness.

Lazarus's definition implies that for something to be psychologically stressful, it has to be appraised in some way as a threat. Yet we know from experience that there are many times when we are unaware of the degree to which our relationships with our inner or outer environment are taxing our resources, even though they are. For example, much of our lifestyle may be undermining our health, exhausting us physically and mentally without our conscious acknowledgment of it. Moreover, our negative attitudes and beliefs about ourselves and others and about what is possible may also be major factors preventing us from growing or healing or from bringing even a modicum of clarity, wisdom, and agency to times of difficulty. These negative attitudes and beliefs are usually below our level of conscious awareness—but they don't have to be.

Precisely because perception and appraisal or the lack of them play such a major role in our ability to adapt and respond appropriately to change, pain, and threats to our well-being, the major avenue available to us for handling stress effectively is to understand what we are going through. We can best do this by cultivating our ability to perceive our experience in its full context, as we did with the problem of the nine dots in Chapter 12. In this way, we can discern connections and relationships and be tuned in to feedback that we may not have been aware of before. This allows us to see our life situation more clearly and thereby influence how much we get caught up in our habitual and automatic reactions in difficult situations, thus allowing us to reduce our overall level of stress. It also frees us from the tight grip of our many unconscious beliefs and emotional schemas that ultimately inhibit our growth. So it can be particularly helpful to keep in mind from moment to moment that it is not so much the stressors in our lives but how we see them and what we do with them, how we are *in relationship* to them, that determines how much we are at their mercy. If we can change the way we see, we can change the way we respond and thereby dramatically lower our stress and its short- and long-term consequences for our health and well-being.

18

Change: The One Thing You Can Be Sure Of

The concept of stress suggests that, in one way or another, we are continually faced with the necessity of adapting to all the various pressures we experience in life. Basically this means adapting to *change*. If we can learn to see change as an integral part of life and not as a threat to our well-being, we will be in a much better position to cope effectively with stress. The meditation practice itself brings us face-to-face with the undeniable experience of continual change within our own minds and bodies, as we watch our constantly changing thoughts, feelings, sensations, perceptions, and impulses, as well as continual change in the outer realm of everything and everybody with whom we are in relationship. The former alone should be enough to demonstrate to us that we live immersed in a sea of change, that whatever we choose to focus on changes from one moment to the next.

Even inanimate material is subject to continual change: continents, mountains, rocks, beaches, the oceans, the atmosphere, the earth itself, even stars and galaxies all change over time, all evolve, and are spoken of as being born and dying. We humans live for such a brief time, relatively speaking, that we tend to think of these things as permanent and unchanging. But they are not. Nothing is.

If we consider the major forces that impinge on our lives, the first thing we will have to acknowledge is that nothing is absolutely stable, even when our lives seem to be on an even keel. Just being alive means being in a continual state of flux. We too evolve. We go through a series of changes and transformations to which it is difficult to affix an exact beginning or an exact end. We emerge as discrete individuals out of a stream of preceding beings of whom our parents are only the most recent representatives. And at a certain point, usually unknown to us in advance, our life as a discrete individual comes to an end. But unlike inanimate matter and most living things, we know the inevitability of change and of our own death. We are able to think about the changes we experience, wonder about them, and even fear them.

Consider just the physical changes we go through. During our lives, the body is constantly changing. A discrete human life begins its journey as a single cell, the fertilized human egg. This microscopic entity contains all the information necessary to become a new human being. As it descends through a fallopian tube and becomes implanted in the wall of the uterus, it begins dividing: from this one cell come two, then those two divide to make four, then those four divide to make eight, and so on. As the cells continue to divide, they gradually develop from a clump into a hollow sphere. The cells at the top differentiate slightly from those at the bottom of this tiny sphere that is to become the body. The sphere grows as the cells continue to divide. As it does, it also changes its shape. It folds in upon itself, creating different layers and regions that ultimately differentiate into specialized cells, which then generate our tissues and organs—brain, nervous system, heart, bones, muscles, skin, sensory organs, hair, teeth, and everything else—all with highly specialized functions, and all ultimately integrated into the one seamless whole that is us.

Yet even in the body's earliest stages, death is part of the process. Some of the cells that are originally laid down to form the structures of the hands and feet die selectively to give rise to the spaces between the fingers and toes so that we don't wind up with paddles at the ends of our arms and legs. And many cells within the developing nervous system die before we are born if they don't find other cells to connect up with. Even on the cellular level, connectedness to the whole appears to be of vital importance.

By the time we are born, our body consists of more than ten trillion cells, all doing their jobs, all more or less in the right place. If they are, we come out whole, ready for the ongoing transformations we will experience during infancy, toddlerhood, preadolescence, adolescence, and young adulthood. And if we are receptive to the idea, growth, development, and learning need not stop at young adulthood. In fact, there is no need for us ever to stop growing and learning. We can continue to cultivate and develop ourselves (the root meaning of the Pali word for meditation, *bhavana,* is "to develop") at every level of the body, mind, and heart, becoming more and more integrated in the process.

At the other end of this seamless process, if we make it that far, our bodies grow old and die. Death is part of their nature, built into the body. The life in individuals always comes to an end, even as the potential for life continues on in the flow of the genes and the emergence of new members of the family and the species.

The point is that life is constant change from the word go. Our bodies change in countless ways as we grow and develop over the course of a lifetime. So do our views of the world and of ourselves. Meanwhile, the external environment in which we live is also in continual flux. In fact, nothing at all is permanent and eternal, although some things appear that way since they change so slowly.

Living organisms have developed impressive ways of protecting themselves from all the unpredictable fluctuations in the environment and of preserving the basic internal conditions for life against too much change. The concept of inner biochemical stability was first articulated by the French physiologist Claude Bernard in the nineteenth century. He hypothesized that the body has evolved finely tuned regulatory mechanisms that are controlled by the brain and mediated by the nervous system and the secretion of hormone messenger molecules into the bloodstream to ensure that optimal conditions for cell functioning are maintained throughout the body in spite of large fluctuations in the environment. These fluctuations may involve temperature changes, lack of food for long stretches of time, and of course threats from predators and competitors. The regulatory responses, all accomplished via feedback loops, preserve the dynamic internal balance, called *homeostasis,* or now, more precisely, *allostasis,* by keeping the corresponding fluctuations of the organism within certain limits. Body temperature is regulated in this way, as are the concentrations of oxygen and glucose in the blood. The distinction between homeostasis and allostasis is that homeostasis refers to maintaining tight ranges of variability on physiological systems that promote *immediate survival,* such as temperature, blood chemistry, and blood oxygen levels. Other physiological systems, however, such as blood pressure, cortisol secretion, and fat storage in body tissues have much wider "operating ranges" and can vary much more between wider limits. These ranges are regulated in part by our brain, and by how we adapt to our ever-changing environment on the longer time scale of days, weeks, months, and years—a time frame characteristic of chronic stress. These physiological "health-maintenance" systems are regulated through "allostasis" rather than through homeostasis. However, both these systems that work to keep us optimally healthy can be seriously disregulated under the pressure of chronically stressful lifestyles.

We have evolved drives and instincts that support homeostasis and allostasis by directing our behavior to satisfy our body's needs. In this category are instincts such as thirst when the body needs water and hunger when the body needs food. Of course, we can also regulate our physiological state to some extent through our own conscious actions, such as putting on or taking off clothes, depending on the outside temperature, or opening a window to cool things off.

So while constant change is the hallmark of the world outside the individual organism, including both the natural and social environments, to a large extent our bodies are biologically protected and buffered from outside changes. We have built-in mechanisms for stabilizing our inner chemistry in order to increase our chances of survival under changing conditions. We also have built-in repair mechanisms that allow biological mistakes to be recognized and corrected—cancer cells to be detected and neutralized, broken bones to mend, blood to clot over a wound, and wounds to seal over and heal. We even have an enzyme, telomerase, that can repair the telomeres at the ends of all of our chromosomes, lengthening the life span of our cells. It is sensitive even to the thoughts we think, especially when we feel threatened.

The myriad regulatory pathways of our biology function in response to specific signals within the organism, our body's inner chemical language. We never have to think about our liver chemistry; fortunately for us, it self-regulates. We never have to think about taking the next inbreath; it takes care of itself. We don't have to remind the pituitary to secrete growth hormone on a certain schedule so that we grow to be the right size in adulthood. And when we are cut or injured, we don't have to think about making the blood clot to form a scab or making the skin heal underneath.

On the other hand, if we abuse the system too much, say by drinking more alcohol than the body can tolerate, then later on we may wind up having to give some thought to our liver. But by that point it may be disregulated beyond repair. The same goes for smoking and the lungs. Even with elaborate repair capabilities and built-in protective and purifying systems, the body can take only so much abuse before it is overwhelmed.

We may find it comforting to know that our bodies have very robust and resilient built-in mechanisms, developed over millions of years of evolution, for maintaining stability and vitality in the face of constant change. This biological resilience is a major ally when it comes to facing stress and change in our lives. It helps us to remember that we have every reason to trust our bodies, even when they are under severe stress, and to work in harmony with them rather than against them.

As we have seen, Hans Selye emphasized that a stress-free life is impossible, that the very process of being alive means that there will be wear and tear associated with the need to adapt to changing outer and inner environments. The question that concerns us is this: how much wear and tear does there have to be?

The modern terminology for biological wear and tear is *allostatic load,* a term introduced by Bruce McEwen, a renowned stress researcher at Rockefeller University. Earlier researchers had introduced the concept of *allostasis* to extend Claude Bernard's notion of *homeostasis,* which literally means "remaining stable by staying the same" and make it more precise in relationship to stress physiology and, in particular, the brain's role in the regulating stress response. The body's beneficial short-term response to stress can in itself become damaging in the longer term. Our bodies have built-in allostatic mechanisms for regulating and optimizing these complex interactions we face under different conditions of stress. The word "allostasis" literally means "remaining stable by being able to change." According to McEwen, "nowhere are these changes more dramatic than in the systems that comprise the stress response," which, taken to the extreme, becomes the fight-or-flight reaction. Responding to stress with greater mindfulness instead of reacting to it habitually and automatically can dramatically reduce the negative effects of stress on the organism (its allostatic load). This is a topic we will take up in the next two chapters.

In the 1960s, researchers began to investigate whether there was a relationship between how much change a person goes through in a year and what happens to his or her health at later times. Drs. Thomas Holmes and Richard Rahe of the University of Washington Medical School listed a number of life changes, including the death of a spouse, divorce, imprisonment, personal injury or illness, getting married, getting fired from work, retirement, pregnancy, sexual problems, death of a family member or close friend, change in line of work or work responsibilities, taking out a mortgage, outstanding personal achievement, change in living conditions, change of personal habits, going on vacation, and getting a traffic ticket. They ordered these "life events" in terms of what they thought was the degree of adjustment they would require and gave them arbitrary numerical values, starting with 100 for death of a spouse and going down to 11 for a minor violation of the law. They found that a high score on their life-change index was associated with a higher probability of illness in the following year than a low score. This suggested that change itself could predispose a person to illness.

Many of the life changes on their list, such as getting married, getting promoted, or having an outstanding personal achievement, are usually considered happy occasions. They are included because even events that may appear positive are nevertheless profound life changes that require adaptation and are therefore stressful. In Selye's terminology, they are examples of *eustress,* or "good stress." Whether they later lead to *distress,* or "bad stress," depends in large measure on how you adapt to them, which hinges on what they really mean to you and whether that meaning changes over time. If you adjust easily, then the eustress is relatively harmless and benign; it may even be beneficial and growth-enhancing, both psychologically and physically. It certainly will not threaten to tax, exceed, or overwhelm your ability to handle the changes. But it is all too easy to see how a positive life change might turn from eustress to distress if you have a hard time adjusting to your new circumstances.

For instance, you may have been looking forward to retirement for years and be happy at first when it comes and you can finally stop getting up early and going to work. But after a while, you may not know what to do with all the time you have. You may come to miss the people, the sense of connectedness and belonging, and the feeling of larger purpose and meaning that you may have felt when you were working. Unless you are forming new connections and finding new opportunities for meaning in your life, you may be failing to adapt to this major life change and it could wind up being a source of stress for you, even though you couldn't wait for it to happen.

The high divorce rate in our society attests to the fact that the happy occasion of marriage can also lead to major distress and suffering. This is particularly so if the initial match was less than compatible or if the individuals are unable to adjust to the changes associated with living together, including, of course, allowing for growth and change on the part of the other. The stress on a marriage is compounded if the couple is unable to adjust to the enormous demands of parenthood and the changes in roles and lifestyle that it brings. The eustress of having children can easily turn to distress and worse. The same is true of job promotions, graduating from school, aging, and all other positive life changes. They require adapting to the change itself.

The meaning that life changes have for you will strongly depend on their total context. If your spouse has been suffering from a long, wasting illness or if your relationship to that person has been one of extended misery, exploitation, or alienation, then the meaning of his or her death may be very different and the difficulty of adjusting to it also very different than if the death occurred suddenly and the relationship was extremely close. Assigning "death of a spouse" a score of 100 in all cases, as Drs. Holmes and Rahe did, does not take into account the *meaning* of the experience for the surviving spouse and the degree of adjustment or adaptation that he or she will have to make as a result.

It is not only the major turning points in our lives that require us to adapt. Every day we face a range of moderately important to trivial obstacles and occurrences with which we have to deal, whether we want to or not, and which we may turn into much larger problems than they need to be if we lose our perspective and balance of mind just when we need them the most.

The Holmes and Rahe life events scale was an important contribution in its day, but it had major weakness, as we have just seen. Another was that it left out entirely the dimension of trauma, and the consequences of highly traumatic events that can befall any of us—in particular, big-T trauma—especially when they occur early in life. Traumatic experiences can themselves compound, negatively distort, and sometimes even trivialize other important life events that have the potential to provide new meaning and life satisfaction but which require being recognized, met, and worked with in creative ways so that the connection with one's own original wholeness can be recovered and restored. A range of therapeutic approaches have been and are continuing to be developed as trauma therapies, including the use of mindfulness and yoga in imaginative ways.*

* See, for example, the recent work of Dr. Bessel van der Kolk at the Trauma Center in Boston.

The ultimate effect on our health of the stress we experience depends in large measure on how we come to perceive change itself, in all its various forms, and how skillful we are in adapting to continual change while maintaining our own inner balance and sense of coherence. This in turn depends on the meaning we attribute to events, on our beliefs about life and ourselves, and particularly on how much awareness we can bring to our frequently mindless and automatic reactions when our buttons are pushed. It is here, in our mind-body reactions to the occurrences in our lives that we find stressful, that mindfulness most needs to be applied and where its power to transform the quality of our lives can best be put to work.

19

Stuck in Stress Reactivity

When you stop and think about it, we human beings are actually remarkably resilient creatures. One way or another we manage to persevere, to survive, sometimes in the face of the full catastrophe writ horrifyingly large, and still have our moments of pleasure, peace, and fulfillment in spite of all the stress, pain, and grief. For one, we are expert copers and problem solvers. We cope through sheer determination, through our creativity and imagination, through prayer and religious beliefs, through involvements and diversions that feed our need for purpose, meaning, joy, and belonging, and for stepping outside of ourselves and caring for others. We cope and are buoyed up by our own tenacious love for life, and by receiving love, encouragement, and support from our family, our friends, and our larger community.

Underlying our conscious engagement with many of the challenges we face is an unconscious biological intelligence that is nothing short of awe-inspiring. This system, which has been honed over millions of years of evolution, functions at the level of perception, motor responses, and allostatic mechanisms, and it can operate extremely rapidly. Neuroscientist Cliff Saron of the Center for Mind and Brain at the University of California, Davis emphasizes that we humans have a marvelous innate capacity to complete patterns on the basis of very partial information. This is an example of the wisdom of the entire body—brain, nervous system, muscles, heart, the works. Everything collaborates for the sake of the whole. As we just saw, some of these systems exert their restorative influences within the body over hours and days, well beyond the immediacy of many threats. When this system is functioning adaptively, our automatic reactions can be life-saving in an emergency in which we have virtually no time to think—for example, when we are driving and the car begins to skid. What this means is that there is nothing wrong with some kinds of automaticity within ourselves. These reactions are biologically trustworthy.

At the same time, however, our innate psychophysiological balance and dynamism, our overall allostasis, stable though it is by virtue of being so adaptable, so flexible, so multifaceted, so reliable without our having to pay conscious attention to it, can be pushed over the edge into disregulation and disorder at every level of our organism if it is driven beyond its capacity to respond and adapt in healthy ways. We see examples of this in the hospital every day. Health can be undermined by a lifetime of ingrained behavior patterns that compound and exacerbate the pressures of living we continually face. Ultimately, our habitual and automatic reactions to the stressors we encounter, particularly when we get in the habit of reacting maladaptively, determine in large measure how much stress we experience. Automatic reactions triggered out of unawareness—especially when the circumstances are not life-threatening but we take them that way all the same—can compound and exacerbate stress, making what might have remained basically simple problems into worse ones over time. They can prevent us from seeing clearly, from solving problems creatively, and from expressing our emotions effectively when we need to communicate with other people or even understand what is going on within ourselves. Ultimately they close down our ability to experience peace of mind, which, when all is said and done, is probably what we most desire. Instead, each time we react habitually in unhealthy ways, without awareness of the patterns of behavior we have fallen into, we stress our intrinsic capacity for well-being and balance a little more. A lifetime of unconscious and unex-

FIGURE 9

THE STRESS-REACTION CYCLE
(Automatic/Habitual)

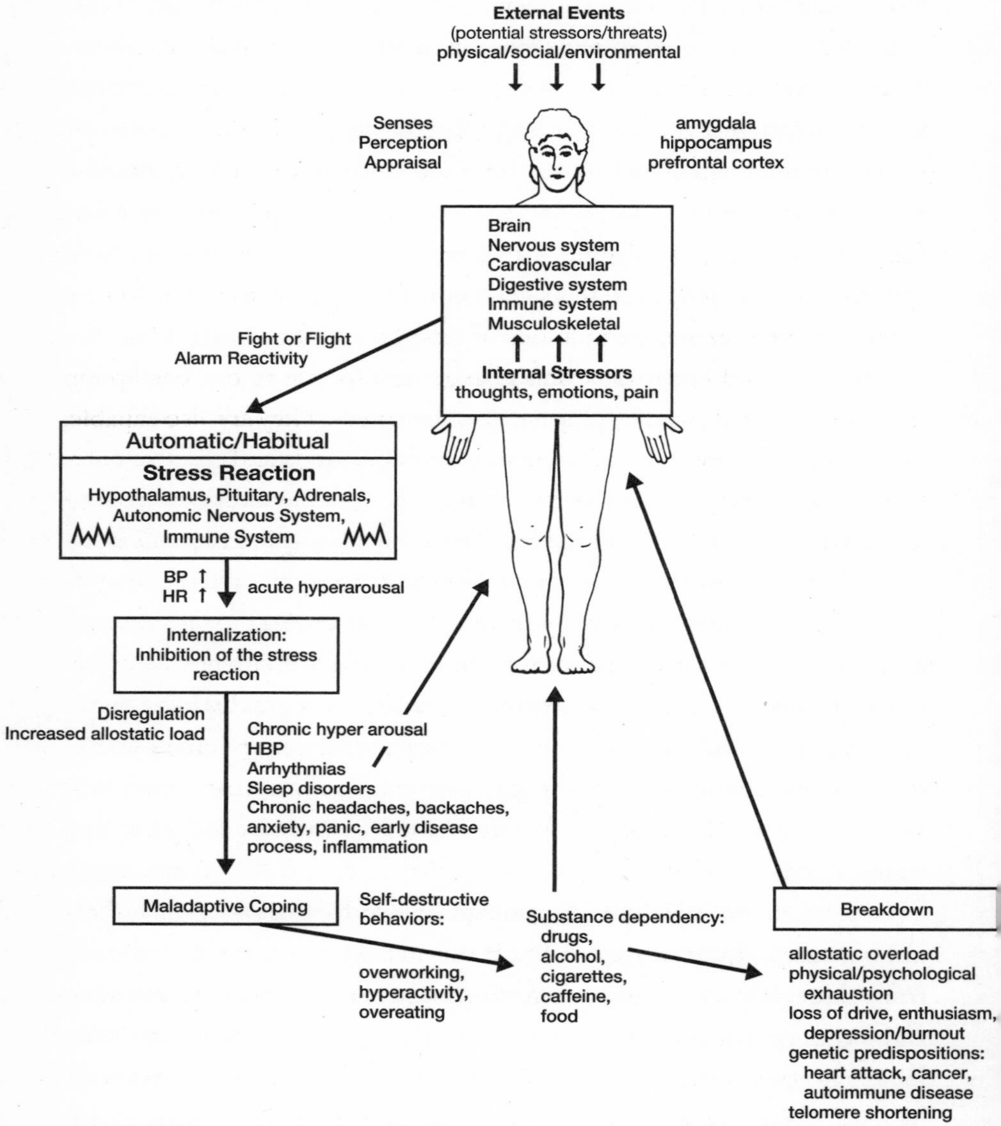

amined habitual reactivity to challenges and perceived threats is likely to increase our risk of eventual breakdown and illness significantly. More and more evidence suggests that this is indeed the case.

Consider yourself for a moment to be the person depicted in the center of Figure 9. External events that might be potential stressors—whether environmental, physical, societal, social, emotional, economic, or political—can bear down on us and generate changes in our bodies, our lives, and our social status. These potential stressors are depicted by the small arrows above the person in the figure. All these forces impinge on us from the outside to one degree or another. They are usually perceived and appraised very rapidly as to the level of threat they pose to the organism, especially under extreme conditions of danger.

Our mind and body don't only change in response to our perception and appraisal of this complex array of outer forces. They are also capable, as we all well know, of generating their own demands and reactive energies, producing another whole set of pressures on the organism. In Figure 9 these are labeled "Internal Stressors" (small arrows inside the box). As we have seen, even our thoughts and feelings can act as major stressors if they tax or exceed our ability to respond effectively to whatever they bring up for us. This is true even if the thought or feeling has no correspondence with "reality." For example, the mere *thought* that you have a fatal disease can be the cause of considerable stress and could become disabling, even though it may not be true. In the extreme, it can profoundly disregulate your physiology, as we saw in the story recounted by Dr. Bernard Lown in Chapter 14.

Some stressors affect us over extended periods of time. We call these *chronic stressors.* For instance, taking care of a family member with a chronic disease or disability is usually an inevitable source of chronic stress for the caregiver. It often goes on for many years, and so requires profound adaptation in order to minimize its rending effects. Of course, having a chronic medical condition yourself is also a source of ongoing stress. On the other hand, some stressors come and go over relatively short periods of time. We call these *acute stressors.* Deadlines, such as getting your income taxes done on time, are an example of this kind of pressure. Other types of acute stressors stem from daily life and may seem minor, but they occur frequently and thus their effects can add up over time: rushing in the morning, driving in traffic, being late for appointments or meetings, having an argument with a child or spouse. Still others are unusual or onetime matters, such as accidents, losing one's job, or the death of someone close to you. All can create acute stress for us and require effective adaptation so that we can eventually heal, through a process of coming to terms with what happened. Without such a process, we might fall into longer-term patterns of behavior that result in additional sources of chronic stress.

UCSF stress researcher Elissa Epel describes our interface with acute stress as a kind of sprint. One way or another, it is soon over, and we can go back to our baseline well-being.* Extending the metaphor, Dr. Epel sees chronic stress as a marathon that usually includes multiple sprints within it. For instance, even within an ongoing situation such as being the primary caregiver for a family member suffering with a chronic condition, there will still always be acute events popping up that need to be dealt with. If we don't realize that we are actually engaged in an ongoing marathon, it is easy to run out of energy, what could be thought of as *coping energy,* and wind up feeling chronically exhausted and burned out. Long-term stress of this kind requires pacing oneself, and maybe even periodic respite, to preserve the resources in our "bank account" and continue making the occasional bigger deposit when we can. Epel makes the point that one way that an acute stressor can become chronic is though intrusive thoughts, worry, and rumination. These thought patterns themselves become the internal stress events that compound and extend the stress. She points to evidence suggesting that rumination itself is thought to be a pathway through which chronic stress causes hypertension. As we have seen, and will see again, her own research on telomeres and telomerase in

* Think of acute stress as like a gazelle that mobilizes a huge fight-or-flight reaction to escape from a lion on the savanna; once a safe distance has been attained, it goes back to quiet grazing as if nothing had happened. For us humans, it is somewhat different, because we can think about what might have happened, even after the immediate threat is over, and drive ourselves crazy in the process. The trauma of the near miss can stay with us for a long time, and needs a certain kind of attention if we are to effectively work with it and resolve it to one degree or another.

chronically stressed populations provides strong evidence for the toxic effects of such ruminative processes when they are unmodulated via more adaptive and intentional psychological processes, such as mindfulness practice.

Some stressors are highly predictable, such as taxes. Others are less predictable, such as accidents or other things that come up unexpectedly and that you have to deal with. In Figure 9, the small arrows represent all these internal and external stressors, both acute and chronic, as they are felt *at any moment in time.* The figure of the person stands for all aspects of your being, the totality of your organism—body *and* mind. This includes all of your organ systems, of which only a few are labeled (the brain and the nervous system, the cardiovascular system, the musculoskeletal system, the immune system, and the digestive system), as well as the conventional psychological sense of yourself as a person, including your perceptions, beliefs, thoughts, and feelings. Of course, the brain plays a critical and commanding role in regulating the functioning of all these processes that contribute to our being alive and to our integrated experience of life unfolding: the organ systems of the body, including our perceptual systems and neuroendocrine systems, as well as our thoughts and emotions, and the meaning we attribute to events.

When you are stressed in some moment to the extent that your mind identifies, anticipates, or imagines a threat to your being, whether it is a threat to your physical well-being, to the integrity of your sense of self, or to your social standing in relationship to others, usually you will react in a particular way. If it is a passing threat or turns out to be neutral when reappraised in the next moment, then either there will be no reaction at all or your reaction will be minimal. But if the stressor is highly charged for you emotionally, or if you consider it to be threatening, then you usually go through some kind of automatic *alarm reaction.*

The alarm reaction is our body's way of clearing the decks for defensive or aggressive action. It can help us in threatening situations to protect ourselves and to maintain or regain control. Our brains and nervous systems are wired to perform in this way under certain circumstances. The alarm reaction enables us to call on the full power of all our internal resources in life-threatening situations. As we shall see, a little bilateral structure deep in the brain, called the amygdala, has a lot to do with it.

Walter B. Cannon, the great American physiologist who worked at the Harvard Medical School in the early part of the twentieth century and who extended Claude Bernard's original concept of the internal stability of our physiology, studied the physiology of this alarm reaction in a number of experimental systems. In one, he studied what a cat goes through when threatened by a barking dog. Cannon termed the cat's reaction the *fight-or-flight response* because the physiological changes the threatened animal goes through are those that mobilize the body for fighting or fleeing.*

We human beings are subject to the same physiological reactions that other animals exhibit. The basic pattern is deeply rooted in our biology. When we feel threatened, the fight-or-flight reaction occurs almost instantly, mediated, as we shall see in a moment, by the autonomic nervous system. It hardly matters whether it is a physical threat or a much more abstract threat to our social well-being and sense of self. The resulting outcomes are very similar: an overall state of physiological and psychological *hyperarousal,* characterized by a great deal of muscle tension, including in the face, and the activation of strong emotions, which may vary from terror, fright, or anxiety, shame, or embarrassment to rage and anger. The fight-or-flight reaction involves a very rapid cascade of brain and nervous system firings and the release of a bevy of stress hormones, the most well known of which are the catecholamines [epinephrine (adrenaline) and

* For our purposes here, I am labeling it a *reaction* to emphasize its often automatic and relatively unconscious nature. That way, I can reserve the term *response* for a relatively more conscious course of action in the face of a challenge or threat. But the fact is that whatever we choose to call it, fight or flight is an extremely complex phenomenon in both the brain and the body. It has highly evolved and vital elements of perception, appraisal, evaluation, thought, and choice associated with it, even though we may be, on the whole, unaware of these processes—unless we cultivate the capacity to pay close attention from moment to moment, through the application of mindfulness, to our actual experiencing of what is unfolding in our mind and body. In this way, we can transform habitual and unexamined reactions—many of which we may have acquired and reinforced through repetition over the course of years and decades and only recently realized are unhelpful, if not toxic, in particular life situations—into more appropriate, skillful, and mindfulness-mediated responses..

norepinephrine (noradrenaline)], which are unleashed very rapidly in response to an immediate acute threat, and cortisol, which is released a bit more slowly. Hyperarousal includes a heightening of sense perceptions so that we can take in as much relevant information as possible as quickly as possible: the pupils of our eyes dilate to let in more light, our hearing becomes more acute, the hair on our body stands erect so that we are more sensitive to vibrations in the air around us. We become very alert and attentive. The heart rate rises and the strength of the heart muscle contractions (and thereby the blood pressure) increases, causing the output of the heart to jump by a factor of four or five so that more blood and therefore more energy can be delivered to the large muscles of the arms and legs, which will be called upon if we are to fight or run.

At the same time the blood flow to the digestive system shuts down, as does digestion itself. After all, if you are about to be eaten by a tiger, there is no point in continuing to digest food in your stomach. It will get digested in the tiger's stomach just as well if you are caught. Both fighting and running require that your muscles get as much blood as possible. You may feel this rerouting of your blood flow in times of stress as "butterflies in your stomach."

Many of these rapid changes in your body and in your emotions come about because of the activation of a particular branch of what is called the *autonomic nervous system* (ANS). The autonomic nervous system is that part of your nervous system that regulates the internal states of your body such as your heart rate, blood pressure, and the digestive process. The particular branch of the ANS that is stimulated in the fight-or-flight reaction is known as the *sympathetic branch*. Its overall function is to speed things up. The other branch, known as the *parasympathetic branch,* acts as a brake. Its overall function is to slow and calm things down. It is the parasympathetic branch that shuts down digestion when we have a fight-or-flight reaction. The sympathetic branch stimulates the heart when we react to stress, and the parasympathetic branch slows it down during the recovery. The parasympathetic branch of the ANS, and in particular the highly evolved vagus (meaning *wandering* in Latin) nerve, plays an essential role in how we deal with stress. When stressed, most people show a decrease in vagal tone, meaning the nerve is less activated, and that decrease is related to greater threat reactivity. Having a higher vagal tone is associated with greater calm and resilience, as well as recovering from stress more rapidly, greater social engagement, and positive emotions. Interestingly enough, just bringing awareness to your breathing and allowing it to slow down on its own, particularly the outbreaths, increases vagal tone. The ANS is regulated by the *hypothalamus,* a gland that lies just below the region of the brain known as the *limbic system,* and above the brain stem. The hypothalamus is the master control switch of the autonomic nervous system, or more accurately, the principle conductor of the ANS orchestra.

The limbic system is a collection of highly interconnected regions located underneath the cerebral cortex and right above the hypothalamus. It has many discrete structures, including the amygdala, the hippocampus, and the thalamus. The limbic system used to be thought of as the "seat of the emotions," but that view is no longer considered entirely valid, as some of the regions of the limbic system, such as the hippocampus, are known to be essential for higher cognitive functions as well, including spatial cognition and declarative memory. Moreover, the prefrontal cortex, the region right behind your forehead and site of the so-called *executive functions,* such as perspective taking, impulse control, decision making, long-term planning, postponement of gratification, and working memory, among others, is now known to have an influence on how emotionally resilient a person is in the face of stress and adversity. It has been said that the prefrontal cortex is the part of the brain that confers on us our uniquely human capacities and qualities. Evolutionarily, it was the last part of the brain to develop. It can downregulate stress reactivity via its massive neuronal connectivity with the various structures and regions of the limbic system (including the amygdala, which plays a major role when we feel anxious, afraid, or threatened, as well as in decoding emotional expression on the faces of others). This bidirectional connectivity between the prefrontal cortex and multiple limbic areas allows for both emotion recognition and emotion regulation. The prefrontal cortex is the region where Richard Davidson's work, including his studies of long-term meditators and with MBSR practitioners, has shown that the left and right sides of the prefrontal cortex regulate emotions differently. Resilience in the face of emotional challenges is characterized by greater activation of the left side of the prefrontal cortex, which is associated with a reduction of fear, anxiety, and aggression (in part perhaps by damping down activity in the amygdala). Recall that a shift in activation from right to left in this region was observed in our collaborative study of MBSR in a corporate work setting. According to Davidson, "the amount of activation in the left prefrontal region of a resilient person can be thirty times that in someone who is not resilient."*

One of the major jobs of the various structures within the limbic system is to regulate the functioning of the hypothalamus. In turn, the hypothalamus influences not only the autonomic nervous system, and thus all the organ systems in the body, but also the endocrine system (the system of glands that secrete stress hormones) as well as our musculoskeletal system. The interconnections among these pathways allow us to experience our emotions *viscerally,* that is, in and through the body and how it is feeling, and at the same time to hold them in awareness and be able to respond in a coordinated and integrated fashion to both external and internal events.

Taken altogether, the deep connectedness of the prefrontal cortex and the limbic system allows for an integrated experience of living, and for the possibility of both using emotional information and regulating our emotional reactivity or responsivity on the basis of a deeper understanding of particular situations and stressors we might be facing. This deeper understanding derives from our values, our sense of who we are (sense of self), and our ability to be aware with intentionality and modulate accordingly the actions we ultimately choose to take. In other words, we can cultivate greater resiliency and well-being, and also wisdom and equanimity, in the face of stressful circumstances. This quality of well-being is sometimes spoken of as *eudaemonia.* All it takes is practice, practice, practice. We will certainly get plenty of opportunities for that, given how much stress there is in our lives on a daily basis.

When the sympathetic branch of the ANS is triggered via limbic stimu-

* Davidson and Begley, *The Emotional Life of Your Brain,* 69.

lation of specific areas in the hypothalamus, the result is a massive discharge of neuronal signals that influence the functioning of every organ system in our body. This is accomplished in two ways: direct neuron (nerve cell) connections to all the internal organs—including the vagus nerve—and the secretion of hormones and neuropeptides into the bloodstream. Some hormones are secreted by glands, others by nerve cells (these are called neuropeptides), still others by both. These hormones and neuropeptides are chemical messengers that travel far and wide in the body to transmit information and trigger specific responses from different cell groups and tissues. When they arrive at their targets, they bind to specific receptor molecules and transmit their message. You might think of them as chemical keys, turning on or off specific control switches in the body. It may well be that all of our emotions and feeling states are dependent on the secretion of specific neuropeptide hormones under different conditions.* Some of these hormone messengers are released as part of the fight-or-flight reaction. For example, epinephrine and norepinephrine are released into the bloodstream by the adrenal medulla (part of the adrenal glands located on top of your kidneys) when the adrenal glands are stimulated by signals from the hypothalamus via sympathetic nerve pathways. These hormones give you the "rush" and sense of extra power in emergency situations that we have labeled the habitual or automatic "Stress Reaction" in Figure 9. In addition, the pituitary gland right below the hypothalamus is also stimulated (via the hypothalamus) when we are stressed. The pituitary triggers the release of other hormones (some from a region of the adrenal glands called the adrenal cortex) that are also part of this habitual stress reaction, including cortisol and a molecule called DHEA (dehydroepiandrosterone). The amygdala is a major player too, as was mentioned earlier, activating whenever there is a sense of threat or challenge, or when one feels thwarted or even potentially thwarted.

* For instance, dopamine is secreted by the hypothalamus, as well as other regions of the brain, and is known to function in attention, learning, retaining information in working memory, and pleasurable experiences. Serotonin regulates mood, appetite, and sleep and is associated with feelings of well-being and happiness. It is primarily secreted in the intestinal tract.

A news item that ran in the *Boston Globe* illustrates the remarkable power inherent in the stress reaction. It read as follows:

> Arnold Lemerand, of Southgate, Mich., is 56 years old and had a heart attack six years ago. As a result, he doesn't like to lift heavy objects. But this week, when Philip Toth, age 5, became trapped under a cast iron pipe near a playground, Lemerand easily lifted the pipe and saved the child's life. As he lifted it, Lemerand thought to himself that the pipe must weigh 300 to 400 pounds. It actually weighed 1800 pounds, almost a ton. Afterward, Lemerand, his grown sons, reporters and police tried to lift the pipe but couldn't.

This anecdote illustrates the power of the fight-or-flight reaction and the surge of energy it provides in acute life-threatening situations. It also demonstrates that in an emergency, you really don't stop to think. If Mr. Lemerand had thought about the weight of the pipe before he tried to lift it, or about his heart condition, he probably would not have been able to lift it. But the necessity for action in the face of a life-threatening situation triggered an immediate state of hyperarousal in which his thinking shut down for a moment and sheer, complex, beautiful reacting took over, operating much faster than conscious thought, and bringing with it its own uncanny power and skill—a feat of instantaneous compassion in action. But once the immediate threat was over, he was unable to perform the same feat, even with lots of help.

It is easy to see how the built-in fight-or-flight reaction increases an animal's chances of survival in a dangerous and unpredictable environment. It works the same way for us. The fight-or-flight reaction may help us to survive when we find ourselves in life-threatening situations. It is not a hardwired reflex of the knee-jerk variety, but a highly evolved intelligent capacity to steer us though complex situations that threaten our survival. So it is not at all bad that we have this vital capacity. We never would have survived as a species without it. What is problematic is when we can't control it and don't know how to modulate it, or when we use its energies across a range of situations where there is no immediate and acute threat to life or well-being but we act as if there were. Then it starts to control us.

Most of the time we do not find ourselves encountering life-threatening situations in civil society and everyday life. We are not running into mountain lions or other threats as we go to work or deal with family life and social situations. But we are still prone, if not hardwired, to go into fight-or-flight mode when we feel threatened or thwarted in our goals, feelings of safety, or sense of control even if we're just driving on the freeway or walking into work and finding something unexpected that we are going to have to deal with. Our minds still perceive events in terms of mortal threats to our well-being and sense of self, even when there is none. When we go that route, then every stressful situation, even if it is potentially manageable in countless other ways, becomes a threat to the system. Our fight-or-flight pathways no longer shut down, even when there is no life-threatening situation. They can become chronically activated.* And when they are, they change our biology as well as our psychology. We become primed, so to speak, for all the problems associated with chronic hyperarousal, right down to the level of which genes in our chromosomes get turned on and upregulated, such as the gene for the glucocorticoid receptors that make us chronically susceptible to stressors, and the genes that produce pro-inflammatory cytokines, which themselves promote a whole range of diseases of inflammation if chronically stimulated. Chronic arousal also shortens our telomeres, as we have seen, and thus accelerates the aging process at the cellular level. All of these consequences of chronic arousal may be avoidable, or at least reducible and ultimately resolvable, if

* This is also the case for social stress, which can also be hugely threatening. One of the most common ways in which we feel threatened is when our social identity, our sense of how others are perceiving us, is threatened. Embarrassment, shame, being rejected by others, and negative thoughts about ourself are all potent triggers of the habitual stress reaction and of its downstream consequences in the body. We understandably take all this very very personally. Yet it might not be the complete story of who we are. This will be a major theme in Part 4.

we learn how to recognize the tendency to go directly into a full-blown stress reaction and modulate it with a more mindfully based response. In part, this will involve recognizing that our instantaneous appraisals of threat are often inaccurate and generate unnecessary fear and suffering for ourselves. As we will see in Part IV, just discovering that we don't always have to believe our own thoughts or emotions or take them so personally when the circumstances and potential challenges we are facing are not in essence personal, even when we are absolutely convinced that they are, gives us other degrees of freedom in terms of responding skillfully to ever-changing life situations. This new way of being in relationship to stress and potential stressors can be hugely liberating.

The fight-or-flight reaction is triggered in animals when they encounter members of another species that might want to eat them for lunch. But it also comes into play when animals are defending their social standing within their own species, and when they are challenging the social status of another animal in their group. When an animal's social position is challenged, the fight-or-flight reaction is unleashed and the two animals in question fight until one either submits or runs away. The hierarchy of dominance and submission is established. Once an animal submits to another, it "knows its place" and doesn't keep going through the same reaction every time it is challenged. It readily submits, and that calms its internal biology so that it is not continually hyperaroused.

People have many more choices in situations of social stress and conflict, but often we get stuck in these same patterns of dominance and submission, fleeing, or fighting all the same. Or as some animals do, we can freeze up completely and simply go numb when threatened. Our reactions in social situations are often not that different from those of animals. That is not surprising, given that much of the stress biology is the same. Yet animals of the same species seldom kill each other in social conflicts the way humans do.

As we just noted, much of our stress comes from threats, real or imagined, to our social status, to our sense of how others perceive us. The fight-or-flight reaction kicks in *all the same,* even when there is no life-threatening situation facing us. It is sufficient for us just to feel threatened.*

By causing us to react so quickly and so automatically, the fight-or-flight reaction often creates problems for us in the social domain rather than giving us additional energy for resolving our problems. Anything that threatens our sense of well-being—challenges to our social status, our ego, our strongly held beliefs, or our desire to control things or to have them be a certain way—can trigger it to some degree. We can be catapulted into a state of hyperarousal, ready for fight or flight, whether we like it or not.

Unfortunately, as we just saw, hyperarousal can become a permanent way of life. Many of our patients in the MBSR program start out by describing themselves as tense and anxious virtually all the time. They suffer from chronic muscle tension, usually in the shoulders, the face, the forehead, the jaw, and the hands. Everybody seems to have particular areas that store muscle tension. Heart rate is also frequently elevated in a state of chronic hyperarousal. You can feel shaky inside, feel "butterflies" in your stomach, experience skipped heartbeats or palpitations, or have chronically sweaty palms. The urge to flee may surface frequently, as can impulses to lash out in anger or to get into arguments and fights.

Certainly these are common responses to everyday stressful situations, not just to life-threatening ones. They come about because our body and mind are wired to react automatically to perceived threat or danger, even though we do not usually run into large carnivore predators in our daily lives. Since the capacity to trigger a fight-or-flight reaction is part of our

* The situation may be a bit more complicated than this model suggests, since women may react differently than men in some kinds of challenging situations. The psychologist Shelley Taylor of UCLA suggests that women also have a tendency to "tend and befriend" in threatening situations—taking care of their young and seeking social support. For more on this and on the complexities of stress biology and psychology, see Sapolsky R. *Why Zebras Don't Get Ulcers.* 3rd ed. St. Martin's Griffin, New York; 2004.

nature, and since, as we have been exploring, it is liable to have major unhealthy consequences biologically, psychologically, socially, and therefore health-wise if it runs chronically out of control, it is essential for us to be aware of this inner tendency and how easily it can be triggered, if we hope to reverse a lifelong pattern of automatic stress reactivity and the heavy burdens that accompany it. As you will see shortly, awareness is the critical element in learning how to free yourself from your stress reactions at those moments when you feel threatened and your first impulse is to run or take some other kind of evasive action, freeze up, or become aggressive and gear up for a fight. These are not good baseline attitudes and patterns of relating to wake up with and to carry into work in the morning or to bring home at the end of a long and frustrating day. They are not so healthy for others, and they obviously are not in your best interest.

At this point it might be useful to ask, "What do we usually do in all those countless situations when the internal pressures that could lead very quickly to a full-blown fight-or-flight reaction are building up inside of us but we know that fighting (or its equivalent) and/or running (or its equivalent) are simply not options, because both are socially unacceptable and, besides, we already know neither will solve our problems?" We still feel threatened, hurt, fearful, angry, resentful. We still have the stress hormones and neurotransmitters clearing the decks for fight or flight. Our blood pressure is rising, our heart is pounding, our muscles are tense, our stomach is churning.

One common way we often deal with our stress reactions in social situations is to suppress these feelings as best we can. We wall them off. We pretend we are not aroused. We dissimulate, hiding our feelings from others and sometimes even from ourselves. To do so, we put the arousal the only place we can think of: deep inside us. We internalize it. We inhibit the outward signs of the stress reaction as best we can (even though any observant person is going to see it or feel it) and try to carry on as usual, holding it all inside. We suppress our emotions and avoid dealing with them and with the actuality of our situation. You can just feel how toxic that might be, especially if it becomes your default mode for getting through the day.

The nice thing about fighting or running is that, at the very least, both are exhausting, so that ultimately, after the stressful situation is over, you rest. Your parasympathetic pathways take over. Blood pressure and heart rate return to baseline, your blood flow readjusts, your muscles relax, your thoughts and emotions cool, and you move toward an overall condition of recovery and recuperation, right down to the level of your biology, your chromosomes, and the families of genes that are getting turned on or off.* When you internalize the stress reaction, however, you don't get the resolution that fighting or running brings. You don't peak, and you don't get the physical release and recovery afterward, like the gazelles on the savanna. Instead, you just carry the arousal around inside you, both in the form of stress hormones, which are wreaking havoc with your body, and in the form of your agitated thoughts and emotions. This is not your brain's fault, nor your body's. High stress and strong amygdala activation simply shut down the activity in the prefrontal cortex, so your executive functions crash and you can't really think clearly and make emotionally intelligent decisions just when you most need to. But when you bring awareness to the unfolding of such stressful situations in the present moment, and to your unconscious and habitual reactions to them, then the totality of your organism is capable of much, much more. The prefrontal cortex can be reclaimed and its activity bolstered, another signature of resilience.

We encounter a lot of different situations from day to day, many of which tax our resources to one degree or another. If each time we run into some aspect of the full catastrophe our automatic response is a mini (or not so mini) fight-or-flight reaction, and if most of the time we inhibit its expression outwardly and just contain its underlying energies, by the end of the day we will be incredibly tense. If this pattern becomes a way of

* See for example: Bhasin MK, Dusek JA, Chang, BH, et al. Relaxation response induces temporal transcriptome changes in energy metabolism, insulin secretion and inflammatory pathways. PloS ONE 8(5): e62817; May, 2013. doi10.1371/journal.pone. 0062817.

life, and if we have no healthy ways of releasing the built-up tension, then over a period of weeks, months, and years we will more than likely drift into a perpetual state of chronic hyperarousal from which we rarely get any break and that we might even come to think of as "normal." We are normalizing a huge allostatic load that we are carrying around, *without even knowing it in many cases,* and certainly without having any kind of systematic and reliable antidotes in the form of practices and skills that we can call upon at such times to restore us to a stress-free baseline. This really compounds unnecessary wear and tear on both the body and the mind.

There is mounting evidence that chronic stimulation of the sympathetic nervous system can lead to long-term physiological disregulation, resulting in problems such as increased blood pressure, cardiac arrhythmias, digestive problems (usually due to inflammatory processes), chronic headaches, backaches, and sleep disorders, as well as to psychological distress in the form of chronic anxiety, depression, or both. When this level of damage happens, we call it *allostatic overload.* Of course, having any of these problems creates even more stress. They all become additional stressors that just feed back on us, compounding our problems. This is illustrated in Figure 9 by the arrow going from these symptoms of chronic hyperarousal back to the person.

We see the results of this way of living every day in the Stress Reduction Clinic. People come to us when they have had enough, when they get desperate enough, when they finally decide that there just has to be a better way to live and a better way to handle their problems. Nowadays, maybe it is because they have read something about mindfulness and the science of meditation in the newspaper, or seen something about it on television or on YouTube. In the first class, we sometimes invite people to describe what they are like when they are their most relaxed selves. Many say, "I can't remember, it's been so long," or "I don't think I have ever felt relaxed!" They instantly recognize the hyperarousal syndrome sketched out in Figure 9. Many say, "This describes me to a T."

We all use various coping strategies to stay on an even keel and to deal with the pressures in our lives. Many people cope remarkably well with extremely trying personal circumstances and have developed their own strategies for doing so. They know when to stop and take time out; they exercise regularly, meditate or do yoga, they pray; they share their feelings with close friends, have hobbies and other interests to take their mind off things; and they remind themselves to look at things differently and not to lose perspective. People who do this tend to be the stress-hardy ones.

But many people cope with stress in ways that are actually self-destructive and just make matters worse on virtually every front. These attempts at control are labeled "Maladaptive Coping" in Figure 9 because, although they may help us to tolerate stress and give us some sense of control in the short run, in the long run they wind up compounding the stress we experience. Maladaptive means that these responses are unhealthy. They cause more stress and only compound our difficulties and our suffering.

One very prevalent maladaptive coping strategy is to deny that there is any problem at all. "Who me, tense? I'm not tense," says the denier, all the while radiating body language and facial expressions that speak of stored muscle tension and unresolved emotions. For some people it takes a long time to even come *close* to admitting to themselves that they are carrying around a lot of body armor or that they feel hurt and angry inside. It's very hard to release tension if you won't even admit that it is here. And if you are challenged by others regarding your patterns of denial, your unwillingness to even take a look at certain areas of your life, strong emotions can surface that can take many forms, including anger and resentment. These are sure signs that you are indeed resisting looking at something deeper within yourself. Therefore, if you are serious about finding a new way of being in your life and in the world, these signs of resistance are really worth paying attention to. They can become your friends and allies if you can turn toward them, make space for them, and welcome them into awareness with kindness and self-compassion. You could experiment with tending (or better, attending) and befriending them, intentionally. It's not as hard as you might think.

All the same, it is important to keep in mind that denial is not always maladaptive. It is sometimes an effective temporary strategy for coping with relatively unimportant problems until you can't deny them anymore and have to pay attention to them and to their consequences, and find more effective ways of dealing with them. And, sadly, heartbreakingly, sometimes denial is the only recourse a person may have or believes he or she has in the face of an impossibly harmful situation, such as the child who is being sexually abused and threatened with death or some other awful consequence if she divulges anything. Some of the patients we see who had such experiences as children had no other options when they were young, especially if their tormentor was a parent or someone whom they were supposed to love—and often did. This was the case for Mary, whose traumatic experiences as a young girl were discussed in Chapter 5. Denial allowed her to keep her sanity in a world of madness. But sooner or later denial stops working and you have to come up with something else. And in the end, even if denial was the best you could do at the time, there is usually a serious price to be paid for it. This is where trauma-oriented therapies can be so valuable, and where mindfulness-based approaches may be of particular value. More and more research in both animals and in people is showing that early stressful and traumatic experiences predispose an individual to a heightened vulnerability later in life if he or she encounters high-stress situations. In low-stress situations, a person can be fine and healthy. But in high-stress situations it can all come crashing down, unless, that is—and now we are talking about people, not animals—they cultivate mind-body strategies such as mindfulness for consciously regulating their emotions, thoughts, and body states.

There are many unhealthy ways we seek to control or regulate the stress in our lives in addition to denying that it exists and pretending that everything is fine. They are unhealthy precisely because, in one way or another, they avoid naming, facing, and dealing with the real problems. *Workaholism* is a classic example. If you feel stressed and dissatisfied by family life, for instance, then work can be used as a wonderful excuse for never being home. If your work gives you pleasure and you get positive feedback from colleagues, if you feel in control when you are there, if you have power and status and feel productive and creative, it is easy to immerse yourself in work. It can be intoxicating and addicting, just like alcohol. And it provides a socially acceptable alibi for not being available for the family, since there is always more work to do than you can possibly get done. Some people drown themselves in their jobs. Most do it unconsciously, with all the best intentions in the world, because deep down they are reluctant to face other aspects of their lives and the need to strike a healthy balance. This maladaptive pattern is powerfully documented in Arlie Hochschild's book *The Time Bind: When Work Becomes Home and Home Becomes Work.*

Filling up your time with *busyness* is another self-destructive avoidance behavior. Instead of facing up to your problems, you can run around like crazy doing good things until your life is overflowing with commitments and obligations and you can't possibly make time for yourself. Despite all the running around, you may not really know what you are doing. This kind of hyperactivity sometimes functions as an attempt to hold on to a feeling of control or deeper meaning in your life when it seems to be slipping away. But it may do just the opposite by obliterating our opportunities for rest and reflection, for non-doing.

We also love to look outside ourselves for quick fixes when we feel stressed or uncomfortable. One popular way of handling stress is to use *chemicals* to change our body-mind state when we don't like how we are feeling, or just to make our moments "more interesting." To cope with the stress and distress in our lives, we use alcohol, nicotine, caffeine, sugar, and all sorts of over-the-counter and prescription drugs. The impulse to go in this direction usually comes from a strong desire to feel different at a low moment. And we have lots of low moments. The level of substance dependency in our culture is dramatic testimony to our individual pain and our yearning for moments of inner peace.

Such low moments or moods are also at the root of the thought pattern known as *depressive rumination.* If not recognized and held lovingly in awareness, such low moments can trigger a downward spiral of toxic and highly inaccurate thoughts leading to episodes of major depressive disorder in some people—especially those who are predisposed to this condition from earlier life events and experiences that were not fully met and resolved on an emotional and cognitive level. This is now the domain of much fruitful research and clinical work in the field of *mindfulness-based cognitive therapy* (MBCT), described in Chapter 24.

Many people do not feel that they can get through the day, or even the morning, without a cup of coffee (or two or three). Having a cup of coffee becomes a way of taking care of yourself, a way of stopping, a way of connecting with others or with yourself. It has its own beauty, its own inner logic, its own culture, and in moderation it can be very effective at helping you pace yourself as you face the demands of the day. Such daily rituals can deepen a sense of pausing to take in the moment. Other people use cigarettes in a similar way. Cigarettes are commonly, if unconsciously, used to get through moments of stress and anxiety. For many years, one tobacco company ubiquitously advertised its brand as "the pause that refreshes." You light up, take a deep breath, the world stops for a moment, there is a momentary sense of peace, of satisfaction, of relaxation, and then you move on . . . until the next stressful moment. Alcohol is another chemical means that is widely used in attempts to cope with stress and emotional pain. It offers the added elements of muscle relaxation and temporary escape from the weight of your problems. With a few drinks inside you, life can seem more tolerable. Many people feel optimistic, social, self-confident, and hopeful when they have been drinking. The people you drink with are likely to provide emotional and social comfort and to reinforce the idea that drinking can help you to feel in control and is a normal and good thing to do. Of course, that may be true, again in moderation and under circumstances that are not habitually self-destructive.

Food can also be used to cope with stress and emotional discomfort in a similar way, almost as if it were a drug. Many people eat whenever they feel anxious or depressed. Food becomes a crutch for getting through uncomfortable moments and a reward afterward. If you have a feeling of emptiness inside, it's only natural to try to fill it. Eating is an easy way to do it. At least you are literally filling yourself. The fact that it doesn't really make you feel better for long does not prevent lots of us from continuing to do it to one degree or another. Using food for comfort can become a powerful addiction. It has been shown biochemically to stimulate the reward center in the brain to release opioids that damp down the hypothalamic-pituitary pathway that triggers stress reactivity. That makes us feel at ease, comfortable, good. And guess what? The foods that deliver this stress-reducing feeling are precisely those foods that are highest in fat and sugar, the so-called comfort foods that we are usually most drawn to, especially when we feel down or stressed. As with any addiction, it is very hard to break out of such cycles of eating to reduce the feelings of stress temporarily, then having to eat some more when they return all too soon, even when you are aware of the pattern. That is, unless you have a strategy for doing so and the strong determination to stick with it over the long haul. More on this subject in the chapter on food stress.

People are also accustomed to using *drugs* to regulate their levels of psychological well-being. Pain medications (such as the narcotic Vicodin) and tranquilizers are among the most widely prescribed medications in the United States, and the most widely abused. In Britain, there is a widely acknowledged epidemic of doctor-prescribed tranquilizer use, with people often suffering extremely debilitating side effects and developing addiction to the drugs, making it very difficult to taper off of them. Tranquilizers (such as Valium and Xanax) are most often prescribed for women, and for longer periods of time than for men. The message is that if you are feeling some discomfort, are having trouble sleeping, are anxious, are yelling at the kids all the time, or are overreacting to little things at home or at work, swallow a pill to take the edge off things, to be your old self, to get things under control. This attitude toward using prescription drugs as the first line of defense to regulate anxiety reactions, depression, and symptoms of stress is very prevalent in medicine. Drugs are convenient and they work, at least for a while. Why not use them? Why not give someone a convenient and effective way of feeling more in control?

For the most part this perspective goes unquestioned in medicine. It is a tacit framework within which the daily work of medicine is conducted. Doctors are bombarded with drug advertisements in medical journals, and drug salespeople are always dropping off free samples of the latest drugs to try out on their patients, as well as notepads, coffee cups, calendars, and pens, all emblazoned with drug names. The pharmaceutical companies make sure that medicine is practiced within a sea of highly visible drug messages.

There is nothing wrong with drugs per se. In fact, as we all know, medications play an extremely important role in medicine. But the climate that is created by aggressive advertising and sales tactics can have strong subconscious influences on the practitioners of the art, leading them to think first and foremost about *which* drug they should be prescribing rather than *whether* they should be prescribing any drug at all as the first line of approach to a particular problem—especially if there is a major lifestyle component to the condition or illness, or if the problem and troubling symptoms have been shown to be positively and in some cases dramatically affected by non-pharmacological means, such as mindfulness practices for pain and anxiety (see Part IV, and in particular, Claire's story in Chapter 25).

Of course, this attitude toward drugs pervades the entire society, not just medicine. We are a drug-ingesting culture. Patients often come to the doctor with the expectation that they will be "given something" to help them. If they don't leave with a prescription, they might feel the doctor is not really trying to help. The over-the-counter products for pain relief, for controlling cold symptoms, and for speeding up or slowing down movement through the colon alone constitute a multibillion-dollar industry in this country. We are inundated with messages telling us that if our body or mind is not feeling the way we would like it to feel, we should just take X and we will be in control once again.

Who could resist? Why would anyone go through the discomfort of a headache when you could take an aspirin or a Tylenol? The fact that we take drugs on many occasions just to suppress symptoms of disregulation usually goes unnoticed. We use them to avoid paying attention to the headache or the cold we have, or to our GI tract when it is problematic, instead of asking ourselves whether there is a deeper pattern and meaning underneath our immediate symptoms and discomfort that might be worth attending to. That doesn't necessarily suggest you shouldn't take the aspirin or the Tylenol. But you could bring awareness to the impulse to go for the quick fix (and your strong desire to suppress the symptoms), and before you take the drug you could at least experiment with bringing a self-compassionate and non-judging awareness to the experience you are having as best you can, at least for a time, and see what happens.

Given the dominant attitude toward drugs in our society, it is little wonder that there is an epidemic of illegal drug use in our country. The driving force among the consumers of illegal drugs is ultimately the same mindset: that is, if you don't like things as they are, take something that will put you in a better state. When people feel alienated or excluded from the dominant social institutions and norms, they are likely to explore ways of relieving those feelings of alienation through the most convenient and immediately powerful means available. Drugs are convenient and they have very immediate effects. Illegal drug use is presently occurring at all levels of society, beginning with widespread abuse of drugs and alcohol among teenagers. According to a 2010 National Survey on Drug Use and Health, more than twenty-two million Americans age twelve and older—nearly 9 percent of the population—use illegal drugs.

Many of the ways people use chemicals, legal and illegal, for attaining a sense of control, peace of mind, relaxation, and that good feeling inside themselves are potential examples of maladaptive coping attempts, especially when they are unexamined or lead to an unhealthy dependency. They become particularly unhealthy when they drift into the realm of the habitual and become the only or the dominant means we employ for controlling our reactions to stress. They are maladaptive because they can compound stress in the long run, even if they provide some relief in the short run. They can rapidly become impediments to adapting effectively to the stressors we live with and to the world as it is. In the long run, as a rule, they don't make us healthier or happier because they don't help us to optimize our own capacity for self-efficacy, self-regulation, emotional balance, and the cultivation of our own deep biological capacity for homeostasis and allostasis.

In fact, they ultimately add to and compound the stress and pressure we are under. This is indicated in Figure 9 by the arrow going from substance dependency back to the person. Reliance on chemicals easily leads to a false sense of well-being, distortions in perceptions, and clouding our ability to see clearly, thus undermining our motivation to find healthier ways to live. In these ways, they can prevent us from growing and healing—at least until we realize that there are other options.

The substances we seek out to relieve stress are also stressors on the body in their own right. Nicotine and the other chemicals in cigarette smoke are implicated in heart disease, cancer, and lung disease; alcohol plays a role in liver, heart, and brain disease; and cocaine can result in cardiac arrhythmias and sudden cardiac death. All are psychologically addicting; nicotine, alcohol, and cocaine are physiologically addicting as well.

A person can live for many years cycling through episodes of stress and stress reactivity followed by maladaptive attempts to keep body and mind under control, followed by more stress, followed by more maladaptive coping, as shown in Figure 9. The habits of overworking, overeating, hyperactivity, and substance dependency can keep you going for a long time. If you choose to look, it is usually evident that things are getting worse, not better. Your body can tell you a thing or two, if you are willing to listen. And if you are in this situation, the people closest to you are probably trying to get you to see it and seek professional help. But when your habits have become a way of life, it is very easy to discount what other people are telling you, and even to deny what your body or mind is trying to tell you. Your habits provide a certain comfort and security that you don't want to give up, even if they are killing you. Ultimately, all maladaptive coping is addictive, and we pay a huge price for it both physically and psychologically. Basically, it keeps us disregulated and prevents us from living our way into the potential fullness of our lives and loves and into freedom from untold delusion and suffering.

As Figure 9 suggests, sooner or later the accumulated effects of stress reactivity, compounded by inadequate and ultimately toxic ways of dealing with it, lead inevitably to breakdown in one form or another. Mostly it will happen sooner rather than later because our internal resources for maintaining homeostasis can take only so much overload and abuse before they succumb and collapse. Research in the new field of epigenetics is showing this very clearly. It is in the *interaction* of our genes with our environment—which includes our lifestyle choices, how we behave, even how and what we habitually think, and, it appears, whether or not we practice mindfulness and other forms of meditation—that the genome is regulated and our susceptibility to various diseases made more or less likely.

When we are not optimizing our epigenetic options to promote and nurture our overall health and well-being through the choices we make about how to be in wiser relationship to our own body and mind and to the world—in the face of our chronic stress reactions and our often less-than-helpful attempts at coping—what gives out first will depend to a large extent on our genes, on our environment, and on the particulars of the way of living we have settled on. The weakest link is what goes first. If you have a strong family history of heart disease, you might have a heart attack, especially if other factors that increase the risk of heart disease—such as smoking, a high-fat diet, high blood pressure, and cynical and hostile behavior toward others—are prominent features of your life.

Alternatively, you may reach a state of disregulation of immune functioning, which may make cancer of some kind, or an autoimmune condition, the more likely outcome. Here too the interaction of your genes, your exposure to carcinogens during your lifetime, your diet, and your relationship to your emotions might make this pathway either more or less likely. A stress-provoked drop in immune function could also lead to greater susceptibility to infectious diseases.

Any organ system could be the ultimate weak link that leads to disease. For some it might be the skin, for others the lungs, for others the cerebral vasculature leading to a stroke, for others the digestive tract or the kidneys. For others it might be an injury, such as a disk problem in the neck or lower back, made worse by an unhealthy lifestyle. Or it might be the burden the body faces by carrying unnecessary weight and excess fat in the wrong places, in particular the abdomen.

Whatever the actual form of the crisis, maladaptive attempts to cope with stress ultimately culminate in breakdown of one kind or another. If the breakdown does not result in death, then it just becomes one more major stressor that you now have to face and work with on top of all the others you already had in your life. In Figure 9, breakdown itself becomes the source of one more arrow feeding back on the person, necessitating even greater adaptation.

There is another branch of the stress reaction pathway, not depicted in Figure 9, that becomes important when a person is faced with unavoidable stress sustained over long periods of time. Examples might be caring for an elderly parent who is ill or who has Alzheimer's disease, or caring for a disabled child. Here all the stressors of daily living are compounded by a whole other set of potentially overwhelming stressors associated with the long-term demands of the situation. If adequate short- and long-term strategies for adapting to the situation are not developed, the pressures of daily living can mount to the point where the person is constantly in a state of hyperarousal, reacting repeatedly to even insignificant stressors with tension, irritability, and anger. Continued arousal with little ultimate control over the fundamental stressor can reach the point where feelings of helplessness and hopelessness begin to dominate. Rather than hyperarousal, chronic depression can set in, leading to a different spectrum of hormonal and immune system changes that, over time, can also undermine health and lead to breakdown. This is clearly demonstrated in a study of mothers caring for children with chronic health problems, in which the rate of degradation of telomeres in leukocytes and of oxidative damage were significantly higher than in mothers of healthy children—but, amazingly, *only* for those mothers who reported high levels of perceived stress. In other words, those who had found ways to see stress as an expected part of life and manage it effectively and therefore did not report high levels of perceived stress, did not show the high rate of telomere shortening, nor did they show oxidative damage.*

* Epel ES, Blackburn EH, Lin J, Dhabhar FS, et al. Accelerated telomere shortening in response to life stress. PNAS. 2004;101:17312–17315.

Breakdown in the stress reaction pathway does not have to be primarily physical. Too much stress and not enough effective coping can lead to a depletion of our emotional and cognitive resources to the point where you might experience what is sometimes called a *nervous breakdown,* a feeling of being completely unable to function in your ordinary life anymore. This condition may reach the point of requiring hospitalization and drug treatment. Nowadays it is fashionable to use the word *burnout* to describe a similar state of near or total psychological exhaustion with an accompanying loss of drive and enthusiasm for the details of your life. What used to give you pleasure no longer does, and your very thought process and emotional life are severely disregulated.

A person experiencing burnout feels alienated from work, family, and friends; nothing seems meaningful anymore. A deep depression can set in under these conditions and can lead to a loss of ability to function effectively. Joy and enthusiasm disappear. As with the physical examples of breakdown, if psychological breakdown occurs, it becomes one more major stressor that the person now has to deal with, one way or another.

This cycle of a stressor triggering a stress reaction of some kind, often accompanied by an internalizing of the stress reaction, leading to inadequate or maladaptive attempts to keep things under control, leading to more stressors, more stress reactions, and ultimately to an acute breakdown in health, perhaps even to death, is a way of life for many of us. When you are caught up in this vicious cycle, it seems that this is just the way life is, that there is no other way. You might think to yourself that this is just part of getting older, a normal decline in health, a normal loss of energy or enthusiasm or feelings of control.

But getting stuck in the stress-reaction cycle is neither normal nor inevitable. As we have already seen, we have far more options and resources for facing our problems than we usually know we have—creative options, imaginative options, healthy options. The healthy alternative to being caught up in any of our self-destructive patterns is to stop *reacting* to stress and to start *responding* to it. There are lots of ways to do this, not one. This is the path of mindfulness in daily life.

20

Responding to Stress Instead of Reacting

And so we are brought back to the key importance of mindfulness. The very first and most important step in breaking free from a lifetime of stress reactivity is to be aware of what is actually happening while it is happening. In this chapter we will look at how we might do this.

Let's consider once again the situation of the person in Figure 9 that we analyzed in the last chapter. As we have seen, at any moment in time this person may be encountering a combination of internal and external stressors that can trigger a cascade of feelings and behaviors we have been calling the *habitual or automatic stress reaction.* Figure 10 shows the same stress-reaction cycle as in Figure 9, but now includes an alternative pathway, which we will call the *mindfulness-mediated stress response,* to differentiate it from the automatic stress reaction. The stress response is the healthy alternative to the stress reaction. We can think of the mindfulness-mediated stress response, which we will sometimes refer to as the *stress response* for short, as the generally healthier alternative to the more unconscious stress reaction. The stress response represents collectively what might be called *adaptive,* or healthy, coping strategies as opposed to maladaptive attempts to cope with stress.

You do not have to go the route of the fight-or-flight reaction nor the route of helplessness, overwhelm, and depression every time you are stressed. With training, practice, and intentionality, you can actually experiment with choosing not to react in those ways when the opportunity arises. This is where mindfulness comes in. Moment-to-moment nonjudgmental awareness allows you to engage in and influence the flow of events and your relationship to them at those very moments when you are most likely to react automatically, and plunge into hyperarousal and maladaptive attempts to keep things under some degree of control.

By definition, stress reactions happen automatically and unconsciously, even though, as we have seen, many different, highly evolved, integrated, and useful cognitive processes may be at play beneath the surface of our awareness. Still, as soon as you intentionally bring awareness to what is going on in a stressful situation, you have already changed that situation dramatically and opened up the field of potentially adaptive and creative possibilities just by virtue of not being unconscious and on automatic pilot anymore. You are now committed to being as present for it as you can be while the stressful event is unfolding. And since you are an integral part of the whole situation, *simply by holding whatever is happening in awareness, you are actually changing the matrix of the entire situation even before you do anything overt, such as take action, or even open your mouth to speak.* This interior shift to embrace what is unfolding in awareness in the present moment can be extremely important, precisely because it gives you a range of options for possibly influencing what will happen next. Bringing awareness to such a moment takes only a split second, but it can make a critical difference in the outcome of a stressful encounter. In fact, it is the deciding factor in whether you go down the path of the "Stress Reaction" in Figure 10 or whether you can navigate over to the path of the "Stress Response."

Let's examine how you would do this. If you manage to remain centered in that moment of stress and recognize both the stressfulness of the situation *and* your impulses to react, you have already introduced a new dimension into the situation. Because of this, you neither have to react automatically with your usual habitual patterns of emotional expression, whatever they are, nor do you have to suppress all your thoughts and feel-

FIGURE 10

COPING WITH STRESS RESPONDING VS. REACTING

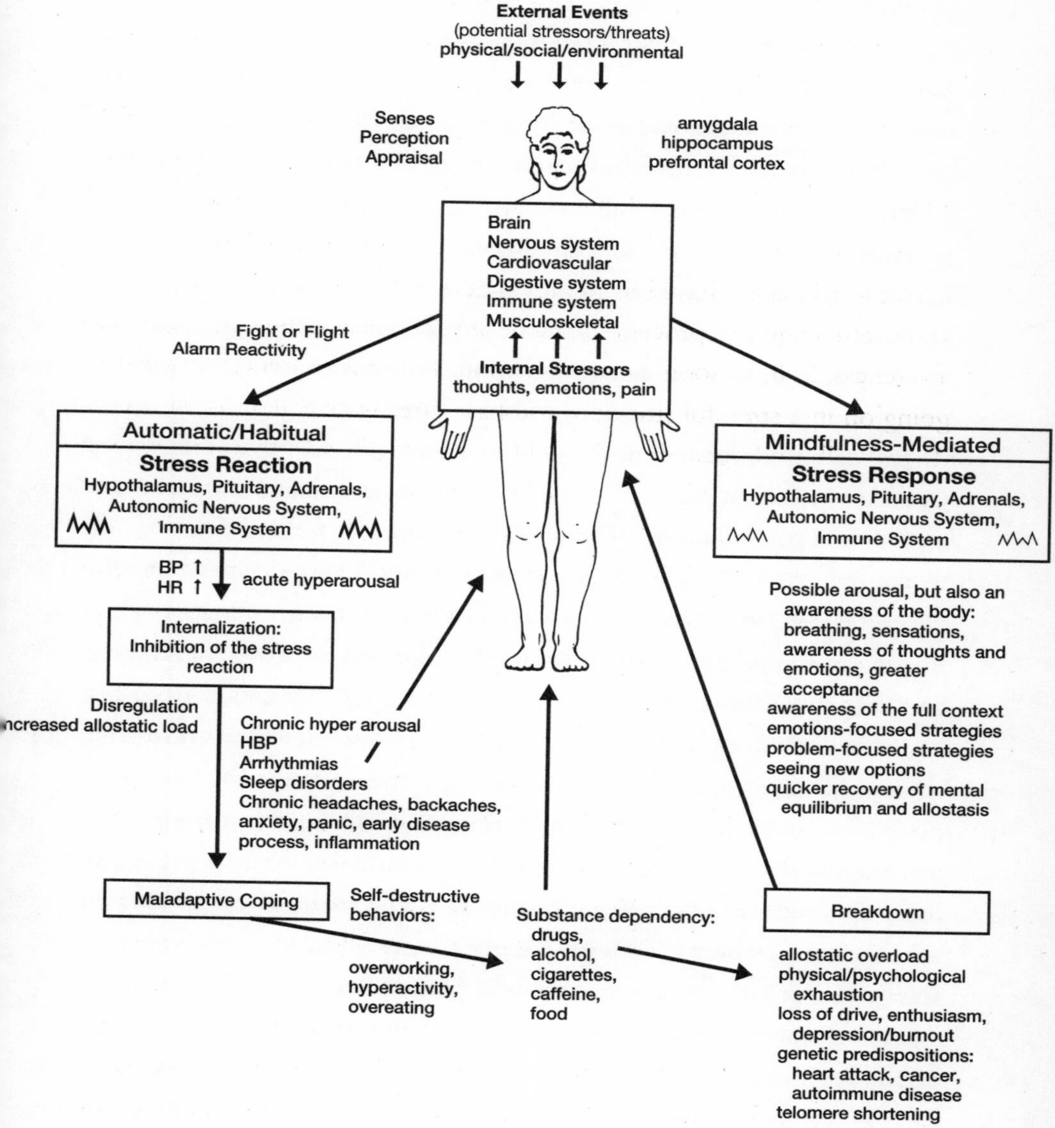

ings associated with heightened arousal to prevent yourself from going out of control. *You can actually allow yourself to feel threatened, fearful, angry, or hurt and to feel the tension in your body in these moments.* Being conscious in the present, you can easily recognize and identify these agitations and contractions for what they are: *thoughts, emotions, and sensations.*

This simple momentary shift from mindless reaction to mindful recognition of what is unfolding inwardly and outwardly can reduce the power of the stress reaction and its hold over you. In that moment, you now have a very real choice. You can still go the route of the stress reaction, but you no longer have to. You no longer have to react automatically in the same old way every time your buttons get pushed. You can *respond* instead—out of your greater awareness of what is happening, and the larger perspective and new options and openings that frequently accompany an expanded perspective, as with the puzzle of the nine dots.

This inner response would be an awful lot to ask of ourselves in a stressful situation if we had the expectation that awareness and centeredness should just come out of nowhere whenever we needed them or that we should simply be able to will our mind and body to be calm when they are not. But in fact, through the formal meditation practices, we have been training our mind and body to respond in this way all along, developing and deepening these very qualities. You have probably experienced any number of small emotional and cognitive reactions, including impatience or annoyance, at places in the body scan, for instance, or in the sitting meditation, or in the mindful yoga. Practically speaking, only through regular training to develop the "muscle" of mindfulness could we possibly hope that our calmness and awareness would be strong enough and reliable enough to assist us in responding in more balanced and imaginative ways when we find ourselves in stressful situations.

The capacity to respond mindfully develops each time we experience discomfort, pain, or strong emotions of any kind during formal meditation and we just observe them and work at allowing them to simply be here as they are, without reacting. As we have seen, the practice itself grounds us in alternative ways of seeing and responding to reactive states within ourselves, moment by moment. It introduces us to an entirely different way of being *in relationship* to what we find unpleasant or aversive or difficult. It offers a new way of being, one that allows us to feel more in touch with what is unfolding moment by moment. It therefore expands our sense of being anchored and stable, at least to some degree, in our recognition and appraisal of an event or circumstance within the larger field of our awareness. This is akin to a new way of being, and thus a new way of feeling more in touch and in control in relationship to our experience, even when things are difficult. We come to see from our own experience that wise relationality—and therefore more appropriate and effective responsivity—can come out of inner calmness, clarity, acceptance, and openness. We come to see that we don't have to struggle with our thoughts and emotions, and that we can't and don't have to try to force things to be as we want them to be in that moment—or ever.

One thing is certain: we know where the fight-or-flight reaction and its various sequellae will lead if it is left to play itself out automatically, as in the left side of Figure 10. We have been going that route most of our lives. The challenge now is for us to realize that, in any moment, we are in a position to actually decide to do things differently by intentionally shifting how we are in relationship to our experience, whatever it is, in that very moment.

Choosing to go the route of the stress response rather than the stress reaction obviously does not mean that you will never react automatically by feeling threatened or fearful or angry, or that you will never do anything silly or self-destructive. What it does mean is that more of the time you might be more aware of those feelings and impulses as they are arising. Your awareness may or may not temper the intensity of the arousal you feel. That will depend on the circumstances, and on the strength of your practice. But in general, either awareness reduces arousal at the time by situating things in a larger perspective, or it helps you to recover from it more quickly afterward. This is indicated in Figure 10 by the smaller squiggles in the box labeled "Stress Response" as compared with the box labeled "Stress Reaction." These represent the summation of all the stress hormones, autonomic nervous system activity, and pathways within the brain and body that are at play to either amplify or damp down the stress reaction in any given moment.

And let's face it—in some situations, emotional arousal and physical tension are totally appropriate. At other times, though, they may be unhelpful, inappropriate, or even destructive. In either case, how you handle whatever arises in the present moment will depend on your ability to rest in and trust in awareness itself, and to disengage, to whatever degree is possible for you, from how personally you might be taking things, especially at times when, in actuality, they are not at all personal.

In some situations, feeling threatened may have more to do with your state of mind and the context in which you find yourself rather than with the triggering event itself. If you bring awareness to your most stressful moments with a sense of openness and curiosity, you might see a bit more clearly how your unbalanced view or emotional upset left over from an earlier event could be contributing to an inappropriate overreaction on your part, one that may be out of proportion to what the actual circumstances warrant. Then you might remind yourself to try letting go of your self-limited view, right in that moment—which means letting it simply be here without feeding it—just to see what would happen. You might try trusting that things will become more harmonious if you make the effort to meet the situation with a more open and spacious frame of mind, with a bit more calmness and clarity and even self-compassion. Why not test this possibility for yourself once or twice? What do you have to lose? This is how we come to a larger perspective taking.

As you bring mindfulness to a stressful moment, you can see if, in effect, it winds up creating something of a *pause,* a moment in which it feels like you have a bit of extra time to assess things more completely. By intentionally orienting yourself in this way to the present moment, challenging as it may be, you have an opportunity to buffer the impending effects of a major stress reaction. This buffering arises by recognizing the early warning signs of the stress reaction in your body and in your mind, and allowing them to be felt and embraced, even welcomed to the degree you can manage that, and held with kindness in awareness. This in turn gives you a bit more time within the pause you have taken to opt for a more mindful and perhaps more emotionally nuanced response, one that will indeed buffer the full brunt of the physiology of the stress reaction and provide you with more creative openings, right in the moment of pausing. Even though it may last only a fraction of a second by the clock, the duration of this pause in the mind can seem expanded, even timeless, and your choices much more vivid and available. It recruits multiple intelligences that we all already possess but frequently forget we have. Of course, responding to the unwanted and unexpected is a skill that develops with practice, and with remembering to implement it in those moments when it might be most beneficial. Indeed, that remembering is a large part of the practice itself.

When you experiment in this way, you may be surprised at how many things that used to push your buttons no longer get you aroused. They may no longer even seem stressful to you, not because you have given up and become defeated or resigned but because you have become more spacious, more relaxed and trusting of yourself.

Responding in this way under pressure is an empowering experience. You are maintaining and deepening your own balance of mind and of body, your capacity for remaining centered, even in difficult situations. This is not some romantic idealization. It is hard work, and we can fail at it repeatedly, getting caught in our own reactivity time and again in spite of our best intentions. This itself is an essential part of practice. In the ongoing cultivation of mindfulness, what we think are our failures are not failures. They are gifts—revealing extremely useful information—if we are open to being mindful of everything that unfolds in our lives, in a day, or in a moment, and putting it all to good use as grist for the mill.

How do we consciously cultivate the mindfulness-mediated stress response in daily life? The same way we cultivate mindfulness in the formal meditation practices: moment by moment, grounding ourselves in our body, in our breathing, in awareness itself. When your buttons are pushed or you find yourself feeling overwhelmed, when feelings of fight or flight come up, you might try bringing your awareness to your jaw as it clenches, to your brow as it furrows, to your shoulders as they tense up, to your fists as they start to clench, to your heart as it begins to pound in your chest, to your stomach as it begins to feel funny, to whatever you might notice about how your body feels at that moment. See if you can be aware of your feelings of anger or fear or hurt as you feel them rising inside you. Locating your emotions in a particular place in your body can be extremely telling, and very useful.

In such moments, you might even try saying to yourself, "This is it" or "Here is a stressful situation" or "Now is a time to tune in to my breathing and center myself." Mindfulness sets the stage for you to respond appropriately right here in this very moment. If you are quick enough, you can sometimes catch the stress reaction before it develops completely and turn it into a more imaginative and creative response instead.

It takes practice to catch stress reactions as they are emerging. But don't worry. If you are like most of us, you will have plenty of opportunities to practice. When you are willing to bring awareness to them, each situation you encounter becomes another occasion for you to practice responding mindfully instead of reacting habitually. You can be certain that you won't be able to respond to *every* situation. It is unrealistic to expect that of yourself. And you will probably find yourself playing catch-up a good deal of the time because you didn't detect the signs of the stress reaction when they first arose. But just by remembering to bring a larger perspective to each one of these moments, you are learning something important about the landscape of emotional reactivity, and transforming the stressors you are experiencing into challenges and passageways for growth.* Now whatever stressors you are facing become like wind for a sailor, here for you to use skillfully to propel you where you want to go. As with any wind, you may not be able to control the entire situation. But perhaps, by experimenting in this way, you will be better able to assume a wiser and more

* Recall happiness researcher Dan Gilbert's comment quoted in the Introduction: "People blossom when challenged and wither when threatened." It is an important distinction.

creative relationship to the circumstances and put its energies to work for you to navigate the difficult conditions and minimize some of the more dangerous or potentially harmful elements of what you are facing.

Probably the best place to start is with your breathing. If you can manage to bring your attention to your breathing for even the briefest of moments, it will set the stage for facing that moment and the next one with greater clarity. As we have seen, the breath itself is calming, especially when we can tune in to it at the belly. It's like an old friend; it anchors us, gives us stability, like the bridge piling anchored in bedrock as the river flows around it. Alternatively, it can remind us that ten or twenty feet below the agitated surface of the ocean there is calmness. What is more, we carry it everywhere, so it is always here, no matter what the circumstances, and thus exquisitely convenient for us to call upon—a true ally in the cultivation of emotional balance.

The breath readily reconnects us with calmness and awareness when we lose touch with them momentarily. If you have been practicing, no doubt you will have experienced that the breath can bring you to an awareness of your body in a particularly stressful moment, including any increase in visceral tension or muscle tightness. After all, the breath sensations are themselves an intimate part of the sensory field of the body and can put you back in touch with the whole of it. Resting in an awareness of breathing, even for one or two breaths, can also remind you to check in with your thoughts and feelings and become aware of them and how they may be expressing themselves in particular regions of the body in the form of tightness or tension of some kind. Perhaps you will see how reactive they are. Perhaps you will question their accuracy.

In maintaining a modicum of stability and groundedness in the face of a potentially threatening stressor, to whatever degree you can manage it, and then turning *toward* it rather than turning away, it is much more likely that, right in that moment, you will have an awareness of the fuller context of the situation, whatever it is. Your impulses to run or to fight, to struggle or protect yourself, or perhaps to panic, freeze, or fall apart, will be seen within this larger picture, along with all other relevant factors in that moment. Perceiving things in this way allows you to remain calmer from the start or to recover your inner balance more quickly if it is thrown off initially by your reaction. One middle manager who completed the MBSR program put the nine dot problem (see Chapter 12) in a prominent place on the wall in her office to remind her to remember to look for the whole context when she feels stressed at work (see Laurie's story on pages 406–410).

When you are stabilized and grounded in calmness and moment-to-moment awareness, you are more likely to be creative and to see new options and openings where the moment before there didn't seem to be any. You are more likely to see new solutions even to old and tiresome challenges, and ways to manage new but unwanted and difficult situations. You are more likely to be aware of your emotions and less likely to be carried away by them. It will be easier for you to maintain your balance and sense of perspective in trying circumstances—what we might call *equanimity*.

If the original cause of your stress has already passed, you will be more likely to see that, at that moment, whatever happened has *already* happened. It is over. It is already in the past. This perception frees you to put your energies into facing this new present moment and dealing with whatever problems or challenges require your immediate attention.

When you channel and modulate your attention in this way, you will experience a quicker recovery of your mental equilibrium, even in very stressful situations, and also of your physiological equilibrium (allostasis) as your bodily reactions calm down. Notice in Figure 10 that, unlike the path of the automatic stress reaction, *the mindfulness-mediated stress response doesn't generate more stress.* It doesn't feed back more stress arrows onto the person. You respond and then it's finished. You move on. The next moment will have less carryover from the preceding one because you faced it and dealt with it when it came up. Plus you have strengthened the muscle of mindfulness a tiny bit. What is more, recognizing and responding mindfully to stressors from moment to moment will minimize the tension that we allow to build up inside of us, both in the body and in the mind, thereby reducing our need to find ways to cope with the discomfort that accompanies internalized tension.

Having an alternative way of handling pressure can reduce our dependence on the common maladaptive coping strategies we so often resort to and get stuck in when we feel tense. One returning graduate said at the end of an all-day session that she figured out that her strongest impulses to go for a cigarette lasted about three seconds. She noticed that a few breaths took about the same time. So she thought she would try bringing awareness to her breathing and just ride the wave of her impulse, watching it crest and then fall, without taking the cigarette. When I last spoke with her, she hadn't had a cigarette in two and a half years.

As relaxation and peace of mind become more familiar to you through the formal meditation practice, it becomes easier to call upon them when you need them. When you are stressed, you can allow yourself to ride the waves of the stress. You will neither have to shut if off nor run away. True, you may be going up and down some, but much less than if you are always at the mercy of your automatic reactivity.

Each week people in the Stress Reduction Clinic come to class with anecdotes—sometimes inspiring, sometimes amusing—of the ways in which they found themselves handling stress differently than before. Phil reported he used the stress response to successfully control his back pain and concentrate better when he took his exams to become an insurance salesman. Joyce was able to remain calm in the hospital and deal with her anxious feelings about her surgery by reminding herself to breathe. Pat actually used it to stay collected and cope with the humiliation of the police coming to her house and taking her off in the middle of the night in front of her neighbors because, it turned out, her psychiatrist was going away for the weekend and mistakenly thought from a phone conversation that Pat was suicidal. Janet, the young doctor, was able to control her nausea and fear and fly medical missions in the Life Flight helicopter. When her sister started in on her with her usual hostility, Elizabeth decided to just remain silent rather than being hostile in return; it surprised her sister so much that they started talking about it, which led to their first good communication in years.

Doug was involved in an automobile accident in which no one was hurt. The accident was not his fault. He said that previously he would have been furious at the other driver for ruining his car and for the inconvenience it caused him on a very busy day. Instead he just said to himself, "No one was hurt, it has already happened, let's go from here." So he tuned in to his breathing and proceeded, with a calmness that was totally uncharacteristic of him, to deal with the details of the situation.

Marsha drove her husband's new van to the hospital for her MBSR class one night. The last thing her husband said to her before she left was "For God's sake, be careful with the van." And she was. She drove very carefully all the way to the hospital. To make sure the van would be safe during the class, she thought she would park it in the garage rather than in one of the open lots. So she drove into the garage. As she did so, she heard a funny noise coming from the top of the van. Too late—the low overhang at the entrance had sheared off the skylight bubble on the top of the van, which she had forgotten about. For a second, when she realized what she had done and what her husband's reaction was going to be, she almost panicked. Then she laughed instead and said to herself, "The damage is done. I don't believe I did this, but it's already done." So she came to class and told us about it, saying how surprised she was that she was able to control her panic, be calm, see the humor in it, and realize that her husband would just have to accept that it had happened.

Keith reported that he discovered he could meditate at the dentist's office. Usually he was terrified of going and always put it off until he just had to go because of the pain. He found himself focusing on his breathing and the feeling of his body sinking into the chair. He found he could do it even as the dentist was drilling in his mouth. Instead of being white-knuckled, he was calm and centered. He was astonished at how well this worked for him.

In Part IV we will be discussing in detail a range of applications of mindfulness practice. There you will find many more examples of people who were able to see and to cope with things differently after they learned to respond to stress with greater mindfulness instead of reacting to it on autopilot, or, we could say, mindlessly. Perhaps by this point, if you have been practicing on your own, you may be finding that you are also responding differently in some ways to the pressures and problems in your life. This, of course, is what is most important!

Greater resilience in the face of stressors and reduced stress reactivity are characteristic of people who practice meditation regularly. This has been demonstrated in a number of studies. Daniel Goleman and Gary Schwartz showed in the early 1970s at Harvard that meditators not only had a heightened sensitivity and emotional involvement compared with non-meditators when both were shown a very graphic film of industrial accidents, but also recovered their physical and mental equilibrium more quickly afterward than did non-meditators.

More recently, the Shamatha Project, the most comprehensive study of the effects of an intensive meditation retreat ever conducted (the retreat was three months long), reported major differences on both psychological and biological measures between the meditators and a wait list control group in a randomized clinical trial under the overall direction of Cliff Saron of the University of California at Davis. These differences included 30 percent higher levels of the anti-aging enzyme telomerase in the meditators, as well as changes in psychological factors such as an increase in perceived control and a reduction in what is called neuroticism (vulnerability to stress and difficult emotions), which were in turn related to increases in measures of mindfulness and purpose in life. Those who increased the most in mindfulness by the end of the study (as measured by a mindfulness self-report scale) had the greatest decreases in cortisol production. Since, generally speaking, higher telomerase levels reflect lower stress reactivity, and greater perceived control is just what you want for responding to stress more mindfully rather than reacting to it automatically, the results of this study that have been reported to date* are a good indication that intensive meditation practice (this study focused in particular on mindfulness of breathing and other objects of attention, as well as the cultivation of lovingkindness and compassion) can lead to a major shift away from stress reactivity that is reflected at both the level of biology and psychology.

In an early seminal study conducted by Dr. Dean Ornish and his colleagues, related to work that will be discussed in more detail in Chapter 31, people with documented coronary heart disease who completed a twenty-four-day intensive lifestyle-change program that involved a low-fat, low-cholesterol vegetarian diet and daily meditation and yoga practice greatly reduced their previously elevated blood pressure responses to a range of tasks inducing psychological stress—such as doing mental arithmetic under time pressure—whereas people in a control group who did not change their diet or practice these techniques did not show a lowered blood pressure reactivity to stress when retested. While, as we have seen, it is normal for blood pressure to go up when we are stressed, it is remarkable that the people who went through the program were able to change their stress reactivity so dramatically within such a short time.

As we have seen, the fact that you can learn to respond to stress with awareness does not mean that you will never react anymore or that you will not sometimes be overwhelmed by anger or grief or fear. We are not trying to suppress our emotions when we respond mindfully to internal or external stressors. Rather, we are learning how to work with all our reactions, emotional and physical, so that we may be less controlled by them and see more clearly what we should do and how we might respond more effectively. What occurs in any particular situation will depend on the seri-

* So much data was acquired during this study that the results will continue to be analyzed and reported for years to come. See http://mindbrain.ucdavis.edu/labs/Saron/shamatha-project.

ousness of what is happening and on its meaning to you. You cannot develop one plan in advance that will be your strategy in all stressful situations. Responding to stress requires moment-to-moment awareness, taking each moment as it comes. You will have to rely on your imagination and trust in your ability to come up with new ways of seeing and responding in every moment. You will be charting new territory every time you encounter stress in this way. You will know that you no longer want to *react* in the old way, but you may not know what it means to *respond* in a new and different way. Each opportunity you get will be different. The range of options available to you will depend on the circumstances. But at least you will have all your resources at your disposal when you encounter the situation with awareness. You will have the freedom to be creative. When you cultivate mindfulness in your life, your ability to be fully present can come through even under the most trying of circumstances. It can cradle and embrace the full catastrophe itself. Sometimes this may reduce your pain and sometimes it may not. But awareness brings comfort of a certain kind even in the midst of suffering. We could call it the comfort of wisdom and inner trust, the comfort of being whole.

IV

The Applications: Taking on the Full Catastrophe

21

Working with Symptoms: Listening to Your Body

The relief of symptoms of various kinds is a multibillion-dollar industry. The slightest sniffle, headache, or stomachache sends people scurrying to the medicine cabinet or drugstore in search of the magic something to make it go away. There are over-the-counter medications to make the digestive tract slow down, others to make it speed up, others to relieve heartburn or neutralize excess stomach acid. With a prescription from a physician, you can obtain drugs to reduce anxiety, such as Valium and Xanax, and drugs to relieve pain, such as Percodan. As we have seen, tranquilizers are among the most prescribed medications in the country. For a long time, so are drugs that decrease the secretion of stomach acid, such as Tagamet and Zantac. Now they are available over the counter. Most of these medications are used primarily to relieve symptoms of discomfort, and they work very well in most instances. But the trouble with the widespread use of many such drugs is that the underlying problems that are producing the symptoms may not be getting addressed just because the symptoms are temporarily relieved.

This practice of immediately going for a drug to relieve a symptom reflects a widespread attitude that symptoms are inconvenient, useless threats to our ability to live life the way we want to live it and that they should be suppressed or eliminated whenever possible. The problem with this attitude is that what we call symptoms are often the body's way of telling us that something is out of balance. They are feedback about dis-regulation of one sort or another. If we ignore these messages or, worse, suppress them, it may only lead to more severe symptoms and more serious problems later on. What is more, the person doing this is not learning how to listen to and trust his or her body.

Before people begin our program, they fill out a questionnaire in which they check off from a list of more than a hundred common physical and emotional symptoms those they have experienced as problematic in the preceding month. They do the same thing again after completing the program eight weeks later.

Over the past three decades of teaching MBSR, we have observed some interesting things when we compare these two symptom lists. First, most people come into the program with a relatively high number of symptoms. The average number of symptoms is 22 out of about 110 possible ones. That is a lot of symptoms. When people leave, they are checking off on average about 14 symptoms, or 36 percent fewer symptoms than when they started. This is a dramatic reduction in a short period of time, especially for people who have that many symptoms in the first place and have had them for quite a long time. This effect is reproducible. We have seen it in virtually every eight-week cycle of MBSR over the past thirty-plus years.

You might wonder whether this reduction in the number of symptoms is a non-specific effect of having some attention paid to them, since it is well known that people can feel better temporarily when they receive almost any kind of professional attention in a medical setting. You might ask whether perhaps the reduction in symptoms is just due to their coming to the hospital every week and being part of a positive group setting, rather than to anything special that they are doing in their stress reduction classes, such as practicing meditation.

While that is a credible supposition, in this case it is unlikely. The participants in the Stress Reduction Clinic have been receiving professional medical attention from the health care system for their problems all along. On average, the chief medical complaint for which they are referred to us has been a problem for them for about seven years. It is unlikely that just coming to the hospital and being in a room full of other people with chronic medical problems and having attention paid to them would, by itself, result in these substantial reductions in their symptoms. But certainly one element contributing to their improvement might well be that they are challenged to do something for themselves for a change to enhance their own health. This facet of their experience in MBSR is a radical departure from the passive role most people assume or are forced into during treatment in the health care system. As we have been emphasizing, this is one example of a more participatory medicine.

Another reason to suspect that the symptom reduction we see among the participants in MBSR results from something that people actually learn in the program is that the reduction is maintained and even improves further after people leave. We know this from several follow-up studies in which we obtained information from more than four hundred people at different times for up to four years after they completed the program.

We also know from these studies that over 90 percent of the people who complete the program say that they are keeping up their meditation practice in one form or another for up to four years after they graduate. Most rate their training in the stress reduction clinic as very important to their improved health status.

Although we see dramatic symptom reduction during the eight weeks of MBSR, we actually focus very little on symptoms in the classes, and when we do, it is not to try to reduce them or make them go away. For one thing, the classes are a mix of people with many different medical problems and life situations. Each person has an entirely different and unique constellation of symptoms and concerns as well as a specific medical treatment plan they are following. In a room with twenty to thirty-five people, all of whom are anxious and concerned about their symptoms and wanting to get rid of them, to focus primarily on the details of each person's situation would simply encourage self-preoccupation and illness behavior. Our minds being what they are, such a forum would in all likelihood give rise to never-ending discussions of what is "the matter" rather than focusing on the possibility of personal transformation. This avenue would be of little real benefit to the participants except for the sympathy and group support it would evoke, which, while certainly therapeutic, are unlikely to lead to profound changes in either view or behavior. By choosing to focus in MBSR on what is "right" with people rather than on what is "wrong" with them, *without denying what is wrong,* we are able to go beyond self-involved preoccupations with the details of what is wrong, however important these concerns might be in other circumstances, and come to the heart of the matter, namely, how people can begin to taste their own wholeness *as they are, right now.*

Instead of discussing symptoms as woes and how to get rid of them, when we do focus on symptoms of one kind or another it is to tune in to the actual *experience* of the symptoms themselves in those moments when they most dominate the mind and body. We do this in a particular way, which might be called giving them *wise attention.* Wise attention involves bringing the stability, calmness, and clarity of mindfulness to our symptoms and to our reactions to them, and not taking personally events and circumstances that are not really personal. We call it "wise" to distinguish it from the usual type of attention we pay to our problems and crises, which tends to be very self-centered and wrapped up in a story or narrative we tell ourselves that may not be entirely accurate and thus not conducive to a larger seeing of options and avenues for relating differently to the unpleasant and the unwanted.

For example, when you have a serious chronic illness, it is only to be expected that you will be very concerned and perhaps even frightened and depressed about the ways in which your body has changed from what it once was and about what new problems you might have to face in the future. The result is that a lot of a certain kind of attention is spent on your symptoms, but it is likely not to be helpful or healing attention, so much as anxiety driven self-absorption and preoccupation. More often than not, that kind of attention is reactive, judgmental, and fearful. There is little room in the mind for acceptance, or for recognition of a larger field of possibilities for relating to one's circumstances and challenges. This is the opposite of wise attention.

The way of mindfulness is to accept ourselves right now, as we are, symptoms or no symptoms, pain or no pain, fear or no fear. Instead of rejecting our experience as undesirable, we ask, "What is this symptom saying, what is it telling me about my body and my mind right now?" We allow ourselves, for a moment at least, to go right into the full-blown feeling of the symptom. This takes a certain amount of courage, especially if the symptom involves pain, a chronic illness, or fear of death. But the challenge here is can you at least "dip your toe in the water" by trying it just a little, say for ten seconds, just to move in a little closer for a clearer look? Can we metaphorically put out the welcome mat for what is here, simply because it is already here, and take a look, or even better, allow ourselves to *feel* our way into the full range of our experience in such moments?

As we experiment with adopting this unusual stance toward our momentary experience, we may also become aware of emotions we may be feeling *about* the symptom or situation we are experiencing. Whether it is anger or rejection or fear or despair or resignation, we hold whatever arises in awareness, as dispassionately as possible. Why? For no other reason than that it is *here now.* It is already part of our experience. To move to greater levels of health and well-being, we have to start from where we actually are today, now, in this moment, not from where we would like to be. Movement toward greater health is only possible because of now, because of where we are. Now is the platform of all further possibilities. So looking closely at our symptoms and our feelings about them and then coming to accept them as they are is of utmost importance.

In this light, symptoms of illness or distress, plus your feelings about them, can be viewed as messengers coming to give you important and useful information about your body or about your mind. In the old days, if a king didn't like the message he was given, he would sometimes have the messenger killed. This is tantamount to suppressing your symptoms or your feelings because they are unwanted. Killing the messenger and denying the message or raging against it are not intelligent ways of approaching healing. The one thing we don't want to do is to ignore or rupture the essential connections that can complete relevant feedback loops and restore allostasis, self-regulation, and balance. Our real challenge when we have symptoms is to see if we can listen to their messages and really hear them and take them to heart, that is, make the connection fully.

When a patient in an MBSR class reports he or she had a headache during the body scan or during a sitting meditation, my response might be, "All right. Now, can you tell us how you *worked* with it?"

What I am looking for is whether, if you became aware that you had a headache during the time you were meditating, you used the occasion as an opportunity to look into this experience you are calling a headache, which is often a problem for you in your life anyway, even when you aren't meditating. Did you observe it with wise attention? Did you bring mindfulness, acceptance, and perhaps a bit of kindness to feeling the sensations themselves? Did you watch your thoughts at that moment? Or did the mind jump automatically into rejection and judging, perhaps to thinking that somehow you were failing at meditation, or that you "can't relax," or that meditation "doesn't work," or that you are a "bad meditator," or that nothing can cure your headaches?

Anybody can have any or all of these thoughts and many others as well. They may come into and go out of your mind at different times in reaction to the headache. As with any other reaction, the challenge here is to shift your attention so that you can see them as *thoughts* and, in doing so, welcome the headache into the present moment because it is here anyway—like it or not. Can you decipher its message by directing careful attention to how your body feels right now? Are you aware *now* of a mood or emotion that may have preceded your realizing that you had a headache? Was there an event that triggered it that you can identify? What are you feeling right now emotionally? Are you feeling anxious, depressed, sad, angry, disappointed, discouraged, annoyed? Are you able to be with whatever you are feeling in this moment? Can you breathe with the sensations of the headache, the pounding feeling in the temples, or whatever it is? Can you see your reactions with wise attention? Can you just watch your feelings and thoughts and see them simply as feelings and thoughts—as impersonal events in the field of awareness? Can you catch yourself identifying with them as "my" feelings, "my" anger, "my" thoughts, "my" headache, and then let go of the "my" and just accept the moment as it is?

When you look into the headache, seeing the constellation of thoughts and feelings, the reacting, the judging, and the rejecting of how you are feeling, the wishing to feel differently that may be going on in your mind, perhaps you will realize at a certain point that you are not your headache unless you go along with this inner process of identification, unless you yourself make it *your* headache. Maybe it is just *a* headache, or maybe it is just a feeling in the head that doesn't need a name at all right now.

The ways we use language tell us a lot about the automatic way we personalize our symptoms and illnesses. For instance, we say "I *have* a headache" or "I *have* a cold" or "I *have* a fever," when it would be more accurate to say something like "The body is headaching" or "colding" or "fevering." When we automatically and unconsciously link each symptom we experience to *I* and *my,* the mind is already creating a certain amount of trouble for us. In order to listen more deeply to a symptom's message, free from our exaggerated reactions to it, we have to perceive our own strong identification with the symptom when it occurs and purposefully let go of it. By seeing the headache or the cold *as a process,* we are acknowledging that it is dynamic and not static, that it is not "ours" but is rather an unfolding process that we are experiencing. Then we may realize, even just a tiny bit, that the narrative we are telling ourselves, whatever it is, is not the whole story—and that by staying caught up in it and believing it as "the truth of things" regarding our pain, we are actually constraining our options for learning and growing, and thus for healing.

When you look into a symptom with the full power of mindfulness, whether it is muscle tension, a rapid heartbeat, shortness of breath, fever, or pain, it gives you much more of a chance to remember to honor your body and listen to the messages it is trying to give you. When we fail to honor these messages, either through denial or by an inflated and self-involved preoccupation with symptoms, we can sometimes create serious dilemmas for ourselves.

Usually your body will try desperately to get its messages through to you despite the bad connection with conscious awareness. A priest described his medical history in class one day by saying he realized, after having been practicing the meditation for a few weeks, that his body had been trying to get him to slow down his fast-paced, high-stress lifestyle by giving him headaches at work. But he hadn't listened, even though the headaches got worse. So his body gave him an ulcer. But still he didn't listen. Finally it sent him a mild heart attack, which scared him so much that he started to listen. He said that he felt grateful for his heart attack now and took it as a gift, because it could have killed him but it didn't. It gave him another chance. He felt this could well be his *final* chance to start taking his body seriously, to listen to its messages and honor them.

22

Working with Physical Pain: Your Pain Is Not You

The next time you hit your thumb with a hammer or bang your shin on the car door, you can perform a little experiment in mindfulness. See if you can observe the explosion of sensations and the expanding shell of screamed epithets, groans, and violent body movements that ensue. It all takes place within a second or two. In that time, if you are quick enough to bring mindfulness to the sensations you are feeling, you may notice that you stop swearing or yelling or groaning and that your movements become less violent. As you observe the sensations in the hurt area, notice how they are changing, how sensations of stinging, throbbing; burning, cutting, rending, shooting, aching, and many others may flow in rapid succession through the region, blending into each other like a play of multicolored lights projected willy-nilly on a screen. Keep following the flow of sensations as you hold the area or put ice on it, put it under cold water or hold it above your head, wave it around in the air, or whatever you are drawn to do.

In conducting this little experiment, you may notice, if your concentration is strong, a center of calmness within yourself from which you can observe the entire episode unfold. It can feel as if you are completely detached from the sensations you are experiencing, as if it were not "your" pain so much as just pain, or even not pain at all but intense sensation, not capturable by any words. Perhaps you felt a sense of being calm "within" the pain or "behind" the pain. Perhaps you observed that your awareness of the pain was not in pain at all, and became a place of refuge, not an escape, but merely a vantage point. If you didn't, you can always investigate how your awareness and intention are in relationship to what we usually call "pain" the next time you are unfortunate enough to bang some part of your body really hard.

Hitting your thumb with a hammer or banging your shin on something brings on immediate intense sensation. We use the term *acute pain* to describe pain that comes on suddenly. Acute pain is usually very intense, but it also only lasts a relatively short while. Either it goes away by itself, as when you bang some part of your body, or it forces you to take action of some kind to make it go away, such as seeking medical attention. If you experiment with trying to bring mindfulness to exactly what you are feeling in those moments when you hurt yourself accidentally, you will probably find that how you relate to the sensations you experience makes a big difference in the degree of pain you actually feel and how much you suffer. It also affects your emotions and your behavior. It can be quite a revelation to discover that you have a range of options for dealing with physical pain, even very intense pain, aside from just being automatically overwhelmed by it.

From the standpoint of health and medicine, chronic pain is a much more intractable problem than acute pain. By *chronic pain,* we mean pain that persists over time and that is not easily relieved. Chronic pain can be constant or it can come and go. It can also vary greatly in intensity, from excruciating to dull and aching.

Medicine manages acute pain far better than it does chronic pain. The underlying cause of an acute pain can usually be identified rapidly and treated, resulting in its elimination. But sometimes pain persists and does not respond well to the most common remedies, which are drugs and surgery. And its cause may not be well defined. If it lasts more than six months or keeps coming back over extended periods of time, then a pain problem that started out as acute is said to have become chronic. In the rest of this chapter and in the one that follows, we will be mostly discussing chronic pain and the specific ways in which you can use mindfulness to befriend your pain, strange as that might sound, and explore options for being in wiser relationship with it. This is what is really meant by *coping* with pain, or learning how to live with it. But we will also touch on what has been learned about pain and suffering from laboratory studies of purposefully induced discomfort.

It is important for the reader to keep firmly in mind the fact that all patients who have medical conditions and diagnoses of one kind or another and are referred to the Stress Reduction Clinic by a health care provider have had a full medical work-up *before* they are permitted to pursue MBSR training. This is critically important in order to rule out or confirm disease processes that may require immediate medical attention. Listening to your pain includes making intelligent decisions about getting proper medical attention. The work of mindfulness needs to be carried out in conjunction with other medical treatments that may or may not be required to relieve pain. MBSR was never meant to be a substitute for medical treatment. It is designed to be a vital complement to it.

Just as we saw earlier that stress per se is not bad, it is important to remember that pain per se is not a bad thing either. Pain is one of your body's most important messengers. If you didn't feel pain, you could do great harm to your body by touching a hot stove or radiator and not even know it. Or you could have a ruptured appendix, for example, and not know that anything was the matter internally. The acute pain we experience under these and similar circumstances tells us that something is the matter. It tells us in no uncertain terms that we need to pay immediate attention and to take action in some way to rectify the situation. It is a healthy alarm reaction. In one case we quickly withdraw our hand from the stove; in the other we get to a hospital as quickly as possible. The pain literally drives our actions because it is so intense.

People born without intact pain circuitry have a terrible time learning the basic safety skills that we all take for granted. Without our knowing it consciously, our experiences with physical pain over the years have taught us a great deal about the world and about ourselves and our bodies. Pain is a very effective teacher. Yet if you were to ask, my guess is that most people would say that pain is categorically bad.

As a society, we seem to have an aversion to pain, even to the *thought* of pain or discomfort. This is why we are so quick to reach for medicine as soon as we feel a headache coming on and why we shift our posture as soon as a little muscle stiffness generates some discomfort. As you will see, this aversion to pain can be an obstacle to learning how to live with a chronic pain condition.

Aversion to pain is really a misplaced aversion to suffering. Ordinarily we do not make a distinction between pain and suffering, but there are very important differences between them. Pain is a natural part of the experience of life. Suffering is one of many possible responses to pain. Suffering can come out of either physical or emotional pain. It involves our thoughts and emotions and how they frame the meaning of our experiences. Suffering too is perfectly natural. In fact, the human condition is often spoken of as colored by inevitable suffering. But it is important to remember that suffering is only *one* response to the experience of pain. Even a mild pain can produce great suffering in us if we fear that it means we have a tumor or some other frightening condition. That same pain can be seen as nothing at all, a minor ache or inconvenience, once we are reassured that all the tests are negative and there is no chance that it is a sign of something serious. So it is not always the pain per se but the way we see it and react to it that determines the degree of suffering we will experience. And it is the suffering that we fear most, not the pain.

In fact, very elegant research by the Nobel laureate psychologist Daniel Kahneman and others has shown that we are very poor reporters of our pain after the fact. How much pain we report experiencing in retrospect, say during a colonoscopy procedure, depends not on the pain's overall intensity or duration but rather, surprisingly, on its peak and on its level at the end of the procedure. This has also been shown to be true for pain induced in a laboratory setting. This observation has profound implications for *how* we remember painful experiences from the past, and therefore how much suffering we ascribe to them. Kahneman points out that how we remember an event is really our only record of it because the experience itself does not have a voice. "The *experiencing self* [as he calls it] is the one that asks the question: "Does it hurt now?" The *remembering self* [his terminology] is the one that answers the question: How was it on the whole?" Our memory tends to generate a narrative that Kahneman's research has shown is very unreliable. We are highly biased and fickle reporters of past experience, whether of suffering or of levels of well-being or happiness. It is far more accurate to have people report on their momentary experiences and then add them up, rather than to ask them to evaluate an experience retrospectively.*

Of course, nobody wants to live with chronic pain. But it is very widespread. The costs to society as a whole from chronic pain as well as to the people who suffer with it are very high. According to a 2011 report of the Institute of Medicine, chronic pain conditions cost our society between $560 billion and $635 billion per year in treatment and lost productivity. The psychological costs, in terms of emotional distress, are equally staggering.

A lingering pain condition can be totally disabling. Pain can erode the quality of your life. It can grind you down bit by bit, making you irritable, depressed, and prone to self-pity and feelings of helplessness and hopelessness. You may feel that you have lost control of your body and of your ability to earn a living, to say nothing of enjoying the activities that usually give pleasure and meaning to life.

What is more, the treatments for chronic pain conditions are all too often only partially successful. Many people are ultimately told by their doctor or by the staff of a pain clinic at the end of a long and often frustrating treatment course, sometimes involving surgery and usually numerous drug treatments, that they are going to have to learn to live with their pain. But too often they are not taught *how* to do this. *Being told that you have*

* Kahneman D. *Thinking Fast and Slow.* New York: Farrar, Straus and Giroux; 2012.

to learn to live with pain should not be the end of the road—it should be the beginning. This is one of the most important roles that an MBSR program can play in a person's life—and in medical care more generally. It may be particularly important for soldiers and veterans returning from war zones such as Iraq and Afghanistan with physical wounds and blast injuries resulting in traumatic brain injury of varying severity as well as post-traumatic stress, particularly when pain is a part of the picture.

In the best of cases, which is probably still the exception rather than the rule, a person with chronic pain will receive the ongoing support of a highly trained multidisciplinary pain clinic staff. Psychological assessment and counseling will be integrated with the treatment plan, which might include everything from surgery to nerve blocks, trigger-point injections with steroids, intravenous lidocaine drips, muscle relaxants, analgesics, physical and occupational therapy, and, with luck, acupuncture and massage. The goal of counseling is to help the person work with his or her body and to organize his or her life to keep what pain there is under some degree of control, to maintain an optimistic, self-efficacious perspective, and to help the person engage in meaningful activities and work within his or her capacity.

In the early days of our hospital, before the Pain Clinic, run by the Department of Anesthesiology, was ironically shut down for budgetary reasons in spite of pain being one of the central concerns of medical patients, it referred many of its patients to the Stress Reduction Clinic for training in MBSR. The deciding factor in who was referred was a willingness on the part of the patient to try to do something for himself or herself to cope with some of the pain, particularly when it had not responded fully to medical treatment alone. In general, those who harbor the attitude that they just want the doctor to "fix it" or to "make it go away" are obviously not good candidates for mindfulness training. They won't understand the need to take some responsibility themselves for working with their condition. They might also interpret the suggestion that the mind can play a role in the regulation of their pain to mean that their pain is imaginary, that it is "all in their head" in the first place. It is not uncommon for people to think that the doctor is implying that their pain is not "real" when he or she proposes a mind-body approach to pain therapy. People who know they are in pain usually want to have something *done* to the body to make the pain go away . . . in other words, to be fixed.

This is only natural when the model you are working with is that your body is like a machine. When something is wrong with a machine, you find out what the problem is and you "fix" it. By the same token, when you have a pain problem, you would go to a "pain doctor," expecting to get what is wrong fixed, just as you would if something were wrong with your car.

But your body is not a machine. One problem with chronic pain conditions is that often it is not clear exactly what is causing the pain. Doctors, even specialists, may not be able to say with certainty why a person is experiencing pain. Diagnostic tests, such as X-rays, myelograms, CT scans, and MRI scans, frequently don't show very much, even though the person may be in a lot of pain. And even if the cause of the pain was known precisely in a particular case, surgeons rarely attempt to cut specific nerve pathways to lessen pain anymore. This is only attempted as a last resort in cases of unremitting, excruciating pain. This kind of surgery used to be performed more frequently, but it usually failed, for the simple reason that pain signals do not travel in exclusive and specific "pain pathways" in the nervous system.

For these reasons, people with chronic pain conditions who seek medical treatment thinking of their body as being pretty much like an automobile and that all the doctor needs to do is to find out why they are in pain and then make it go away by cutting the right nerve or giving them some magic pills or injections are usually in for a rude awakening. Things are rarely that simple with chronic pain conditions.

In the new paradigm, pain is not just a "body problem," it is a whole-system problem. Sensory impulses originating both at the surface of your body and internally are transmitted via nerve fibers to the brain, where these messages are registered and interpreted as pain. This has to happen before they are considered painful by the organism. But there are many well-known pathways and way stations within the brain and the central nervous system by which higher cognitive and emotional functions can modify the perception of pain. The systems perspective on pain opens the door for many different possible ways to use your mind intentionally to influence your experience of pain. This is why meditation can be of such great value in learning to live with pain. So if a doctor suggests that meditation might help you with your pain, it does not mean that your pain is not "real." It means that your body and your mind are not two separate and distinct entities and that, therefore, there is always a mental dimension to pain. This means that you can always influence the pain experience to some extent by mobilizing the inner resources of your own mind, one of which is kindness toward yourself.

The above perspective has been corroborated and amplified by recent laboratory studies looking at the effects of mindfulness training on pain induced in volunteers who have no prior experience of meditation, as well as in long-term meditation practitioners. The pain is usually induced by heat or by cold, and in each case great care is taken to insure that no harm or tissue damage is done to the subjects. Overall, the results are showing that meditative practices similar or identical to those used in MBSR can have dramatic effects on pain reports. Much of the research is now trying to identify the brain mechanisms by which pain modulation might occur. One study, conducted by Antoine Lutz, Richard Davidson, and their colleagues at the Center for Investigating Healthy Minds at the University of Wisconsin, found that long-term meditators (with over ten thousand hours of lifetime practice) using a meditative practice known as "open monitoring"—similar to the choiceless awareness we use in MBSR—showed significant reduction in the degree of unpleasantness they reported for a particular level of painful stimulus compared to the control group. However, the long-term meditators did not report any less intensity than did the control group.* In another study, these findings were

* Perlman DM, Salomons TV, Davidson RJ, Lutz A. Differential effects on pain intensity and unpleasantness of two meditation practices. *Emotion.* 2010;10:65–71.

shown to be associated with changes in brain activity in the experienced meditators in a network known to be associated with the assessment of "salience." Apparently the meditators were able to reduce fearful anticipatory thinking by staying in the present moment, and thus showed reduced reactivity to the painful stimulus.*

Such findings underscore the well-known fact that there are different dimensions to the experience of pain: the sensory, the emotional, and the cognitive, all of which contribute to the overall sense of suffering that accompanies physical discomfort. When we recognize these distinct components of the global experience of "pain" within ourselves and can differentiate between them, as we learn to do in MBSR, this can significantly reduce the experience of suffering, as we found in our early studies of people with chronic pain conditions taking the MBSR program,† and as described in detail in this chapter and the following one.

Other studies, looking at Zen meditation practitioners, have shown that long-term practitioners are less sensitive to both unpleasantness and intensity, and that they show gray matter thickening in specific regions of the brain known to be involved in experiencing pain.‡

Some laboratory studies are even showing that very brief training in mindfulness with the primary focus on breathing, along the lines of four 20-minute training sessions, can dramatically reduce pain ratings of unpleasantness (by 57 percent) and intensity (by 40 percent) and show changes in the brain in areas known to modulate the experience of pain.§

* Lutz A, McFarlin DR, Perlman DV, Salomons TV, Davidson RJ. Altered anterior insula activation during anticipation and experience of painful stimuli in expert meditators. *Neuroimage.* 2013;64:538–546.

† Kabat-Zinn J. An outpatient program in behavioral medicine for chronic pain patients based on the practice of mindfulness meditation: Theoretical considerations and preliminary results. *General Hospital Psychiatry.* 1982;4:33–47; Kabat-Zinn J, Lipworth L, Burney R. The clinical use of mindfulness meditation for the self-regulation of chronic pain. *Journal of Behavioral Medicine.* 1985;8:163–190. Kabat-Zinn J, Lipworth L, Burney R, Sellers W. Four-year follow-up of a meditation-based program for the self-regulation of chronic pain: Treatment outcomes and compliance. *Clinical Journal of Pain.* 1986;2:159–173.

‡ Grant JA, Courtemanche J, Duerden EG, Duncan GH, Rainville P. Cortical thickness and pain sensitivity in Zen meditators. *Emotion.* 2010;10:43–53.

§ Zeidan F, Martucci KT, Kraft RA, Gordon NS, McHaffie JG, Coghill RC. Brain mech-

It remains to be seen why different laboratories are reporting somewhat different findings for different meditation practices. This is often the case in science, especially in fields such as this one, which is really in its infancy. However, overall such studies are corroborating and extending the clinical findings from our early studies, now replicated by other groups, which showed dramatic and long-term positive effects of training in MBSR on patients with a wide range of chronic pain conditions.

PAIN OUTCOMES IN THE STRESS REDUCTION CLINIC

Before looking further into the ways we can use mindfulness to work with pain, let's review some of the results obtained in our early studies of people with chronic pain conditions undergoing training in MBSR in the stress clinic. These studies showed that there is a dramatic reduction in the average level of pain during the eight weeks of MBSR as measured by a pain questionnaire called the McGill-Melzack Pain Rating Index (PRI). This is a reproducible finding. We see it in every class, year after year, among patients with chronic pain conditions.

In one study, 72 percent of the patients with chronic pain conditions achieved at least a 33 percent reduction on the PRI, while 61 percent of the pain patients achieved at least a 50 percent reduction. This means that the majority of people who came with pain experienced clinically significant reductions in their pain levels over the eight weeks they were practicing the meditation at home and attending weekly classes at the hospital.

In addition to pain, we looked at how much these people changed in terms of their negative body image (the degree to which they rated different parts of their body as problematic). We found that by the end of the program, on average they perceived their bodies as approximately 30 percent less problematic. This implies that negative views and feelings about one's body, which are especially strong when people are limited in

anisms supporting modulation of pain by mindfulness meditation. *Journal of Neuroscience*. 2011;31:5540–5548.

what they can do because of pain, can improve markedly in a short period of time.

At the same time, these same individuals also showed a 30 percent improvement in the degree to which pain interfered with their ability to engage in the normal activities of daily living, such as preparing food, driving, sleeping, and sex. This improvement was accompanied by a sharp drop (55 percent) in negative mood states, an increase in positive mood states, and major improvements in anxiety, depression, hostility, and the tendency to somatize, that is, to be overly preoccupied with one's bodily sensations. By the end of the program, people with chronic pain in this study were reporting taking less pain medication, being more active, and feeling better in general.

Even more encouraging, these improvements lasted. In a follow-up study that examined how people with pain conditions were coping up to four years after their experience training in MBSR, we found that, on average, most of the gains they had achieved by the end of the program were either maintained or improved still further.

In addition, the follow-up study showed that the pain patients continued to keep up their meditation practice, many to a very strong degree. Ninety-three percent said that they continued to practice the meditation in one form or another at some level. Almost everybody reported still using awareness of their breathing in their daily lives, as well as other informal mindfulness practices. Some were practicing formally as well when they felt a need. About 42 percent were still practicing formally at least three times a week for at least fifteen minutes at a time three years later, although by four years this figure dropped to 30 percent. All in all, this represents an impressive level of discipline and commitment, considering they had learned the mindfulness practices years earlier.

The pain patients in the follow-up study were also asked to rate how important the training they received in MBSR was to them at the time they were being asked to respond. Forty-four percent (at three years) and 67 percent (at four years) rated the program between 8 and 10 on a 1-to-10 scale (where a rating of 10 meant "very important"), and over 50 percent rated it 10 at four years. Responses for six months, one year, and two years of follow-up fell between these values, from 67 percent rating it between 8 and 10 at six months to 52 percent giving it that rating at two years.

In terms of how much what they learned in the clinic was responsible for their pain reduction at follow-up, 43 percent reported that 80 to 100 percent of their pain improvement at follow-up was due to what they had learned in the MBSR program. An additional 25 percent attributed 50 to 80 percent of their pain improvement to what they learned in MBSR. So by their own reports, the meditation training had lasting effects in terms of their pain improvements.

In another study, we compared two groups of pain patients. All forty-two people in this study were being treated in our hospital's pain clinic using standard medical protocols as well as supportive therapies such as physical therapy. But one group of twenty-one patients was also referred for MBSR training in the Stress Reduction Clinic in addition to their pain clinic treatments, while the other group had not yet been referred to the stress clinic. Both groups were followed over a ten-week period, the meditators between the time they started and the time they finished the MBSR program; the other group between the time they started their pain clinic treatments and ten weeks later.

We knew from previous studies that we could expect the meditators to show large reductions in pain and psychological distress on our rating scales. The question was, How would the meditators compare with other patients in the pain clinic who were not practicing meditation but who were receiving powerful medical treatments for pain such as lidocaine injections?

What we found was that the non-meditators showed little change over the ten weeks that they were being treated in the pain clinic, while the meditators showed major improvements. For example, the MBSR group showed an average 36 percent improvement in pain on the McGill-Melzack Pain Rating Index, while the non-meditators showed no improvement. The MBSR group showed a 37 percent improvement in negative body image, while the non-meditators had a 2 percent improvement. The

MBSR group also showed an 87 percent improvement in mood, the nonmeditators only a 22 percent improvement; and the MBSR group had a 77 percent improvement in psychological distress, while the nonmeditators had an 11 percent improvement.

Even though this pilot study was not a randomized trial, these results suggested quite powerfully that doing something for yourself—as the people in the Stress Reduction Clinic were doing by engaging in the MBSR classes and in the various mindfulness meditation practices assigned for homework each week in addition to receiving medical treatment for their pain conditions—can result in many positive changes that may not occur or occur as powerfully with medical treatment alone. This finding underscores the potential power of a more participatory medicine, in which the patients are full collaborators and participants in all attempts to help them to move toward greater levels of health and well-being, tapping into their deep interior resources for learning, growing, healing, and transformation through their own systematic efforts to cultivate wise attention and greater intimacy and familiarity with their minds and bodies.

One of the most interesting discoveries we made in the MBSR classroom is that medical patients with very different kinds of pain problems all show similar improvements in their condition when they engage in the regular cultivation of mindfulness. People with low-back pain, neck pain, shoulder pain, face pain, headache, arm pain, abdominal pain, chest pain, sciatic pain, and foot pain, caused by a range of problems including arthritis, herniated disks, and sympathetic dystrophies, were all able to use the meditation practices to achieve major reductions in their pain that endured over time. This suggests that many different kinds of pain conditions and experiences might be positively affected by the MBSR curriculum, which involves, above all, a willingness *to turn toward, lean in,* and *open to* the moment-to-moment experience of pain with great self-compassion and kindness, and to learn from it instead of closing oneself off from it and trying to make it go away—in a word, in inviting even unpleasant and unwanted experiences to become your teacher.

USING THE MEDITATION PRACTICE TO WORK WITH PAIN

Some people have difficulty understanding why we emphasize that they try to enter *into* their pain when they simply hate it and just want it to go away. Their feeling is, "Why shouldn't I just ignore it or distract myself from it and grit my teeth, and just endure it when it is too great?" One reason is that there may be times when ignoring it or distracting yourself doesn't work. At such times, it is very helpful to have other tricks up your sleeve besides just trying to endure it or depending on drugs to ease it. Several classic laboratory experiments with acute pain showed that *tuning in* to sensations is a more effective way of reducing the level of pain experienced when the pain is intense and prolonged than is distracting yourself. In fact, even if distraction does alleviate your pain or help you to cope with it some of the time, bringing mindfulness to it can lead to new levels of insight and understanding about yourself and your body, which distraction or escape can never do. Understanding and insight, of course, are an extremely important part of the process of coming to terms with your condition and really learning how to live with it, not just endure it. One of the ways we speak about it is that the sensory, the emotional, and the cognitive/conceptual dimensions of the pain experience can be *uncoupled* from one another, meaning that they can be held in awareness as independent aspects of experience. Once you see that your thoughts about the sensations, for instance, are not the sensations themselves, both the experience of the sensory and the cognitive dimensions of the pain experience may change independently. This is also true for our emotional reactions to unpleasant sensory experience. This phenomenon of uncoupling can give us new degrees of freedom in resting in awareness and holding whatever arises in any or all of these three domains in an entirely different way, and dramatically reduce the suffering experienced.

So, where do you begin? If you have a chronic pain condition, hopefully by this point you have already started experimenting with some of the mindfulness exercises suggested in Part I. Perhaps during your reading or during your experiments with the MBSR practices, you found yourself thinking about your own situation from a different angle or feeling a desire to pay attention to things you may have taken for granted before, maybe even letting yourself become genuinely *curious* about this phenomenon we call pain. Perhaps you have also begun to practice one or more of the formal guided meditations on the schedule outlined in Chapter 10. If you haven't, the first thing to do now, if you want to commit to making the MBSR curriculum a part of your life, at least for the next eight weeks, is to make a firm commitment to yourself that you will set aside and protect a stretch of time in your day, every day (or at least six days a week), to practice, whether you feel like it or not! It is best to start with the body scan. Practically speaking, that means using the guided mindfulness meditation practice CD or download of the body scan and giving yourself over to doing what it says to do—again, for at least forty-five minutes a day, six days a week. It also means forming the intention to practice as if your life depended on it, whether you find that you like the body scan or not on any given day, and even if you don't feel you are "getting anywhere" with it right away.

All of the suggestions in Part I will be just as relevant to you for working with pain as they are to people who do not have chronic pain. This includes cultivating the attitudes described in Chapter 2. Be aware of the tendency to identify yourself as a "chronic pain patient." Instead, remind yourself on a regular basis that you are a whole person who happens to have to face and work with a chronic pain condition as intelligently as possible—for the sake of your quality of life and well-being. Reframing your view of yourself in this way will be especially important if you have a long history of pain problems and feel overwhelmed and defeated by your current situation and by your past experiences.

Of course, you will be more aware than anybody that having pain doesn't free you from all the other kinds of problems and difficulties people have. Your other life problems need to be faced too. You can work with them in the same way you will face and work with pain. It is important to remind yourself, especially if you feel discouraged and depressed at times, that you still have the ability to feel joy and pleasure in your life. If you remember to cultivate this wider view of yourself, your efforts in the meditation will have a much more fertile soil in which to take root and give rise to new ways of seeing and being in relationship to your experience, including the presence and intensity of your pain condition. The meditation practice may also wind up helping you in unsuspected ways having nothing to do with your pain.

As we saw when we discussed symptoms in the last chapter, making the pain go away is not a very useful immediate goal. Pain can disappear altogether at times, or it can subside and become more manageable. What happens depends on a great many different circumstances, only some of which are under your potential control. A lot depends on the kind of pain you have.

For instance, headaches are more likely than low-back pain to disappear in a short period of time and not recur. In general, improving low-back pain takes more work over a longer period. But whatever your pain problem, it is best to immerse yourself in practicing the meditation regularly, keeping in mind and even cultivating the attitudinal factors we considered in Chapter 2, and see what happens. Your daily meditation practice will be your pain laboratory. *Your ability to regulate or modulate your experience of pain and develop a healthier relationship with it will grow out of practicing the body scan, the sitting meditation, the yoga (if it is advisable for you to be doing it), and out of the mindfulness you are bringing to everyday living, moment by moment by moment and day by day by day.*

The body scan is by far the practice that works best at the beginning for people with chronic pain, especially if sitting still or moving is difficult. You can do it lying on your back or in any other convenient outstretched position. Just close your eyes, tune in to your breathing, and feel your belly expand gently on the inbreaths and recede on the outbreaths. Then, as described in Chapter 5, use your breathing to direct your attention down to the toes of your left foot. Start working from there, maintaining moment-to-moment awareness. When your mind is on one region of your body, the idea is to keep it focused on that region as best you can, feeling any and all sensations (or lack of sensations if you don't feel anything), and breathing in to and out from that region. Every time you breathe out, see if you can let your whole body sink a little more deeply into the surface you are lying on as the muscles all over your body release their tension and relax. When it comes time to leave that region and move on to the next, letting go of it completely in your mind's eye and dwelling in stillness for at least a few breaths before tuning in to the next region on your journey up through your left leg, then your right leg, then through the rest of your body. The basic meditation instructions about how to work with your mind when it wanders still apply (except when you are in so much pain that you cannot concentrate on anything other than the pain itself; working with this situation is described on pages 379–380): when you notice at a certain point that your mind is somewhere else, observe where it has gone, and then gently escort your attention back to the region you are focusing on. If you are using the guided body-scan CD, when your mind wanders off and you realize it, then bring your attention back and pick up wherever my voice or the voice of your instructor is suggesting that you focus.

Move slowly, scanning in this way through your entire body. As you move through a particularly problematic region, perhaps one in which the sensations of discomfort and pain are quite intense, or have been in the past, see if you can treat it like any other part of your body that you come to focus on—in other words, gently breathing in to and out from that region, carefully observing the sensations, allowing yourself to feel them and open up to them and letting your whole body soften and relax each time you breathe out. The basic invitation is to "inhabit" each region of your body with full awareness and put the welcome mat out for whatever arises in the way of sensations, again, with gentleness and kindness toward yourself and toward your body. At the same time, you can invite whatever thoughts and emotions are associated with this region of your body to also be fully acknowledged, felt and met, without having to fix anything at all in this moment, or solve any problem or difficulty. You are simply taking up residence in the region in question, and resting in awareness. Then, when it comes time to let go of that region and move on (you can decide for yourself when that moment is if you are practicing without the guidance), letting go of it completely (if it helps, try saying "good-bye" in your mind silently on an outbreath), and see if you can simply rest in calmness and stillness in this moment. Even if the pain sensations don't change at all or become more intense, just move on to the next region as best you can, inhabiting it now with full awareness.

If the painful sensations in a particular region do change in some way, see if you can note precisely what the qualities of that change are. Let them register fully in your awareness and keep going with the body scan.

It is not helpful to *expect* pain to disappear. In fact, it is helpful not to expect anything at all. But you may find that the experience of pain changes in intensity, sometimes getting momentarily stronger or weaker, or that the sensations change, say from sharp to dull, or to tingling or burning or throbbing. It can also be helpful to be aware of any thoughts and emotional reactions that you may be having about either the pain, your body, the guidance on the CD, the meditation itself, or anything else. Just keep up the perceiving and letting go, perceiving and letting go, breath by breath and moment by moment.

Anything you observe about your pain or about your thoughts and emotions is to be noted *non-judgmentally* as you maintain your focus in the body scan. In the MBSR program, we do this every day for weeks. It can be boring, sometimes even exasperating. But that is okay. Boredom and exasperation can also be seen as thoughts and feelings and let go of. As we have mentioned a number of times, and it is certainly true in regard to the body scan practice in particular, we tell our patients, "You don't have to like it; you just have to do it." So whether you find the body scan to be very relaxing and interesting, difficult and uncomfortable, or exasperating, is irrelevant to whether it will serve you well. As we have seen, it is probably the best place to get started in this whole process of befriending your experience and inhabiting your awareness with the body just as it is. After a few weeks, you can switch over to alternating the body scan with both the sitting meditation and with the yoga if you like. But even then, don't be too quick to give up on the body scan.

Also, it is important not to be overly thrilled with "success" or overly disappointed by lack of "progress" as you go along. Every day will be different. In fact, every moment and every breath will be different, so it is helpful not to jump to conclusions about either the practice or its value to you after one or two sessions. *The work of growth and healing takes time.* It requires patience and consistency in the meditation practice over a period of weeks, if not months and years. If you have had a problem with pain for a number of years, it is not exactly reasonable to expect that it will magically go away in a matter of days just because you have started to meditate. But, especially if you have tried everything else already and still have pain, what do you have to lose by practicing the meditation on a regular basis for eight weeks, or even longer? Is there something better you could be doing in those forty-five minutes a day than touching base with yourself, no matter what you think or feel at those moments, and, with some degree of kindness and self-compassion (very different from self-pity), dwelling in the domain of being? At times of discouragement, just watch the feelings of discouragement themselves, letting them be and then letting them go too, as best you can, as you keep practicing, practicing, practicing.

When you encounter moments when the pain is so intense that it is impossible for you to direct your attention to any other part of your body, let go of the body scan, shut off the CD if you are using it, and just bring your attention to focus directly on the pain itself in that moment. There are a number of ways to approach pain besides those we have already discussed. The key to all of them is your unwavering determination to direct your attention gently, delicately, but firmly on and into the pain, no matter how bad it seems. After all, it is what you are feeling right now, so you might as well see if you can at least accept it a little bit, just because it is here.

In some moments when you go into your pain and face it openly, it may seem as if you are locked in hand-to-hand combat with it or as if you are undergoing torture. It is helpful to recognize that these are just thoughts. It helps to remind yourself that the work of mindfulness is not meant to be a battle between you and your pain and it won't be unless you make it into one. If you do make it a struggle, it will only make for greater tension and therefore more pain. Mindfulness involves a determined effort to observe and accept your physical discomfort and your agitated emotions, moment by moment. Remember, you are trying to find out about your pain, to learn from it, to know it better, to become familiar, even intimate with it, not to stop it or get rid of it or escape from it. If you can assume this attitude and be calmly *with* your pain, looking at it in this way, "befriending" it for even one breath or even half a breath, that is a step in the right direction. From here, you might be able to extend your embrace and remain calm and open while facing the pain for maybe two or three breaths or even longer.

In the clinic we like to use the expression "putting out the welcome mat" to describe how we work with pain and discomfort during meditation. Since pain (or perhaps we should start referring to it as intense and unwanted sensation) is already present in a particular moment, we do what we can to be receptive and accepting of it. We try to relate to our experience of discomfort in as neutral a way as possible, observing it nonjudgmentally, feeling what it actually feels like in detail. This involves opening up to the raw sensations themselves, whatever they may be. We breathe with them and dwell with them from moment to moment, riding the waves of the breath, the waves of sensation, resting in our attending, in awareness itself.

We might also investigate a little bit further by asking ourselves the question, "How bad is it right now, in this very moment?" If you practice doing this, you will probably find that most of the time, even when you are feeling terrible, when you go right into the sensations and ask, "*In this moment,* is it tolerable? Is it okay?" the chances are you will find that it is. The difficulty is that the next moment is coming, and the next, and you "know" they are all going to be filled with more pain.

The solution? You might experiment with taking each moment as it comes, seeing if you can be 100 percent in the present in one moment, then do the same for the next, right through the forty-five-minute practice period if necessary or until the intensity subsides, at which point you can go back to the body scan. You may also discover that the experience of what we call "pain" is not monolithic, that the sensations are sometimes changing moment by moment by moment as we hold them in awareness.

As we have already noted, there are two other very important dimensions of the pain experience that you can investigate in addition to observing the bare bodily sensations themselves. You can also bring awareness to any thoughts or feelings you may be having about the sensations. For one thing, you may come to notice that you are referring to the entire constellation of your experience silently in your mind as "pain." This too is a thought, just a name. It is not the experience itself. Notice it if you are labeling the sensations in this way. Maybe it is not necessary to call them "pain." Perhaps it even makes them seem stronger. Why not look and see for yourself whether this is so? Then perhaps you will approach them in a more open, curious manner, with a very light and gentle touch, again, much as you might approach a shy animal sunning itself on a tree stump in a forest glade.

When you start looking in this way at your experience, you may discover that there are also all sorts of other thoughts and emotions milling about, appearing and disappearing, commenting, reacting, judging, catastrophizing, feeling depressed or anxious, yearning for relief. Statements such as "This is killing me," "I can't stand it any longer," "How long will this go on?" "My whole life is ruined," "There is no hope for me," or "I'll never get the better of this pain," may all move through your mind at one time or another. You may find such thoughts coming and going constantly. A lot of them are fear-based, anticipatory thoughts about how bad the future may be. It is good to notice that *none of them is the pain itself.*

Can you be aware of this as you practice? It is a key realization. Not only are these thoughts not the pain itself, they are not you either! Nor, in all likelihood, are they particularly true or accurate. They are just the understandable reactions of your own mind when it is not ready to accept the pain and wants things to be different from the way they are, in other words, pain-free. When you see and feel the sensations you are experiencing *as sensations,* pure and simple, you may see that these thoughts about the sensations are useless to you *at that moment* and that they can actually make things worse than they need be. Then, in letting go of them, which, you may recall, means allowing them to be as they are, you come to accept the sensations simply because they are already here anyway. Why not just accept them—for now?

However, you cannot reliably let go into accepting the sensations until you realize that it is your thinking that is labeling the sensations as "bad." It is your thinking that doesn't want to accept them, now or ever, because it doesn't like them and just wants them to *go away*. But notice, now it is not *you* that won't accept the sensations, it is just your thinking, and you already know, because you have seen it for yourself firsthand, that your thoughts are not you.

Does this shift in perspective show you another option for facing your pain? What about letting go of those thoughts on purpose, as a little experiment, when you are in a lot of pain? What about letting go of that part of your mind that wants things to be the way it wants them to be, even in the face of incontrovertible evidence that they are not that way right now? What about accepting things just as they are right now, in this very moment, even if you hate them, even if you hate the pain? What about purposefully stepping back from the hatred, the anger, and the catastrophizing and instead not judging things at all, just accepting them, which means, remember, simply letting them be? This is a very courageous stance to take in relationship to intense sensation. It has nothing to do with passive resignation or giving up.

It may also strike you at a certain point, particularly if there is a moment of calmness in the midst of the inner turmoil, that your *awareness* of sensations, thoughts, and emotions is different from the sensations, the thoughts, and the emotions themselves—that aspect of your being that is aware is not itself in pain or ruled by these thoughts and feelings at all. It knows them, but it itself is free of them. You can check this out for yourself the next time you experience intense sensation or an intense emotion. You can rest in awareness and ask yourself, "Is my awareness of the pain in pain?" or "Is my awareness of the feelings of fear, or anger, or sadness frightened, or angry, or sad?" Even one brief moment of investigation by asking yourself this question and looking to see what is actually so for you can be very helpful in cultivating a greater intimacy and understanding concerning the nature of your suffering and possibly revealing new options for shifting your relationship to it right in this moment.

When engaged in the body scan or any of the other mindfulness practices, you may come to notice that when you identify with your thoughts or feelings or with the sensations in your body, or with the body itself for that matter, there is much greater turmoil and suffering than when you inhabit the domain of alert and affectionate attention, the domain of non-judgmental spaciousness, and simply rest in awareness with no agenda other than to be awake.

We adopt this perspective of open presence and acceptance throughout the meditation practice. However, toward the end of the body scan, you may recall that there is an explicit sequence that encourages the cultivation of *choiceless awareness,* a disidentifying with the entire play of inner experience, whether it be the breath, sensations, perceptions, thoughts, or feelings. Toward the end of the body scan, after we have intentionally let go of the body, we sometimes invite our thoughts and feelings, our likes and dislikes, our concepts about ourself and the world, our ideas and opinions, even our name, into the field of awareness and we intentionally let go of them as well, as we simply rest in awareness itself. On the CD, it suggests that you tune in to a sense of being complete in the present moment, as you are, without having to resolve your problems or correct bad habits or pay your bills or get a college education or anything else. Can you identify with yourself as being whole and complete in this moment and at the same time part of a larger whole? Can you sense yourself as pure "being," that aspect of you that is bigger than your body, beyond your name, beyond your thoughts and feelings, your ideas and opinions and concepts, even beyond your identification of yourself as a certain age or as male or female?

In the letting go of all of this, you may come to a point at which all concepts dissolve into stillness and there is just awareness, a knowing beyond any "thing" to be known, a non-conceptual and not merely cognitive knowing. In this stillness, you might come to know that whatever you are, "you" are definitely not merely your body, although it is yours to work with and to take care of and make use of. It is a very convenient and miraculous vehicle, but it is hardly you. Nor are your thoughts and emotions. Don't your ideas and opinions evolve over time? You may no longer think or like things that earlier you might have been extremely self-identified with. This suggests that your essential self might be more akin to awareness than to anything else in the ever-changing constellation of aggregates that is you, especially when you learn to inhabit awareness as your "default mode," your natural baseline condition of being, and embody it in your own friendly way from moment to moment, and day by day, through thick and through thin.

If you are not your body, then you cannot possibly be your body's pain. Your essential nature has to be bigger than the pain. As you learn to take up residency and dwell in the domain of being, your relationship to pain and to intense uncomfortable sensation in your body can undergo profound transformative and healing changes. Such experiences, even fleeting tastes and intimations, can guide you in developing your own ways of coming to terms with the pain you experience, to make room for it, to befriend it, to live with it—as so many of our patients have learned to do.

Of course, regular practice is necessary, as we have been emphasizing all along. The domain of being is easier to talk about than to experience. To make it real in your life, to get in touch with it in any moment, takes a degree of intentionality and effort, as well as determination and, dare I say it, discipline. A certain kind of digging, a kind of inner archaeology, is required to uncover your intrinsic wholeness, covered over as it may be with layer after layer of opinions, likes and dislikes, and the heavy fog of automatic, unconscious thinking and habits, to say nothing of pain from the past, as well as present-moment pain. There is nothing romantic or sentimental about the work of mindfulness, nor is your intrinsic wholeness a romantic or sentimental or imaginary construct. It is here now, as it always has been. It is part of being human, just as having a body and feeling pain are part of being human.

If you suffer from a chronic pain condition and you find that this way of looking at things resonates with you, then it may be time to test this approach for yourself, if you haven't already. The only way to go about it is to start practicing and keep practicing. Find and cultivate moments of calmness, stillness, and awareness within yourself using your pain as your teacher and guide.

It is hard work, and there will be times when you will feel like quitting, especially if you don't see quick results in terms of pain reduction. But in doing this work, you must also remember that it involves patience and gentleness and lovingkindness toward yourself, and even toward your pain. It means working at your limits, but gently, not trying too hard, not exhausting yourself, not pushing too hard to break through. The breakthroughs will come by themselves in their own good time if you put in the energy in the spirit of self-discovery. Mindfulness does not bulldoze through resistance. You have to work gently around the edges, a little here and a little there, keeping your vision alive in your heart, particularly during the times of greatest pain and difficulty.

23

More on Working with Pain

Dear Jon and Peggy: I have many aches and pains but I feel great. I was able to shovel my driveway, which is 250 feet long. Breathing, meditating, and frequent breaks for arms, legs, back, and neck exercises. I had muscle soreness but nothing to incapacitate me. In thirty years I never before attempted to shovel my driveway. Thank you. Pat.

WORKING MINDFULLY WITH CHRONIC LOW-BACK PAIN AND BACK PROBLEMS

People who have never had a problem with chronic pain have no idea how much living with a pain condition changes your whole life and everything you do. Many people with back injuries are unable to work, especially at jobs that require lifting or driving or standing for long periods. Some spend years on workman's compensation while trying to recover sufficiently to be able to get back to work and lead something resembling a normal life, or to be certified as disabled so that they can receive disability payments. Often there are legal problems and battles in order to receive benefits. Living on a fixed and very reduced income, coupled with being stuck in the house in pain for days, weeks, months, sometimes even years, unable to do what one once could, is extremely frustrating and depressing, not just for the person in pain but for his or her entire family and circle of friends. It can make everybody feel angry, defeated, and helpless.

Whether you are disabled by your pain at all times or just have a chronic "bad back" that you have to be careful of, the effects of low-back pain on your life can be debilitating and depressing. Just bending over the sink when brushing your teeth, or picking up a pencil, or getting into the bathtub or out of a car can trigger days or even weeks of intense pain that may force you onto your back in bed just to bear it. Not only pain but also the threat of pain if you make a wrong move constantly affects your ability to lead a normal life. Thousands of things have to be done slowly and carefully, taking nothing for granted. Lifting heavy objects may be out of the question. Even lifting very light objects can cause major problems. And at those times when you are not in pain, the strange feeling of instability and vulnerability in that central region of your body can still lead you to feel insecure and precarious. You may not be able to stand up straight or turn or walk in a way that feels normal. You may feel a need to brace yourself or guard yourself against people or circumstances that might throw your body off balance. It is very hard to have your body feel "right" when its central fulcrum feels unstable and vulnerable.

Sometimes your back can go out even when you are being careful. You may not have noticed anything in particular that you did, but even so, there are times when your back muscles can go into spasm, triggering a setback that may last for days or weeks. One minute you can be relatively okay, the next minute you are in trouble.

People with chronic back pain tend to have "good days" and "bad days." Often there are very few good days. It can be very discouraging to live from day to day uncertain about how you will feel tomorrow or what you will or won't be able to do. It is hard to make definite plans, which makes it almost impossible to work at a regular job and makes it hard socially as well. And if you do have a good day now and again, you can feel so exuberant because your body feels "right" or normal for a change that you might well overdo things to compensate for all the times you were unable to do anything. Then you wind up paying for it later. This can be a vicious cycle.

A back problem almost forces you to be mindful because the result of being unaware of your body and what you are doing can be so debilitating. In order to work systematically around the edges of your limitations, in order to get stronger and healthier and to be able to do at least some of the things you want to do, mindfulness becomes absolutely essential.

The people in the Stress Reduction Clinic with chronic pain who are the most successful in learning to live with and regulate their pain cultivate a long-term perspective on rehabilitating themselves. Big improvements in mobility and pain reduction may or may not come about in the eight weeks of the MBSR program. You are better off thinking in terms of six months, or even a year or two, and proceeding patiently and persistently, no matter how well things go at first. However, the quality of your life can begin to improve from the very first time you practice the body scan, as we saw in the case of Phil (Chapter 13). This is especially true if you are willing to work with your body and your back problems slowly and systematically. Such a commitment and strategy should include a reasonable vision of what you might be able to accomplish with consistent work. It may help to imagine how your back might be in three years or five years if you were to keep up a steady, mindful physical exercise program, encouraging your whole body, not just your back, to grow stronger and more flexible. One very successful scientist I know who has severe pain "puts his body back together" for an hour every morning before he goes out to face the world.

It might help if you think of yourself as in long-term training, like an athlete. Your project is rehabilitating yourself. Your starting point, of course, is your condition in the moment you decide to engage in befriending your body as it is and to work with it from here on out, for life, if necessary, all puns intended. There is simply no other place to begin. The deep meaning of the word *rehabilitation* comes from the French verb *habiter,* which means "to dwell," "to inhabit." So rehabilitation doesn't just mean to reenable. At an even deeper level, it means *to learn to live inside again.* That, it turns out, is profoundly reenabling.

A long-term approach to rehabilitating your body as a whole, and in particular your back if you have a chronic back condition, might include mindfully working to strengthen your back by doing the physical therapy exercises prescribed for you or by practicing as much of the yoga as you are able to manage. First check with your physical therapist or doctor to make sure that these specific exercises are appropriate in your case. Modify them in whatever ways seem appropriate, even day by day, including skipping certain postures entirely and adding others. You don't have to do it all. Just do the exercises that you are able to do and avoid those that your doctor says are unwise for you or that you sense are not right for you now. As we have seen, any moving you do is yoga, and any postures you adopt are as well, if you engage in them mindfully and lovingly.

Any program of mindful body work that you decide to engage in needs to be approached particularly slowly and gently, especially when you have a back problem. A physical therapist who works with many of our patients once commented that she loves to work with people after they have been through MBSR. She says they are noticeably more responsive, relaxed, and tuned in to their bodies during their physical therapy sessions than people who do not know about mindfulness—people who have never been taught how to *breathe with* their stretches and their movements, and how to work *with* the body and *with* painful sensations instead of against them. And the participants themselves say the same thing: that physical therapy changes once they know how to use their breathing as they lift and bend and stretch.

Taking care of the whole of your body through regular exercise is even more important if you have a back problem than for someone without one. Remember, "If you don't use it, you lose it." It is important not to let your back problem become an excuse for not taking care of the rest of your body. As a complement to whatever you find useful within the practice of the mindful yoga, perhaps you could strengthen your body overall by walking regularly or by using a stationary bicycle a few times a week, or by swimming or doing flowing movement exercises in a pool. In the spirit of MBSR, if you intend to do whatever you can to rehabilitate your body, it is important to do something to stretch and strengthen your body every day, or at least every other day, as described in detail in Chapter 6, even if it is just for five minutes at first.

On top of working with your body in these ways as best you can, we suggest you practice the body scan daily, as described in Chapters 5 and 22, as the core of your rehabilitation strategy. Use the body scan, whether you like it at first or hate it, as a time to "rebody" yourself by getting deeply in touch with your body from moment to moment, in stillness, working with whatever sensations arise, and putting the welcome mat out in particular for whatever discomfort or pain you may encounter, and befriending them as best you can. It is helpful to keep bringing to mind the foundational attitudes of MBSR, and in particular, a willingness to be kind and gentle with yourself. Even though you may be very attached to "making progress," which of course is only natural, seeing if you can bring yourself to practice the body scan moment by moment and day after day for its own sake, without any attachment to outcome. This may be the best short- and long-term strategy for having things grow and deepen over time in the direction of true healing and true rehabilitation.

If you are out of work or retired, you will have plenty of time for this. Time can weigh very heavily on us when we are stuck in the house or feel in any way that life is passing us by. You may find yourself feeling bored and frustrated, uncomfortable and irritable, or even sorry for yourself. Anybody would. But none of those assessments is based on the truth of things. They are themselves just more thinking. If you intentionally make up your mind to use some of the time that you have during the day in the service of your own rehabilitation and healing, by practicing the meditation and the yoga, you can transform a bad or isolating or fear-inducing situation into a creative one. You obviously didn't ask for your back problem to happen, but as long as it has, you may as well decide that you will use your time to good advantage in order to rehabilitate yourself as best you possibly can and taking a long-term perspective on how that will unfold. Remember, it's your body and nobody knows it as well as you do, and nobody depends on it as much as you do for your well-being, whatever your circumstances, whatever your age.

One of the most healing things you can do for your body during the day is to use your breath periodically to bathe and embrace the region of pain or discomfort and invite it to soften in the same way that we use the breath in the body scan practice itself, as described in the previous chapter. You can do this by consciously directing your breath in to the painful region, feeling it as it moves into and blends with your back, for instance, and then visualizing and/or feeling the painful sensations softening and dissolving as the breath releases and the whole body, including this region, relaxes to whatever degree it does. It is important to take a day-by-day, even moment-by-moment perspective, purposefully reminding yourself to take each day as it comes, each moment as it comes, and letting go as best you can of any expectations that you should feel a certain way or that the pain should lessen. Instead, we are just watching the breath do its work, and bringing as much kindness and compassion and acceptance to ourself and our situation as possible, moment by moment by moment, and breath by breath by breath. If you need to modify the position of your body in the body scan so that it works more effectively for you, then by all means, be creative in this regard. That would include your decision about what surface you choose to lie on, whether the floor on a thick pad or on your bed, or whether you sometimes feel the need to practice curled up on your side rather than lying on your back in the corpse pose, or anything else that you intuitively feel would be of help in supporting your ongoing practice. Remember, I am not joking when I say that it is important to practice as if your life depended on it. It does.

Healing is truly a journey. The road has its ups and downs. So you should not be too surprised if you have setbacks and sometimes feel as if you are taking one step forward and then sliding two steps backward. This is the way it always is. If you are cultivating mindfulness and seeking ongoing advice and encouragement from your doctor and others who are supporting your efforts, you will be able to catch things as they change and be flexible enough to modify what you are doing when necessary to accommodate your changing situation and the limitations of the moment, whatever they might be. We all have limitations. They are worth befriending. They teach us a lot. They can show us what we most need to pay attention to and honor. They become our cutting edge for learning and growing and gentling ourselves into the present moment as it is. The most important thing is to believe in your own ability to persevere through the many ups and downs, and to not lose sight of your intrinsic wholeness, right in this moment, and your commitment to realizing it fully in the only moment you possibly can, this one. For beyond all efforts at progress and getting someplace better—even though progress and healing can and do unfold over time—the fact of the matter is that in some very deep way, whatever you are looking for or hoping for is already here. You are already whole, you are already perfect, including all your supposed imperfections. There truly is no place to go, nothing to do, nothing to attain. When you practice with this attitude, it is like an oxygen line straight into the heart. Then, paradoxically, great attainment is possible. This is the power of non-doing and non-striving embodied. Another word for it would be *wisdom.*

Bringing mindfulness to your daily activities is particularly valuable, in fact indispensable, when you have a back condition and back pain. As we have seen, sometimes even lifting a pencil or reaching for the toilet paper the wrong way (isn't it amazing that there may be a "wrong way" for you to reach for the toilet paper?), opening a window, or getting out of a car can trigger back spasms and acute pain. So the more you are aware of what you are doing while you are doing it, the better. Doing things on automatic pilot can lead to serious setbacks. As you probably know, it is particularly important to avoid lifting and twisting simultaneously, even with very light objects. First lift, always bending the knees and keeping the object close to your body, then turn. It helps to couple all your movements with awareness of your breathing and your body position. Are you twisting and standing up simultaneously when you get out of the car? Don't. Instead, do one first, then the other. Are you leaning over at the waist to push up a window? Don't. Instead, get in close to it before you attempt to lift it. Mindfulness of little things like this can make a big difference in protecting yourself from injury and pain.

Then there is the challenge of getting things done around the house.

There will be times when you can't do any work at all. But there may be other times, depending on the severity of your back condition, when it may be possible to do things if you do them in moderation and see them as part of your program to build up your strength and flexibility. Take vacuuming, for instance. Lifting and pulling the vacuum cleaner can be dangerous if you have a back condition. But if you are going to do it, you can devise ways to do it mindfully. The movements involved in vacuuming can be very hard on the back. But with a little attention and imagination, you can make the movements of vacuuming into a kind of mindful yoga. You can do under the bed and under the couch on your hands and knees or squatting if that is possible, bending and reaching with awareness, using your breath to guide your movements, just as you would when doing the yoga exercises. If you vacuum this way, and you do it slowly and mindfully, chances are you will know when the body has had enough, and you will listen to its message. Then you might stop and do a little more in a day or two. After you stop, try doing some yoga for five or ten minutes to relax and "distress" your body and stretch some of the muscles that may have tensed up.

Needless to say, this is not the way most people vacuum, or do anything else. But if you experiment, you are likely to find that a little awareness, coupled with the skills that come from your regular yoga and meditation practice, can go a long way toward transforming drudgery into therapy and frustrating limitations into healing opportunities. You work at the edges of what is possible, listening to your body. As you do, you might find yourself growing stronger over the weeks and months. Of course, people who don't have pain might avoid back injuries by vacuuming in the same way. And if vacuuming is out of the question for you, you might try some other household chore and work with it in a similar way.

In the Stress Reduction Clinic, we suggest that people with back pain take a very cautious, experimental approach toward reclaiming those areas in their lives that are most compromised by their condition. Just because you have pain doesn't mean you should give up on your body. It is all the more reason to work with it to make it as strong as it can possibly be so that it can come through for you when you need it. Giving up on sex or walking or shopping or cleaning or hugging is not going to make things better.

Experiment mindfully! Find out what works for you and how to modify things so that you can engage in the most important activities of daily living, at least for short periods. Don't automatically deprive yourself, out of fear or self-pity, of the normal activities that make life meaningful and that give it coherence. Remember, as we saw in Chapter 12, if you say "I can't . . . ," then you certainly won't. That thought or belief or statement becomes a self-fulfilling prophecy; it creates its own reality. But since it is only a thought, it is not necessarily completely accurate. Wouldn't it be better to catch yourself at those moments, see through the "I can't . . ." or the "I could never . . ." thoughts and try instead "Maybe, somehow, it just might be possible. Let me try it . . . mindfully." I cannot tell you the number of people who, over the years, have come up to me and told me that working in this way "saved my life."

Recall Phil, the French Canadian truck driver who had injured his back and whose experience with the body scan in the first few weeks of the program is recounted briefly in Chapter 13. It took him several weeks before he learned how to be in his body during the body scan in such a way that his relationship to intense discomfort shifted, and he experienced a dramatic and enduring reduction in his pain. He experienced many ups and downs in those first weeks but kept up the practice anyway. Finally he wound up feeling much more able to modulate his back pain, and also more in control in other areas of his life as well.

Before he started meditating, Phil had been wearing a TENS unit daily, which the pain clinic had prescribed for him as part of his treatment.* He had felt he couldn't get along without it and wore it all day long, every day. But after a few weeks practicing the body scan, he found he could go two or three days without wearing it. He was very pleased to be able to regulate his pain on his own like that. To him it was a sign of his own power.

But when it came time for the class to do the yoga, once again he came

* A transcutaneous electrical nerve stimulator (TENS) is a device worn on the belt that delivers mild electric shocks to the skin that reduce the experience of pain.

to a crossroads. After the program was over, he described it this way: "You know, I almost gave it up again in the third week when you started talking about yoga and all that stuff. I said, 'Oh my God, that's going to kill me to do that,' but then you said that if it bothers you, don't do it, so I mostly did the body scan. But I did do some yoga too, and I did a lot during the all-day session. It bothered me at times, some of the exercises bothered me to do them, like the leg raising and the folding yourself up and rolling backward on your neck. I can't do a whole lot of that. The things I can do that don't bother me, I do them every so often. I am definitely feeling more flexible."

In reviewing his experience at the end of the eight weeks, Phil said, "No, the pain is not gone, it's still there, but you know, when I start feeling it too much, I just sit aside somewhere, take ten, fifteen, twenty minutes, do my meditation, and that seems to take over. And if I can stay at least fifteen or thirty minutes or better, I can walk away and not even think about it for maybe three, four, five, six hours, maybe the whole day, depending on the weather."

He also noticed that things were different at home with his wife and children. In his own words: "We had a bit of a problem when I first came here [to the clinic]. We had problems, ya know. I had this pain problem so much on my mind and about finding another kind of a job without the education I figured I needed for most jobs or whatever . . . this stuff all built up pressure and, without realizing, I was like a madman, ya know? I mean, my wife was just like a slave working for me, more or less, and we sat down one night and I got kinda frustrated and I told her, 'We gotta talk.' There wasn't much sex life going on, and that's driving me up a wall. I'm not a person who goes weeks without it, ya know, and so I said, 'Come on now, let's . . . ,' so she finally made me realize what was going on. She says, 'How long since you told me you love me? How long?' We sit down—we've got a double recliner, ya know, like a love seat—and she says, 'Let's sit down and watch TV together.' But when I'm watching TV, I'm watching TV. She'll talk and I go, 'Uh-huh, uh-huh,' but it goes right through me, ya know. She'll say, 'Well, I told you . . . ,' and I'll say, 'Well, I'm sorry, I wasn't listening, I was watching my boxing' or whatever. Well, she finally made me realize what's going on. After I started in the Stress Reduction Clinic, I says, 'Wow, ya know, I do realize it now, ya know. So we got away from the TV now. At night we don't sit down and watch TV no more. We go outside. We have a campfire every night when it's nice, with the neighbors. We sit down and talk, ya know, and sometimes we're with another couple, sometimes just talking or sitting watching the fire, and it just draws my attention. And the first thing you know, they're talking, but it's just like they're a distance far away. I can find myself getting to the breathing exercise automatically, and I feel so much better after this. And it beats watching that boob tube. My relationship with my wife has improved a hundred percent, and with the kids too.'"

On the subject of trying new things, Phil also observed, "One other thing I got from the program . . . Before, I was never able to talk in public the way I did in the classes. Anytime I ever tried before, I could feel my face burning, turning as red as a tomato, because I am bashful and shy, I always was. I don't know what made me be able to talk in the classes the way I did. You see, what I did say, whenever I said something, I had a good feeling about it. It didn't come from my mouth, it came from inside, ya know? From the heart."

INTENSIVE MEDITATION AND PAIN

It is no accident that meditation practice has something to teach us about coping with pain. Over the past 2,500-plus years, practitioners of meditation have had a lot of experience learning from pain and developing methods to transcend it. Intensive training in meditation has traditionally been the province of monasteries and retreat centers set up for that explicit purpose. Long-term meditation practice can be very painful physically and emotionally, as well as uplifting and liberating. Imagine going off somewhere and doing what we do in our all-day session (see Chapter 8), but staying in silence for seven days or two weeks or a month or three months. People do just that on meditation retreats set up for that very purpose. In fact, it is a very profound gift you might give yourself, when you are ready.

When you sit without moving, especially cross-legged on the floor, for extended periods of time, typically for between half an hour and an hour, and sometimes even longer if you choose, and you do this maybe ten hours a day for days or even weeks at a time, your body can begin to hurt with excruciating intensity, primarily in the back, shoulders, and knees. The physical pain eventually diminishes by itself most of the time, but sitting through even a few days of it can be quite challenging. You tend to learn a lot about yourself and about pain from putting yourself in this kind of situation on purpose. If you are willing to turn toward the pain, accept it, observe it, and not run from it, it can teach you a great deal. Above all, you learn that you can work with it. You learn that pain is not a static experience; it is constantly changing. You come to see that the sensations are just what they are and that your thoughts and feelings are something apart from the sensations. You come to see that your mind may play a large part in your own suffering, and it can play a large role in freeing you from suffering as well. Pain can teach you all of these things.

People attending meditation retreats invariably have to face the physical pain that comes up during long sittings. It is unavoidable in the early stages of a retreat. It comes out of sitting still in postures we are not used to. It also arises when we become aware of the accumulated physical tension we carry around with us, unnoticed, in our bodies. In many ways, the qualities of this type of pain strongly resemble the spectrum of sensations that occur in many chronic pain conditions: the aching, the burning, the episodes of sharp, shooting sensations in the back or the knees or the shoulders. You could stop the pain at any time by getting up and walking, but mostly, if you are a meditator, you choose to stay and be mindful of it as just another experience. In return, it teaches you how to cultivate calmness, concentration, and equanimity in the face of discomfort. But it is not an easy lesson to learn. You have to be willing to face the pain over and over again, day in and day out, and observe it, breathe with it, look into it, accept it. In this way, meditation practice can be a laboratory for exploring pain, for learning more about what it is, how to go deeply into it, and ultimately how to come to terms with it.

As we saw in the previous chapter, recent studies of experienced meditators suggest that they may have a much higher tolerance for pain intensity than novice meditators, since they rate the sensations as much less unpleasant than the novices at the same degree of intensity. They also show thickening in certain parts of the brain associated with mapping sensation and regulating emotional expression in the body. Meditators seem to be able to uncouple the sensory dimension of the pain experience from the emotions and thoughts that so often accompany it and that compound the experience of suffering. They see it as bare sensation, and do not take it so personally. This uncoupling of the sensory from the emotional and cognitive dimensions of the pain experience may result in significant reductions in the degree of suffering associated with exposure to a painful experience. We see this happening every day in the MBSR classes.

ATHLETES AND PAIN

Like meditators, endurance athletes also know a certain kind of self-induced pain firsthand. They too know the power of the mind in working *with* their pain so that they are not defeated by it. Athletes are constantly putting themselves into situations that are bound to produce pain. You cannot run a marathon at your fastest pace and not face pain. In fact, few people could run a marathon at any speed and not encounter pain.

Then why do they do it in the first place? Because runners, and all other athletes, know from firsthand experience that pain can be worked with and transcended. When the body is screaming out to stop because the metabolic pain (from the muscles not being able to get enough oxygen fast enough) toward the end of a race is so great, whether it is a 100-meter sprint or a 26.2-mile marathon, or an ultramarathon or a triathlon, whether it is swimming or biking, or running, or something else, an athlete has to reach into himself or herself and decide virtually moment by moment whether to back off the pace or to find new resources for going beyond what a normal person would consider an absolute limit.

In fact, unless a physical injury occurs (producing an acute pain-of-injury that makes you stop, and rightly so, to prevent further injury), it is invariably the mind that decides to quit first, not the body. Athletes can be plagued by lapses of concentration, by fears and self-doubts, and by the knowledge that they face certain pain during training and competition. For these reasons as well as many others, many athletes and their coaches now believe that systematic mental training is every bit as necessary as systematic physical training if they hope to be able to perform at their peak. In fact, in the new paradigm, there cannot be complete physical fitness and optimal performance of any task without mental fitness. These need to be cultivated together.

In 1984, I had an opportunity to work with the United States Olympic men's rowing team, training the rowers in the same meditation practices that the pain patients use in MBSR to cope with their chronic pain conditions. These world-class athletes were able to use mindfulness strategies to improve their ability to face and cope with pain during training and competition, just as the patients are able to use it to work with their pain, even though these two different groups of people are working at opposite ends of the physical fitness spectrum.

Readers with chronic low-back problems might be interested to know that John Biglow, the single sculler on the 1984 U.S. Olympic rowing team, achieved his position as the best male American sculler that year in spite of a chronic back problem resulting from a herniated disk when he injured himself rowing in 1979. Following his injury, and then a serious setback in 1983 when he reinjured himself, he was never able to row hard for more than five minutes at a time, after which he would have to rest for three minutes before he could row hard again. Yet he was able to rehabilitate himself by training very carefully using the knowledge of his own limits, to the point where he was able to demand of his back the enormous effort required to compete at the world-class level. In order to be the single sculler on the Olympic team, Biglow had to race against and beat all the fastest, strongest, and most competitive rowers in the country. (Races are 2,000 meters and are completed in about five minutes.) Imagine the faith, determination, bodily intelligence, and mindfulness necessary for someone with a chronic back problem to even set out to work toward such a goal, not to mention achieve it. But the goal he set for himself was meaningful enough to sustain him along the extremely arduous, painful, and lonely road he followed.

In the 2012 Olympics, held in London, an Iranian super-heavyweight lifter, Behdad Salimikordasiabi, lifted 545 pounds in his first try in what is called the clean and jerk. Along with his score in the event called the snatch, his total score was so high that he had clearly already won the gold medal for that event. Since he was still entitled to two more attempts, the crowd went wild, urging him to go for breaking the world record, which had been set by his own teacher and mentor. After one failed attempt, he declined to go for it, in spite of the crowd's urging, the intoxicating heat-of-the-moment feeling, and the fact that he had lifted much heavier weight in practice sessions. He said later that he had rested too long between lifts and that his body had "gotten cold," making it unwise to go for the world record. He said there would be plenty of other occasions to attempt to break the world record. This is a remarkable example of someone being mindful of his body and being able to both recognize and respect its limitations of the moment, in spite of all the emotion from the crowd and perhaps in his own mind. We may not be capable of lifting much in the way of weight, but each one of us has that very same capacity to heed our own interior messages from the body and work with them in ways that further our overall goals. In that way, we are all athletes of the possible.

Each of us, in our own way, no matter what our situation or disability, is capable of such achievements if we can define meaningful goals for ourselves and then work intelligently toward their fulfillment. Even if we don't achieve the goal completely, the effort itself can be sustaining and healing if we find meaning in the process itself and work with awareness, moment by moment and day by day, honoring our limitations but not being imprisoned by them. If you have any doubts about this, just watch the wheelchair athletes in local road races, or the Paralympics on YouTube. It could bring you to tears of uplift and admiration.

HEADACHES

Most headaches are not signs of brain tumors or other serious pathological conditions, although such thoughts can easily enter your mind if you suffer from headaches that are constant, chronic, and severe. But if headaches persist or are extremely severe, it is always important to go through at least one full diagnostic work-up to rule out such pathology before trying to control them either with medication or meditation. In such cases, a well-trained physician will make sure this is done before referring a headache patient for MBSR training. Most of the patients in the Stress Reduction Clinic who have problems with chronic headaches come with diagnoses of either tension headaches, migraines, or both. All have had a full neurological examination, which usually includes a CAT scan to rule out a brain tumor.

The majority of people who are referred to the clinic with chronic headaches respond well to the meditation practice. One woman came to the program with a twenty-year history of migraine headaches, for which she took Cafergot every day. She had been treated at numerous headache clinics with no relief. Within two weeks of entering the program, she had a two-day stretch with no headaches. This had not happened to her in twenty years. She remained headache-free for the duration of the course and for some time afterward.

You only need one experience of having a headache disappear that has been chronic and constant to know that it is within the realm of possibility for such a thing to happen. This can completely change the way you think about your body and your illness, and can provide you with renewed faith in your ability to control and regulate what previously seemed uncontrollable and unmanageable.

One elderly woman told her class recently that the idea of putting out the welcome mat for her migraine struck her as particularly appropriate. So the next time she felt one coming on, she sat down to meditate and "talked" to her headache. She said things like "Come in if you want to, but you should know that I am no longer going to be ruled by you. I have a lot to do today and I just can't spend much time with you." This worked quite well for her and she seemed pleased with this discovery.

There is a place on the body-scan CD, after we have gone through the entire body, that suggests breathing through an imaginary hole at the top of your head, much as a whale breathes through a blowhole. The idea is to feel as if your breath could actually move in and out through this hole and then be present for how it actually feels, however that is, with full awareness and acceptance. You are not trying to make anything happen, but just being playful and experimenting.

Many people with headaches have used that "hole" as a release valve for their headaches. You just breathe in and out through the top of your head and let the tension or pressure or whatever the sensations are in that region flow right out of the body through the hole, to whatever degree they do. Of course it is harder to do this if you have not been developing your ability to concentrate through regular meditation practice. But if you have been practicing breathing this way every day as part of your work with the body scan, when you do have headache-like symptoms, you may find that they can be dispelled easily, before they build into a full-blown headache. But even if you have a full-blown headache, this method can be effective in taking the edge off it or shortening its duration, or even dissolving it.

As they get into practicing the meditation on a regular basis, whether they have a headache or not at the time they do it, most people who come to the Stress Reduction Clinic with headache problems report that both the frequency and the severity of their headaches decrease.

As your practice deepens, you may notice that your headaches do not come out of nowhere. There are usually identifiable preconditions that trigger their onset. The problem is that we only poorly understand many of the physiological triggers, and we often ignore or deny the psychological or social triggers. Certainly, stressful situations can give rise to headaches, and many people, especially those with muscle tension headaches, are at least aware of this connection. But many other people report that they wake up with headaches or that they get them when they are not under obvious stress, when everything is going well for them, on the weekends, or at other times in which they don't feel stressed.

A few weeks of mindfulness practice often generate new insights in these individuals about their headaches and why and when they get them. Sometimes people discover that they may be a lot more tense and keyed up than they thought they were, even on the weekends. Sometimes they see that a particular thought or worry might precede the onset of a headache. This can even happen as you wake up in the morning and are getting out of bed. One anxious thought can make you tense before your feet touch the floor, although you may be completely unaware of the thought. All you know is that you "woke up with a headache."

This is another way that being mindful as you go through the day can be useful. It helps you to tune in to your body and to your breathing from the very first moment that you know you are awake in the morning. You might even try saying to yourself as you wake up, "I am waking up now" or "I am awake now," and *feel how it feels* by bringing awareness to your body as a whole, lying in bed, for at least a few breaths, before you move to get up. You can even remind yourself that you are greeting a brand-new day, filled with possibilities that you cannot possibly know but can be ready for by being open and awake for whatever may transpire as the day unfolds.

Over time, this ability simply to rest in awareness can lead you to make connections that may have previously gone unnoticed, such as realizing the link between a thought you wake up with or a situation that occurs early in the day, perhaps even in the first few minutes that you are up, and a headache later on. This can lead you to intentionally try to short-circuit a possible headache-producing chain of events by bringing awareness right to the thought as it arises, seeing it as a thought, and letting it go. Or you can take action to change your relationship to a bothersome stressful situation and monitor the results of your efforts. It may also be that you will become aware of times and places where you are more likely to get a headache and in this way identify environmental factors such as pollution and allergens that might play a role in triggering some kinds of headaches.

For some people, chronic headaches may really be a metaphor for everything that is disconnected and disregulated in their lives: body, family, work, environment, the full catastrophe. Their whole life could be described as a headache. They usually have so much stress in their day-to-day lives that it is difficult to know where to start thinking about why they might be getting headaches. If this describes your present situation, it may be helpful for you to know that you do not have to *solve* any of your problems in order to get started. All that you really need to do is begin paying more careful attention from moment to moment during your day to what is really going on, headache or no headache. In other words, practice being more fully present and more fully embodied, awake, and aware. With time, movement toward self-regulation happens naturally, as we have seen. Allostasis is restored, and you may find that the headaches literally and even metaphorically *dissolve* as if on their own. It may take years to work yourself out of such a situation completely, but the attempt itself, coupled with a willingness to accept where you already are and be patient, can lead to dramatic improvements in your headaches long before the rest of your problems have been resolved.

The two stories that follow are examples of ways in which chronic headaches may serve as a metaphor for a person's entire life situation at a particular point in time, and how this dilemma can be worked with and perhaps turned around to lead, ultimately, not only to relief of the headaches but, even more importantly, to some insight and resolution of the larger situation.

Fred, a thirty-eight-year-old man, was referred for anxiety associated with sleep apnea, a condition characterized by temporary cessation of breathing during sleep. The apnea was due to his obesity. Fred was five foot ten, and at the time he weighed 375 pounds. In addition to his anxiety and his sleep apnea, Fred had chronic headaches. Whenever he felt stressed, he got a headache. Getting on a bus would always result in a headache. He hated buses ("they make me sick"), but he had no car and depended on them to get around. He lived with a roommate and worked managing a concession stand. His weight was so great that his neck would prevent him from breathing properly when he was lying down. This is what caused his sleep apnea. His pulmonary doctor had told him he would have to have a tracheotomy if he didn't lose weight right away. This prospect caused Fred a great deal of anxiety. He did not want to have a tracheotomy. A colleague of ours who was counseling him for weight reduction suggested he attend the Stress Reduction Clinic's classes in MBSR to deal with his anxiety.

Fred came to the first class and didn't like it at all. He said to himself, "I can't wait till this session is over. I won't be back." At the time he had agreed to go, it hadn't quite hit him what it would be like to be in a class with about thirty other people. He had always been uncomfortable in crowds and had never been able to talk in a group. He was shy and instinctively avoided any kind of situation that might lead to conflict. But as he described it to me when the program was over, some "gut feeling" brought him back to the second class. He found himself saying, "If I don't do it now, I'll probably never do it" and "Everyone else has got problems or else they wouldn't be here." So, in spite of his feelings about the first class, Fred decided to keep coming. He started practicing the body scan that first week because it was assigned for homework, and by the next class he already knew that it was "going to work" for him. As he put it, "I really got into it right away." He was even able to say something in the class about how relaxing he had found it to tune in to his body.

From the time he started doing the body scan, Fred's headaches disappeared. This happened in spite of the fact that the stress in his life was increasing as it became more and more obvious that he was gaining weight, not losing it, and would have to have the tracheotomy. Yet by just "relaxing and going with the flow and enjoying it," he was able to ride on the buses without getting headaches or feeling sick.

He also became more assertive. He was able to ask his roommate to leave when he stopped contributing to the rent. This was something he felt he would have never been able to do before. As he became more self-confident, Fred also started feeling more relaxed in his body. The yoga bothered him because of his weight and he didn't do much of it. But although he gained some weight during the program, he did not get depressed. Previously, gaining even a minuscule amount of weight would send him into a severe depression.

Fred also had high blood pressure. At one point prior to joining the MBSR program, his blood pressure was measured at 210/170, which is dangerously high. Usually it averaged around 140/95 on blood pressure medication. When he completed the program, it was averaging around 120/70, lower than it had been for fifteen years.

As a postscript, he underwent not one but two attempts at a tracheotomy in one week, but they didn't work because his neck was so thick they couldn't get the tube to stay in. Both times it fell out after a few days. So he never did get the tracheotomy.

When I saw him again a month after the course ended, he was on a diet and had lost a noticeable amount of weight. He was continuing with his meditation practice. He said he had never felt so sure of himself in his life. Losing the weight gave him a major boost in self-confidence. He said he was feeling happy for the first time in years and that his sleep apnea had diminished with his weight loss. And he had had only one headache since he finished the course.

In another class, a forty-year-old divorced woman named Laurie was referred by her neurologist for migraine headaches and work stress. She had had migraines since she was thirteen, often four times in a single week. These included seeing lights in front of her eyes, usually followed by nausea and vomiting. Although she was on medication, the drugs often did not help her headaches unless she took them at exactly the right time, before the headache built up. This time was always hard for her to judge. In the four months preceding her referral to the clinic, Laurie's headaches had gotten worse, to the point where several times she had sought help in the emergency room of the hospital.

When Laurie took MBSR, on occasion we asked the class participants in the fourth week to fill out the Holmes and Rahe Social Readjustment Rating Scale, in addition to continuing with their daily meditation practice. As we saw in Chapter 18, this scale is simply a list of life events. The assignment was to check off those items that happened to you in the past year. The list includes such things as death of a spouse, change in work status, illness in the family, marriage, taking out a large mortgage, and a number of other events. Each item has a particular score, which is supposed to be related to how stressful it would be to have to adapt to such a change in one's life. In the instructions for this scale it says that a total score of over 150 means that you are under considerable stress and need to make sure you are taking steps to adapt to these situations effectively.

On the day we discussed that homework assignment in class, Laurie had the highest score on the life-events scale of anyone in the class. She told us how she and her boyfriend had both tallied their scores one night in disbelief. She scored 879 and he scored in the 700s. Their response was to laugh when they saw how high their scores were. They figured they must be stronger than they thought because, as she put it, looking at their scores, "It's a miracle we are not both dead." She knew they could easily have been crying rather than laughing. She said that she saw laughing as a good sign, a healthy response in itself.

Laurie's life at that time was dominated by fear that her ex-husband was trying to kill her, which, according to her, he had actually attempted to do. On top of this, her two sons had recently been injured in a car accident, although not seriously, and she was going through a very stressful time at work.

She worked as a middle manager in a large corporation that was going through a major restructuring that made everybody feel insecure and under a lot of pressure. Her situation was made more complex by the fact that she, her boyfriend, and her ex-husband all worked for the same company.

In the fifth class, she said that during that week she had seen the prodromal "lights" that usually signal the onset of a big migraine headache. But for the first time, she had become aware of them early on. There were only a few lights, not the overwhelming array that usually meant that the headache was less than an hour away and already, as she put it, "unstoppable." She decided then and there to take one pill and then get into bed and do the body scan, thinking that maybe she could avoid taking the other three pills that she was supposed to take in sequence over several hours to control the headaches with medication.

What Laurie reported with some pride was that for the first time since she was a girl, she had been able to short-circuit a headache on her own. She never took the other three pills. She did the body scan, fell asleep toward the end, and woke up feeling completely refreshed. She attributed her success to two things: First, she felt that practicing the meditation over the preceding weeks had helped her to become more sensitive to her body and to what she was feeling. This is why, she surmised, she was able to be aware of the early warning signs of the migraine several hours before the full-blown headache was upon her and to take some action. Second, she now had something she could do at such a moment when she recognized the warning signs early enough. At least she felt she now had something she could try out as an alternative to taking a drug to control her headache. She had approached the impending headache in a new way, experimenting with drawing on her own inner resources for regulating it and herself through her mindfulness practice.

Laurie continued to be headache-free over the next four weeks, even though her life was in a state of perpetual upheaval. She put the problem of the nine dots up on the wall in her office, and she tried to respond to the stressors in her life instead of reacting to them.

In the week following the end of the program, Laurie had another big migraine headache. It came on the day before Thanksgiving and continued through the next day. She wouldn't let herself be taken to the emergency room, although she was in the bathroom throwing up more than she was with her family. They were begging her to let them take her to the hospital. But in her mind, her sons had come home for Thanksgiving dinner and she could only think of how awful it was that she was so sick on the one day that she was getting to see them.

When I saw her the next morning, she was pale, distraught, and tearful. She said she felt like a "failure" after all the good results she had had during the course. She had been hoping that her doctor would take her off Inderal if she was able to remain headache-free. Now she felt she had "blown that possibility completely." Even worse, she also felt like a failure because she had no idea why she had gotten the headache. She said that she hadn't felt stressed by the thought of Thanksgiving. On the contrary, she had been looking forward to it. But as we talked more about the days leading up to the holiday, it became clearer to her that it did have a special meaning for her that year, and that she had had higher expectations than usual because her boys were coming and she had been feeling that she hadn't been seeing enough of them. She also recalled that on Tuesday, before the headache came on with full force, she had been seeing the lights and spots of the prodrome but that they just hadn't really registered in her awareness. She recalled that her boyfriend had asked her at a certain point what she wanted to do for dinner and she had said, "I don't know, I can't think. My mind is a blank."

This was probably the critical point for her. It was an early warning signal from her body that a migraine was coming on. But this time, for whatever reason, the message just did not get through. She said later that she was probably feeling too busy, rushed, and tired to listen to her body, even though she had had the successful experience of short-circuiting the last one by taking immediate action when she had felt the early warning signs.

After her upset with herself had subsided, she was able to realize that this horrible headache did not mean that she was a failure. If anything, it meant that she might benefit from being even more tuned in to her body's messages. She began to see that perhaps it was unrealistic to expect that after twenty-seven years of problems with migraine headaches, she would learn to control them in four weeks to the point where they would never be a problem for her again, especially given the current upheavals in her life.

By not generalizing from this one headache into making herself a failure, Laurie was able to see that having this particular headache at this particular time was teaching her something she hadn't yet fully realized and that, in that sense, it could be seen as helpful. It was teaching her that she needed to honor how much of a crisis her life was in at that time, what with court dates coming up, her problems at work, and her anger at her ex-husband. It was teaching her that such pressures don't go away just because a holiday is coming up. In fact, they can make the holiday more of a loaded situation emotionally and lead to unconscious but strong expectations and desires that things go a certain way.

And most importantly, the headache was teaching her that, at that point in her life especially, she couldn't afford to ignore or override her body's messages. She needed to honor them and be even more prepared than she had been to stop what she was doing when the early warning signs came on, take her medication, and practice the body scan immediately. If this was what the full catastrophe of her situation demanded of her, she realized that nothing less would do if she hoped ultimately to come to greater harmony in her life and to free herself from her headaches, literally and metaphorically.

24

Working with Emotional Pain: Your Suffering Is Not You . . . But There Is Much You Can Do to Heal It

The body has no monopoly on suffering. Emotional pain, the pain in our hearts and minds, is far more widespread and just as likely to be debilitating as physical pain. This pain can take many forms. There is the suffering of self-condemnation, such as when we blame ourselves for something we did or for something we didn't do, or when we feel unworthy or stupid and lack confidence in ourselves. If we caused others harm, we might also experience the pain of guilt, a combination of self-blame and remorse. There is pain in anxiety, worry, fear, and terror. There is pain in loss and grief, humiliation and embarrassment, despair and hopelessness. We may carry one kind of emotional pain or another deep within our hearts and bodies, often for much of our lives, like a heavy and sometimes secret burden, at times unknown even to ourselves.

Just as with physical pain, you can be mindful of emotional pain and can use its energy to grow and heal. The key is to be willing to make room for your suffering, to welcome it, observe it without trying to change it, to befriend it intentionally, to invite it to be present, in other words, to be with it just as you would with a symptom, with physical pain, or with a thought that surfaces repeatedly.

It is difficult to convey the importance of being able to shift your perspective to an acceptance of the present moment, whatever is happening, when emotional pain surfaces. Whether, as has happened to people who were in the clinic, it is feeling frightened by a medical emergency that takes you to the ICU, or angry and humiliated because the police came to your door and took you away in the middle of the night to commit you against your will, or frustrated and depressed because a new doctor yelled at you in front of a waiting room full of people and refused to fill a prescription you had been given routinely in the same clinic for years, it is your willingness to cultivate mindfulness *in these moments* and in the aftermath of such moments that is most important. Bringing awareness to whatever is unfolding *while* you are experiencing pain is critical to working with your emotions.

Of course, the natural tendency is to avoid feelings of pain whenever possible and to wall ourselves off from as much of it as we can, or to be automatically swept away by a tidal wave of emotion. In either case, we are too preoccupied, our minds too turbulent, to remember to look directly, with eyes of wholeness, in such moments—that is, unless we have been training the mind to see its own upsets, whatever they may be and however painful, as opportunities to respond in new ways rather than becoming a victim of our own reactions. In the end, the damage that is done when we deny or avoid our feelings or become lost in them only compounds our suffering.

As with physical pain, our emotional pain is also trying to tell us something. It too is a messenger. Feelings have to be acknowledged, at least to ourselves. They have to be encountered and felt in all their force. There is no other way through to the other side of them. If we ignore them, repress them, suppress them, or sublimate them, they fester and yield no resolution, no peace. And if without any awareness of what we are doing we exaggerate them, dramatize them, and preoccupy ourselves with their turmoil and the stories we generate about them to validate our experience, they too linger and cause us to become stuck in patterns that may go on for an entire lifetime.

Even in the tortured throes of grief or anger, in the gnawing remorse of guilt, in the slack tides of sadness and hurt, and in the swells of fear, it is still possible to be mindful, to know that in this moment I am feeling grief and grief feels just like *this,* I am feeling anger and anger feels like *this,* I am feeling guilty or sad or hurt or frightened, or confused and it feels like *this.*

Strange as it may sound, the intentional *knowing* of your feelings in times of emotional suffering contains in itself the seeds of healing. Just as we saw with physical pain, that aspect of you that can *know* your feelings, that sees clearly what they are, that can accept them in the present, while they are happening, no matter what they are, in their full, undisguised fury if such is the case, or in their many disguises, such as confusion, rigidity, or alienation, that awareness itself has an independent perspective that is outside of your suffering. It is not buffeted by the storms of the heart and of the mind. The storms still have to run their course; their pain has to be felt. But they actually unfold differently when cradled in awareness. The awareness is not part of the pain. It is what holds the pain, as the weather unfolds within the space of the sky.

For one thing, when held in awareness, the storm is no longer just happening *to* you, as though you are the victim of an outside force. You are now taking responsibility for feeling what you are feeling in this moment, because this is what is arising in your life right now. These moments of pain are as much moments to be lived fully as are any others, and they can actually teach us a great deal, although few of us would seek out these lessons willingly. But relating to your pain consciously, as long as it is here anyway, allows you to engage fully with your emotions rather than be a victim of them.

And even though the pain you feel may be as great as if there were no seeing, no conscious awareness of a larger picture at all, this bringing of attention to emotion allows you to see and embrace your feelings with a certain degree of wisdom. The pain may be as great, but at least the edge comes off the suffering when we inquire into who is suffering, when we observe our mind flailing about, rejecting, protesting, denying, clamoring, fantasizing, hurting, and generating narratives that may be less than wholly accurate and therefore not really helpful.

Mindfulness allows us to see more clearly into the nature of our pain, and the stories we construct about it. Sometimes it helps us to cut through confusion, hurt feelings, and emotional turmoil, caused perhaps by misperceptions or exaggerations and our desire that things be a certain way. When you next find yourself in a period of suffering, try listening for a calm inner voice that might be saying, "Isn't this interesting? Isn't it amazing what a human being can go through? Isn't it amazing how much pain and anguish I can feel or create for myself or get bogged down in?" In listening for a calmer and clearer voice within your own heart, within your own pain, you will be reminding yourself to observe the unfolding of your emotions with wise attention, with a degree of non-attachment. You may find yourself wondering how things will finally be resolved, and knowing that you don't know, that you will just have to wait and see. Yet you can be certain that a resolution will come, that what you are experiencing is like the crest of a wave—it can't keep itself up indefinitely, so it has to release. And you will know as well that how you handle what is going on at the crest of this wave can influence what the resolution will be. For instance, if, in a fit of anger, you say or do something that deeply harms another person, you have compounded the suffering of the moment even more and ensured that the resolution will be even further away, and perhaps much less to your liking. So in moments of great emotional pain, perhaps you will come to accept not knowing how things will resolve in the present moment, maybe not even generating or believing the usual story you tell yourself, and in that acceptance, you can begin the process of healing.

You may discern within your pain, even as you feel it, that some of it is coming from non-acceptance, from rejecting what has already happened or what was said or done, from wanting things to be some other way, more to your liking, more under your control. Perhaps you would like another chance. Perhaps you want to turn back the clock and do something differently, or to say something you didn't say, or to take back something you did say. Perhaps you are jumping to conclusions without knowing the whole story and feeling hurt unnecessarily because of your own premature reactions to things. There are many ways in which we suffer, but usually they are variations on a few basic themes.

If you are mindful as emotional storms occur, perhaps you will see in yourself an unwillingness to accept things as they already are, whether you like them or not. Perhaps that part of you that does see this has, in one way or another, already come to terms with what has happened or with your situation. Perhaps, at the same time, it recognizes that your feelings still need to play themselves out, that they are not ready to accept the situation or to calm down, and that this too is all right.

Just as in the meditation practice, our minds have a strong tendency to reject things as they are when it comes to *my* pain, *my* dilemmas, *my* grief. As Einstein pointed out (see Chapter 12), this locks us into an identification with our separateness. As we have seen, such a view can cut us off from our ability to see clearly and to heal, just when we might need it most.

If a momentary insight into the process of your pain unfolding should arise, let it be simply an observation. Do not jump from it to a blanket condemnation of yourself for not being able to accept what is or to connect with a larger whole. This is all just more thinking, and judgmental, romantic, and idealistic thinking at that. What we need in such moments is simply to feel what is here to be felt and let it wash through us, however long the process may take, as best we can resting in awareness and watching our thoughts and our emotions do whatever they may do with a degree of equanimity. An unwillingness to accept what has transpired may be totally appropriate in this moment. You may feel threatened by an impending calamity or sense of doom. Or perhaps you have suffered a grievous loss, have been wronged by someone, or made some error in judgment that you feel remorse for and are unwilling to "just accept."

As we saw in Chapter 2, acceptance does not mean that you *like* what has occurred or that you are merely passively resigned to it. It does not mean capitulation or surrender. The way we are using the word here, it means only that you admit the bare fact that whatever has happened has *already* happened and is therefore in the past. More often than not, acceptance can only come with time, as the storm plays itself out, as the winds die down. But how much healing takes place after the devastation depends on how much you are able to be awake, face the storm's energies, and observe them with wise attention while they are raging, however painful that may be.

Profoundly healing insights may arise if you are willing to look deeply into your emotional pain as it is occurring, as well as in its aftermath. One major realization you might come to is the inevitability of change, the direct perception that, whether we like it or not, *impermanence is in the very nature of things and relationships.* We saw this within physical pain when we observed changes in its intensity and the coming and going of different sensations, even the shifting of the pain from one place to another in the body, as sometimes happens. We also noted it in our changing thoughts and feelings and attitudes toward our pain.

When you look deeply into emotional pain at the time you are feeling it, it is hard not to notice that here too your thoughts and emotions are in a state of extreme turbulence, coming and going, appearing and disappearing, changing with great rapidity. In times of great stress, you may notice certain thoughts and feelings recurring with unrelenting frequency. They return over and over again, causing you to keep reliving what happened or wondering what you might have done differently or how what happened could have come about. You may find yourself blaming yourself or someone else over and over again, or reliving a particular moment again and again, or wondering over and over what will happen next or what will become of you now.

But if you can be mindful at such times, if you are watching carefully, you will also notice that even these recurring images, thoughts, and feelings have a beginning and an end, that they are like waves that rise up in the mind and then subside. You may also notice that they are never quite the same. Each time one comes back, it is slightly different, never exactly the same as any previous wave.

You may also notice that the intensity of your feelings cycles as well. One moment there may be a dull hurt, the next moment intense anguish and fury, the next moment fear, then dullness again or exhaustion. For brief moments you may even forget altogether that you hurt. In seeing these changes in your emotional state, you may come to realize that none of what you are experiencing is permanent. You can actually see for yourself that the intensity of the pain is not constant, that it changes, goes up and down, comes and goes, just as your breath comes and goes.

That part of you that is mindful is just seeing what is transpiring from moment to moment, nothing more. It is not rejecting the bad, it is not condemning anything or anybody, it is not wishing that things were different, it is not even upset. Awareness, like a field of compassionate intelligence located within your own heart, takes it all in and serves as a source of peace within the turmoil, much as a mother would be a source of peace, compassion, and perspective for a child who was upset. She knows that whatever is troubling her child will pass, so she can provide comfort, reassurance, and peace in her very being.

As we cultivate mindfulness in our own hearts, we can direct a similar compassion toward ourselves. Sometimes we need to care for ourselves as if that part of us that is suffering is our own child. Why not show compassion, kindness, and sympathy toward our own being, even as we open fully to our pain? To treat ourself with as much kindness as we would another person in pain is a wonderfully healing meditation in its own right. It cultivates lovingkindness and compassion, which know no boundaries.

A "WHAT IS MY OWN WAY?" MEDITATION

One of the major sources of suffering in our lives is that we usually want to have things our own way. Thus when things happen that we like, we feel that everything is going our way and we feel happy. And when things feel like they are going against us, when they do not happen the way we want or the way we expected or planned for, then we tend to feel thwarted, frustrated, angry, wounded, and unhappy, and we suffer.

The irony is that often we really don't know what our way is, even though we want to have it all the time. If we get what we want, we usually want something else in addition. The mind keeps finding new things that it needs in order to feel happy or fulfilled. In this regard, it is rarely satisfied for long with the situation as it is, even if things are relatively peaceful and satisfying.

When little children get upset because they can't have everything they see that they would like to have, we are apt to tell them, "You can't always have your own way." And when they say, "Why not?" we say, "Because" or "You'll understand when you grow up." But this is a fiction we perpetrate on them. In fact, most of the time we grown-ups don't behave as if we understand life any better than our children do. We want to have things our own way too. We just want different things than they do. Don't we get just as upset when things don't turn out as we want them to? We find it easy to smile at their childishness or to get angry at it, depending on our own state of mind. Perhaps we have just learned how to hide our feelings better.

To break out of this trap of always being driven by our own desires, it is not a bad exercise to ask yourself from time to time, "What *is* my own way?" "What do I really want?" "Would I know it if I got it?" "Does everything have to be perfect right now, or under my total control right now, for me to be happy?"

Alternatively, you might ask yourself, "Is everything already basically okay right now?" "Am I just *not noticing* the ways in which things are good because my mind keeps coming up with ideas for what it has to have or has to get rid of before I can be happy, just like a child?" Or, if that is not the case, you might go on to ask, "Are there specific steps that I can take, seeing my unhappiness right now, that would help me to move toward greater peace and harmony in my life?" "Are there decisions I could make that would help me to find my own way?" "Do I have any power to chart my own course, or am I fated to live out the rest of my life unable to experience happiness or peace because of fate, because of decisions I made or that were made for me decades ago, perhaps when I was young and silly, or blind, or insecure, or more unaware than I am now?"

If you practice incorporating questions about your own way into your meditation practice, you will find that it is very effective in bringing you back to the present moment. You might try sitting with the question "Right now, what is my way?" It is sufficient to ask the question. Trying to answer it is not necessary. It is more fruitful just to ponder the question, keeping it alive from moment to moment, listening for the response from within your heart. "What is my own way?" "What is my own way?"

Many of the people in the Stress Reduction Clinic rapidly discover that their own way may be the life that they are actually living. What other way could be theirs? They come to see that their pain is a part of their own way too, and not necessarily an enemy. They also come to see that at least some of their emotional pain, if not most of it, comes from their own actions or inaction and is thus potentially manageable. In seeing with eyes of wholeness, they come to realize that they are not their suffering, just as they are not their symptoms, their physical pain, or their illness.

These realizations are not some abstract philosophy. They have very practical consequences. They lead directly to an ability to do something about your emotional suffering, right in the intensive care unit, right in the police van, right in the doctor's office, right at work, or wherever else your life takes an unexpected turn and you find yourself in uncharted territory with very strong emotions surfacing in you or in others. Taking responsibility for your own mind at such times provides comforting passageways through what may have seemed like impenetrable barriers, imprisoning walls of fear or hopelessness or lack of confidence. Such passageways out of suffering appear in those moments when it dawns on you that "this is it," that the life you are actually living right now is your life, the only one you have. When you are willing to see in this way, it becomes possible to accept your life fully in this moment, just as it is, whatever the particulars. For the moment at least, what is happening is what is happening. The future is unknown and what happened in the past is already over.

By dropping into the present moment as it is, however it is, by settling into awareness and acceptance, grounded in some degree of calmness and clear seeing, you become less susceptible to the feelings of fear and hopelessness that might arise in such moments. Right inside the pain, you can already be taking steps toward doing what needs to be done, toward affirming your own integrity, toward healing.

Suggesting that such a course is both possible and practical, that it is implementable, is not to belittle either your pain or your suffering. They are all too real. Rather, it is to say that as the emotional upheavals come and go, or our bad feelings linger and weigh on us, we also know, because we are tasting it, that our strength and our ability to grow and to make changes, to transcend our hurts and our deepest losses, do not depend on outside forces or on chance. They reside here already, within our own hearts, right now.

PROBLEM-FOCUSED COPING AND EMOTION-FOCUSED COPING

Working mindfully with your emotions begins by acknowledging to yourself what you are actually feeling and thinking in the present. It is helpful to come to a complete stop and, even for short periods, to *sit with the hurt,* breathing with it, feeling it, not trying to explain it or change it or make it go away. This in itself brings calmness and stability to the mind and heart.

Once again, harking back to Chapter 12, it helps to remember to look at your situation with eyes of wholeness. From a systems perspective, there are two major interacting components to emotional pain. One is the domain of your *feelings;* the other is the domain of the situation or *problem* that lies at the root of the feelings. In being with your hurt, you might ask yourself whether you can see your emotional state as separate from the details of what has actually happened or is happening. If you can differentiate between these two components of your dilemma, you are more likely to chart your way through to an effective resolution of the entire situation, including your feelings. If, on the other hand, the domain of feelings and the domain of the problem itself get mixed up and confounded, as they often do, it is very difficult to see clearly and to know how to act decisively. This confusion itself generates more pain and more suffering.

To begin with the problem-focused coping approach, you might take a moment and simply try focusing on the problem aspect of a situation you are experiencing. Ask yourself if you are seeing it in its fullness, apart from your strong feelings about the problem. Then ask yourself whether there might be practical actions you could take that would help address and solve things in the domain of the problem. If the whole problem seems too big to handle, try breaking it down into manageable parts in your mind. Then act. *Do something.* Listen to and trust your intuition, your heart. You might attempt to correct the problem or to reduce the extent of the damage as best you can.

On the other hand, you might see that there are times when absolutely nothing can be done. If this is your perception, then really do nothing. *Do* non-doing! Simply rest in awareness itself, with things exactly as they are. In this way, you can use your understanding of non-doing just to be with what is in such moments, with full intentionality. This quiet holding of what is unfolding, in the field of your own heart, is as much of a response as anything you might do. Sometimes it is the most appropriate response possible.

By acting mindfully when you can, whether it results in doing or non-doing, you are putting the past behind you. As you act in the present, things change in response to what you choose to do, and this in turn will affect the problem itself. This way of proceeding is sometimes called *problem-focused coping.* It can help you to function effectively in spite of strong emotional reactions; and it can prevent you from doing things that might make matters worse than they already are.

On a parallel track, you can bring awareness to what you are *feeling*. Try to be aware of the source of your suffering. Is it from guilt or fear or loss? What are the thoughts going through your mind? Are they accurate? Can you just watch the play of your thoughts and feelings with full acceptance, seeing them as a storm system or a cresting wave that has a structure and life of its own? Are they affecting your judgment and your ability to see clearly? Are they telling you to do things that you are aware might make things worse rather than better? Bringing wise attention to the domain of feelings is part of what is sometimes called *emotion-focused coping.* As we have seen, just bringing mindfulness to the storm system itself influences how it resolves and so helps you to cope with it. A further step in this process comes when you are able to entertain alternative ways of seeing and being with your feelings, when you are able to hold them and yourself in an embrace of self-compassion, as if you were a loving parent to yourself, with a heart big enough to bring gentleness and lovingkindness and a wider perspective to yourself in the midst of your pain and suffering, whatever forms they might take.

Let's look at a concrete example that combines problem-focused and emotion-focused coping and see how they might be used together:

> Many years ago, I was climbing a mountain in western Maine with my son, Will, in the spring when he was eleven years old. We had on heavy packs. It was late in the afternoon and it looked like a storm was coming. We were halfway up a difficult series of high ledges and found the going quite rough, especially with the packs. At a certain point we found ourselves holding on to a small tree that was growing out of the rock, looking at the valley beneath us and the storm clouds gathering. All of a sudden we both got scared. It wasn't at all clear how to get up and over the next ledge. It really felt as if one of us could slip and fall very easily. Will was shaking, at that moment frozen by fear. He definitely did not want to go higher.
>
> Our fear was very strong, but it was also an embarrassment. Neither of us wanted to admit to feeling frightened, but there it was. To me, it seemed as if we had only two choices. We could push on and "tough it out" and not pay attention to our feelings, or we could honor them. Especially with the storm coming, it seemed as if our feelings of fear and uncertainty might be telling us something very important. We clung to the little tree and purposefully tuned in to our breathing and to our feelings, suspended somewhere between the top of the mountain and the bottom and not knowing what to do.
>
> As we did this, we calmed down some and were able to think more clearly. We talked about our options, about our strong desire to push on to the top, about not wanting to feel that our

fear was "defeating" us, but also weighing our sense of danger and vulnerability at that moment. It didn't take long for us to decide to honor our feelings and to back off from our original intent. We cautiously went back down and found shelter just as the winds and heavy rains let loose. We spent the night snug in a shelter, happy that we had had the sense to honor what we were feeling. But we still wanted to try to climb the mountain. In fact, we wanted to do it more than ever so that, if possible, we would not be left with the feeling that it was our fear that had ultimately prevented us from reaching the summit.

So the next day, as we ate breakfast, we developed a strategy that broke the problem down into pieces. We decided to take each phase of the path up as it came, agreeing that we didn't know how difficult it would be for us to get over the ledges with our packs on. We also agreed that we didn't know what would happen or whether it would be possible for us to make it to the top but that we would try anyway and deal with any problems as we encountered them.

It was very slippery on the rock because of all the rain. This made the going even more difficult than the day before. Almost right away we decided to try going barefoot to see if that would improve our traction. It did. A lot. We climbed as far as we felt comfortable with the packs. When we reached the ledges again, it seemed that Will's pack was just too big and heavy for him and was causing him to be pulled backward as he tried to find fingerholds and footholds in the rock. So we decided to leave the packs and go up as far as we could and just see what things looked like. We got to the little tree again and this time there was no sense of fear in either of us. Barefoot and without the packs, we felt completely secure. What had seemed like an insurmountable obstacle the day before now seemed easy. Now we could see exactly how to go higher from where the tree was. So we climbed on until we reached a place beneath the top where the going got a lot easier.

> The view was spectacular. We were above rapidly dissipating storm clouds, watching the mountains as they became bathed in the morning sunlight. After a while I left Will there. He was perfectly happy to be alone. He sat perched on a rock in the stillness of the morning, looking out over the valleys and the mountains for well over an hour while I went down to get the packs and bring them up, one at a time. Then we went on our way.

I tell this story because I saw so clearly when we were stopped at the little tree how important it was for us that we got frightened and that we were able to acknowledge it. Our fear kept us from acting foolishly. I also saw in that moment how important it was going to be *for both of us* to attempt that same route up again the next day, under better conditions and taking a problem-solving approach. When we did so, we dealt with the slipperiness and the weight of the backpacks in imaginative ways. This allowed us to come once more to the point where we had experienced our fear the day before and to see whether we could move through it and beyond it at a different moment in time.

What I imagined Will took away from this experience, and what was certainly reinforced in me, was a sense that fear could be worked with—that he could attend to and honor feeling frightened, that fear could even be helpful and intelligent, that it was neither a sign of weakness on his part nor an inevitable result of going up the mountain that way. One day things could be frightening, the next day not. Same mountain, same people, but also different. By our willingness to see the problem as separate from our feelings and to honor *both,* we had been able to be patient and to not let the fear mushroom and become dangerous in itself or to defeat our confidence. This strategy enabled us to break down the problem of getting to the top of the mountain into smaller problems that we then took on one at a time, experimenting, seeing how things would go, not knowing whether we would make it but at least trying again and using our imagination, taking things moment by moment.

When you find yourself in times of emotional turmoil and pain, it can be very therapeutic to proceed simultaneously on parallel tracks. One track involves awareness of your thoughts and feelings (the emotion-focused perspective). The other involves working with the situation itself (the problem-focused perspective). Both are essential for responding effectively in stressful and threatening situations.

In the problem-focused approach, as we have just seen, we try to identify the source and scope of the problem with some clarity, independent of our feelings—as with the problem of the nine dots in Chapter 12. We try to discern what might need to be accomplished, what actions might need to be taken, what the potential obstacles to progress are, and also what inner and outer resources might be available to us to bring to bear on the problem as we understand it. To proceed in this way, you may need to try things you have never tried before, seek other people's advice and help, even acquire new skills yourself in order to deal with certain problems. But if you break the problem down into manageable pieces and then take them on one at a time, you may find that you can act effectively even in times of emotional pain and turbulence. In some cases, approaching things in this way can diminish your emotional arousal or suspend it long enough to prevent it from blinding you or compounding your problems.

There can also be pitfalls to a problem-focused coping approach, especially if you forget that it is only one of two parallel tracks. There are some people who tend to relate to everything in life in an objective, problem-solving mode. In the process, they may cut themselves off from their own feelings about the situations they face, as well as fail to recognize and respond appropriately and with emotional intelligence to the feelings of others. This habit will hardly lead to a balanced way of life. It can create much unnecessary suffering.

Focusing on our emotions, we observe our feelings and thoughts from the perspective of mindfulness and remind ourselves that we can work with our feelings, just as Will and I did at the little tree. You discover, through ongoing practice, that emotional crises are "workable," that you can usually intentionally expand your perspective around your feelings, right in the midst of a very difficult and trying moment, and thus cradle them in awareness. You may sometimes hear this strategy referred to as *reframing,* that is, putting a larger or different frame around the issue in question. Reframing can be done with either your emotions, the problem itself, or both. Seeing a problem as an opportunity or challenge is an example of reframing. So is seeing your hurt in the frame of the suffering of other people who may be worse off than yourself. Mindfulness itself is the ultimate frame within which to perceive the actuality of things as they are. I call it undergoing an "orthogonal rotation in consciousness."* In one moment, because of awareness and the insights that can arise from its openhearted and innately intelligent spaciousness, everything is different. New openings and options can now arise, even though everything is still exactly as it was, except for you.

Times of great emotional upheaval and turmoil, times of sadness, anger, fear, and grief, moments when we feel hurt, lost, humiliated, thwarted, or defeated—all these are times when we most need to know that the core of our being is stable and resilient and that we can weather these moments and become more human in the process. It helps to come to stillness in such moments. When we observe our emotional pain as it unfolds, with acceptance, with openness and with kindness toward ourselves, and at the same time take a problem-focused approach toward the situation itself, we strike a balance between facing, honoring, and learning from our emotional pain moment by moment as it is expressing itself, and acting effectively in the world. This in itself minimizes the many ways in which we can get stuck in and blinded by emotion in any moment—this blindness only potentiated and compounded by our deeply engrained and often unexam-

* See *Coming to Our Senses,* 347–358.

ined emotional patterns of a lifetime. Mindfulness of our thoughts and feelings, particularly those that arise from our relationships with others and in stressful, threatening, and emotionally charged situations, can play a major role in helping us to act effectively in the midst of our deepest emotional pain. At the same time, it sows seeds that heal the heart and the mind.

MINDFULNESS AND DEPRESSION

These seeds of mindfulness can be sown and watered in many different ways. As you probably know, among the disregulations of emotion that can cause us enormous suffering, depression is the most prevalent. It has been described as the black dog of the night. Black hole would be another appropriate metaphor. Depression is a major public health concern throughout the world, especially in more highly technologized societies, and an endless source of chronic unhappiness. In the past twenty years, a very important development has occurred, using the same paradigm, meditative practices, and overall format as MBSR, with the aim of effectively addressing the risks of relapsing into an episode of major depression once one has been successfully treated. I am referring to the development and widespread use of mindfulness-based cognitive therapy.

MBCT was developed by three world-renowned emotion researchers and cognitive therapists with a primary interest in depression: Zindel Segal of the University of Toronto, Mark Williams, of Oxford University, and John Teasdale, formerly of Cambridge University. The story of how they developed MBCT is dramatically told in their book *Mindfulness-Based Cognitive Therapy for Depression.** MBCT follows the same eight-week format as MBSR, but it is designed specifically for people who have suffered from multiple episodes of clinical depression (otherwise known as major depressive disorder) but who are not currently depressed, having been

* Segal, ZV, Williams JMG and Teasdale, JD *Mindfulness-Based Cognitive Therapy for Depression.* 2nd ed. New York: Guilford; 2012.

treated successfully by cognitive therapy or with antidepressants. The risk of relapsing once someone has had three or more episodes is over 90 percent, and the costs, including the costs in terms of human suffering, are enormous. What Teasdale, Segal, Williams, and their colleagues were able to show, in a randomized trial first reported in the year 2000, is that people with a prior history of three or more episodes of major depression taking the MBCT program relapsed at half the rate of the control group, which only received routine health care from their doctor and continued with their regular regimen of treatment, whatever it was. This was a staggering result, given the prevalence of major depressive disorder and the high risk of relapsing after successful treatment. Interest in mindfulness and MBCT spread rapidly through the cognitive therapy community, based on the excellent science behind their findings. Their first book, written primarily for cognitive therapists, was then followed by a second, which I wrote with them, directed to a broader readership.* The key to the MBCT approach is to recognize that any efforts to talk yourself out of depression, or fix it in one way or another through changing the way you think about things or feel about yourself, only compounds its grip. What is required is just what we have been exploring from the beginning: a shift from an attitude of "fixing" what you think is wrong with you (one more misguided element of the domain of doing) to a mode of mind that is much more *allowing* and *accepting* and simply *aware*. This is precisely what we have been experimenting with in the meditation practices and perhaps experiencing, at least to some degree, namely *the domain of being*. In this domain, as we have been emphasizing repeatedly, we simply see thoughts, whatever their content and emotional charge, as "events in the field of awareness" that come and go like clouds in the sky. They are not to be taken personally and are not to be taken as true. As mentioned earlier, MBCT is the recommended treatment for relapse prevention in the guidelines of the United Kingdom's National Health Service for people with a history of three or

* Williams M, Teasdale J, Segal Z, Kabat-Zinn J. *The Mindful Way Through Depression: Freeing Yourself from Chronic Unhappiness.* New York: Guilford; 2007.

more episodes of chronic depression. There is a growing research literature on MBCT and its effects in preventing recurrence of depression. It is even being used successfully as a therapy for people with so-called treatment-resistant depression. Applications of MBCT to other conditions, such as chronic anxiety, have also been developed.*

* Orsillo S, Roemer L. *The Mindful Way Through Anxiety: Break Free from Chronic Worry and Reclaim Your Life.* Berkeley: New Harbinger; 2011. Semple R, Lee J. *Mindfulness-Based Cognitive Therapy for Anxious Children: A Manual for Treating Childhood Anxiety.* Oakland: New Harbinger; 2011.

25

Working with Fear, Panic, and Anxiety

There is a wonderful scene in a movie from the late 1970s, *Starting Over,* in which Burt Reynolds is in the furniture section of a big department store with a young woman (Jill Clayburgh) when she proceeds to have an anxiety attack right there in the store. As he struggles in a bewildered fashion to help her pull herself together and get her emotions under control, he looks up to find that they are surrounded by a horde of gawking shoppers. He shouts out, "Quick, does anyone have a Valium?" at which point a hundred hands fish frantically into their coat pockets and purses.

This is certainly an age of anxiety, and it hasn't gotten any less so in the thirty years since that movie came out. Quite the contrary, given the speed at which we now live our lives and at which we ask our minds to function in the digital age. Many people in the Stress Reduction Clinic come because they have problems related to anxiety, caused by the rampant stress in their lives and compounded by their medical problems. Anxiety is one of the most pervasive mind states we encounter in the clinic. This is hardly surprising, since most of our patients are sent precisely because either they or their doctors think they need to learn how to relax and how to handle stress better.

If we are honest with ourselves, most of us will have to admit that we live out our lives on an ocean of fear, much of the time trying to avoid recognizing that fact. Every once in a while those feelings of fear will surface in even the hardiest of us. They may be about death or about being abandoned or betrayed. They may stem from previous traumas we have experienced, both big-*T* and little-*t* traumas, such as having being chronically disregarded and neglected, or outrightly abused, violated, or even tortured. They may arise from feeling pain or from anticipating it, or from being alone, or sick, or disabled. We can fear for someone we love, that he or she may be hurt or killed. We may harbor fears of failure or fears of success, fears of letting other people down, or fears about the fate of the earth. Most of us carry such fears within us. They are always present, but they usually surface only under certain circumstances.

Some people handle fearful feelings much better than others do. Commonly, we cope with our fears by ignoring such feelings when they surface, or by denying them altogether, or by concealing them from other people. But to cope in this way increases the likelihood that damage will be done in some other way, either by developing habitual maladaptive behavior patterns such as passivity or aggressiveness to compensate for our insecurities, by becoming overwhelmed and incapacitated by the very feelings themselves when they do surface, or by focusing on physical symptoms or other less threatening aspects of our lives that we feel more able to control. And many people are unable to cope even in these questionable ways. They may find it difficult if not impossible to deny or ignore or conceal their anxiety. Without effective means for dealing with it, their anxiety can have significant detrimental effects on their ability to function. Chronic anxiety can also fuel severe patterns of what is called *experiential avoidance, in which people attempt to avoid at all cost any thoughts, feelings, memories, or physical sensations that might cause distress. This is tantamount to holding themselves back from life itself, out of fear of their own inner experience.* Chronic anxiety can also trigger depression in some people. And of course, in all its forms, it tends to cause us to succumb to many of the maladaptive coping avenues we reviewed in Chapter 19 to avoid or mitigate our distress.

The cultivation of mindfulness can have a positive impact on anxiety reactions via the stress-response pathway discussed in Chapter 20. In several studies conducted in collaboration with our colleagues in the Department of Psychiatry, we showed that MBSR significantly reduced both anxiety and depression scores in those patients who had both a medical diagnosis and a secondary diagnosis of generalized anxiety disorder or panic disorder over the course of the eight weeks of the program, and that their improvement was maintained at a three-year follow-up.*† We will discuss these two studies in more detail below.

As you might imagine, the application of mindfulness to chronic anxiety involves allowing the anxiety itself to become the object of our nonjudgmental attention. We intentionally observe fear and anxiety when they come up, just as we do with pain. When you move in close to your fears and observe them as they surface in the form of thoughts, feelings, and bodily sensations, you will be in a much better position to recognize them for what they are and know how to respond to them appropriately. Then you will be less prone to becoming overwhelmed or swept away by them, or to feel you have to compensate in ways that are ultimately self-destructive or self-limiting.

The word *fear* implies that there is something specific that is causing this emotional state to arise. Under certain threatening circumstances, all of us might experience fear, even terror. It is a major characteristic of the fight-or-flight reaction. To be suddenly unable to breathe would trigger it, for example. People with chronic obstructive lung disease have to face this kind of fear and learn to work with the panic it induces. Being the object of an attack, or learning that you have a fatal disease would be other examples. On a more pedestrian level, impending deadlines can also trigger fear.

Under such circumstances, frightening thoughts or experiences can easily lead to a state of panic, driven by desperation and feelings of com-

* Kabat-Zinn J, Massion AO, Kristeller J, Peterson LG, et al. Effectiveness of a Meditation-Based Stress Reduction Program in the Treatment of Anxiety Disorders *Am J Psychiatry.* 1992;149:936–943.

† Miller JJ, Fletcher K, and Kabat-Zinn J. Three-Year Follow-Up and Clinical Implications of a Mindfulness Meditation-Based Stress Reduction Intervention in the Treatment of Anxiety Disorders *General Hospital Psychiatry* 1995;17:192–200.

plete loss of control. But to panic in a threatening situation is a very dangerous and unfortunate reaction, because it is disabling just at the time that you most need to keep your wits about you and problem-solve with extreme rapidity and clarity.

When we speak of "anxiety," we are talking about a similar strongly reactive emotional state but without a clearly identifiable impending cause or threat. Anxiety is a generalized state of insecurity and agitation that can be triggered by almost anything. Sometimes it seems as if there is nothing triggering it at all. You can feel anxious and not really know why. As we saw in Chapter 23 when we discussed headaches, it is possible to wake up feeling shaky, tense, and frightened. If you are plagued by anxious feelings, your anxiety may frequently seem out of proportion to the actual pressures you are under. You may have a hard time putting your finger on the root cause of your feelings. You may find yourself worrying all the time, even when there is nothing the matter or there is no major threat. You may be tense all the time, chronically tense. You may find yourself catastrophizing, stuck in a default mode of feeling that "if it's not one thing, then it's another," that there is always *something* to be worried about. When this state of mind becomes pervasive and develops into a chronic condition, it is referred to as generalized anxiety disorder (GAD). Its symptoms may include trembling, shakiness, muscle tension, restlessness, easy fatigability, shortness of breath, rapid heartbeat, sweating, dry mouth, dizziness or light-headedness, nausea, the feeling of a lump in the throat, feeling keyed up, being easily startled, difficulty concentrating, trouble falling asleep or staying asleep, and irritability.

In addition to generalized anxiety, some people suffer from what are called anxiety attacks, or panic attacks. These are episodes in which a person experiences a discrete period of intense fear and discomfort for no apparent reason. Often people who suffer from panic attacks have no idea why they get them or when one will happen. The first time it happens, you can think you are having a heart attack, since it is frequently accompanied by acute physical symptoms including chest pains, dizziness, shortness of breath, and profuse sweating. There may be feelings of unreality, and you may also think that you are dying or going crazy or that you may lose control of yourself. It may be very disconcerting, rather than reassuring, if your doctor tells you that you are not having a heart attack and you are not going crazy, because it is apparent that *something* is very wrong. If you are cared for by a doctor who can recognize these symptoms as a panic attack, you may be on the road to getting the right kind of help in bringing them under control. Unfortunately, many people with panic attacks continue to visit emergency rooms and wind up being told that "there is nothing wrong" and being sent home with no assistance or with a prescription for tranquilizers.

While it can be reassuring to know what a panic attack is and that you are not going to die from it or go crazy, what is most important is to know that you can work with these mind-body storms by changing the way you see and pay attention to the very processes of thought and reactivity within your own mind. It is to undertake such work that physicians, psychiatrists, psychologists, and psychotherapists send their patients with chronic panic attacks to the Stress Reduction Clinic for training in MBSR.

As noted earlier, in the early to mid-1990s, in collaboration with our colleagues in the department of psychiatry, we conducted a study to look at the effects of MBSR training on twenty-two patients referred to the clinic for a range of medical diagnoses and who were also shown, through further testing, to have a secondary condition of generalized anxiety disorder and/or panic disorder. This study came about because we were seeing dramatic improvements in people reporting high levels of anxiety in their lives, improvements that we thought merited a more systematic investigation. In addition to people's reports that they were feeling more in control of their panicky feelings, they were showing major reductions on self-reported measures of anxiety, phobic anxiety, and medical symptoms following the program. We wanted to put these results to a more stringent test, using more sophisticated measures to monitor psychological status. We also felt the need to confirm independently that those people who were being referred to the Stress Reduction Clinic by their medical doctors primarily for their symptoms of anxiety and panic were being correctly diagnosed. This was possible by collaborating with expert psychologists and psychiatrists in confirming a secondary anxiety diagnosis in addition to their medical diagnoses and monitoring their progress over time. We began the study by inviting people referred to the stress clinic who were reporting high levels of anxiety on a questionnaire to participate. Each person who agreed to be in the study was interviewed at length by either a psychiatrist or a clinical psychologist to establish a precise psychological diagnosis. Their levels of anxiety, depression, and panic were also assessed weekly as they went through the eight weeks of MBSR training and for three months after the program ended. Twenty-two people were followed in this way. Three years later, we conducted a follow-up study as well.

We found that both anxiety and depression dropped markedly over the eight weeks of the MBSR program in virtually every person in the study. So did the frequency and severity of their panic attacks. A three-month follow-up found that they had maintained their improvements after completion of the program. Most individuals were virtually free of panic attacks at the three-month follow-up. The same was true after three years. The three-year follow-up study also showed that most people were still practicing the meditation in one way or another, in ways that were significant and meaningful to them.

These studies, although on a small number of individuals and without a randomized control condition for comparison, clearly showed that people who suffer from panic attacks and anxiety disorders are able to put mindfulness training to practical use in regulating their feelings of anxiety and panic. They also showed that what the participants learned in the program over eight weeks had a lasting benefit, just as we saw with the people with chronic pain conditions in Chapter 22.

During the period when the people in the anxiety study were receiving MBSR training, the instructors did not treat these patients any differently from anybody else who was taking the program. In fact, the instructors didn't even know who was in the study, and the study itself was never mentioned in the classes. Nor was the MBSR curriculum altered in any way to try to get good results specifically with anxiety patients. The study participants were indistinguishable from everybody else—people with chronic pain, heart disease, cancer, and all the other medical problems for which people were referred. And although the results of the study showed major improvements among the twenty-two people who were followed in this way on the various symptom measures we used, the most interesting part is that ultimately, as with every person who goes through the clinic, they all had their own unique experiences and stories to tell. Although the results suggest that practicing mindfulness can dramatically reduce anxiety and the frequency and severity of panic attacks, it is in their individual stories that we can best see how mindfulness meditation practice might be of profound use and benefit to someone who is suffering from anxiety. The following is an account of how one person successfully resolved her problems after eleven years of chronic anxiety and panic.

CLAIRE'S STORY

Claire, a thirty-three-year-old happily married woman with a seven-year-old son, came to the Stress Reduction Clinic when she was six months pregnant with her second child. She had been having feelings of panic and actual panic attacks on and off for the past eleven years, ever since her father died. In the last four years, the attacks had gotten much worse and were preventing her from living a normal life. Claire described herself as having been raised in an overprotective ethnic family. She was twenty-two and engaged to be married when her father died. She had promised him that she would get married right away, even if he were to die before the wedding, which is what happened. Her father died on a Thursday, he was buried on Saturday, and on Sunday she was married. She said she knew nothing about the world at that time, having always been protected from problems by living at home.

Until that time, Claire had thought of herself as happy and well adjusted. Her problems with anxiety started shortly after her father's death and getting married. She would find herself feeling nervous and worked up about little things that she knew weren't important or even real, and she felt unable to either explain or control these feelings. She began to think she was "going crazy." This pattern of anxious thoughts and feelings got worse over the years. She felt less and less in control. Four years prior to her coming to the clinic, she began having episodes in which she actually passed out. At that point she went to see a neurologist, who gave her tranquilizers and told her that her problems were due to anxiety.

From then on, her biggest fear was that she would make a fool of herself by fainting in a crowd of people. She was afraid to drive or to go places alone. She began seeing a psychiatrist, who continued her on the tranquilizers. He also urged her to take antidepressants as well, but she refused.

After some time in treatment, Claire and her husband came to feel that the therapeutic approach being taken with her amounted to trying to "brainwash" her into taking medication rather than taking her seriously as a person.

Her psychiatrist saw her only to change her medication and worked in conjunction with a counselor who saw Claire regularly. She recalled that both the psychiatrist and the counselor repeatedly told her that the medication was the solution to her problems, that she was "just that kind of person," the kind who needs to take tranquilizers every day to get through the day. They used the argument that her situation was no different from that of people with high blood pressure or a thyroid condition. These people need to take medication every day to keep their conditions regulated, and she did too. The message was that she should stop resisting their efforts to help her and just be cooperative. They kept insisting that her panic attacks could be controlled only if she took the drugs. And for the most part she did, at least at first.

But in her heart Claire was feeling that her doctor and counselor had no interest in her unless she was willing to accept their position on her need for medication. When she would go in and tell them that the medication wasn't working, that she was still having panic attacks, the psychiatrist would simply increase the dose. She just didn't feel heard as a person at all.

She also felt blamed. She was accused of being stubborn and unreasonable for refusing to go on antidepressants and for questioning the need to be on the tranquilizers for an indefinite period. It bothered her that they would never tell her how long she would have to be on them. She felt they were implying that she would probably be on them for decades and that she would always have to be in counseling. When she asked about alternative approaches that might replace the drugs, such as stress reduction, yoga, relaxation, and biofeedback, she was told that she could do that if she wanted, that "it won't hurt, but it won't help your problem."

The last straw for her came when she learned she was pregnant. Looking back, she felt that this pregnancy was a blessing because it resulted in a dramatic change in her relationship to the medical world. She insisted on getting off all her medication as soon as she found out she was pregnant, against the advice of her psychiatrist and counselor. She saw another counselor for a while who supported her position, and she finally decided to stop seeing the psychiatrist altogether because it was always such a battle of viewpoints about the medication. So she started looking for alternatives. She found someone who did hypnosis with her to control the anxiety, and that helped some. At least she felt supported in the therapy itself. But she was still very nervous and panicky. Finally her neurologist suggested that she go to the Stress Reduction Clinic.

By this time, she was at a point where her anxiety made it difficult for her to get in her car and go anywhere. She couldn't stand being in crowds. Her heart was always pounding. She was totally unused to dealing with any kind of stress on her own. So, six months pregnant, Claire enrolled in the stress reduction program.

In the first class, she found that she was able to relax into the body scan. She had no anxiety while she was doing it, even though she was lying on the floor, pregnant, with thirty total strangers packed in like sardines on foam mats. Her usual anxious thoughts and feelings had somehow disappeared for those two and a half hours in the first class.

Claire was thrilled to have such an experience. It confirmed her belief that there was something she could do herself to free herself from her chronic nervousness. She practiced every day with the guided meditations, and each week had some progress to report. She was ebullient and enthusiastic and appeared quite confident when she spoke in class. She told us one day that she had stopped playing the radio in her car and was following her breathing instead. She said she felt calmer that way.

No one had told her to do that. She came to it on her own as she experimented with integrating her meditation practice into her everyday life.

When she felt herself getting tense, she would let herself go into the tension and observe it. During the eight weeks of the program, she had only one very mild panic attack, a dramatic change from the period when she was on the tranquilizers and having several every day.

At the end of the eight weeks, she said she felt a lot better. She was much more confident and was no longer preoccupied with the fear that she might lose control in public. She no longer feared parking in parking lots or walking on a crowded street. In fact, she began making it a point to deliberately park her car several blocks away from wherever she was going so she could walk mindfully the rest of the way. She was also sleeping soundly, which she had been unable to do before.

Claire said that, all in all, she felt better about herself now than she had ever felt in her life, although she pointed out that her problems hadn't really changed. Somehow, even though she had fears about the baby she was expecting because of the drugs she took in the early weeks of her pregnancy, her fearful thoughts were not leading to nervousness and panic. Things did not seem so overwhelming anymore. She had confidence in her ability to cope with things if she had to, "when the time comes." This was something she had never been able to feel or say before. In the past, the slightest negative thought would have sent her right into a state of nervous agitation and panic.

Although she was nine months pregnant, she was practicing her meditation every day. She got up an hour early to do it. She set her alarm for 5:30 a.m., lay in bed for fifteen minutes, and then went into another room and did one of the guided mediations using the CDs. She alternated the mindful yoga one day with the sitting meditation the next day. She preferred the sitting meditation over the body scan and utilized it the most.

I spoke with Claire a year later and got an update on her life. At that point, she had been off all medications for a year and had not had a panic attack. She did have about six mini episodes of anxiety, all of which she was able to control on her own. It turned out that her baby had to have surgery eighteen days after birth for repair of a pyloric stenosis (a condition in which there is a narrowing of the valve between the stomach and the intestines that causes the baby to vomit up feedings and may prevent adequate nourishment and weight gain). During that time, Claire virtually lived at the hospital to be with her baby, and found herself concentrating almost constantly on her breathing to remain calm and clear-sighted and to remind herself not to let her mind wander to what-ifs. After the surgery, her baby was fine and grew normally. Claire felt she could never have effectively handled such an intensely stressful situation had she not learned what she did in the MBSR program.

Claire's story illustrates that chronic anxiety and panic are potentially controllable through the practice of mindfulness meditation, at least for a highly motivated person. Her experience and that of many other people in the Stress Reduction Clinic suggest that a mindfulness-based approach might be a good first line of treatment for such conditions in general, rather than going to drug treatment right away, especially for people who do not want to take medications.

This is not to suggest that there are not appropriate uses of medications in the treatment of anxiety and panic. Certain tranquilizers and antidepressants have proved extremely useful in managing acute anxiety disorders and panic attacks and helping to bring people out of them and back to a condition of allostatic self-regulation. Medications can also be used effectively in combination with good psychotherapy and behavioral counseling, using a range of different approaches such as cognitive therapy, hypnosis, and, increasingly, mindfulness-based interventions. However, Claire's experience with her medical treatment is far from atypical, unfortunately. Many patients with anxiety disorders feel that the drugs they are on do not help them that much, and that medication is often used *instead* of listening to people and guiding them to locate for themselves and learn to inhabit the domain of self-regulation and inner balance. Claire was determined to face her anxiety and try to manage it herself because she saw so clearly how it was ruining her life. She felt that her dependency on tranquilizers was just reinforcing the view of herself as a nervous wreck, a basket case. And she proved to herself that her instincts had been correct all along, that she didn't have to live her whole life as an invalid, taking medication forever to manage her mental states as if they were a thyroid deficiency.

Now let's explore in detail how the meditation practice might be used to work with feelings of panic and anxiety so that they no longer control your life. These suggestions go hand in hand with the approaches we explored in the last chapter on opening to and working with emotional pain of all kinds.

HOW TO USE MINDFULNESS PRACTICE TO WORK WITH ANXIETY AND PANIC

Your meditation practice is a perfect laboratory for working with anxiety and panic. In the body scan, the sitting meditation, and the mindful yoga, we work at recognizing and accepting any feelings of tension we find in our body and any agitated thoughts and emotions that arise as we dwell in the domain of being. The meditation instructions emphasize that *we don't have to do anything* about bodily sensations or anxious feelings except to become aware of them and desist from judging them and condemning ourselves.

In this way, cultivating moment-to-moment non-judgmental awareness amounts to a systematic way of teaching your body and mind to develop calmness and equanimity within or beneath any anxious feelings that might be present. This is exactly what Claire did in her practice. The more you practice, the more comfortable you come to be in your own skin. The more comfortable you feel, the closer you come to perceiving that *your anxiety and fears are not you and that they do not have to rule your life.*

As you come to taste even brief moments of comfort, relaxation, and clarity, you may notice, both during formal meditation and at other times, that you do not feel anxious all the time. In observing this, you see that anxiety varies in intensity and that it comes and goes just like everything else. You discover that it is impermanent, a temporary mental state, just like boredom or happiness. This is an important insight, a potentially liberating insight, because it shows you that it is possible to live free from such oppressive mental states, in part by not taking them personally, and adopting a much broader perspective on what they are in relationship to who you are in your fullness.

Recall from Chapter 3 the story of Gregg, the firefighter, who was incapacitated by anxiety and unable to breathe when he tried to put on his mask. When he started the MBSR classes, just watching his breathing during the body scan would induce feelings of agitation and panic. Yet by working with his aversive reaction to his own breathing, he quickly saw that there were ways to *shift his relationship* to what was most scary without fighting with himself. In other words, he learned how to go "underneath" his agitation without trying to get rid of it or fix it, and drop into present-moment awareness and reside in calmness, clarity, and equanimity. Originally Gregg had no idea that this would even be possible.

Through ongoing mindfulness practice, you learn to get in touch with and draw upon your deep interior resources for physiological relaxation and calmness, even at times when there are problems that have to be faced and resolved, and sometimes even in the face of crises and serious threats to your well-being. In doing so, you also learn that it is possible to trust a stable inner core within yourself that is reliable, dependable, and unwavering. Gradually the tension in your body and the worry and anxiety in your mind become less intrusive and lose some of their force. While the surface of your mind can still be choppy and agitated at times, like the surface of the ocean, you can learn to accept the mind being that way and at the same time experience an underlying inner peace in a domain that is always right here, a domain in which the effect of the waves is damped to gentle swells at most. This is what we have been calling the domain of being. Through ongoing practice, you learn to rest in the depths of awareness itself, fully awake, grounded in non-doing and non-striving. You also learn, through ongoing practice, to act with clarity and purpose (when it is appropriate to take action) out of this ground of awareness, as the fully integrated human being you already are and always have been.

A critical part of this learning process is coming to see, as we have now emphasized many times, that you are not your thoughts and feelings and that you do not have to believe them, react to them, or be driven or tyrannized by them. As you practice focusing on whatever you are giving primary attention to in your meditation practice, you are likely to come to see your thoughts and feelings as discrete, short-lived events, much like individual waves on the ocean. These waves arise in awareness for a moment and then recede. You can watch them and perceive them as discrete "events in the field of your consciousness." They come, and they go. And when they go, they are—for that moment at least—gone. If not fed, they dissolve, and for that moment, you are free.

When you observe the unfolding of your own thinking moment by moment, you may come to notice that thoughts carry different levels of emotional charge. Some are highly negative and pessimistic, loaded with anxiety, insecurity, fear, gloom, doom, and condemnation. Others are positive and optimistic, joyful and open, accepting and caring. Still others are neutral, neither positive nor negative in emotional content, just matter-of-fact thoughts. Our thinking proceeds in rather chaotic patterns of reactivity and association, elaborating on its own content, building imaginary worlds, and filling the silence with busyness. Thoughts with a high emotional charge have a way of recurring again and again. When they come up, they grab hold of your attention like a powerful magnet, carrying your mind away from your breathing or from awareness of your body.

When you look at thoughts as just thoughts, purposefully not reacting to their content and to their emotional charge, you become at least a little freer from their attraction or repulsion. You are less likely to get sucked into them quite as intensely or as often. The more powerful the emotional charge, the more the content of the thought is likely to capture your attention and draw you away from just being in the moment. Your work is simply seeing and letting go, seeing and letting go, sometimes ruthlessly and relentlessly if need be, always intentionally and courageously. Just seeing and letting go, seeing and letting be.

When you practice in this way with all of the thoughts that come up during meditation, whether they are "good," "bad," or "neutral" in content, whether they are highly emotionally charged or not, you will find that the ones that are anxious and fearful in content will seem less powerful and less threatening. They will have less of a hold over your attention because now you are seeing them as "just thoughts" and no longer as "reality" or "the truth." It becomes easier to remind yourself that you don't have to get caught up in their content. It becomes easier to see how you contribute to the ongoing strength of certain thoughts by fearing them and, ironically, by holding on to them.

Seeing them in this light breaks the insidious chain by which one anxious thought leads to another and to another until you become lost in a self-created world of fear and insecurity. Instead, it will be just one thought with anxiety content, seeing it, letting it go, returning to calmness and open spaciousness; another thought with anxiety content, seeing it, letting it go, returning to calmness and open spaciousness; over and over and over, thought by thought by thought . . . holding on to the breath (for dear life if you must) to get you through the choppier times.

Working mindfully with highly charged thoughts and emotions does not mean that we do not value the expression of strong emotions or that strong feelings are bad, problematic, or dangerous and that every effort should be made to "control" them or get rid of them or suppress them. Attending to your emotions mindfully, accepting them, and then letting go of them without necessarily reacting does not mean that you are trying to invalidate them or get rid of them. It simply means that you know what you are experiencing. You are fully aware of them as emotions, recognizing that anger feels like this, fear feels like this, sadness feels like this. Your awareness of the anger is not angry. Nor is your awareness fearful. Nor is it sad. Being grounded in present-moment awareness of strong emotions also does not mean that you won't act on your thoughts and feelings or express them in their full power. It simply means that when you do act, you are more likely to do so with clarity and inner balance because you now, in this very moment, have some perspective on your experience and are not just being driven by mindless reactivity. In the embrace of awareness, the force of your feelings can be applied creatively, as appropriate, to solve or dissolve problems, rather than compounding difficulties and causing harm to yourself or others, as so often happens when you lose your center. This is another example of the way in which the emotion-focused perspective and the problem-focused perspective can complement each other in mindfulness. It is also an example of how the meditation practice, brought to everyday life and its emotional ups and downs, is its own yoga, inviting us to work fluidly with whatever tensions we find, and putting them to good use in the service of seeing through our habitual ways of imprisoning ourselves by taking our strong feelings so personally and reacting to them so automatically.

As we change our relationship to our thoughts by paying attention to the process of thinking, we will also come to see that perhaps we should change the way we think and speak about our thoughts and feelings altogether. Rather than saying "I am afraid" or "I am anxious," both of which turn "you" *into* the anxiety or fear, it would actually be more accurate to say "I am experiencing a lot of fear-filled thoughts," so there is not such a strong identification of them with who or what "you" are—since you are much bigger than any thought or emotion you might be having. You are more akin to awareness itself, especially if you learn through ongoing practice to *inhabit* awareness as your default mode or ground of being. You could go even further and say something to yourself such as "It is fearing at the moment," along the lines of "It is raining." It might help in reminding yourself of the impersonal nature of these emotions and the thoughts that are so tightly coupled to them. In this way you are emphasizing to yourself that you are not the content of your thoughts, nor are you your emotions. If that is so, then you do not have to identify with either the content of your thoughts or with their emotional charge, however powerful they may be. Instead you can just be aware of all of it, accept it, and listen to it caringly, feeling perhaps how and where it is expressing itself in the body in any moment. Then your thoughts will not drive you toward even more fear, panic, and anxiety, but can be used instead to help you see more clearly what is actually *on* your mind. You could call this a fundamental gesture of befriending the mind, a way of becoming intimate with its comings and goings without being trapped by them. This intimacy is not an ideal, as we have noted before. It is a *practice*. Indeed, it is *the* fundamental practice of mindfulness.

As you look more deeply into the process of your own thinking from the perspective of calmness and mindfulness, you may come to see, as we noted in Chapters 15 and 24, that much of your thinking and your emotions occur in recognizable patterns that are driven by discomfort of one kind or another. There is the discomfort of being dissatisfied with the present and wanting something more to happen, to possess something more that would make you feel better, more complete, more whole. This pattern could be described as the impulse to get what you want and to hold on to it, much like the monkey we saw in Chapter 2, which holds on to the banana and is thereby trapped, although all he needs to do to be free is to release the banana from his grip.

If you look even more deeply into it, you will probably find that, beneath it all, such impulses are driven, much as we might hate to admit it, by a kind of greediness, the desire for "more for me" in order to be happy, a craving for what we don't have and want to have to feel complete. Perhaps it is money, or more money, or time, or control, or recognition, or love that you want, or more food even though you have already eaten. Whatever it is you are craving at the moment, to be driven by such impulses implies that, in reality, you don't believe that you are whole as you are, that you are already complete. You can easily become a slave of your own craving. We are all at risk of this.

Then there is the opposite pattern, dominated by thoughts and feelings of wanting certain things *not* to happen or to stop happening, the desire to get rid of certain things or elements in your life that you think are preventing you from feeling better, happier, more satisfied. These patterns of thought can be described as driven by hatred, dislike, aversion, rejection, a need to get rid of what you don't want or don't like so that you can be happy. In this case, you become a prisoner of your aversion.

Mindfulness brought to our actual behavior may drive home the realization that we can be caught, in our mind and in our actions, between these two driving motives of liking/wanting (greed) and disliking/not wanting (aversion)—however subtle and unconscious they may be—to the point that our lives become one incessant vacillation between pursuit of what we like and flight from what we don't like.* Such a course will lead to few moments of peace or happiness. How could it? There will always be cause for anxiety. At any moment you might lose what you already have. Or you might never get what you want. Or you might get it and find out it wasn't what you wanted after all. You might still not feel complete.

Unless you can be mindful of the activity of your mind, you won't even notice that this is going on. A blanket of unawareness, our old acquaintance the automatic pilot mode, will ensure that you will continue to bounce from pillar to post, feeling out of control much of the time. This is basically because you think your happiness is solely dependent on whether you are getting what you want. (See the section "A 'What Is My Own Way?' Meditation" in Chapter 24.)

This way of living winds up consuming a great deal of our energy. It

* This dichotomy of motives or drives is reflected in the basic "approach" and "avoidance" patterns of behavior that are characteristic of all living organisms. Our brain structure seems to reflect this dichotomy in its functional asymmetry. Approach behaviors are primarily associated with activation in particular regions of the left prefrontal cortex, while avoidance is associated with activation of similar areas in the right prefrontal cortex. Note that this asymmetry is relevant to the results we obtained in our study of MBSR in a corporate setting, where we found a shift in the emotional setpoint, from more right activation to more left activation, or from more of an avoidance/aversion mode to a more approach/allowing/accepting mode characteristic of greater emotional intelligence. That does not mean that "approach" is always healthy and "avoidance" unhealthy, especially when they take the form of greed and hatred, rather than when both impulses are held in a discerning awareness that can differentiate what is wholesome from what is unwholesome—in other words, wisdom.

also blankets so much of our life with unawareness that we hardly ever perceive that we may actually be basically okay right now, that it may be possible to find a locus or a core of harmony within ourselves in the midst of the full catastrophe of our fear and anxiety, in this very moment. In fact, when you think about it, where else could harmony and well-being possibly be found?

The only way to free yourself from a lifetime of being tyrannized by your own thought processes, whether you suffer from excessive anxiety or not, is to come to see your thoughts for what they are and to discern the sometimes subtle—but most often not-so-subtle—seeds of craving and aversion, of greed and hatred, at work within them. When you can successfully step back and see that you are not your thoughts and feelings, that you do not have to believe them, and that you certainly do not have to act on them, when you see vividly that many of them are inaccurate, judgmental, and fundamentally greedy or aversive, you will have found the key to understanding why you feel so much fear and anxiety. At the same time you will have found the key to maintaining your equilibrium. Fear, panic, and anxiety will no longer be uncontrollable demons. Instead you will see them as natural mental states that can be worked with and accepted just like any others. Then, lo and behold, the demons may not come around and bother you so much. You may find that you don't see them at all for long stretches. You may wonder where they went or even whether they ever existed. Occasionally you may see some smoke, just enough to remind you that the lair of the dragon is still occupied, that fear is a natural part of living, but not something you have to be afraid of.

Believing in your capacity to take on whatever comes up is fundamental to the healing power you are cultivating. Beverly came to MBSR because she was living with the uncertainty of a very frightening situation. She had had a cerebral aneurysm (broken blood vessel in the brain) the year before, which was surgically repaired but left a weakened place in an artery that might lead to a second aneurysm. She came to the stress clinic because she was experiencing a lot of anxiety. She felt that she was no longer her old self and that her body and her nervous system were sometimes out of control. She was having unpredictable, frightening seizures, dizzy spells, and problems with her eyes. She felt unsure of herself now with other people. She also thought that she was much more emotional than she had been before, but she wasn't sure of this. She was confused and frightened.

Numerous CAT scans of her brain were required to monitor her condition. They made her anxious and uncomfortable. She did not like having her head inside a big machine and having to lie perfectly still for long periods. Of course she also feared the results of these tests.

Two weeks into the stress reduction program, another CAT scan was scheduled. She was not looking forward to it at all. Yet as her head was being slowly glided into the cavity of the machine, somehow the thought came to her to try to put her mind in her toes, as she had been practicing in the body scan for two weeks. She wound up keeping it there for the entire test and breathing in and out from her toes, which were farthest from the machine. Focusing on her toes, she felt more in control and could stay relaxed. She came through the procedure totally calm and panic-free. Her uncharacteristic calmness amazed both her and her husband. She came to the next class thrilled with the discovery of her newfound ability to control what had seemed uncontrollable.

Beverly's body still continues to do strange things that worry her a great deal. But she now feels that she has some tools she can use daily to keep her in greater balance. In particular, she finds helpful the image of the mountain, stable and unmoving amidst all the changes in the weather that engulf it, and she often invokes this "inner mountain" during her meditation and at other times.* She says that she is now able to accept the uncertainty of her condition. This alone gives her more peace of mind. The full catastrophe hasn't gone away. But she is handling it in a way that enables her to feel better about herself now, more optimistic about the future.

Having the confidence and the imagination to take on and work with

* For more on the mountain meditation, see *Wherever You Go, There You Are,* and the guided mountain meditation in the Series 2 Guided Mindfulness Meditation Practice CDs.

whatever comes up requires that you have powerful tools to work with and enough experience with them to know how to use them, as well as the flexibility and presence of mind to remember to call on them under trying circumstances. Beverly displayed these qualities when she decided to focus her mind on her toes and use her meditation while she was in the scanner.

A few weeks following her CAT scan, she had to undergo another type of brain imaging, this time an MRI. She thought she would use the same method that had helped during the CAT scan, but when she tried to concentrate on her toes, she found she couldn't do it because the MRI scanner made very loud banging sounds (from its magnets), which bothered her too much. Instead of panicking, she switched her attention to the sounds themselves and again found that she was able to dwell in a state of calm during the procedure. So, in addition to developing a set of tools to handle her anxiety, Beverly also managed to be imaginative and flexible in her use of them. She responded to the novel challenge of the clanging sounds of the MRI scanner instead of merely reacting automatically in what was for her a very stressful situation. Flexibility of this kind is essential if you hope to be able to maintain your balance in the face of the unexpected. Again, it is all part of the practice of mindfulness, part of which, as we have now seen on more than a few occasions, involves bringing it into every aspect of your everyday life, even, or especially, in difficult situations that you may not have even anticipated would become problematic.

Another example of successfully working with anxiety comes from a man who told the following story to his class in the Stress Reduction Clinic. He had always had a tendency to panic and to feel frightened in crowds, but had not had a panic attack in about six months. He was taking the program for a medical problem unrelated to anxiety. At one point during the program he went with friends to a Celtics basketball game on their home court, the old Boston Garden. As he sat down in his seat, high above the parquet floor, he felt the old familiar feelings of claustrophobia and fear of being trapped in a closed space with a throng of people. In the past, that feeling would have presaged a full-blown panic attack. It would have caused him to bolt for an exit. In fact, fear of it would have kept him from going to the game in the first place.

Instead of bolting, he reminded himself that he was breathing. He sat back and rode the waves of his breathing for a few minutes, focusing on them and letting go of his panicky thoughts. After a few minutes the feeling passed and he enjoyed the rest of the evening thoroughly.

These are just a few examples of how people have used the mindfulness meditation practice and its applications in everyday life to work with and calm anxiety and panic. Together with some of the other stories in this book, they may give you a handle on how to come to your own center of stability and calmness of mind within the storms of fear, panic, and anxiety that sometimes blow in our lives, and on how to emerge from their hold wiser and freer.

26

Time and Time Stress

Practice not-doing and everything will fall into place.

—LAO-TZU, *Tao Te Ching*

In our society, time has become one of our biggest stressors—and then some. With the advent of the digital age, the Internet, wireless devices, and social networking, we have entered an amazing world of 24/7 connectivity. It was supposed to make our lives much easier—and in so many ways it has. But we may also find that we have developed a dependency on the technology, and that it can become oppressive as well as convenient because the communications never stop coming. Plus everything is happening faster and faster, making it hard to keep up, even with the really important things. So the technology is both hard to live with at times (just think about email overload) and impossible to live without. And this is only the very beginning. The younger among us have never known the purely analog world and are thus, along with the rest of us, immersed in a novel and ever-changing world that never existed before, with all its promise and also potential costs, costs that may not even be noticeable if you never knew anything else.

In any event, there is no question that time is moving faster and faster as we juggle more and more communications. We may be in touch with everybody else in the world through our devices, Facebook pages, Twitter feeds, and the like, yet not so much in touch with ourselves. And we may be far too busy or absorbed even to notice.

Still, time has always been a huge mystery, and there is no sign that that will ever not be the case. At some stages of life, it may feel as if there is never enough time to do what we need to do. Often we don't know where time has gone, the years pass by so fast. At other stages, time may weigh heavily upon us. The days and the hours can seem interminable. We don't know what to do with all our time. Crazy as it may sound, I am suggesting that the antidote to time stress is intentional non-doing, and that non-doing is applicable whether you are suffering from not having "enough time" or suffering from having "too much time." The challenge here is for you to put this proposition to the test in your own life, to see for yourself whether your relationship to time can be transformed through the practice of non-doing—in other words, though the cultivation of mindfulness.

If you feel completely overwhelmed by the pressures of time, you might wonder: how could it possibly help to take time away from everything you "have to do" in order to practice non-doing? And on the other hand, if you are feeling isolated and bored and have nothing but time on your hands, you might wonder how it could possibly help to fill this burden of unfilled time with "nothing."

The answer is simple and not at all far-fetched: *well-being, inner balance, and peacefulness exist outside time.* If you commit yourself to spending some time each day in inner stillness, even if it is for two minutes, or five, or ten, for those moments you are stepping out of the flow of time altogether. The stillness and calm, the sense of well-being and wakeful presence that come from letting go of time transform your experience of time when you move back into it. Then, simply by bringing awareness to present-moment experience, it becomes possible to flow along with time during your day rather than constantly fighting against it or feeling driven by it.

The more you practice making some time in your day for non-doing, the more your whole day becomes non-doing; in other words, the more it is suffused with an awareness grounded in the present moment and therefore outside of time. Perhaps you have already experienced this if you have been practicing the sitting meditation or the body scan or the yoga. Perhaps you have observed that being aware takes no extra time, that awareness simply rounds out each moment, restores its fullness, breathes life into it, makes it embodied. So if you are pressed for time, being in the present gives you more time by giving you back the fullness of each moment that you already have. No matter what is happening, you can be centered in perceiving and accepting things as they are. Of course, you can also be aware of what still needs to be done in the future, without it causing you undue anxiety or loss of perspective. Then you can move to do it, with your doing coming out of your being, out of groundedness, out of integration, out of a moment of interior balance, of equanimity, of peace.

You can even bring this orientation to your electronic communications, whether it is texting, email, spending time on Facebook or Twitter, or sharing photos and videos—whatever your preferences. How? First by being in your body as you use your devices, and thus being in the present moment. Second, you can construct texts mindfully, with full awareness of what you are doing. If you are responding to tons of email, you can pace yourself so you are not feeling like you are playing Whac-A-Mole and running faster and faster to respond, even as you fall further and further "behind." You are only falling behind in your own mind, especially if you lose touch with who is doing all the doing, namely, with who you are, and the whole domain of being. Otherwise, as you well know, you can click send before you even realize that you didn't want to say what you said, or forgot the most important point. Also, you can become aware of the impulse to tweet, to share a moment or a thought, and how easily it can come between you and the experience you think you are having (and broadcasting to others) but aren't really having because you are too busy advertising your location and impressions to take a moment to drop in on your experience and actually feel it, and let it develop unevaluated and unshared, at least for a moment. These are all ongoing challenges brought on by the speed-up of virtually everything, and the endless appetite and impulses for recording and sharing our experience even before we allow ourselves to have it, breathe with it, digest it, and assimilate it in our own heart and mind. These are all new occupational hazards of carrying wireless multipurpose micro-supercomputers in our pockets and purses. We do this stuff just because we can. But do we ever stop and ask ourselves, even for one moment or one breath, what might be lost in this process of documenting and sharing so quickly?

Now that we have at least touched on what it feels like to never have enough time, and what we might do about that, let's suppose that you find yourself in the exact opposite life situation, in which you don't know what to do with all the time you have. Sad to say, this is too often the case as we get older and perhaps move into being more isolated and frailer, perhaps with some of our senses less acute than they used to be, putting us even more out of touch. Time can weigh on your hands. Perhaps you feel empty, disconnected from the world and from all the meaningful things being done in it. Perhaps you can't go out, or hold down a job, or get out of bed for long, or even read much to "pass the time." Perhaps you are alone, without friends and relatives, or far from them. Perhaps you don't even understand the Internet and don't want to. How could non-doing possibly help you? You are already not doing anything and it is driving you nuts!

Actually, you are probably doing a lot even though you are unaware of it. For one thing, you may be "doing" unhappiness, boredom, and anxiety. You are probably spending at least some time, and perhaps a great deal of time, dwelling in your thoughts and memories, reliving pleasant moments from the past or unhappy events. You may be "doing" anger at other people for things that happened long ago. You may be "doing" loneliness, resentment, self-pity, or hopelessness. These inner whirlpools of the mind can drain your energy. They can be exhausting and make the passage of time seem interminable. Loneliness is a risk factor in and of itself for both ill health and mortality. As we saw in the Carnegie Mellon study, training in MBSR can reduce loneliness, and seems to make a difference right down to the level of our genes and our cells. One way it may be doing this is by transforming our relationship to time.

Our subjective experience of time passing seems linked to the activity of thought in some way. We *think* about the past, we *think* about the future. Time is measured as the space between our thoughts, and in the never-ending stream of them. As we practice mindfully watching our thoughts come and go, we are cultivating an ability to dwell in the silence and stillness beyond the stream of thought itself, in a timeless present. Since the present is always here, now, it is already outside of time passing. T. S. Eliot put it this way at the very end of the first of *Four Quartets,* "Burnt Norton":

Ridiculous the waste sad time
Stretching before, and after.

The whole of *Four Quartets,* his last and greatest poem, is about time, its beauty, its mystery, and its "indignities."

Non-doing is a radical stance to adopt, even for one moment. It means letting go of our attachment to *everything.* Above all, it means seeing and letting go of your thoughts as they come and go. It means letting yourself be. If you feel trapped in time, non-doing is a way for you to step out of all the time on your hands by stepping into timelessness. In doing so, you also step out, at least momentarily, from your isolation, your unhappiness, and your desire to be engaged, busy, a part of things, doing something meaningful. By connecting with yourself outside the flow of time, you are already doing the most meaningful thing you could possibly do, namely to come to peace within your own mind, coming into contact with your own wholeness, reconnecting with yourself. Here is Eliot, again from "Burnt Norton":

Time past and time future
Allow but a little consciousness.
To be conscious is not to be in time . . .

You could look at all the time you have as an opportunity to engage in the inner work of being and growing. Then, even if your body doesn't work "right" and you are confined to the house or to a bed, even if you feel somewhat diminished from your former self, the possibility is still here to turn your life into an adventure and to find meaning in each moment. If you commit yourself to the work of mindfulness, your physical isolation might take on a different meaning for you. Your inability to be active in outer ways and the pain and regret that you may feel from it may become balanced by the joy of other possibilities, by a new perspective on yourself, one in which you are seeing optimistically, reframing the time that weighed on your hands as time to do the work of being, the work of non-doing, the work of self-awareness and understanding, the work of being present for and with others with kindness and compassion.

There is no end to this work, of course, and no telling where it might lead. But wherever that is, it will be away from suffering, away from boredom and anxiety and self-pity, and toward healing. Negative mental states cannot survive for long when timelessness is being cultivated. How could they when you are already embodying peace? Your concentrated and stable awareness serves as a crucible in which negative mental states can be contained and then transmuted.

And if you are able-bodied enough to do at least some things in the outside world, dwelling in non-doing will likely lead to insights as to how you might connect up with people and activities and events that might be meaningful to you as well as helpful and useful to others. Everybody has something to offer to the world—in fact, something that no other person can offer, something unique and priceless. And that, of course, is *one's own unique being*. If you practice non-doing, you may find that, rather than having all this time on your hands, the days may not be long enough to do what needs doing. But that requires that you let the doing come out of being. In this work, you will never be unemployed, whether you have a job or not.

If you take a more cosmic perspective on time, none of us is here for very long anyway. The total duration of human life on the planet has itself been the briefest of eye blinks, our own individual lives infinitesimal in the vastness of geological time. Stephen Jay Gould, the late Harvard University paleontologist, pointed out that "the human species has inhabited this planet for only 250,000 years or so—roughly 0.0015 percent of the history of life, the last inch of the cosmic mile." Yet the way our minds represent time, it feels as if we have a long time to live. In fact, we often delude ourselves, especially early in life, with feelings of immortality and of our own permanence. At other times we are only too keenly aware of the inevitability of death and the rapidity of the passage of our lives.

Perhaps it is the knowledge of death, conscious or unconscious, that ultimately drives us to feel pressed for time. The word *deadline* certainly carries the message. We have many deadlines, those imposed by our work and by other people and those we impose on ourselves. We rush here and there, doing this and that, trying to get it all done "in time." Often we are so stressed by the squeeze of time that we do what we are doing just to get through with it, to be able to say to ourselves, "At least *that* is out of the way" as we check it off our never-ending to-do list. And then it's on to the next thing that needs doing, pressing on, pressing through our moments, until we are in the Whac-A-Mole situation again, just doing, doing, doing, as speedily as possible, to get it all done, knowing that we will never get it all done—and also sometimes realizing that if we are not careful, we will miss what is most precious and most important, and most easily forgotten in our own lives—namely, an embodied experience of who is doing all of this doing. In other words, once again: the domain of being!

Some doctors believe that time stress is a fundamental cause of disease in the present era. Time urgency was originally featured as one of the salient characteristics of coronary-disease-prone, or type A, behavior. The type A syndrome is sometimes described as "hurry sickness." People who fit into this category are driven by a sense of time pressure to speed up the doing of all their daily activities and to do and think more than one thing at a time. They tend to be very poor listeners. They are constantly interrupting and finishing other people's sentences for them. They tend to be very impatient. They have great difficulty sitting and doing nothing or standing in lines, and they tend to speak rapidly and to dominate in social and professional situations. Type A's also tend to be highly competitive, easily irritated, cynical, and hostile. As we have seen, the evidence points to hostility and cynicism as the most toxic elements of coronary-prone behavior, although others view those elements as coming out of time urgency. But even if continuing research shows that time urgency by itself is not a major factor in heart disease, it nevertheless has a toxicity all its own. If not handled well, time stress can easily erode the quality of a person's life and threaten health and well-being.

Robert Eliot, a cardiologist and stress researcher, described his own mental state and his relationship to time prior to his heart attack—and this in the era before the Internet—as follows:

> My body cried out for rest, but my brain wasn't listening. I was behind schedule. My timetable read that by the age of forty I should be the chief of cardiology at a major university. I was forty-three when I left the University of Florida at Gainesville and accepted the position of chief of cardiology at the University of Nebraska in 1972. All I had to do was run a little faster and I'd be back on track.

Yet he found himself running into roadblocks of various kinds in his efforts to establish an innovative cardiovascular research center.

> I came to feel that the walls were closing in on me and that I would never break free to make my dream a reality.
>
> Desperately I did what I had been doing all my life. I picked up the pace. I tried to force things through. I crisscrossed the state to provide on-the-spot cardiology education to rural Nebraska physicians and build support among them for the university's cardiovascular program. I scheduled academic lectures across the country, continually flying in and out at a moment's notice. I remember that on one trip on which my wife, Phyllis, helped with the business arrangements, a seminar went superbly, and on the plane ride home Phyllis wanted to savor the

> memory. Not me. I was rushing through the evaluation forms, worrying about how to make the next seminar better.
>
> I had no time for family and friends, relaxation and diversion. When Phyllis bought me an exercise bike for Christmas, I was offended. How could I possibly find time to sit down and pedal a bicycle?
>
> I was often overtired, but I put that out of my mind. I wasn't concerned about my health. What did I have to worry about? I was an expert in diseases of the heart, and I knew I didn't have any of the risk factors. My father had lived to be seventy-eight and my mother, at eighty-five, showed no sign of heart disease. I didn't smoke. I wasn't overweight. I didn't have high blood pressure. I didn't have high cholesterol. I didn't have diabetes. I thought I was immune to heart disease.
>
> But I was running a big risk for other reasons. I had been pushing too hard for too long. Now all my efforts seemed futile. . . . A feeling of disillusionment descended on me, a sense of invisible entrapment.
>
> I didn't know it then, but my body was continuously reacting to this inner turmoil. For nine months I was softened for the blow. It came two weeks after my forty-fourth birthday.

As he described it, after a disappointing confrontation one day, he got very angry and was unable to calm down. After a sleepless night and a long drive to a speaking engagement, he gave a medical lecture. Following a heavy lunch, he tried to diagnose cases, but his mind was foggy and his eyes blurry. He felt dizzy. These were the conditions that immediately preceded his having a heart attack.

Dr. Eliot's heart attack led him to write a book called *Is It Worth Dying For?* in which he described how he came to answer that question with a resounding "No" and went on to change his relationship to time and to stress. He described his life leading up to his heart attack as "a joyless treadmill." And this from a person who in some way obviously loved his work.

Norman Cousins, the prominent magazine editor and leading intellectual, described the conditions leading up to his heart attack in much the same way in his book *The Healing Heart*—in the era *before* the airport security instituted following the attacks of September 11, 2001:

> The main source of stress in my life for some years had been airports and airplanes, necessitated by a heavy speaking and conference schedule. Battling traffic congestion en route to airports, having to run through air terminals . . . having to queue up for boarding passes at the gate and then being turned away because the plane had been overbooked, waiting at baggage carousels for bags that never turned up, time-zone changes, irregular meals, insufficient sleep—these features of airline transportation had been my melancholy burdens for many years and were especially profuse in the latter part of 1980. . . . I returned from a hectic trip to the East Coast just before Christmas only to discover that I was due to leave again in a few days for the Southeast. I asked my secretary about the possibility of a postponement or a cancellation. She carefully reviewed with me the special facts in each case that made it essential to go through with the engagements. It was obvious . . . that only the most drastic event would get me out of it. My body was listening. The next day I had my heart attack.

Notice the sense of time pressure and urgency in the words themselves in both these passages: "behind schedule," career "timetable," "I picked up the pace," "I tried to force things through," "no time for family or friends," "joyless treadmill," "battling traffic," "having to run" to make the plane, "having to queue up," "waiting" for baggage, dealing with "time-zone changes."

Time pressures are not solely the province of successful executives, physicians, and academicians who travel a lot. In our post-industrial and now totally digital society, all of us are exposed to the stress of time. We strap on our watches in the morning, pocket our smart phones with our calendars and appointments, our emails and our Twitter feeds, and we get going. We conduct our lives by the clock, and squeeze everything else into the "in-between" or "on-the-way-to" moments. The clock dictates when we have to be where, and woe to us if we forget too often. Time and the clock drive us from one thing to the next. It has become a "way of life" for many of us to feel driven every day by all our obligations and responsibilities and then to fall into bed exhausted at the end of it all. If we keep up this pattern for long stretches without adequate rest and without replenishing our own energy reserves, breakdown will inevitably occur in one way or another. No matter how stable and robust your allostatic circuits, they can eventually be pushed over the edge if they are not reset and recalibrated from time to time—to reduce the allostatic load, the everyday wear and tear.

Nowadays we even transmit time urgency to our children. How many times have you found yourself saying to little children, "Hurry up, there's no time" or "I don't have time"? We hurry them to get dressed, to eat, to get ready for school. By what we say, by our body language, by the way we rush around ourselves, we are giving them the clear message that there is simply never enough time.

This message has been getting through to them all too clearly. It is not uncommon now for children to feel stressed and hurried at an early age. Instead of being able to follow their own inner rhythms, they are scooped up onto the conveyor belt of their parents' lives and taught to hurry and to be time-conscious. This may ultimately have deleterious effects on their biological rhythms and cause various kinds of physiological disregulation as well as psychological distress, just as it does in adults. For instance, high blood pressure begins in childhood in our society, with small but significant elevations detectable even in five-year-olds. This is not true in nonindustrial societies, where high blood pressure is virtually unknown. Something in the stress of our way of life beyond just dietary factors is probably responsible for this. Perhaps it is the stress of time.

In earlier times, our activities were much more in step with the cycles of the natural world. People stayed put more. They didn't travel very far. Most died in the same place they were born and knew everybody in their town or village. Daylight and darkness dictated very different life rhythms. Many tasks just could not be done at night for lack of light. Sitting around fires at night, their only sources of heat and light, had a way of slowing people down—it was calming as well as warming. Staring into the flames and the embers, the mind could focus on the fire, always different, yet always the same. People could watch it moment by moment and night after night, month after month, year after year, through the seasons, and see time stand still in the fire. Perhaps the ritual of sitting around fires was mankind's first experience of meditation.

In earlier times, the rhythms of people were the rhythms of nature. It was a wholly analog world. A farmer could only plow so much by hand or with an ox in one day. You could only travel so far on foot or even with a horse. People were in deep connection with their animals and their needs. The animals' rhythm dictated the rhythms of the day and the limits of time. If you valued your horse, you knew not to push it too fast or too far. You could only communicate to people face-to-face, or, in a pinch, through drumming or smoke signals.

Now we can live largely independent of those natural rhythms. Electricity has given us light in the darkness, so that there is much less of a distinction between day and night—we can work after the sun goes down if we have to, or want to. We never have to slow down because the light has failed. We also have cars and tractors, telephones and jet travel, radios and televisions, photocopying machines, laptops and tablets and ever smaller and more powerful wireless devices of all kinds, and an alternate universe of sorts in the Internet. These have shrunk the world and reduced by a staggering amount the time that it takes to do things, find things out, communicate, go someplace, or finish a piece of work. Computers have amplified to such an extent the ability to get paperwork and computations done that, although they are tremendously liberating in some ways, people can find themselves under more pressure than ever to get more done in less time. The expectations of oneself and of others just increase exponentially as the technology provides us with the power to do more and more and do it faster and even faster. Instead of sitting around fires at night for light and warmth and something to look into, we can throw switches and keep going with whatever we have to do. We can also watch television and YouTube videos, surf the Web, or live in the blogosphere and think we are relaxing and slowing down. Actually, it may be just more sensory bombardment.

And in the near future, what with the next waves of technological products either here already or on the way—online shopping, "smart" television, narrowcasting of advertisements, electronic homes with voice-activated functions, and of course personal robots you can talk to and have look after whatever needs looking after—we will have more and more ways to distract ourselves, more and more ways to stay busier and busier and to do more and more things simultaneously, with expectations rising accordingly. Already, we can drive *and* do business (and increase the accident rate enormously through inattention and multitasking behind the wheel), we can exercise *and* process information, we can read *and* watch programs on split screens on our tablets, we can watch two or three or four things at once on television. We will never be out of touch with the world and with the content and demands that we can easily become addicted to. But will we ever be in touch with ourselves?

FOUR WAYS TO FREE YOURSELF FROM THE TYRANNY OF TIME

Just because the world has been speeded up through technology is no reason for us to be ruled by it to the point where we are stressed beyond all limits and perhaps even driven to an early grave by the treadmill of modern life. There are many ways you might free yourself from the tyranny of time. The first is to remind yourself that time is a product of thought. Minutes and hours are conventions, agreed upon so that we can conveniently meet and communicate and work in harmony. But they have no absolute meaning, as Einstein was fond of pointing out to lay audiences. To paraphrase what he was supposed to have said in explaining the concept of relativity, "If you are sitting on a hot stove, a minute can seem like an hour, but if you are doing something pleasurable, an hour can seem like a minute."

Of course we all know this from our own experience. Nature is in fact very equitable. We all get twenty-four hours a day to live. How we see that time and what we do with it can make all the difference in whether we feel we have "enough time," "too much time," or "not enough time." So we need to look at our expectations of ourselves. We need to be aware of just what we are trying to accomplish and whether we are paying too great a price for it or, in Dr. Eliot's words, whether it is "worth dying for."

A second way of freeing yourself from the tyranny of time is to live in the present more of the time. We waste enormous amounts of time and energy musing about the past and worrying about the future. These moments are hardly ever satisfying. Usually they produce anxiety and time urgency, thoughts such as "Time is running out" or "Those were the good old days." As we have seen now many times, to practice being mindful from one moment to the next puts you in touch with life in the only time you have to live it, namely, right now. Whatever you are engaged in takes on a greater richness when you drop out of the automatic pilot mode and into awareness and acceptance. If you are eating, then really eat during this time. It might mean choosing not to read a magazine or watch TV while half consciously shoveling food into your body. If you are babysitting for your grandchildren, then really *be* with them. Do what it takes to become fully engaged. Time will disappear. If you are helping your children with their homework or just talking with them, don't do it on the run or while talking on your phone or checking your email surreptitiously. Make the effort to be fully present. Make eye contact. Own those moments. Slow time down. Be in your body. Then you will not see others as "taking time" away from you. All your moments will be your own. And if you want to reminisce about the past or plan for the future, then do *that* with awareness as well. Remember *in the present.* Plan *in the present.*

The essence of mindfulness in daily life is to make every moment you have your own. Even if you are hurrying, which is sometimes necessary, then at least hurry mindfully. Be aware of your breathing, of the need to move fast, and do it with awareness until you don't have to hurry anymore; then let go and relax intentionally, as best you can, and give yourself time to recover if you need to. If you find your mind making lists and compelling you to get every last thing on them done, then bring awareness to your body and the mental and physical tension that may be mounting, and remind yourself that some of it can probably wait. If you get really close to the edge, stop completely and ask yourself, "Is it worth dying for?" or "Who is running where?"

A third way of freeing yourself from the tyranny of time is devote some of it intentionally each day just to be, in other words, to meditate. We need to carve out and protect our time for formal meditation practice because it is so easy to write it off as unnecessary or a luxury; after all, it is empty of doing. When you do write it off and give this time over to doing, you wind up losing what may be the most valuable part of your life: time for yourself to just be.

As we have seen, in practicing mindfulness meditation in all the ways we have been exploring and engaging in, you are basically stepping out of the flow of time and residing in stillness, in an eternal present. That doesn't mean that every moment you practice will be a moment of timelessness. That depends on the degree of concentration and calmness that you bring to each moment. But just making the commitment to practice non-doing, to let go of striving, to be non-judgmental about how judgmental you are at times, slows down that time for you and nourishes the timeless in you. By devoting some time each day to slowing down time itself, and by giving yourself the gift of a formal time dedicated to just being, you are strengthening your ability to act out of your being and fully inhabit the present moment throughout the rest of your day, when the pace of the outer and inner worlds may be much more relentless. That is why it is so important to organize your life around preserving some time each day for just being, for resting in awareness with no agenda other than to be awake.

A fourth way of freeing yourself from time is to simplify your life in certain ways. As recounted earlier, I once conducted an eight-week MBSR program just for judges. Judges tend to be sorely stressed by overwhelming caseloads. One judge complained that he never had enough time to review cases or to do extra background reading to prepare for them, and that he didn't feel he had enough time to be with his family. When he explored how he used his time when he was not at work, it turned out that he religiously read three newspapers every day and also watched the news on television for an hour each day. The newspapers alone took up an hour and a half. It amounted to a kind of addiction.

Of course he knew how he was spending his time. But for some reason he hadn't made the connection that he was choosing to use up two and a half hours a day with news, almost all of which was the same in each newspaper and on TV. When we discussed it, he saw in an instant that he could gain time for other things he wanted to do by letting go of two newspapers and the TV news. He intentionally broke his addictive news habit and now reads one paper a day, doesn't watch the news on TV, and has about two more hours a day to do other things.

Simplifying our lives in even little ways can make a big difference. If you fill up all your time, you won't have any. And you probably won't even be aware of why you don't. Simplifying may mean prioritizing the things that you have to and want to do and, at the same time, *consciously choosing to give certain things up*. It may mean learning to say no sometimes, even to things you want to do or to people you care about and want to help, so that you are protecting and preserving some space for silence, for non-doing—and for everything you have already said yes to.

After the day-long silent mindfulness mini retreat at the hospital in week six of the MBSR program, a woman who had been in pain for a number of years discovered that the next day she had no pain at all. She also woke up that morning feeling differently about time. It felt precious to her in a new way. When she got a routine call from her son, saying that he was bringing over the children so that she and her husband could babysit for them, she found herself telling him not to bring them, that she couldn't do it just then, that she needed to be alone. She felt she needed to protect this amazing moment of freedom from pain. She felt she had to preserve the preciousness of the stillness she was experiencing that morning rather than to fill it, even with her grandchildren, who she of course loved enormously. She wanted to help her son out, but this time she needed to say no and to do something for herself. And her husband, sensing something different in her, perhaps her inner peacefulness, uncharacteristically supported her.

Her son couldn't believe it. She had never said no before. She didn't even have anything she was doing that day. To him it seemed nuts. But she knew, perhaps for the first time in quite a while, that some moments are worth protecting, just so that nothing can happen—because that "nothing" is a very rich nothing.

There is a saying: "Time is money." But some people may have enough money and not enough time. It wouldn't hurt them to think about giving up some of their money for some time. For many years I worked three or four days a week and got paid accordingly. I needed the full-time money, but I felt the time was more important, especially when my children were little. I wanted to be there for them as much as I could. Then I worked full-time at the hospital and medical school for many years. This meant I was away from home more, and I felt the pressure of time more in many ways. As best I could, I practiced non-doing moment by moment within the domain of all the doing, and tried, mostly unsuccessfully, to remember not to overcommit myself.

I am lucky to have a lot of say in how much I work, as well as what I do. And the work that I do, in all its guises, is a labor of love. Most people don't have that much of a say in what they do and how much they work. Still, there are many ways in which it is possible to simplify your life. Maybe you don't need to run around so much or have so many obligations or commitments. Maybe you don't have to have the TV on all the time in your house. Maybe you don't need to use your car so much. Maybe you don't need to be on your cell phone as much as you are. And maybe you don't really need so much money. Giving some thought and attention to the ways in which you might simplify things will probably start you on the road toward making your time your own. It is yours anyway, you know.

You might as well enjoy it. You might as well inhabit all your moments. They are not "yours" forever.

Mahatma Gandhi was once asked by a journalist, "You have been working at least fifteen hours a day, every day for almost fifty years. Don't you think it's about time you took a vacation?" To which Gandhi replied, "I am always on vacation."

Of course, the word *vacation* carries within it the meaning of "vacant, empty." When we practice being completely in the present, life in its fullness is totally accessible to us at all times, precisely because we are outside of time. Time becomes empty and so do we. Then we too can always be on vacation. We might even learn how to have better vacations if we practiced all year long.

But only in time can the moment in the rose-garden
The moment in the arbour where the rain beat,
The moment in the draughty church at smokefall
Be remembered; involved with past and future.
Only through time time is conquered.

T. S. Eliot, "Burnt Norton," *Four Quartets*

27

Sleep and Sleep Stress

Of all the things we do on a regular basis, sleeping is one of the most extraordinary and least appreciated. Imagine: once a day, on average, we lie down on a comfortable surface and leave our bodies for hours at a time. It is sacred time too. We are very attached to sleeping, and we almost never consider giving up some sleep on purpose to accomplish personal goals. How many times have you heard people say, "I need my eight hours or I'll be a basket case"? And if you suggest to people that they might get up an hour earlier or even fifteen minutes earlier to make time to do other things that they value but have no time for, you will find lots of resistance. People feel threatened when you tamper with their sleep time.

Yet ironically, one of the most common and earliest symptoms of stress is trouble with sleep. Either you can't get to sleep in the first place because your thinking mind won't shut down, or you wake up in the middle of the night and can't get back to sleep. Or both. Usually you toss and turn, trying to clear your mind, telling yourself what a big day you have tomorrow, how important it is to be rested, all to no avail. The more you try to get back to sleep, the more awake you are.

As it turns out, you can't *force* yourself to go to sleep. It is one of those dynamical conditions, like relaxation, that you have to let go into. The more you try to get to sleep, the more you create tension and anxiety, which wake you up.

When we talk about "going to sleep," the language itself suggests "getting somewhere." Perhaps it would be more accurate to say that sleep "comes over us" when the conditions are right. Being able to sleep is a sign of harmony in your life. Getting enough sleep is a basic ingredient of good health. When we are sleep-deprived, our thinking, our moods, and our behavior can become erratic and unreliable, our body becomes exhausted and we become more susceptible to "getting" sick.

Our sleep patterns are intimately related to the natural world. The planet turns on its axis once every twenty-four hours, giving us cycles of light and darkness, and living organisms seem to cycle with it, as seen in the diurnal changes known as *circadian rhythms.* These rhythms show up in daily fluctuations in the release of neurotransmitters in the brain and nervous system and in the biochemistry of all our cells. We have these basic planetary rhythms built into our systems. In fact, biologists speak of a "biological clock," controlled by the hypothalamus, which regulates our sleep-wake cycle and which can be disrupted by jet travel, by working the night shift, and by other behavior patterns. We cycle with the planet, and our sleep pattern reflects this connection. When it is disrupted, it takes us some time to readjust, to get back to our normal pattern.

A seventy-five-year-old woman was sent to the Stress Reduction Clinic with a sleep problem that had started a year and a half previously. She had also had a recent onset of hypertension that was under control with medication. She had been employed in the public schools and had retired ten years before. She reported that most nights she just wasn't able to sleep and would spend the whole night "perfectly comfortable, not restless" but awake. Her doctor had prescribed a very low dose tranquilizer to help her relax, but she still thought of the medication with "fear and trembling." She tried it a few times, taking half a pill. It did help her to sleep, but she hated taking it and stopped. She came to the Stress Reduction Clinic hoping she could learn to sleep better without depending on medication.

She did. She kept up the meditation practice faithfully throughout the course. She didn't like the sitting meditation because she said her mind wandered too much, but she loved the yoga and did it every day, much more than we required. By the end of the eight weeks, she was sleeping, as she put it, "marvelously" every night, and was very pleased with her ability to do it without medication.

If you are having a lot of trouble sleeping, your body may be trying to tell you something about the way you are conducting your life. As with all other mind-body symptoms, this message is worth listening to. Usually it is just a signal that you are going through a stressful time in your life and you can expect that if and when it is resolved, your sleeping pattern will improve by itself. Sometimes it helps to look at how much exercise you are getting. Regular exercise, such as walking or yoga or swimming, can make a major difference in your ability to sleep soundly at any age, as you can discover by experimenting for yourself.

Sometimes people get caught up in thinking they need more sleep than they really do. Our need for sleep changes as we grow and is known to diminish as we get older. Some people can function well on four, five, or six hours of sleep per night, but they may feel that they "should" be able to sleep longer.

When you can't sleep, you might try getting out of bed and doing something else for a while, something you like doing or that you might feel good about getting done. I like to assume that if I can't sleep, it may be because I don't need to be sleeping just then, even if I really want to be. When I have trouble sleeping, the second thing I do is meditate. (The first is toss and turn and feel upset until I realize what I'm doing.) If I don't manage to fall back asleep after a time, I get out of bed, wrap myself up in a warm blanket, sit on my cushion, and just watch my mind. This gives me a chance to look carefully at what is so pressing and agitating that it is keeping me from peaceful sleep. Alternatively, I might just assume the corpse pose lying on my back in bed and practice the body scan.

Sometimes meditating for a half hour or so in this way will calm the mind to the point where you can go back to sleep. Other times it may lead you to do something else, such as work on a favorite project, make lists, read a good book, listen to music, take a walk or go for a drive, or just accept the fact that your mind is simply agitated, upset, angry, fearful, or whatever it may be in the moment and embrace it in awareness without having to do anything with it. The middle of the night is also a good time to do yoga if you happen to be up, although that might wake you up even more.

To handle sleeplessness in this way requires that you recognize and accept that, like it or not, you are already awake. Catastrophizing about how bad your day is going to be because you'll be so exhausted if you don't get back to sleep doesn't help—and may not even be true. You just don't know. And forcing yourself to try to sleep doesn't help either. So why not let the future take care of itself, especially since the fact is that right now you are already awake? Why not be fully awake?

As was mentioned briefly in the Introduction, mindfulness practice comes primarily out of the Buddhist meditative tradition, although it is found in one form or another in all contemplative traditions and practices. Interestingly enough, there is no God in Buddhism, which makes it a very unusual religion. Buddhism is really based on reverence for a principle, embodied in a historical person known as the Buddha. As the story goes, someone approached the Buddha, who was considered a great sage and teacher, and asked him, "Are you a god?" or something to that effect, to which he replied, "No, I am awake." The essence of mindfulness practice is to work at waking up from the self-imposed half sleep of unawareness in which we are so often habitually, but not inevitably, immersed.

We tend to function on automatic pilot so much of the time that it might well be said that we are more asleep than awake, even when we are awake. In *Walden,* which is really a rhapsody to mindfulness, Henry David Thoreau said: "We must learn to reawaken and keep ourselves awake, not by mechanical aid, but by an infinite expectation of the dawn, which does not forsake us in our soundest sleep."

If we make a commitment to ourself to be *fully* awake when we are awake, then our view of not being able to sleep at certain times will change along with our view of everything else. Whenever we happen to be awake in the twenty-four-hour cycle of the planet's turning can be seen as an opportunity to practice being fully awake and accepting things as they are, including the fact that your mind may be agitated and you are unable to sleep. When you do this, more often than not, your sleeping will take care of itself. It just may not come when you think it should and it may not last as long as you think it should, or it is more broken up than you think it should be. So much for "shoulds."

If this approach sounds radical to you, it might be valuable to think of the alternatives for a moment. There is a multimillion-dollar industry built around drugs to regulate sleep. This industry is a testament to our collective loss of homeostasis or allostasis, to how widespread this single example of the disregulation of our basic biological rhythms is. Many people regularly rely on pills to help them to get to sleep or to stay asleep. Control and regulation of their natural internal rhythms and cycles are given over to a chemical agent to restore homeostasis. Shouldn't this be the recourse of last resort, after all else has failed?

In the Stress Reduction Clinic, we put a lot of people to sleep, not that we mean to. It's just that the body scan can be very relaxing. If you do it when you are at all tired, it is amazingly easy to fall asleep rather than to "fall awake," even though falling awake is the basic invitation of the body scan in the first place—to drop into a condition of open and relaxed awareness as we visit and inhabit each region of the body in turn. This is why some people have to really work at staying awake through the entire body scan, and maybe even practice with their eyes open, or even sitting up. Some people may not hear the end of the CD for weeks. Some are even "out" by the time they reach the toes of the left foot, which is where we usually start, or by the left knee for sure! When we practice together in class, the instructor's guidance is sometimes punctuated by snoring. That brings a lot of smiles and giggles, but it is only to be expected. Most of us are sleep-deprived to one degree or another, and when we get at all relaxed, the tendency is to go unconscious. So we have to *learn* how to fall awake as we get more and more relaxed. But it is a learnable skill, and a very valuable one at that. It just takes practice, practice, practice.

When people come to the clinic primarily for help with sleep problems, we give them explicit permission to play the body scan CD at bedtime to help them to fall asleep—that is, as long as they make the commitment to themselves also to use the CD once a day at some other time to fall awake. And it works! Most people with sleep disturbances report a marked improvement after a few weeks practicing the body scan (for one example, see Mary's sleep graphs in Figure 3, Chapter 5), and many give up their sleeping pills before the eight weeks are up. Homeostasis is being restored, and you can feel it in the room as the weeks go on.

Some people in the MBSR program find it equally effective and easier when they want to go to sleep or to get back to sleep to just focus on their breathing as they lie in bed, letting the mind follow the breath as it moves into the body, and then following it back out all the way and letting the body just sink or melt into the mattress with each outbreath. You can think of it as breathing out to the ends of the universe, and breathing in from there, all the way back into your body.

Let's think for a moment in a bit more detail about how we manage to "go to sleep" at night. At a certain time, we lie down on a padded surface in a darkened room, close our eyes, and let the mattress hold us as we settle into the sheets. Things start to feel a bit hazy, and hopefully, off we go as delicious sleep comes over us. Because we are so practiced at falling asleep under certain conditions, when we come to practice the body scan, particularly because it is done lying down on a comfortable surface with the eyes closed, we have to learn to travel along the road of deepening relaxation as we settle into the present moment with awareness, wherever we are focusing in the body, and recognize when we are coming to a fork. In one direction lies haziness, loss of awareness, and sleep. As we have seen, this is an extremely good road to take on a regular basis. It helps us to stay healthy and to restore our physical and psychological resources. Sleep is a blessing. In the other direction lies wakefulness, heightened awareness, and deep well-being, outside of time. This is also an extremely restorative condition to inhabit, worth cultivating on a regular basis. Physiologically and psychologically it differs greatly from sleep. The ideal is to cultivate both sleep and wakefulness in your life on a daily basis, and to know when one is more important than the other. They are both blessings, in different ways.

Our great attachment to sleep usually causes us to worry a lot about the consequences of losing sleep. But if you subscribe to the view that your body and mind can self-regulate and correct for some of the disturbances in sleep patterns we experience from time to time, then you can use your sleep imbalance as a vehicle for further growth, just as we have seen that you can use other symptoms, even pain or anxiety, to experience deeper levels of wholeness. But it requires a whole lot of deep listening in your life.

In my own case, I got few nights of totally uninterrupted sleep when our children were little. This meant learning to live with getting up a lot during the night. Every once in a while I would go to bed really early and catch up that way. But mostly my system seemed to adjust to getting less sleep and less dreaming, and I managed quite well during that time.

I think one reason it didn't exhaust me completely and that I didn't get sick as a result was that I didn't fight it. I accepted it and used it as part of my meditation practice. I mentioned in Chapter 7 that I frequently found myself walking the floor at night with them when they were babies—comforting, chanting, rocking—and, using the walking, the singing, the rocking, and the patting to be aware of them as my children, to be aware of their feelings, their bodies, my own body, their breath, my breath, to be aware of being their father. True, I would just as soon have been back in bed, but since I wasn't and couldn't be, I used being awake as an opportunity to practice being as awake as possible. Seeing it this way, being up at night became just another form of training and growth as a person and as a father.

And now that our children are long grown up and living lives of their own, there are still times that I find myself waking up in the middle of the night. I sometimes relish them. When I do, I get out of bed and I sit or do some yoga or both. Then, depending on how I feel, I might either go back to bed or work on projects that I want to complete. I find it very peaceful in the middle of the night. No phone calls, no disturbances, especially if I stay away from my email, tempting as it is to check and then get seduced into communicating with the world. That can also be wonderful, especially if done with at least a modicum of mindfulness and joy in connecting with people I want to connect with. But the night offers other gifts too precious to ignore. For one, the silence. The stars and the moon and the dawn can be spectacular and give a feeling of connectedness that you don't get if you are unaware of the heavens at night. The mind usually relaxes once I stop trying to get back to sleep and focus instead on using the precious gift of these hours to be as present for them as possible.

Of course, people are different and we have different rhythms. Some people function best late at night, others early in the morning. It's very useful to find out how you might use the twenty-four hours you have each day in the way that works best for you. And you can only find this out by listening carefully to your mind and your body and letting them teach you what you need to know—in the hard moments as well as the easy ones. As usual, this means letting go of some of your resistance to change and experimentation, and perhaps giving yourself permission to get enthusiastic about exploring the unexamined and often limiting conditions of your life. Your relationship to sleep and to all the hours of the day and night is a very fruitful object of mindfulness. It will teach you a lot about yourself if you worry less about losing sleep and instead pay more attention to being fully awake.

28

People Stress

Maybe you've noticed: other people can be a big source of stress. We all have times when we feel that others are controlling our lives, making demands on our time, being unusually difficult or hostile, don't do what we expect them to do, or don't seem to care about us or take our feelings into account. We can probably all think of particular people who cause us stress, people we prefer to avoid if we can but often can't because we live with them or work with them or have obligations that involve them and which have to be met. In fact, many of the people who cause us the most stress may be people we love very deeply. We all know that love relationships can occasion deep emotional pain as well as joy and pleasure.

Our relationships with other people provide us with unending opportunities for practicing mindfulness and thereby reducing what I sometimes refer to as "people stress." As we saw in Part III, our stress cannot be said to be due solely to external stressors, because psychological stress arises from the *interaction* between us and the world. So in the case of people who "cause us stress," we need to take responsibility for our part in those relationships, for our own perceptions, thoughts, feelings, and behavior. Just as in any other unpleasant or threatening situation, we can react unconsciously with some version of the fight-or-flight reaction when we are having a problem with another person, and this usually makes matters worse in the long run.

Many of us have developed deeply ingrained habits for dealing with interpersonal unpleasantness and conflict. These habits are often our inheritance, molded by the ways our parents related to each other and to other people. Some people are so threatened by conflict or angry feelings in others that they will do anything to avoid a blowup. If you have this habit, you will tend not to show or tell people how you are really feeling but will try to avoid conflict at all costs by being passive, placating the other person, giving in to them, blaming yourself, dissimulating—whatever it takes.

Others may deal with their insecure feelings by creating conflict wherever they go. They see all their interactions in terms of power and control. Every interaction is made into an occasion for exerting control in one way or another, for getting their own way, without thinking or caring about others. People who have this habit of relating tend to be aggressive and hostile, often without any awareness of how it is perceived from the outside. They can be abrasive, abusive, insensitive out of sheer habit. Their speech tends to be harsh, both in their choice of words and in their tone of voice. They may act as if all relationships are struggles to assert dominance. As a result they usually leave a wake of bad feelings behind them in other people.

All of us probably have a mix of these different ways of being within us, perhaps not in the extreme, but nevertheless, present or latent—at one pole, experiential avoidance, and at the other, the capacity for aggression, heavy-handedness, and insensitivity. As we saw in Chapter 19, the deeply automatic impulse for fight-or-flight influences our behavior even when our lives are not in danger. When we feel that our interests or our social status is threatened, we are capable of reacting unconsciously to protect or defend our position before we know what we are doing.* Usually this

* Daniel Goleman refers to this as an "amygdala hijack." It happens when the prefrontal cortex, responsible for executive functioning, perspective taking, and emotion regulation, among other things, doesn't modulate the incoming signals that the amygdala sends out when it detects a threat to the organism, even if it is imagined.

behavior compounds our problems by increasing the level of conflict, both inwardly and outwardly. Or alternatively, we might act submissively. When we do, it is often at the expense of our own views, feelings, and self-respect. But since we also have the ability to reflect, to think, and to be aware, we have a range of other options available to us that go well beyond our most unconscious and deeply ingrained instincts. But for the most part, we need to cultivate these options purposefully. They don't just magically surface, especially if our mode of interpersonal relating has been dominated by automatically defensive or aggressive behavior that we have not really bothered to look at. Again, it is a matter of choosing a response rather than being carried away by a reaction.

Relationships are based on connectedness and interconnectedness, on what we could call *intrinsic relationality.* When people are willing to communicate with honesty and candor, and at the same time with mutual respect, an exchange of perspectives can take place that may lead to new ways of seeing and being together for the people involved. We are capable of communicating far more than fear and insecurity to each other when our emotions become part of the legitimate scope of our awareness. Even when we are feeling threatened, angry, or frightened, we have the potential to improve our relationships dramatically if we bring mindfulness into the domain of communication itself. As we saw in Chapter 15, the motive of affiliative trust, for instance, which got stronger in people who took the stress reduction program, might be a healthy alternative to the relentlessly one-pointed pursuit of power in relationships.

The word *communication* suggests a flow of energy through a common bond. As with *communion,* it implies a union, a joining or sharing. So to communicate is to unite, to have a meeting or union of minds. This does not necessarily mean agreement. It does mean seeing the situation as a whole and understanding the other person's view as well as one's own, to whatever degree we can manage such openness of heart and presence.

When we are totally absorbed in our own feelings and attached to our own view and agenda without recognizing it, it is virtually impossible to have a genuine communication. We will easily feel threatened by anyone who doesn't see things our way, and we will tend to be able to relate to only those people whose view of the world coincides with our own. We will find our encounters with people who hold strongly opposing views to be stressful. When we react by feeling personally threatened, it is easy to draw battle lines and have the relationship degenerate into "us" against "them." This makes the possibility of communication very difficult. When we lock in to certain restricted mind-sets, we cannot go beyond the nine dots and perceive the whole system of which we and our views are only a part. But when both sides in a relationship expand the domain of their thinking and are willing to consider the other side's point of view and keep in mind the system as a whole, then extraordinary new possibilities emerge as imaginary but all-too-limiting boundaries in the mind dissolve.

The possibility of attaining harmony in communication applies to large collections of people, such as nations, governments, and even to political parties, as well as to individuals, once they realize the price of treating the other as the enemy, and therefore less than human. How else to explain that countries that were previously at war trying to kill one another's citizens only two generations ago, such as the United States and Germany and Japan, are now so closely allied and their economies so intertwined? Or that apartheid could be ended in South Africa without a race war but with a vital Truth and Reconciliation Commission to reveal, name, confront, and hold in public awareness without recrimination the individual instances of enormous brutality and suffering that were perpetrated over decades—with the victims and the perpetrators voicing their pain and their sorrow face-to-face? How else to explain the greater channels of communication and trade between the United States and China, which were closed off to each other for so many years?

Even when one party takes responsibility for thinking of the whole system and the other does not, the whole system is altered and new possibilities for conflict resolution and mutual understanding may emerge. Of course, these potential openings can be short-lived, punctuated, even threatened and closed off by unilateral reversions to older and more autocratic ways of thinking and acting. We see examples of this every day in the news. Still, in spite of huge levels of resistance from those benefiting from the status quo, or who are ideologically fixated by a particular perspective, the overall picture for mutual understanding through communication is optimistic, I believe, as increasing virtual and real-life vehicles for sharing information and promoting social, economic, educational, and cultural exchange come to influence communication on a global scale, not only government to government, but group to group and individual to individual—witness the so-called Arab Spring in 2011 and its complex but hopeful aftermath, and the movements for greater democracy that are taking root, sometimes painfully so and against sometimes seemingly insurmountable obstacles, in so many countries. More and more, serious economists and political scientists are looking for overarching frameworks to understand these social, economic, and geopolitical trends, their origins and long-term promise. As one example, in his recent book *The Price of Civilization,* Jeffrey Sachs, a macroeconomist from Columbia University, makes a compelling case that mindfulness can serve as the primary vehicle for reconciling so many of the fundamental discordant elements that are threatening the well-being of the world and individual nations at every level. We will visit this subject in more detail in Chapter 32, on world stress.

When we arrive at the topics of people stress and difficulties in communication in the MBSR curriculum, usually in week six, we sometimes have the whole class divide up into pairs to engage in a series of awareness exercises originally adapted from the martial art of aikido by the late author and aikido practitioner George Leonard. These exercises help us to act out *with our bodies,* in partnership with another person, the experience of responding instead of reacting in threatening and stressful situations. We get to simulate different possible emotional action scenarios between two people, explore the energies of these different ways of being in relationship, and experience firsthand how they feel from the inside.

In aikido, the goal is to practice maintaining your own calm and grounded center while you are under physical attack. The challenge is to make use of the attacker's own irrational and imbalanced energy to dissipate his or her aggression without getting hurt yourself and also without harming the attacker. This involves being willing to move in close to the attacker and actually make contact with him or her while at the same time not placing yourself directly in the path of greatest danger, that is, right in front of the oncoming person.

The way we do these exercises in class, people take turns playing the role of the attacker and of the person who is the receiver of the attack. The way we structure it, in each scenario the attacking partner always represents a situation or person who is "running you over"—in other words, causing you stress, in other words, representing the stressor. The person being attacked (or stressed) then has various options that he or she can play out in response to the stressor. In each one, the attacker comes at the other person the very same way, that is, with arms stretched out in front and walking quickly straight toward the other person's shoulders, with the intention to give that person a significant "hit" or collision, in other words, as we said, to run the person over.

In the first scenario, as the attacker comes at you, you just lie down on the floor and say something like, "It's okay, do whatever you want, you're right, I'm to blame," or "Don't do it, it wasn't my fault, someone else did it." We observe what that feels like with a partner, with each of us taking each role in turn. People invariably find this scenario distasteful in both roles but admit that it is frequently acted out in the real world. Many people spontaneously share stories of feeling like the doormat in the family or feeling trapped in their own passivity, intimidated by powerful others. The attackers usually admit feeling pretty frustrated by this scenario, when the other person just submits and surrenders. They are seeking some connection and impact, and it just doesn't happen.

We then proceed to a scenario in which, when the attacker comes at you, you move out of the way at the very last minute, as fast as you can, so that he or she goes right by you. There is no physical contact. This usually causes the attackers to feel even more frustrated. They were expecting contact and they didn't get it. The people who got out of the way feel pretty good this time. At least they didn't get run over. But they also realize that you can't relate like this all the time or you will be avoiding and running away from stressful situations and people constantly. Couples often get into this kind of behavior with each other, one pursuing contact, the other rejecting or avoiding it at all costs. These aggressive and passive (and sometimes, as when you are always avoiding contact as a way of getting back at another person, passive-aggressive) roles, when they become deep habits, can be very painful for both parties because there is no contact, no communication. It is lonely and frustrating. Yet people can and do live out their lives relating habitually to other people through these basic passive and aggressive stances, even with those they are closest to.

In another scenario, instead of getting out of the way, you push back when you are attacked. You dig in your heels and resist. Both parties wind up pushing against each other's shoulders with straight arms. To intensify the situation and make it more emotionally charged, we might have people yell "I'm right, you're wrong" at each other as they are doing this. It rapidly becomes exhausting. When we stop action, close our eyes, and bring our attention to our bodies and our emotions in the moment, people invariably say, after they have caught their breath, that this scenario feels better than the one in which one person was being passive. At least in this one there is contact. They discover that while struggling is exhausting, it can also be exhilarating in its own way. We are making contact, standing up for ourselves, and letting our feelings out, and that feels good. When we do this exercise, it always seems a little clearer why so many of us are virtually addicted to—and stuck in—this way of relating. It can actually feel good, in a limited way.

But this exercise leaves us feeling empty too. Usually both people in a struggle think they are right. Each is trying to force the other to see it "my way." Both know deep down that the other person is not likely to come to see it differently, not out of forcing and intimidation and struggle. What does happen is that either we adjust to a life of perpetual struggle or one person submits every time, usually claiming that he or she is doing it to "save the relationship." We can even get caught in thinking that these patterns in our relationships are the way things have to be. Even if they are painful and exhausting, in some ways we might tend to feel comfortable and secure with what we already know, with the familiar. At least we don't have to face the unknown risks of choosing to see or do things differently and thereby threaten the status quo.

Too often we forget the physical and psychological costs of living like this, not only for the two parties in the relationship but for others who are connected to it as well, such as children and grandparents, who may be observing this kind of relating day in and day out and even taking the brunt of it. In the end, our lives can become bogged down in a very limited view of ourselves, our relationships, and our options. Perpetual struggle hardly seems a very good model for communication or for growth or change.

The last exercise in this series is called *entering and blending* in aikido. This option represents the mindfulness-mediated stress response as opposed to the various habitual stress reactions we have just touched on in the other scenarios. The gesture of entering and blending is based on being centered, on being awake and mindful. It requires that we be aware of the other person as a stressor without losing our own balance of mind or grounding in the body as a whole. We are also grounded in our breathing and in our seeing the situation in its entirety without reacting totally out of fear, even if fear is present, which it very likely is in our real-life stressful encounters with people. On a physical level, the entering and blending involves stepping *into* the attacker, positioning your feet so that you step toward but also slightly to the side of the attacker at the same time that you take hold of his or her outstretched wrist on the arm closest to you. In aikido this movement is the *entering*. By entering the attack, you manage to sidestep the brunt of it at the same time that you move in close and make secure and authoritative contact. You are fully engaged. The very positioning of your body is making a statement that you are willing to encounter and work with what is happening, that you will not be run over. You don't try to control the attacker with brute force. Instead you take hold of his or her wrist and then proceed to "blend" with the attacker's energy by rotating your body, turning with his or her momentum so that you wind up with both of you facing in the same direction. You still have the other's wrist firmly in hand. At this moment you are both seeing the same thing because you are looking in the same direction. For a moment you are sharing the same perspective—that of the attacker.

One of the virtues of entering and blending in this way is that you avoid a head-on impact, in which you might be badly hurt or overwhelmed by the sheer momentum of the other person, yet you also are also engaging fully and making firm contact. And by being willing to *move* with his or her momentum by *turning,* you are communicating, metaphorically, with your body, that you are willing to see things from his or her perspective, that you are receptive and willing to look and listen. This allows the attacker to maintain his or her integrity, but at the same time, it communicates that you are not afraid of making contact, nor are you willing to let his or her energy overwhelm or harm you. At this moment you become partners rather than adversaries, whether the other person (the attacker) knows it or not, or wants to or not.

Of course, having gotten to this point through entering and blending, you still have no idea what will happen in the next moment—but now you have a number of options. One possibility is to turn the attacker as his or her energy winds down, using your point of contact, your grip on the attacker's wrist, to effect another turn of the two of you together, so that now you are showing that person how *you* see things—since you are now both facing in another direction. What happens next becomes a dance. We actually don't know what will transpire. You are not totally in control and neither is the other person. But by maintaining your center, you are at least in control of yourself in the present moment and therefore much less vulnerable to harm. You can't have much of a plan for what to do next because so much depends on the situation itself. You have to trust in your imagination and your ability to come up with new ways of seeing right in that moment.

Of course, you shouldn't try this in real life if you are under physical attack unless you a highly trained in the martial art of aikido. Even then, the most evolved response would be to turn and walk away, or run away if you have to. This would be true even among high-ranking black belts. It is called wisdom.

The exercises I am describing here are meant metaphorically. If you can remember to enter and blend, to step slightly to the side and take hold and turn when you are feeling under assault by this or that communication or circumstance, you will find you have many more options for responding rather than reacting in highly charged, stressful situations, especially when they involve communicating with other people who have a perspective or agenda very different from your own.

I once had an immediate supervisor in the hospital, when I had just started the Stress Reduction Clinic and before I joined the faculty of the medical school, whose way of relating was to say things like "you son of a bitch" with a big smile on his face. He caused me a lot of stress because his hostility prevented us from having an effective working relationship. But I came to realize, after a few very unsatisfying attempts at communicating my needs to him, that he had no idea he was being hostile. He would drive the people who reported to him to distraction and despair. Often they would have terrible arguments with him and go away feeling angry, hurt, and, above all frustrated at not being supported, or even seen and acknowledged. It was exceedingly unprofessional. One day in his office, when I met with him to have him sign off on something routine that I needed for the clinic, he smiled as he said something hostile to me. There and then, I decided to call him on it. Very gently but matter-of-factly, I asked him if he was aware that every time he related to me, he said something that put me down. I also took the opportunity to tell him, with as much candor as I could muster, that I kept getting the sense that he didn't like me personally and that he disapproved of the work I was doing with meditation and yoga and my attempts to build an effective Stress Reduction Clinic for the hospital.

His response to this was utter amazement. He genuinely had no idea that he had been calling me names and had been giving me the feeling that he didn't like me and disapproved of what I was doing. As a result of this one conversation, our working relationship improved a good deal and became much less stressful for me. We came to understand each other better, in part because I chose to name, and then enter and blend with his unconscious attacks rather than resist them and mount an all-out assault of my own in return because I was feeling angry, hurt, and frustrated. The other people he supervised also found him to be easier to relate to after that incident. And when he left the hospital for another job, he actually asked me to write a letter of recommendation for him. I did, happily.

The path of entering and blending in moments when you feel attacked or threatened in some way obviously involves taking certain risks, since you can't know what the protagonist will do next nor how you will respond. But if you are committed to meeting each moment mindfully, with as much calmness and acceptance as possible, and with a sense of your own integrity and balance, fresh and imaginative solutions that might lead to a new level of understanding and to greater harmony often come to mind as you need them. Partly this requires being in touch with your feelings and accepting them, even acknowledging them and sharing them, as appropriate, in ways that are not hostile and defensive in their own right. This capacity for being in wise relationship to your thoughts and feelings and to the thoughts and feelings of others who might see things very differently from the way you do is known as *emotional intelligence.* When one person in an adversarial relationship takes responsibility for relating differently, the entire dynamic of the relationship changes, even if the other person is completely unwilling to engage in this way. The very fact that you are seeing differently and holding your own center in the face of the unwanted and the difficult and the threatening means that you yourself are much less caught up in emotional reactivity and in trying to force an issue or an outcome, even one that is desirable for you. Why let the momentum of another person's agenda catapult you into a severe imbalance of body and mind just at the moment when you need all your inner resources for being clear and strong?

The patience, wisdom, and firmness that can come out of a moment of mindfulness in the heat of a stressful interpersonal situation yield fruit almost immediately, because the other person usually senses that you cannot be intimidated or overwhelmed. He or she will feel your calmness and self-confidence and willingness to step in, to enter, and engage—and will in all likelihood be drawn *toward* it because it embodies openhearted presence and equanimity, an inner peacefulness and balance that is in subtle ways contagious. Again, we are not speaking of an ideal state here, but of a way of being in relationship, an ongoing, ever-unfolding practice in its own right—simply mindfulness brought to relationality. We may "fail" at it over and over again, yet each time, if we stay open, we learn and grow stronger, and wiser.

When you are willing to be secure enough in yourself to listen to what other people want and how they see things without constantly reacting, objecting, arguing, fighting, resisting, making yourself right and them wrong, they will feel heard, welcomed, accepted, met. This feels good to anybody. They will then be much more likely to hear what you have to say as well, maybe not right away, but as soon as the emotions recede a little. There will be more of a chance for communication and for an actual communion of sorts, a meeting of minds, and an acknowledging and coming to terms with differences. In this way, your mindfulness practice can have a healing effect on your relationships.

Relationships can heal just like bodies and minds can heal. Fundamentally, this is done through love, kindness, and acceptance. But in order to promote healing in relationships or to develop the effective communication such healing depends on, you will have to cultivate an awareness of the *energy* of relationships, including the domains of minds and bodies, thoughts, feelings, speech, likes and dislikes, motives, and goals—not only other people's but also your own—as they unfold from moment to moment in the present. If you hope to heal or resolve the stress associated with your interactions with other people, whoever they may be, whether they are your children or your parents, your spouse, your ex-spouse, your boss, your colleagues, your friends, or your neighbors, mindfulness of communication becomes of paramount importance. It is the heart of emotional intelligence.

One good way to increase mindfulness of communication is to keep a log of stressful communications for a week. We have people do this in the week preceding the class on communication (fifth week). The assignment is to be aware of one stressful communication a day at the time that it is happening. This involves an awareness of the person with whom you are having the difficulty, how it came about, what you really wanted from the person or situation, what the other person wanted from you, an awareness of what was actually happening and what came out of it, as well as how you were feeling at the time it was happening. These items are recorded each day in a workbook and we then share and discuss them in class. (See the sample calendar in the Appendix.)

People come in with many rich observations about their patterns of communication that they had not been very conscious of before. Just keeping track of stressful communications and your thoughts, feelings, and behavior while they are happening provides major clues about how you might behave differently to optimize your aspirations more effectively. By this point in the program, some people are realizing that much of their stress comes from not knowing how to be assertive about their own priorities when interacting with others. They may not even know how to communicate what they are really feeling, or they feel that they don't have a right to feel what they are feeling. Or they may feel afraid about expressing their feelings honestly. Some feel absolutely incapable of ever saying no to other people, even though they know that to say yes means that their own resources will be taxed to the limit or beyond. They feel guilty doing something for themselves or having plans of their own. They are always ready to serve others at the expense of themselves, not because they have transcended their own physical and psychological needs and have become saints, but because they believe that that is what they "should" do to be a "good person." Sad to say, this often means that they are always helping other people but feel incapable of nourishing or helping themselves. That would be too "selfish," too self-centered. Thus, they put other people's feelings first, but for the wrong reasons. Deep down they may be running away from themselves by serving other people, or they may be doing it to gain approval from others or because they were taught and now think that that is the way to be a "good person." This is a kind of faux selflessness.

This behavior can create enormous stress because you are not replenishing your inner resources, nor are you aware of your attachments to the role you have adopted. You can exhaust yourself running around "doing good" and helping others, and in the end be so depleted that you are incapable of doing any good at all and unable to help even yourself. It's not the doing things for others that is the source of the stress here. It is the lack of peace and harmony in your mind as you engage in doing all the doing.

If you decide that you have to say "No" more often and define certain limits in your relationships so that you might bring your life into greater balance, you will discover that there are a lot of ways you might do it. Many ways of saying no cause more problems than they solve. If you react to demands from others by saying no in an angry way, you create bad feelings all around and more stress. Often when we feel put upon, we automatically attack the other person in return, making him or her feel blamed, or threatened, or inadequate. The use of abrasive language and tone of voice contribute to this attack. Usually the first thing we do is react by saying no. Adamantly. In some circumstances you might even find yourself calling the other person names. Here is where assertiveness training can be very useful. What assertiveness training amounts to is mindfulness of feelings, speech, and actions.

Assertiveness is predicated on the assumption that you can be in touch with what you are actually feeling. It goes far beyond whether you can say no when you want to. It concerns your deepest ability to know yourself and to read situations appropriately and face them consciously. If you have an awareness of your feelings as feelings, then it becomes possible to break out of the passive or hostile modes that so automatically rear up when you feel put upon or threatened. So the first step in becoming more assertive is to practice knowing how you are actually feeling. In other words, practice mindfulness of your own feeling states. This is not so easy, especially if you have been conditioned your whole life to believe that it is wrong to have certain kinds of thoughts or feelings in the first place.

Every time they come up, the reflex is to go unconscious and lose your awareness completely. Alternatively, you may condemn yourself inwardly, feel guilty about what you are feeling, and try to hide what you are really feeling from others. You may get stuck in your own beliefs about good and bad and end up denying or suppressing your feelings.

The first lesson in assertiveness is that your feelings are simply your feelings! They are neither good nor bad. "Good" and "bad" are just judgments that you or others impose on your feelings. To act assertively really requires a non-judgmental awareness of your feelings just as they are. This is itself an embodiment of self-compassion, kindness, and ultimately, wisdom.

Many men grew up in a world in which there was an overriding message that "real men" don't have—and therefore should not show—certain kinds of feelings. This social conditioning makes it very difficult for boys and men to be aware of their true feelings a lot of the time because their feelings are "unacceptable" and therefore very quickly edited out, denied, or repressed. This makes it particularly difficult to communicate effectively at highly emotionally charged times, such as when we are feeling threatened or vulnerable and when we experience grief or sorrow or hurt.

Our best chance of breaking out of this dilemma is for us to suspend the judging and editing of our emotions as we become aware of doing this, and instead to risk listening to our feelings and accepting them as they are, because they are already here. But, of course, this means we have to want to be more open and more honest, at least with ourself, and then perhaps to communicate differently out of our own more embodied awareness of how we see things and how we feel about them.

Even in situations that are not threatening, men can have a hard time communicating their feelings. We have been so conditioned to devalue communicating our true feelings that we often forget that it is even possible. We just plunge ahead with what we are doing and expect people to *know* what we want or what we are feeling without our having to say it. Or we don't care; we do what we do and let the consequences fall where they may. It can threaten our autonomy to tell other people our plans or our intentions or our feelings. This behavior can be a source of endless exasperation to women.

When you know what you are feeling and have practiced reminding yourself that your feelings are just feelings and that they are okay to have and to feel, then you can begin to explore ways of being true to your feelings without letting them create more problems for you. They create problems both when you become passive and discount them and when you become aggressive and inflate and overreact to them. To be assertive and act out of emotional intelligence means to know your feelings *and* to be able to communicate them in a way that allows you to maintain your integrity without threatening the integrity of others. For example, if you know that you want to or need to say no in a particular situation, you can practice saying it in such a way that you are not using it as a weapon. You might first try informing the other person that you would be glad to fulfill the request if the circumstances were different (if this is in fact the case), or you might in some other way acknowledge that you respect the other person and his or her needs. You do not have to tell the other person why you are saying no, but you can choose to if you want to.

When being assertive, it is very helpful to remember to say how you are feeling or seeing the situation by making "I" statements rather than "you" statements. "I" statements convey information about your feelings and views. Such statements are not wrong; they are simply statements of your feelings. But if you are uncomfortable with your feelings, you might wind up blaming how you are feeling on the other person without even knowing it. Then you may find yourself saying things like "You make me so angry" or "You are always making demands on me."

Can you see that this is saying that the other person is in control of *your* feelings? You are literally handing power over your feelings to another person and not taking responsibility for your end of the relationship, a dynamic that obviously includes both of you.

An alternative might be to say something like "I feel so angry when you say this or do that." This is more accurate. It says how you feel in response to something. This leaves the other person room to hear what you are saying about how you see and feel without feeling blamed or attacked and without being told that he or she has more power than he or she actually has.

Maybe the other person won't understand. But at least you have made the attempt to communicate without doing battle. This is where the dance begins, just as with the aikido. What you do or say next will depend on the particular circumstances. But if you maintain mindfulness of the entire situation and of your own thoughts and feelings, you will be much more likely to steer your way through to some kind of understanding, accommodation, or agreement to disagree without losing or surrendering your dignity and integrity—either through being passive or through being aggressive.

The most important part of effective communication is to be mindful of your own thoughts, feelings, speech, and body language, as well as of the situation. It is also crucial to remember that you and your "position" are part of a larger social system. If you expand the field of awareness to include the whole system, this will allow you to see and honor the other person's point of view as well as to *feel with* (i.e., empathize with) his or her thoughts and emotions. Then you may be better able to listen and really hear, to see and comprehend, to speak and know what you are saying, and to act effectively and assertively, with dignity and with respect for the other as a whole human being. Most of the time cultivating this approach—which we might call *The Way of Awareness*—can resolve potential conflicts and create greater harmony and mutual respect. In the process, you are much more likely to get what you want and what you need from your encounters with other people. And so are they!

29

Role Stress

One of our biggest obstacles to effective communication, one that prevents us from even *knowing* our true feelings, is that we easily get stuck in our various personal and professional roles. Either we have no awareness of this or we feel helpless to break out of the rigid constraints they can impose on our attitudes and behaviors. Roles have a momentum of their own, the momentum of the past, the way other people have done things, the expectations we hold for ourselves and how we should do things or that we think other people hold for how we should act. Men can unconsciously take on habitual roles with women, and women with men, parents with their children, and children with their parents. Work roles, group roles, professional roles, social roles, roles we might adopt in illness—all can be confining if we have no awareness of them and how they mold our behavior in so many different situations.

Role stress is a side effect of our ingrained habits of doing when the domain of being gets eclipsed. It can be a major obstacle to our continued development as a human being, what some might call psychological or even spiritual growth, and a source of much frustration and suffering as well. We all have strong views about who we are, about our situations, about what we do and how things should be done, what the parameters are within which we can work, what the rules of the game are, and also how confining they can be. Usually these are colored by very strong beliefs about what can and cannot be done, what constitutes appropriate behavior in a particular situation, what we would feel comfortable with, and what it means to be a ___________, where you fill in the blank: mother, father, child, sibling, spouse, boss, worker, lover, athlete, teacher, lawyer, judge, priest, patient, man, woman, manager, executive, leader, doctor, surgeon, politician, artist, banker, conservative, radical, liberal, capitalist, socialist, older person, grandparent, elder.

All these ways of acting in the world can have a stylized component to them, often a set of unwritten expectations that we have of ourselves about what it means to be "good" at what we do. Each role can convey an identity, as well as a mantle of importance or authority or power. While some of this is basic to knowing the role or the calling, much of it is merely posturing, a creation of our own mind more than anything else, an attaching of a particular view and expectation to ourself that we then act out and get caught up in. If we fail to perceive that we may be treading this path, such entanglements can wind up causing us much distress and prevent us from being who we really are while doing what we need to do. The momentum and demands of our roles, coupled with these self-imposed unconscious expectations, can drive us to the point where our roles can feel highly constraining, sometimes even like prisons of our own making, rather than vehicles for expressing the fullness of our being and our wisdom and the unique ways in which we might share it with the world.

Mindfulness can help us to extricate ourselves from the negative effects of excessive role stress because, once again, much of the stress comes from unawareness, partial seeing, or misperception. When we are able to observe our own involvement in the stress that we blame on our roles, then we will be able to act in imaginative ways to restore balance and harmony and get unstuck.

This happened dramatically in class one day during the pushing exercises. Abe, a sixty-four-year-old rabbi who came to the clinic with heart disease and who was recently having a lot of trouble in his relationships with people, had a difficult time with the entering and blending exercise described in the last chapter. After attempting it with a partner, he just stood still, looking bewildered. His body reflected his state of confusion. Then all of a sudden he exclaimed out loud, "That's what it is! I never turn! I'm afraid I will get hurt if I turn!"

He had realized that he wasn't turning when he was being attacked, that his body was rigid when he attempted to take hold of the other person's wrist. This was why there was no harmonious blending of his energy with his "attacker's."

Then, in a metaphorical flash of insight, he connected this to his relationships in general. He saw that he never "turns" in his relationships, that he is always rigid, that he only holds his point of view, even as he plays at seeing the other person's. And all because he has a fear of being hurt.

Then Abe took it one step further. He said, pointing to his partner in the exercise, "I could trust him. He's trying to help me."

Abe shook his head, dumbfounded, as the whole experience took hold and he saw its ramifications. He called it a new type of learning for him. His body had taught him something in a matter of minutes that words could never have accomplished. For one moment, it had released him from a role he is so enmeshed in that he can almost never see it. Now he has to keep this newfound awareness alive and find alternative ways of relating to people and to potential conflict.

Sometimes it is easy to feel that the role you feel confined in is the worst possible role. We readily project that other people in other roles or even in the same role never have the kinds of problems that we do—but it's not true. Just talking with other people who are in your situation or to people who are feeling stress in entirely different situations can be healing, because it puts things in a larger perspective. We feel less isolated and less alone in our suffering. We learn that other people feel as we do, that they too are in or have been in similar roles and circumstances.

If you are willing to discuss your roles, other people can mirror your situation back to you and help you to see new options, ones your mind may have edited out for you as being "unthinkable." They are unthinkable only because your mind is so attached to one way of seeing or because you are so unconscious of your roles that you can't see them at all.

One day in class, a woman in her mid-forties who was referred with heart disease and panic attacks recounted her trials with one of her grown-up sons, who was being extremely abusive of her but who refused to move out of the house, although she and her husband wanted him to. They were in an ongoing stalemate, with the son refusing to leave, and the mother alternatively telling him to leave and feeling guilty about not wanting him around and fearful about what might happen to him if he did leave. Her disclosure occasioned a spontaneous outpouring of sympathy and advice from other people in the class who had been through similar situations. They tried to help her to realize that her love for her child was preventing her from seeing clearly that he needed to leave and was even asking her, by his behavior, to kick him out into the world. But the love of a parent is so strong that often it can lead to being stuck in a role and dynamic that is no longer working, no longer helpful to either the child or the parent.

We suffer in all sorts of roles. Usually it is not the role per se but rather our relationship to it that makes it stressful. Ideally we want to make use of our roles as opportunities; opportunities to do good work, to learn and to grow, and to help others. But we need to be wary of identifying so strongly with one view or one feeling that it blinds us to seeing the full extent of what is actually happening and narrows our options, confining us to self-created ruts that ultimately frustrate us and prevent us from growing.

Every role has a particular set of potential stressors that goes with the territory. For instance, let's say you are in a role at work that identifies you as a leader and innovator, as a hard-driving problem solver. If you succeed in bringing your enterprise to the point where things are more or less under control, it may leave you feeling uncomfortable and out of sorts. You may be one of those people who function best under pressure, with constant threats, crises, and impending disasters to which they can devote their full energies. You may not know how to accommodate yourself to situations in which you have already succeeded at bringing some stability to the scene. You may continue to be hard-driving and seek out new windmills to tilt at, just to feel comfortable and engaged. Such a pattern may be a sign that you are becoming stuck in a particular role. Perhaps by this point you are only feeding a chronic addiction for work while devaluing your other roles and obligations.

If this work addiction results in an erosion of the quality of family life, for instance, it may be sowing the seeds of much unhappiness. You may find that you are very successful in some arenas while at the same time you are not relating well to your children or to your spouse anymore, or your grandchildren, just as we saw with Dr. Eliot, the cardiologist in Chapter 26 on time stress. You may find a gulf broadening between you. Your mind may be full of details about work, absorbed in your own problems that they don't even know about or wouldn't find interesting. You may not be around very much, either physically or psychically. You may not even know that much about their lives anymore, about what they are feeling and what they are going through each day. Without even knowing it, you may gradually have lost your ability to tune in to the people you love and who love you the most, perhaps even your ability to express your feelings for them. You may have become stuck in your work role and unable to operate in your many other life roles comfortably. And you may even have forgotten what is most important to you. You may even have forgotten who you are.

All people who are in positions of power and authority in their work lives run the risk of this kind of alienation. We call this "the stress of success." The power, control, attention, and respect you get in your professional role can become intoxicating and addicting. It's hard to make the transition from being the authority who commands, dictates, and makes consequential decisions that influence people and institutional policies to being a father or mother, a husband or wife, a role in which you are just a regular person. Your family won't be too impressed that you make million-dollar decisions or are an important and influential person. You still have to take out the garbage, do the dishes, and spend time with the kids, be a regular human being, just like everybody else. Your family knows who you really are. They know the good, the bad, and the ugly, the kind of things you can conceal in your work life to make yourself look a certain way, more perfect, more authoritative. They see you when you are confused and unsure of yourself, stressed, sick, upset, angry, depressed. They love you for who you are, not for what you do. But they may miss you deeply and become alienated from you if you undervalue your role in the family and forget how to let go of your professional persona. In fact, if you get too lost in your work role, or too attached to it and what it satisfies in you, you may wind up jeopardizing your relationships to the point where the gulfs you create may become impossible to bridge. By that time, of course, no one may want to even make the effort anymore.

The clash of your multiple roles and their tug in different directions is one ongoing manifestation of the full catastrophe in this brave new world we are continually reinventing at warp speed now. It has to be faced and worked with. Some kind of balance has to be struck. Without awareness of the potential dangers of role stress, the damage may be done long before you come to realize what is happening. This is one reason there is so much alienation between men and women in families, between parents and young children, and between adult children and elderly parents. It is certainly possible to grow and change within our roles without abandoning them. But roles can become confining and can limit further growth if we lock ourselves or each other into them.

If we bring awareness to our various roles, we will be more likely to function effectively without getting stuck in them. We might even risk being ourselves in all our various roles. We might at some point feel secure enough to be true to ourselves and be more authentic in everything we choose to do. Of course, this means being willing to see and let go of old baggage that no longer works for us. Perhaps you have gotten stuck in a bad-guy role, a victim role, a doormat role, a weak-person role, the role of the incompetent one, the dominant one, the big authority, the hero, the one who is always busy, the one who is always rushing, who has no time, or the role of the sick person, or the sufferer. Whenever you have had enough of this, you can decide to bring an element of wise attention to these roles. You can practice letting go of them and allowing yourself to expand to the full extent of your being by changing the way you actually do things and respond to things. There is really only one way to do this. It takes a ruthless and, at the same time, kind and self-compassionate commitment to seeing your own impulses to go for the familiar, to fall into habitual patterns and confining mind-sets, and a willingness to let go of them in the very moments when they arise. As Abe saw so clearly, you have to turn, turn, turn to stay fresh and avoid the ruts.

Maybe there is something to be learned from the fact that the Chinese character for "breakthrough" is written as "turning."

30

Work Stress

All the potential stressors that we have examined so far, including time pressures, other people, and confining roles, converge in the work arena. They can be sorely compounded by our need to make money. Most of us have to do something to earn a living, and most jobs are at least potentially stressful in a variety of ways. But work is also a way of connecting with the larger world, a way of doing something useful, of making some kind of contribution of labor and effort to a meaningful endeavor, which hopefully has its own rewards beyond those of merely a paycheck. The sense of contributing something, perhaps by feeding people, or helping them get where they need to go, or caring for their health, or being of help in other ways—a sense of creating, of putting our knowledge and skills to work—can help us to feel a part of something bigger, something worth working for. If we could see our own work in this way, it might make it more tolerable, even under difficult circumstances, or better still, deeply satisfying.

People who can't work at all because of illness or injury often feel they would give anything to be working again, to not have to stay in bed or go stir-crazy around the house. When you are limited in your ability to get out and connect in this way, almost any job can seem worth having. We often forget or take for granted that work can lend meaning and coherence to our lives. The meaning and coherence it provides are in proportion to how much we care about and believe in it. And in periods of high unemployment, of course, the need for work and the indignities and travails of being laid off and of not being able to find another job, or to have to work for a much lower salary than before at something one may not want to be doing, creates enormous levels of personal as well as family and social stress in our society.

As we know, some jobs are particularly demeaning and exploitative. Some working conditions are highly toxic to either physical or psychological health or both. Work can be dangerous to your health. Some studies show that men (these particular studies were done on men) in jobs that have little decision-making latitude but high standards of performance—such as a waiter, an office computer operator, or a short-order cook—show a higher prevalence of heart attacks than men in jobs with more control. This is true independent of age and other factors, such as cigarette smoking.

But even if you have a job with a lot of autonomy and a good salary and you are doing things that you care about, even love to do, work always presents its unique challenges and lets you know that you are never completely in control, even if you think you are. The law of impermanence still applies. Things still change. You can't control that. There are always people or forces that can disrupt your work, threaten your job and your role, or make what you said one day "inoperable" the next, no matter how much power you may think you have accumulated. Moreover, there are usually intrinsic limits to how much you can do to change things or resist certain changes within organizations and industries, even if it objectively looks as if you have a lot of power and influence. Just think for a moment about how difficult it is, even if you wanted to, to regulate Wall Street and the global financial industry for the sake of stability. Even the president of the United States is unable to do it, and may not want to. Think of the recession of 2008, triggered and then compounded by clever people in the banking industry and the housing market intoxicated by the prospect of selling houses on a massive level to people who they knew couldn't afford them, ultimately draining the savings of so much of the world's middle class and putting so many people out of work. Balance and a measure of sanity may eventually be restored, but the harm to individual people can be colossal, and lasting. And this tends to happen in cycles because the collective memory for such object lessons in business and finance is very short. This itself is a kind of disease, brought on by the human mind when it loses its moral compass, as can happen so easily in work settings under all the competing pressures to "succeed," and to "grow the business."

At the level of the individual person at work, job stress, insecurity, frustration, and failure can be experienced in any job and at any pay grade, from janitor to chief executive, from waiter, factory worker, or bus driver to lawyer, doctor, scientist, police chief, or politician. Many jobs are intrinsically stressful, as we have seen, because of the combination of low decision-making latitude and high responsibility. To correct this requires reorganizing the job itself or compensating the employees better to make it more tolerable. Yet, given that many job descriptions will not be rewritten in the short run to lower employee stress, people are forced to cope as best they can using their own resources. The degree to which you are affected by such stressful circumstances can be influenced positively by your own coping skills. As we saw in Part III, the level of psychological stress you experience depends on how you interpret things—in other words, on your attitude, on whether you are able to flow with change or, on the other hand, make every ripple in the way things are unfolding into an occasion for fighting or worrying or falling into despair.

If we are not careful, we can burn out at any job, no matter how much control and decision-making authority it looks like we have. Often it is because we are entrained over time to try to get more and more and even more done in the finite twenty-four hours that each of us has, no matter what. This is especially so in this era of the unending barrage of electronic communications that are driving work, or more likely, if we are not careful, impeding it, in the sense of our getting any real work done, so caught up are we in self-distraction and in multitasking, which just reduce our capacity to get anything done well. Tony Schwartz, author and longtime student of performance and excellence in business, writes in the *New York Times* that studies show that "paradoxically, the best way to get more done may be to spend more time doing less. . . . strategic renewal—including daytime workouts, short afternoon naps, longer sleep hours, more time away from the office, and longer and more frequent vacations—boosts productivity, job performance, and, of course, health." In other words, we have to develop personal strategies for conserving our energy and attention, renewing those resources, and avoid perpetually distracting ourselves, or working so continuously that our actual performance suffers. And obviously, it takes moment-to-moment awareness of what is happening within us and around us to be able to shift our relationship to it all in a healthier direction. But it is easier said than done unless we are practicing mindfulness in all aspects of our lives.

If you have a job, to cope effectively with work stress practically requires that you look at your situation with eyes of wholeness, no matter what the particulars of your employment may be. It can help keep things in perspective if you ask yourself from time to time, "What is the job I am really doing and how can I best do it under the circumstances I find myself in?" As we have seen, we can easily fall into ruts in our roles, especially if we have held the same job for a long time. If we do not guard against it, we may stop seeing each moment as new, each day as an adventure. Instead, we may become susceptible to feeling drowned in the repetitiveness and predictability of each day. We may find ourselves resisting innovation and change and becoming overly protective of what we have built because we feel threatened by new ideas or changing standards and rules, or by new people coming in.

It is not uncommon for us to operate on autopilot in our work in the same way that we do at other times in our lives. Why should we expect to be fully awake and living in the moment at work if mindfulness is not something we value in our lives as a whole? As we have seen, the automatic pilot mode may get us through our days, but it won't help us with the feeling of being worn down by all the pressures, the routines, the monotony and sameness of what we may be doing from day to day, especially if we feel alienated from its larger purpose. We can feel just as stuck at work as in other domains in our lives. Or even more so. We may feel that we don't have alternatives, that we are limited by economic realities, by our own earlier life choices, by all sorts of things that prevent us from changing jobs or advancing or doing what we really want to be doing. But we may not be as stuck as we think. Work stress can be greatly reduced in many cases simply by an intentional commitment to cultivate calmness and awareness in the domain of work and by letting mindfulness guide our actions and our responses to all the stressors we have to deal with or tolerate. We can become less reactive and rely more on our sense of agency.

As we have seen over and over again, our own mind can produce more limitations for us than there are in actuality. While we all live within certain economic realities and the need to make a living doing what we are able to do, we often don't know what those limits really are, just as we don't know what the limits of our body's ability to heal really are. What we do know is that clarity of vision usually doesn't hurt, and it may provide fresh insights as to what might be possible. We can train ourselves to see openings, and not just limitations and barriers to satisfying change.

Bringing the meditation practice into your work life can make for major improvements in the quality of your life at work no matter what your job. You do not always have to get out of a stressful job for your work life to start to change in positive ways. Sometimes simply deciding, as an experiment, to make your work part of your meditation practice, part of your work on yourself, can shift the balance from a sense of being done in by the job to a sense of knowing what you are doing and choosing to do it. This change in perspective can lead directly to a change in what your job means to you. Work can become a vehicle that you are purposefully using to learn and to grow. Obstacles then become challenges and opportunities, frustrations occasions to practice patience and compassion, what other people are doing or not doing occasions to be assertive and communicate effectively, and power struggles occasions to watch the play of greed, aversion, and unawareness in other people and in yourself. Of course, sometimes you may have to leave a job because it is not worth the effort to pursue such a path, given the circumstances.

When you introduce mindfulness as the thread guiding your seeing and your actions from moment to moment and from day to day, at work, as you get up in the morning and prepare to go to work, and as you leave to come home, work really becomes something you are *choosing* to do, every day, in a way that goes beyond the necessity of having a job to make money or to "get somewhere" in life. You are bringing the same attitudes that we have been cultivating as the foundation of mindfulness in other aspects of life into your work life in a seamless merging of moments. Rather than having work run your life completely, you are now in a position to be in greater balance with it.

True, there are obligations and responsibilities and pressures that you have to face and deal with, which may be beyond your control, and which may cause you stress, but is that not the same in every other aspect of your life as well? If it were not one set of pressures, would it not be another after a short time? You need to eat. You need connection to the larger world one way or another. There will always be some aspect of the full catastrophe to be faced somewhere, sometime. It is *how* you face it that matters.

When you begin to look at work mindfully, whether you work for yourself, for a big institution, or for a little one, whether you work inside a building or outside, whether you love your job or hate it, you are bringing all your inner resources to bear on your working day. This will allow you to take more of a problem-solving approach as you go along, and thus to cope better with the stressors at work. Then, even if you come to a point where you have to face a big life transition, perhaps because you were fired from your job or were laid off or you decided to quit or to go out on strike, you will be better prepared to meet these changes, hard as they are, with balance, strength, and awareness. You will be better prepared to handle the emotional turmoil and reactivity that invariably accompany major life crises and transitions. Since you have to go through difficult times anyway if such things happen to you, you might as well have all your resources and strength at your disposal to deal with them as best you can.

Many people come to the Stress Reduction Clinic because of stress-related problems stemming from pressures at work. Not uncommonly, they may first see their primary care physician for one or more persistent physical complaints, such as palpitations, nervous stomach, headaches, and chronic insomnia, with the expectation that the doctor will diagnose the problem and treat it, fixing what is wrong with them. When the physician suggests that it is nothing serious, "just stress," it is very easy to feel incensed and indignant.

One man, the plant manager of the largest high-tech manufacturing firm of its kind in the country, came to the clinic with complaints of dizzy spells at work and a feeling that his life was "spinning out of control." When his doctor suggested that his symptoms were due to job stress, he wouldn't believe it at first. Even though he had responsibility for the production efficiency of the entire plant, he denied feeling stressed. While there were certainly things that bothered him at work, they were "no big deal." He suspected he might have a brain tumor or something "physical" causing his problems. He said, "I thought there had to be something wrong with me internally. . . . When you feel like you're about to fall down on the job and you're looking to grab something, you say, 'Stress is one thing, but there has got to be something really wrong for this to happen.'" He felt so bad physically at work and was wound up so tight mentally by the time he left to go home at night that he would frequently have to pull his truck over to the side of the road to regain control of himself. He thought he was losing his mind. He also thought he was going to die from lack of sleep. He described himself as being up for days at a time. He would watch the news until 11:30 and then go to bed. He might sleep for one hour, perhaps from 2:00 to 3:00 a.m. Then he would be awake thinking about what the next day was going to bring. His wife recognized that he was under a lot of stress, but somehow he was unwilling to see it that way, perhaps because he just couldn't believe that stress could make him feel so bad. It was also inconsistent with his role, and with his image of himself as a strong leader. When he was referred to the clinic, he had been having problems at work for about three years, and things were reaching a breaking point.

By the time the course ended, he was no longer having dizzy spells and he was sleeping soundly through the night. Things changed in about the fourth week, when he heard other people in his class describing the same things he was feeling and their success at regulating them and feeling more in control. He began to entertain the notion that perhaps he too could do something to regulate his own body and bring the symptoms he was having under greater control. He came to realize that, indeed, his symptoms really were directly related to stress at work. He began to see that he felt worse toward the end of the month, when the shipments had to go out, the profits had to be tallied, and the pressure was on. At those times, he would find himself running around like crazy getting his employees "cooking," as he put it. But because he was practicing the meditation daily, he was now aware of what he was doing and feeling, and he found he could use awareness of his breathing to relax and break the automatic stress reaction cycle before it built up too much.

Looking back on it when the course was over, he felt that it was his attitude toward his work, more than anything else, that had changed. He attributed this to the fact that he was paying more attention to his body and to what was bothering him. He began to see himself and his mind and behavior in a new light, and realized that he didn't have to take things so seriously. He would tell himself, "The most they can do is fire me. Let's not worry about it. I'm doing the best I can. Let's take it day by day." He would use his breathing to keep himself calm and centered, to keep himself from reaching what he called "that point of no return." When he recognizes that he is in a stressful situation, now he finds that he can immediately feel himself tensing up in the shoulders and say to himself, "Slow down, let's gear it back a little." As he explained to me, "I can back right off it now. I don't even have to go sit down. I can just do it. I can be talking to someone and go right into a state of relaxation."

His change in perspective is reflected in how he goes to work in the morning. He started taking back roads, driving more slowly, doing his breathing on the way in to work. By the time he gets there, he is ready for the day. He used to take the main roads through the city, as he put it, "fighting with people at the lights." Now he can see and admit to himself that in the past he was actually a nervous wreck even before he reached work. He feels like a different person now, he says, ten years younger. His wife can't believe it and neither can he.

He was shocked to think that things could have gotten as bad as they did, that he could have gotten into such an "unbelievable state of mind." "I used to be the calmest person when I was a kid. Then gradually things at work crept up on me, especially as the money got bigger and bigger. I wish I had taken this program ten years ago."

But it wasn't just his attitude toward work and his awareness of his reactivity that changed. He took steps to communicate more effectively with his employees and made real changes in the way things were getting done. "After I was practicing the meditation for a few weeks, I came to the decision that it was time to start putting more trust into the people who work for me, that I just had to. I called a big meeting and said, 'Look, you guys, you are getting paid a lot of money to do these jobs and I'm not carrying you anymore. This is what I expect, bang bang bang bang, and if it's too much, we'll get more people, but this is what has to be done and we're all going to get it together and we are going to work as a team.' And it's working out all right. They don't do it 100 percent the way you'd like, but it gets done anyway and you have to be willing to bend and live with that. That's life, I guess. I am able to be much more efficient, and we are making big money." So now he feels that he is more productive on the job even though he is experiencing far less stress. He had seen that he was wasting a lot of time doing things that other people should have been doing. "To be a manager of a plant, you have to be doing the right things to keep the ship floating and going in the right direction all the time. I find that although now I'm not working as hard, I get more done. Now I have time to sit at my desk and plan, whereas before I used to have fifty people always on my back, constantly coming to me with this or that."

This is an example of how one person was able to bring the meditation practice into his work life. He came to see what was actually happening at work with greater clarity and, as a result, was able to reduce his stress and rid himself of his symptoms without having to quit his job. If we had told him at the beginning that this would have happened as a result of lying down and scanning his body for forty-five minutes a day for eight weeks or from following his breathing, he would have thought we were crazy, and with good reason. But because he was at his wits' end, he made the commitment to do what his doctor and we were recommending in spite of its apparent "craziness." As it was, it took four weeks for him to begin to see how the meditation practice was relevant to his situation. Once that connection was made, he was able to tap into his own inner resources. He was able to slow down and appreciate the richness of the present moment, listen to his body, and put his intelligence to work.

Few of us on the planet, regardless of the work we do, would not benefit from greater awareness. It is not just that we would be calmer and more relaxed. In all likelihood, if we saw work as an arena in which we could hone inner strength and wisdom moment by moment, we would make better decisions, communicate more effectively, be more efficient, and perhaps even leave work happier at the end of the day.

HINTS AND SUGGESTIONS FOR REDUCING WORK STRESS

1. When you wake up, take a few quiet moments to affirm that you are choosing to go to work today. If you can, briefly review what you think you will be doing and remind yourself that it may or may not happen that way.
2. Bring awareness to the whole process of preparing to go to work. This might include showering, dressing, eating, and relating to the people you live with. Tune in to your breathing and your body from time to time.

3. When leaving the house, don't say good-bye mechanically to people. Make eye contact with them, touch them; really be "in" those moments, slowing them down just a bit. If you leave before other people wake up, you might try writing them a brief note to say good morning and express your feelings toward them.
4. If you walk to public transportation, be aware of your body breathing, walking, standing and waiting, riding, and getting off. Walk into work mindfully. As best you can, leave your cell phone alone. Try smiling inwardly. If driving, take a moment or two to come to your breathing before you start the car. Remind yourself that you are about to drive off to work now. Some days, at least, try driving without the radio on. Just drive and be with yourself, moment by moment. Leave your cell phone alone. When you park, take a moment or two to just sit and breathe before you leave the car. Walk into work mindfully. Breathe. If your face is already tense and grim, try smiling, or try a half smile if that is too much.
5. At work, take a moment from time to time to monitor your bodily sensations. Is there tension in your shoulders, face, hands, or back? How are you sitting or standing in this moment? What is your body language saying? Consciously let go of any tension as best you can as you exhale and shift your posture to one that expresses balance, dignity, and alertness.
6. When you find yourself walking at work, take the edge off it. Walk mindfully. Don't rush unless you have to. If you have to, know that you are rushing. Rush mindfully.
7. Try doing one thing at a time and giving it the full attention that it deserves for as long as it deserves, without distracting yourself or allowing yourself to be distracted, such as by incoming emails and texts. Overall, the evidence from studies shows that not only does multitasking not work, it degrades performance on every task you are trying to juggle.
8. Take frequent breaks if you can and use them to truly relax and

renew. Instead of drinking coffee or smoking a cigarette, try going outside the building for three minutes and walking or standing and breathing. Or do neck and shoulder rolls at your desk (see Figure 7). Or shut your office door if you can and sit quietly for five minutes or so, following your breathing.

9. Spend your breaks and lunchtime with people you feel comfortable with. Otherwise, maybe it would be better for you to be alone. Changing your environment at lunch can be helpful. Choose to eat one or two lunches a week in silence, mindfully.
10. Alternatively, don't eat lunch. Go out and exercise, every day if you can, or a few days a week. Exercise is a great way of reducing stress. Your ability to do this will depend on how much flexibility you have in your job. If you can do it, it is a wonderful way of clearing the mind, reducing your tension, and starting the afternoon refreshed and with a lot of energy. Many workplaces now have wellness centers that provide organized employee exercise programs both at lunchtime and before and after work. If you have the opportunity to exercise at work, take it! But remember, an exercise program takes the same kind of commitment that the formal meditation takes. And when you do it, do it mindfully. That changes everything.
11. Try to stop for one minute every hour and become aware of your breathing. We waste far more time than this daydreaming at work. Use these mini meditations to tune in to the present and just be. Use them as moments in which to regroup and recoup. All it takes is remembering to do it. This one is not easy, since we so easily get carried away by the momentum of all the doing.
12. Use everyday cues in your environment as reminders to center yourself and relax—the telephone ringing, downtime before a meeting convenes, waiting for someone to finish something before you can start in on it. Instead of relaxing by "spacing out," relax by tuning in.
13. Be mindful of your communications with people during the

workday. Are they satisfying? Are some problematic? Think about how you might improve them. Be aware of people who tend to relate to you in a passive or a hostile mode. Think about how you might approach them more effectively. Try seeing your fellow employees with eyes of wholeness. Think about how you might be more sensitive to their feelings and needs. How might you help others at work by being more mindful and more heartful? How might awareness of tone of voice and body language, your own and that of others, help you when communicating?

14. At the end of the day, review what you have accomplished and make a list of what needs to be done tomorrow. Prioritize the items on your list so that you know what is most important.
15. As you are leaving work, bring your awareness to walking and breathing again. Be aware of the transition we call "leaving work." Monitor your body. Are you exhausted? Are you standing erect or bent over? What expression is on your face? Are you in the present moment, or are you getting out ahead of yourself in your thinking mind?
16. If you are taking public transportation, bring your attention to your breathing, walking, standing, and sitting. Notice if you are rushing. Can you back it down a bit and own those moments between work and home as much as any of your other moments to live? Be aware of the impulse to fill them up by being on your phone. As much as possible, be aware of the impulse to use it, and leave it alone to whatever degree possible. Just see if you can be in your own good company for at least some of this time. Or, if you are driving, take a moment or two once again to sit in your car before you start it up. Drive home mindfully. Leave the cell phone alone unless it is hands-free and essential that you make the call then and not later. Can you be aware of that decision? Can you be aware of the impulse to simply ignore your decision and make the call anyway?
17. Before you walk in the door, realize that you are about to do

so. Be aware of this transition we call "coming home." Try greeting people mindfully and making eye contact rather than shouting to announce your arrival.

18. As soon as you can, take your shoes off and get out of your work clothes. Changing to other clothes can complete the transition from work to home and allow you to integrate more quickly and consciously into your non-work roles. If you can make the time, take five minutes or so to meditate before you do anything else, even cooking or eating dinner.
19. Keep in mind that the real meditation is how you live your life from moment to moment. In this way, everything you do can become part of your meditation practice, if you are willing to inhabit the present moment and embrace it in awareness, in your body, "underneath" thinking.

The foregoing are offered merely as hints and suggestions for bringing your mindfulness practice into the domain of work. Ultimately, of course, the challenge is yours to decide what might best help you reduce any stress related to your work. Your creativity and imagination in this regard will be your most important resource.

31

Food Stress

You cannot live a healthy life in our complex globalized society without paying at least some attention to what you are putting into your body. Our relationship to food has changed so much in the past few generations that the exercise of a new form of intelligence, still developing, may be necessary to sort out what is of value and nourishing from the incredible choices that are presented to us.

For example, gone are the days when we ate directly off the land, consuming a small number of foods that had been the exclusive and unchanging staples of the culture over millennia. Until early in the twentieth century, our diet had changed little from generation to generation. It was intimately dependent on an individual's ability to acquire food through hunting and gathering and/or for cultivating it through farming and the raising of livestock. Over the years, we came to know what was edible in nature and what was not, and our bodies adapted to the diet of particular isolated regions, climates, groups, and cultures. Getting or growing food took most of the energy of all of the members of the social group. We ate what we could obtain from the local environment, to live as best we could. For better or for worse, subject to all its unpredictability and fickleness, we lived in an intrinsically homeostatic balance with the natural environment. We lived within nature, not apart from it.

We are still very much a part of nature, but we may be less aware of our intimate connections with it now because we are able to manipulate it so much of the time to our own ends.

Our relationship to food in first-world countries has undergone an enormous transformation toward greater complexity, with infinitely more choices for what we now call "the consumer." In the old days, we were pretty much all producers of food, in one way or another. Now the vast majority of society lives physically and psychologically far from food production. Although biologically we still eat in order to live, psychologically many people could be said to live in order to eat instead, so great are our psychic preoccupations with food that have little to do with actual hunger.

Moreover, we are now continually exposed to foods that didn't exist even a decade or two ago, foods that are synthesized or processed in factories, that are only distantly related to anything we might recognize as gathered from the wild or cultivated locally. In the developed countries, it is now possible to obtain any food we want in any season, thanks to a distribution system that transports it over huge distances in a matter of days. Very few people in these societies any longer depend completely on growing food for themselves or hunting or foraging it off the land. We no longer have to expend all our time and energy acquiring food to have enough to eat.

We have become a nation of food consumers. Only a small percentage of the population is involved in food production, a great change from earlier days. Now we buy food in large stores, veritable cornucopias, temples of abundance and consumerism. Our experience is that there is always food on the supermarket shelves, thousands of different kinds of foods to choose from. This arrangement liberates us from having to acquire it every day. All we need is enough money to purchase it. Refrigeration and freezing, canning and packaging, and of course the addition of preservatives have made it possible for us to store food in our homes so that we can actually eat whatever we want whenever we want. These developments have been miraculously liberating, and we all benefit from them as we enjoy the availability of so many foods that are the product of careful genetic breeding and cultivation over the past century or two, including many of the fruits and vegetables in our markets: think of beautifully formed oranges, grapefruit, apples, plums, avocados, kale, carrots, beets, and so on.

Our food production and distribution system is a perfect example of our collective interdependence and interconnectedness. The conduits of food distribution are the arterial circulation of the social body, and the refrigerator trucks, railroad cars, and planes are the specialized transport vehicles for supplying the tissues and cells of the society with vital nourishment, putting aside for a moment the issue of their huge carbon footprint and whether it is sustainable to continue to live in this way. A massive trucker strike would result in cities empty of food within a matter of days. There would simply be no food left in the stores for people to acquire. We tend not to think about such things.

Another thing we don't think about so much is that our food supply has become concentrated in a small number of gigantic corporations, agribusinesses that supply almost everything you find stocked on supermarket shelves. Our grandparents would not recognize perhaps 70 percent of what is on those shelves as food. But they might become addicted to it pretty quickly, both to the miraculous convenience of food acquisition in modern life (what we call shopping) and to the marvels of unimaginably seductive high-calorie and high-fat foods.

There is no question that, as a population, we are probably healthier than ever before. While many people would ascribe much of this to our diets, it turns out that this may be only partially true. Clean water and sanitation played an enormous role in lowering mortality and extending our longevity. And we may be at a critical inflection point in the health of our society. There is mounting and very convincing evidence that health in America and in many other first-world countries that are unfortunately following our lead is now being impaired by diseases associated with an overconsumption of food in general and of certain foods in particular, diseases occasioned by our affluence and abundance. For the first time in history, it is said, our children may not be healthier and more robust than their parents. Witness the obesity epidemic that has been mushrooming inexorably since the mid-1970s, driven by many different factors, but primarily by the supersizing of meals and the consumption of huge numbers of empty calories in non-nutrient-rich, highly synthesized "foods" such as sodas.

Our health is also being threatened by exposure to hundreds if not thousands of chemicals in our environment that human bodies were never exposed to before over the entire span of our evolution as a species, because they were only invented in the past decades. Many of these chemicals are residues from fertilizers and pesticides associated with agribusiness, as well as pollutants from other industries that make their way into the food chain from an increasingly contaminated environment. Or they are additives and preservatives put there by the food industry, sometimes without sufficient testing. Altogether, these chemicals are placing our exquisitely evolved homeostatic biochemical networks at some unknown degree of risk for cellular and tissue disruption and damage. We simply do not know, no matter what the experts say, what exposure to some of these chemicals in food will lead to in coming generations or over a lifetime of ingestion. What we do know is that we are playing a kind of chemical Russian roulette with our own bodies and those of our children, in almost all instances without the consumer knowing that he or she is an involuntary participant in this game. As part of a public television program on this subject in conjunction with the Mount Sinai School of Medicine, the highly respected television journalist, Bill Moyers, had his own body burden of toxic chemicals tested. The results revealed eighty-four distinct chemicals in his blood and urine, including hazardous chemicals in common use, such as dioxin, PCBs, and phthalates, as well as compounds such as DDT, the use of which has been banned in the United States for more than forty years. Many of those chemicals enter our body through what we eat, although there are also many other environmental exposure routes as well, including everyday household and consumer products.

Since the food we eat over a lifetime has a major influence on our health, we need to pay attention in a sensible, non-alarmist, non-fanatical way to the whole domain of what we put in our bodies, if we haven't already begun to do so. The adage "you are what you eat" has more than a modicum of truth to it. We simply have to bring some degree of mindfulness to what we purchase and put in our bodies in order to navigate and modulate the potential dangers to our health across the life span, especially during particularly vulnerable windows of time, such as during pregnancy and breast-feeding, during childhood, and in adolescence.

Obesity is rapidly becoming a global epidemic in both children and adults, and diabetes, metabolic syndrome, and cardiovascular disease along with it. In 1990, the year this book was first published, ten states in the United States had a prevalence of obesity of less than 10 percent, and no state had a prevalence equal to or greater than 15 percent, according to the Centers for Disease Control and Prevention. By the year 2000, no state any longer had a prevalence of obesity of less than 10 percent. Twenty-three states had a prevalence of between 20 and 24 percent, and no state had a prevalence equal to or greater than 25 percent. By 2010, no state had a prevalence of less than 20 percent, and thirty-six states had a prevalence of 25 percent, with twelve of these states (Alabama, Arkansas, Kentucky, Louisiana, Michigan, Mississippi, Missouri, Oklahoma, South Carolina, Tennessee, Texas, and West Virginia) showing a prevalence of 30 percent or more. This is a mind-boggling phenomenon, for which there are no definitive answers about how to slow it down or reverse it. The new 2012 health care law in the United States devotes billions of dollars to a full-court press over multiple years on this issue, including grassroots efforts to organize classes to teach people at highest risk, in their own communities, about healthy eating, exercise, and other lifestyle choices.

Diet clearly comes into play in a range of chronic diseases, even newly described ones such as metabolic syndrome, which seems to be at the root of many different diseases due to inflammatory processes at the cellular and tissue levels. Diet-based disease is more a factor in some populations and social groups than in others. Of course, it is also strongly related to poverty.

It is well known that a diet high in animal fat and cholesterol is a major factor in coronary artery disease, in which the arteries of the heart become blocked by fatty plaques that then calcify. This process begins in childhood. Cardiovascular diseases are more prevalent than all other diseases put together, so paying attention to what we eat and to our entire relationship to food is extremely important if we hope to live a healthy life and experience robust well-being. Luckily, there is more and more evidence that there are many things we can do to live in a healthier way when it comes to food.

When scientists want to create coronary artery disease in animals, they put them on a diet that is the equivalent of bacon, eggs, and butter for six months or so. This diet is very effective in clogging the arteries of the heart. There are very high levels of cholesterol and saturated fat in butter, red meat, hamburgers, hot dogs, and ice cream—all popular staples of the American diet. In countries such as China and Japan, which have diets with less meat and animal fat and more fish and rice, the incidence of heart disease is much lower. However, these countries have high rates of certain cancers, such as esophageal and stomach cancer, which are thought to be related to a high consumption of cured, pickled, and smoked foods. Interestingly enough, as these Asian societies adopt more of an American diet, they are now seeing dramatic increases in heart disease and obesity. This doesn't mean that you can't have bacon or eggs in your diet, only that, given your individual situation and risk, it is a good idea to find some kind of reasonable balance, to be aware of your most unexamined and potentially unhealthy shopping and eating habits and find healthier ways of nourishing yourself and your family.

While the relationship of diet to cancer is less clear than in the case of heart disease, there is considerable evidence that points to a role for diet in cancers of the breast, colon, and prostate. Here too, the total amount of fat in the diet seems to play a significant role. There is some evidence that people who have a high-fat diet have lower levels of some immune functions (for instance, natural killer cell activity, which, as we have seen, is thought to play a role in protecting the body against cancer) and that when they change to a diet with a lower total fat content (including fats of both animal *and* vegetable origins), they show increases in natural killer cell activity. Many studies in animals also show a link between diet and cancer, and dietary fat plays the largest role. Excessive consumption of alcohol, particularly in conjunction with cigarette smoking, also appears to increase the probability of some cancers in people.

Way back in 1977, the Senate Select Committee on Nutrition declared that Americans were killing themselves by overeating. Little did they know how prescient their warning call would be. At the time, it recommended that we reduce the calories we obtain from fat from about 40 percent to about 30 percent, of which only 10 percent should come from saturated fat and the other 20 percent from mono- and polyunsaturated fats. They recommended that the loss of calories from fat should be compensated for by increasing the calories we obtain from complex carbohydrates. They made this recommendation because they thought it was achievable, not because they thought that 30 percent was the optimal level of fat in the diet. The traditional Chinese diet derives only 15 percent of total calories from fat. In traditional native cultures such as the Tarahumara Indians of Mexico, famous for their ultramarathon runners, only about 10 percent of total calories come from fat, and almost none of it is from animal fat. Studies of the Tarahumara have shown that they have virtually no heart disease or high blood pressure in their population. In this country, Seventh-day Adventists have been studied by scientists interested in nutrition because most of them are vegetarians and they too have a very low incidence of heart disease and cancer.

It turns out that there are many ways in which we can become aware of our relationship to food on all levels, and transform our relationship to it. While we no longer explicitly include the subject in the formal curriculum of MBSR, as we did for the first ten years of the program, bringing mindfulness to the food we buy, how we prepare it, what we eat, and how we feel after eating—and to the messages that our body gives us after we have eaten—can make a very big difference in the quality of our lives, and in how healthy we are, and even how long we live.

One piece of advice that might go a long way if we are able to keep it in mind when we are shopping and thinking about what to prepare for our meals comes from Michael Pollan, the author of *The Botany of Desire* and

The Omnivore's Dilemma, among other important and influential works on the nation's food crisis. He framed it rather elegantly and succinctly:

"Eat food, mostly plants, not too much."

It is good advice. However, it is easy to say, not so easy to do. It might be a good phrase for us to keep in mind, and put into action, if we dare. For one thing, it challenges us to ask ourselves whether what we are putting into our bodies is actually *food* or something else. Pollan's prescription, while simple, is vitally important for us to fathom and then put into practice in our everyday eating patterns. The phrase is what Zen practitioners would call a *koan.* It reveals more and more to us over time if we keep it in mind. It can actually teach us and shape our experience and our choices if we keep it in the forefront of our awareness over days, weeks, months, and years.

Pioneering work over more than thirty years by Dr. Dean Ornish and his collaborators at the Preventive Medicine Research Institute in Sausalito and the University of California, San Francisco, has consistently demonstrated that by changing your lifestyle in a comprehensive way—including what you choose to eat and what you choose not to eat—you can slow down, stop, and even reverse the progression of severe coronary heart disease as well as early-stage prostate cancer.

The Ornish approach involves changing not only the way you eat, but equally important, the way you live. The regimen consists of eating a whole-foods, high-fiber, mostly vegetarian diet that is low in fat and refined carbohydrates such as sugar and white flour and high in fruits and vegetables, whole grains, legumes, and soy products, supplemented with fish oil or flaxseed oil. In addition, it calls for moderate exercise in the form of walking, as well as the ongoing practice of yoga, and meditation. It also emphasizes the cultivation of love and intimacy in one's relationships. In both heart patients and prostate cancer patients, cholesterol levels dropped substantially without the need for cholesterol-lowering drugs. This same approach has been shown to reverse the progression of type 2 diabetes, one of the major consequences of obesity-generating diets.

Subjects in the prostate study showed dramatic epigenetic changes as a result of eating this way, evidence that our very chromosomes are positively influenced by such lifestyle changes, as we saw earlier in the work of Elissa Epel, Cliff Saron, David Creswell, and others. In particular, the expression of large numbers of what are called "pro-inflammatory genes" was turned off (down-regulated is the technical term), thereby reducing disease-producing inflammatory processes within the body. Hundreds of oncogenes known to promote prostate cancer, breast cancer, and colon cancer were also turned off. At the same time, the expression of genes that have been shown to be health-enhancing was increased (up-regulated).

These changes were seen in just three months on the program in randomized clinical trials, and constitute strong evidence that our bodies are actually responding to our lifestyle choices, and in particular our food choices, on a molecular level that can be health-enhancing if we pay attention to those choices and modify how we live.

What is more, our old friend telomerase, which you will recall is the enzyme that controls aging by repairing and lengthening the tips of our chromosomes, increased significantly in men with early stage prostate cancer who followed the Ornish program. This suggests that the comprehensive lifestyle changes they undertook may be tilting their cellular biology in the direction of greater longevity and lower stress. In people who spent at least five years on the program, telomeres actually increased in length.

Dr. Ornish's work is a dramatic demonstration of the resiliency and flexibility of the human body and its ability to heal itself if given a chance. Since these diseases progress over decades in our bodies before we suffer any ill effects or come to be diagnosed, his research findings are exceedingly important. They tell us that even after years of a chronic and pathological process going on within the body, we can do something not only to stop it but to reverse its damage. And this something can be accomplished not with drugs but by people becoming more aware of their own ability to change their lives and their health in crucial ways—and then actually *changing* the way they live their lives and what and how they choose to eat.

In Dr. Ornish's heart disease study, those people who were in the control group received excellent traditional medical care for their disease over the course of the study period. They followed the latest conventional recommendations espoused by most cardiologists, namely, to lower their intake of fat in their diet to about 30 percent and to exercise regularly. However, they did not make the radical lifestyle changes that the other group did, including a commitment to the ongoing daily practice of yoga and meditation. In spite of following those conventional medical guidelines for heart disease patients, the people in the control group showed progression of their disease. Their coronary arteries were, on average, more clogged a year later, as might be expected in such a progressive disease.

Dr. Ornish's work with patients with coronary artery disease demonstrated for the first time that changing the way you live can improve the functioning of your heart and actually reverse atherosclerosis without high-tech medical intervention—which in any event cannot reverse heart disease. You might say that these men and women were able to induce their hearts to heal by changing the way they lived: routinely practicing meditation and yoga (one hour a day), walking often (three times a week), getting together regularly to practice and to support each other, and of course changing what they ate.

Follow-up studies over periods of up to five years have shown that the regression of the disease continues if people maintain these lifestyle changes. Medicare now covers the Ornish program as an approved lifestyle intervention. Remember, it is not a matter of weight loss. It is a matter of healthy eating and mindful choices. When we eat for health rather than for weight loss, we are much more likely to be healthy, as well as to lose weight and keep it off. Not all diets that result in weight loss are actually healthy. One study of more than forty thousand Swedish women who were followed over sixteen years showed that "low carbohydrate-high protein diets . . . are associated with increased risk of cardiovascular disease";

another, published in the *New England Journal of Medicine,* showed that high-protein, low-carbohydrate diets promote coronary artery disease even if they don't increase traditional cardiac risk factors like blood pressure or cholesterol levels.

One of the most interesting and important findings in Dr. Ornish's studies was this: the more people changed their diet and lifestyle, the more they improved—at any age. What seems to matter most is your *overall* way of eating and living, and the degree of kindness and self-compassion you bring to the whole undertaking. Dr. Ornish likes to emphasize that with a kind and mindful approach, you cannot really fail. Rather than thinking of yourself as "going on a diet"—because diets are by definition all about what you can't have and what you must do—all it takes is a willingness to move in a healthier direction and make incremental changes. The fact that his patients keep to these newly adopted lifestyle changes for many years is in part a testament to their yoga and meditation practice, at least in my opinion. The discipline and intentionality blend into a way of being. Rather than thinking of it as "This is the diet I have to stick to" or "This is the meditation or yoga I have to do," it becomes instead merely a matter of "This is how I live my life." All else follows much more easily with such an attitude, as discussed in detail in Chapter 2.

Even so, changing your relationship to food is not so easy, even if you decide that you want to or that you need to in order to be healthier. This is evident from all the failed efforts that people make to lose weight. If, for whatever reason, you decide that you need to change your diet in order to promote increased health and to prevent or slow down disease processes, you will have to go about it with a profound commitment and inner discipline that is born of intelligence rather than fear, paranoia, or an overriding preoccupation with how you look or how much you weigh. Your looks and weight will take care of themselves, to a first approximation, if you give yourself over to the process itself and trust it. This will involve becoming mindful of your relationship to food at all levels. You will need to become more aware of your automatic and even addictive behaviors around eating, of your thoughts and feelings, and of the social customs associated with food and eating. These are areas in which we are unlikely to observe our behavior systematically and non-judgmentally unless we make a strong commitment to liberate ourselves from our maladaptive, habit-driven relationships to food and to develop a healthier, more coherent, and integrated way of living.

As we have seen, the systematic training of the mind can be profoundly beneficial when we seek to encounter and free ourselves from our automatic and unconscious behaviors and from the underlying motivations and impulses that drive them and cause us increased suffering in so many different domains. Our relationship to food is no exception. For this reason, the practice of mindfulness can be particularly useful for making and then maintaining healthy changes when it comes to food and the ways we shop and cook and eat. In fact, awareness, and to a certain extent change as well, come naturally to the domain of food and eating as your meditation practice grows stronger and as you practice bringing mindfulness to all the activities of daily living. Perhaps you have already noticed this for yourself. We can hardly avoid looking at the domain of eating when we start paying attention in daily life. The raisin exercise may have been illuminating, but it contained the seeds for a much deeper investigation of our relationship to what we put into our bodies in the way of nourishment.

Food certainly occupies a central role in most of our lives. Effort and energy go into buying food, preparing it, serving it, eating it, attending to the physical and social environments in which we eat, and cleaning up afterward. All of these activities involve behaviors and choices that we might bring attention to. In addition, we might be more conscious of domains such as the quality of the food we eat, how it was grown or made, where it comes from, and what is in it. We might also pay attention to how much we eat, how frequently we eat, when, and how we feel as a consequence of eating. For instance, we could be mindful of how we feel after we eat certain foods or certain amounts of food, and whether we feel differently when we eat quickly or slowly or at particular times. We can bring mindfulness to the attachments and cravings we may have for particular foods, to what we, as well as our children, will and won't eat, and to the habits the family has toward food. We might also benefit from bringing awareness to how much, when, and where we talk about food and eating. All of these areas come into vivid focus when we bring mindfulness to the domain of food.

So do the most elemental aspects of eating, such as the joy and pleasure we derive from it, the experiencing of delicious and nutritious food through how it looks when we really take it in through our eyes, how it smells, and how it tastes when we savor it before moving on to the next mouthful. The social aspects of food preparation and eating are equally elemental and nurturing. The joy of sitting down to a meal with family and friends, of being in community at work and at home over food, is one of the most profound and human dimensions of life.

Most of us find it quite difficult to change our habits, and our dietary habits are no exception. Eating can be a highly emotionally charged activity for us both socially and culturally. Our relationship to food has been conditioned and reinforced over our entire lifetime. Eating holds many different meanings for us. We have emotional associations with particular types of food, with eating a certain amount of food, with eating in particular places and at particular times and with particular people. These associations with food can be part of our sense of identity and well-being. When we are inordinately attached to them or feel we may be abandoning something deeply meaningful to us if we change how we eat, these understandable concerns can make changing our diet even more difficult than making other kinds of lifestyle changes. That is why the gentle, non-forcing approach of mindfulness, brought to eating, can be both transformative and healing. Rather than losing what you most fear to lose, you may come to see that you are reestablishing and reconfiguring the connections that are most meaningful to you, making them potentially even more meaningful, joyful, and satisfying.

Perhaps the best place to begin is not by trying to make any changes at all but simply by paying close attention to exactly what you are eating and how it affects you. Try observing exactly what your food looks like and how it tastes as you are eating it. The next time you sit down to a meal, really look at what is on your plate. What is its texture? Look at the colors and the shapes of the food. How does it smell? How do you feel as you look at it? How does it taste? Is it pleasurable or unpleasant? How do you feel right after eating it? Is it what you wanted? Does it agree with you?

Notice how you feel an hour or two after eating. How is your energy level? Did eating that food give you energy or did it make you feel sluggish? How does your belly feel? What do you think now about what you ate then?

When people in the stress clinic start paying attention to their eating in this way, they report some interesting observations. Some discover that they eat particular foods more out of habit than from liking them or wanting to eat them. Others notice that eating certain foods upsets their bellies or results in fatigue later on, connections they never noticed before. Many report that they now get more enjoyment out of eating, because they are aware of it in a new way.

In the early years of the program, we noticed that some participants were reporting making changes in their eating patterns well before we touched on the subject of mindfulness and diet in any detail, which only came toward the end of the eight weeks. Perhaps this came about as a result of the raisin eating meditation in the first class and the conversation around that experience. These spontaneous changes in eating patterns still occur, as the participants in the program bring greater mindfulness to their eating as part of the daily informal meditation practice.

Almost none of our patients come to the clinic seeking to lose weight or change their diets. Nevertheless, many naturally start eating more slowly, again perhaps a legacy of the raisin-eating meditation. In later weeks, they often report finding that they are satisfied eating less and are more aware of their impulses to use food to satisfy psychological needs.

Some people actually lose weight over the eight weeks simply by paying attention in this way and without consciously trying to lose weight.

For example, Phil, the truck driver with back pain whom we met in Chapters 13 and 23, also changed his relationship to food while he was in the MBSR program. In fact, he lost fourteen and a half pounds. In his words: "Actually I'm not on any special diet. I'm paying attention when I eat. I catch myself sometimes after I start to eat; get the breathing down pat, slow down a bit. Life is such a rat race even if you're not going anywhere, always running, running, running. You do everything fast, you just slop the food in your mouth and two hours later you're hungry again because you didn't taste nothing, you just went right by it. You're full but, like I say, the taste bud has a lot to do with everything. If you didn't taste it, you'll be hungry again because you didn't taste anything you had. That's the way I look at it now. I eat less if I slow myself down because I chew my food better, I taste it. I've never been able to do that before, ya know. I'd like to lose another fifteen pounds. If I keep slowing down, ya know, losing just a little like I am now every week, then I'll probably be able to keep it down after, ya know. It's like, if you lose in a hurry, when dieting is over, you put it right back on. With the meditation I learned that you gotta set goals for yourself, ya know, and once you set your goal, go for it, don't get away from it. When you go somewhere, you see it all the time, it's in your mind. You reflect on it."

It is important for all of us to pay at least some attention to our relationship to food and to what is known about the connections between diet and health. That way, we can begin to make more informed decisions about how we are choosing to live. As usual, it is awareness itself that is primary here. In MBSR, we do not advocate a particular diet. We do advocate that people pay attention to this domain of their lives as well as to all others, instead of leaving it in the control of the automatic pilot mode. We do encourage people to inform themselves and to make whatever changes they think are important, and to do so over a relatively long period of time in order to shift the odds more in their favor in terms of overall health. Most people we work with are convinced that there is room for making healthy changes in their diet, and MBSR is often a turning point in this regard for them.

But even if you have decided that you want to make changes in your diet to improve your health and to reduce the risks of heart disease and cancer, or even simply to enjoy your food more, to feel better, and to have more energy, it is not always easy to know how to initiate healthy changes. Nor is it easy to stick with them over time. Our habits and customs of a lifetime have a momentum of their own that needs to be respected and worked with intelligently. In Dr. Ornish's heart disease study, the participants received a great deal of support in changing their diets and in sticking with their new regimen. They were taught vegetarian cooking, had to give up many foods entirely, and were initially supplied with a range of prepared healthy foods and snacks to keep in the freezer to use while they were learning how to cook and shop for the new foods.

It's hardly the same if you want to make changes on your own to lower your cholesterol and fat intake or to cut down on the amount of certain foods you eat or the amount of food you eat, period. Habits and customs of a lifetime are hard to change without outside support. To change your eating patterns, you need to really know why you are trying to make those changes in the first place. Then you will have to *remember* why from day to day and even from moment to moment, as you encounter a myriad of impulses, opportunities, and frustrations that can throw you off the track. In other words, you will need to believe really deeply in yourself and in your vision of what is healthy and important for you. You will certainly need reliable information about food and nutrition and an awareness of your relationship to food and to eating so that you can make intelligent choices about where to shop, what to buy, and how best to prepare it.

This is where simply applying moment-to-moment awareness to food and to eating can be crucial for bringing about positive changes. In the same way that mindfulness can have a positive influence on our relationships with pain, fear, time, and people, it can also be used to transform our relationship to food.

For instance, many people use eating as a major form of stress reduction. When we are anxious, we eat. When we are lonely, we eat. When we are bored, we eat. When we feel empty, we eat. When all else fails, we tend to eat. That is a lot of automatic eating. We don't do it to nourish the body or to quench real hunger. We mostly do it to make ourselves feel better emotionally, and also to fill up time.

What we eat at those times can add up to an unhealthy diet. The rewards and treats we give ourselves to feel better tend to be rich and sweet, such as cookies, candy, cake, pastries, and ice cream. These are all high in hidden fat and loaded with sugar. Or they tend to be salty, such as chips and dips of various kinds. These are also loaded with hidden fat.

We also have to make our own way navigating what is available and convenient. Fast-food chains specialize in foods that are high in animal fat, cholesterol, salt, and sugar, although even they are now changing to provide more healthy alternatives, such as salad bars and baked instead of fried foods. Although many restaurants are now highlighting heart-healthy foods, such as baked fish and chicken, most still do not pay attention to such matters and prepare food in ways that can make it higher in fat than it need be. It is still not easy to find healthy food if you are away from home and trying to find something to eat. Sometimes it may be healthier not to eat until you find what you really want to put into your body. At such times we can fall back to practicing patience and work at letting go of feeling incomplete or deprived.

If you want to improve your health, looking at your diet becomes extremely important. It's not just a question of animal fat and cholesterol, heart disease and cancer. There is considerable evidence that Americans overeat, period, and that our high-sugar diet promotes chronic inflammatory processes throughout the body. There is a whole new field, called *functional medicine,* that is trying to elucidate these kinds of issues and to relate them to our genetic individuality, since each of us has a unique configuration of genes that can predispose us to particular food allergies, food sensitivities, or inflammatory processes.

Other lifestyle factors come into play that can interact with our diets for better or for worse. Men ordinarily eat about 2,500 calories a day, women about 1,800. Yet as a society we are relatively sedentary. We don't burn up calories working to the same extent as people did in previous generations. We do a lot of driving in cars to go places and a lot of sitting at work. Driving and sitting do not burn calories the way walking and manual labor do. The Centers for Disease Control and Prevention reported in 2006 that calorie consumption among women had increased in the thirty years between 1971 and 2000 by 22 percent, whereas among men it increased by 7 percent. These figures mirror the increase in portion size over the past thirty-plus years, as well as the obesity epidemic itself, and they underscore why other lifestyle factors are so important in facing this crisis. All the evidence suggests that it is highly likely that you will be healthier, even if you don't change your diet in any other way, just by eating a little less.

However, in our society it has become dangerous even to suggest that we might be overeating. The prevalence of eating disorders, especially among young girls and women, has sensitized us to how disregulated people can become about their body image. Sometimes people's relationship to eating becomes pathological, to the point of either starving themselves and thinking that their emaciated bodies are still overweight *(anorexia nervosa)* or bingeing on food they cannot resist eating and then purposefully purging by vomiting so that they won't gain weight *(bulimia)*. There is a strong underlying emotional component to these disorders, and often a history of trauma. The ongoing suffering and self-loathing is enormous and heartbreaking, and cannot be approached and dealt with without radical honesty, enormous compassion, and the reestablishing of trustworthy connectedness and interconnectedness following trauma.

Eating disorders may be, in part, an unhappy consequence of the gross preoccupation of our postindustrial society with outward appearance as well as its tendency to objectify bodies and notions of beauty, especially in women. Rather than paying attention to inner experience and being kind and accepting of oneself, we tend to condemn ourselves if we do not fit the established norms of weight, height, and outward appearance. So we have become a society largely alienated from our bodies as they are and in search of some eternal and ideal image. We are a society of crash dieters and failed dieters, of consumers of chemical cocktails known as diet sodas—all in the quest for the "perfect" body.

Yet there is little wisdom in all the fads associated with food and dieting. Why don't we drink water instead of diet soda? Why do we go on elaborate diets and then binge on what we have deprived ourselves of? Perhaps it is time to realize that our energy is being misdirected. Perhaps we are overly preoccupied with our weight and our appearance rather than with healing ourselves and optimizing our well-being and our happiness. If we start paying attention to the basics, such as what the mind is up to in the present moment and what we are putting into our bodies and why, we might make more substantial progress toward realizing greater health with a lot less neuroticism and wasted energy. This shift in lifestyle can be approached by starting a process of becoming much more aware of what it feels like to inhabit your body with kindness and self-acceptance throughout the day, or even in brief moments, if that is all you can manage, and then, more specifically, bringing awareness to the moment-to-moment experience of selecting what you choose to eat, seeing it, smelling it, chewing it, and tasting it, as well as how you feel before, during, and after each mouthful. Mindful eating has more to do with striking a gentle and flexible balance than with being artificially rigid. The more you can stay in the experiencing of the *process,* accepting whatever feelings and emotions might arise, however aversive they may be, the more your body, your mind, and the food itself will teach you what you need to know. The shift toward eating in a healthier way will unfold out of that process.

When we do touch on the subject of mindfulness in relation to diet and health, we sometimes review with our patients the guidelines from the national scientific and professional societies that concern themselves with the American diet. For example, the Institute of Medicine of the National Academy of Sciences recommends that people reduce their consumption of pickled foods, smoked foods, and prepared meats, or avoid them altogether, because of their likely relationship to certain cancers. In practical terms this means giving up or drastically reducing consumption of salami, bologna, corned beef, sausage, ham, bacon, and hot dogs. The American Heart Association recommends reducing consumption of red meat, drinking low-fat or skim milk and eliminating whole milk and cream, cutting down on fatty cheeses, and restricting the intake of eggs, which contain about 300 milligrams of cholesterol per egg. (The Ornish diet for reversing heart disease contains about 2 milligrams of cholesterol a day.) However, I eat eggs pretty much every day, and have for many years. Yet I naturally have a very low cholesterol level and a good ratio. So a lot of the specific dietary choices you make may be a matter of your genetic makeup, when following particular dietary guidelines for optimal health.

What do these organizations suggest you eat to replace the foods they are telling you to avoid or cut down on? They recommend increasing your consumption of fresh fruits and vegetables, preferably raw or carefully cooked so that their nutrients are not destroyed or dissolved away. Some vegetables, such as broccoli and cauliflower, seem to have a protective effect against certain kinds of cancer, perhaps from the naturally occurring antioxidants they contain. These organizations also recommend introducing more whole grains, such as wheat, corn, rice, and oats into your diet, although corn and rice are high on the glycemic index and may not be good for some individuals, especially in large quantities. Whole grains are found in breads, as cereals for breakfast or snacks, and as an important part of dinners. They are the best sources of complex carbohydrate, which should constitute approximately 75 percent of the calories in our daily intake of food. Gluten sensitivities also need to be taken into account, since so many people are now sensitive to gluten-containing grains and processed foods that contain gluten. In general, an anti-inflammatory diet is most conducive to health.

In addition to providing complex carbohydrate and nutrients, whole grains, fruits, and vegetables also lend bulk to the diet because they contain the outside husks of the grain and plant tissues, known as roughage or fiber. Fiber helps move food through the intestinal tract, reducing the amount of time that the tissues of the digestive tract are exposed to the waste products of digestion, which can be toxic and which the body needs to eliminate efficiently.

In summary, paying attention to your relationship to food is important for your health. Listening to your body and observing the activity of your mind in relationship to food can help you to make and maintain healthy changes in your diet. If your meditation practice is strong, you will naturally be more in touch with your food and how it affects you. You will naturally be more mindful of your cravings for certain foods, you will be able to see those desires more readily *as thoughts and feelings,* and you will perhaps be better able to let them go *before* you act on them.

When we are on automatic pilot, we tend to act (in this case, eat) first and only then become aware of what we have done and remember why we actually didn't really want to do it in that fashion. Mindfulness of when we eat, what we eat, how it tastes, where it comes from, what is in it, and how we feel after we eat it, if practiced consistently, and with a light touch and a sense of humor, not as an obsession, can go a long way toward bringing healthy change naturally to this extremely important and too often highly emotionally charged domain of our lives.

HINTS AND SUGGESTIONS FOR MINDFULNESS OF FOOD AND EATING

1. Start paying attention to this whole domain of your life, just as you have been doing with your body and your mind.
2. Try eating a meal mindfully, in silence. Slow down your movements enough so that you can watch the entire process carefully. See the description of eating the raisins mindfully in Chapter 1. Try shutting off your phone while you are eating.
3. Observe the colors and textures of your food. Contemplate where this food comes from and how it was grown or made. Is it synthetic? Does it come from a factory? Was anything put into it? Can you see the efforts of all the other people who were involved in bringing it to you? Can you see how it was once connected to nature? Can you see the natural elements, the sunlight and the rain, in your vegetables and fruits and grains?
4. Ask yourself if you want this food in your body before you eat it. How much of it do you want in your belly? Listen to

your body while you are eating. Can you detect when it says "enough"? What do you do at this point? What impulses come up in your mind?

5. Be aware of how your body feels in the hours after you have eaten. Does it feel heavy or light? Do you feel tired or energetic? What might this be trying to tell you? Do you have unusual amounts of gas or other symptoms of disregulation? Can you relate these symptoms to particular foods or combinations of foods to which you might be sensitive?
6. When shopping, try reading labels on food items such as cereal boxes, breads, frozen foods. What is in them? Are they high in fat, in animal fat? Do they have salt and sugar added? What are the first ingredients listed? (By law they have to be listed in decreasing order of amounts, with the first ingredient the most plentiful).
7. Be aware of your cravings. Ask yourself where they come from. What do you really want? Are you going to get it from eating this particular food? Can you eat just a little of it? Are you addicted to it? Can you try letting go of it this once and just watch the craving as a thought or a feeling? Can you think of something else to do at this moment that will be healthier and more personally satisfying than eating?
8. When preparing food, are you doing it mindfully? Try a peeling-potatoes meditation or a chopping-carrots meditation. Can you be totally present with the peeling, with the chopping? Try being aware of your breathing and your whole body as you peel or chop vegetables. What are the effects of doing things this way?
9. Look at your favorite recipes. What ingredients do they call for? How much cream, butter, eggs, lard, sugar, and salt is in them? Look around for alternatives if you decide that a particular recipe is no longer what you want to be cooking. Many delicious recipes are now available that are low in fat, cholesterol, salt, and sugar. Some use low-fat yogurt instead of cream, olive oil instead of lard or butter, and fruit juices for sweetening.

32

World Stress

Our world, the celestial body we call planet Earth, has apparently come down with a fever. The diagnosis is serious, the prognosis not good, and things could get a lot worse, according to the majority of planetary scientists, who, for all their knowledge and supercomputer modeling, have never seen a case like this before and so cannot be certain about how the patient needs to be treated. Some of the symptoms that led to this diagnosis are a temperature rise worldwide, thanks to an enormous increase of carbon dioxide and other greenhouse gases in the atmosphere from our burning of carbon-containing fuels, and a very rapid melting of glaciers and the polar ice caps. This fever is primarily a result of our activity as human beings, now that there are so many of us on the planet. Our agriculture, livestock, and industries, coupled with our destruction of the rain forests and pollution of the oceans, is disrupting the natural cycles that have kept the planetary homeostasis finely balanced for tens of thousands of years. As a result, the world itself, our very home, is now being stressed in ways that have never happened before in the span of human history. The potential consequences of this accelerating trend for the future, and for the future of our children and their children and their children's children, indeed, for our entire species and other species as well, are largely unknown but do not portend well.

So perhaps it is time for us to wake up to the unforeseen consequences and costs of our actions not merely as individuals, but also as a species, not only for our own health, but also for the health of the whole world going forward. For all these phenomena are interconnected. All stem from the human mind and human activity. When the human mind knows itself, we get wisdom and all the beauty and understanding and compassion that human history has given us—the arts, the sciences, architecture, technological wonders, music, poetry, medicine, everything that is found in the world's great museums, universities, and concert halls. And when the human mind does not know itself, we get ignorance, cruelty, oppression, violence, genocide, holocausts, death, and destruction on a colossal scale. For this reason, mindfulness writ both large and small is not a luxury. Writ small, it is a liberative strategy for being healthier and happier as an individual. Writ large, it is a vital necessity if we are to survive and thrive as a species, if we are to fully embody and enact our species' name: *Homo sapiens sapiens* . . . the species that knows, and knows that it knows, in other words, the species that is aware and knows that it is aware. Whatever unfolds from here out in human history, given the condition of our fragile planet and its ecosystems and homeostatic cycles, mindfulness will of necessity be an important, potentially critical factor. So it is a good thing that it seems to be finding its way into both political and economic discourse and action, as we will see.

Harking back to the previous chapter on food and food stress, we tend to take the abundance of wholesome food for granted in the first world. But planetary changes such as drought are severely straining the food supply in certain parts of the world, and with the warming of the planet, the pressures on our food sources will only increase. So again, given that we live in a highly interconnected world, we would do well to begin to recognize how much our individual well-being and health, and that of our families and descendents, will depend on these larger ecological and geopolitical forces. For instance, in the future it will be increasingly difficult for us to choose a healthy diet in a polluted and food-stressed world. There are too many factors we don't know about that might have long-term negative effects on our health.

For instance, you could be eating a low-cholesterol, low-fat, low-salt, low-sugar diet high in complex carbohydrates, fruits, vegetables, and fiber and still be at risk for illness if your water supply is contaminated with chemicals from illegal dumping, or if the fish you eat is polluted with mercury or PCBs, or if there are pesticide residues on the fruits and vegetables you are eating.

So when we think about the relationship of health to diet, it is important to think about diet in a broader sense than the way we usually do. The quality of the food we buy, where it was grown or caught, how it was raised, and what was added to it are important variables. Awareness of these interconnected aspects of diet and health will at least allow us to make intelligent decisions about what to eat a lot of and what to eat only once in a while, to hedge our bets so to speak in the absence of absolute knowledge about the state of particular foods. The writings of Michael Pollan, mentioned earlier, are very helpful in this regard.

Perhaps, in this day and age, we need to expand our definition of food altogether, and what we include within it. I like to think of anything that we take in and absorb, that gives us energy or allows us to make use of the energy in other resources, as food. If you think in this way, you certainly need to consider water in this category. It is an absolutely vital food. So is the air we breathe. The quality of the water we drink and the air we breathe directly affects our health. In Massachusetts, some water supplies have been contaminated to the point where towns have had to import water from other localities. Many wells in the state are now highly polluted too. There are many days in Los Angeles when there are air pollution alerts due to high concentrations of chemicals in the air. Children, elderly people, and pregnant women are advised to stay indoors on those days. And if you drive into Boston from the west, there are many days when you can see a mass of yellowish brown air hanging over the city. It is hard to believe that it is healthy to be breathing such air day in and day out, as a steady diet over a lifetime. Many of our cities are like this now, some even most of the time. In some other countries, it is a much bigger problem.

Clearly we have to start thinking about our air and water as food and pay attention to their quality. You can filter the tap water you use for drinking and cooking just to be on the safe side, or buy bottled water. While it seems a shame to have to pay even more for water than you might be paying now, in the long run it may be intelligent to do so, especially if you are pregnant or if you are trying to encourage your children to drink water rather than soda. Of course, this will depend on knowing how good your water is and whether bottled water is any better. In some cases it may not be, depending on what the bottle is made of.

Protecting yourself from air pollution is another concern. If you live downwind from power plants or other industry, or even just live in a city, there is little you can do at an individual level except to stay away from people who are smoking and maybe hold your breath when a city bus goes by. Only legal and political action over an extended period will have an effect on air and water quality. These are dramatic reasons why people who care about their health might want to put some of their energy into action for social change. It is in everybody's self-interest to care for the natural world. The environment is easily polluted, but it is not so easy to clean it up. We as individuals cannot detect pollution in our food. We have to depend on our institutions to keep the food supply uncontaminated. If they do not, or if they fail to establish appropriate standards or testing procedures, our health and the health of future generations may be at significantly greater risk in countless ways that we are only now coming to realize.

For instance, pesticides such as DDT and industrial chemicals such as PCBs from the electronics industry are now found everywhere in nature, including, as we saw, in our own body fat and in breast milk. Pesticides that have been banned in the United States, such as DDT, continue to be sold by American manufacturers to third world countries. Ironically, these pesticides are used on crops that are grown for export to the United States, such as coffee and pineapples, so we get back, in our own food, residues of the poisons we exported for use elsewhere. (This has been described in a compelling account in *Circle of Poison,* by David Weir and Mark Schapiro.)

The trouble is that while the manufacturers of the pesticides know about this, consumers in general do not. We think we are being protected by our laws about what can be used on crops and what cannot, but our laws do not govern pesticide levels used on food grown in other countries, such as Costa Rica, Colombia, Mexico, Chile, Brazil, and the Philippines, where our coffee, bananas, pineapples, peppers, and tomatoes often come from. What is more, pesticides used in the third world are usually applied in the field by farm workers who are not given any instruction in the safe use of these products to minimize the contamination of the food, nor are they told how to protect themselves while using these chemicals. According to the World Health Organization, there are over one million cases of people being poisoned by pesticides in the third world each year, with thousands dying. Meanwhile, the global environment is rapidly becoming overloaded with pesticides. The Environmental Protection Agency reports that 5.1 billion pounds of pesticides are used each year in the United States alone. The continued effect of this kind of saturation of the environment and of our food chain with pesticides is unknown, but is not likely to be beneficial.

Coming back to the earth itself, it is only relatively recently that we have come to realize that we live on and share a small and fragile planet that can be stressed and ultimately overwhelmed by the activities of our very precocious species. We now know that our interconnectedness extends to the planet itself. Its ecology, just like that of the human body, is a dynamical system, robust but also delicate, with its own homeostatic and allostatic mechanisms that can be stressed and disrupted. It has its own limits, beyond which it can rapidly break down. If we fail to realize that our collective human activity is capable of throwing its cycles out of balance, then we may very well be creating the seeds of our own destruction.

The vast majority of environmental scientists think we have already gone dangerously far along that road. The world is slowly coming to recognize that human activity can pollute the oceans to an unthinkable extent, create acid rain that denudes the forests of Europe, and raze the remaining tropical rain forests, which provide a significant fraction of the oxygen we breathe and that cannot be replaced except by rain forests. Human activity also degrades croplands to the point where they cannot produce food. It pollutes the atmosphere with carbon dioxide, thereby raising the average temperature of the earth's surface. It destroys the ozone layer of the earth's atmosphere by releasing fluorocarbons, thereby increasing our exposure to dangerous ultraviolet radiation from the sun. It pollutes our water and the air we breathe, and contaminates the soil and the rivers and wildlife with toxic chemicals.

While such issues may seem remote to us or appear to be the quaint saber-rattling of romantic and hysterical wildlife and nature lovers, the effects of these practices on us may not be remote at all in the next decade or two if the destruction of the environment is not slowed and if our release of greenhouse gases is not drastically reduced. We are already apparently seeing the consequences of this in storms of increasing severity, such as Hurricane Katrina, which devastated New Orleans in 2005, and Hurricane Sandy, which inundated so many parts of New York City and New Jersey in 2012. Such storms may become much more common in the coming years, major stressors in our lives and in the lives of future generations. We may see an increased incidence of skin cancer if the atmosphere becomes less and less able to filter out the harmful ultraviolet rays in the sun's light due to destruction of its ozone layer, and increased rates of cancer, miscarriages, and birth defects from greater lifetime exposures to chemicals in the environment and perhaps in food as well.

Although you can find these issues discussed and reported on in the newspapers daily, as well as on the Web, much of the time we pay them little heed, as if they don't really concern us or as if it is hopeless. Sometimes it does feel as if there is nothing that we as individuals can do.

But just becoming more aware and informed about these problems and their relationship to our health as individuals and to the health of the planet as a whole may be a significant positive first step toward bringing about change in the world. At the very least you have changed yourself when you become more informed and aware. You are already a small but significant part of the world, perhaps more significant than you think. By changing yourself and your own behavior in even modest ways, such as recycling reusable materials and being mindful of your consumption of energy and non-renewable resources, you do change the world.

These issues affect our lives and our health even now, whether we know it or not. And they are a source of psychological as well as physical stress. Our psychological well-being may depend on being able to find someplace in nature where we can go and just hear the sounds of the natural world, without the sounds of human activity, of airplanes, cars, and machines. And, more ominously, knowing that a nuclear accident or attack could in just minutes destroy large swaths of life as we know it is a psychological stressor we all live with but don't like to think about. But our children know it, and some studies show that they are deeply disturbed by the possibility of nuclear destruction.

Unless we radically change the course of history with a new kind of thinking based on understanding wholeness, the examples of the past give us little cause for optimism. After all, there has never been a weapons system that has been invented that has not been used, except for the intermediate-range ballistic missiles. The destruction of these weapons by the United States and the former Soviet Union, coupled with measured nuclear arms reductions and attempts to secure existing stockpiles, was certainly a step toward eliminating the possibility of nuclear war, but it was only a first step. We ourselves, under other circumstances, of course, found it possible and morally defensible, we thought, to incinerate two entire cities of people. This shows that it is not just "others" who are capable of unleashing violence, even nuclear violence, on civilian populations, given the right combination of circumstances. We are "the other side." Perhaps what is required is to stop thinking in terms of "us" and "them," "good guys" and "bad guys," and to start thinking more in terms of "we." When we don't think deeply and feel deeply in terms of "we," it is entirely possible, as many experts assert, that our policies are more likely to create enemies and people who wish us harm than to create conditions for true healing on a global level.

We also need to be more conscious as a society of the threat to the environment and to our health posed by the radioactive wastes produced in nuclear weapons manufacturing and in nuclear power plants. We have no realistic ways at present of preventing contamination of the environment from these highly radioactive wastes, which remain toxic for hundreds of thousands of years. The nuclear industries and the government have always downplayed the danger to civilian populations from radioactivity, and they continue to do so to this day. But the danger is undeniable. The plutonium our weapons plants have made is the most toxic substance known to humankind. One atom of it inside your body can kill you. Hundreds of pounds of it, enough to make many homemade nuclear bombs, have disappeared from stockpiles here and abroad.

Such concerns are definitely deserving of our conscious attention. We encounter information about these issues every day, whether we are aware of it or not. Perhaps we should expand our concept of our diet to recognize that it also includes the information, images, and sounds that we take in and absorb in one way or another, usually without the least awareness. We live immersed in a sea of information. The digital revolution has made this the age of information. Are we not exposed to a steady "diet" of information, which we take in daily through newspapers, the radio, television, and wireless platforms of all kinds? Does this "diet" not influence our thoughts and feelings and shape our view of the world and even of ourselves much more than we are apt to admit? Does not information constitute, in and of itself, a major stressor in many ways? Why else would the phrase "TMI," for "too much information," be so prevalent in our colloquial discourse? It is the truth. We are drowning in information, and it is too much. But at the same time, we do not cultivate enough knowledge, which could lead to understanding, which in turn could lead to wisdom. We are a long way from "too much" understanding or wisdom.

Take, for example, the fact that we are constantly immersed in a sea of mostly bad news from all around the world, a sea of information about death, destruction, and violence. It is a steady diet, so much so that we hardly notice it. During the Vietnam War, many American families thought nothing of eating dinner while watching the battle footage of the day and hearing about the body counts. It was surreal. The networks and the military reconfigured how the news is reported from war zones, so that we weren't exposed in the same way to such images from Iraq or Afghanistan, although they can probably be found on YouTube if you want to see them. Keep your radio on for a while on any day and it is likely that you will hear graphic details of rape, murder, and, every so often, unthinkable school shootings. And that is to say nothing of the news from abroad.

We consume this diet daily. You can't help but wonder what kind of effects it has on us, individually and collectively, to have such graphic and up-to-the-minute knowledge of all these disturbing upheavals and catastrophes, but with virtually no immediate capacity to influence them, other than our efforts, sometimes striking and uplifting, through social networking, to support those in crisis, both materially and morally. Still, one likely effect of drinking in all the bad news is that we might gradually become insensitive to what happens to other people. The fate of others may become just another part of the sea of background violence within which we live. Unless it is particularly gruesome, we may not even notice it at all.

But it does go inside us, just as all the advertisements we are exposed to are taken in. You can't help noticing this when you meditate. You begin to see that your mind is full of all sorts of things that have crept into it from the news or from advertisements. In fact, advertising people are paid very high salaries to figure out effective ways of getting their message inside your head so that you will be more likely to want and buy what they are selling.

Television, movies, and our celebrity-obsessed culture also figure as a large part of our standard diet nowadays, brought to us 24/7 via cable, satellite, YouTube, downloads, and streaming to our television sets and mobile devices. In the average American household, the television is on for seven hours a day, according to some studies, and many children watch four to seven hours a day, more time than they spend doing anything else in their lives except sleeping. They are exposed to staggering amounts of information, images, and sounds, much of it frenetic, violent, cruel, and anxiety-producing, and all of it artificial and two-dimensional, not related to actual experiences in their lives other than TV watching itself.

And that is just television. Children are also exposed to images of extreme violence and sadism in popular horror movies. Grotesque and graphic simulations of reality involving killing, raping, maiming, and dismemberment have become extremely popular among the young. These vivid simulations have now become part of the diet of young minds, minds that have few defenses against this kind of reality distortion.

These images have enormous power to disturb and distort the development of a balanced mind, particularly if there is nothing of equal strength in the child's life to counterbalance them. For many children, real life pales in comparison to the excitement of the movies and computer games, and it becomes harder and harder, even for the moviemakers, to maintain their viewers' interest unless they make the images more graphic and more violent with each new release.

This pervasive diet of violence for American children must be having effects on their psyches. It is certainly having its effects in the society—witness the epidemic of bullying in our schools, and the horrifying litany of mass killings in schools and public places. Just think of Columbine, Aurora, Tucson, and Milwaukee, the latter three within a few years of each other, and the latter two within a few weeks. And then came the massacre of children at the Sandy Hook Elementary School in Newtown, Connecticut. There are already far too many reports of adolescents and young adults killing other people, some after seeing movies that they used as inspiration, as if real life were just an extension of the movies in their own minds, and as if other people's lives and fear and pain were of no value or consequence. This diet seems to be catalyzing a profound disconnection from human feelings of empathy and compassion, to the point where many children no longer identify with the pain of someone who is being victimized. One recent news article on teenage violence reported that by the time they are sixteen years old, American children have passively witnessed on average approximately 200,000 acts of violence, including 33,000 murders on television and in the movies.

The bombardment of our nervous system with images, sounds, and information is particularly stressful if it never lets up. If you switch on the television the moment you wake up, you have the radio on in the car on the way to work, you watch the news when you get home, and then you watch television or movies in the evening, you are filling your mind with images that have no direct relationship to your life. No matter how wonderful the show or how interesting the information, it will probably remain two-dimensional for you. Little of it has enduring value. But in consuming a steady diet of this stuff, which feeds the mind's hunger for information and diversion, you are squeezing out of your life some very important alternatives: time for silence, for peace, for just being without anything happening; time for thinking, for playing, for doing real things, for socializing with people face-to-face. The constant agitation of our thinking minds, which we encounter so vividly in the meditation practice, is actually fed and compounded by our diet of television, radio, newspapers, magazines, movies, and the Internet. We are constantly shoveling into our minds more things to react to; more things to think, worry, and obsess about; and more things to remember, as if our own daily lives did not produce enough on their own. The ultimate irony is that we do it to get some respite from our own concerns and preoccupations, to take our mind off our troubles, to entertain ourselves, to carry us away, to help us relax.

But it doesn't work that way. Watching television hardly ever promotes physiological relaxation. Its purview is more along the lines of sensory bombardment. It is also addicting. Many children are addicted to TV and don't know what to do with themselves when it is off. It is such an easy escape from boredom that they are not challenged to find other ways of dealing with time, such as through imaginative play, drawing, painting, and reading. Television is so mesmerizing that parents use it as a babysitter. When it is on, at least they might get a few moments of peace. Many adults are themselves addicted to soap operas, sitcoms, or news programs. One can't help wondering about the effects of this diet on family relationships and communication. Same for the gaming devices that now are a must to keep children entertained and learning.

All these observations and perspectives are merely offered as food for thought. Every issue I have raised here can be seen in many different lights.

There are no "right" answers, and our knowledge of the intricacies of these issues is always incomplete. They are presented here as examples of our interface with what we might call *world stress.* They are meant to provoke and challenge you to take a closer look at your views and behaviors and at your local environment, so that you might cultivate greater mindfulness and perhaps a more deliberate and conscious way of living in relationship to these phenomena that so color and shape our lives, whether we know it or not, whether we like it or not.

Each one of us needs to come to our own way of seeing world stress. It affects us all, even if we think we can ignore it. We touch on these issues in the Stress Reduction Clinic precisely because we do not live in a vacuum. The outer world and the inner world are no more separate than the mind and the body. We believe that it is important for our patients to develop conscious approaches to recognizing and working with these problems as well as their more personal problems if they are to bring mindfulness to the totality of their lives and cope effectively with the full range of forces at work within them.

World stress will only become more intense in the future. In the early 1970s, Stewart Brand of *Whole Earth Catalog* fame predicted narrowcasting and smart televisions, delivering only the information you want to know when you get home at the end of the day. That day is already here, but it is likely that, in terms of what is coming, we have seen nothing yet. Still, we are already in a world in which our access to information never sleeps, and goes with us everywhere through our various portable wireless devices, Twitter feeds, Facebook posts, and automatic downloads. Personal robots are on the horizon, their prototypes already at work in specialized venues such as the Mars rovers and available commercially in toys such as Furbys. Fully digitized houses are on the way. While these and other emergences may turn out to be liberating in some ways and give us more freedom and flexibility, we will also have to be on our guard against being sucked into a mode of living in which each of us is reduced to being a walking information processor and entertainment consumer.

The more complicated the world gets and the more intrusive it becomes on our own personal psychological space and privacy, the more important it will be to practice non-

doing. We will need it just to protect our sanity and to develop a greater understanding of who we are beyond our roles, beyond our PIN numbers, user names, and passwords, our Social Security and credit card numbers. It is very likely that meditation will become an absolute necessity in order for us to recognize, understand, and counter the stressors of living in such an age of ever-accelerating change, and to remind ourselves of what it means to be human.

None of the impending changes and the challenges they might augur that we have touched on here is insurmountable. They have all been created by the human mind and by its expressions in the outer world. Such challenges can equally well be met and navigated by the human mind if it learns to value and develop wisdom and harmony and to see its own interests in terms of wholeness and inter-connectedness. To do so requires us to leap beyond the impulses of mind we call fear, greed, and hatred. We can all play significant roles in making this happen by working on ourselves and on the world too. If we can come to understand that we cannot be healthy in a world that is stressed beyond its capacity to respond and to heal, perhaps we will learn to treat our world and ourselves differently. Perhaps here too we will learn not to merely treat the symptoms we are experiencing, whatever they may be, and try to make them go away, but rather, to understand and come to grips with their underlying causes. As with our own inner healing, the outcome will depend on how effectively we tune our own instrument—the body, the mind, the heart, our relationships with others and with the world itself. To have a positive effect on the problems of the larger environment, we will need continually to tune and retune to our own center, to our own hearts, cultivating awareness and harmony in our individual lives and in our families and communities. Information itself is not the problem. What we must learn is to bring wise attention to the information that is at our disposal and to contemplate it and discern order and connectedness within it so that we can put it to use in the service of our health and healing, individual, collective, and planetary.

There are a few hopeful signs on the political, economic, and technological fronts. Mindfulness is increasingly making its way into the mainstream of society and its institutions, becoming a part of the colloquial discourse, and, we can only hope, increasingly becoming embodied in actual daily practice. For example, as was mentioned in the chapter on people stress, the highly respected macroeconomist Jeffrey Sachs has recently made an impassioned and well-argued case in his book *The Price of Civilization* that mindfulness needs to be at the heart of any attempt to resolve the major problems we face as a country and, by implication, as a world. Interestingly enough, he calls what he does "clinical economics," very much parallel to and inspired by how a doctor approaches a patient. Based on a remarkable career treating economic crises in Latin America, Eastern Europe, and Africa over the past twenty-five years, he diagnoses the problem of our economy as follows:

> At the root of America's economic crisis lies a moral crisis: the decline of civic virtue among America's political and economic elite. A society of markets, laws, and elections is not enough if the rich and powerful fail to behave with respect, honesty, and compassion toward the rest of society and toward the world. America has developed the world's most competitive market society but has squandered its civic virtue along the way. Without restoring an ethos of social responsibility, there can be no meaningful and sustained economic recovery . . .
>
> . . . We need to be ready to pay the price of civilization through multiple acts of good citizenship; bearing our fair share of taxes, educating ourselves about society's needs, acting as vigilant stewards for future generations, and remembering that compassion is the glue that holds society together. . . . The American people are generally broad-minded, moderate, and generous. These are not the images of Americans we see on television or the adjectives that come to mind when we think of America's rich and powerful elite. But America's political institutions have broken down, so that the broad public

> no longer holds these elites to account. And alas, the breakdown of politics also implicates the broad public. American society is too deeply distracted by our media-drenched consumerism to maintain the habits of effective citizenship.

Citing both the Buddha and Aristotle, Sachs makes the case for a "middle path," a path of moderation and balance between work and non-work (what he calls, quaintly in this day and age, "leisure"), savings and consumption, self-interest and compassion, individualism and citizenship. He writes: "We need a *mindful society,* in which we once again take seriously our own well-being, our relations with others, and the operation of our politics." He then goes on to show in detail how this can be brought about, and he explains how urgent it is that all of us take responsibility for its success. In the second half of the book, Sachs enumerates eight dimensions of our lives in which mindfulness is crucial for individual fulfillment and happiness, and for social and economic well-being:

Mindfulness of self: personal moderation to escape mass consumerism
Mindfulness of work: the balancing of work and leisure
Mindfulness of knowledge: the cultivation of education
Mindfulness of others: the exercise of compassion and cooperation
Mindfulness of nature: the conservation of the world's ecosystems
Mindfulness of the future: the responsibility to save for the future
Mindfulness of politics: the cultivation of public deliberation and shared values for collective action through political institutions
Mindfulness of the world: the acceptance of diversity as a path to peace

This is a remarkable prescription for bringing both ethics and sanity to the body politic in practical ways that can restore its homeostasis, its health, and its promise. We can only hope that it will have a widespread influence, especially on what he calls the "millennial generation," the children of the Internet (ages eighteen to twenty-nine in the year 2010), among whom he sees the greatest potential for transformation and healing. May we all, young and not so young alike, wake up to this new opportunity and inhabit it fully in the way we live our lives and pursue our work and our dreams. The alternatives are too grim and too horrific to contemplate. So maybe we should, in the spirit of knowing the full extent of what we threaten ourselves with. Perhaps the magnitude and urgency of what we face will motivate us to choose to live more mindfully on a global level.

There are other inspiring efforts we can point to that are already bringing greater mindfulness into various aspects of the body politic, in this country and abroad. One is the work of Tim Ryan, a six-term Democratic congressman from Ohio, mentioned in Chapter 14. Congressman Ryan is himself a committed practitioner of mindfulness meditation and yoga and a tireless advocate in Congress for mindfulness-based programs in areas as diverse as health, education, the military, economics, business, the environment, energy, and criminal justice. He says:

> As a political leader, I know that to make the world a better place, we need practical applications that have been tried and tested. And when I find applications that work, I like to let people know about them. I believe I would be derelict in my duty as a congressman if I didn't do my part to make mindfulness accessible to as many people as possible in our nation.*

Now there is at least one person in Congress, out of 435 members of the House of Representatives and 100 senators, who is committed to the practice of mindfulness in his life and to its adoption and long-term application in critical areas of the body politic. With time, I can envision a lot more of his colleagues joining him. Tim Ryan may be a few years too old to be a member of the millennial generation that Jeffrey Sachs is counting on, but he is showing the way for the younger generation as he advocates for effective material support—both for more research studies and for strategic implementation of mindfulness-based programs to promote the deep well-being of the nation. He describes his vision as follows:

* Tim Ryan, *A Mindful Nation: How a Simple Practice Can Help Us Reduce Stress, Improve Performance, and Recapture the American Spirit*. New York: Hay House; 2012; xxii.

> As a country of immigrants, innovators, and risk takers, we understand how to adapt and change and find the edge. Now we need to change our collective neuropathways and create a new dynamic in America. We need to join together and update our economic and governmental systems. The industrial model, which has resulted in large, overly bureaucratic organizations that don't communicate well with each other and lose touch with events on the ground, is an outdated method for organizing and governing our society. We need new ways of thinking and new ways of mobilizing ourselves. We need to reinvest in the people of our country so that we can tap into their deep capacity for innovation to help us craft a new model to organize our society. We need systems that support our citizens to creatively participate in helping us meet these challenges. We may not know today precisely what ideas will positively transform the way we live, but mindfulness will help us to see the best emerging ideas in our rapidly changing time. . . . Mindfulness alone will not make this happen, but it will allow us to tap into the potential of every citizen and marshal all of the talents of this great country. A mindful nation is more able to change course and cut a new path when circumstances require it.*

Ryan's is a profoundly inspiring narrative. I hope the millennial generation, and all other generations, are not only listening but also falling in love with what might be possible if they stay true to themselves within the larger embrace of interconnectedness.

This is certainly true for the movement of mindfulness in various ways into the domain of the new technologies, as recounted by Congressman Ryan in his book. For instance, Google has several mindfulness programs for its staff and promotes greater mindfulness not only at its headquarters in Silicon Valley but at its centers around the world. Chade-Meng Tan, one

* Ibid pp. 143–144 in Tim Ryan's *A Mindful Nation.*

of the early Google engineers who originally helped develop Google searches in Asian languages, has, along with an august group of advisors that includes Mirabai Bush, Daniel Goleman, Norman Fischer, Marc Lesser, and Philippe Goldin, developed a mindfulness-based program for Google and for business environments worldwide called Search Inside Yourself (SIY). Meng recently came out with a book by the same name, which is a bestseller in the United States and in many other countries. In addition, Google has had an MBSR program for its employees for many years, conducted by Renee Burgard. Employees often go back and forth between these two programs as they deepen their mindfulness practice and seek out new ways of using mindfulness not only to regulate the stress in their own lives but also to catalyze greater insight and creativity in the next promising areas of innovation. Innovative leaders, such as Jenny Lykken and Karen May, Meng's boss at Google, are bringing mindfulness to the challenges of creating an optimal work climate and work-life integration.

In Silicon Valley, interest in mindfulness and its applications is not limited to Google. There are MBSR and other mindfulness programs at Apple, also taught by Burgard. Arturo Bejar and other engineers at Facebook are building mindfulness elements into their platform to address conflicts when they arise among Facebook's 1.1 billion users, helping people become more aware of their state of mind, their emotions, and how they are communicating. They have a strong collaborative research program with Dacher Keltner at the University of California, Berkeley, and his group that is studying the effects of mindfulness and compassion in reducing such conflicts and improving communications among users. There are leaders at Twitter, such as Melissa Daimler, and other companies who are bringing mindfulness into the domains of organizational effectiveness and learning.

Some of the most respected innovators in Silicon Valley are incorporating mindfulness in their companies. For example, Medium (started by one of the founders of Twitter) and Asana (started by one of the founders of Facebook) regularly support mindfulness in their companies through programs, talks, and other efforts. Dustin Moskovitz and Justin

Rosenstein, cofounders of Asana, put it this way: "Companies that are not mindful lose their way, lose their best people, become complacent, and stop innovating." They have said that in the same way mindfulness and reflection help individuals with personal growth, these practices also help organizations evolve and find their full potential.

Each year a meeting called Wisdom 2.0, initiated, organized, and hosted by Soren Gordhamer, brings together the leadership of the tech world with the leaders of the mindfulness movement to promote greater dialogue and innovation. This meeting is especially meaningful and poignant because the inventors and stewards of the new Web-based technologies—for the most part members of the millennial generation, and in many cases extremely wealthy at a very early age—also understand the potential shadow sides of their own creations and are interested in how to use mindfulness to help identify new ways of using and living with digital innovation that do not promote addiction and a loss of the priceless analog elements of a meaningful life. Major philanthropists associated with Silicon Valley, such as Joanie and Scott Kriens of the 1440 Foundation (named for the number of minutes in each day), are using their resources to support mindfulness, and more broadly, authentic relationship skills in the schools, in wellness, and in the workplace.

To return to the domain of politics for a moment, mindfulness is also becoming part of the politics of the United Kingdom. A number of members of the House of Commons and the House of Lords are interested in mindfulness and its societal and economic potential, and have been practicing together in an eight-week mindfulness course led by Chris Cullen and Mark Williams of the Oxford University Centre for Mindfulness. One of the principals in this group is Chris Ruane, a former schoolteacher and member of the House of Commons representing a constituency in North Wales. Another is Richard Layard, an economist at the London School of Economics and a member of the House of Lords. On December 4, 2012, Chris Ruane gave an impassioned and forceful speech in the House of Commons describing the potential of mindfulness for dealing with high youth unemployment, a gigantic problem in the United Kingdom. Lord Layard is engaged in advocating for a new economic metric, beyond gross domestic product, that would take into account psychological human elements in assessing the health of the economy and of the nation. He is championing this societal change through a group he founded called Action for Happiness. Many of Lord Layard's views are expounded on in his book, *Happiness: Lessons from a New Science.* Together, Ruane and Layard are championing another cycle of the mindfulness program to meet the growing interest of their colleagues in Parliament. A similar flowering of interest and practice is taking place in the Swedish parliament, led by a filmmaker who is also an MBSR instructor, Gunnar Michanek.

As of February 2013, there is a mainstream magazine, *Mindful,* and its website, Mindful.org, exclusively devoted to covering this emerging field in all its various manifestations, especially the global community of practitioners and its efforts, taking so many different forms, to transform and heal our world. I receive emails from friends and colleagues who are MBSR teachers in such far-flung places as Beijing, Tehran, Capetown, Buenos Aires, and Rome, all reporting on what they are doing, how things are going, and when we will next be crossing paths at various international mindfulness meetings and training programs.

All the unfoldings that I have been recounting here would have been unimaginable even a few short years ago. Taken together, they give the distinct impression that what may have seemed impossible only a few years ago is already happening. And that is indeed the case. The movement of mindfulness into the mainstream of medicine, health care, psychology, and neuroscience itself would have been seen as inconceivable in 1979.

Yet it has already happened. Equally impossible would have been the notion that the National Institutes of Health in the United States would be funding mindfulness research to the tune of tens of millions of dollars annually, which it now is, or that the National Health Service in the United Kingdom would recommend mindfulness, in the form of mindfulness-based cognitive therapy, as the treatment of choice in the prevention of depressive relapse, which it has. I sometimes say that from the perspective of 1979, these occurrences were somewhat less probable than that the expanding universe—triggered by the big bang 13.7 billion years ago, according to cosmologists—would have suddenly ground to a halt and begun to collapse back onto itself in a "big crunch." Yet they all happened, and much more as well. I see all these emergences as very promising signs, ones that I hope are only the beginning of a major global movement that will spur us to come to our senses as a species and cultivate greater intimacy with and understanding of various hidden dimensions of our own being.

I have written elsewhere that the human species can be seen in some sense as the autoimmune disease of the planet. We are both the cause of the earth's distress and its victim. But this does not need to continue. We are the cause when we are unaware of the multiple effects our activity has on the world, many of which have become toxic. But we can also be the agent of healing and flourishing if we wake up. Then we will be a huge beneficiary of our own embodied and enacted wisdom. This work has hardly begun, and it will need virtually all of us on the planet to contribute in whatever ways we can. Perhaps this is our common work and our common calling, to discover and embody that which is deepest and best within us as human beings—for the sake of the world, and for the sake of all beings, human and otherwise.

And so we come full circle, from the outer world back to the inner world, from the larger whole back to the individual person, each one of us facing our own life, with our own breath and body and mind. The world we live in is changing at warp speed, and we are inexorably enmeshed in those changes, whether we like it or not, whether we know it or not. Many of the changes in the world today are definitely in the direction of greater peace and harmony and health. Others clearly undermine it. All are part of the full catastrophe.

The challenge, of course, is how we are to live. Given world stress and food stress, work stress and role stress, people stress, sleep stress, time stress, and our own fears and pain, what are we going to do this morning when we wake up? How will we conduct ourselves today? Can we be a center of peace, sanity, and well-being right now? Can we live in harmony with our own minds and hearts and bodies right now? Can we put our multiple intelligences to work for us in our inner lives and in the outer world, which have never really been entirely separate?

The thousands of extraordinary ordinary people who have been through the Stress Reduction Clinic over the past thirty-four years, along with perhaps millions of others who have encountered mindfulness through MBSR and other mindfulness-based programs throughout the world, have come to face these challenges of living with greater confidence, resilience, and wisdom by systematically and lovingly cultivating awareness in their lives, and thus discovering for themselves that there is indeed a healing power in mindfulness.

We cannot predict the future of the world, even for a few days, yet our own futures are intimately connected to it. But what we can do, and so often fail to do, is to own our present, fully, as best we can, moment by moment. As we have seen, it is *here* that the future gets created, our own and the world's. How we choose to be and what we choose to do are important. They make a difference. Indeed, they make all the difference.

Having now looked at a number of concrete applications of mindfulness in this part of the book, it is time for us to come back to the practice itself, and to close with a final section in which you will find further practical suggestions for how to fine tune your cultivation of mindfulness, bring it further into your life, and find other like-minded communities and people who share a love for this way of being and doing.

HINTS AND SUGGESTIONS FOR DEALING WITH WORLD STRESS

1. Pay attention to the quality and source of your water and your food. How is the air quality where you live?
2. Be aware of your relationship to information. How much do you read newspapers and magazines? How do you feel afterward? When do you choose to read them? Is this the best use of these moments for you? Do you act on the information you receive? In what ways? Are you aware of cravings for news and information, to the point where it suggests addiction? How often do you check your email? Your phone for messages and texts and tweets? How is your behavior affected by your need to be stimulated and bombarded with information, or to broadcast what you are doing and thinking? Do you keep the radio or TV on all the time, even when you are not watching or listening? Do you read the newspaper for hours just to kill time? How frequently do you actively distract yourself, and how?
3. Be aware of how you use your television. What do you choose to watch? What needs does it satisfy in you? How do you feel afterward? How often do you watch? What is the state of mind that brings you to turn it on in the first place? What is the state of mind that brings you to turn it off? How does your body feel afterward?
4. What are the effects on your body and on your psyche of taking in bad news and violent images? Are you ordinarily aware of this domain at all? Notice if you are feeling powerless or depressed in the face of the stress and anguish in the world.
5. Try to identify specific issues that you care about, and which, if you worked on them, might help you to feel more engaged and more powerful. Just doing *something,* even if it is a very little something, can often help you to feel as if you can have an effect, that your actions count, and that you are connected to the greater world in meaningful ways. You might be able to feel effective if you identified an important health, safety, or envi-

ronmental issue in your neighborhood or town or city and worked on it, perhaps to raise other people's consciousness of a potential problem or to alleviate one that has already been identified. Since you are a part of the larger whole, it can be inwardly healing to take some responsibility for outward healing in the world. Remember the dictum "Think globally, act locally." It works the other way around too: "Think locally, act globally." And as best you can, find other like-minded people to do it in community with, since you are always already part of a much larger whole, even as you are whole yourself.

V

The Way of Awareness

33

New Beginnings

As another cycle of the Stress Reduction Clinic's MBSR program comes to a close, I look around one last time and marvel at these people who embarked together on this journey of self-observation, acceptance, and healing eight short weeks ago. Their faces look different now. They sit differently. They know how to sit. We started out this morning with a twenty-minute body scan, then went from that into sitting for twenty minutes or so. The stillness was exquisite. It felt as if we could sit forever.

It feels as if they know something very simple now that somehow eluded them before. They are still the same people. Nothing much has changed on a big scale in their lives—except, in some subtle way that comes out as we review what it has meant for them to come this far on the journey, everything.

They do not want to stop at this point. This happens each time an eight-week cycle comes to an end. It always feels as if we are just getting started. So why stop? Why not keep meeting weekly and continue practicing together?

We stop for many reasons, but the most important one has to do with developing autonomy and independence. Our learning in these eight weeks needs to be tested in the world, when we have nothing to fall back on except our own inner resources. This is part of the learning process, an important part of making the practice one's own.

The practice need not stop just because the MBSR program is over. In fact, the whole point is for the practice to keep going. This journey is a lifelong one. It is just beginning. The eight weeks is just to get us launched or to redirect the trajectory we are on. By ending the classes, we are simply saying, "All right, you have the basics. Now you are on your own. You know what to do. Do it." Or better yet, "Live it." We are purposefully taking away the external supports so that people can work at sustaining the momentum of mindfulness on their own and at fashioning their own ways of putting it to work in their lives. If we are to have the strength to face and work with the full catastrophe in our lives, our meditation practice needs a chance to develop on its own, to depend only on our own intentionality and commitment, not on a group, not on a hospital program.

When I started the clinic and what became known as MBSR thirty-four years ago, the thinking was that after eight weeks of training, people would go out on their own. Then, if they wanted to come back after six months or a year or more, we would make this an option by holding graduate programs in which they could take the practice deeper. This model has worked well over the years. The graduate classes are well attended, and clinic graduates also come back regularly to sit with us during our all-day sessions. These graduate classes have taken many different forms, sometimes five sessions, sometimes six or more, sometimes spaced out monthly, sometimes weekly. Sometimes they have specific themes. But they are all fundamentally about keeping up or reigniting the momentum in one's practice, deepening it, and integrating mindfulness more and more into every aspect of daily life and living our way fully into what we most love.

For you, the reader, it is important to remind yourself that classes, groups, follow-up sessions, guided meditation CDs, downloads, apps, and books can be very helpful at certain junctures, but they are not essential. What is essential is your vision and your commitment to practice today and to get up and practice tomorrow too, no matter what else is on your agenda. If you follow the outline of the MBSR program our patients follow, as described in Chapter 10, eight weeks should be a sufficient time to bring your meditation practice to the point where it begins to feel natural and like a way of life that you might want to continue with. You certainly will have seen before the eight weeks are over that the real learning comes from within yourself. Then, by rereading sections of this book, by diving into the books on the reading list in the Appendix, and, when possible, by locating like-minded people and groups to meditate with, you can reinforce and support your practice as it grows and deepens. There have never before been more opportunities for doing so, both locally and globally, in the flesh and online, no matter where you live.

Looking around the room now, I am struck by the high level of enthusiasm everyone seems to have about what they have accomplished in this brief period of time and by how much they obviously respect and admire each other's strength and determination as well as their own. Their superb attendance reflected that commitment.

Edward didn't miss one day of practice. Since he had started off with the body-scan CD at my suggestion when I first saw him two months before the program began, his effort is even more impressive to me. He feels his life depends on it. He takes time to practice sitting meditation every lunchtime at work, either in his office or in his car in the parking lot. Then he practices with the body-scan CD when he gets home from work, before he does anything else. Only then does he make dinner. He says that practicing this way has lifted his spirits and helps him to feel that he can handle the physical and emotional ups and downs he is going through as a result of having AIDS—including the fatigue he often feels and the numerous tests and protocols to which he is subjected.

Peter feels he has made major changes in his life that will help him to stay healthy and prevent another heart attack. His realization when he caught himself washing his car at night in his driveway was a major eye-opener for him. He too continues to practice every day.

Beverly, whose experiences were described in Chapter 25, feels that the program helped her to be calmer and to believe that she can be herself in spite of her bad days. As we saw, she thought to use her meditation training in imaginative ways to maintain control during medical diagnostic procedures that frightened her.

Marge had surgery for removal of a non-malignant mass in her abdomen right after the program ended, so I didn't get to talk with her until several months later. I had lent her a copy of the hospital stress reduction video program that I had made years ago, *The World of Relaxation,* which she used at home to prepare herself mentally for the surgery and to help her with her recovery in the weeks afterward, in addition to her regular meditation practice.* She later told me that she was awake for the one-hour operation with an epidural block and meditated through the whole thing. She heard them talking about dissecting the tumor off the large intestine but was able to remain calm. When she went home, she used the meditation over and over again in the hope of speeding and deepening her recovery process. She said that she had no problems with pain after the anesthesia wore off, as she had had with other surgeries in the past. She says that before she started in the program, she was wound up like a tight spring. Now she feels much more relaxed and easygoing, even though she still has as much pain in her knees as ever.

Art has fewer headaches now and feels he can use his breathing to prevent them from happening in stressful situations. He feels more relaxed, even though the particular pressures of police work are still there. He is looking forward to retiring from it. He liked the yoga best of all and said he experienced a new level of relaxation on the all-day session, when time fell away completely.

Phil, the French Canadian truck driver we have met a number of times along the way, went through some dramatic experiences with the practice.

* Available in DVD and CD form at www.betterlisten.com.

His way of speaking and his willingness to share what he was going through touched everyone in the class. He now feels he will be better able to concentrate and will not be so ruled by his back pain when he takes the exam for his insurance broker license. He feels that his pain is more manageable and that his ability to appreciate his time with his family has made life richer.

Eight weeks later, Roger remains more or less bewildered about his life situation. He made it through the program, which surprised me, and he says he is more relaxed and less dependent on drugs for pain, but he still does not have much clarity about how to face his domestic situation. He lost his temper on at least one occasion, and his wife had to get a court order to keep him away from the house. He clearly needs some individual attention. However, he has been in therapy before and rejects the suggestion of any more at this time, much as I encourage him to pursue it again.

Eleanor is glowing like a lightbulb this morning. She came to the clinic because she was having panic attacks. She hasn't had one since the program started, but she feels that if one comes up, she will know how to handle it now. The all-day session was extremely important for her. She touched areas of inner peace she said she has never known in sixty years.

And Louise, who told us on the first day that her son "made" her take the program by saying to her, "Mom, it worked for me and now you absolutely *have* to do it," found it started helping right away with her whole attitude toward her life, as well as with her pain from rheumatoid arthritis and the restrictions it was imposing on her ability to live the way she wanted to. She found she was able to "get behind her pain" in the body scan, and then learned to pace herself throughout her day. A few weeks ago, she triumphantly told the class of going in the car to Cooperstown for the weekend, something she would never have thought possible before. Of course she visited the Baseball Hall of Fame with family and friends, and each time that she felt she had had enough of the crowds and the press of people, she went outside, found a place to sit, closed her eyes, and just did her meditation, completely unselfconsciously, in spite of all the people milling around. She knew that that was what she needed to do to stay balanced during this potential ordeal for her. She did it a number of times that day and that weekend, and was able to sail through her trip. She exclaimed, "My son was absolutely right. I thought he was crazy, but this has given me another chance at life."

Loretta, who came for hypertension, found her life changed as well. She works as a consultant to corporations and public agencies. She said before the program that she was always afraid to show her clients the reports she had prepared for them. Now she feels much more confident about her work, declaring, "So what if they don't like it? For that matter, so what if they *like* it? Now I see that it's whether *I* feel good about it that is most important. It's made for a lot less anxiety about my work, and a lot better work too."

This insight, "So what if they *do* like it?" speaks volumes about Loretta's growth in the past eight weeks. She has clearly seen that she can be trapped by the positive, by approval, by acclaim, as much as by criticism and failure. She has seen that she must define her experiences on her own terms for them to hold real meaning for her. The rest is just an elaborate fiction, an illusion, although one it is easy to become stuck in.

Loretta's insight and her ability to embody it in her life are a perfect example of how easy it is to get stuck in our story and think that it represents reality when it does not.* Her realization is a reflection of what we mean by the word *wisdom*. It reflects the clarity and new possibilities that can arise when you no longer mistake the story it is so easy to fabricate in your head for the actuality of things, and choose instead to shift from the default mode of narrative self-referencing to a more embodied, present-moment mode of not-knowing, of being grounded in the body, and of gentle and open awareness. The more you practice, the more this happens effortlessly.

* Recall the University of Toronto study mentioned in the Introduction, which discussed the function of the midline narrative network in the prefrontal cortex, and how its activity diminished and the present moment lateral network activity increased following MBSR training. Loretta's experience is a graphic illustration of that phenomenon—two distinct modes of self-referencing, which can be influenced through training in mindfulness.

And Hector leaves feeling he has learned to control his anger better. Since he was a wrestler and carries his three hundred pounds effortlessly, like a massive but delicate bird, it was great fun for me to do the aikido exercises with him. He knew how to hold his center physically, and now he knows how to hold it emotionally as well.

All these people, and the many others who are completing the program this week with other instructions, have worked hard on themselves. Most changed in one way or another, even though our emphasis was and continues to be on non-striving and self-acceptance. The gains most of them made did not come out of idleness or passivity. They didn't come solely from attending class each week and giving each other support. They came, for the most part, out of what you might call the loneliness of the long-distance meditator, out of their willingness to practice on their own, by themselves, when they felt like it and when they didn't feel like it—to sit and to be, to dwell in silence and stillness and encounter their own minds and bodies. Any gains they experienced came out of practicing non-doing, even when their minds and bodies resisted and clamored for something more entertaining, something that required less effort.

Before we close, Phil, who has by this time become the class storyteller, shares the following memory with us, which he says he has been carrying around since he was twelve years old, not knowing exactly why. Suddenly its meaning struck him this week as he was practicing:

> We were going to a Baptist church in Canada. It was a small church, there was maybe about ninety people going to that church, ya know. There was a lot of problems at the church at that time. And my father isn't the type of person to go to a church where there was always a kind of problem. The church is supposed to be united, ya know, and working together. And so he says, "Let's get away from here for a while." We knew this small church out in the country, in the middle of nowhere. It's

like a four-corner, and there was the church and that was about it. There was all farmers around there. They only had a group of maybe ten, fifteen, twenty people at the most going to the church and, well, we figured we'd go there for support, ya know. They'll increase their people and we'll meet new people and make new friends.

So we went there and they had no ministers there. Ministers would come in from here and there different Sundays and just kinda do the service. And that Sunday we were there waiting and waiting. No minister. It was way past time, so somebody decided that maybe we should start singing some hymns, ya know. And so we got together and sang a few hymns and still no minister, and it's getting late. So one guy says, well maybe someone would like to read something from the Bible and say something, ya know. Nobody said anything, wanted to do anything. But this guy stood up. He didn't have no education, didn't know how to read or nothing. He was a farmer, very plain, very maybe what some people would call uneducated, which he was, for one thing, but not dumb, ya know, just plain, not having an education. So he could not read the Bible to say something. But he asked if somebody could read the Bible for him, he knew of the passage. It was about giving. And then, being a farmer, he gave this example, he says: "It's just like the pig and the cow had a conversation one day together. And the pig said to the cow, 'How come you get grain, bought grain from the store, ya know, all the best of everything, and I get garbage from the table, garbage to eat?' And the cow says, 'Well, I give every day, but you, we have to wait till you're dead to get anything good out of you.'" So he says, "This is what the Lord wants you to do . . . give to the Lord every day, ya know, give your soul to the Lord, ya know, give praise to the Lord every day and you will be rewarded more ways than one, ya know. And don't be like the pig and wait until you're dead for God to get anything out of you."

So that was what the message was all about. And this is what kept on coming to my mind as I'm doing the body scan . . . and finally one day it came to me that it's the same thing with the stress reduction program. You have to give something, you have to really work at it, you have to give thanks to your body, ya know, recognize your eyes. Don't wait until you go blind and say, "Oh my God, my eyes." Or your feet, don't wait until you're almost crippled, or anything like this . . . your mind, I mean, they say if you had enough faith, the size of a grain of salt, you could move mountains. The same thing . . . most doctors say we use a very little bit of our brain. The brain is a very powerful thing, just like a battery in a car. It's got all kinds of power, but if you don't have good connections, you're not going to get anything out of it, ya know. You have to practice your brain to put it to work, in other words, so you'll get something out of it, ya know.*

And I says, "My God, this is more or less what this [MBSR] is all about," ya know. I kinda pictured that together. But this message that farmer gave us in church that day, this spiritual message was very powerful. I got goose bumps when I heard it and I still do. Like I say, it came to me and I just translated it, as it's the same for your own body. You have to give to be able to receive. I gave this program a lot of effort and time. Sometimes I didn't feel like driving one hundred miles just for this thing. But I came to every class, never missed a meeting, always on time. But, see, it's easy once you start getting something out of it. If you put in your mind that you want to try, give it the best there is, all the attention you can, you'll get something out of it, ya know.

* Phil's intuitions preceded the scientific studies showing positive effects of MBSR on the brain by several decades.

It is clear as they leave the room today that most people understand that although the classes may be over, this is only the beginning. The journey really is a lifelong one. If they have found an approach that makes sense to them, it is not because someone sold it to them but because they explored it for themselves and found it of value. This is the simple path of mindfulness, of being awake in one's own life. Sometimes we call it the Way of Awareness.

Walking the path of awareness, which means living a life of awareness, requires that you keep up the meditation practice. If you don't, the Way tends to get overgrown and obscured. It becomes less accessible even though, at any moment that you choose, you can come back to it again because it is always right here. Even if you have not been practicing for some time, as soon as you are back with your breathing, back in the moment, resting in awareness itself as your new default mode, your home base, your home, you are right here again, back on the path—which is also no path, because there is truly nowhere to go, nothing to do, and nothing to attain. You are already whole, already complete, just as you are—and that is perfect—for now—in the warm embrace of your own awareness.

With this perspective, once you are cultivating mindfulness systematically in your life, it is virtually impossible to stop. Even not practicing is practicing in a way, if you are aware of how you feel compared with when you do or did practice regularly, and how it affects your ability to handle stress and pain.

The way to maintain and nurture mindfulness is to develop a daily momentum in your meditation practice and keep it going as if your life depended on it. Now you *know* directly from your own experience, not as a concept, that it actually does. The next two chapters give you some concrete and practical recommendations for keeping up both the formal and the informal mindfulness practice so that this Way of Awareness can lend ongoing clarity, direction, meaning, and beauty to your life as it continues to unfold.

34

Keeping Up the Formal Practice

The most important part of the work of mindfulness is to keep your practice alive. The way you do that is to do it. It needs to become part of your life, in the same way that eating is or working is. We keep the practice alive by making time for being, for non-doing, no matter how much rearranging it takes. Making a time for formal practice every day is like feeding yourself every day. It is that important.

The various specific practices you might choose to work with at any given time, or whether you use CDs, apps, or downloads for guidance, are not as important as keeping up your practice. Period. The various practices you engage in on your own and when you do make use of the guided meditations are just ways of bringing you back to yourself, and to remind you that it is possible now, in this moment, with whatever is happening, to rest in awareness itself. The important thing is to keep coming back to this moment. The best advice for any kind of question in the meditation practice is to keep practicing, to just keep looking at whatever arises in non-judgmental awareness and with kindness, especially if it is a recurring pattern, conundrum, thought, or feeling. Over time, the practice tends to teach you what you need to know next. If you sit with your questions and your doubts, they tend to dissolve in subsequent weeks. What seemed impenetrable becomes penetrable, what seemed murky becomes clear. It is as if you are really just letting your mind settle and learning how to rest in its essential nature, which is pure awareness. Thich Nhat Hanh, the venerable and highly respected Vietnamese meditation teacher, poet, and peace activist, uses the image of cloudy apple juice settling in a glass to describe meditation. You just sit with whatever is present, even discomfort, anxiety, or confusion, with whatever is present, and the mind settles all by itself. It is like that—if you are patient enough, and if you remind yourself to simply *rest . . . rest . . . rest* in awareness, without doing anything at all but staying awake and spacious.

It may be helpful to reread Part I, "The Practice of Mindfulness," from time to time as your meditation practice deepens, as well as the chapters on the applications of mindfulness in Part IV that are most relevant to you. Many things that you might have thought were obvious at first may become less so as your practice develops. And some details that might not have been meaningful to you at the beginning can become much more meaningful. The instructions are so simple that it is easy to misunderstand them. We have to hear them and read them over and over again. All of us do. And when we do revisit the instructions, it tends to take us more and more deeply into understanding and clarity, not so much about the details of practice but more about who we actually are as human beings. It can also be quite useful to hear the way different MBSR teachers guide the same meditation practices. Often just hearing it from a different person can open up a new way of understanding what you are asking of yourself.

Even the instructions on being aware of the breath can be easily misunderstood. For example, many people hear the instruction to "watch" your breath or to "pay attention to your breathing" to mean "think about" your breath. They are not the same. The practice is not asking you to think about your breathing. It is inviting you to explore experientially *being with* your breathing, observing it, *feeling it*. True, when the mind wanders away, thinking about your breath will bring it back into awareness. However, at that point, you go back to *feeling* the breath sensations, to riding on the waves of the breath with full awareness moment by moment and breath by breath. Remember, it the awareness that is most important, not the breath, nor any other object of attention.

The instructions on how to handle thinking are also often misunderstood. We are not suggesting that thinking is bad and that you should suppress your thoughts so that you can concentrate on your breathing or on the body scan or on a yoga posture. The way to handle thinking is to just observe it as thinking, *to be aware of thoughts as events in the field of your consciousness.* Then, depending on your practice, you can do various things. For example, if you are working at developing calmness and concentration using your breathing as the primary object of attention, you can purposefully let go of the thoughts and go back to the breath as soon as there is an awareness that thinking has carried your attention off the breath. Letting go is not a pushing away, a shutting off, a repression, or a rejection of your thoughts. It is more gentle than that. You are allowing the thoughts to do whatever they do as you keep your attention on the breath as best you can, moment by moment.

Another way of working with thinking is to watch it instead of your breath, to let the process of thinking become the primary object of attention, along with the individual thoughts. In this practice, which we do for a short while toward the end of the guided sitting meditation CD, you simply bring your attention to the flow of thought itself. In doing this, we are not oriented toward the content of our thoughts, even though we are aware of their content. We simply let the content and the emotional charge a thought may carry register in our awareness, and we work at just seeing thoughts as thoughts, as spontaneous arisings within the mind, like clouds and weather patterns in the atmosphere, observing them come and go, without getting pulled into their content.

In mindfulness practice, it is okay to have any thoughts at all. We don't try to censor our thinking, nor do we judge it as we observe it. You may find this difficult to do, especially if as a child you were brought up to believe that certain thoughts were "bad" and you were bad for having them. The work of mindfulness practice is very gentle. If a thought or a feeling is here, why not admit it and look at it? Why suppress the content we dislike and favor the content we like when, in the process, we are compromising our chance to see ourselves clearly and know our minds more as they really are?

Here is where the work of acceptance comes in, what some people call *radical acceptance.* We need to remember to be gentle and kind with ourselves as we allow ourselves to be receptive not only to the breath but to any moment and whatever it might bring. At the same time, we can recognize that some thoughts are potentially helpful and will reduce our suffering, and others are less than helpful, even toxic, generating extra suffering all by themselves. None of your thoughts is the enemy. Each one has something valuable to teach us if we see it for what it is, a thought, and if we rest in awareness of its comings and goings, without getting caught up in it and tortured by its content and emotion.* As we have emphasized over and over again, this orientation itself is a practice that deepens over time if nurtured regularly.

As we cultivate mindfulness systematically in our lives and in formal meditation practice, we will see over and over again that the pull of the mind is invariably away from looking deeply within, away from awareness of your internal experience of being. The pull of our minds tends toward externals, what we have to do today, what is going on in our lives, how many emails we haven't responded to that are weighing on us with each passing moment and day. But when such thoughts, whatever they are, capture our attention and we momentarily become involved in their content, our awareness ceases at that moment. So the real practice is not what technique you are using but your commitment to accord wise attention to your experience, inwardly and outwardly, from moment to moment—in

* This is a domain where mindfulness-based cognitive therapy has made profound contributions. As we have seen, people who have experienced a number of episodes of major depression in their lives are at very high risk of relapsing, even when they are well and not depressed, due to a disregulated pattern of thought and emotion known as depressive rumination. Mindfulness gives them a new way of being in relationship to their thoughts by not believing their content but just seeing them as events in the mind, like clouds coming and going that they do not have to get caught up in. See Williams M, Teasdale J, Segal Z, Kabat-Zinn J. *The Mindful Way Through Depression: Freeing Yourself from Chronic Unhappiness.* New York: Guilford; 2007. This approach is also being used now for people suffering from generalized anxiety, panic, and other oppressive emotional conditions.

other words, on your willingness to see and let go, to see and let be, no matter what thoughts or emotions may be preoccupying the mind at any given time.

Other problems, in addition to those stemming from misunderstanding the meditation instructions, may arise that can also undermine your practice. A big one is thinking that you are getting someplace. As soon as you notice that you are feeling proficient at the meditation or that you are getting into "special states" or "good spaces," you have to be careful and watch very, very closely what is going on in your mind. While it is only natural to be pleased by signs of progress, such as deeper concentration and calmness, insights that feel meaningful and even liberating, feelings of relaxation and self-confidence, and of course changes in your body and in body awareness itself that feel new and good to you, it is very important to just let them happen without generating a big story or narrative about them, and without taking too much credit for them either. For one thing, as we have seen, as soon as the mind comments on an experience, it distances you from it and makes it into something else—a narrative. Also, it is not really accurate for the mind to claim that "you" are responsible, that you did something. After all, the essence of the practice is non-doing.

The mind runs after anything and everything. One minute it might be saying how wonderful the meditation practice is, the next it is convincing you of the opposite. Neither thought really comes from wisdom. What is important is to recognize the impulse to build up the story of how good your meditation practice is when it comes up and to work with it in awareness as you would work with any other thought, by seeing it clearly as a thought, as a narrative, and by letting it be, and letting it go. Otherwise, practically speaking, you could easily get into talking a great deal, in your own head and to others, about how wonderful mindfulness meditation and mindful yoga are, how much they have helped you, how everybody else should do them. Bit by bit, you might become more of a proselytizer rather than a practitioner. The more you talk, the more energy you dissipate that might serve you better if it went into your practice. If you keep an eye out for this common pitfall of meditation, your practice will grow in depth and maturity and your mind will become less ruled by its own little delusions. For this reason, we actually recommend to the people taking the MBSR program in the clinic, at the very beginning of the eight weeks, that they not tell a lot of people that they are meditating, and also that they try not to talk about their meditation but just do it. This is the best way to make use of those well-intentioned and enthusiastic but often diffuse, confused, and impulsive energies of mind that want to immediately share a novel experience with others, rather than to make use of the enthusiasm by putting those energies right back into your practice. In other words, when the impulse arises to talk about how wonderful meditation is and how much you are benefiting from it, it's best to keep silent and sit some more. This goes for tweets and Facebook posts as well.

This brief review has covered some of the most common misunderstandings about the formal practice. They are all easily corrected by reminding yourself of what I saw on a T-shirt one day. It said, "Meditation—it's not what you think!"

In Chapter 10, we outlined the schedule of the eight-week program of MBSR. For convenience, the formal practice schedule is summarized below. It is probably best if you practice using the Series 1 Guided Mindfulness Meditation Practice CDs, just as our patients do. Then you will know exactly what is expected of you moment by moment, and will have the benefit of the tonal dimension the verbal guidance provides. We suggest that you follow this program for eight weeks and then continue on your own, with or without the CDs. Further suggestions for keeping up your momentum and commitment are given following the eight-week schedule.

Eight-Week Practice Schedule

Weeks 1 & 2	Practice the body scan at least 6 days per week, 45 minutes a day (CD #1). Practice sitting with awareness of breathing 10 minutes per day at a different time from the body scan practice.
Weeks 3 & 4	Alternate the body scan with Mindful Yoga 1 (CD #2) (45 minutes) if that is possible for you, 6 days per week. Continue sitting with awareness of breathing, now for 15 to 20 minutes per day. If you care to, try expanding the field of awareness to include a sense of the body as a whole sitting and breathing.
Weeks 5 & 6	Practice the sitting meditation (CD #3) 45 minutes per day, alternating with either the body scan or the Mindful Yoga 1. Experiment with mindful walking meditation on your own if you haven't already. In Week 6, you can introduce standing yoga and a few other postures (Mindful Yoga 2) into the mix. Keep up the Sitting Meditation (CD #3) every other day.
Week 7	Practice 45 minutes per day using your own choice of methods, either alone or in combination. Try not using the CDs this week and practicing as best you can on your own. Feel free to go back to the CDs if it proves too difficult for whatever reason at this point in time.
Week 8	Go back to using the CDs. Do the body scan at least twice this week. Continue the sitting meditation practice and the mindful yoga on whatever schedule feels best to you. Include formal mindful walking if you care to.

BEYOND EIGHT WEEKS:

- Sit every day. If you feel that sitting is your major form of practice, sit for *at least* twenty minutes at a time, and preferably thirty to forty-five minutes. It may help deepen your practice if you use the CD for guidance at least once or twice a week for the first few months. If you feel the body scan is your major form of practice, then make sure you sit as well for at least five to ten minutes a day. If you feel like you are having a bad day and have absolutely no time, then sit for three minutes or even one minute. Anybody can find three minutes or one minute. But when you do it, let it be a minute of concentrated non-doing, letting go of time for that minute. Keep your focus on the breath and a sense of the body as a whole sitting and breathing.

- If at all possible, try to sit in the morning. It will have a positive effect on your whole day. Other good times to practice are (a) as soon as you get home from work, before dinner; (b) before lunch, at home or in your office; (c) in the evening or late at night, especially if you are not tired; (d) any time at all—every moment is a good time for formal practice.

- If you feel the body scan is your major form of practice, then do it every day for *at least* twenty minutes at a time and preferably thirty to forty-five minutes. Again, it might be good to use the CD for guidance once or twice a week for the first few months.

- Practice the yoga four or more times a week for thirty minutes or more. Check to make sure you are doing it mindfully, especially with awareness of breathing and bodily sensations and resting between postures. I do it in the early morning before I sit, pretty much every day, in a space set up for that purpose.

- Experiment with the Series 2 and Series 3 Guided Mindfulness Meditation Practice CDs, which have a range of mostly shorter guided meditations.

- See what happens as your practice evolves and deepens. Explore the various books on the reading list that strike your interest to support your ongoing practice.

You may also find it helpful to practice together with other people from time to time. Practicing with others, especially if you have only been practicing by yourself, can be a wonderfully supportive and deepening experience. I make a point of going to talks or classes or group sittings as much as I can, and I also try to make time for periods of extended intensive practice, times when I go off on teacher-led meditation retreats, similar to our all-day sessions but longer, sometimes for a week or ten days at a time, sometimes for longer. Retreats can be an extremely important part of deepening your practice and making it your own. Also, being exposed to a range of different highly experienced and effective mindfulness teachers, each with his or her unique way of articulating the practice of mindfulness and the universal dharma framework in which it arose and developed, can be incredibly valuable in invigorating your practice as well as deepening your perspective on non-doing and the endless depths of mindfulness when it is fully embodied.

In addition to retreats, you might try searching out groups in your area with whom you could sit and practice on occasion or more regularly. That is very easy to do on the Internet. You can also find resources of all kinds for deepening your practice, including talks on YouTube and listings of sitting groups and events. There are even MBSR programs online that you can participate in.

I tend to go on retreat at two different mindfulness centers: the Insight Meditation Society (IMS) in Barre, Massachusetts, and the Spirit Rock Meditation Center in Woodacre, California. Both offer mindfulness meditation retreats led by some of the most effective and experienced meditation teachers in the world. Many of these teachers travel and lead retreats in different parts of the country as well. You can find out about their programs and retreats at the following websites: www.dharma.org and www.spiritrock.org.

Both IMS and Spirit Rock have a somewhat Buddhist orientation. However, as a rule, their emphasis is on the universal and human relevance of mindfulness and its practical applications in everyday life. They do not proselytize, and you can easily take what appeals to you and leave the rest. Anyone with training in MBSR or other mindfulness-based programs will immediately recognize that the basic practice of mindfulness they are familiar with is at the core of these centers' offerings, even though some of the forms and rituals, such as occasional chanting and bowing, might be different. Both centers provide excellent supportive environments for deepening one's meditation practice and for meeting other people who are committed to living mindfully.

In addition to retreats, you might want to search for MBSR programs in the vicinity of where you live. Many hospitals and community education centers now offer MBSR and other mindfulness-based programs. My suggestion is to speak with the instructor and see if you feel a sense of rapport and connection. Don't be shy about asking about the instructor's own relationship with mindfulness practice and what kind of professional training he or she has received (MBSR, MBCT, etc.). I suggest you enroll only if you get a feeling of authenticity, integrity, and presence from the teacher. In New York City, there is a longstanding collaborative of MBSR teachers who share a common website and support each other: www.mindfulnessmeditationnyc.com. Places such as the Open Center in New York City and the Omega Institute in Rhinebeck, New York, also offer occasional programs on mindfulness, as do many other centers across the United States and around the world. If you live in the Boston area, I also recommend the Cambridge Insight Meditation Center for meditation classes and group meditations. Here the practice is taught from the perspective of the Thai forest tradition. While it too has a Buddhist orientation, the quality of the teaching is excellent and the community it serves is broad and varied. Of course, there are many wonderful Buddhist centers in the United States and around the world that could be invaluable resources for supporting you in your practice. In addition to the Theravada tradition, there are also Zen and Tibetan centers with highly respected teachers from whom you might benefit if you don't find the rituals and forms to be impediments. Indeed they can be powerful aids if understood properly.

Finally, just sit, just breathe, just rest in being present, being aware. And if you feel like it, allow yourself to smile inwardly, just a tad.

35

Keeping Up the Informal Practice

Dear Jon: I could write a book on how my anxieties have become controllable since I have taken the stress reduction program. . . . Moment to moment has been a real key for me, and every day I get more confident in my abilities to cope with stress. Regards, Peter.

As we have seen, the essence of mindfulness is paying attention on purpose, in the present moment, non-judgmentally. So keeping up the informal practice means paying attention, being awake, and owning your moments as best you can, and as often as you can. This can be great fun. You can ask yourself at any point, "Am I fully awake?" "Do I know what I am doing right now?" "Am I fully present in the doing of it?" "How does my body feel right now?" "My breathing?" "What is my mind up to?"

We have touched on numerous strategies for bringing mindfulness into daily life. You can tune in to standing, walking, listening, speaking, eating, and working. You can tune in to your thoughts, your mood states and emotions, your motives for doing things or for feeling a certain way, and, of course, the sensations in your body. You can tune in to other people, children and adults, their body language, their tension, their feelings and speech, their actions and the consequences of those actions. You can tune in to the larger environment, the feel of the air on your skin, sounds of nature, light, color, form, movement, shadows.

As long as you are awake, you can be mindful. All it takes is wanting to and remembering to bring your attention into the present moment. Once again, it is important to emphasize that paying attention does not mean "thinking about." It means directly perceiving what you are attending to. Your thoughts will only be a part of your experience. They may or may not be an important part. Awareness means seeing the whole, perceiving the entire content and context of each moment. We can never grasp this entirely through thinking. But we can perceive it in its essence if we get beyond our thinking, and come in touch with direct seeing, direct hearing, direct feeling. Mindfulness is seeing and knowing that you are seeing, hearing and knowing that you are hearing, touching and knowing that you are touching, going up the stairs and knowing that you are going up the stairs. You might respond, "Of course I know I am going up the stairs when I am going up the stairs," but mindfulness means not just knowing it as an idea, it means *being with* going up the stairs, it means moment-to-moment awareness of the experience. Mindfulness is a *non-conceptual* knowing, or better yet, a *more-than-conceptual* knowing, the essence of awareness. By practicing in this way, we can break loose from the automatic-pilot mode and gradually bring ourselves to live more in the present moment and know its energies more fully. Then, as we have seen, we can respond more appropriately to change and to potentially stressful situations, because we are aware of the whole and of our relationship to it. You can practice this anytime, anywhere, as long as you are willing to be awake.

Chapter 9 explored the topic of mindfulness in daily life in some detail and should be reviewed for ideas for keeping up this aspect of the practice. You might want to supplement that with *Wherever You Go, There You Are,* a book I wrote on the subject of mindfulness in everyday life. Chapter 10 suggests a number of informal awareness exercises that we do in MBSR along with the formal mindfulness practices. First and foremost is practicing tuning in to our breathing at various moments throughout the day. As we have seen, this anchors us in the present. It grounds us in our body and helps us to be centered and awake to the moment.

We also practice being mindful of a whole range of routine activities, such as waking up in the morning, washing, getting dressed, taking out the garbage, doing errands. The essence of the informal practice is always the same. It involves inquiring of yourself, "Am I here now?" "Am I awake?"

"Am I in my body?" The very asking usually brings us more into the present, puts us more in touch with what we are doing.

The informal homework assignments for the eight weeks of MBSR are listed below. These informal practices are meant to accompany the weekly assignments for formal practice from the previous chapter. Of course, you can make up your own. When that starts happening spontaneously, it is a good sign that the practice is taking root. Life offers endless creative opportunities. Every aspect of your day and your life has the potential to be part of your informal practice. Ultimately, the real practice, as we have emphasized repeatedly, is how you live your life in the only moment you are ever alive, this one.

Week 1: Eat at least one meal this week mindfully.

Week 2: For this week, be aware of one pleasant event a day while it is happening. Record these, as well as your thoughts, feelings, and bodily sensations, in the Awareness of Pleasant or Unpleasant Events Calendar (see Appendix) and look for patterns. What, if anything, do you notice about what makes an experience "pleasant"? In addition, bring awareness to at least one routine activity a day: i.e., getting out of bed in the morning, brushing your teeth, taking a shower, cooking, washing the dishes, taking out the garbage, shopping, reading to your children, putting them to bed, walking your dog, and so on. With a light touch, just see if you can be present with whatever you are doing, including the feeling of being in your body.

Week 3: For this week, be aware of one unpleasant or stressful event a day while it is happening. Record the event and your bodily sensations, thoughts, feelings, and reactions/responses in the Awareness of Pleasant or Unpleasant Events Calendar (see Appendix). Look for underlying patterns. What, if anything, do you notice about what makes an experience "unpleasant"? During this week, also make an effort to "capture" your moments at different times during the day. Be aware of the tendency to fall into automatic pilot mode and notice under what circumstances it occurs. In general, take note of what pulls you off center. What do you most not want to look at? What thoughts and emotions dominate the day? What happens to your awareness of your body when the automatic pilot takes over?

Week 4: Be aware of any stress reactions during the week, without trying to change any of them. Bring awareness to any times you might find yourself feeling stuck, blocked, closing off emotionally, or numbing out, if such feelings arise. Don't try to fix them in any way, but just hold them in awareness with as much kindness toward yourself as you can muster.

Week 5: Bring awareness to moments in which you find yourself reacting, as well as falling into old habits of thought and emotional contraction. Experiment with responding rather than reacting if you see the reaction coming in time. If not, see if you can shift a reaction that is already happening into a more mindful response, even if it is not very elegant. Try to be as creative as possible in this regard, perhaps noticing whether you sometimes take things personally when they really are not personal, and whether that may trigger the emotional reaction. Notice reacting during formal meditation practice when it arises. Do you find yourself reacting during the body scan, or the yoga, or the sitting meditation? If so, hold those moments in awareness as best you can. The formal practices provide a very rich soil for discerning reactivity in the mind and cultivating alternative responses. Bring awareness to one difficult communication a day during this week and record on the Awareness of Difficult or Stressful Communication Calendar (see Appendix) what happened, what you wanted from the communication, what the other person wanted, and what actually transpired. Look for patterns over the week. Does this exercise tell you anything about your mental states and their consequences as you communicate with others?

Week 6: Bring awareness to what you choose to eat this week: where it comes from, what it looks like, how much you choose to eat, your reactions to eating it or anticipating eating it, and how you feel afterward. Try to do this with interest, curiosity, and kindness rather than any sense of judging yourself. Be aware of other ways in which you take in and "digest" the world, such as through the eyes, the ears, the nose—in other words, your diet of sights and sounds, the news, TV, air pollution, and so on. Be particularly aware of other people and the quality of your relationships with them. Experiment with silently generating lovingkindness toward those you love and toward those you don't even know as you interact with them or pass by them on the street.

Week 7: Bring particular awareness to waking up in the morning and lingering in bed long enough to realize for yourself that you are awake and it is a brand-new day, a brand-new beginning in your life—maybe even staying in bed for a few minutes, resting in awareness with no agenda, perhaps in the corpse pose. If it seems important to you, you might try waking up a bit earlier than you otherwise would so you meditate in bed for a time, lying down, without feeling the pressures of time. At the end of the day, as you are once again finally lying in bed, when you are ready to go off to sleep, see if you can touch base ever so gently with the breath, just one or two inbreaths and one or two outbreaths, as you release yourself from the day and allow sleep to come over you. Continue to experiment with directing lovingkindness silently toward others and toward yourself.

Week 8: This is the last formal week of the MBSR program. It follows the eighth class. For this reason, we often say that the eighth week is the rest of your life. In other words, it has no end. Just as with the practice and with your life, it extends itself out in present moments until it doesn't any longer. You have only moments to live. We all do. So why not live our way into them as best we can, for as long as we have? Is that not what it means to live a full and potentially happy and wise life?

ADDITIONAL AWARENESS EXERCISES YOU MAY FIND USEFUL

1. Try to be mindful for one minute in every hour. You can take this on as its own formal practice.
2. Touch base with your breathing throughout the day wherever you are, as often as you can.
3. Bring awareness to the connections between physical symptoms of distress that you might be having, such as headaches, increased pain, palpitations, rapid breathing, muscle tension, and preceding mental states. Keep a calendar of these for one full week.
4. Be mindful of your needs for formal meditation, relaxation, exercise, a healthy diet, enough sleep, intimacy and affiliation, and humor—and honor them. These needs are the mainstays of your health. If adequately attended to on a regular basis, they will provide a strong foundation for health, increase your resilience to stress and lend greater satisfaction and coherence to your life.
5. After a particularly stressful day or event, make sure that you take steps to decompress and restore balance that very day if at all possible. In particular, meditation, cardiovascular exercise, sharing time with friends, tending and befriending in general, and getting enough sleep will help in the recovery process.

In summary, every moment of your waking life is a moment to which you might bring greater stillness, awareness, and embodied presence. Our suggestions for how to do this will pale next to your own as you cultivate mindfulness in your life.

36

The Way of Awareness

In our culture, we are not so familiar with the notion of ways or paths. It is a concept that comes from ancient China, the notion of a universal lawfulness of all things, including being, non-being, and the changing nature of everything. This is known as the Tao, or simply "the Way," with a capital *W*. The Tao is the world unfolding according to its own lawfulness. Nothing is done or forced, everything just comes about. To live in accord with the Tao is to understand non-doing and non-striving. Your life is already doing itself. The challenge is whether you can see in this way and live in accordance with the way things are, to come into harmony with all things and all moments. It has nothing to do with either passivity or activity. It transcends opposites. This is the path of insight, of wisdom, and of healing. It is the path of acceptance and peace. It is the path of the mind-body looking deeply into itself and knowing itself. It is the art of conscious living, of knowing your inner resources and your outer resources and knowing also that, fundamentally, there is neither inner nor outer. It is profoundly ethical.

There is still far too little of this in our education. As a rule, our schools do not emphasize being, or the training of attention, although this situation is changing rapidly.* When mindfulness is not taught in school, we are left to sort out the domain of being for ourselves. It is *doing* that is still the dominant currency of modern education. Sadly, though, it is often a fragmented and denatured doing, divorced as it is from any emphasis on who is doing the doing and what we might learn from the domain of being. And often, far too often, our doing is under the pressure of time, as if we were being pushed through our lives by the pace of the world, without the luxury of stopping and taking our bearings, of knowing who is doing all the doing, and why. Awareness itself is not highly valued, nor are we taught the richness of it and how to nurture, use, and inhabit it—how it can round out the limitations and sometimes the tyranny of thinking, and provide a counterbalance to our thinking and our emotions, serving as the independent dimension of intelligence that it actually is.

It might have helped us considerably to have been shown, perhaps through some simple exercises in elementary school, that we are not our thoughts, that we can watch them come and go and learn not to cling to them or run after them. Even if we didn't understand it at the time, it would have been helpful just to hear it. Likewise, it would have been helpful to know that the breath is an ally, that it leads to calmness just by watching it. Or that it is okay to just be, that we don't have to run around all the time doing or striving or competing in order to feel that we have an identity—that we are fundamentally whole as we are.

We may not have gotten these messages as children, except perhaps those generations who watched *Mister Rogers' Neighborhood* or *Sesame Street,* but it is not too late. Anytime you decide that it is time to reconnect with the domain of your own wholeness is the right time to start. In the yogic traditions, age is measured from when you started practicing, not from when you were born. So, by this point, if you have started practicing, you may now be only a few days or weeks or months old! How nice.

Strange as it may seem, this is the real work we invite the people who are referred by their doctors to the Stress Reduction Clinic to engage in. It

* Now there is a strong and growing movement to bring mindfulness into primary and secondary education, as well as into the curriculm of colleges and universities.

is the exploring of the notion that there is a way of being, a way of living, a way of paying attention that is like starting afresh, that is liberating in and of itself, right now, within all one's suffering and the turmoil of life. But to explore it as an idea or a philosophy would be a dead exercise in thinking, just more ideas to fill our already overcrowded minds.

You are invited, in the same spirit as our patients are invited, and in the abiding spirit of mindfulness and MBSR, to work at making the domain of being an ally in your life, to walk the path of mindfulness and see for yourself how things change when you change the way you are in relationship to your body, to your mind, to your heart, and to the world. As we saw at the very beginning, it is an invitation to embark on a lifelong journey, an invitation to see life as an adventure in awareness.

This adventure has all the elements of a heroic quest, a search for yourself along the path of life. It may sound far-fetched to you, but we see our patients as heroes and heroines in the Greek sense, on their own personal odysseys, battered about by the elements and the fates, and now, having embarked upon this journey of healing and the realization of wholeness, finally treading the path toward home.

As it turns out, we don't have to look very far to reconnect with our deepest selves on this quest. At any moment, we are very close to home, much closer than we think. If we can simply realize the fullness of *this* moment, of *this* breath, we can find stillness and peace right here. We can be at home right now, in our body as it is, in this moment as it is.

When you walk the path of awareness, you are bringing a systematic consciousness to the experience of living that only makes living more vibrant, more real. The fact that no one ever taught you how to do this or told you that it was worth doing is immaterial. When you are ready for this quest, it finds you. It is part of the Way for things to unfold like this. Each moment truly is the first moment of the rest of your life. Now really is the only time you have to live.

Mindfulness practice provides an opportunity to walk along the path of your life with your eyes open, awake instead of half unconscious, responding consciously in the world instead of reacting automatically, mindlessly. The end result is subtly different from the other way of living in that we know that we are walking a path, that we are following a way, that we are awake and aware. No one dictates to you what that path is. No one is telling you to follow "my way." The whole point is that there is only one way, but that way manifests in as many different ways as there are people and customs and beliefs.

Our real job, with a capital J, is to find *our own way,* sailing with the winds of change, the winds of stress and pain and suffering, the winds of joy and love, until we realize that we have also in some sense never left port, that we have never been separate from our truest self—that we are always at home in our own skin, or can be if we simply remember.

There is no way to fail in this work if you approach it with sincerity and constancy. Meditation is not relaxation spelled differently. If you do a relaxation exercise and you aren't relaxed at the end, then in some sense you have failed. But if you are practicing mindfulness, then the only thing that is really important is whether you are willing to look and to be with things as they are in any moment, including discomfort and tension and your ideas about success and failure. If you are, then there is no failure.

Similarly, if you are facing the stress in your life mindfully, you cannot fail in your responses to it. Just being aware of it is a powerful response, one that changes everything and opens up new options for growth and for doing.

But sometimes those options don't manifest right away. It may be clear what you don't want to do but not clear yet what you do want to do. These are not times of failure either. They are creative moments, moments of not knowing, moments to be patient, centered in *not knowing*. Even confusion and despair and agitation can be creative. We can work with them if we are willing to be in the present from moment to moment with awareness. This is Zorba's dance in the face of the full catastrophe. It is a movement that carries us beyond success and failure, to a way of being that allows the full spectrum of our life experiences, our hopes and our fears, to play itself out within the field of life itself unfolding, flowering in each moment we are fully present with it, for it, and in it.

The Way of Awareness has a structure to it. In this book we have gone into that structure in some detail. We have touched on how it is connected to health and healing, to stress, pain and illness, and to all the ups and downs of the body, the mind, the heart, and life itself. It is a path to be traveled, to be cultivated through daily practice. Rather than a philosophy, it is a way of being, a way of living your moments and living them fully. This way only becomes yours as you travel it yourself.

Mindfulness is a lifetime's journey along a path that ultimately leads nowhere, only to who you are. The Way of Awareness is always here, always accessible to you, in each moment. After all is said and done, perhaps its essence can only be captured in poetry, and in the silence of your own mind and body at peace.

So, having arrived at this point on our journey together, let's let the moment be cradled in the vision of the great Chilean poet, Pablo Neruda, in a poem he called "Keeping Quiet."

Now we will count to twelve
and we will all keep still.

For once on the face of the earth,
let's not speak in any language;
let's stop for one second,
and not move our arms so much.

It would be an exotic moment
without rush, without engines;
we would all be together
in a sudden strangeness.

Fishermen in the cold sea
would not harm whales
and the man gathering salt
would look at his hurt hands.

Those who prepare green wars,
wars with gas, wars with fire,

victories with no survivors,
would put on clean clothes
and walk about with their brothers
in the shade, doing nothing.

What I want should not be confused
with total inactivity.
Life is what it is about;
I want no truck with death.

If we were not so single-minded
about keeping our lives moving,
and for once could do nothing,
perhaps a huge silence
might interrupt this sadness
of never understanding ourselves
and of threatening ourselves with death.
Perhaps the earth can teach us
as when everything seems dead
and later proves to be alive.

Now I'll count up to twelve
and you keep quiet and I will go.

Afterword

A great deal has happened on so many fronts since this book first appeared in 1990. For one, the Stress Reduction Clinic described here, since the year 2000 under the direction of my longtime colleague and friend Dr. Saki Santorelli, has continued to thrive at UMass for another thirteen years, thanks in large measure to his remarkable leadership and vision and skill in negotiating the waters during a very turbulent and trying time in medicine. In September 2013 the clinic celebrated its thirty-fourth year in continual operation. More than twenty thousand medical patients have completed the eight-week MBSR program. The present teachers and staff of the clinic are unsurpassed in their devotion to articulating the practice of mindfulness effectively, in the quality of the work they do, and in the profound effects they have on the people who take the program in helping them to know themselves better and grow more fully into themselves to whatever degree might be possible. As a community, we share a deep gratitude for all the past MBSR instructors and staff who contributed to the successes of the program over the years—they are listed in the Acknowledgments.

In the past twenty years, the work described in this book, in the form of MBSR and other mindfulness-based programs, has spread around the world. While from one perspective this may have seemed improbable, from another perspective it makes a lot of sense, and can be seen as a very positive development, perhaps arriving at just the perfect moment for the world to take note of the power of mindfulness and harness its transformative and healing potential. At first it happened relatively slowly, and then increasingly rapidly. It spread to hospitals, medical centers, clinics, and a range of other institutions such as schools, businesses, prisons, the military, and beyond. It part, this was propelled by the work of the Stress Reduction Clinic having been featured in the 1993 public television special *Healing and the Mind,* with Bill Moyers, seen by more than forty million viewers over the years. Since the entire forty-five-minute segment was crafted as a guided meditation in its own right by the talented producer David Grubin and by the editors—a very unusual use of television—it had a profound impact on the viewers, entraining them right into the process and practice of mindfulness along with the patients who were taking the class.

Our work in the clinic has also been featured in many other television news programs and articles in the media over the years, and now, increasingly, in the foreign media as well.

The development of mindfulness-based cognitive therapy, with its powerful theoretical rationale and its well-designed and executed clinical trials demonstrating and confirming its efficacy, also played a major role in the spread of interest in mindfulness in psychological circles and in psychotherapy. So has the development of self-report instruments that purport to "measure mindfulness" and have given rise to a rich and growing body of research. Studies on the effects of MBSR and other forms of meditation practice on both brain activity and brain structure and connectivity have also accelerated work in this growing area of neuroscience, now known as contemplative neuroscience. Many of these studies have been conducted on monks and other practitioners with tens of thousands of hours of meditation practice and training. Richard Davidson and his collaborators at the University of Wisconsin in the Laboratory of Affective Neuroscience and the Center for Investigating Healthy Minds have been pioneers in this area. The University of Wisconsin has its own Center for Mindfulness and a fine team of MBSR instructors, led by its founder, Katherine Bonus.

The Mind and Life Institute and its annual Summer Research Institute have catalyzed a growing community of young scientists and clinicians at the highest levels. It has also made it much more acceptable as a career path to do research in this area, by making strategic funding available for young investigators through Varela Research Grants (named after the late Francisco Varela—the co-founder of the Mind and Life Institute, a polymath neuroscientist, philosopher, and highly committed meditation practitioner) as well as larger grants for senor investigators.

In 1995 we inaugurated an umbrella institute, known as the Center for Mindfulness in Medicine, Health Care, and Society (CFM), to house not only the Stress Reduction Clinic but the wellspring of initiatives and projects that were emerging out of our work by that time, well beyond the work in the clinic itself. The CFM now offers mindfulness-based programs of all kinds in schools and businesses in addition to its work with medical patients. It also houses an institute, Oasis, for educating and training interested health professionals and others in the intricacies of mindfulness practice and its delivery in a range of different institutional settings. Oasis offers an MBSR instructor certification program that professionals are participating in from around the world.

The CFM also collaborates with other institutions in a range of ongoing research projects, and hosts an annual international mindfulness conference that, in 2013, is in its eleventh year. Hundreds of scientists, clinicians, and educators from around the world attend these meetings and share their initiatives and studies with each other—a beautiful and growing global community. Many of these mindfulness teachers are now writing both professional and trade books to express their own unique perspectives on mindfulness, MBSR, MBCT, and other mindfulness-based interventions. They are also studying and writing about meditation practices which cultivate lovingkindness and compassion, as well as the cultivation of what some psychologists are calling *virtuous human qualities,* such as generosity, forgiveness, gratitude, and kindness.

All these efforts from different groups around the world are driving and deepening the growing interest and understanding of mindfulness as an actual *practice,* and not merely as a philosophy or good idea. The field of mindfulness-based interventions is increasingly multifaceted. MBSR programs and other programs modeled on it are even being offered now by Buddhist meditation centers such as InsightLA.

From 1992 to 1999, we ran a free MBSR clinic in the inner city in Worcester, with free on-site mindful child care, free transportation, and in which classes were taught in Spanish as well as in English. This clinic and the hundreds of people it served demonstrated the universality of MBSR and its adaptability to multicultural settings. We also conducted a four-year program for inmates and staff of the Massachusetts Department of Corrections, and demonstrated an ability to reach large numbers of inmates with MBSR and reduce measures of hostility and stress. One of our colleagues, George Mumford, who co-led our inner city clinic, also trained both the Chicago Bulls and then the Los Angeles Lakers in mindfulness during their championship seasons.

You can find out more about the CFM and the Stress Reduction Clinic, its professional training opportunities, and where MBSR programs that we know about are located around the world by visiting the CFM's website at www.umassmed.edu/cfm.

In his Preface, Thich Nhat Hanh describes this book as "a door opening both on the dharma (from the side of the world) and on the world (from the side of the dharma)." Although you will not find the word *dharma* in this book, other than in this paragraph, in the Preface, and in two other places, I would say that we need it in our vocabulary, as there is no way to translate it. For many years, I was hesitant to use it at all, and there is certainly no need for it in the teaching of MBSR, nor do we ever use it in that context. Still, it is necessary in the training of MBSR teachers, because, as Thich Nhat Hanh saw, MBSR is deeply rooted in dharma. If prospective MBSR teachers think that mindfulness is just another cognitive-behavioral "technique" developed within the intellectual framework of Western clinical psychology, they would be sorely mistaken. That would be a profound misunderstanding of the origins of mindfulness and of MBSR, and the depths of its healing and transformative potential. For obvious reasons, one cannot teach what one does not understand, and mindfulness cannot be understood outside of its embodied cultivation through practice without attachment to any outcomes, however desireable. For anybody who is interested in this subject in any detail, I have written an extended piece entitled "Some Reflections on the Origins of MBSR, Skillful Means, and the Trouble with Maps." It can be found in the book *Mindfulness: Diverse Perspectives on Its Meaning, Origins, and Applications,* co-edited by Mark Williams of the Oxford University Mindfulness Centre and myself. You may also want to consult a chapter called "Dharma" that I wrote for *Coming to Our Senses.* These attempts to use the word and locate it within the field of mindfulness-based interventions are meant to give more explicit background to those who care to understand the traditions out of which MBSR emerged and upon which its practices are based. MBSR was meant from the beginning to be an experiment to see whether mainstream America and American medicine and health care would be receptive to this transformative and liberative dharma perspective, if framed in a universal vocabulary and within an easily accessible and commonsensical format and idiom. MBSR and its "cousins" are expressions, however limited they may be in some regards, of the deep wisdom stemming from practices discovered and refined long ago in India and kept alive and refined further over millennia by multiple traditions—mostly but not exclusively Buddhism—in all the civilizations of Asia.

May mindfulness in its most universal expression prove valuable in your life and in all your relationships, both inner and outer. May your mindfulness practice continue to grow and flower and nourish your life and work from moment to moment and from day to day. And may the world benefit from this potentially boundless flowering within your own heart.

Acknowledgments

In an undertaking such as this one, there are a great many people to thank because the work of MBSR is so distributive and widespread now, and based not only in collegiality but in deeply meaningful dharma friendship. Space will not permit me to individually thank by name all my colleagues and friends who have contributed to the nurturance of mindfulness-based interventions and contemplative practices more broadly throughout the world in the twenty-five years since this book first appeared, and those who contributed to the work of MBSR in the years before that. You know who you are. Please know how deeply I honor what you have done, what you are doing, and even more, who you are. Your work and our past or ongoing connections in this growing community of purpose and practice have been an inspiration for revising and updating this book. I hope it contributes in some small way to furthering your work and to the ongoing flowering of mindfulness in the world.

Many people contributed directly and indirectly to this book at different stages. Going back to the very beginning, without the faith and support of Tom Winters, Hugh Fulmer, and John Monahan, the Stress Reduction Clinic would never have existed. They were the first doctors to send their patients. James E. Dalen, chief of medicine at UMMC until 1988, then dean of the University of Arizona College of Medicine, was a staunch supporter and champion from the very start, and has remained a friend ever since.* Judith K. Ockene, director of the Division of Preventive and Behavioral Medicine at the University of Massachusetts Medical School, has given continuing support and encouragement for more than thirty years now, first during my tenure as director of the stress reduction clinic and, beginning in 1995, also as executive director of the Center for Mindfulness in Medicine, Health Care, and Society (CFM); and since 2000, to Saki Santorelli in his role as executive director of the CFM. I am grateful for Judith's longstanding commitment and hard work to transform medicine and health care through changing how we as individuals choose to live our lives—the lifestyle choices we make—and how we might develop enlightened policy to optimize the health of the society as a whole.

Words cannot express my gratitude and my appreciation for my longtime friend and colleague, Saki Santorelli, who I have known since 1981, when he attended my classes as the first intern in what became, over time, the Center's training curriculum for health professionals. Saki joined the clinic in 1983 as an instructor, and has worked there continually since. I bow to him for his vast heart, his vision, his creativity, and his exceptional leadership of the Center for Mindfulness in an era fraught with challenges to the Center, which he navigated with great insight, fortitude, and wisdom. In this same era, he was also able to preside over and guide a period of remarkable deepening and expansion of the CFM's activities and impact via collaborative research, expanded professional education programs offered by the Oasis Institute, which he founded and developed, and his initiation of an Annual International Scientific Conference: Investigating and Integrating Mindfulness in Medicine, Health Care, and Society, held every year since 2003. These visionary initiatives have contributed to a

* Jim interviewed me and several physician colleagues who teach mindfulness for the inaugural issue of a new journal, *The Medical Round Table*. Dalen J; Kabat-Zinn, J; Krasner M; and Sibinga E. Guidance clinicians can give their patients for identifying and reducing stress. *The Medical Round Table* 2012, 1: 7-16.

profound furthering of MBSR and of mindfulness research and education in many different domains throughout the world.

I would also like to thank the thousands of physicians and other health professionals at the University of Massachusetts Medical Center, now known as the UMass Memorial Medical Center, and in the greater New England community who have referred their patients to the Stress Reduction Clinic over the years. Their faith in the clinic and, above all, in their patients' abilities to grow, change, and, ultimately, to influence the course of their own health as a complement to their medical treatments sets an essential tone for our efforts to help their patients to mobilize their own interior resources for healing through MBSR and a more participatory medicine.

My wife, Myla Kabat-Zinn, contributed enormously to the first edition, which she read in its entirety, bringing to every page her sensitivity to language, to excess, and to lapses in clarity. I am hugely grateful for her abiding patience, stalwart support, and forbearance over the extended periods when I was absorbed in revising it, and for her editorial advice on the Introduction to this edition.

Heartful and deep appreciation to Elissa Epel and Cliff Saron for schooling me so patiently in the latest views on stress reactivity. If there are any inaccuracies, oversimplifications, or vaguenesses in the stress section, it is certainly not due to their vigilance and recommendations, but to my attempts to keep things relatively simple. I want to thank Paul Grossman for his very helpful input on the stress section as well. I am also indebted to Dean Ornish for his help in describing his pioneering work. And I thank Zindel Segal, Mark Williams, and John Teasdale for the privilege of working with such remarkable and modest beings, whose impact on the world has been so enormous through their development of MBCT and its foundational research base. I am grateful for the many wonderful years of personal and professional conversations, collaborations, and adventures, from which I have learned and continue to learn so much.

I want to thank Priyanka Krishnan, my editor at Random House, for the pleasure of working with her and her team, including Shona McCarthy.

Priyanka gave careful and wise consideration to every element of this book, and was a huge exponent of efficiency in the process while making generous room for her author's agency. I also want to thank the editor of the first edition, Bob Miller—who originally acquired this book when it was a radical and brave act to publish a mainstream book on meditation—for his friendship and support over the past twenty-five years.

A deep bow of appreciation, gratitude, and debt to my teaching colleagues in the clinic, past and present, for their dedication to MBSR, their embodiment of mindfulness and heartfulness, and for the examples they set for the professionals they train around the world, simply by being who they are: Melissa Blacker, Adi Bemak, Katherine Bonus, Kasey Carmichael, Jim Carmody, Meg Chang, Jim Colosi, Fernando de Torrijos, Pam Erdmann, Paul Galvin, Cindy Gittleman, Trudy Goodman, Britta Hölzel, Jacob Piet Jacobsen, Diana Kamila Lynn Koerbel, Florence Meleo-Meyer, Kate Mitcheom, David Monsour, George Mumford, Peggy Rogenbuck-Gillespie, Elana Rosenbaum, Larry Rosenberg, Camila Skold, Rob Smith, David Spound, Bob Stahl, Barbara Stone, Carolyn West, Ferris Urbanowski, Zayda Vallejo, Susan Young, and Saki F. Santorelli. Peggy Roggenbuck-Gellispie was the very first teacher I hired in the clinic. It was her suggestion to incorporate the pleasant and unpleasant events calendars into the homework in Weeks 2 and 3.

A special bow of gratitude to Bob Stahl for the longstanding and supremely loving role he has played in organizing and nurturing the development of the San Francisco Bay Area MBSR teachers community for more than twenty years, and for his work with the CFM, and in particular, with Florence Meleo-Meyer, in training MBSR instructors around the world.

I am deeply grateful to and often awed by the deep caring all of the administrative staff, past and present, who have so consistently and so creatively powered the work of the clinic and the CFM: Jean Baril, Kathy Brady, Leigh Emery, Monique Frigon, Dianne Horgan, Brian Tucker, Carol Lewis, Leslie Lynch, Roberta Lewis, Merin MacDonald, Tony Maciag, Kristi Nelson, Jessica Novia, Norma Rosiello, Amy Parslow, Anne Skillings, and Rene Theberge.

I also want to acknowledge and thank the members, past and present, of the Advisory Board of the CFM under Saki's tenure: Lyn Getz, Cory Greenberg, Amy Gross, Larry Horwitz, Maria Kluge, Janice Maturano, Dennis McGillicuddy, and Tim Ryan. Larry has been a friend and keen advisor of the CFM since 1995, when he came to help us with our first strategic planning process. Maria Kluge has been a major supporter of the Center, as well as being an MBSR teacher in the US and in Germany.

I wish to thank all my teachers for the many gifts they have given me.

And finally, I thank all the people who came to the stress reduction clinic as patients, shared their stories in class, and were then willing to have them appear in this book. They did so expressing a virtually unanimous hope that their personal experiences with the meditation practice and the MBSR curriculum might help inspire others who suffer from similar life challenges to find wellbeing, peace, and relief in their lives.

Appendix

Awareness Calendars

Reading List

Resources

Guided Mindfulness Meditation Practice CDs with Jon Kabat-Zinn: Ordering Information

Awareness of Pleasant or Unpleasant Events Calendar

Instructions: One week, be aware of one pleasant event or occurrence each day *while it is happening*. At a later time, on a calendar such as the one provided here, record in detail what it was and your experience of it. The next week, be aware of one unpleasant or stressful experience each day, and record it in a similar way.

	What was the experience?	Were you aware of the pleasant (or unpleasant) feelings *while* the event was happening?	How did your body feel, in detail, during this experience? Describe the sensations you felt.	What moods, feelings and thoughts accompanied this event at the time?	What thoughts are in your mind now as you write this down?
Monday					
Tuesday					

Wednesday					
Thursday					
Friday					
Saturday					
Sunday					

Awareness of a Difficult or Stressful Communication Calendar

Instructions: One week, be aware of one difficult or stressful communication each day *while it is happening*. At a later time, record the details of your experience on a calendar such as the one provided here.

	Describe the communication. Who was it with? What was the subject?	How did the difficulty come about?	What did you really want from the person or situation? What did you actually get?	What did the other person[s] want? What did they actually get?	How did you feel during and after this time?	Has this issue been resolved yet? If not, how might it be?
Monday						
Tuesday						

Wednesday						
Thursday						
Friday						
Saturday						
Sunday						

Reading List

MINDFULNESS MEDITATION: ESSENCE AND APPLICATIONS

Alpers, Susan. *Eat, Drink, and Be Mindful.* Oakland, CA: New Harbinger, 2008.

Analayo, Satipatthana. *The Direct Path to Realization.* Cambridge: Windhorse Publications, 2008.

Amero, Ajahn. *Small Boat, Great Mountain.* Redwood Valley, CA: Abhayagiri Monastic Foundation, 2003.

Bardacke, Nancy. *Mindful Birthing.* San Francisco: HarperCollins, 2012.

Bartley, Trish. *Mindfulness-Based Cognitive Therapy for Cancer.* Oxford: Wiley-Blackwell, 2012.

Bauer-Wu, Susan. *Leaves Falling Gently: Living Fully with Serious and Life-Limiting Illness Through Mindfulness, Compassion, and Connectedness.* Oakland, CA: New Harbinger, 2011.

Bays, Jan Chozen. *Mindful Eating.* Boston: Shambhala, 2009.

——. *How to Train an Elephant.* Boston: Shambhala, 2011.

Beck, Joko. *Nothing Special.* New York: HarperCollins, 1995.

Bennett-Goleman, Tara. *Emotional Alchemy: How the Mind Can Heal the Heart.* New York: Harmony, 2001.

Biegel, Gina. *The Stress Reduction Workbook for Teens.* Oakland, CA: New Harbinger, 2009.

Bodhi, Bhikkhu. *The Noble Eightfold Path.* Onalaska, WA: BPS Pariyatti Editions, 2000.

Boyce, Barry, ed. *The Mindfulness Revolution: Leading Psychologists, Scientists, Artists, and Meditation Teachers on the Power of Mindfulness in Daily Life.* Boston: Shambhala, 2011.

Brantley, Jeffrey. *Calming Your Anxious Mind: How Mindfulness and Compassion Can Free You from Anxiety, Fear, and Panic.* Oakland, CA: New Harbinger, 2003.

Carlson, Linda, and Michael Speca. *Mindfulness-Based Cancer Recovery.* Oakland, CA: New Harbinger, 2011.

Chokyi Nyima, Rinpoche. *Present Fresh Wakefulness.* Boudhanath, Nepal: Rangjung Yeshe Books, 2004.

Davidson, Richard J., with Sharon Begley. *The Emotional Life of Your Brain.* New York: Hudson Street Press, 2012.

Davidson, Richard J., and Anne Harrington. *Visions of Compassion.* New York: Oxford University Press, 2002.

Didonna, Fabrizio. *Clinical Handbook of Mindfulness.* New York: Springer, 2008.

Epstein, Mark. *Thoughts Without a Thinker: Psychotherapy from a Buddhist Perspective.* New York: Basic Books, 1995.

Feldman, Christina. *Silence: How to Find Inner Peace in a Busy World.* Berkeley, CA: Rodmell Press, 2003.

———. *Compassion: Listening to the Cries of the World.* Berkeley, CA: Rodmell Press, 2005.

Germer, Christopher. *The Mindful Path to Self-Compassion.* New York: Guilford, 2009.

Germer, Christopher, Ronald D. Siegel, and Paul R. Fulton, eds. *Mindfulness and Psychotherapy.* New York: Guilford, 2005.

Gilbert, Paul. *The Compassionate Mind.* Oakland, CA: New Harbinger, 2009.

Goldstein, Joseph. *Mindfulness: A Practical Guide to Awakening.* Boulder, CO: Sounds True, 2013.

———. *One Dharma: The Emerging Western Buddhism*. San Francisco: HarperCollins, 2002.

Goldstein, Joseph, and Jack Kornfield. *Seeking the Heart of Wisdom*. Boston: Shambhala, 1987.

Goleman, Daniel. *Focus: The Hidden Driver of Excellence*. New York: HarperCollins, 2013.

———. *Destructive Emotions: How We Can Heal Them*. New York: Bantam, 2003.

———. *Healing Emotions: Conversations with the Dalai Lama on Mindfulness, Emotions, and Health*. Boston: Shambhala, 1997.

Gunaratana, Bante Henepola. *The Four Foundations of Mindfulness in Plain English*. Boston: Wisdom, 2012.

———. *Mindfulness in Plain English*. Somerville, MA: Wisdom, 2002.

Hamilton, Elizabeth. *Untrain Your Parrot and Other No-Nonsense Instructions on the Path of Zen*. Boston: Shambhala, 2007.

Hanh, Thich Nhat. *The Heart of the Buddha's Teachings*. Boston: Wisdom, 1993.

———. *The Miracle of Mindfulness*. Boston: Beacon Press, 1976.

Kabat-Zinn, Jon. *Mindfulness for Beginners: Reclaiming the Present Moment—and Your Life*. Boulder, CO: Sounds True, 2012.

———. *Letting Everything Become Your Teacher: 100 Lessons in Mindfulness—Excerpted from Full Catastrophe Living*. New York: Random House, 2009.

———. *Arriving at Your Own Door: 108 Lessons in Mindfulness—Excerpted from Coming to Our Senses*. New York: Hyperion, 2007.

———. *Coming to Our Senses: Healing Ourselves and the World Through Mindfulness*. New York: Hyperion, 2005.

———. *Wherever You Go, There You Are*. New York: Hyperion, 1994, 2005.

Kabat-Zinn, Jon, and Richard J. Davidson, eds. *The Mind's Own Physician: A Scientific Dialogue with the Dalai Lama on the Healing Power of Meditation*. Oakland, CA: New Harbinger, 2011.

Kabat-Zinn, Myla, and Jon Kabat-Zinn. *Everyday Blessings: The Inner Work of Mindful Parenting*. New York: Hyperion, 1997.

Kaiser-Greenland, Susan. *The Mindful Child: How to Help Your Kid Manage Stress and Become Happier, Kinder, and More Compassionate*. New York: Free Press, 2010.

Krishnamurti, J. *This Light in Oneself: True Meditation.* Boston: Shambhala, 1999.

Levine, Stephen. *A Gradual Awakening.* New York: Random House, 1989.

McCowan, Donald, Diane Reibel, and Marc S. Micozzi. *Teaching Mindfulness.* New York: Springer, 2010.

McQuaid, John R., and Paula E. Carmona. *Peaceful Mind: Using Mindfulness and Cognitive Behavioral Psychology to Overcome Depression.* Oakland, CA: New Harbinger, 2004.

Mingyur, Rinpoche. *The Joy of Living.* New York: Three Rivers Press, 2007.

——. *Joyful Wisdom.* New York: Harmony Books, 2010.

Olendzki, Andrew. *Unlimiting Mind: The Radically Experiential Psychology of Buddhism.* Boston: Wisdom, 2010.

Orsillo, Susan, and Lizbeth Roemer. *The Mindful Way Through Anxiety.* New York: Guilford, 2011.

Packer, Toni. *The Silent Question: Meditating in the Stillness of Not-Knowing.* Boston: Shambhala, 2007.

Penman, Danny, and Vidyamala Burch. *Mindfulness for Health: A Practical Guide to Relieving Pain, Reducing Stress and Restoring Wellbeing.* London, UK: Piatkus, 2013.

Richard, Matthieu. *Why Meditate? Working with Thoughts and Emotions.* New York: Hay House, 2010.

——. *Happiness: A Guide to Developing Life's Most Important Skill.* New York: Little, Brown, 2007.

——. *The Monk and the Philosopher.* New York: Schocken, 1998.

Rosenberg, Larry. *Breath by Breath.* Boston: Shambhala, 1998.

——. *Living in the Light of Dying.* Boston: Shambhala, 2000.

Ryan, Tim. *A Mindful Nation.* New York: Hay House, 2012.

Salzberg, Sharon. *Real Happiness.* New York: Workman, 2011.

——. *A Heart as Wide as the World.* Boston: Shambhala, 1997.

——. *Lovingkindness.* Boston: Shambhala, 1995.

Santorelli, Saki. *Heal Thy Self: Lessons on Mindfulness in Medicine.* New York: Bell Tower, 1998.

Segal, Zindel V., Mark Williams, and John D. Teasdale. *Mindfulness-Based Cognitive Therapy for Depression: A New Approach to Preventing Relapse.* 2nd ed. New York: Guilford, 2012.

Semple, Randye J., and Jennifer Lee. *Mindfulness-Based Cognitive Therapy for Anxious Children.* Oakland, CA: New Harbinger, 2011.

Shapiro, Shauna, and Linda Carlson. *The Art and Science of Mindfulness: Integrating Mindfulness into Psychology and the Helping Professions.* Washington, DC: American Psychological Association, 2009.

Shen-Yen, with Dan Stevenson. *Hoofprints of the Ox: Principles of the Chan Buddhist Path as Taught by a Modern Chinese Master.* New York: Oxford University Press, 2001.

Siegel, Daniel J. *The Mindful Brain: Reflection and Attunement in the Cultivation of Well-Being.* New York: Norton, 2007.

Silverton, Sarah. *The Mindfulness Breakthrough: The Revolutionary Approach to Dealing with Stress, Anxiety, and Depression.* London, UK: Watkins, 2012.

Smalley, Susan, and Diana Winston. *Fully Present: The Science, Art, and Practice of Mindfulness.* Philadelphia: Da Capo, 2010.

Snel, Eline. *Sitting Still Like a Frog: Mindfulness for Kids Aged Five Through Twelve and Their Parents.* Boston: Shambhala, 2013.

Spiegel, Jeremy. *The Mindful Medical Student.* Hanover, NH: Dartmouth College Press, 2009.

Stahl, Bob, and Elisha Goldstein. *A Mindfulness-Based Stress Reduction Workbook.* Oakland, CA: New Harbinger, 2010.

Sumedo, Ajahn. *The Mind and the Way.* Boston: Wisdom, 1995.

Suzuki, Shunru. *Zen Mind Beginner's Mind.* New York: Weatherhill, 1970.

Thera, Nyanoponika. *The Heart of Buddhist Meditation.* New York: Samuel Weiser, 1962.

Tolle, Eckhart. *The Power of Now.* Novato, CA: New World Library, 1999.

Trungpa, Chogyam. *Meditation in Action.* Boston: Shambhala, 1970.

Urgyen, Tulku. *Rainbow Painting.* Boudhanath, Nepal: Rangjung Yeshe, 1995.

Varela, Francisco J., Evan Thompson, and Eleanor Rosch. *The Embodied Mind: Cognitive Science and Human Experience.* Cambridge, MA: MIT Press, 1991.

Wallace, Alan B. *The Attention Revolution: Unlocking the Power of the Focused Mind.* Boston: Wisdom, 2006.

———. *Minding Closely: The Four Applications of Mindfulness.* Ithaca, NY: Snow Lion, 2011.

Williams, J. Mark G. and Jon Kabat-Zinn, eds. *Mindfulness: Diverse Perspectives on Its Meaning, Origins, and Applications.* London: Routledge, 2013.

Williams, Mark, and Danny Penman. *Mindfulness: A Practical Guide to Finding Peace in a Frantic World.* London: Little, Brown, 2011.

Williams, Mark, John Teasdale, Zindel Segal, and Jon Kabat-Zinn. *The Mindful Way Through Depression.* New York: Guilford, 2007.

FURTHER APPLICATIONS OF MINDFULNESS AND OTHER BOOKS ON MEDITATION

Brown, Daniel P. *Pointing Out the Great Way: The Stages of Meditation in the Mahamudra Tradition.* Boston: Wisdom, 2006.

Loizzo, Joe. *Sustainable Happiness: The Mind Science of Well-Being, Altruism, and Inspiration.* New York: Routledge, 2012.

McLeod, Ken. *Wake Up to Your Life: Discovering the Buddhist Path of Attention.* San Francisco: HarperCollins, 2001.

HEALING

Bowen, Sarah, Neha Chawla, and G. Alan Marlatt. *Mindfulness-Based Relapse Prevention for Addictive Behaviors.* New York: Guilford, 2011.

Byock, Ira. *The Best Care Possible: A Physician's Quest to Transform Care Through the End of Life.* New York: Penguin, 2012.

——. *Dying Well: Peace and Possibilities at the End of Life.* New York: Riverhead Books, 1997.

Fosha, Diana, Daniel J. Siegel, and Marion F. Solomon, eds. *The Healing Power of Emotion: Affective Neuroscience, Development, and Clinical Practice.* New York: Norton, 2009.

Gyatso, Tenzen. *The Compassionate Life.* Boston: Wisdom, 2003.

——. *Ethics for a New Millennium.* New York: Riverhead Books, 1999.

Halpern, Susan. *The Etiquette of Illness: What to Say When You Can't Find the Words.* New York: Bloomsbury, 2004.

Lerner, Michael. *Choices in Healing: Integrating the Best of Conventional and Complementary Approaches to Cancer.* Cambridge, MA: MIT Press, 1994.

McBee, Lucia. *Mindfulness-Based Elder Care: A CAM Model for Frail Elders and Their Caregivers.* New York: Springer, 2008.

Meili, Trisha. *I Am the Central Park Jogger: A Story of Hope and Possibility.* New York: Springer, 2003.

Moyers, Bill. *Healing and the Mind.* New York: Broadway Books, 1993.

Ornish, Dean. *Love and Survival: The Scientific Basis of the Healing Power of Intimacy.* New York: HarperCollins, 2008.

——. *The Spectrum: A Scientifically Proven Program to Feel Better, Live Longer, Lose Weight, and Gain Health.* New York: Ballantine Books, 2007.

Pelz, Larry. *The Mindful Path to Addiction Recovery: A Practical Guide to Regaining Control over Your Life.* Boston: Shambhala, 2013.

Remen, Rachel. *Kitchen Table Wisdom: Stories That Heal.* New York: Riverhead Books, 1997.

Simmons, Philip. *Learning to Fall: The Blessings of an Imperfect Life.* New York: Bantam, 2002.

Sternberg, Esther M. *Healing Spaces: The Science of Place and Well-Being.* Cambridge, MA: Harvard University Press, 2009.

——. *The Balance Within: The Science Connecting Health and Emotions.* New York: W. H. Freeman, 2001.

Tarrant, John. *The Light Inside the Dark: Zen, Soul, and the Spiritual Life.* New York: HarperCollins, 1998.

Wilson, Kelly. *Mindfulness for Two: An Acceptance and Commitment Therapy Approach to Mindfulness in Psychotherapy.* Oakland, CA: New Harbinger, 2008.

STRESS

LaRoche, Loretta. *Relax—You May Have Only a Few Minutes Left: Using the Power of Humor to Overcome Stress in Your Life and Work.* New York: Hay House, 2008.

Lazarus, Richard S., and Susan Folkman. *Stress, Appraisal, and Coping.* New York: Springer, 1984.

McEwen, Bruce. *The End of Stress as We Know It.* Washington, DC: Joseph Henry Press, 2002.

Rechtschaffen, Stephen. *Time Shifting: Creating More Time to Enjoy Your Life.* New York: Random House, 1996.

Sapolsky, Robert M. *Why Zebras Don't Get Ulcers.* New York: St. Martins/Griffin, 2004.

Singer, Thea. *Stress Less: The New Science That Shows Women How to Rejuvenate the Body and the Mind.* New York: Hudson Street Press, 2010.

PAIN

Burch, Vidyamala. *Living Well with Pain and Illness: The Mindful Way to Free Yourself from Suffering.* London: Piatkus, 2008.

Cohen, Darlene. *Finding a Joyful Life in the Heart of Pain: A Meditative Approach to Living with Physical, Emotional, or Spiritual Suffering.* Boston: Shambhala, 2000.

Dillard, James M. *The Chronic Pain Solution: Your Personal Path to Pain Relief.* New York: Bantam, 2002.

Gardner-Nix, Jackie. *The Mindfulness Solution to Pain: Step-by-Step Techniques for Chronic Pain Management.* Oakland, CA: New Harbinger, 2009.

Levine, Peter, and Maggie Phillips. *Freedom from Pain: Discover Your Body's Power to Overcome Physical Pain.* Boulder, CO: Sounds True, 2012.

McManus, Carolyn A. *Group Wellness Programs for Chronic Pain and Disease Management.* St. Louis, MO: Butterworth-Heinemann, 2003.

Sarno, John E. *Healing Back Pain: The Mind-Body Connection.* New York: Warner, 2001.

TRAUMA

Emerson, David, and Elizabeth Hopper. *Overcoming Trauma Through Yoga: Reclaiming Your Body.* Berkeley, CA: North Atlantic Books, 2011.

Epstein, Mark. *The Trauma of Everyday Life.* New York: Penguin, 2013.

Karr-Morse, Robin, and Meredith S. Wiley. *Scared Sick: The Role of Childhood Trauma in Adult Disease.* New York: Basic Books, 2012.

———. *Ghosts from the Nursery: Tracing the Roots of Violence.* New York: Atlantic Monthly Press, 1997.

Levine, Peter. *Healing Trauma: A Pioneering Program for Restoring the Wisdom of Your Body.* Boulder, CO: Sounds True, 2008.

———. *In an Unspoken Voice: How the Body Releases Trauma and Restores Goodness.* Berkeley, CA: North Atlantic Books, 2010.

Ogden, Pat, Kekuni Minton, and Claire Pain. *Trauma and the Body: A Sensorimotor Approach to Psychotherapy.* New York: Norton, 2006.

Sanford, Matthew. *Waking: A Memoir of Trauma and Transcendence.* Emmaus, PA: Rodale, 2006.

van der Kolk, Bessel, Alexander McFarlane, and Lars Weisaeth, eds. *Traumatic Stress: The Effects of Overwhelming Experience on Mind, Body, and Society.* New York: Guilford, 1996.

POETRY

Bly, Robert. *The Kabir Book.* Boston: Beacon, 1971.

Bly, Robert, James Hillman, and Michael Meade. *The Rag and Bone Shop of the Heart.* New York: HarperCollins, 1992.

Eliot, T. S. *Four Quartets.* New York: Harcourt Brace, 1977.

Hafiz. *The Gift: Poems by Hafiz.* Trans. David Ladinsky. New York: Penguin, 1999.

Hass, Robert, ed. *The Essential Haiku.* Hopewell, NJ: Ecco Press, 1994.

Lao-Tsu. *Tao Te Ching.* Trans. Stephen Mitchell. New York: HarperCollins, 1988.

Mitchell, Stephen. *The Enlightened Heart.* New York: Harper and Row, 1989.

Neruda, Pablo. *Five Decades: Poems 1925–1970.* New York: Grove Weidenfeld, 1974.

Oliver, Mary. *New and Selected Poems.* Boston: Beacon, 1992.

Rilke, R. M. *Selected Poems of Rainer Maria Rilke.* New York: Harper and Row, 1981.

Rumi. *The Essential Rumi.* Trans. Coleman Barks. San Francisco: Harper, 1995.

Ryokan. *One Robe, One Bowl.* Trans. John Stevens. New York: Weatherhill, 1977.

Shihab Nye, Naomi. *Words Under the Words: Selected Poems.* Portland, OR: Far Corner Books, 1980.

Tanahashi, Kaz, *Sky Above, Great Wind: The Life and Poetry of Zen Master Ryokan.* Boston: Shambhala, 2012.

Whyte, David. *The Heart Aroused: Poetry and the Preservation of the Soul in Corporate America.* New York: Random House, 1994.

Yeats, William Butler. *The Collected Poems of W. B. Yeats.* New York: Macmillan, 1963.

OTHER BOOKS OF INTEREST, SOME MENTIONED IN THE TEXT

Abrams, David. *The Spell of the Sensuous.* New York: Vintage, 1996.

Blakeslee, Sandra, and Matthew Blakeslee. *The Body Has a Mind of Its Own: How Body Maps in Your Brain Help You Do (Almost) Everything Better.* New York: Random House, 2007.

Bohm, David. *Wholeness and the Implicate Order.* London: Routledge and Kegan Paul, 1980.

Chaskalson, Michael. *The Mindful Workplace: Developing Resilient Individuals and Resonant Organizations with MBSR.* Chichester, West Sussex: Wiley-Blackwell, 2011.

Doidge, Norman. *The Brain That Changes Itself; Stories of Personal Triumph from the Frontiers of Brain Science.* New York: Penguin, 2007.

Gilbert, Daniel. *Stumbling on Happiness.* New York: Vintage, 2007.

Goleman, Daniel. *Ecological Intelligence: How Knowing the Hidden Impacts of What We Buy Can Change Everything.* New York: Broadway Books, 2009.

——. *Social Intelligence: The New Science of Human Relationships.* New York: Bantam, 2006.

——. *Emotional Intelligence: Why It Can Matter More than IQ.* New York: Bantam, 1995.

Kaza, Stephanie. *Mindfully Green: A Personal and Spiritual Guide to Whole Earth Thinking.* Boston: Shambhala, 2008.

Kazanjian, Victor H., and Peter L. Laurence. *Education as Transformation: Religious Pluralism, Spirituality, and a New Vision for Higher Education in America.* New York: Peter Lang, 2000.

Lantieri, Linda. *Building Emotional Intelligence: Techniques to Cultivate Inner Strength in Children.* Boulder, CO: Sounds True, 2008.

Layard, Richard. *Happiness: Lessons from a New Science.* New York: Penguin, 2005.

Marturano, Janice. *Finding the Space to Lead: A Practical Guide to Mindful Leadership.* New York: Bloomsbury, 2014.

Nowak, Martin. *Super Cooperators: Altruism, Evolution, and Why We Need Each Other to Succeed.* New York: Free Press, 2011.

Osler, William. *Aequanimitas.* New York: McGraw-Hill, 2012.

——. *A Way of Life.* Springfield, IL: Charles C. Thomas, 2012.

Sachs, Jeffrey D. *The Price of Civilization: Reawakening American Virtue and Prosperity*. New York: Random House, 2011.

Snyder, Gary. *The Practice of the Wild.* San Francisco: North Point, 1990.

Watson, Guy, Stephen Batchelor, and Guy Claxton, eds. *The Psychology of Awakening: Buddhism, Science, and Our Day-to-Day Lives.* York Beach, ME: Weiser, 2000.

Resources

There are a great many mindfulness associations and programs throughout the world, taught in many different languages. You can find them readily on the Internet through Google and other search engines. This list is simply a few of the centers we know about in the English-speaking world, and other websites that may be sources of information or support.

Center of Mindfulness in Medicine, Health Care, and Society
University of Massachusetts Medical School
Worcester, Massachusetts
http://www.umassmed.edu/cfm/index.aspx

Oxford Mindfulness Centre
University of Oxford, United Kingdom
http://oxfordmindfulness.org

Centre for Mindfulness Research and Practice
Bangor University, North Wales
http://www.bangor.ac.uk/mindfulness

Mindfulness Research Guide

A free online publication, published monthly, to keep abreast of the scientific research studies on mindfulness and its applications

http://www.mindfulexperience.org/research-centers.php

Clinical Education and Development and Research

University of Exeter, United Kingdom

http://cedar.exeter.ac.uk/programmes/pgmindfulness

University of California Center for Mindfulness

San Diego, California

http://health.ucsd.edu/specialties/mindfulness/Pages/default.aspx

University of Wisconsin Center for Mindfulness

UW Health Integrative Medicine

Madison, Wisconsin

http://www.uwhealth.org/alternative-medicine/mindfulness-based-stress-reduction/11454

Mindful Birthing and Parenting

University of California, San Francisco

San Francsico, California

http://www.mindfulbirthing.org

Duke University Medical Center

Integrative Medicine

Durham, North Carolina

http://www.dukeintegrativemedicine.org/classes-workshops-and-education/mindfulness-based-stress-reduction

Jefferson University Hospitals

Philadelphia, Pennsylvania

http://www.jeffersonhospital.org/departments-and-services/mindfulness/public-programs

Awareness and Relaxation Training
San Francisco, California
http://www.mindfulnessprograms.com

MBSR British Columbia
Vancouver, BC Canada
http://www.mbsrbc.ca

Open Ground Mindfulness Training
Sydney, Australia
http://www.openground.com.au

Mindful Psychology
Auckland, New Zealand
http://www.mindfulpsychology.co.nz/trainers.html

Institute for Mindfulness South Africa
Capetown, South Africa
http://www.mindfulness.org.za

Guided Mindfulness Meditation Practice CDs with Jon Kabat-Zinn: Ordering Information

There are three sets of Guided Mindfulness Meditation Practice CDs, which can be ordered directly from the websites:

www.mindfulnesscds.com
or
www.jonkabat-zinn.com

Digital download is available for each series.

Series 1 (4 CDs) These are the guided meditations and yoga practices described in this book that constitute the formal practice curriculum of MBSR (the Body Scan Meditation, Mindful Yoga 1, Sitting Meditation, and Mindful Yoga 2). Each program is 45 minutes in length. They are the original guided meditations used by Dr. Kabat-Zinn's patients in his classes in the Stress Reduction Clinic.

Series 2 (4 CDs) These guided meditations are designed for people who want a range of shorter guided meditations to help them develop and/or expand a personal mindfulness meditation practice. This series includes the Mountain and Lake Meditations (each 20 minutes) as well as a range of other 10-minute, 20-minute, and 30-minute sitting and lying down practices. This series was originally developed to accompany *Wherever You Go, There You Are.*

Series 3 (4 CDs) These guided meditations were originally developed to accompany *Coming to Our Senses* and use the unique sensory language of that book. The practices include mindfulness of breathing (Breathscape) and of other body sensations (Bodyscape), mindfulness of sounds and hearing (Soundscape), of thoughts and emotions (Mindscape), the practice of choiceless awareness (Nowscape), and a lovingkindness meditation (Heartscape). It also includes a brief guided walking meditation. All programs are 20 to 30 minutes in length.

Index

Approach/avoidance behavior, 447n
Assertiveness, 491–94
Athletes, 398–400, 602
Attitudes, 184–85
health and, 230–31, 243–49, 253–54, 265–68
Attitudinal foundation of mindfulness practice, 19–30
acceptance, 27–29
beginner's mind, 24–25
importance of, 19–20
letting go, 29–30, 31
non-judging, 21–23, 76–77, 256, 330
non-striving and non-doing, 21, 26–27, 31, 91, 92–95, 101, 112, 209, 267, 392, 442, 571, 592
other qualities of, 30–31, 601
patience, 23–24, 31, 55, 61, 379
trust, 25–26, 31

About the Author

JON KABAT-ZINN, PH.D., is a scientist, writer, and meditation teacher. He is Professor of Medicine emeritus at the University of Massachusetts Medical School, where he founded MBSR, the Stress Reduction Clinic, and the Center for Mindfulness in Medicine, Health Care, and Society.

In addition to this book, he is the author of *Wherever You Go, There You Are: Mindfulness Meditation in Everyday Life* (Hyperion, 1994, 2005), *Everyday Blessings: The Inner Work of Mindful Parenting* (co-authored with Myla Kabat-Zinn; Hyperion, 1997, 2014), and *Coming to Our Senses: Healing Ourselves and the World Through Mindfulness* (Hyperion, 2005). He is also co-author, with Williams, Teasdale, and Segal, of *The Mindful Way Through Depression: Freeing Yourself from Chronic Unhappiness* (Guilford, 2007); author of *Arriving At Your Own Door: 108 Lessons in Mindfulness* (Hyperion, 2007); *Letting Everything Become Your Teacher* (Random House, 2009); *The Mind's Own Physician: A Scientific Dialogue with the Dalai Lama on the Healing Power of Meditation* (editor, with Richard Davidson, New Harbinger, 2011); *Mindfulness for Beginners: Reclaiming the Present Moment and Your Life* (Sounds True, 2012); and *Mindfulness: Diverse Perspectives on its Meaning, Origins, and Applications* (editor, with Mark Williams, Routledge, 2013). His books are published in over thirty-five languages.

Dr. Kabat-Zinn received his Ph.D. in molecular biology from MIT in 1971 in the laboratory of Nobel Laureate Salvador Luria. His research career focused on mind/body interactions for healing and on the clinical applications of mindfulness meditation training for people with chronic pain and stress-related disorders. Dr. Kabat-Zinn's work has contributed to a growing movement of mindfulness into mainstream practices and institutions such as medicine, psychology, health care, schools, corporations, prisons, and professional sports. Hospitals and medical centers around the world now offer clinical programs based on training in mindfulness and MBSR.

He is a founding fellow of the Fetzer Institute, and a fellow of the Society of Behavioral Medicine. He received the Art, Science, and Soul of Healing Award from the Institute for Health and Healing, California Pacific Medical Center in San Francisco (1998); the 2nd Annual Trailblazer Award for "pioneering work in the field of integrative medicine" from the Scripps Center for Integrative Medicine in La Jolla, California (2001); the Distinguished Friend Award from the Association for Behavioral and Cognitive Therapies (2005); an Inaugural Pioneer in Integrative Medicine Award from the Bravewell Philanthropic Collaborative for Integrative Medicine (2007); the 2008 Mind and Brain Prize from the Center for Cognitive Science, University of Torino, Italy; and a Pioneer in Western Socially Engaged Buddhism Award (2010) from the Zen Peacemakers Association.

He is the founding convener of the Consortium of Academic Health Centers for Integrative Medicine (CAHCIM), and a member of the Board of the Mind and Life Institute, a group that organizes dialogues between the Dalai Lama and Western scientists to promote deeper understanding of different ways of knowing and probing the nature of mind, emotions, and reality. He and his wife, Myla Kabat-Zinn, are engaged in supporting initiatives to further mindfulness in K-12 education and to promote mindful parenting.